LORDS AND LANDLORDS:
THE ARISTOCRACY AND THE TOWNS
1774–1967

Lords
and Landlords:

the Aristocracy and the Towns 1774-1967

David Cannadine

LEICESTER UNIVERSITY PRESS 1980

First published in 1980 by Leicester University Press
Distributed in North America by Humanities Press Inc., New Jersey

Copyright © Leicester University Press 1980

Designed by Douglas Martin
Phototypeset in V.I.P. Baskerville by Western Printing Services Ltd, Bristol
Printed in Great Britain by Unwin Brothers Limited, Old Woking, Surrey
Bound by Redwood Burn Ltd, London and Esher

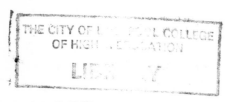
British Library Cataloguing in Publication Data

Cannadine, David
Lord and landlords.
1. England – Nobility – Case studies
2. Devonshire family
3. Calthorpe family
I. Title
301.44'2   HT653.G7

ISBN 0–7185–1152–2

Contents

List of Tables

List of Graphs

List of Illustrations

FOR MY MOTHER

AND

IN MEMORY OF MY FATHER

Preface

It is arguable that the most fundamental changes to have occurred in Britain during the last two centuries concern the decline of the hereditary, aristocratic, landed elite on the one hand, and the rise of a mass, industralized, urban society on the other. This book is concerned, not so much to examine these themes in isolation, but to see how they are interrelated. Of course, there was much more to the decline of the aristocracy than the rise of towns, and there were many other influences on urban development besides those grandees who owned the land on to which some of the industrial and leisure towns of nineteenth-century England expanded. But the links between those who owned the land and those who lived on it – collaborative in some instances, conflicting in others – form the most precise point of contact between the old, pre-industrial elite on the way down, and the new, industrial mass on the way up. The paradoxes, contradictions and ambiguities of this encounter form the subject of this book.

Two symbolic dates may be taken to mark the beginning and the end of the period under examination: 1774 and 1967. The first was the occasion of the passing of the London Building Act, whose regulations concerning house-building were to govern the metropolis for the next 70 years. And, in the same year, the fifth duke of Bedford began to develop the remaining virgin land on his Bloomsbury estate. At the time, there was nothing particularly remarkable about this (except the novel use of 99-year building leases): it was simply another of those upturns in the building cycle and in metropolitan estate development which had occurred intermittently since the construction of the Covent Garden Piazza by Inigo Jones for the fourth earl of Bedford in 1631–5. But in retrospect, this date best pinpoints the beginning of the greatest phase of aristocratic involvement in urban development – initially in London, then in the great provincial towns, and finally at the seaside – which did not spend itself until the closing decades of the nineteenth century.

In each case, urban estates were developed by the aristocracy on the basis of certain presuppositions about the nature of landed society: the sanctity of property, especially of land; the duty of a landowner to augment his estates; and the permanence of society in which landowners should be not only powerful, but able to pass on the landed base of that power to their descendants. The past 100 years, however, have seen the gradual erosion of almost all those assumptions. And so, while the aristocracy has adapted and survived to a greater extent than many would have predicted at the close of the nineteenth century, the result nevertheless has been to change fundamentally the nature of their involvement in the urbanization process. Accordingly, the best terminal date for this second, conservative phase is the Leasehold Reform Act of 1967. For, while this was not designed as a specifically anti-aristocratic measure, the idea behind it, of obliging the landowner to sell the freehold when his tenant so wishes, strikes at the very heart of the remaining landed estates in our great towns. The last barrier safeguarding their sanctity has been breached.

No book covering a theme as broad as this over so long a period of time can hope to examine it comprehensively. Accordingly, I have limited myself to five general, interpretative chapters, which seek to outline the arguments and problems as I see them, and draw heavily on other people's work in the process. Sandwiched between them are two detailed case studies – each concerning an estate and family of intrinsic fame, interest and importance – which form the basis of the generalizations offered elsewhere in the book. Even if my conclusions do not stand up to subsequent testing, perhaps they will serve to stimulate others to delve more deeply where I have only been able to skim the surface.

In the course of writing this book, I have incurred many debts of gratitude. In particular, I am grateful to Brigadier Sir Richard Anstruther-Gough-Calthorpe for his kindness in allowing me to see the Calthorpe papers in the Edgbaston Estate Office, and to Mr H. E. Greening and Mr J. P. Meering for their hospitality while I worked there. In this regard, I must also thank Mr A. J. M. Baker of Walters, Vandercom and Hart, for allowing me to consult the Calthorpe family papers in his firm's possession. To His Grace the Duke of Devonshire and the Trustees of the Chatsworth Settlement, my debt is no less great. I am also indebted to Mr Wragg and Mr Day at Chatsworth, and to Mr Rowsell and Mr O'Callaghan of the Compton Estate Office in Eastbourne. My thanks are also due to Mr T. J. Burrows of Currey and Company, for making available important papers concerning the Devonshire family, and for accommodating me as an intruder into a busy office.

I must also thank the librarians and archivists of the Public Record Office, the House of Lords Record Office, the Hampshire, Kent, East Sussex and Greater London Record Offices, Birmingham Reference Library, Birmingham University Library and Eastbourne Public Library. I am also most grateful to Mr Joseph Gillott, Eastbourne Corporation, Sydney Mitchell and Company, the Governors of Eastbourne College and of the Schools of King Edward VI in Birmingham, and the Secretaries to the Birmingham General Hospital, the Birmingham and Midland Institute, the Birmingham Botanical Gardens, the Eastbourne Pier Company and the Eastbourne Water Works Company, for allowing me to consult material in their possession. I have also to thank the editors of the *Historical Journal*, *Social History* and the *Agricultural History Review*, for kindly allowing me to use material which originally appeared in their journals in article form.

I first became interested in this problem in my undergraduate days, and I am grateful to the Master and Fellows of Clare College, Cambridge, for their generosity in enabling me to undertake some important early research. Since then, my work has been most generously supported by the President and Fellows of St John's College, Oxford, the Trustees of the Jane Eliza Procter Fund, the Master and Fellows of St John's College, Cambridge, and the Master and Fellows of Christ's College, Cambridge. To all of these institutions, I am most appreciatively indebted.

My intellectual obligations are no less great. To Graham Butler and Richard Hughes, who originally stimulated my interest in history, my gratitude is profound and abiding. Derek Beales was the most formative influence in my undergraduate days, and has been a constant source of inspiration and encouragement thereafter. Peter Mathias was a most generous and helpful research supervisor in Oxford, as was Lawrence Stone at Princeton. Since my arrival at Christ's, Jack Plumb has been a stimulating and influential mentor, to whose enthusiasm and encouragement I owe a great deal. Jim Dyos smoothed for me the difficult path between the thesis and the book, and it is a source of particular sorrow that my thanks can now only be to his memory. Peter Boulton and the staff of Leicester University Press have been unfailingly generous and helpful.

At home, my mother and sister have provided encouragement and support in boundless quantities. But it is only right that the last word of acknowledgment should be to my late father. He, more than anyone, encouraged my historical studies, and eagerly awaited the appearance of this book, in which, with all its manifold imperfections, he would have taken such pride and delight.

D.N.C.
Christ's College, Cambridge
28 February 1979

Part One
Themes and Problems

1 The aristocracy and the towns: ambivalence and ambiguity

At least in part, the history of modern England is the history of the passing of aristocratic society – the story of 'a great – perhaps the greatest – senatorial order that was passing away'.[1] By the years after the Second World War, this departure was almost complete: the gentry had shrivelled, the grandees had shrunk, never to return. Arguably from the 1920s, and certainly from the 1940s, England has been a nation without a landed aristocracy at its apex.[2] Like the fall of the empire which they and their associates created and ruled, this change is one of the most fundamental to have occurred in recent English history. But how exactly did the landed aristocracy decline? What were the reasons for it? When precisely did it happen? The questions multiply, and so do the answers: the rise of mass parties and the fall of agricultural revenue; the proliferation of honours and the erosion of self-confidence; success in pursuing chorus girls and failure to avoid death duties; the cumulative poison of income tax and the instant catastrophe of two world wars. Assuredly, it was no easier to kill off the aristocracy than it was to assassinate Rasputin . . .

1

So it is altogether appropriate that historians should on occasions cast themselves in the role of coroner and try to establish the causes of death. Considering the straitened circumstances of many aristocrats by the 1940s, the questions are as legitimate as they are important. But if such scholars were able to journey back through time, and investigate the Belgravia of 'Chips' Channon or the country house world of the seventeenth earl of Derby, to say nothing of the more extravagant régime which existed in the years before 1914, they might begin to wonder whether a funeral oration which placed the aristocracy's demise somewhere in the last quarter of the nineteenth century was not, perhaps, a little premature. For it was not until 1905 that the lavish creation of non-landed peerages began; not until 1908 that the first prime minister took office who did not own a landed estate; not until 1911 that the House of Lords lost its powers of absolute veto over Commons legislation; not until 1922 that the aristocratic grip on the countryside relaxed; not until 1945 that peerages were given to those who had no large income; not until 1958 that life peerages were introduced; not until 1963 that hereditary peers were allowed to disclaim their titles; not until 1964 that the last hereditary peerages of non-royal lineage were created; and not yet that the composition of the House of Lords has been fundamentally reformed by legislation.[3] Collectively, these events and non-events are eloquent testimony to aristocratic decline. Yet they are strung out over half a century. Although many occurred before the First World War, their cumulative effect was only made manifest much later.

Certainly, as late as 1914, no *parvenu* entrepreneur – however fabulous his fortune, however celebrated his achievements – could hope to rival the social prestige of those 'rulers of principalities' and 'miniature empires' at whose 'ubiquitous' influence and power T. H. S. Escott was still able to marvel in 1885.[4] The seventh duke of Devonshire once admitted that he had more houses than he knew what to do with: Chatsworth and Hardwick in Derbyshire, Holker Hall in Lancashire, Bolton Abbey in Yorkshire, Lismore Castle in Ireland, Compton Place in Sussex, Devonshire House and Chiswick House in London, and Beaufort House at Newmarket. But even he was outdone by the sixth duke of Buccleuch, who boasted six houses in Scotland and as many again in England. In one year alone, 1888, the Buccleuch estates in Scotland provided 7,726 grouse, 1,121 black game, 2,342 partridge, 2,961 pheasant, and 3,639 hare, which were either consumed by the family and their guests, or given away.[5]

Nor were these grandees exceptional. It took 38 domestic servants and 39 gardeners to maintain the Derbys' lavish hospitality at Knowsley in 1900 – figures surpassed both by the Duke of Marlborough at Blenheim (who was not particularly wealthy), and by the Duke of Westminster at Eaton (who most decidedly was).[6] The fifth earl of Lonsdale is reputed to have spent £13,000 a year on cigars alone, and also numbered among his playthings his own private orchestra and two steam yachts at Cowes.[7] The first duke of Westminster's horses won the Derby five times, and his collection of 183 paintings included six by Rubens, three Titians, one Raphael and two Rembrandts. His grandson, who became second duke in 1900, and combined the grandeur of Henry VIII with the extravagance of Lorenzo the Magnificent, shot, fenced, danced, golfed and motored his way through the Edwardian era.[8] And if the endless round of country house weekends palled, there was always the London season to provide diversion. The great houses, with their sumptuous balls, receptions and parties, in rooms cascading with jewels, orders and works of art, captivated even such opponents of the aristocracy as Joseph Chamberlain, Asquith (to say nothing of his daughter Violet), and Lloyd George himself.[9] Newcomers like Lipton and Cowdray might aspire to equal the social prestige of these august grandees; but however careful and painstaking their studied emulation, they remained socially inferior to the aristocracy of birth.

In politics, too, the landed aristocracy's tenacity was remarkable. Despite the attacks of Bright, Chamberlain and Lloyd George, the repeal of the Corn Laws, the Free Trade in Land campaign and the People's Budget, they were still *there* at the top in 1914. Each great concession which the landed classes made to popular pressure in the nineteenth century was hailed by radical leaders as portending the eclipse of aristocratic government. Yet in reality it was radicalism itself which was doomed: to constant frustration. Reform and repeal came and went, but it was another generation before the middle classes reached the Commons in appreciable numbers, let alone the cabinet. At the general election of 1830, it was claimed that 'The aristocracy has been taught a lesson . . . The secret had been imparted, . . . the secret of their weakness'.[10] Thirty years later, Bright was certain that 'the fort of selfishness and monopoly cannot be held forever'.[11] But for all that, aristocrats of three generations' standing were in a majority in every cabinet until 1895; landowners generally were dominant until 1906; ambassadors to the courts of Europe and viceroys and governors general of the great dominions were drawn almost entirely from this class; and, despite claims about 'unmoderated democracy', England in 1914 still had one of the narrowest electoral franchises in Europe.[12]

Even the effects of the Second and Third Reform Acts were delayed by at least a generation. Aristocrats who had entered politics as young men before these measures were passed continued to dominate Westminster well into the new century. The cabinet career of the great Marquess of Salisbury lasted from 1866 to 1902, when he was succeeded as prime minister by his nephew Arthur Balfour; the eighth duke of Devonshire resigned his last ministerial appointment in 1903, having first held office under Earl Russell in 1866; and the Marquess of Ripon sat in every Liberal cabinet between 1863 and 1908.[13] The battle for the control of the Conservative party in the 1880s was fought between a Cecil and a Churchill, and the advent of a prime minister in 1908 who did not own a landed estate was much less significant at the time than in retrospect. In local affairs, too, the gloomy prognostications of the late 1880s, when it was feared that the reform of county government would deprive the gentry of their most important bastion of power, were found to have been grossly exaggerated. As with the passing of the Great Reform Act, the same men continued to dominate the system, even if they were now chosen by more democratic means.[14]

Most impressive of all, however, was the aristocracy's continued wealth. Some families may have tottered on the brink of ruin in the early nineteenth century, but by the mid-Victorian period many aristocrats were acquiring wealth of a type, and in amounts, which even their richest ancestors had never experienced. When visiting England in the 1860s, H. A. Taine was taken to the House of Lords, where he observed some of these financial superpowers:

> The principal peers present were pointed out to me, and named, with details of their enormous fortunes: the largest amounting to £300,000 a year. The Duke of Bedford has £220,000 a year from land; the Duke of Richmond has 300,000 acres in a single holding; the Marquess of Westminster, landlord of a whole London quarter, will have an income of one million pounds a year when the present long leases run out.[15]

Indeed, it seems that the most affluent of the English artistocracy not only far outshone their entrepreneurial rivals in the mid-Victorian period, but were also, in all probability, the wealthiest ruling class in Europe:

In point of wealth, the House of Lords exhibits a standard which cannot be equalled in any other country. Take the Dukes of Northumberland, Devonshire, Sutherland and Buccleuch, the Marquesses of Westminster and Bute, the Earls of Derby, Lonsdale, Dudley and Leicester and Baron Overstone, and where (in the manner of wealth), will you find their equals collectively?[16]

Of these, the Westminsters were the most famous. By the 1860s their wealth had become legendary, earning them this description from incredulous contemporaries:

The wealthiest family in Europe – perhaps, due regard being had to security, the wealthiest uncrowned house on earth. The Lichtensteins have a throne; the Rothschilds are still exposed to the chances of the market. There is no other family which certainly possesses a larger income.[17]

Expenditure was on an equally epic scale. Between 1870 and 1882, the second marquess lavished £600,000 on the re-building of Eaton Hall.[18]

Certainly, until the 1880s, the majority of the richest men in the land owed their opulence to the possession of broad acres and all that went with it[19] and, however worrying the agricultural depression was for many, those super-rich aristocrats, comfortably buttressed by their urban rentals, mineral royalties and the like, remained high in the wealth tables. In 1883, John Bateman counted four families – the Buccleuchs, the Derbys, the Devonshires and the Northumberlands – whose land was valued at in excess of £150,000 annually. Not far behind came the Fitzwilliams, the Bedfords, the Sutherlands, the Butes, the Dudleys and the Norfolks. And this excluded families like the Portmans, Cadogans and Westminsters, whose acres were narrow but whose metropolitan rents were enormous.[20] When the seventeenth earl of Derby succeeded in 1908, the gross rental of his estates was little short of £300,000 a year. Even that was surpassed by the Bedfords, the Portlands, the Butes, the Sutherlands and the Northumberlands. Predictably, the Westminsters topped the list: in 1914 the second duke was reputed to enjoy an income of £1,000 *a day*.[21]

It is clear that neither in politics, society nor wealth did 'feudalism' surrender to 'industry' with the rapidity that *The Times* had feared when Edward Strutt was created Baron Belper in 1856, an event which had seemed to portend the eclipse of the old order.[22] Assuredly, the gentry and the poorer aristocracy were increasingly separated off from their super-rich cousins as a result of the agricultural depression. It may well be that the landed elite as a whole took its duties less seriously at the local level in the 1900s than it had done hitherto.[23] Politically, they were weaker than they had been a century before; socially, their ranks were less exclusive; their wealth, too, was less Himalayan compared with the fortunes being made in industry by the last quarter of the nineteenth century. But their hold on the land, their leading role in politics, their near monopoly in the Lords, and their firm grip on the highest posts in empire and embassy, meant that they were still incomparably the most dominant single class in 1914.

Since, like Charles II, the English aristocracy has been 'an unconscionable time a dying', it is as important to inquire how they were able to remain so powerful for so long as it is to seek explanations for their decline. The singular adaptability of the English landed establishment 'is a feature that above all others has distinguished the history of England from that of her continental neighbours in recent centuries': how did this continue to be so during the nineteenth and twentieth centuries?[24] Given that the forces at work against the aristocracy appear in retrospect so overwhelming, how did they succeed in resisting them so successfully for so long? Considering that so much of the social, political and economic climate of England since the classical phase of the Industrial Revolution has been increasingly hostile to the ethos of an aristocratic polity, how did the landowning classes manage not only to survive but also to prosper in the world's most advanced industrial society?

This book seeks to explore one major aspect of the aristocracy's ambiguous position by investigating their relationship with the towns of England between the late eighteenth and mid-twentieth centuries. In part it is concerned to examine how the towns affected the aristocracy: undermining their power in some ways, prolonging their influence in others. At the same time it seeks to investigate the reciprocal influence which the aristocracy exerted on evolving urban communities, either as the incarnation of hostile privilege or as the embodiment of all that ambition could desire. For just as the towns were both poison and pillar, blunderbuss and buttress for the aristocracy, so the aristocracy were both idol and evil, example and enemy, for the towns. In this lengthy process of interaction, both elements exerted influence and were themselves subject to it and changed by it. 'Though the capitalist elements in the town "rose", the landed classes did not "fall" – at least for a very long time.'[25] By examining that confrontation within the specific context of urban growth, this book may help to explain why the landed classes have often been declining, but have never fallen completely, and why the middle classes have always been rising, but have never fully triumphed.

2

Insofar as the aristocracy in Britain *has* declined, some of the explanation undoubtedly lies in the facts and consequences of the massive urban growth experienced by Britain in the last 200 years. For, as Ralph Nevill put it, surveying the scene despondently from the vantage point of the 1920s, 'the political influence of the English landowning class must in any case have disappeared with the development of the great towns and the increase in population'.[26] Indeed, the unique resilience of the English aristocracy was tested to the full by the growth in urban population which was without precedent or rival for, in the nineteenth century, Britain was incomparably the most urbanized society in the world. By 1900, the American urban population was only 40 per cent, the Scandinavian less than one-quarter, the Austrian only slightly above one-third, the Russian a mere 20 per cent, and the French barely double that. Yet in England, one-third of the population had been officially classified as urban as long ago as 1800, and one-half were town dwellers by mid-century. Britain's closest rivals – Belgium and Germany – did not reach that stage until the end of the century – when already over three-quarters of the inhabitants of England were town dwellers.[27]

So when, at mid-century, Robert Vaughan noted that it was 'pre-eminently an age of great cities' and when, 50 years later, A. F. Weber observed that 'the most remarkable social phenomenon of the present century is the concentration of the population in great cities', it was the English urban experience which provided the most eloquent example.[28] Contemporaries were amazed by the proliferation of squares and slums, streets and suburbs. 'Our metropolis has become such as the world has not seen', wrote Vaughan. 'Our leading towns in the provinces equal the capitals of ordinary kingdoms.'[29] And he was quite correct. In the course of the nineteenth century, the number of towns in England with over 20,000 inhabitants rose from 15 to 185. In 1800, 3 out of 9 million people lived in towns; in 1900 the figure was 24 out of 30 million. Between 1821 and 1831 alone, Sheffield, Birmingham, Manchester, Liverpool and Leeds all grew by more than 40 per cent, and for no decade from 1811 to 1851 did the growth of Bradford fall below 50 per cent. London itself expanded from 1.8 million inhabitants in 1841 to 4.2 million at the turn of the century, making it incomparably the largest metropolis in the western world. Ruskin hardly exaggerated when he spoke of the ever-growing population being 'thrown back in continually closer crowds upon the city gates'.[30]

Not surprisingly, there was much in this which the aristocracy found alarming. In particular, they were frightened by the evidence of urban squalor, by the realization that a new and apparently barbaric world had come into being which threatened to swamp their own comfortable existence. The best-selling Royal Commission reports of the 1840s, with their grotesque revelations of stinking cemeteries and leaking coffins, the 'condition of England' novels of the same period, the detailed press accounts from the 1880s, and the careful investigations of Booth and Rowntree at the end of the century, revealed an urban society riddled with poverty, crime, drunkenness, prostitution and vice.[31] So it was hardly surprising that writers described English towns in the same vocabulary that they lavished on the horrors of 'darkest Africa'. Even Robert Vaughan, who was in some ways inclined to take an optimistic view of urban society, conceded that the city nurtured an unprecedentedly luxuriant growth of depravity. And he was far surpassed in eloquent pessimism by John Knox. 'Wretched, filthy, haggard, dissolute, profligate, careworn, outcast', was how he described 'the masses who inhabit the dingy courts, dingy cellars and miserable garrets of our great towns'.[32] Not until the end of the century, when measures were taken to improve slum conditions, and housing and town planning became important political issues for the first time, was fear replaced by effective and active concern.

However, it was not just urban squalor which the landed classes feared: it was also the new style of urban politics. 'For the first time in modern history, a body politic had got itself into a mainly urban condition', which brought with it a society whose values were in many senses hostile to those of an aristocratic polity.[33] Ideally, the aristocratic world was static, oligarchic, hierarchical, limited and intimate. Urban society, by contrast, was mobile, democratic, egalitarian, broad and impersonal: 'a system of life constructed on a wholly new principle'.[34] In the middle of the century, Edward Baines of Leeds gave this antithesis a specifically anti-aristocratic articulation when he noted how his generation, 'born and bred in the cities', displayed 'middle-class, noncon-formist dislike and suspicion of the rural-based, anti-urban aristocracy'.[35] And, although the townsmen could not compete for a long time in terms of confidence, education or wealth, they did – by definition – possess *numbers*, which introduced an entirely new element into the political equation. Indeed, the *Edinburgh Review* recognized this as early as 1824, when it noted how 'Men only feel their consequences, and they can only act in a collective capacity and with vigour and effect, after they have been condensed into masses and collected in cities.' Or, as Joseph Cowen put it 30 years later: 'The gathering of men into crowds has some drawbacks, yet the concentration of citizens, like the concentration of soldiers, is a source of strength.'[36]

Indeed it was. The Reform Bill agitation, the campaign against the Corn Laws, and the Chartist threat vindicated these observations, as different urban groups sought to storm the citadel of aristocratic privilege. In retro-spect, we know just how little these enterprises accomplished; but at the time, the picture appeared very different. As Derek Fraser has noted, 'the Victorian town halls were fortresses in the battle against country estates'. For Vaughan, writing in the 1840s, the clash between the haves and the have nots, between the aristocrat and the town dweller, was everywhere apparent:

> In no part of Europe is this struggle between the feudal and the civic, as generally represented by the landed class and the mercantile class, so pervading, so organised or so determined as among ourselves . . . The elements of social life which tend necessarily to collision are nowhere so powerful, nowhere so nearly balanced; and as the natural consequence of such a relation of parties we are, perhaps, at this moment, the most contentious people upon earth.[37]

It was all very alarming for, as he went on to explain, there was more at stake than the outcome of specific political controversies:

> Those who possess the prizes of life betray their jealousy of all appear-ances which seem to prognosticate that others who have hitherto been

excluded from them may be raised to participate in them. Hence the great object of the upper portions of society is stationariness and repose, while that of the lower is wakefulness and movement. The one sees everything to fear in change; the other looks to it in the buoyancy of hope.[38]

Nor did they look in vain: the repeal of the Corn Laws seemed to symbolize emphatically the triumph of numbers over nobles, of the urban interpretation of the national interest over the rural.

Nor was this the end of the affair. 'We have a revolution slumbering, but gathering power in all our cities', observed E. P. Hood in 1851. Radical, urban-based politicians like Baines, Roebuck and Mundella

> did not argue on the defensive. They persistently carried the attack into the countryside, comparing contemptuously the passive with the active, the idlers with the workers, the landlords with the businessmen, the voluntary initiative of the city with the 'torpor' and 'monotony' of the village, and urban freedom with rustic 'feudalism'.[39]

Indeed, with the advent of the Birmingham caucus and Joseph Chamberlain, the high priest of exuberant, urban radicalism, stridently anti-aristocratic in tone, who likened the landlords to the lilies of the field 'who toil not, neither do they spin', it seemed to some as though Hood's 'revolution' was not far off. The foundation of the National Liberal Federation, followed by the National Union of Conservatives, marked a real turning point, announcing as it did the advent of a new age of mass, urban-dominated, politics. Even Gladstone, a self-confessed 'out and out inequalitarian', with a reverence for landed estates which only just stopped short of idolatry, admitted that the 'masses' would ultimately prevail against the 'classes'. Summarizing the landowners' fears at the end of the century, G. F. C. Masterman observed how

> They dread the fermenting, in the populous cities, of some new, all-powerful explosive, destined one day to shatter into ruin all their desirable social order. In these massed millions of an obscure life, but dimly understood, they behold a danger to security and to all pleasant things.[40]

The late nineteenth-century attacks on urban leaseholds, followed by Lloyd George's more general broadside against the landed classes, only served to show how well grounded their fears were.[41]

Nor was the attack limited to matters of power, politics and principle. For in the battle of moral values, the sobriety, probity and rectitude of evangelical, bourgeois, urban England triumphed overwhelmingly over the hedonistic extravagance more characteristic of the Regency aristocracy. From the 1820s, if not before, taking on a bourgeois hue became almost obligatory for any aristocrat seeking either popular acclaim or royal approval.[42] The greatest ornaments of the late nineteenth-century peerage – men like the seventh duke of Devonshire or the first duke of Westminster – were as respectable, pious and benevolent as the most abstemious, upright and virtuous middle-class family.

Embourgeoisement was not a process limited to certain groups within the working class. Many of the aristocracy succumbed with equal commitment to this new and essentially urban ideal. In the triumph of the creed of 'Godliness and Good Learning', the counting house vanquished the country house as the arbiter of morality.

3

However, such a picture – 'the city in arms against a countryside tenaciously opposed to reform' – for all its useful insights, is too simple in seeing class and geographical conflict at the roots of nineteenth-century politics, just as it is too unequivocal in depicting a defensive and declining aristocracy gradually and inexorably overwhelmed by a united and increasingly confident urban society.[43] For neither the landowners nor the town-dwellers have been as monolithic as this antithesis suggests; nor have they been so hostile to one another as is sometimes supposed. In the case of the landowners in particular, their own internal divisions, and their strong links with the evolving urban community, severely undermine so agreeable but unsubtle a view.

To begin with, however monolithic and united landed society might have looked to those who viewed it from the *outside*, it looked decidedly different when surveyed from *within*. As Professor Burn has noted, 'the Duke of Omnium and the small squire were half a world apart', and this could be as true of their politics and social life as of their finances.[44] Nor did the internal divisions always follow the same lines. A great magnate and a lesser squire might be seen together riding to hounds, paying their joint respects to the corporate nature of county society. Likewise, on the local bench, they might collaborate in the enforcement of law and order, affirming their shared belief in hierarchy and deference. But the very next week, either at the local hustings or at Westminster itself, they might be at daggers drawn over some particular issue of party-political significance for, on most major questions in nineteenth-century politics, the landed classes were split from top to bottom. The passing of the First Reform Act, and the repeal of the Corn Laws, for example, were not so much a triumph of the middle classes but, in Parliament at least, the victory of one part of landed society over another since both issues were resolved in a legislature where both parties were preponderantly landed in composition.[45] Even families were split. Indeed, over the Corn Laws, as over every major political issue from the time of the Fox-North Coalition to Home Rule, fathers in the Lords and sons in the Commons could be seen going through different lobbies.[46] However strong might have been their sense of family, of county community, or of national group solidarity, the fact remains that in nineteenth-century politics, *both* parties were captained and supported by members of the landed classes.[47]

Indeed, it was the fact that land conferred the right to participate in politics, and that politics was played both in the shires and in London, which helps explain why the English aristocracy was, in Sir Lewis Namier's memorable adjective, 'amphibious': neither totally rural nor yet fully urban.[48] They may have been happier and more at ease, as Lord Eustace Percy implies, in the country;[49] but any landowner who, in 1800, could claim an income in excess of £10,000 a year, was fully able to participate in metropolitan 'society' as well.[50] Even the greatest of magnates spent half of the year deep in the countryside, renewing contacts with the local landowners and the 'pseudo' gentry of the county towns. For the other half, they repaired to the great metropolis, there to enjoy the pleasures of the season and the excitement of Parliament, and to perpetuate that carefully-fostered illusion that everyone really knew everyone else. 'Society', the centre of the aristocracy's world, the clearing house for gossip and political information, the marriage market *par excellence*, was by definition an *urban* phenomenon. So, while the Prussian aristocracy spent most of its year in the countryside, and while their Russian cousins loitered immovably in the cities of Moscow and St Petersburg, the English landowning classes divided their time between each arena, and so came to dominate both.[51] It is not altogether surprising, therefore, that, while the definition of a gentleman might be *rural*, the location of 'society' was *urban*.

Accordingly, the interests of the English aristocracy were never limited to farms, fields and agriculture. However much they may have affected to despise trade, they were rarely averse to increasing their income from non-agricultural sources if an opportunity presented itself on or near their estates. The participation of the English aristocracy in ventures as varied as docks and harbours, mines and markets, urban estates and East Indiamen, canals, turnpikes and railways, is a platitude of English social history for all periods since the time of Elizabeth. Indeed, during the century from the 1780s – the classical phase of the Industrial Revolution – their involvement was greater than ever before.[52] No landed class so well disposed towards the making of money by such means could ever be completely hostile to urban expansion. Moreover, the practice of primogeniture served to forge another link between the aristocracy and the towns. Many younger sons, it is true, took to the army, the navy, the law and the Church, the traditional sources of outdoor relief for those who did not ensnare an heiress; but for others, the East India Company and a host of similar trading ventures beckoned.[53] Indeed, the founder of the Calthorpe dynasty, to whose descendants' activities a large part of this book is devoted, began his career in just this way.

So, at one and the same time, the English landed classes were downwardly mobile, entrepreneurially adventurous, and also well integrated into the London money market. A peer would marry an heiress provided the terms were right, although her father might be a banker or a merchant or even an ironmaster. A landowner would have no hesitation is using his estate as security for a loan whether from a London bank like Hoares' or Childs', which dealt almost exclusively with the aristocracy and shunned entrepreneurs, or from an insurance company like the Royal Exchange or the Equitable, whose funds were mainly derived from the lower-class savings of the urban community.[54] The money thus acquired could be spent on rural or urban ventures. It might be channelled into the countryside for house building, land purchase or agricultural improvement, or it might be used to finance other, more 'amphibious' enterprises, such as making a dock, sinking a mineshaft, or constructing a market. In the same way, the revenue derived from such sources could either be re-cycled as a further instalment of investment, or channelled back to the landowner's rural holdings in the form of agricultural improvement. When it came to borrowing money or to investing income, the aristocracy paid little heed to the barriers between the country and the town.[55] To them, indeed, the barriers were largely invisible.

However, the most eloquent evidence of the 'amphibious' nature of the aristocracy was their active involvement in the physical expansion of urban England from the 1770s. Before then, their activity had been necessarily confined to the development of estates in Dublin and London, where the creation of the Covent Garden Piazza by Inigo Jones for the fourth earl of Bedford between 1631 and 1635 initiated the process.[56] Further development was intermittent: Bloomsbury and St James's Squares followed the Restoration; Hanover, Grosvenor and Cavendish Squares came after the peace with France and the Hanoverian succession; and Berkeley Square took shape at a more desultory pace in the 1730s.[57] But the major turning point came in 1774, 'a key year in the history of London building', when the London Building Act was passed, for its regulations concerning the making of new streets and the construction of houses continued to govern metropolitan building for the next 70 years.[58] Simultaneously, new developments were initiated in Portland Place and Portman Square, and a further offensive was contemplated on the Bedford Estate. Again, the results were to be of momentous, long-term significance. In part, this was because the building agreements made in 1776 for Bedford Square were the first to make extensive use of 99-year leases, thereby creating a precedent which was soon to be followed almost universally on other building estates. But in addition, they also initiated a new phase of development which was not to run its course until 1860, with the completion of Gordon Square. And by then, the development of other great aristocratic estates, ranging from the Grosvenors in nearby Belgravia to the Ladbrokes more distant in Notting Hill, had completely transformed the western face of the metropolis.[59] As a result, when those two self-consciously radical lovers, Lady Ottoline Morrell and Bertrand Russell, walked the streets of London together in the early years of the twentieth century, it proved unnecessary for them to stray beyond the confines of land owned either by his family (the dukes of Bedford) or hers (the dukes of Portland).[60]

Where the London landowners led, their provincial colleagues soon followed, equally eager to garner the rich harvest of urban rentals. From the 1810s and 1820s, when the rate of population growth of the provincial towns first became spectacular, until the closing decades of the nineteenth century, aristocratic landowners were busy cutting up their fields into plots, laying out roads, and leasing out land to speculative builders. The Calthorpes were amongst the earliest in Birmingham, but soon the Butes at Cardiff, the Norfolks and Fitzwilliams in Sheffield, the Derbys, Seftons and Salisburys in Liverpool all followed suit.[61] Already, too, in the early decades of the century, enterprising landowners, men like Lord Radnor at Folkestone and Sir Lawrence Palk at Torquay,[62] took their first, faltering steps in the process of resort creation. Indeed, by the middle decades of the nineteenth century, aristocratic involvement in seaside towns had become commonplace, with the Tapps-Gervises at Bournemouth, the Devonshires at Eastbourne, the Scarisbricks and Heskeths at Southport and the Mostyns at Llandudno following enthusiastically where the pioneers had led.

If the century from the 1770s saw the aristocracy at their most involved in the urbanization process, the years which followed brought the added comforts of income and prestige. However uncertain urban estate development might be in its initial stages, and however long the process of letting out all the plots might take, by the last quarter of the nineteenth century the well-secured income derived from such sources buttressed many an aristocratic rent roll. Indeed, as early as 1804, W. H. Marshall had noted how 'if an estate verged on a populous town, building sites, garden grounds and paddocks may enhance its value', and by the end of the century, this prediction had been spectacularly vindicated.[63] The Westminsters' legendary riches were almost wholly derived from those precious acres in Pimlico, Belgravia and Mayfair, which had come to them as the result of a fortunate marriage and which were, by 1914, the most expensive and fabulous real estate in the world. No less significant were the Bedfords' London rentals. For, as the tenth duke put it towards the close of the nineteenth century, the losses he incurred on his agricultural estates were only made bearable because he owned 'some lodging houses in Bloomsbury'. The Portlands, Portmans and Cadogans would have understood exactly what he meant. In the provinces, too, many landed families whose acres were not particularly broad, but which happened to be advantageously located, shared in this urban bonanza, such as the Ramsdens in Huddersfield, the Derbys in several towns in Lancashire, the Palks at Torquay and the Radnors at Folkestone. Not surprisingly, from the 1880s, radical opinion began to harden against the massive 'unearned increment' which accrued to these families when the original 99-year leases began to fall in and new higher rentals were fixed. But it was only in 1909, with Lloyd George's 'People's Budget', that such gains were actually taxed for the first time. The aristocracy squawked as never before, emphatic proof that they had been hit on a tender and lucrative spot.

Although the years from the 1880s saw increased hostility in some quarters, they also provided evidence of a very different urban attitude. In a book published in 1897 entitled *Social Transformations of the Victorian Age*, T. H. S. Escott drew attention to 'the civic association of the titular aristocracy with the new democracy of England', by which he meant the novel but increasingly

prevalent custom whereby town councils – often immediately after incorporation – invited the most prominent local landowner to become mayor.[64] As
table 1 shows, the abruptness with which this trend began is remarkable. Before

Table 1. Aristocratic mayors of English provincial towns, 1880–1969

Decade	Number
1880–9	0
1890–9	18
1900–9	14
1910–19	12
1920–9	8
1930–9	15
1940–9	7
1950–9	4
1960–9	3
Total	81

Source: *Whitaker's Almanack*, 1880–1969.
Note: An aristocrat is defined as a hereditary peer or close relative (wife, child, sibling, niece, nephew).

1890 there had been no aristocratic mayor of a major provincial town for over a
century, and even smaller communities could boast few since the passing of the
Municipal Corporations Act. However, in the 1890s and the decades which
followed, towns of all sizes welcomed blue-blooded first citizens. At one
extreme were those small country towns, 'the Banburys of England', where
the parliamentary dominance of a local landowning family often survived the
Second Reform Act, and where the habit of deference might therefore be
expected to die hard. Indeed, all those marked with an asterisk in table 2
are to be found on Professor Gash's list of proprietary boroughs and, with the
exception of Arundel, all were still in existence in the later period examined by
Professor Hanham.[65] For the rest, the aristocratic mayors were without exception important local landowning or political figures, or both. At Durham, for
example, the Earl of Durham (fig. 1) and Marquess of Londonderry were not
only mayors but also chancellors of the local university, as was the Duke of
Northumberland, the other major landowner in the neighbourhood.[66] At the
other extreme, London itself affords similar examples. Lord Rosebery was the
first chairman of the London County Council and when, a decade later, Lord
Salisbury sought to clip the council's wings by elevating the old vestries to
positions of competing power, the ninth duke of Bedford became the first
mayor of Holborn, the fifteenth duke of Norfolk the first mayor of Westminster, and the fifth Earl Cadogan the first mayor of Chelsea – a position also
filled by his grandson, the seventh earl, as late as 1964.

The reasons for this sudden proliferation of aristocratic mayors remain
something of a mystery. For many small towns such as Whitehaven in

Table 2. Aristocratic mayors of small English provincial towns, 1890–1969

Town	Family	Terms as mayor (1)	(2)	(3)	(4)	(5)
*Altrincham	Stamford	1938				
Appleby	Hothfield	1896	1938–46			
*Arundel	Norfolk	1903	1936			
Aylesbury	Courtown	1928				
Buckingham	Addington	1933–4	1944–6	1952		
Burton-on-Trent	Anglesey	1912				
Buxton	Devonshire	1921	1952–3			
Chesterfield	Devonshire	1912				
Chipping Norton	Brassey	1899–1902				
Durham	Durham	1900				
	Londonderry	1911	1937			
Grantham	Brownlow	1910	1925	1935		
Honiton	Devon	1930–3				
*Huntingdon	Sandwich	1897–8				
Kings Lynn	Fermoy	1932				
	Townshend	1929				
Monmouth	Llangattock	1897–8	1907–8			
*Peterborough	Fitzwilliam	1901				
*Richmond	Zetland	1896–7				
*Ripon	Ripon	1896				
Romsey	Shaftesbury	1899–1903				
Salisbury	Burnham	1928				
*Stamford	Exeter	1910	1962			
Thetford	Fisher	1963–4				
*Warwick	Warwick	1895–6	1902	1916	1930–1	1952
Watford	Clarendon	1923				
*Wenlock	Forester	1899–1900	1910	1922	1937	1962
*Whitehaven	Lonsdale	1895–6				
*Wilton	Pembroke	1900	1933–4	1934–6		
*Woodstock	Marlborough	1908–9	1938–42	1947–53		
Worcester	Beauchamp	1896				
	Coventry	1930				

Source: *Whitaker's Almanack*, 1890–1969.

Note: A mayor's term of office includes parts of two calendar years, beginning in November until 1948, and from May since 1949. To avoid confusion, this and the two following tables record the single year as reported in *Whitaker's*. A succession of years accordingly indicates more than one term of office. Where such long-term mayoralties overlap two decades, they were counted twice in table 1.

* indicates inclusion in the list of proprietary boroughs given in N. Gash, *Politics in the Age of Peel: a study in the technique of parliamentary representation* (1953).

Fig. 1. The third earl of Durham as mayor of Durham, 1900 (by courtesy of the Sheldon Press).

Cumberland, incorporation was supposed to have removed aristocratic influence after a long and painful battle against powerful, predatory families like the earls of Lonsdale.[67] So it seems all the more curious that many such towns should celebrate their freedom by voluntarily submitting once more to those very families whose influence they had sought to escape. Perhaps it was because the aristocracy by then was so weak that it no longer represented a real threat as it once had. Or perhaps it was because, even among town councils of an ostensibly radical hue, love of rank and title remained. Either way, such municipal obsequiousness enabled the aristocracy to enjoy a further innings of pomp and prestige, as the old world was called in to redress the balance of the new.

4

In the same way that the aristocracy's relationship with the towns was ambiguous, changing and multi-faceted, so a similar picture emerges when the problem is examined from the other side. Just as the landowning classes had no collective, corporate attitude towards the towns, so the ever-expanding urban population had no single telescope through which it viewed the aristocracy. Categories like 'urban', 'middle class' and 'working class', and all-embracing, mutually-exclusive descriptions of behaviour, like 'conflict' or 'collaboration', almost invariably break down on closer inspection, leaving in their place an over-riding impression of irritating vagueness and fluidity.

Part of the reason for this is that, for a longer period than is sometimes recognized, *urban* England was preponderantly *Trollopian* England. The sudden, shocking, strident growth of Leeds, Birmingham and Manchester may have staggered Vaughan and his contemporaries, but it is important to remember that in 1851 – the year in which half of England's population was for the first time declared officially urban – a town like York was still a more representative example of urban England than a town like Liverpool.[68] And with this world of the cathedral close, the assembly rooms and the local races, in towns like Exeter and Lincoln, the local gentry enjoyed as close and 'amphibious' a relationship as did their more wealthy cousins with the great metropolis itself. Local loyalties were strong, intimate and hierarchical. Such industry as there was remained small-scale. Class consciousness was localized and ephemeral. Even in the last decades of the nineteenth century, when its heyday was past, this particular element of the urban world remained an appendage rather than a threat to aristocratic, landed England.[69] Not surprisingly, it was these towns which elected aristocratic mayors in the greatest numbers and over the longest period of time.

Moreover, even the inhabitants of the great industrial towns were less isolated from the countryside and the values which prevailed there than is sometimes assumed: a preponderantly urban population with no first-hand experience of rural life is a relatively recent development in this country. Nineteenth-century working-class family networks straddled the rural-urban divide, making them as 'amphibious' as the aristocracy, albeit in a different way. Towns such as Preston in 1851 contained a high proportion of working-class inhabitants born in the countryside. Under these circumstances, it is hardly surprising that hostility to factory discipline, and the survival of practices such as 'St Monday' should be a constant feature of nineteenth-century industrial life.[70] Even as late as the 1900s, domestic servants, who by then formed the largest single occupational category, were chiefly recruited from the countryside.[71] And, however much Vaughan and his contemporaries may have been staggered by the spread of urban sprawl compared with what had gone before, until the closing decades of the nineteenth century at least, the actual physical extent of cities remained relatively limited, so that the countryside was never far away.[72]

Perhaps this in part explains why, for the nineteenth and the twentieth centuries, the landed aristocracy has been a source of irresistible fascination to many members of the urban working class. All too often, working-class history and working-class consciousness are implicitly equated with *radical* political activity. But, as Geoffrey Best reminds us, that ignores the 'flag-saluting, foreigner-hating, *peer-respecting*' (my italics) side of working-class culture, in which the landed aristocracy loomed large: the embodiment of all that was most fabulous, splendid and *heroic*, living their lives at a level of intensity and grandeur denied to ordinary, lesser mortals.[73] 'In their day', notes W. L. Burn, 'they shone with the radiance of the television "star" in ours' – Hollywood figures half a century before the big screen had been invented.[74] The very real popularity, among the urban working classes, of men like the first duke of Westminster ('He could pass from the racecourse to the chair at a missionary meeting without incurring the censure of the strictest') and the seventeenth earl of Derby ('Racing is my greatest amusement'), derived from the fact that their grand, genial lives *fulfilled* rather than affronted popular expectations as to how the aristocracy should behave.[75]

Such attitudes were pandered to and exploited by those late-Victorian creators of plebeian suburbia, with their 'monotonous but purposeful recital of Debrett – Burlington, Montague, Addington, Melbourne, Devonshire, Bradford' – in the street names which attracted the socially ambitious to whom the aristocracy was Mecca.[76] But beyond that, the occasional glimpse of a grandee passing by in procession was all they could hope for. For the middle classes, however, the Industrial Revolution greatly increased the opportunities for material success, thereby opening up new and unprecedented possibilities for social emulation. Ever since Tudor times, those who acquired money in large amounts had sought to convert it into land, and the Industrial Revolution, while opening up new avenues for making money, in no sense fundamentally altered that objective. Families like the Peels, Arkwrights, Gladstones and Overstones bought their way into land on an epic scale, as if determined to support Coleridge's belief that 'To found a family and to convert his wealth into land are twin thoughts in the mind of an opulent merchant, when he thinks of reposing from his labours.'[77] For if one platitude of English social history is that 'gentility is nothing but ancient riches', another is that, for all the entrepreneurial buoyancy of nineteenth-century England, it conspicuously failed to evolve a correspondingly autonomous, urban-based, entrepreneurial culture in successful opposition to the aristocratic.[78] The ultimate proof of success in business was the ability to leave it. The middle classes were more taken in by the aristocracy's public hostility to trade than they were themselves. As a result, many became – albeit in a different way – as 'amphibious' as their betters.

Of course, the solid splendours of Hawarden or Drayton were only open to the greatest and most wealthy entrepreneurs. Those who were less successful had to content themselves with emulation on a less extravagant, but no less important, scale. The suburban villa, with its coach house and large garden, creating the 'illusion of *rus in urbe*', was merely a replica of the country house, 'democratised and rendered accessible to a large part of the nation'.[79] In the same way, the two or three domestics who were the necessary pre-condition for being considered respectable, were but a scaled-down version of the retinues of specialized servants to be found in the great country houses.[80] And the middle classes' growing liking for fox-hunting, racing and cricket – all in origin aristocratic pursuits – demonstrated that even in the realms of recreation, the aristocracy's cultural predominance was unbroken.[81] However much the urban bourgeoisie acquired their wealth from the 'modern' sectors of the economy, they spent it anachronistically.[82] For what other purpose did nonconformist businessmen send their sons to public school and Oxbridge, unless it was to convert them into gentlemen, proconsuls and bishops?[83]

So, while urban middle-class politics were on occasions anti-aristocratic, they took place in a cultural nexus where the aristocracy remained supreme. Even Joseph Chamberlain, for all his attacks on the landed classes, bought a large, well-servanted house outside Birmingham, and sent his sons to public school. And in any case, exactly how class-conscious *were* the urban middle classes? Recent research increasingly suggests that they were no more monolithic than the landowners: to see them in any other way is merely to accept the rhetoric of successive urban, radical movements at their own self-evaluation. As Derek Fraser has shown, issues such as parliamentary and municipal reform and the repeal of the Corn Laws were bitterly and fiercely fought over by middle-class figures, even in Birmingham and Manchester.[84] Like the landowners, the middle classes saw these questions in party terms: they identified more closely with the aristocratic leadership on the same side than with their middle-class colleagues on the other. So, like the landowners, the middle classes were united as a class in some ways, but divided in others.[85] A bourgeois, nonconformist businessman might feel bound to his fellow entrepreneurs by civic pride and religious loyalty one day, and then defer to aristocratic leadership in matters of party politics the next. Yesterday's radical businessman became today's deferential voter.

Indeed, it seems clear that in certain factory towns during the later decades of the nineteenth century, party politics was in practice but an extension of rivalry between different factories and employees, just as in the countryside, they had earlier resembled battles between different estates and landowning families. Workers voted Tory or Whig, not out of any feeling of class solidarity, but out of respect for the political opinions of their employers. 'At a contested election in a Lancashire borough', noted W. A. Abrams, 'one may see the entire body of workers at two rival factories pitted against each other.'[86] Nor did the affinity with the rural estate end here, for displays of employer paternalism – a celebration of the coming of age of a son, treats and feasts at Christmas, the provision of houses and churches and chapels – were also strong. Not surprisingly, under these circumstances, it became fashionable for employers to represent the town in which their works were located, in the same way that landlords represented those county constituencies in which their estates were to be found: the Pilkingtons and Hornbys in Blackburn, Harland and Wolff in Belfast, and Brunner and Mond for Cheshire constituencies.[87] In a very real sense, such partisan and paternal activity embodied the ethos of the rural elite transferred to an urban setting.

5

These, then, are some of the paradoxes, ambiguities and contradictions in a nation preponderantly urban but obsessively rustic,[88] revelling in competition yet admiring hierarchy, winning democracy while buttressing aristocracy. In every sense, the aristocracy and the towns in the nineteenth century enjoyed a love-hate relationship.[89] One element in this was the survival of a landed establishment, which was both the beneficiary and victim of urban growth, a declining agrarian elite which survived as the ruling class in an industrial, urban, property-owning democracy. The other was an evolving urban society, both energetic and successful in its assaults on landed dominance, yet at the same time diffident and divided in its attitude towards the patricians. How else, indeed, can be explained the curious evolution of a country at once the first industrial nation and earliest urban society, yet also the last in western Europe to possess a legislature one-half of which is still preponderantly composed of those who sit there by hereditary right?

The two case studies with which this book is primarily concerned illustrate in detail many of these general themes. The first examines the Calthorpe family and their development of Edgbaston, Birmingham's most exclusive suburb. It shows how a relatively poor and insignificant landed family achieved aristocratic fulfilment largely on the basis of urban revenue, only to incur criticism from those very Birmingham politicans who in fact constituted their most illustrious tenants. Yet, by their suburban life-style and frequent displays of civic obsequiousness, these middle-class people themselves displayed an attitude to the aristocracy which was as ambivalent as the Calthorpes' position in Birmingham was ambiguous.

The second case study concerns the creation of Eastbourne by the dukes of Devonshire: a smaller, less radical town, and a greater, more powerful family.

Again, though, contradictions and paradoxes abound. On the one hand, the middle-class inhabitants emulated the aristocracy in their desire for social segregation and in their leisure pursuits, and collaborated entrepreneurially in the creation of the town. But, as the corporation's strength and financial resources grew, the Devonshires were gradually ousted from their previously paramount position. Nevertheless, they were able to console themselves with the agreeable palliatives of increased income and exalted social position: what they lost on the roundabouts of power they gained on the swings of status.

Between them, these examples – the 'Belgravia of Birmingham' and the 'Empress of Watering Places' – provide two classic instances of aristocratic involvement with urban growth at its most famous and best documented: but first, in order to lessen the steep descent from general themes to local detail, it is important to establish a more specific chronology and precise sense of place.

2 The great provincial towns: confrontation and compromise

The most specific point of contact between the old, agrarian elite and the new urban society took place in those large provincial towns to which the aristocracy were linked by economic interest. Some drew rentals from building estates on top of the land; others enjoyed mineral royalties from beneath. They lived off the land while the town dwellers lived on it or worked below it. In the first category were the Calthorpes in Birmingham, the Derbys in Liverpool, Bury and Bootle, the Donegalls in Belfast, the Ramsdens in Huddersfield, the Seftons and Salisburys in Liverpool, the Norfolks and Fitzwilliams in Sheffield, and the Butes in Cardiff. In the second came the Sutherlands in the Potteries, the Hathertons, Dudleys and Dartmouths in the Black Country and – once more – the Butes in Glamorganshire. In these districts, contact between the aristocracy and the towns was highly personalized. The landowners necessarily formed their views of the threats and promises of urban society on the basis of their own local experience. And for the town dwellers, the aristocracy was not some vague, distant abstraction, but was personified by the local landlord or employer. For economic contact necessarily led to political and social interaction. This chapter seeks to examine that encounter, first by looking at individual families, and then by drawing out some general themes.

1

Of all the great provincial towns with which the aristocracy was connected, pride of place must go to Cardiff, which was almost entirely the creation of the Butes. During the first half of the nineteenth century, the second marquess, 'in a manner of speaking the ruling monarch of the town', exercised supreme control over local government and parliamentary selection, dominated local philanthropy and the bench, and initiated the town's expansion by his decision, in 1828–34, to build the docks.[1] But his death in 1848, which left administration in the hands of absent and unloved trustees, combined with a growth in civic wealth, power and confidence, gradually undermined the family's position, so that by the time the third marquess came of age in 1868, their old dominance was gone. Yet even so, he too left an indelible mark, partly because he was 'the town's most distinguished resident', partly because of the extravagance and gusto with which he and William Burgess re-built and restored Cardiff castle, and partly because, in 1890, he agreed to serve as mayor. Even as late as the 1930s the family still owned half of the land on which Cardiff stood, a fact which more than anything explains the continuing and vociferous Welsh antipathy to urban leaseholds after the First World War.[2]

A similar picture emerges of aristocratic involvement in Belfast, another great urban creation of the nineteenth century and Celtic capital of the twentieth. There, during the early decades of the nineteenth century, the second marquess of Donegall was the dominant figure – resident, lord of the Castle, major philanthropist, and undisputed arbiter of local and parliamentary affairs.[3] However, unlike the Butes, severe financial embarrassment curtailed the family's activities, and obliged them to sell off, or lease out on 999-year terms, most of their Belfast estate in the 1820s and 1830s.[4] The reform of national and local representation in 1832 and 1842 further weakened their position: one member of the family was unseated by petition after the 1837 election, and another was defeated outright in 1841. After the death of the third marquess in 1883, the remaining Belfast estates passed, via his daughter, to the ninth earl of Shaftesbury, who went some way to restoring the family's position in the town. He re-occupied and re-opened Belfast Castle as a centre of local society, served as president or patron of many local charities, was lieutenant (1903–11) and then lord mayor (1907) of Belfast, and the first chancellor (1909–23) of the reformed Queen's University.[5]

Only in Huddersfield, among English towns, was there an example of one family in such a position of preponderant territorial power – in this case the Ramsdens, Yorkshire gentry and baronets. The building of the Ramsden Canal had been their doing in the 1770s, and again in the 1840s they profoundly influenced the town's development by bringing in the railway and re-building the area adjacent to the station.[6] Moreover, local government remained almost entirely in their hands until the passing of the Huddersfield Improvement Act in 1848. Indeed, the creation of the Huddersfield parliamentary constituency 16 years before had actually served to increase their power, giving them what amounted initially to a nomination borough where previously there had been none. Even if not 'coming quite into the category of proprietary boroughs', notes Norman Gash, 'Huddersfield in the 1830s was sufficiently under the control of the Whig Sir John Ramsden to defy the efforts of Radicals and Tories to capture the seat'.[7] Indeed, as late as the 1880s, the family still counted for something in local politics. And even if there was no Ramsden mayor at the close of the century, they were still in demand to lend dignity to civic events such as the laying of the cornerstone of the Jubilee Tower in 1898 (fig. 2).[8]

In no other English town was the dominance of one single family so great: individual owners were weaker, or influence was shared between several families. Liverpool provides the best example of this second alternative. For, in addition to the corporation, which was itself a large landowner within the city, the earls of Derby and Sefton and the marquesses of Salisbury had large holdings.[9] Certainly, the Derbys and Seftons were extensively involved – both politically and financially – in the affairs of the Liverpool & Manchester

Railway in the 1830s, and there were constant references among local politicians to the influence exerted by the fourteenth earl of Derby in the town in the 1850s.[10] His younger son, the sixteenth earl, was mayor of Preston, lord mayor of Liverpool, and chancellor of the town's new university. 'His Lordship', observed one local paper on his death in 1908:

> had been so closely linked with the city and its multifarious aspirations – civic, commercial and philanthropic – that it became almost a custom to look to him, if not for actual initiation of important movements, at least for hearty co-operation and, in some instances perhaps, for direction.[11]

Not to be outdone, his successor the seventeenth earl, 'king' of Lancashire, served as lord mayor of Liverpool, chancellor of the university, president of the Liverpool Chamber of Commerce and, on his death in 1948, was mourned as 'the grand old man of Merseyside'.[12]

Fig. 2. The laying of the cornerstone of the Victoria Jubilee Tower, Huddersfield, June 1898. Sir John William Ramsden is at front row, centre, with his son directly behind him, and with the mayor on his left (by courtesy of Advertiser Press Ltd).

Across the Pennines in Sheffield, the Fitzwilliam and Norfolk families were equally involved in local affairs. From the 1800s until the 1830s, there was close collaboration between the relatively radical Lord Milton, son of the fourth Earl Fitzwilliam, and the manufacturing classes of the town, on whose behalf he presented petitions in Parliament and championed causes such as parliamentary reform and the repeal of the Corn Laws.[13] But then in the 1840s, the townsmen and the family clashed over control of the local West Riding Whig party organization and, although they made peace in the 1850s, the Fitzwilliams were never again as dominant.[14] Thereafter, they took less interest in local politics and turned to the development of their Eccleshall estate on the outskirts of the town.[15] Later the sixth earl became renowned as a local philanthropist, and in 1910 his successor was lord mayor.

However, by then the Fitzwilliams had yielded first place to the Norfolks as a node of reverential politics in the town. During the first half of the century they had kept a relatively low public and political profile, concentrating their endeavours on the creation of nearby Glossop and the development of part of their Sheffield building estate.[16] But during the time of the fifteenth duke, who held the title from 1860 to 1917, they became much more publicly involved in the affairs of the town. Indeed, in his anachronistic splendour he was closely akin to his relative the third marquess of Bute: a Roman Catholic, an extravagant builder of churches and castles, and a great philanthropist. He was closely connected with Sheffield's celebrations of Victoria's Diamond Jubilee, persuaded the queen to open its new town hall, and served as mayor and then lord mayor in 1896–7. He was also the first freeman of the city and, like his colleagues in Liverpool and Belfast, became chancellor of the local university.[17]

No less important were the dukes of Sutherland, whose relations with that clutch of unlovely towns known as the Potteries fluctuated violently during the course of the nineteenth century. For the first two decades, they were a major political power, controlling the local county seat and the boroughs of Newcastle-under-Lyme and Lichfield, as well as being an important and direct employer of labour in their mines and iron works. However, growing hostility towards the 'Trentham interest' caused them to abdicate both their political and entrepreneurial roles during the 1820s, and never again did they interfere energetically in local party politics.[18] But the rebuilding of Trentham by the second duke in the late 1840s, on a scale of unprecedented magnificence, was hardly the conduct of a family bent on withdrawal, and their presence in the Potteries remained important until the closure and demolition of Trentham in 1911. In Longton, the success of the waterworks in the middle of the century owed much to their participation and support, and in the 1890s, the fourth duke was not only mayor of that town, but also an important figure behind the scenes in the moves for confederation.[19] Even more well known was his wife, 'Meddlesome Millicent', who had opened her first bazaar at the age of six in Newcastle-under-Lyme, and never stopped thereafter. With her 'exhaustless passion for philanthropy, bazaars and platforms' and her active concern for those suffering from industrial diseases, she found herself gloriously but affectionately parodied as 'Interfering Iris, Countess of Chell', in Arnold Bennett's *The Card*.[20]

Although there was no single magnate of comparable stature to the 'Leviathan of Wealth' in the southern half of Staffordshire, aristocratic involvement in the towns of the Black Country was extensive. In Dudley itself, the influence of the titular family, both as politicians and philanthropists, remained strong: criticism of 'the castle influence' was still voiced in the 1840s and 1850s.[21] In subsequent decades they gave money extensively for churches, schools and hospitals; in the 1890s, both the second earl of Dudley and his agent were mayors of the town; and the earl became the borough's first freeman in 1899.[22] In West Bromwich, where the earls of Dartmouth were the foremost local family, a similar picture emerges. In the 1830s and 1840s, they were vigorous – if not always successful – opponents of reform. By the 1880s they enjoyed the relative serenity and security of being philanthropists and figure-heads. The fifth earl presented the borough with its mayoral chain, and his portrait was placed in the council chamber. Even in the years prior to the First World War, they were still conspicuous in West Midland Conservative and Unionist circles.[23]

By contrast, the Calthorpes in Birmingham were never a major political force in the town, even if their ownership of the Edgbaston estate made them the largest landowners there. Although prosperous as a result of Edgbaston's development, they were probably the poorest family to be described here: certainly not in the same league as super-powers like the Butes or Sutherlands. Nor were they august grandees of ancient lineage, who had been in and out of cabinets and governments for generations, like the Fitzwilliams or the Derbys. This, combined with their absenteeism, the size of Birmingham and the vigour of its middle-class politics, meant that their impact on the town's affairs was necessarily muted. Before the Great Reform Act, they were important – but never dominant – as philanthropists, collaborators and intermediaries, presenting petitions at Westminster and adorning and supporting local charities. Thereafter their social leadership and patronage remained significant and appreciated in some local voluntary societies, but was never indispensable. And in the 1870s and 1880s, even this limited position was largely eroded by the energetic and anti-aristocratic endeavours of Joseph Chamberlain and his colleagues. Only with gifts of land to the new university in 1900 and 1907 did they re-emerge as local worthies of note and public figures of minor interest.

Finally, there is a twentieth-century transatlantic joker in this patrician, nineteenth-century and very British pack. The Astors were American plutocrats, English newspaper proprietors, and the recipients of a peerage from Lloyd George. Yet their link with Plymouth between the wars was reminiscent of more traditional and venerable modes of aristocratic involvement with the great provincial towns. Waldorf became M.P. for Plymouth in 1910 and continued to serve in that capacity until he succeeded as second Viscount Astor in 1921. He was then followed by his wife, the redoubtable Nancy, who held the seat until 1945. Waldorf was made a freeman in 1936, was lord mayor from 1939–44, and Nancy herself became a freeman in 1959.[24] Indeed, it was not until the late 1950s that the family's political involvement with the town came to an end. Although they only owned a single house in the city for most of the time they were connected with it, these transatlantic patricians forged links with Plymouth which place them firmly in an older – and now defunct – tradition.

The best summary of the families and towns thus described remains that of Asa Briggs:

> In the provincial cities, the owners of protected estates like the Calthorpe Estate, which owned and managed Edgbaston in Birmingham, had a strategic influence on the whole development of the city. The owners of such estates, served by solicitors, and themselves serving as patrons of urban parishes, governors of grammar schools, and presidents of charitable associations, often provided the backbone of a 'conservative' interest in cities whose flavour was essentially radical.[25]

In the light of the evidence available, it is possible to suggest a tentative chronology of such involvement, with the important proviso that the exact phases varied, depending as they did both on the size and nature of the town on the one hand, and the wealth, energy and interests of individual members of the particular aristocratic family on the other. With this reservation in mind, it is possible to distinguish six consecutive phases of development. The first, lasting until the 1820s in some instances, and the 1840s in others, was a period of aristocratic dominance, collaboration and importance never to be equalled again. Then, from the 1820s to the 1840s came a time of crisis and confrontation, after which several of the families withdrew residentially from the towns with which they were connected. In the light of this the third period, lasting from the 1840s to the early 1870s, was a phase of remarkable calm, compromise, balance and mutual admiration, abruptly terminated in many instances by outbursts of controversy and criticism which continued intermittently through the 1880s. But then, once more, peace was made, and a phase of ceremonial importance and social prestige ensued which lasted until the First World War and beyond. Only in the inter-war years, and more dramatically after 1945, did the extensive sales by the aristocracy of their urban estates bring this final period to a close.

The first phase was characterized by extensive aristocratic involvement, either in the form of direct control or of collaboration and influence. At one extreme – as in Cardiff or Belfast – towns expanded spectacularly, but within a framework of outdated administrative machinery, which left the lord of the manor in a powerful position regarding both local and parliamentary affairs. Every M.P. for Cardiff was a Bute nominee, and representation at Westminster of Belfast was constantly in the hands of one member or another of the Donegall family.[26] At the other end of the spectrum, men like the future fifth Earl Fitzwilliam and the third Lord Calthorpe occupied an important place in Sheffield and Birmingham, not as all-powerful lords of the manor, but as intermediaries prepared to convey middle-class, urban opinion to Westminster in the absence of more direct representation. At some mid-point were the Leverson-Gowers in Newcastle-under-Lyme and the Mosleys at

Manchester: lords of the manor, but already beginning to feel the chill blast of middle- and working-class hostility.

From the 1820s, these winds blew with increased vigour and intensity. The reform of Parliament and of local government, the incorporation of some large towns for the first time, and the urban-based, anti-aristocratic rhetoric of the Anti-Corn Law League all betokened a hostile general climate. 'The battle of the day', noted Cobden, 'is still against the aristocracy . . . In a word, *Incorporate Your Borough.*'[27] More specifically, in towns where the aristocracy had maintained a territorial or residential presence, they became the focal point for protest and confrontation, from which they often withdrew into the comforting distance and relative isolation of the country. In the Potteries, fearful for the safety of Trentham, overwhelmed by the ferocity of the attacks on the 'Trentham Interest', and bruised by their spectacular electoral defeat in the North Staffordshire constituency in the 1820 general election, the Sutherlands abandoned both their entreprenurial and boroughmongering activities.[28] In Birmingham, the third Lord Calthorpe alienated much of his middle-class support by his hostility to the Reform Bill. In Belfast the Donegalls fell out with the townsmen over the harbour and water supply. And the Fitzwilliams were humiliatingly defeated by the strength of the West Riding townsmen in the election of 1848.[29] Not surprisingly, retreat was the order of the day. The Dudleys withdrew to Witley Court in 1839, because Himley, their old home, was too close to the Black Country for comfort. The Mosleys, vanquished by the citizens of Manchester, abandoned the town for Rolleston, over the horizon in Staffordshire. After the death of the second marquess of Bute in 1848, his successor was an infant, so the family ceased to appear in Cardiff castle. And the Dartmouths, following the Dudleys, abandoned their ancestral home at Sandwell, and bought Patshull Hall in 1847.[30]

Yet this retreat, however spectacular, was far from total: for the whole of the mid-Victorian period, helpfully but inadequately labelled a time of 'equipoise', 'boom' and 'deference', saw a *rapprochement* between the aristocracy and the towns, on the basis of mutual regard and esteem, which would have seemed quite unthinkable in the acrimonious days of the 1830s and early 1840s. With the repeal of the Corn Laws, the demise of Chartism, and the disintegration of the Free Trade in Land Campaign, Cobden was left to rant and rave alone against the iniquities of aristocratic privilege. 'We are a servile, aristocrat-loving race', he noted despondently in the 1860s; and he was right. When, for example, the second duke of Sutherland died in 1861, the whole of the Potteries was plunged into mourning. On the day of the funeral, blinds were drawn, shops closed, bells tolled in Stoke, Newcastle and Longton, and a huge crowd gathered to watch the funeral procession at Trentham. The local paper excelled itself in its eulogy of the great man:

> The charities of the Duke, both public and private, were very great, as he contributed liberally, but in the least ostentatious manner, not only to

local objects of a religious, educational or benevolent kind, but to most of those of a national character likewise . . . The Trentham family deservedly enjoy great popularity throughout the populous manufacturing district of North Staffordshire, the Duchess having long taken a deep interest in the beautiful manufactures of the Potteries and promoted their advancement . . . Another source of this good feeling towards the family arises from the Duke having always permitted the public to have free access to the healthful grounds of Trentham . . . We conclude these remarks by saying that the Duke's death will be sincerely and generally lamented; and mixed with that feeling will be the wish that his successor may inherit his virtues and faithfully discharge the duties which high position and great wealth throw upon their possessor.

How different were these sentiments from those which had prevailed 40 years before: then, the 'Trentham Interest' had been the incarnation of arbitrary power and aristocratic despotism. 'If a mob were to arise', one radical had threatened, 'in these parts, the first objective of it would be to destroy Lord Stafford's property.' Now, by contrast, the people of the Potteries stood, orderly, mournful and respectful, as the ducal coffin passed by.[31]

At times of celebration, too, entire towns joined in the family party. When Sir William Ramsden came of age in 1852, Huddersfield rejoiced. Fourteen years later, when the third marquess of Bute reached his majority, Cardiff gave itself over to a week of junketing. Banquets were held, memorials presented, benefactions given, and loyal toasts drunk. In 1872, the third marquess reappeared in even greater triumph, for he had his bride with him. Once more, the town was *en fête*. For three days the celebrations continued, each more extravagant than that which had gone before. On the last night, there was a firework display and a formal banquet at which a song, specially composed in the marquess's honour, was sung amid loud acclaim:

Let all be merry, all be glad
That they have wedded been!
The young but stalwart Stuart lad
To lovely Gwendoline.

A hearty welcome let us give
The Marquess and his queen.
And let us pray that long may live
Lord Bute and Gwendoline.[32]

More generally, even in towns with no large aristocratic landowner, the patronage of a grandee or two was the almost indispensable prerequisite for the successful launching and maintenance of any middle-class charitable association or voluntary society.[33] A peer like the seventh duke of Devonshire, for example, who was neither a public figure of the first rank, nor an orator of

Periclean accomplishment, could flit from one urban engagement to another: a *conversazione* at Sheffield in 1863 to promote the local School of Practical Science, a procession at Leeds in 1868 after which the Prince of Wales opened the Art Treasures Exhibition, and a ceremony at Manchester in 1873, when the duke himself opened the new buildings of Owens College.[34] Not surprisingly, when in 1857 the Duke of Norfolk visited Sheffield, he was assured by the mayor on behalf of the townspeople that he could expect to find 'amongst them all, the respectful attachment which was due from them to those occupying His Grace's exalted rank'.[35] Indeed, the *Spectator*, taking up a remark of Gladstone's, went even further and suggested that, if the duke had been a Protestant, he would make the strongest Conservative candidate for the town.[36]

In this regard, the Norfolks were unusual, for one important element in this mid-Victorian *rapprochement* between the aristocracy and the great industrial towns, apart from a love of rank and title which transcended politics, was a shared and partisan commitment to some form of Whiggism or Liberalism. This was not universally the case. Besides the Norfolks, the Derbys in Liverpool were normally Tory as of course were many townsmen. Elsewhere, though, the local grandee tended to take up a political position sufficiently to the left of centre to be acceptable to towns of a generally Liberal hue. This was so in the case of the Calthorpes in Birmingham, where the fourth lord was a Palmerstonian, and whose son and heir voted for the abolition of church rate and extension of the franchise while he was an M.P. It was also true of the Ramsdens in Huddersfield, the Sutherlands in the Potteries, of Lord Dudley, who abandoned Toryism between 1845–7, and of the Fitzwilliams in Sheffield. Even in Cardiff, where the Bute trustees continued the second marquess's policy of stern and unwavering Toryism, the family was not entirely beyond the pale in a Liberal town because, in open hostility to his relatives, James Crichton-Stuart, nephew of the second marquess, served as the town's Liberal M.P. from 1857 to 1880. In this way, in many towns where the aristocracy were important landowners, shared party political loyalties combined with abiding social prestige to enhance their position.

This honeymoon, however, only endured for a generation. From the late 1860s, and with growing stridency in the 1870s, 'a new variety of rude noises began to make themselves heard in Birmingham', which ushered in two further decades of hostility and conflict.[37] Again, as in the 1830s, and early 1840s, the general climate of opinion was anti-aristocratic: the Third Reform Act, Home Rule, the establishment of the county councils, the Settled Land Act, the campaign for leasehold enfranchisement, the Select Committee on Town Holdings, and the Royal Commission on the Housing of the Working Classes, to say nothing of the more general worry engendered by the agricultural depression. For the first time, the actual management of the great urban estates, both metropolitan and provincial, was exposed to close public scrutiny. Again and again, agents from the Northampton Estate in Clerkenwell, the Norfolk Estates in Sheffield and the Derby Estates in Bury, appeared before the committees, in attempts to contradict the latest disagreeable story which locals had reported. At Bury, the town council passed a unanimous resolution against the leasehold system, and in Sheffield the opposition to the Norfolks' management of their estates was led by the mayor.[38] Elsewhere the scene was little better. In the late 1860s and early 1870s, the Duke of Sutherland was locked in a protracted legal battle in which he sought an injunction to restrain the corporations of Newcastle and Burslem from allowing their sewage to pollute the grounds of Trentham, and at the same time, Lord Norton, owner of Saltley, was in similar conflict with the Birmingham Corporation. As A. J. Mundella put it, specifically apropos of the issue of sewerage, 'the number of landlords who have some grudge against, or litigation pending with, boroughs is really surprising, and *they hate them*'.[39]

More alarming still was the fashion of big-spending, self-confident, financially expert town councils which was ushered in by Joseph Chamberlain's Birmingham mayoralty from 1873–6. Thereafter, many town councils, hitherto timid and miserly, now began to cast covetous, acquisitive eyes on docks or markets or water companies or manorial rights still owned by aristocrats. In addition, newly confident of the intrinsic importance of civic government, their reliance on the old order to give antique legitimation to their municipal endeavours markedly lessened. In Birmingham itself, matters came to a head in the general election of 1880 when, although the Conservatives did unusually well, the defeat of Augustus Calthorpe at the hands of Chamberlain himself was a bitter humiliation for the family. Elsewhere, confrontation increased. In 1876, the Huddersfield Corporation bought out the Ramsdens' market rights, and the Sheffield Corporation tried a similar move – albeit unsuccessful – against the Duke of Norfolk. In 1880–1, Cardiff Corporation, which had once been the second marquess of Bute's to command, tried to take over the docks from his successor, and in Bury, the council, after a titanic struggle with Lord Derby, finally secured an Improvement Act which enabled them to buy out the water works, which Derby owned.[40] In one way and another, it was all very alarming.

3

Once more, however, the battle between the aristocracy and the towns was not to be fought to the death. Again, after two decades of crisis, confrontation and conflict, there took place another *rapprochement*, most eloquently illustrated in the proliferation of titled mayors and lord mayors of the great industrial towns. For, although the majority of aristocratic first citizens were to be found in those small towns which they had previously dominated as rotten boroughs, there were many examples in the great cities too, which understandably attracted more attention, as can be seen from table 3.

Table 3. Aristocratic mayors and lord mayors of industrial towns, 1890–1969

		Terms as mayor or lord mayor	
Town	Family	(1)	(2)
Belfast	Shaftesbury	1907	
Bolton	Leverhulme	1919	
Cardiff	Bute	1891	
	Windsor	1896	
Dudley	Dudley	1896–7	
Longton	Sutherland	1896	
Liverpool	Derby	1896	1912
	Sefton	1945	
Plymouth	Astor	1940–4	
Preston	Derby	1902	
Sheffield	Norfolk	1896–7	
	Fitzwilliam	1910	

Source: *Whitaker's Almanack*, 1890–1969.
Note: Neither Cardiff nor Belfast appears in table 1.

Indeed, if certain town councils had had their way, this list would have been even longer, for there were many cases where the requests of the local municipal body were declined. Swansea, for example, approached the Duke of Beaufort; Rotherham asked Earl Fitzwilliam; and Cardiff, not satisfied with two titled mayors, wanted Lord Tredegar, who had already refused an invitation from Newport.[41]

But the most important event here was the decision by the third marquess of Bute to accept the mayoralty of Cardiff in 1890, on the occasion of the visit of the British Association to the town – 'the first peer to hold the highest municipal office in any English or Welsh borough for several generations – certainly since the Reform Act'. In his case, as with the remainder, the territorial links will be obvious. Apart from the Butes, the Windsors were the other major landowners in Cardiff; Lord Leverhulme bought his way extensively into Cheshire and Lancashire after the time of Bateman; and the Astors' close political connections with Plymouth have already been mentioned. Equally revealing are the obvious omissions: Birmingham, where the Calthorpes' unquestioned landed importance was not reflected in the political balance in the town; Leeds, predominantly a freehold town, with no great aristocratic estate within its boundaries; and Manchester, where the combination of strong civic consciousness and 'highly fragmented units of ownership in the central area' again precluded extensive aristocratic participation in local affairs.[42]

While contemporaries were impressed by these 'fresh opportunities of public service offering themselves to the nobility', they were less sure why they had come about. Escott thought it represented 'the titular association of the great aristocracy with the new civic democracy of England'.[43] But, seen in the context of links between the grandees and the great industrial towns going back for a century, this was perhaps less remarkable than he thought. 'Association' there had always been. Why should it suddenly have taken this particular form at this precise moment? Considering that most of the towns listed here had been incorporated for at least 50 years, why did they wait until the end of the nineteenth century before offering their highest civic office to their most illustrious citizens?

At the most general level, it may be seen as an aptly novel expression of the new *rapprochement*. In social terms, England from the 1880s was increasingly a class-dominated society, with a growing working class and trades union movement on one side, and on the other a middle class ever more preoccupied with the defence of property, merging into a new plutocracy of big business and wealthy landowners.[44] The advent of aristocratic mayors, alternating as many of them did with local big businessmen, perfectly exemplifies this trend. And, at the level of party politics another, complementary explanation suggests itself: for while the previous *rapprochement* had frequently been on the basis of some shared Whig or Liberal assumptions, this new accommodation was increasingly rooted in a Conservative consensus. 'Villa Toryism' in the towns merged with 'country-house Toryism' among the grandees.[45] The Calthorpes, Fitzwilliams, Dudleys, Sutherlands and Ramsdens, all of whom had in an earlier generation been Whig or Liberal, now espoused or returned to Toryism, joining the Butes and the Derbys and the Norfolks in the process. For different reasons, the urban middle classes and the great landowners were, politically, moving in the same direction at the end of the nineteenth century. The proliferation of aristocratic mayors in the great industrial towns was just one indication that they had both arrived at a similar destination.

More specifically, this trend may be explained with direct reference to the evolution of local government itself. Despite the strident, radical, anti-aristocratic rhetoric of Chamberlain's municipal revolution, one of its more paradoxical effects in the long term was to encourage highly anachronistic displays of civic pride and grandeur. The purchase of gas and water companies was one side of the coin; the construction of a grand, baroque Council House, and the making of a wide boulevard deliberately named Corporation Street, was the other. Whereas the reformed but tight-fisted corporations of the 1840s had despised municipal glamour, the revived and extravagant councils at the close of the century regarded civic pomp, ritual and ceremonial as altogether appropriate to their new, exalted status. The period from the late 1880s to the First World War was the golden age of civic glamour – of concern with maces and regalia, coats of arms and robes for aldermen, of the construction of new grand civic buildings like the town halls in Cardiff and Belfast – which proclaimed to the world the greatness of the municipality.[46] As the radical cutting edge of local government became blunted, so its public image was increasingly presented in atavistic terms. Under these circumstances, what could be more fitting than to import the human embodiment of anachronism and tradition: the landed aristocracy themselves?

But there were other local reasons as well. Within a civic setting of such contrived and self-conscious grandeur, it was advantageous if the mayor could be a man of high social standing and glamorous reputation, able to carry off the ceremonial side of the job with dignity: and, since most mayors received little or no payment for their services, it was also important that he should be wealthy enough to entertain lavishly on behalf of the town, to give money freely to local charities, and to patronize the town's good causes. Not surprisingly, under these circumstances, many councillors were reluctant or unsuited to be mayor, and a council could be forced to seek an outsider. Local and prosperous businessmen, like Sir Charles Mander in Wolverhampton, could well meet the second of these criteria; but only the landed aristocracy could meet the first as well. For landlords with urban estates and mines were not only rich, they were still *heroic*. As Lawrence Lowell observed, a town council would ask a peer to become mayor, 'for the lustre of his title and with a view to hospitality at his castle'.[47] More than any local businessmen, titled mayors could provide glamour, sparkle, romance and security, personally embodying those attributes which the council wanted for itself. They donated maces and chains of office, brought their friends Victoria or Edward VII to dignify civic functions, provided feasts, banquets and balls of unimagined lavishness and splendour and then, at the end of it all, grandly donated their mayoral salary to charity. They behaved, as expected, *heroically*. Such a prospect was enough to set even the most hard-headed businessmen a-twitter, as Arnold Bennett noted in *The Card*:

> The Earl (of Chell), a mild, retiring man, when invited by the Town Council to be the ornamental Mayor of Bursley, accepted the invitation . . . The Mayor and Mayoress gave an immense afternoon reception to practically the entire roll of burgesses . . . A little later, the Mayoress let it be known that she meant to give a municipal ball. The news of the ball thrilled Bursley more than anything had thrilled Bursley since the signing of Magna Charta.

For, as he later explained, 'a municipal ball given by a titled mayor' was 'the most exciting event that can happen in any town'.[48]

All this is well illustrated by the junketings at Dudley in January 1899, to celebrate Lord Dudley's election as the first freeman of the borough.[49] The events of that day capture delightfully the rich amalgam of civic glamour, platitudinous oratory, sumptuous feasting, and smug self-congratulation which invariably characterized such proceedings. At the town hall, an enormous crowd of excited onlookers was assembled, and the mayor presented Dudley with a gold casket containing a scroll on which his name was inscribed. To tumultuous applause, he then replied:

It is impossible for me to express in adequate terms my appreciation of the
high honour which you have just bestowed on me. From the earliest days
of my life, down to the present time, I and my family have been the
constant recipients of the most generous and courteous favours at the
hands of the inhabitants of this town and its representatives. My birth,
the attainment of my majority and my marriage, in fact each step in the
ladder of life, has been made the occasion for a renewed expression of
neighbourly regard and good will, and now again today, when the experience of past years has increased and ripened our mutual acquaintance-
ship, you have crowned the long list of your previous favours by confer-
ring upon me the highest mark of honour and esteem which it is in your
power as burgesses to grant.

After the ceremony was over, a nine-course meal was enjoyed in the evening,
during which six toasts were drunk: the queen and royal family, the army,
navy and auxiliary forces, the Earl of Dudley, the mayor and corporation of
Dudley, our visitors, and the town and trade of Dudley. While the health of the
earl was drunk, the orchestra played 'For he's a jolly good fellow'. In replying,
the earl said he could not 'find words which would in any way express the
gratitude which I feel'. But this sudden onset of taciturnity was soon overcome, and his speech, in which he once again extolled 'the cordial and
harmonious relations which, I am happy to think, exist between the inhabitants of this district and myself', occupied nearly a whole column in the local
paper's report of the proceedings. Finally, as the orchestra played 'Auld lang
syne', this 'red letter day in our local history' came to a close. But the
comfortable feeling of self-congratulation was not yet ended for, the following
day, the local paper delivered its verdict on the proceedings:

> One of the most striking features of English life is the absence of that deep
> gulf which exists in many countries between the aristocracy and democ-
> racy. It is a most healthy sign when a nobleman like Lord Dudley, blessed
> with ample possessions, instead of living a life of mere selfish, luxurious
> isolation, comes down into the arena of common life and takes more than
> his full share of municipal work.

Although a Black Country occasion, this could have been Bute or Sutherland
or Norfolk or Fitzwilliam or Derby, in Cardiff, Longton, Sheffield or Liverpool. The oratory and the sentiments would have been identical. The combination of aristocratic condescension and civic pretentiousness took the same
form wherever it occurred.

Clearly, those 'great reserves of goodwill, tradition and respect for aristocratic mystique', however much they had been eroded in the 1830s and 1840s, and
further assailed in the 1870s and 1880s, were still deeply engrained in the
subconscious of many a town dweller at the end of the nineteenth century.[50]
And as in the 1850s, 'honoured and flattered in their lives, the deaths of such

grandees produced a *crescendo* of glorification', as much in the towns they had once adorned as on the estates where they lived.[51] Indeed, if press coverage is any guide, interest in such events actually *grew*, rather than diminished, as the nineteenth century advanced. The fifth Earl Fitzwilliam, who died in 1857, had one whole column announcing his death, and then another on the following day reprinting material from the *Leeds Mercury* and *The Times*. But when his son died in 1902, he received a full-page obituary, and the report of his funeral took up a further three and a half columns.[52] Clearly, this increased coverage reflected changed attitudes as much as changed techniques of newspaper reporting and production. At the fifth earl's death Sheffield, officially, paid little heed; but in 1902, not only the lord mayor but also the mayors of Doncaster, Rotherham and Peterborough attended the funeral. In the case of the Norfolks, the change was even more pronounced. The fourteenth duke, who died in 1860, got six column inches on the day of his death, and a further six, ten days later, describing the funeral at Arundel. A memorial service was held in Sheffield, but the council was not represented. When his successor died in 1917, he received a whole page obituary, the lord mayor sent a telegram to his widow, the town council passed a unanimous motion of condolence, the lord mayor attended the funeral at Arundel, and a memorial service held simultaneously in Sheffield was attended by representatives of all major local bodies.[53]

These examples could be multiplied: the reports of the deaths of successive earls of Derby and dukes of Sutherland give exactly the same impression.[54] At the end of the nineteenth century, the public's demand for detail about the lives of the aristocracy, and the press's capacity to satisfy it, was greater than ever before. Every wreath, every mourner, every tear shed by a sorrowing widow: the urban public wanted to know about it all. But what, in fact, did it all stand for? Assuredly, these grandees were 'ornamental' in the sense that they lent glamour and dignity to civic occasions; but they were also ornamental in that by this time they adorned, though did not fundamentally influence, civic affairs. For in the main, the aristocracy had exchanged real power in the towns for social prestige and – in many cases – ample rental. Indeed, the choice of ornamental mayors by town councils may well be seen as the recognition, by both parties, that such a change had taken place, since 'only when aristocratic influence had become a spent force would the prestige of the peerage be exploited to further civic dignity'. Even radicals – as in Cardiff in 1890 – would accept a titled mayor, if he was effectively politically impotent.[55]

For it would be mistaken to suppose that in this last phase of their relationship with the great industrial towns the aristocracy exercised 'strategic influence' in any formidable way. Their attendances at council meetings were infrequent; they were almost invariably ignorant of the agenda; and they normally got through the year by a combination of orotund and bland phrases, the occasional feast and ball, and perhaps the donation of a piece of plate or a park in commemoration. Their own speeches, and the platitutidinous phrases of their biographers and obituarists, about taking 'a deep interest in all that concerned the welfare and prosperity of the city', of 'long standing connexions' with the district, or of never being 'a mere figurehead', ring hollow.[56] For, as the third marquess of Bute explained, in a letter of devastating candour written while he was mayor of Cardiff, it was all really rather a sham:

> I get on pretty well with my civic government here. My official confidants are nearly all radical dissenters, but we manage in a quite friendly way. They only elected me as a kind of figurehead; and although they are good enough to be glad whenever I take part in details, I am willing to leave these in the hands of people with more expertise than myself.[57]

Or, as that perceptive but anonymous writer in the *Quarterly Review* warned:

> A merely ornamental discharge of . . . Municipal functions, coupled from time to time with expressions of sympathetic interest in the masses, will not serve, and ought not to serve.[58]

The same picture emerges when the links between the aristocracy and the new provincial universities founded at the turn of the century are examined. From the 1870s, families like the Ripons, Norfolks, Spencers, Derbys and Devonshires had been associated with the movements in higher education of which the new civic universities were the final product. So, when the federal university of Victoria was disbanded, allowing Leeds, Liverpool and Manchester to go it alone, when Sheffield received its own charter, and when Queen's, Belfast was reformed, they all stayed loyal to local aristocratic chancellors, and indeed continued to do so until the Second World War and beyond (see table 4).[59]

Indeed, as the table shows, Manchester actually became *more* traditional. Although abandoning aristocratic patronage for John Morley in 1908, it then reverted to type in choosing the Earl of Crawford and Balcarres – himself an important local coalowner in Wigan, a town in which his ancestors had been the major political power in the nineteenth century.[60] Only two universities began, and remained, outside this tradition: Bristol, where the selection of H. O. Wills reflected the massive financial support given to the university by his family; and Birmingham, where the choice of Chamberlain was as much a reflection of his enthusiasm and support for the venture as of his unrivalled local political stature.[61]

Again, however, the question must be posed: what did it all mean? By many criteria, these civic universities were monuments to middle-class, entrepreneurial initiative, promoted out of concern for civic pride, or the desire to make available a more practical type of education to a broader cross-section of society than that which Oxbridge could provide. In every case, gifts from the business community – the brewers in Birmingham, the cutlers in Sheffield, the shipowners in Liverpool – far eclipsed the contributions of the local aristocracy. Nor did they play any greater role as chancellors in the affairs of the

Table 4. Chancellors of provincial universities in England and Northern Ireland, 1900–60

University	Chancellor	Term
Birmingham	Joseph Chamberlain	1900–14
	Viscount Cecil	1918–44
	Sir Anthony Eden	1945–75
Bristol	H.O. Wills	1909–11
	Viscount Haldane	1913–30
	Sir Winston Churchill	1930–65
Leeds	Marquess of Ripon	1904–9
	9th duke of Devonshire	1909–38
	10th duke of Devonshire	1938–50
	Princess Royal	1951–66
Liverpool	16th earl of Derby	1903–8
	17th earl of Derby	1909–48
	Oliver Stanley	1949–50
	5th marquess of Salisbury	1951–71
Manchester	5th earl Spencer	1903–7
	8th duke of Devonshire	1907–8
	Viscount Morley	1908–23
	27th earl of Crawford	1923–40
	1st earl of Woolton	1944–64
Queen's, Belfast	9th earl of Shaftesbury	1908–23
	7th marquess of Londonderry	1923–49
	1st viscount Alanbrooke	1949–63
Sheffield	15th duke of Norfolk	1905–17
	Marquess of Crewe	1917–44
	6th earl of Harewood	1944–7
	1st earl of Halifax	1947–59
	Lord Butler	1959–

Source: *Whitaker's Almanack*, 1900–69.

universities than they did as mayors in the affairs of the towns. When Lord Shaftesbury retired as chancellor of Queen's, Belfast, the Council of the Senate thanked him, rather pointedly, for having fulfilled his role so well 'on those occasions when his many commitments allowed him to'; at one degree congregation at Sheffield, the fifteenth duke of Norfolk closed the proceedings early so as to catch a train for London, leaving some of the graduands unpresented as a result. The official historians of Queen's, Belfast, in describing the chancellorship of Shaftesbury's successor, the Marquess of Londonderry, summarized well the general picture: 'on formal occasions, he had played his part with dignity, and the office demanded little more'.[62]

Why, then, were these grandees appointed? In part for the same reasons which impelled town councils to seek their services as chief magistrate: because they adorned and glamourized any ceremony in which they participated, and because the combination of high aristocratic prestige with limited real influence was ideal for socially ambitious businessmen who were eager to retain the substance of power. In addition, just as the new acquisitive and self-confident town councils were curiously insecure, seeking to clothe their naked newness with invented or acquired traditions, so these redbrick universities, for all their middle-class support and entrepreneurial orientation, were equally unsure and in some ways diffident ventures. In terms of building design, for example – flamboyant Gothic at Manchester, Italianate at Birmingham, Tudor at Sheffield, English Perpendicular at Bristol – 'their derivative harking-back to ancient styles was a means of clothing in respectability institutions which felt themselves to be self-consciously new and seeking status'.[63] What, then could be more appropriate than to appoint as chancellors those grandees who, with their venerable titles, august lineage and historic names, were the personal embodiment of those very same sentiments? Here is exemplified to perfection that conflation of ideals described by H. J. Perkin: 'the entrepreneurial ideal had triumphed, only to throw in its lot with the seemingly defeated aristocratic'.[64]

By the Second World War, this 'Indian Summer' of aristocratic collaboration with the great towns was turning to autumn. The death of the seventeenth earl of Derby in February 1948 was positively the last occasion on which the passing of a territorial grandee plunged a major English town into mourning. Flags were lowered to half mast on all public buildings in Liverpool; the lord mayor attended the funeral; and there was a memorial service in the cathedral attended by all the leading civic dignitaries;[65] but by then such displays, and the links between the aristocracy and the towns of which they were in part the expression, were things of the past.

On the towns' side, the decline in the practice of appointing colourful, wealthy, socially important mayors, and their replacement by professional politicians who were increasingly creatures of the party machine, meant that demand for outsiders – either aristocrats or great local businessmen – lessened. The advent of mayors drawn from the Labour party in the inter-war years, whose purses were smaller and who frowned upon the tradition of civic grandeur and hospitality, necessarily undermined those displays of local pageantry and ceremonial which aristocratic mayors had been uniquely well fitted to enhance. And after the Second World War, when the position of mayor became a salaried and annual appointment, and all effective power lay with the group party chairman, the residual prestige which the job had retained in the 1920s and 1930s largely evaporated. In the council chamber as in county government, the transition from 'social leaders' to 'public persons' greatly undermined the possibilities for aristocratic participation in local affairs.[66]

And, while demand lessened, so did supply, as the traditional links between the aristocracy and the towns gradually began to snap. In parliamentary elections, a member of the Bute family was defeated at Cardiff in 1918 and a

Stanley was forced out at Preston in 1922. Since then no member of either family has stood for, let alone won, an urban constituency with which they could claim close connection. In addition, the Dudleys in the Black Country, the Derbys in Liverpool, the Ramsdens in Huddersfield and the Fitzwilliams in Sheffield were all active in the land market, selling off large parts of their urban estates in the inter-war years. Only the abnormal circumstances of the Second World War, which revived urban loyalty to the established order, and once more called for a mayor with a large purse, brought Lord Sefton to the mayor's parlour in Liverpool and Lord Astor to the same position in Plymouth. Even then, in 1944, Astor was unceremoniously bundled out of office by the Conservative party leader – despite his not unreasonable wish to be mayor in the year of victory – on the grounds that the exceptional circumstances which had justified his appointment were coming to an end.[67]

The post-war years have merely seen an intensification of this trend. No great provincial town has had an aristocratic mayor since Lord Astor stepped down, hurt and begrudgingly, at Plymouth. Territorially, the Butes, Dudleys and Seftons have withdrawn completely from those towns where once they owned so much land. The economic contact, which was the pre-condition for political interaction and social intercourse, has in many cases completely vanished. The new universities of the 1960s, once more founded in conscious opposition to the ethos of Oxbridge, did again take peers as chancellors: Todd at Strathclyde, Robbins at Stirling, Franks at East Anglia, Clark at York. But beneath this façade of decorative continuity, circumstances have in practice changed completely. For these were all life peers, not even hereditary barons of first creation, who owed their elevation to intellectual or public distinction. None of them owned land extensively in the towns of whose universities they became chancellor, or indeed anywhere else, and few possessed country houses in the sense that the seventeenth earl of Derby would have understood. Indeed, recently, this pattern has been followed in redbrick universities as well. Today, the most likely candidates for chancellorships are either members of the Royal Family – the last great figureheads left – or people of genuine intellectual distinction. Only the eleventh duke of Devonshire remains at Manchester, a solitary reminder of a bygone age.

4

These six phases in the links between the aristocracy and the great manufacturing towns – power then conflict, influence then confrontation, ornamental impotence then territorial abdication – illustrate many of the general themes discussed in the previous chapter; but even this outline can do no more than give an overall picture, for three caveats must be entered. In the first place, although these stages of development seem to be valid for all the towns and families discussed, there was also a more general hierarchy of power and influence which only detailed research into single families and individual towns will fully reveal. For example, it seems likely that the Butes, with their massive economic interests in Cardiff and large leasehold building estates, were always more powerful there than the Sutherlands were in the Potteries, where their economic interest was much less and where they were not major ground landlords. And somewhere between these two extremes came the Derbys at Liverpool and the Norfolks and Fitzwilliams in Sheffield. The precise ranking, in terms of the power and influence, which each family wielded in their respective towns, has yet to be established.

Secondly, detailed research into individual examples would probably lay more stress on the importance of party politics for beyond those two phases of consensus – Whiggish in the 1850s and 1860s, then Conservative in the 1890s and 1900s – lie those specific and sudden changes of family allegiance, the result of quirks of personality or the unpredictability of succession, which invariably modify and distort any attempt at neat periodization. Between 1830 and 1868, for example, the holders of the Calthorpe title moved from Liberal Tory to Conservative to Palmerstonian, and when, in 1880, Augustus Calthorpe contested Birmingham as a Conservative, his elder brother, the fifth Lord, was a Liberal. Between 1880 and 1885, the fifteenth earl of Derby, previously a Conservative and subsequently a Unionist, flirted with the Liberals, while his brother and heir remained a staunch Tory. Of necessity, such shifts and changes in a family's public and party political image modify any attempt at clear-cut classification.

Finally, it is important to stress that – whatever their party political allegiance at any given moment – these urban aristocrats were both *above* politics, as the embodiment of the established order, yet often at the same time involved *in* politics as partisan participants. However, just as the middle and working classes could be peer-respecting one day and then privilege-hating the next, so among aristocrats similar contradictions co-existed. At the beginning of the nineteenth century, for example, the second marquess of Bute acted in Cardiff as a philanthropist by virtue of his wealth and social position: he was an aristocrat. But the specific charities to which he gave his name were those which he found politically congenial: he was also a Conservative.[68] Likewise, on one level – that stressed by Randolph Churchill – the seventeenth earl of Derby was a non-partisan grandee, 'king' of Lancashire, friend of George V, an avuncular, established authority figure, 'the incarnation of the best qualities of a Lancastrian'. But at another level – as he appears in the pages of P. F. Clarke's work – he was the 'lynchpin of Lancashire Toryism', a fiercely partisan political boss, not so much a man above the battle as actively involved in it. As his local obituarist recognized, Derby managed to be both 'an uncompromising Conservative' and yet be 'respected by all parties for his fairmindedness'.[69] The skill with which many aristocrats, especially in their relationship with the great towns, managed to reconcile these apparently mutually exclusive roles was remarkable.

So the ambiguities and paradoxes remain, more easily illustrated than resolved. The part of this book devoted to the Calthorpes' attempts to examine that family's fluctuating relationship with the citizens of Birmingham in accordance with the overall outline established here. Of necessity, however, their political and social relationship with the town can only be fully understood if the nature of their economic involvement is explained: therefore, it is as much a study of the Calthorpes as urban landlords and prosperous aristocrats as it is an investigation of changing political and social relationships. Before this detailed account can be given, however, the second main area of aristocratic involvement in provincial urban life in the nineteenth century must be outlined.

3 The holiday resorts: new towns, new opportunities

The themes of conflict and conciliation between the aristocracy and the towns in nineteenth-century England were most extensively developed in those great provincial cities to which some landowners were tied by economic interests; but their sheer size and diversity necessarily limited the real power which the aristocracy could wield. Of the towns discussed in the last chapter, only Cardiff – in this regard a larger version of Barrow-in-Furness – could plausibly be described as an aristocratic creation, almost entirely the product of aristocratic initiative and investment. In the other towns, the aristocracy's economic interests were never paramount. By contrast, the seaside towns were much smaller, had come into being more recently, were much more dependent on landowners' finance and enterprise, and so tended to offer greater scope for the wielding of aristocratic power in an urban context during the second half of the nineteenth century. As Escott noted, with pardonable exaggeration, 'dukedoms have a habit of connecting themselves with water places', and the aristocracy did so in such a way as to maintain a creative link with the urbanization process after their most active phase was passed in London and the great provincial towns.[1]

For although seaside towns grew spectacularly in percentage terms during the first half of the nineteenth century, it was in the years after the establishment of a railway network that their physical expansion was most impressive. While the great industrial monsters like Manchester, Leeds and Birmingham had all expanded most rapidly in the 1820s and 1830s, but thereafter slowed down, the seaside resorts maintained, and even surpassed, their early rates of growth. Indeed, during the 1880s and 1890s towns such as Eastbourne, Hastings, Southport and Folkestone were among the most rapidly expanding in the country.[2] Thus a new type of town came into being with which the aristocracy was connected, more closely and later in the century than was the case with the industrial towns. And, although by definition there was no period of pre-Reform Act dominance or post-Reform Act confrontation, the years from the 1840s to the 1930s bear a striking similarity to the phases of aristocratic involvement with the great industrial towns. Initially, in the seaside resorts, the power of the aristocracy was greater; but by the early 1900s, it had been reduced to a level more akin to that of the Derbys in Liverpool or the Butes in Cardiff at the turn of the century. But who exactly were these seaside aristocrats, and which were the towns that they helped to create?

1

By the early nineteenth century, aristocratic involvement in the making of leisure towns was nothing new. The Georgian spas had not only been designed with an upper-class *clientèle* in view: they had also, in some cases, been the product of aristocratic initiative. With the possible exception of the Pulteney family, who were major landowners in the town, Bath had been developed by speculative builders and an unusually energetic and profit-minded corporation.[3] But in other, lesser spas, the influence of the aristocracy – as entrepreneurs rather than clients – was paramount. Royal Tunbridge Wells, for example, was created by the Abergavenny family, and Buxton in Derbyshire owed its development entirely to the initiative of the dukes of Devonshire. In the 1790s, the fifth duke lavished £63,000 on the making of the Crescent which he hoped would rival Bath, and during the mid-Victorian period, the seventh duke was even more prodigal in his attempts to revive the town's flagging fortunes by financing new ventures such as the pavilion and the winter gardens.[4]

So it was that when fashion drifted away from Bath and the other spas to seaside towns like Brighton, Hastings and Scarborough, during the early decades of the nineteenth century, further opportunities opened up for an aristocracy already familiar with the rudiments of leisure-town creation. And as with spas, so with holiday towns: the greatest was once more the exception which proved the rule. For Brighton owed even less to aristocratic entrepreneurship than did Bath. Its landownership pattern was fragmented, and even the coherent developments of Kemp Town and Brunswick Square were undertaken by spectulators rather than aristocrats.[5] Nevertheless, as the nineteenth century advanced, bringing with it railways and a middle class ever more eager and able to travel and to holiday in exclusive respectability, those many estates whose broad acres bordered on the coast became the setting for the last great episode of aristocratic involvement in the urbanization process. Whereas the great industrial towns were (in most cases) already in being, and expanded onto land which aristocrats owned, the aristocracy owned the land where the seaside towns appeared long *before* they came into being. In the one case they *responded* to urban growth; in the other, they actually *initiated* it.

Of all the great nineteenth-century seaside resorts whose evolution bore an unmistakably aristocratic stamp, Eastbourne stands out as the one where it was most indelible. For the 'Empress of Watering Places', the 'Duke's town', was almost entirely the creation of the House of Cavendish. The resort was begun in the early 1850s, and from then until the late 1880s the Devonshires and their associates dominated the town. They controlled its layout, were the majority shareholders in the public utilities, and were the dominant voice on the local board. Indeed, on incorporation in 1883, it was the duke's agent who became first mayor. In the early 1890s, however, the town began to free itself from Cavendish control, and an ugly and acrimonious battle took place in which the council tried to buy out the water company – the Devonshires' most profitable local investment. Eventually a compromise was reached, and out of this reconciliation was born the mayoralty of the eighth duke in 1897–8. His ornamental year of office was so splendid that his successor became chief magistrate in 1909–10, thereby confirming the new *rapprochement* between family and town.

In its high social tone and aristocratic connections, Eastbourne was rivalled among the resorts of the south coast only by Folkestone, where the earls of Radnor were the dominant landowners. They had bought their way into land as far back as 1697, but it was not until 1807 that the first tentative steps were taken to develop their seaside estates. In that year, the Folkestone Harbour Company was set up by Lord Radnor, with a capital of £22,000, the aim being to establish the town as a major cross-Channel harbour; but by 1842, over £69,000 had been spent to no good purpose, and the enterprise was sold off to the South Eastern Railway Company. In 1825, Lord Radnor obtained a private Act which enabled him to grant building leases, though for the next 15 years development was slow.[6] Only after the 1840s, when his agent Sidney Smirke drew up a new plan, did development really begin to accelerate. Donations of land for parks and churches followed; a Radnor club was founded for the towns's elite; and in the 1890s the Leas or West End was laid out with lawns, pavilions, band stands and shelters as a high-class recreation area. The Radnors themselves remained resident in the town; the private policeman employed by His Lordship to patrol the Leas was a constant reminder of their presence; and in 1902, the sixth earl served as mayor.[7]

By comparison, the influence of the Palk family, later Lords Haldon, over Torquay, was not so long lasting. They bought their seaside estate in 1768, and their earliest forays into urban development included the rebuilding of the harbour in 1803–6 and the construction of a market in 1820 – both entirely at their own expense. In 1825, they too, obtained a private Act to enable them to grant building leases, and effective development dates from this time – although it was not until the 1850s that real progress was made. The baths, constructed between 1852–69, were paid for by the Palks, as were the major extensions to the harbour, undertaken between 1867 and 1870 at a cost of £70,000.[8] In the later 1870s and early 1880s, however, relations between the town and the family rapidly deteriorated, so that on the death of the first Lord Haldon in 1883, it was noted how, in recent years, 'the town and its chief landlord' had not 'been able to reconcile interests', with the result that there had been a 'decline in Lord Haldon's personal popularity'.[9] Moreover, the second lord inherited the estates heavily mortgaged, partly as a result of the high costs of developing Torquay, and so was obliged to begin liquidating his urban holdings in an attempt to reduce his 'terrible encumbrances'. Indeed, between 1887 and 1894, and again after 1906, sales were so extensive that, by the outbreak of the First World War, the family had entirely severed its territorial connection with the town it had done so much to create.[10]

The Tapps-Gervis-Meyrick family, by contrast, maintained a lower but more enduring profile in the affairs of Bournemouth. In 1836 Sir George William Tapps-Gervis commissioned Benjamin Ferry to plan a holiday town, and during the next five years, roads were laid, gardens created, and villas constructed. But in 1842 Sir George died, leaving a son of 15, and his affairs in the hands of trustees. Four years later, they secured a private Act which enabled them to borrow a further £5,000, replace Ferry with Decimus Burton, and initiate another phase of more rapid development.[11] Between 1856 and 1890, the town was administered by Improvement Commissioners, of whom 11 were elected but two were chosen by the lord of the manor. In 1861, Sir George Tapps-Gervis-Meyrick, now of age, opened the pier, and in 1894 he presented both Meyrick Park and his rights as lord of the manor to the council. Finally, in 1903, his son vested his interest in the cliffs and foreshore in the council.[12] As another prominent citizen noted, the family were 'one of the few from whom Bournemouth has really received benefits to any extent'.[13] When Sir George Tapps-Gervis-Meryrick died in 1928, the flags on all the public buildings in the borough were flown at half mast.[14]

As with Liverpool and Sheffield, Southport was under the influence of more than one family – in this case the Heskeths and the Scarisbricks, both Lancashire gentry, of whom the former had been involved, in the 1840s, in the initially optimistic, but subsequently disastrous project to develop Fleetwood as a port and high-class holiday town. But at Southport, where development was initiated in the 1820s, they fared rather better. In the 1830s, the two families collaborated to build the promenade, provided land on advantageous terms for churches and charities, and patronized local sporting events. In 1853 they helped to set up the water company, and between 1865–8, land was donated for Hesketh Park.[15] Incorporation, however, combined with a minority in the Scarisbrick family, which left the estate to be administered by absentee trustees in a manner reminiscent of the Butes in Cardiff, meant that the balance of power began to tilt inexorably towards the local inhabitants. In the early 1880s, the council and the two families clashed bitterly when attempts were made to buy and develop the foreshore for the town, and in 1885 the Southport Improvement Act enabled the council to over-ride the landowners' opposition.[16] Thereafter, however, relations gradually improved, so that two members of the Scarisbrick family served as mayors in 1902 and 1903, and one Hesketh in 1906. More unusually, in each case, they actually stayed on to serve as councillors in their own right.[17]

In the last quarter of the nineteenth century, when aristocratic power and influence in these resorts was visibly on the wane, two entirely new seaside towns came into being under aristocratic auspices. The first of these was Skegness, where the Earl of Scarbrough was so powerful that it is often cited as 'without doubt the finest example of comprehensive resort planning'.[18] Development was begun in the late 1870s, and was supervised by H. V. Tippett, the earl's local agent. A plan was drawn up in 1873; building plots were marked out by 1876; and local companies were set up to provide gas, water, pleasure gardens, hotels, swimming baths and a pier, in which the earl was the majority shareholder.[19] Even after he had begun to sell off some of his land in the early 1920s, he still remained an important figure. He retained control of the pier company, and intervened decisively in 1932 in the question of sewage disposal. Moreover, throughout the inter-war years, the Assistant Clerk to the Town Council was Vivian Tippett, son of the man who had first planned the estate.[20] In 1945, on the death of the tenth earl, he was mourned as 'a good friend' and 'the Fairy Godfather of Skegness'.[21]

Finally, in the 1880s, the de la Warrs, a family of Kentish landowners, began to create Bexhill. In 1883, the seventh earl constructed the sea wall, and thereafter laid out parades and promoted the local gas and water companies. His son, the future eighth earl, lived in the manor house at Bexhill from 1891, and succeeded to the title in 1896. During the 1890s, the family built the Kursal as a centre for local entertainment, and financed the construction of the Sackville, a high-class hotel in the grand manner. The eighth earl turned the manor house into a Mecca for his aristocratic friends, and the parties and entertainments he provided were so brilliant that the 1890s were long remembered as the town's golden decade.[22] He himself was chairman of the Urban Council and the Incorporation Committee, and was unashamedly the most powerful local resident. But his departure for the Boer War and the town's incorporation in 1902 witnessed a major shift in the balance of power, as initiative and influence passed into the hands of local leadership.[23] Yet for another generation and more, the de la Warrs and the Earls Brassey, their near neighbours and relatives, enjoyed an Indian summer of prestige and social leadership, as each family provided, in successive generations, mayors of the borough. When Earl Brassey became mayor in 1970, the local paper exclaimed proudly that 'Bexhill has never had before, and probably never will have again, such a distinguished chief citizen'.[24] And when the eighth earl de la Warr died on active service in 1915, he was mourned as 'the maker of modern Bexhill'.[25]

2

To borrow – but necessarily revise – Asa Briggs' summary of the great magnates' links with the industrial towns and apply it to the holiday resorts, aristocratic landownership there represented a 'conservative interest' in towns whose flavour was itself 'essentially conservative'. Physically distanced from the great centres of population, overwhelmingly middle class, and with the lower orders mainly consisting of retinues of servants, they represented segregated, middle-class suburbia at its most extreme, transported to a coastal location. Assuredly, some towns like Southport had an unusually large population of nonconformists, and in Torquay and Folkestone the popularity of leasehold enfranchisement meant the Liberals enjoyed support there for longer than might otherwise have been expected;[26] but in the main, the party political element was of less significance than in the great industrial towns. The defence of property and respect for the established order were deeply rooted in these overwhelmingly middle-class communities with an aged and leisured population.

Within this general framework, it is again possible to describe a spectrum of aristocratic influence. At one end come the Devonshires in Eastbourne, the Scarbroughs in Skegness and the de la Warrs at Bexhill – territorially predominant, controlling the timing of development, and holding the majority of shares in local public utilities. In their decades of greatest power and influence, little went on in these towns outside their control. At the other extreme were the Scarisbricks and Heskeths in Southport, the Tapps-Gervis-Meyricks in Bournemouth, and the Mostyns at Llandudno. They withdrew from positive entrepreneurship earlier, even before incorporation, leaving the creation and promotion of amenities to local initiative. Hence the local municipal bodies in Southport and Bournemouth tended – indeed were obliged – to be more aggressive and entrepreneurially adventurous than those docile bodies in Eastbourne and Bexhill, who were content to eat out of the proffered aristocratic hand for much longer. Finally, at some half-way point were the earls of Radnor at Folkestone, who shared control of the town with the South Eastern Railway after the company bought up the docks and made them pay, and Sidney Sussex College, Cambridge, who developed Cleethorpes in collaboration with the Manchester, Sheffield & Lincolnshire Railway.[27]

The spectrum ranging from great power via shared influence to abdicated responsibility is more easily delineated than for the great industrial towns, but an account of the phases of development is of necessity more schematic and chronologically less coherent. In each of the great industrial towns, the periods run closely parallel throughout the century, regardless of the specific differences of economic evolution. The seaside towns, however, came into being in two distinct periods – Eastbourne, Folkestone, Bournemouth, Torquay and Southport in the mid-Victorian years, and Skegness and Bexhill at the end of the century – which means that similar phases of development did not always occur simultaneously. Even so, at the necessary cost of abandoning contemporaneity, it is possible to pick out four major periods, which broadly resemble the post-Reform Act divisions suggested in the case of the great industrial towns in the developing relationship between landowners and town-dwellers.

The first coincided, in most cases, with the mid-Victorian era of *rapprochement* between the aristocracy and the great provincial centres, although in the case of Bexhill and Skegness it occurred in the two closing decades of the century. This was the period in which the landowners wielded real power, spent lavishly, and dominated local affairs. It was followed, in the 1880s at Southport, in the 1890s at Eastbourne, and in the early 1900s at Bexhill, by a time of clashes and confrontation, as the new town councils came into being and, perhaps in conscious emulation of Chamberlain, began to mobilize their financial resources in successful opposition to the landlords' hitherto predominant pecuniary power. But then, after the balance of power was fundamentally tilted in favour of the towns, the aristocracy came to enjoy – as they did in the great industrial centres – a long-lasting period of decorative impotence and high social prestige as 'ornamental' mayors. Finally, beginning with the Haldons at Torquay even before the First World War, but in most towns only occurring much later, there was a period of territorial abdication, as the economic links between aristocrats and seaside towns were severed in the same way and at the same time as they were being dissolved in the great provincial cities.

The first phase, that of resort creation, was necessarily characterized by the great power and influence wielded by the local landowner or his representatives. These new resorts were often miles away from the nearest large town, which meant that there was no one but the landlord who could effectively take the initiative as far as development was concerned, so that landowners came to dominate not only the layout of the town, but also those firms set up to provide recreational facilities, and even the local board, whose financial resources were at this time relatively restricted. At Eastbourne, the duke's agent was chairman of the local board; at Bournemouth, the lord of the manor was entitled to a seat on the board of Improvement Commissioners *ex officio*; and at Bexhill, the eighth earl de la Warr was chairman of the Urban Board. At Skegness, by 1882, the local sanitary authority had been able to raise £1,600 to spend on drainage, whereas during the same period, Lord Scarbrough had expended over £5,000.[28] Donations of land for churches or parks, or of money towards drainage, were met with displays of gratitude and obsequiousness which surpassed those recorded in the great provincial towns. And no ceremony – the laying of the foundation stone of the town hall or the opening of the pier – was complete unless it was performed by a representative of the local landowning family to whom the inhabitants felt they owed so much.

However, this was not a phase which lasted indefinitely. Power in resorts tended to be wielded by those who spent the most money, and by the end of the nineteenth century the balance between the aristocracy (hitherto the biggest spenders) and the local municipal body (previously very limited in its resources) was beginning to shift. Among the aristocracy, landowners like the Haldons, who were heavily mortgaged, became increasingly reluctant to invest further in harbours or sea walls or winter gardens on which the return seemed to be so small. On the towns' side, the passing of the Municipal Corporations Act in 1882, which enabled the monarch in council to grant a charter of incorporation to any town on petition by the inhabitants, was a major turning point.[29] Apart from Southport, which had received its charter in 1867, and Folkestone, which was an ancient borough, none of the new seaside towns had charters as the last quarter of the century opened; but then incorporation came in a rush: at Eastbourne in 1883, Bournemouth in 1890, Torquay in 1892 and Bexhill in 1902.

The exact relationship between the achievement of municipal status and emancipation from the influence of the landlord varied. In Torquay, in the early 1880s, the local board had already fallen out with Lord Haldon over the question of tolls levied on produce entering the town by the market company which he owned, and incorporation came in the wake of this hostile feeling.[30] At Bexhill, incorporation seemed to have taken place under the auspices of Lord de la Warr, and it was confidently expected that he would not only serve as Charter Mayor but as first elected mayor of the borough. But, although he was returned at the head of the poll, he was not elected to the mayor's chair, and thereupon resigned as a councillor. His position in the town, 'which he had so suddenly relinquished, was never fully recovered', so it was incorporation itself which was the major turning point.[31] At Eastbourne, by contrast, although incorporation took place in 1883, the town remained a docile lap dog of the Cavendishes for nearly another decade until, in the early 1890s, the council tried unsuccessfully to take over the local water company in which the duke was the majority shareholder. And at Southport, confrontation was even more delayed but also more protracted. Incorporation had taken place in 1867, but the major confrontation with the local landowners on the issue of the foreshore did not take place until 1881–3. Even when that was settled, the question of leasehold enfranchisement provided renewed ground for controversy. A unanimous resolution was passed by the town council against the leasehold system in March 1887, and the town clerk gave evidence to the Select Committee on Town Holdings which was highly critical of the two major ground landlords. In the seaside as much as in the great industrial towns, the balance of power was shifting.[32]

3

Then, once more, there took place that *rapprochement* between the aristocracy and the towns which was marked at the seaside as in the great provincial cities, and which again is best displayed by a list (table 5) of aristocratic mayors.

Table 5. Aristocratic mayors of English seaside towns, 1890–1969

| | | Terms as mayor | |
Town	Family	(1)	(2)
Bexhill	Brassey	1908	1909
	de la Warr	1904–5	1933–5
Deal	Abercorn	1910	
Devonport	St Levan	1891–2	
Eastbourne	Devonshire	1898	1910
Folkestone	Radnor	1902	
Poole	Wimborne	1897	
Winchelsea	Ritchie of Dundee	1925	1935

Source: *Whitaker's Almanack*, 1890–1969.

To this list should be added Sir Charles Scarisbrick, mayor of Southport in 1902; his son, Sir Talbot, who was mayor in 1903; Charles Fleetwood Hesketh, who was mayor in 1906; and his son Roger, who was mayor in 1950, Conservative M.P. from 1952–9, and made a freeman in 1966.[33] Finally, at Colwyn Bay, the local grandee, Lord Colwyn, was both Charter Mayor and first elected mayor after the town's incorporation in September 1934.[34]

Most of the territorial links here are obvious. The Brasseys – descended from the great contractor – did not own an acre in Bexhill. But they were major landowners in Kent, lived near the town at Normanhurst, and a daughter of the first Earl Brassey married the eighth earl de la Warr. Likewise, the Wimbornes were major landowners in Dorset, where they held 17,000 acres, and wielded considerable local influence until the end of the century.[35] And in the case of the dukes of Abercorn, the Hon. George, who was mayor of Deal, was also Captain of Deal Castle from 1899 until 1923. The first Lord St Levan was a major landowner in Cornwall, resident of St Michael's Mount, the chief ground landlord in Devonport and, although his refusal to sell tenants their freeholds aroused local hostility, it was claimed that 'he gave the town land for recreational purposes . . . the churches and chapels and charitable institutions of Devonport benefitted largely by his generosity'.[36] Finally, two industrialist families who had more in common with Lord Leverhulme than with some of the ancient and many-acred titles listed here: the Ritchies were a family of Scottish businessmen, who finally settled at Rye, and Lord Colwyn was a Lancashire industrialist who retired to Colwyn Bay in 1928, and thereafter became closely connected with the affairs of the town.[37]

Equally illuminating are the obvious omissions. Some, such as Southend and Blackpool, are predictable: as at Manchester or Leeds, the fragmented pattern of landownership meant there was no local grandee available.[38] The lack of a Haldon mayor at Torquay is more surprising, but by the time titled mayors had become popular, the sale of the family estate was already well under way, and a nobleman who seemed bent on liquidating his entire local holdings was hardly likely to endear himself to the town. More remarkable, perhaps, is the lack of a mayor of Bournemouth from the Tapps-Gervis-Meyrick family, whose economic links with the town remained strong until after the First World War.[39] Like the Calthorpes in Birmingham, however, their 'conservative interest' had never been very large, and by the end of the nineteenth century they had been eclipsed as the major local grandees by Merton Russell-Cotes and his wife. Russell-Cotes was a local businessman and philanthropist who was himself brought in from outside the council to be mayor in 1894, on which occasion the precedents of Bute at Cardiff and the Earl of Warwick at Warwick were cited.[40] Bournemouth certainly wanted a grandee as mayor; but, like Birmingham in choosing the chancellor of its University, the citizens preferred their most distinguished resident to their most important ground landlord.

Even allowing for such important omissions, the strength and longevity of this phase of decorative aristocratic involvement in the affairs of seaside towns is remarkable. With the exception of the altogether extraordinary wartime mayoralties of Astor at Plymouth and Sefton at Liverpool, titled mayors of the great industrial towns were already out of fashion by the time of the First World War. But in the seaside towns, the movement still had much life in it: Bexhill, Winchelsea, Colwyn Bay and Southport were all to enjoy titled mayors in the inter- and even post-war years. In the same way, there was a greater element of 'apostolic succession', of son following father, in the holiday towns. Only in Liverpool, of the great provincial cities, did this happen; but at Southport (twice), Bexhill (twice), Eastbourne and Winchelsea, the progression of the mayoral chain of office from father to son was commonplace. Indeed, at Bexhill, all the titled incumbents were related. When Earl Brassey opened the local town hall in 1908 (fig. 3), he presented to the town his

Fig. 3. The first Earl Brassey opening Bexhill town hall, 1908. The boy on Brassey's right is his grandson, Lord Buckhurst, himself mayor of Bexhill in 1933–5 (reproduced from the *Bexhill-on-Sea Observer*, 2 March 1908 by permission of the British Library).

grandson, the future ninth earl de la Warr, and placed the mayoral hat on his head as a prophecy that he, too, would one day be first citizen.[41] He duly did serve as mayor, when the incident was often recalled. Indeed, of his three titled predecessors, one was his grandfather, one his father, and one his uncle.[42]

Yet while the tradition of titled mayors was stronger and more enduring in the seaside towns than in the great provincial cities, the reasons why it happened at all were largely similar. To begin with, holiday resorts were even more obsessed with civic dignity than the great provincial towns – not surprising considering that they had had less time to get used to it. At Bournemouth, for example, concern over the proper outfit for the mayor was so great immediately after incorporation that one contemporary suggested the council's ambition was to ensure that 'their Mayor shall be arrayed like Solomon in all his glory'. Five years later, in the same town, there was a debate as to how, precisely, the mayor should be addressed, which caused the town clerk to consult his opposite numbers in Dover, Wolverhampton, Liverpool and Manchester, in search of clarification. Finally, it was agreed that there was no precedent for 'Right Worshipful', and that 'Worshipful' had to suffice by itself.[43] The more recently civic dignity had been acquired, the more zealous were councillors to preserve and enhance it, and there was no better way to accomplish that end than to obtain the services of a titled mayor.

At the same time, to be mayor, even for a year, of a small, recently-incorporated town was expensive. As Merton Russell-Cotes recalled: 'He (the mayor) is expected to be enterprising and hospitable, a subscriber to societies, clubs and associations almost innumerable, and be ready at all times to maintain the honour and dignity of the borough.'[44] But if few such men were forthcoming in the great provincial cities, they were in even shorter supply in seaside towns whose economic base was narrow and precarious. There were no heavy industries, and building, from which many transient fortunes were made, was notoriously risky. Nor was the considerable rentier population of much help – old, retired, and living on fixed incomes. As the *Bexhill-on-Sea Observer* explained, potential mayors 'are not to be picked up on the beach', and did 'not grow on hedges'.[45] Indeed, by the mid-1930s, as the ninth Earl de la Warr's successor pointed out, 'it was becoming increasingly difficult, not only in this borough but elsewhere, to find suitable candidates for the Mayoralty, owing to the tradition of open handed hospitality which the position so often entails'.[46]

So, at the seaside as much as in the great industrial towns, the appeal of an aristocratic mayor was the combination of 'the lustre of his title and with a view to hospitality at his castle'.[47] There were, however, also important local reasons. With their wide, well-planned, tree-lined roads appropriate for parades, their squares, and bandstands and promenades ideal for set-piece speeches and presentations, and their large hotels – the Sackville at Bexhill, the Metropole at Folkestone, the Imperial at Torquay and the Grand at Eastbourne – so well able to accommodate important banquets, seaside towns were in some ways better suited for the staging of civic pageants than industrial towns, whose main streets might be mean, narrow and crowded. And at a time when each seaside resort with pretensions claimed to be more 'respectable' than its rivals, a titled first citizen was thought to be of great publicity value. At a more mundane level, untried, inexperienced town councillors might be genuinely eager to obtain the services of an important public figure as first mayor who would show them by example how to conduct their affairs, as was the case at Colwyn Bay.[48]

Perhaps, too, these titled mayoralties of holiday resorts involved a more self-conscious awareness of reconciliation between town and family than was the case in the great industrial centres. At Southport, for example, the policy of inviting both families to occupy the highest civic office was deliberately undertaken 'with the idea of both recognizing and of improving the relations between the town and the landowning interest'.[49] Likewise, at Eastbourne, the council's invitation to the eighth duke of Devonshire to serve as mayor, and his acceptance of it, were self-consciously seen by both parties as a reconciliation after the quarrel over the water works company. And at Bexhill, after Lord de la Warr had – in some opinions – been slighted by the council in November 1902, when it refused to elect him first mayor, the decision to do so twelve months later was an explicit attempt to 'satisfy those who thought he was unfairly dealt with a year ago'.[50]

As in the great provincial cities, these titled mayors were expected to be grand, generous, impartial, splendid, hospitable and heroic; and in the main they were. Their mayoral banquets reached heights of unimagined magnificence; their speeches were endlessly reported; their houses were lovingly and lavishly described; and their gifts to the town were greeted with acclamation. Sir Charles Scarisbrick, for example, was Coronation Mayor of Southport, and presided over 'a year of brilliance and social functioning'. He was grand enough to donate his mayoral salary of £500 to charity, and gave each councillor a pewter mug as a memento of his year of office.[51] His son, Sir Talbot, who followed him, was even more lavish, entertaining the local police, the postmen, the corporation officials and workmen, as well as giving two childrens' parties and a mayoral reception and ball for 900. During his year of office, the British Association held its annual meeting at Southport, and he entertained all the members at a great banquet in his country house, to which they were conveyed by special trains.[52] In a similar fashion, the sixth earl of Radnor invited Folkestone Council to visit him at Longford Castle, gave a garden party for 400, and presented a badge for the mayoral chain as a farewell gift.[53] At Bexhill, Lord Brassey went one better, and presented the mayoral chain *before* he himself became mayor.[54] He, too, presided over a year of magnificence and his every activity – from fighting a fire at Normanhurst to giving a party at his London town house – was fully reported in the local press.[55] The last fling of such magnificence was during the inter-war mayoralty of his grandson, the ninth Earl de la Warr. He revived the mayoral banquet, which by then had fallen into decline, brought down the Lord Chancellor and the Foreign Secretary (who were his colleagues in the National Government) to address it, and arranged for both the king and queen and the Duke and Duchess of York to visit the town.[56]

Grand social occasions; orotund speeches containing nothing but 'complimentary phrases, agreeable commonplace and acceptable advice'; gifts to the town of civic regalia or open spaces: the recipe never failed, and almost all the titled mayors were asked to remain in office for at least another year.[57] One single episode may be taken as representative of this phase of civic obsequiousness.[58] On 9 November 1907, Lord Brassey received the Freedom of Bexhill, and was subsequently installed as mayor for the ensuing year. At eleven o'clock, the outgoing mayor presented him with the Freedom of the borough in the town hall. 'When I hand you this illuminated copy of the resolution', he said to Brassey, 'and it comes to your turn to say a few words, I know, my lord, that you will modestly claim the honour as yours, but we shall say that the greater honour is ours.' Brassey then received the illuminated scroll 'amid hearty cheers', and made a felicitously bland speech in reply. Then at twelve o'clock he was elected mayor, which was announced with a peal of bells from the local church, and he spoke again:

> My lot has been cast here in Sussex; I have lived here for some fifty years; I am your near neighbour. I ought to be, and I am, a sincere well wisher to this community [applause] and I ought to desire its prosperity. I may regret that I have not more personal power to promote its prosperity. I can only say once more that I must do my best. I shall be glad to do my best . . . and now, I have only to say in conclusion that in connection with the office of mayor, I value very much the opportunity which it affords for making friends with men of all classes.

His speech was greeted with 'loud applause'.

The same evening the mayoral banquet was held at the Hotel Metropole, 'a fitting finale to a most memorable day'. Lord Brassey, 'who wore the crimson ribbon of a Knight Grand Cross of the Most Honourable Order of the Bath, and the chain and badge of his mayoral office, was in the best of good spirits'. The meal was of nine courses, and afterwards there were toasts to the king and royal family, the navy, army and auxiliary forces, the mayor and people of Bexhill, and the visitors. By comparison with other similar occasions, this was a truncated list: however, between the toasts and the replies, various performers sang and played, such as Miss Fanny Wentworth who, for ten minutes, 'caused the hall to reverberate with peals of laughter as she told some amusing stories and sang "Isn't that like a man?"'. In the course of the speeches, Brassey was described as 'a man who has given many long years to the public good, who has worked hard and well, and who has entered actively into your municipal life at a time when he might justly be thinking of a rest from his labours'. In reply, Brassey once more declared that 'on all occasions you shall command my best services', and at eleven o'clock, after the singing of the national anthem, the evening ended, and Lord Brassey 'entered his motor and drove with the Hon. T. A. Brassey' back to London.

Such scenes were repeated in Folkestone, Eastbourne, Southport and Devonport: the same junketings, speeches, and mutual expressions of esteem and regard. But, as with the great provincial cities, what did it all mean?

Again, one peer after another expressed his 'keen interest', his 'sincere concern', his 'benevolent interest' and his 'deep affection' for the town in question.[59] But again, it was all very largely a sham: for they were but ornamental figureheads, decorative, ignorant and impotent. Lord Radnor, for example, accepted the mayoralty of Folkestone with 'great diffidence', because he admitted to having 'little knowledge of the working of municipal affairs'.[60] Sir Charles Scarisbrick, despite his year as mayor of Southport, 'was never in the ordinary sense an intimate associate with local life', and 'did not find municipal work too congenial'.[61] At the beginning of his term, the first earl Brassey was described by a Bexhill paper as 'an exceedingly busy man, who already has his hands full, and . . . in his seventy-second year', and later in his term, the same journal was moved to lament that 'his lordship has not been amongst us as much as we would have liked'.[62] His son was even less in evidence. Three times, when offered the mayoralty by the council, he stressed that he could only be a 'nominal mayor', but so excited were they by the prospect of another aristocratic first citizen, that they waved his doubts aside. However, they were well founded. His business interests in Italy and Sardinia meant he was out of the country for half the year, and while he was in England, he hunted on Mondays, which was the same day the Bexhill Council met. Even the local paper, which had supported his election, had to admit that he was 'unable to give more than an occasional and superficial attention to the work of the office'.[63]

Yet, despite their evident lack of knowledge of local affairs and their inability or unwillingness to play more than a nominal part, aristocratic mayors survived longer in holiday resorts than in any other type of town, with the exception of those small country towns which had often been pocket boroughs, where obsequiousness to the aristocracy survived even the Second World War, and where other, alternative chief magistrates were even harder to come by. But the severing of the territorial links between landowners and the seaside towns which they had done so much to create was remarkably similar in its timing and its effects to that which occurred in the great provincial cities. Indeed, the Haldons at Torquay had begun to sell off their estate in the 1880s, and by the First World War had pulled out of the town entirely.[64] By then, also, Lord Radnor had ceased to reside in Folkestone and Lord de la Warr had leased out the manor house at Bexhill.[65] In 1919, on the death of the second earl, the Brassey line and the title became extinct, and the Normanhurst estate was broken up. In the inter-war years, the Tapps-Gervis-Meyricks sold their central Bournemouth holdings, and both the Scarisbricks and the Heskeths sold out at Southport.[66] After the Second World War the Devonshires ceased to be resident at Compton Place in Eastbourne or to employ a full-time resident agent, and the earls of Scarbrough began to sell out at Skegness. In the seaside towns as much as in the great provincial cities, the age of aristocratic prestige, to say nothing of the real power and dominance which preceded it, has gone. Significantly, when the eleventh earl of Scarbrough died in 1969, he was not described, like his father, as 'the Fairy Godfather of Skegness', but as 'a member of the family which once owned practically all' of the town.[67]

4

As with the great provincial cities, this account of aristocratic involvement in the seaside towns both sets some of the generalizations of the first chapter in a more specific context, and offers a provisional outline of a complex subject. Again, the party political allegiance of the aristocratic families in question needs to be considered more thoroughly. Some families were remarkably consistent: the Haldons, Radnors, St Levans and Scarbroughs were staunch Conservatives throughout. Of the Scarisbricks, though, Sir Charles was a Conservative while his son was a Liberal, and at Eastbourne the Devonshires moved from Liberalism to Unionism and finally to Conservatism as a consequence of Home Rule. Even more peripatetic was the ninth Earl de la Warr. He began his political career as a follower of MacDonald, in whose second Labour government he held minor ministerial office. He then held a variety of posts in the National Government, among them lord privy seal and president of the Board of Education, and was subsequently chairman of the National Labour party from 1931 to 1943. Finally, having represented the Churchill coalition in negotiations with the Emperor of Ethiopia in 1944, he resigned from the Labour party, and served as Postmaster-General in the Conservative governments of 1951–5.

Yet, whatever might be happening at Westminster while these grandees served their terms as mayor, party politics rarely obtruded. The only occasion when this was significant was when the first earl Brassey – a Liberal – refused to serve as mayor of Hastings because the Conservatives on the council made it clear that they would move for his dismissal from the chair on the grounds that he was not a burgess of the borough.[68] But in the main, party political quarrels were suspended, as Lord Radnor explained on becoming mayor of Folkestone:

> It will be my endeavour during the time that I possess the powers conferred by my year of office – while maintaining the views I strongly hold on questions of public interest – to assist you in proving that your interests and my interests are one; and that your interests are mine, and will go as far as possible in front of my own. We all wish to work for the prosperity of the town, both now and in the future.[69]

And so the aristocratic mayors presided as bland, avuncular, established, authority figures, above party politics, representing all that was best in the borough. However partisan they might be at Westminster, in the seaside towns their image was very different. Instead of urging people to vote Liberal or Tory, they constantly exhorted all inhabitants to pull together for the benefit of the borough.

The chapters on the Devonshires and Eastbourne which form a large part of this book will illustrate in detail many of the themes sketched in here. As the most wealthy and powerful family to be concerned with resort creation, the control they initially exercised was very great, and their subsequent period of ceremonial importance was long and successful. But, as with the Calthorpes and Edgbaston, this public role can only be understood in the context of their economic links with the town: how they created it, how they financed it, and how much revenue they drew from it. 'The Empress of Watering Places' was an economic venture as well as providing scope for the estate developers to influence the urbanization process, and so the Devonshires' involvement with Eastbourne will be examined from both standpoints.

Part Two
The Calthorpes
and Birmingham

4 Introduction: the landowners and the land, 1717–1810

Once Arden engreened this rolling country, and even today it has woodland quietude, so that lovers who walk arm in arm along the discreet pavements overshadowed with weeping laburnum and fans of horse chestnuts may hear . . . the whinny of a brown owl ripple through the night – or even, it is said, a casual nightingale, or a garden warbler aping that peerless song . . . The deserted roads do not follow a geometrical pattern, but interlace with long curves and sweeps; the street lamps are far between, and seem to have been erected for the bedazzlement of the summer moths which flutter round them rather than for the direction of mankind; for most people who live in Alvaston are not fly-by-nights, but solid, respectable folk.[1]

Thus Francis Brett Young describes the gracious, elegant and fictional 'North Bromwich' suburb of 'Alvaston' as it appeared during the last quarter of the nineteenth century, when at the zenith of its fame. In part, its reputation reflected the importance of its inhabitants, who included those rich merchant princes, such as the Laceys, Fladburns and Astills, who were 'North Bromwich's' substitute for a hereditary aristocracy, and who made up its civic and intellectual elite. But these august and self-assured people lived in an area whose appearance constituted the second reason for its renown: for, although situated no more than ten minutes' carriage drive from the centre of the town, it stood as an oasis of sylvan tranquillity amid the noise, dirt and squalor of the 'City of Iron' – a region of tree-lined roads and exquisitely tasteful houses, with their libraries and music rooms, tennis courts and croquet lawns, rose trees and rhododendron bushes.

1

Yet this charming and inviting suburb was no figment of the author's imagination. Like most of the places in his books, it was but a thinly disguised version of reality. For just as 'North Bromwich' was modelled on Birmingham, so 'Alvaston' was in fact Edgbaston, 'the aristocratic suburb of Birmingham', its 'Belgravia' or 'West End'.[2] 'Edgbaston is unquestionably the most important suburb of Birmingham', observed *Edgbastonia* on the occasion of its first issue in 1881, 'the favourite place of residence for the professional men, merchants and traders of the busy town which it adjoins, with a population more numerous and wealthy than those of other suburbs.'[3] Such an immodest claim would have been ridiculously conceited, had it not actually been true. At the same time, the magazine began a series entitled 'Edgbastonians past and present', which read like a Birmingham *Who's Who*. Among the first to be featured were Arthur Ryland, Charles Sturge, George Dawson, Thomas Avery and Timothy Kenrick. Nor was this a transient phenomenon. For as the new century dawned, the civic elite showed no inclination to move away: Charles Gabriel Beale, Sir George Kenrick, Sir Oliver Lodge, Charles Gore, and Austen and Neville Chamberlain were all sheltered beneath Edgbaston's residential umbrella. In a very real sense, Edgbaston was but the council house at home.

However, like Brett Young's 'Alvaston', Edgbaston's reputation did not derive merely from the reflected glory of its inhabitants. It was also the result of the suburb's intrinsic merit as a piece of unified, thoughtful and tasteful planning. Indeed, contemporaries outdid themselves in singing a chorus of praise which was sustained for over half a century. Here, for example, is one local opinion of 1853:

> The roads are excellent, and for the most part are bordered with trees of luxuriant growth, behind which are ensconced extremely handsome houses, in every variety of style and dimension. There are certainly few points in England which exhibit an assemblage of architectural beauty amidst a landscape of so strictly rural a character.[4]

Fifty years later, *The Builder* expressed the same view:

> Few towns can boast such an extensive and beautiful residential suburb as Birmingham possesses in the large western district known as Edgbaston. One drives through road after road, broad, well kept and flanked by a series of detached houses, many of them of a picturesque character.[5]

And, in the 1900s, 'John O' London' ventured as far north as Birmingham, where he found most of its suburbs to be wretched, but

> Edgbaston was different. Impossible to miss Edgbaston. And this suburban Eden . . . more than fulfils expectations. Its labyrinth of roads is quiet, exclusive and beautiful. London has no such suburb within the four mile radius. In its way, it is rivalled only by Clifton . . . You scent roses and culture. Here Birmingham is explained, for here she rests and is thankful.[6]

Nor did contemporaries have any doubt as to whom gratitude was due for this altogether delightful suburban oasis. Politically, Birmingham might be radical for much of the nineteenth century, hostile to privilege, rank and even royalty. But the creation of Edgbaston represented one of the most outstanding examples of collaboration between an aristocrat who owned the land and those city dwellers who came to live on it. As Walter Barrow put it in a lecture in 1911:

> Birmingham owes its most enchanting suburb to the fact that it has been

in the hands of one owner who has declined to sell, and who has kept it as a purely residential neighbourhood.[7]

Indeed, half a century before, the *Edgbaston Directory* had noted that

His Lordship has paid such attention to its improvement as to render it, independent of all other advantages, the most eligible spot for building in the neighbourhood of Birmingham.[8]

And, when Thomas Anderton wrote in 1900, he was even more explicit:

Edgbaston is chiefly, I may say almost entirely, the property of the Calthorpes, and the late Lord Calthorpe, also his predecessor, were wise in their day and generation, and they had land agents who were shrewd and far-seeing. They saw the importance of reserving Edgbaston and laying it out as an attractive, quiet suburb.[9]

In other words, Edgbaston was in part 'aristocratic' because it played host to Birmingham's elite. But it was also 'aristocratic' because it was owned, throughout the nineteenth century, by the Lords Calthorpe. Their 2,500-acre estate simultaneously gave them a considerable foothold in the largest nineteenth-century English provincial town, while providing it with a suburb whose renown extended far beyond the confines of the city. In the course of the nineteenth century, Edgbaston's development made the Calthorpes wealthy, famous, respected and disliked; for while their economic links with the town were both important and solid, their social and political relationship with it was far more tenuous and fluctuating. But who exactly were the Calthorpes? Where had they originated? How did they become linked with the town of Birmingham in the first place? And why and when did they begin to develop Edgbaston in this manner?

2

On the sixteenth of April 1717, there took place an agreement between two families: of the one part, Thomas, Lord Ffauconberg and Lady Bridgett, his wife; of the other, Sir Richard Gough. In fact, this single transaction was part of a larger deal between the two families, for in the same year Lady Bridgett's sister, Dame Mary Shelly, sold land to Harry Gough, Sir Richard's nephew.[10] The two selling sisters were the only children of Mary, Lady Gage, herself the only offspring of Thomas Middlemore, the last direct male descendant of that family who had been lords of the manor of Edgbaston and other estates in the Midlands since the fifteenth century. When Lady Gage died, her two daughters partitioned the inheritance; Edgbaston went to Bridgett, while the other family lands scattered in the parishes of Solihull, Knowle, Moseley, Northfield and Kings Norton, passed to Mary. She sold her estates to Harry for £13,000.[11] Sir Richard Gough bought the Edgbaston estate for £20,400, thereby

Fig. 4. Sir Richard Gough, 1659–1727 (by courtesy of the Calthorpe Estate Office).

beginning that connection between Edgbaston and his family which has
continued unbroken to this day.

His ancestors were of Welsh origin, became Wolverhampton wool merchants, and finally, in the mid-seventeenth century, established themselves as
minor gentry by the purchase of the manor of Oldfallings in Staffordshire.[12]
(See genealogical table, Appendix A, p. 431.) John Gough (1608–65) consolidated the family holdings by acquiring estates at Walton and Perry in the same

county. His eldest son, Henry, was educated at Christ Church and the Middle Temple and was knighted in 1678, in belated repayment for services which his grandfather had rendered to Charles I during the civil war. From 1685 to 1687 and 1689 to 1701, he was M.P. for Tamworth, and from 1705 to 1708 for Lichfield. His younger brother, Richard, was born in 1659 and – as was so common for younger sons of the gentry – went into trade at an early age, joining the band of 'dwarfs and pygmies' of whom Sir Josiah Child complained. He was evidently a gifted, industrious and fortunate merchant who, after obtaining experience in the Mediterranean and the Levant, made four extremely successful journeys to the East. He became a director of the East India Company, bought a house in Chelsea in 1715, and was knighted in the same year, when he presented an address to the king expressing delight at the safe establishment of the Hanoverian dynasty.

His merchanting career, his highly liquid wealth, and his metropolitan connections marked Sir Richard out as a member of that new, rising class, the 'pseudo gentry'. But he did not remain among them for long. In 1706 he bought 23 acres of land adjacent to Gray's Inn Road in London. Eight years later he acquired an interest in the borough of Bramber, which he represented as a silent Whig until his death.[13] Then, in 1717, he retired and settled at Edgbaston, thereby returning, after his interlude in trade, to that level of society in which he had been born. There, he played the part of the local squire to perfection. He began to rebuild Edgbaston Hall, and in 1719 enclosed the grounds surrounding it as a deer park. Six years later, he paid for alterations made to Edgbaston church, and in the same year he gave the dean and chapter of Lichfield Cathedral £200 to augment the living, in return for which he and his heirs were granted the right to appoint the vicar in perpetuity.[14]

Ten years after he retired to Edgbaston, he died, and was succeeded by his eldest son Henry, who was created a baronet – the first of George II's reign – in April 1728, perhaps as a result of his father's support for Walpole. He, too, was M.P. for Bramber, shared the seat with his cousin Harry, and took the same stance in politics as his father, voting in favour of Walpole's ill-fated Excise Scheme in 1733, and against an opposition motion in favour of repealing the Septennial Act in the following year.[15] On his death in 1744, he was succeeded by his son, another Henry, who again sat as M.P. for Bramber. Once more, his early recorded votes show a markedly Whiggish tendency – support for Wilkes, for Dunning's motion and for Fox's India Bill of 1783;[16] but thereafter, he moved to support the younger Pitt, to whom he wrote in March 1789, requesting a peerage. This first attempt was unsuccessful, but in June 1796 he was finally ennobled as Baron Calthorpe of Calthorpe in the county of Norfolk.

His choice of title is explained by the matrimonial career of his father, the first Sir Henry. His first wife died in June 1740, having borne him no children. With seemingly uncommon haste, he tried again, and in July 1742 married Barbara Calthorpe. It is not surprising that he moved so rapidly, for the lady in question was an exceedingly attractive propositon on the mid-eighteenth-

Fig. 5. Survey of the Lordship of Edgbaston by William Deeley, 1701 (by courtesy of Cambridge University Library).

century marriage market.[17] Heiress to a clutch of estates and houses which her family had been accumulating during the preceding 200 years, she boasted among her ancestors two high sheriffs of Norfolk and a rector of London. While the Goughs were still selling wool in the market place, her forbears had been attending Cambridge and winning knighthoods. By the 1740s, the family estates comprised 2,000 acres scattered in Norfolk, a mansion at Ampton in Suffolk, a small estate and house at Elvetham in Hampshire, and a half share in the pocket borough of Hindon in Wiltshire. Barbara's brother, Sir Henry Calthorpe, who had the enjoyment of all this accumulated acreage and influence, was unmarried and middle-aged, as were his only two male relatives, his cousins James and Henry. The likelihood that Barbara or her descendants would inherit everything therefore seemed considerable. It was a risk worth taking, and the first Sir Henry Gough wasted no time.

Although Barbara and her husband both pre-deceased Sir Henry Calthorpe, all his estates did indeed pass, on his death in 1788, to Barbara's son, the second Sir Henry Gough, who married Frances Carpenter in 1783. As was commonly the case when land was transferred in this manner, it was conditional on the recipient taking the arms and additional surname of the family which had become extinct. So, in 1788, the second Sir Henry Gough became Sir Henry Gough-Calthorpe, no longer an obscure and *parvenu* country gentleman, but an established landowner, and his choice of title on his ennoblement aptly reflected the means by which this transformation had been accomplished. But the first Lord Calthorpe was still not satisfied, for his will gave his successors power to sell off the outlying estates in Norfolk and Suffolk, provided they invested the proceeds in a consolidated estate centred either on Edgbaston or Elvetham.[18] His death in 1798 – only two years after his ennoblement – denied him personally the opportunity to accomplish this step. Nor did his eldest son Charles, second lord, hold the title long enough to effect any major alterations in the family holdings. But under his successor, George, third lord, who held the title from 1807 to 1851, there was initiated a series of changes which were to transform not only his financial position, but the western side of Birmingham as well.

3

Although collectively the Calthorpe holdings which the second Sir Henry inherited exceeded in acreage the initial Gough purchase made by Sir Richard, Edgbaston remained throughout the century the family's largest single property. The estate as purchased was 1,700 acres, and thereafter, with the transient exception of the years 1823–4, it remained unfalteringly the policy of its owners until the closing decades of the nineteenth century to add to it at every possible opportunity. Already, by 1787, it had been extended to nearly 2,000 acres, largely as a result of the purchases made by the first Sir Henry, and during the first half of the nineteenth century in particular, the Calthorpes

Fig. 6. Edgbaston Hall in the eighteenth century (by courtesy of Birmingham Reference Library).

added to it even more energetically. (Although the family's surname was originally Gough, and Gough-Calthorpe from 1788, it is most convenient to refer to them as the Calthorpes, the name of their title.) From the very beginning, the family were the dominant owners in Edgbaston, and as they consolidated and extended their estate, their position was further strengthened.[19]

By 1819, the only large area of land immediately to the south of the Hagley Road which the Calthorpes did not own within the parish of Edgbaston was the 88-acre Curzon estate. For several years, the third Lord Calthorpe's Birmingham agent, John Harris, had kept a wary eye on it, for he feared that

the mischief that would arise in the event of an obstinate or unaccommodating person obtaining Curzon's land would be considerable, as they might throw out some of your lordship's plans, or excite an injurious competition for the building land.[20]

Accordingly, when the estate came up for sale in 1819, he suggested that no time be lost in acquiring it:

> The opportunity to purchase may never come again, and if it did, it would be under circumstances of increased value in consequence of our building plans coming daily into closer contact with Mr. Curzon's property.[21]

But, although Curzon was 'most desirous that Lord Calthorpe should have this property in preference to any other person', his initial asking price of £22,000 proved unacceptable, for Harris advised Calthorpe that the estate was worth no more than £18,000. Extensive negotiations ensued, and finally in September 1819 Calthorpe obtained it for £18,500.[22] It was a good bargain: Calthorpe needed to buy the property more urgently than Curzon needed to sell it to him, yet it was Curzon who had made the greater concession.

This important purchase effectively completed the rounding-out of the Calthorpes' holdings in the parish of Edgbaston itself and the result is well demonstrated in the tithe commutation award of 1827 (see table 6).

Table 6. The structure of landownership in Edgbaston, 1827 *(to the nearest acre)*

Size of estates (acres)	Landowners		Area occupied	
	nos.	%	(acres)	%
Under 1	5	20.0	2	0.08
1 and under 5	10	40.0	26	1.08
5 and under 10	5	20.0	32	1.32
10 and under 25	3	12.0	55	2.27
25 and under 100	nil	nil	nil	nil
Over 100	2	8.0	2,307	95.25
Total	49	100.0	2,422	100.00

Source: BRL MS. 662,130, Edgbaston Tithe Award 1827.

Compared with other suburbs whose nineteenth-century evolution has been studied, the concentration of landownership as revealed here is quite remarkable. In Hampstead, 70 per cent of the land was shared by five estates, and in Camberwell two-thirds of the land was held by seven landowners. Even the 1,250 acres of Glasgow's West End were owned by 23 different freeholders.[23] But in Edgbaston, by contrast, the power to decide what should be done with the land, as well as when and by whom, rested effectively with one owner: the Calthorpes. For they themselves held 2,064 acres, or 85 per cent of the total acreage of the parish. The only other relatively large holding, which at 243 acres was but a tenth of the Calthorpes', was owned by Mrs Catherine Noel, and her land was exclusively to the north of Hagley Road, effectively separated from the majority of the Calthorpes' acres. In

1852, her estate was sold to Joseph Gillott, the pen manufacturer, himself a resident of the Calthorpe estate, and he subsequently developed the land in conscious imitation of the Calthorpes themselves.[24]

There is no evidence which has survived to suggest that the Calthorpes themselves were in the market for the Noel estate. Hagley Road was a more effective boundary than the undifferentiated border of the Noel estate further north, and in any case by then their schemes for expansion were taking them further westward, beyond the confines of the parish of Edgbaston. Between 1850 and 1854, the Calthorpes spent £38,000 on 176 acres in Harborne, and in the next three years laid out a further £9,150.[25] These purchases between them enlarged the estate to its greatest extent – very nearly 2,500 acres. In 1892 an unsuccessful bid was made for the adjacent Ravenhurst estate in Harborne, which would have further consolidated their westerly holdings:[26] but thereafter, apart from the occasional donation of land for philanthropic purposes, the Calthorpes' Edgbaston acres remained constant until the First World War.

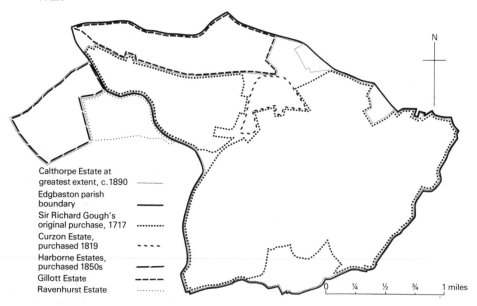

Fig. 7. Edgbaston: landownership and estates in the eighteenth and nineteenth centuries.

As well as being the largest single land holding in Birmingham as defined by the borough boundaries of 1838, the Edgbaston estate was also the most inviting, for there can be no doubt that Sir Richard Gough had selected a most congenial place for his retirement in 1717:

The spot he had chosen was one of great beauty, not only commanding extensive and charming views of the hills and slopes of Frankley and the

Lickeys, but within the park boundary there was undulating and grandly timbered scenery, lightened by the charm of the placid lake, and surrounded by woodland stretching to the vale below.[27]

Although the north-east corner of the estate lay only a mile from the centre of Birmingham, its westerly and south-westerly location made it largely immune from the smoke, noise and pollution of the town – already noticeable in the eighteenth century and only to get worse in the nineteenth – since the prevailing wind carried all such 'noxious vapours' in the opposite direction. Moreover, the soil was sandy and well drained, the estate was well wooded, its altitude – between 300 and 600 feet – ensured that the air was clean and fresh, and the views from the south-facing slopes were excellent.

Such advantages of topography and location made Edgbaston as appealing to the middle-class manufacturers of Birmingham in the nineteenth century as it had been to Sir Richard Gough in the eighteenth. Indeed, all of the great middle-class suburbs of Victorian England – Headingley, The Park, Hampstead or Kelvinside – shared these characteristics of clean air, altitude, good views and trees, however much they may have differed as regards the structure of landownership.[28] And in Birmingham, Edgbaston alone was able to provide them for most of the nineteenth century. On all sides of the town except the west and the south, the land fell sharply away from the sandstone ridge on which the town centre was located, and industry, canals and working-class houses had already congregated there by the end of the eighteenth century.[29] In other words, whatever had been the structure of landownership in nineteenth-century Edgbaston, it is probable that the middle classes of Birmingham would have colonized it sooner or later.

4

However, while location and topography were between them powerful and important forces predisposing Edgbaston towards high-class residential development, the great preponderance of one single landowner makes it more than ever important to study his particular attitudes and decisions: for it was at that level that the precise nature and timing of development was in large part determined. In 1783, the second Sir Henry moved his family from Edgbaston Hall to the Calthorpe home at Ampton in Suffolk. Never again was any member of the Calthorpe family to live at Edgbaston. Two years later, Edgbaston Hall itself was leased out to William Withering, and was thereafter occupied by a variety of distinguished tenants until it was converted into a golf club in the twentieth century. Then, in 1786, the first building lease on the estate was granted.[30] It was for 99 years, at a fixed ground rent, and required the lessee to spend a specified amount on building a house within a limited time. At the end of the period, both land and house would revert to the lessor. By 1796, nine such leases had been granted, filling in the easternmost triangle

of land at the Five Ways between Hagley and Harborne Roads. This policy
was clearly intended as the shape of things to come, for the marriage settlement between the second Sir Henry Gough and Frances Carpenter, drawn up
in 1783, had empowered future tenants for life to grant such leases, and Sir
Henry's will explicitly passed on such power to his successors.[31]

So the lines of future policy for the development of the Edgbaston estate
were clearly laid down at the end of the eighteenth century. Nor was this
confined to the granting of building leases. Opposition to public utilities, for
which Edgbaston was later to become famous, also dates from the time of the
second Sir Henry. In 1791, the Birmingham and Worcester Canal Act was
passed, empowering the company to construct a canal from a wharf in the
centre of the town to the River Severn near Worcester.[32] Unless the route was
to be exceptionally circuitous, it was necessary for the canal to cross the centre
of Edgbaston estate, thereby threatening the prospects for high-class
development unless the interests of the estate were suitably safeguarded.
Accordingly, Sir Henry Gough-Calthorpe – who was in fact a shareholder in
the venture – obtained clauses in the Act prohibiting the building of factories,
workshops or warehouses alongside the canal at Edgbaston, forbidding the
construction of reservoirs for the canal on his land, and placing the towpath on
the western side of the canal, as far away from the hall as possible. Such
successful vigilance was the model which his successors constantly tried to
emulate.[33]

During the lifetime of the young second Lord Calthorpe (1798–1807), the
impact of Napoleonic wars and the slump in the housing market meant
that no more building leases were granted,[34] but this was only a temporary lull.
Between 1810 and 1813 George, third Lord Calthorpe, and his agent, John
Harris, decided to begin a more systematic development of Edgbaston as a
building estate. Two of Harris's long letters about Edgbaston have survived
for this period, and between them they give an almost complete picture of the
scheme envisaged. In his first letter, Harris urged the need, by adopting 'a
general and well-considered plan', to avoid the piecemeal, 'selfish and sordid'
development to which small freeholders, thinking only in terms of short-term
profit, were prone.[35] The aim, he continued, must be to attract the most
important citizens of Birmingham, and to 'introduce that population by a
ready and convenient access'. So, he argued, it would be 'proper, not merely to
set out roads, but to make such of them as appear from their situation to meet
your approbation.' Such 'proper communication' would, Harris claimed,
'bring into the market an immense tract' of building land holding out great
prospects for future development. The estate, he went on, should aim to attract
tenants, not by advertising, but rather by acquiring a reputation for giving
'every indulgence and attention to applicants'. 'Being well pleased themselves', he suggested, 'they will soon communicate their satisfaction to others',
and so the demand for building accommodation would be sure to rise.

In the same letter, Harris went on to enumerate four possible types of tenant: farmers and poor cottagers, already resident on the estate, and gentlemen and tradesmen, so far only occupying those few plots which had been leased out during the time of the first Lord Calthorpe. He had no doubt as to which types of tenants were preferable: 'the accommodation of the gentleman and tradesman must be obtained at the expense of the farmer'. Accordingly, some of the agricultural tenants must be removed, either to the more remote parts of the Edgbaston estate, or to other properties of Lord Calthorpe. This would then leave room for the gentlemen and tradesmen who, 'taking their lands rather for amusement than profit', would constitute the ideal type of tenant.

In his second letter, he went on to discuss the question of how the houses themselves should be built.[36] There were, Harris argued, essentially three types of builder. The first was speculative. He

> has the trouble of taking the land and putting up the house or houses, which he afterwards sells to his client, to whom he likewise transfers his lease. And if a builder has a good connection in this way, he frequently takes a considerable plot of land, and erects villas for sale.

But, as he went on to explain, the other types were rather different:

> The second description of tenants for building land are persons of property, who take a quantity of land for the purpose of building a good house for themselves, and other houses for letting, by which means they secure a neighbourhood of friends and acquaintances.
>
> The third description are those people who, having acquired a moderate competence, wish to retire to a small country house, and therefore take just as much land as would be sufficient for the purpose.

It was, Harris felt, this last type of potential tenant – 'a little man who wishes to take a plot of ground anything under one acre, for his own comfort and retirement' – who was 'most deserving encouragement'.

5

So, before the Battle of Waterloo was won, the future course of Edgbaston's development was outlined and agreed upon. Speculative builders, working-class housing, industry, manufactures and trade were all to be excluded, and the industrial elite of Birmingham were to be welcomed. Like many nineteenth-century aristocratic landowners, the Calthorpes' initial preferences were exclusive and exalted. It remains to be seen precisely how far they were able to implement them.

5 The making of an 'aristocratic' suburb, 1810–1914

During the century which followed the third Lord Calthorpe's decision, Birmingham grew 'from a position of second-rate importance' to be 'the fourth or fifth city of the empire'.[1] From being a physically restricted late eighteenth-century town, with a population of 70,000, it expanded, by the early 1910s, into Greater Birmingham, containing more than half a million inhabitants. In the process, it experienced changes so profound and wide-spread that William Hutton or even Thomas Attwood would have found it practically unrecognizable. In terms of housing, this prodigious growth meant that demand was sustained at a high level but, by setting out with such exclusive intentions, the Calthorpes were necessarily putting themselves beyond the limits which most inhabitants could afford. Conveniently for the historian, however, such a policy also ensured the creation of an ideal index of the estate's progress, for the individual building leases, taken by 'respectable' people, suitably averaged so as to iron out short-term fluctuations, give an exact guide as to the phases of the estate's development (graph 1a). From 1810 to 1842, there was a period of short-term uncertainty and fluctuation, in which, however, real and tangible progress was made. Then, between 1843 and 1880 the estate experienced steady and cumulative expansion, reaching a peak in the unprecedented building boom of the mid and late 1870s. Finally, in sharp contrast, the last 30 years were a phase of stagnation, decline and worry.

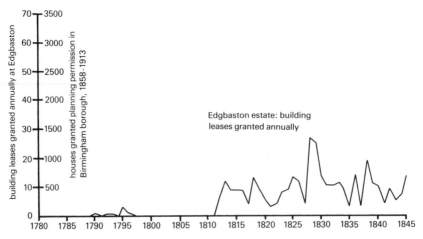

Graph 1a. Building leases granted at Edgbaston, 1786–1914 (EEO MS, Lease Books, I–VIII; J. Parry Lewis, *Building Cycles and Britain's Growth*, 1965, 308).

Graph 1b. Seven-year moving averages of building leases granted on the Edgbaston estate, 1815–1911.

1

In retrospect, the years between 1810 and 1842 showed more emphatic signs of growth and progress than was often apparent at the time. In the 45 years following Lord Calthorpe's decision, the total number of building leases taken went up from 9 to 342. Gross rental more than doubled, from £5,233 in 1810 to £11,673 in 1845, representing an increase of 2.3 per cent annually. Equally emphatic was the rise in population, from 1,155 in 1810 to 3,854 in 1831, and 6,609 ten years later.[2] Of course, these figures were for the entire parish, but the Calthorpes' holdings were so large that they form a reliable guide to the estate's progress (graph 2). By 1846, Edgbaston was well integrated into Birmingham's suburban transport network. Six omnibuses plied daily in each direction along the Hagley and Bristol roads, and five made the journey each

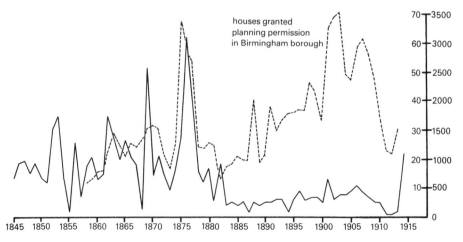

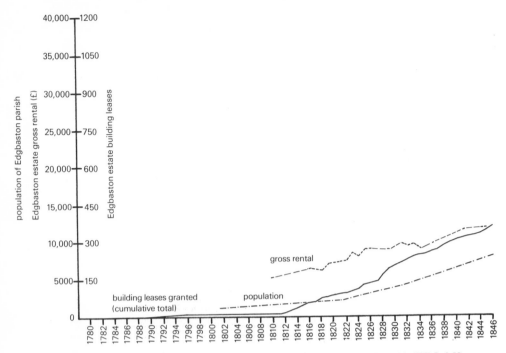

Graph 2. Edgbaston rents, leases and population growth, 1786–1914 (EEO MS, Account Books; Lease Books; I–VIII; *VCH*, VII, 14; breaks in lines indicate no data available).

day to Harborne and back through the centre of the estate.[3] 'As a whole', Harris had written to Calthorpe in 1823, 'the estate bids fair both in beauty and value to exceed anything of the kind in the kingdom'.[4] Such words had been optimistic then; but by the middle of the century, they had been vindicated.

The Calthorpes' own contribution to this development was threefold. In the first place, those agricultural tenants who occupied the land nearest the estate's north-eastern border were moved into other farms as and when they became vacant.[5] Then, in order to bring this land into the building market, roads were laid out (fig. 9) and plots marked. Between 1812 and 1820, Calthorpe Street, George Street (named after the third lord), Frederick Street (named after the fourth lord) and Church Street were laid out in the north-eastern corner of the estate near Five Ways. At the same time, another area was developed on the north side of Bristol Road, where Wellington Road (in honour of the victor of Waterloo) and Sir Harry's Road (in memory of the two eighteenth-century Sir Henrys) were laid down. In the 1820s, development was further continued in a westerly direction, as Westbourne, Vicarage and Chad Roads were constructed. On the eastern side of the Worcester Canal, a small artisan quarter was created, in the region of Sun Street, Spring Street,

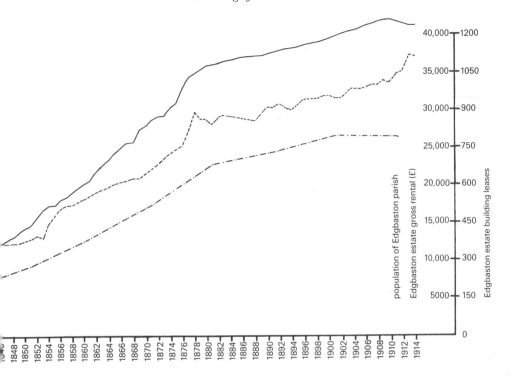

Balsall Heath Road and Yew Tree Road. Finally, the construction of the new turnpike road to Pershore in the late 1820s and early 1830s, to the cost of which Calthorpe himself contributed, opened up another new area of building land east of, but parallel to, the Bristol Road.[6]

The advantage of location, the appeal of topography, and the making of wide, well-laid, tree-lined roads, were powerful forces attracting middle-class tenants. The encouragement of churches and other amenities served further to enhance the area's lofty social tone. Land and money were given for St George's church in 1833, and favourable terms were offered to those local charitable societies anxious for clean air and sylvan surroundings – the Deaf and Dumb Asylum in 1814, the Botanical and Horticultural Society in 1836, and the General Institution for the Blind in 1851.[7] In part, Calthorpe's motives were genuinely philanthropic: as an evangelical he was an active participant in London in many societies concerned with moral and spiritual welfare; but, in the case of Edgbaston, altruism was mingled with self-interest. For example, when urging Calthorpe to offer hospitality to the Deaf and Dumb Asylum, Harris stressed 'the degree of advantage which in all probability would accrue to the estate generally'.[8] And in the same way, he urged that accommodation should be given to the Botanical and Horticultural Society because it would 'greatly promote the interest of the estate'. Thus was Edgbaston early established as 'patron of the charities of life'.[9]

All this energetic activity amazed, and on occasions annoyed, contemporaries. One visitor to Edgbaston in 1825, who had not seen the parish for a quarter of a century, noted: 'How changed the scenery! Many of the fields which at that time were fine pastures of arable land are now covered with dwellings of elegant villas.'[10] Drake went even further, claiming that 'about 1812, it became a fashion, almost epidemic, to build residences in this neighbourhood'.[11] One resident of George Street was so worried by the prospect of encroachment that in 1828 he wrote an account of his house and garden, 'because it is more than probable that from the rapid encroachment of the town there may be hardly, at the end of twenty years, a single vestige by which to trace its present unquestionable beauties'. Indeed, one witness giving evidence before a House of Lords Select Committee in 1846 could argue that 'almost a new town' had arisen there.[12]

However, the amazement of contemporaries was greater than the actual rate of progress (fig. 8). The area of building land which the Calthorpes had initially opened up was far larger than was immediately needed. The last plot in Calthorpe Street was not taken until 1848, and in Frederick Street until 1852: nearly 40 years after the roads had been made. Hardly any plots were taken in Wellington Road until 1837, and it was not entirely filled for another 30 years. In the early 1820s, Sir Harry's Road and Wellington Road were practically devoid of houses, and even as late as 1838, half of all the land in Birmingham undeveloped was located in Edgbaston parish. By the middle of the nineteenth century, 40 years after the third lord's scheme had been

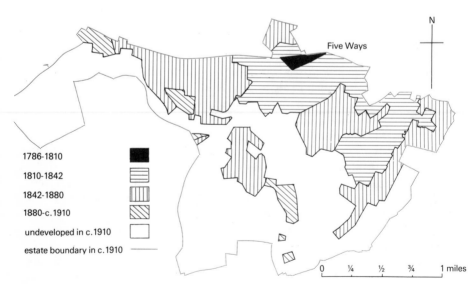

Fig. 8. Edgbaston: chronology of development, 1786–1910.

launched, Edgbaston remained essentially an agricultural region, with houses confined to a narrow strip along the estate's northern and north-eastern boundaries.

Yet even this limited development had not been achieved without difficulty. Of necessity, since the estate set out to attract those 'who have basked in the sunshine of commercial prosperity', the 'opulent inhabitants of Birmingham', it followed that they would only seek large, new houses when trade was good, profits were buoyant, and future prospects bright.[13] Accordingly, there is a close parallel between the line recording the leases granted at Edgbaston and that summarizing business activity. Indeed, the Edgbaston figures only diverge markedly from the national aggregates when economic fluctuations in Birmingham itself were out of step. The post-Waterloo slump, a temporary recovery, a further depression, another brief upturn, and then the great crash of 1826–7 are all revealed. The boom which followed was not in step with national trends, but aptly reflected the pronounced local upturn. Indeed, in 1829, the *Birmingham Gazette* felt able to comment on 'the rapid manner in which this town has been extended on all sides within the last few years'.[14] Thereafter, the peaks and slumps of the 1830s and 1840s once more denoted a return to the pattern of the national business cycle (graph 1b).

Such fluctuations are mirrored precisely in the correspondence between Lord Calthorpe and his agent. 'I am happy to report', wrote Harris shortly after the scheme had been agreed upon, 'that at present everything seems to prosper, and that capital and useful industry are rapidly advancing into your lordship's property'. But by May 1818, he was reporting 'three years of difficulties', and the gloom did not lift until another ten years were passed. 'It is very satisfying', wrote Calthorpe to Harris in July 1828, 'especially in these times in which there seems to be a considerable stagnation of trade in many quarters . . . , to hear so favourable an account of the progress of building at Edgbaston'. The census figures for 1831 gave him further cause for comfort: 'I see by the returns that the population of Edgbaston has increased since the last census far beyond what I had imagined'.[15] Indeed, so optimistic did Harris soon become, that he thought it time that more farmers were removed, so as to bring new land into the market. Finally, after one more period of uncertainty in the early 1840s, the time of troubles was passed, and the era of expansion was in sight.

2

The years between 1843 and 1880 were a period of sustained and almost uninterrupted growth for the Edgbaston estate, appropriately reflecting those mid-Victorian years of optimism, expansion and self-confidence which characterized Birmingham as a whole. Between 1851 and 1881, the town's population grew from 177,922 to 400,744. By 1881, 93 per cent of the pen makers, 78 per cent of the button makers, 61 per cent of the pin makers, and 55 per cent of the small arms manufacturers of England and Wales were located in Birmingham.[16] Although delayed by a generation, this frenzied economic activity found apt political expression in the celebrated mayoralty of Joseph Chamberlain between 1873 and 1876. For the essence of his policy was the mobilization of this accumulated private wealth for municipal purposes, which he accomplished with such style, gusto and success as to win for the town the epithet of 'the best-governed city in the world'.[17]

Predictably, this rising tide of entrepreneurial wealth buoyed the Calthorpes up to unimagined heights as landlords, as the local factory masters, increasing alike in number and prosperity, sought refuge and quiet in Edgbaston. Between 1851 and 1881, the parish's population mushroomed from 9,269 to 22,760.[18] On the estate itself, the Calthorpes gave land for St James' church in 1852, and for Calthorpe Park in 1867. The original Edgbaston parish church was enlarged in 1856, St George's likewise in 1884, and a new estate office was constructed in 1864.[19] The total number of leases granted rocketed from 342 to 1,077, at an annual average of 21, three times the figure for the previous period (graph 2). Between 1810 and 1844, there had been only 14 years in which the number of leases granted rose above 10; between 1845 and 1880, the figure only fell below 10 on four occasions, and for 15 years stood at 20 or above. The estate minute books for this period recording unceasing activity: applications for leases as never before, plots being measured and marked out, new roads being planned and laid, tenders invited and contracts awarded. Most impressive of all, gross rental grew from £12,296 in 1848–9 to £29,919 in 1878, an increase of 3 per cent per annum. So, by the end of this period, the annual revenue from Edgbaston was actually greater than the initial purchase price of the estate.

More prosaically, this meant that all the vacant sites along those many roads optimistically laid down in the 1820s were finally filled up. In the mid-1850s a new working-class area was created north of Hagley Road along Beaufort and Duchess Roads, and in the next decade, a more extensive artisan quarter was established on the eastern corner of the estate, around Varna and Princess Roads. To the south of Calthorpe Park, new and larger houses were constructed along the Bristol and Pershore Roads, and ribbon development also continued along Hagley Road, stimulated by the advent of the Harborne Railway in 1874 and the Birmingham & West Suburban Railway in 1876.[20] And in the large wedge between these arterial roads, development was in every sense more extensive. To the north-west of Edgbaston Park, Arthur, Ampton and Carpenter Roads were laid out, and the plots were quickly taken. The first lease on Arthur Road was granted in 1848; by 1865 it was filled completely; and on Ampton Road, begun in 1850, the last lease was taken only six years later. A second high-class area was to the south of Hagley Road, along Norfolk, Augustus and Westfield Roads, pushing further west after the coming of the railway to Meadow, Woodbourne and Hermitage Roads. Finally, on the high ground to the west of Edgbaston Park,

Fig. 9. Edgbaston roads, c. 1910.

separated from the rest of the estate by a valley, was begun the most splendid development of all, in the region of Farquhar, Somerset and Richmond Hill Roads (fig. 9).

As a result of this unprecedented expansion, by the mid-1880s the estate had largely assumed the appearance which it was to retain for the next 60 years or so (fig. 8). Under these circumstances, the comments of contemporaries lamenting the pace of change were more plausible than they had been half a century before. Comparing Birmingham of the mid-1880s with its early-nineteenth-century predecessor, one observer noted that

> the overflow of its wealthier inhabitants, who were then just commencing to establish themselves among the fields and leaves of Edgbaston, has now spread itself for miles beyond in all directions, surrounding the once half-rural gardens with roads and houses, and bringing them in appearance, if not in reality, much nearer the heart of the town.[21]

Indeed, by the early 1870s, no fewer than three different companies were operating half-hourly omnibus services along the Hagley, Harborne, Bristol and Pershore Roads. In 1876 they were joined by the steam trams along Bristol Road, and by the mid-1880s, there was a train every ten minutes at the Hagley Road station of the Harborne line, and trains called every hour at the Church Road and Somerset Road stations of the West Suburban Railway.[22]

Yet, despite these signs of unprecedented expansion, much of Edgbaston still remained undeveloped. Almost the whole area west of a line from Calthorpe Park to Edgbaston Hall to Metchley remained farmland, as did those new acres acquired in the 1850s in Harborne parish. As another contemporary noted in 1883: 'even now, a peep into the park from over the churchyard wall behind the church makes it difficult to realise the proximity of a great town.'[23] In part this was because some even more extensive schemes of development envisaged by the estate in the heady days of the 1870s had not been implemented. One map shows an elaborate grid system of roads planned for the Metchley Farm area, which it was hoped would be brought into the commuters' orbit by the building of the Birmingham & West Suburban Railway. Another scheme envisaged a road between Edgbaston Pool and Edgbaston Park Road, for which the sewers were actually laid. Similar provision was made for the extension of Farquhar Road north-east to St George's church and finally, in 1880, it was proposed to extend Meadow Road, parallel to Hagley Road, to the westernmost boundary of the new Harborne lands.[24] None of these schemes was ever realized, but they stand as impressive evidence of the expansionist mood of Lord Calthorpe and his agents at the time.

Nevertheless, in the short run, the ups and downs of cyclical fluctuations remained severe, as the number of leases granted at Edgbaston continued to rise and fall in harmony with local business conditions (graph 1b). During the late 1840s and early 1850s – Edgbaston's first really long and sustained phase of growth – building activity was general throughout the country for, as *The*

Builder noted, 'there is no lack of brick or mortar and, west, north and south, our cities are extending themselves into the country'. But the Crimean War ushered in a period of depression, and it was not until the early 1860s that trade generally, and building specifically, revived in Birmingham. Then again, in the early 1870s, building – but not industry – stagnated because of over-production.[25] Finally, later in that decade, there was the massive, unprecedented building boom which engendered that euphoric atmosphere in which both Joseph Chamberlain's Corporation Street and most of modern Edgbaston were born. By the early 1880s, however, the boom had collapsed, leaving both Birmingham's Parisian boulevard and the Calthorpes' new roads with empty plots which were to remain vacant for many years.[26]

3

Although it only became apparent in the 1890s and thereafter, the early 1880s were in fact a major turning-point in the development of Edgbaston. During the previous 70 years, there had been the excitement of the initial problems of promotion and the building mania of the mid-Victorian period; but for the rest of the nineteenth century, and indeed largely until after the Second World War, there was, by contrast, little activity to report. For many years, however, this did not become apparent. In part, this was because the estate continued to think in terms of expansion, interpreting the down-turn in the mid-1880s as a transient fluctuation rather than anything more fundamental. So Yateley Road was built in 1886, and an attempt was made to develop neighbouring Kingscote Road as an artisan quarter.[27] In 1901 Barnsley Road was opened on the north-west tip of the estate, and the large building firm after whom it was named agreed to construct 14 houses there. Other ideas were entertained, such as the development of the land near Selly Oak for small, semi-detached houses and, in 1899, it was even considered cutting up the park of Edgbaston Hall into building plots.[28] One of the attractions of giving land near Selly Oak to Birmingham University in 1900 was that 'it will open up a large area of building land which is at present not available'.[29] Moreover, this illusion of activity was buttressed by continued building on the estate well into the early 1890s. For many of the speculative builders, like the Barnsleys, who had taken large numbers of plots in the 1870s, had been unable to begin construction on them immediately, and were often only able to turn their attention to them some time later.[30] Finally, whatever the contours of development may have been, the 30 years from the late 1870s saw Edgbaston at the zenith of its fame.

However, the reality of long-term stagnation, as distinct from a short-term trough, could not be concealed indefinitely. In 1891, there were still 1,113 acres of agricultural land in Edgbaston, all of them on the Calthorpe estate, and amounting in fact to nearly half of their local holdings. Indeed, so rural did parts of their land remain that in 1902 the Albrighton Hounds caught a fox in Meadow Road.[31] Plots along those roads laid down in the euphoric atmosphere of the late 1870s – Farquhar, Somerset, Westfield, Meadow, Woodbourne and Hermitage – were still unlet in 1910. Rental, which had risen so spectacularly in the previous 30 years, now stagnated at around £30,000 a year (graph 2). Between 1880 and 1910, only 206 leases were granted, an average of below seven a year, lower even than during the first phase of development (graph 1b). And this stagnation was reflected in the population figures: 24,436 in 1891, 26,486 in 1901, and then a decline to 26,398 ten years later.[32]

So the correspondence between the Lords Calthorpe and their agents in these years is largely a catalogue of inactivity. 'Things generally are very quiet now', reported the agent in August 1895. 'It is very difficult, with so many houses available, to get people to build', he observed in the following year.[33] And the new century brought no improvement. 'I have let two small plots of land during the month, but the demand is very slow', Arthur Davies noted in 1901, and circumstances had in no sense altered by 1905: 'I am having no applicants for building land, and things generally are very quiet.'[34] This limited and trivial correspondence contrasts vividly with those letters written in the active years of mid-century. Instead of planning new roads, time was lavished on land to be given up to widen old ones. Rather than applicants for building plots, matters such as the choice of a new tenant for Pebble Mill Farm became major issues. Items such as rent rebates to the three remaining farm tenants and concern over air space in cowsheds assumed unreasonable importance in estate affairs simply by default.[35]

If Edgbaston's development was sluggish by comparison with those golden, mid-Victorian decades in the estate's history, it was positively alarming when compared with building in contemporary Birmingham. For in the town, as elsewhere, the trough of the mid-1880s was soon left behind, so that by the end of the century it was in the grip of a building boom which equalled in both length and intensity that of the late 1870s (graph 1b). The advent of the tram, and the improvement in the real incomes of the most prosperous members of the working class, led to the creation of a new, more distant ring of commuter suburbs, three to four miles from the city centre, largely constructed by those builders who now shunned Edgbaston.[36] The growth of the once-independent small villages, drawn inexorably into the vortex of urbanization, is eloquent testimony to the extent of late nineteenth-century suburban growth: Handsworth grew from 11,000 in 1861 to 70,000 fifty years later; Aston expanded from 16,337 to 82,000 in the same period; Yardley mushroomed from 9,745 in 1881 to 60,000 in 1908; and Erdington, more sedately, tripled from 9,627 in 1891 to 32,000 by 1911.[37] The contrast with Edgbaston, which actually lost residents in this period, could not be more striking.

To the south of the city, on the borders of Edgbaston which had once been open to the country, expansion was equally marked. Between 1881 and 1901, there was a 200 per cent increase in the population of Kings Norton and Northfield. As the *Birmingham Daily Post* put it, ten years later:

In no district has suburban development been more rapid and conspicuous than on the south side of the city. Thirty years ago, the parishes of
Kings Norton and Northfield were formed by villages and hamlets rural
in their simplicity . . . Now they include thickly-populated districts.[38]

Further to the west, Harborne village had reached 14,000 by 1911, and the
prospects for nearby Oldbury, Bearwood, Quinton and Warley seemed
equally bright. Indeed, as early as 1883, the then Edgbaston agent, George
Edwards, had predicted that 'the next twenty years will make a considerable
change in the neighbourhood', and events had proved him right.[39] The incorporation of Harborne, Balsall Heath, Saltley and Ward End in 1891, of
Quinton in 1909, and of Aston Manor, Erdington, Handsworth, Yardley,
Kings Norton and Northfield by the Greater Birmingham Act of 1911, was the
statutory proof that Edwards had forecast correctly.

It seems altogether extraordinary that Edgbaston did not share in this
expansionist phase, as it had done in the previous boom of the 1870s. After all,
there were still 1,100 acres of virgin farmland, and the estate's preference for
residential accommodation seemed exactly appropriate at a time when urban
growth took the form of relatively prosperous suburban expansion. Partly it
was because Edgbaston was beginning to lose its status as the only high-class
suburb of Birmingham, for much of this new phase of suburban growth took
the form of high-standard middle-class development. Erdington, Handsworth, Moseley, and parts of Kings Norton, Northfield, Selly Oak and
Yardley were explicitly geared to cater for the middle class. This description of
Moseley in 1911, for instance, is also a perfect picture of Edgbaston:

Admittedly one of the finest suburbs in the country . . . There are no small
houses there because of the restrictions in regard to building enforced by
the ground landlord. There are no manufactories or works of any kind,
and shops are confined to the vicinity of what was the old village green.[40]

At a time when it was beginning to be whispered that Edgbaston was past its
prime, with out-of-date houses, the intrusion of tramways, and other signs of
decay, such competition was altogether unwelcome.

Moreover, for the very rich, those families who had adorned the centre of
Edgbaston for nearly a century, the advent of the motor car enabled them to
live at a greater distance from the city, once again enjoying that semi-rural
existence which the encroachment of new suburbs around the Calthorpes'
estate meant was ever more difficult to find in Edgbaston. Indeed, as early as
1866, attention was drawn to 'a constantly increasing disposition on the part of
the manufacturers and merchants of Birmingham to live away from the town
at some little distance'.[41] But the new century, which saw the beginnings of
development in the distant villages of Knowle, Solihull, and Barnt Green, saw
this trend carried one stage further. For where once businessmen had moved
from the town centre to Edgbaston, and entertained no thoughts of moving on
again, they now contemplated more distant suburban seclusion:

Like the Arab, they are folding their tents and stealing silently away in the direction of Knowle or Solihull, where the octopus tentacles of expanding Birmingham are as yet in the distance. Silently, and without any show of ostentation, a little revolution is taking place.[42]

As far as the Calthorpes were concerned, it was a revolution which they did not welcome, but could not reverse, for the advent of these new commuter communities at Warley, Selly Oak, Harborne, Bearwood and Bournville, surrounded those parts of Edgbaston which had previously been open to the countryside, and gave rise to a new flow of commuters who daily crossed Edgbaston to work in the city (cf. figs. 10 and 11). Gradually, but inexorably,

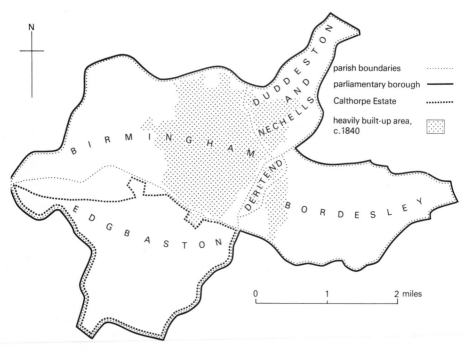

Fig. 10. Edgbaston in Birmingham, *c.*1840.

the forces of urban growth were coming to stifle Edgbaston's open and rustic boundaries. And the demand, by the residents of these new communities, for some form of mass transport in addition to the relatively expensive and exclusive omnibuses, became increasingly strident. As a result, tramlines were laid along the Bristol Road in 1876, and in the 1900s there was a constant campaign to lay them on the routes to Harborne and Quinton for, as one authority put it in 1907: 'in order to serve that population of the outskirts, it is necessary to have a tramway running through Edgbaston'.[43] Even Lord Calthorpe's agent, who took a survey of the traffic using the once-quiet Hagley Road, was obliged to admit how busy it had become:

The traffic along this road is now very heavy. On the seventh inst. I took a census of those [omnibuses] passing here between one and two o'clock. Total sixty two (44 horse-drawn and 18 motor). Between two and three o'clock fifty eight (42 and 16 respectively). As some begin running at seven a.m. and continue until midnight, there must be between eight hundred and nine hundred each day, a very big number for a residential thoroughfare.[44]

And, along the Bristol Road, too, 'there is a great population now travelling between Birmingham and Selly Oak every day – at all times a very heavy traffic along the road, which has quite altered the character of the whole thing'.[45]

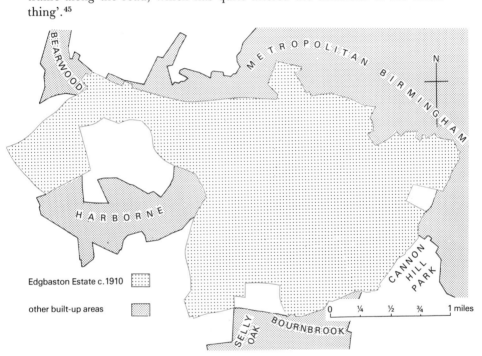

Fig. 11. Edgbaston in Birmingham, *c*.1910.

4

Unfortunately, the Calthorpes themselves were powerless to break this vicious, self-reinforcing and damaging cycle. The more these new suburbs expanded on the estate's borders, the more commuters crossed Edgbaston to and from their work in the city centre, the less pleasant became its once-quiet roads, and the more eager became people of wealth and means to move out to the country. As a result, the belief became more widespread that Edgbaston was declining, the exodus was reinforced, the new suburbs grew even more rapidly, the traffic crossing Edgbaston was further increased, and so the cycle began all over again. Before the suburbanization of the Calthorpes' green acres had even reached the half-way mark, the process of urban growth had leapfrogged beyond, thereby making it harder than ever to complete Edgbaston's development. So, when Augustus, sixth Lord Calthorpe, died in 1910, ·the golden years of the 1870s must have seemed very distant, and the prospects for his most prized estate were distinctly uncertain.

6 The superintendence of development, 1810–1914

In his draft evidence for the Select Committee on Town Holdings in 1888, George Edwards, the then Edgbaston agent, singled out as the most important character of the Calthorpe estate its 'unity of management and control'.[1] In this he was no doubt correct: if the pattern of landownership there had been as fragmented as in the other parishes of Birmingham, Edgbaston would assuredly never have developed in precisely the manner it did; for, coupled with the unified administrative structure which necessarily followed from the Calthorpes' landed predominance in the parish, was a development policy carefully evolved, scrupulously applied, and vigorously enforced. However greatly the number of leases granted annually may have fluctuated in the short or long run, the lines on which the Calthorpes' policy had been laid down remained rigid. In part, the key to success in maintaining Edgbaston as the 'West End' of Birmingham lay in the care with which they let building plots, the strict terms they put in their leases, and the zeal with which they enforced them. Indeed, Thomas Ragg had drawn attention to this at a time when the greatest phase of Edgbaston's development lay ahead:

> The regulations under which the Calthorpe estate is let out on building leases are such as will, for nearly a century at least, keep the parish of Edgbaston open, airy and rural. Only a certain number of houses are allowed on a given quantity of ground (always sufficient to leave good garden room), and no manufactory, tavern or beer house is permitted to be introduced.[2]

At the end of the great building boom, as *Edgbastonia* proclaimed proudly, the same policy still held:

> Lord Calthorpe . . . has exercised the strictest care in preventing the erection of such buildings as would destroy the present character of the locality, and intending investors are enabled to build without fear of detriment to the value of their property.[3]

Even as late as 1910, the 'stringent covenants as to the purpose for which the land may be used' still attracted attention.[4]

1

Yet it would be misleading to imply that the Calthorpes were omnipotent landowners, that the only real constraint on their power was how they chose to wield it, or that Edgbaston was an estate on which they could imprint any

grand design they wished. For despite all the advantages of location, topography and unified control, they – like all great aristocratic urban landlords –
remained at the mercy of countervailing market forces, with which they might
co-operate, but could rarely defy.[5] To begin with, the ever-expanding metropolis of Birmingham was almost daily getting nearer. Certainly, when the
earliest leases were granted, at the end of the eighteenth century, there was half
a mile of virgin land between Five Ways and the town, and the estate was open
to the country on all its borders; but by the early 1820s this had already
changed considerably, for the neighbouring St Martin's estate on the opposite
side of Islington Row, and the Gooch estate at the north end of Bristol Road,
had already been developed by then.[6] And the pace of Birmingham's mid-
Victorian expansion was such that by the 1880s there was a continuous urban
sprawl adjacent to the estate's northern and eastern boundaries, stretching in
an arc from the junction of Hagley and Gillott Roads eastwards to Calthorpe
Park, and including by then some of the town's most squalid slums and
workshops. Finally by 1910, the estate's southern and western borders were
similarly besieged from those new commuter suburbs of Harborne, Selly Oak
and Bournville (fig. 11).

This was the hostile, dynamic urban context within which the Calthorpes
and their agents tried, during the course of the nineteenth century, to develop a
building estate on completely opposed principles. Because it was large, com-
prising one-third of Birmingham's land area between 1838 and 1891, and
because its central regions were comfortably distant from the rest of the town,
it proved relatively easy to maintain the 'tone' over much of its area and for
most of the century. But at those lengthy points of contact between Edgbaston
and the rest of the town, especially on the estate's northern and eastern
boundaries, there was fought a constant – and not always successful – battle, in
which the Calthorpe policy of exclusiveness was pitted against the irresistible
tendency of the adjacent area towards decay. Thomas Ragg, the local poet,
depicted the conflict vividly:

> And to the north the darkly flanking town
> Encroaching constantly like the wild waves
> Of ocean on some tempest-beaten coast,
> Till, by its very heavings, on the very verge
> The swelling tide of population's thrown;
> And, but for barriers by a Calthorpe raised,
> Would sweep the lustre of thy vales away.

Or, as he put it more prosaically, 'the change in passing in any direction out of
the parish of Birmingham into the Calthorpe estate is readily discernible'.[7]

The second major weakness of the Calthorpes' position was that, like all
other landowners anxious to develop urban estates, they were limited by the
size and nature of the market. Of course, if they wished, they could initially
prohibit absolutely both industry and members of the working classes, simply

by refusing to grant them building leases. But if they could keep out those whom they did not want, it did not automatically follow that they could attract those whom they *did* want. Were there, for example, enough wealthy, middle-class people in Birmingham to fill up entirely an estate as large as Edgbaston in the manner which its owners desired? And even if such people did settle in sufficient numbers, there was no way in which the Calthorpes could compel them to stay. Because they did not monopolize Birmingham's potential building land in the way which they monopolized Edgbaston's, the Calthorpes were ultimately as much at the mercy of the market as was any other landlord in the town. The fact that, for 60 years or so, Edgbaston was the only successful and exclusive suburb, guaranteed it no immunity from competition should circumstances alter – a fact of which Edgbaston agents were only too well aware.

Moreover, when the third Lord Calthorpe and John Harris agreed on their development programme, the precedents in Birmingham for the creation and maintenance of a high-class residential estate were not encouraging. In the late eighteenth century, other major landowners had tried to establish their building estates as high-class areas,[8] but they had conspicuously failed to achieve this over any long period of time. In all cases, the building leases initially granted had not contained covenants sufficiently restrictive to give the landlord any effective power to prevent the subsequent decline in the overall tone of the estate. Neither the Colmore nor the Inge leases, for example, prohibited the construction of workshops, and when Sir Thomas Gooch leased land to the Birmingham and Warwick Canal in 1795 to enable the proprietors to construct a wharf, they were empowered to erect buildings 'at their pleasure', and Sir Thomas explicitly agreed not to interfere.[9]

With effete agreements such as these, the quality of housing decayed, the purpose for which it was used was altered, and the landlord in each case was powerless to do anything about it. The Colmore estate, for example, had originally developed the Newhall region, near St Philip's church, as an exclusive area for merchants, with good houses, large gardens, a fine view of the country, and only a rowing boat's distance from the tea gardens at Deritend; but by the turn of the century, workshops had been built in the gardens and orchards, and the once fine houses had degenerated into slums.[10] If there were no covenants in the original lease prohibiting manufacturing, and if the house contained a large garden, it was only too easy for the tenant to construct a workshop, and the landlord was powerless to prevent it. So, by 1826, nearly all the plots leased on the Colmore estate, initially for houses, contained in addition 'offices' or 'other premises' or 'manufactories'.[11] And, until the leases fell in, there was nothing the landlords could do.

Given the adjacent and hostile metropolis, the real limits on their power, and the unfavourable precedents which recent local history afforded, the lavish and exclusive scheme which Lord Calthorpe and John Harris evolved in the early 1810s was not going to be implemented easily, however much the advantages of topography and location might weigh favourably in the balance. How far in practice did the development of Edgbaston in the hundred years which followed witness the implementation of the modification of their grand designs? To begin with, the supervision of the initial development had to be close and rigorous: industry, the working classes and speculative builders must be kept at bay, and good-class houses for the wealthy of Birmingham must be encouraged. How successful were the Calthorpes in achieving this?

2

The most impressively consistent aspect of estate administration was the rejection of any application for land for any purpose other than private housing. Compared with other Birmingham estates, at least until the growth of the new suburbs at the end of the nineteenth century, this was the most distinctive feature of the estate's administration, justified on the unanswerable premise that the best way to keep industry out was not to let it in to begin with. Of course, because of its distance from the town, its altitude, and the absence of adequate and cheap transport facilities, Edgbaston was intrinsically an un-attractive location for workshops or working-class housing. Even so, George Edwards claimed in 1888 that he had rejected an application for land at eight pence a yard 'for a site on lease without restrictions, and afterwards let the same land with restrictions suitable to the character of the neighbourhood at two pence a yard'.[12] And when the Calthorpes gave land for philanthropic purposes, the terms were equally restrictive. When Calthorpe Park was made available to the town, there were clauses in the agreement prohibiting build-ing, shops, trade or steam engines. And the land given to the new university in 1900 and 1907 was donated conditional on its use 'solely for the purpose of a university for ever', with no houses, pubs, smoke, fumes or smells.[13]

Exceptions to this rule were very rare. Of all the leases granted between 1786 and 1914, only 11 gave permission for some form of business activity,[14] and these were restricted to light, non-polluting trades – carpenters' or stonemasons' shops or warehouses – with absolute prohibition on any other form of trading or business activity. Considering that 1,284 leases were granted altogether, these are surely the exceptions which prove the rule. As Ragg had urged them, the Calthorpes had maintained their vigilance:

And may ye long be suburbs, keeping still
Business at a distance from your green retreats,
And the tall chimneys of the Millocrat
Outside your smiling borders.

Indeed, even at the end of the century, Edgbaston was still 'remarkable for the very few licensed houses or shops or factories which are to be found upon it.'[15]

By comparison, the intended embargo on working-class housing was much less completely realized. For Edgbaston's inhabitants were by no means restricted to Birmingham's upper crust, but also encompassed much of the loaf beneath: as table 7 shows, the pattern is obviously that of a pyramid. Less than one-third of all the leases, and only about one-seventh of the houses built, were those lavish dwellings, costing £1,000 or more, which gave the district its reputation as the 'Belgravia of Birmingham'. Slightly more than one-third of the leases, and also about one-third of the houses, were for the solid, respectable, servant-keeping middle classes. The remainder – one-third of the leases but no less than half of the houses – were for the lower-middle and prosperous working classes.

Table 7. Value of houses built on Edgbaston estate, 1786–1914

Value of house (£)	*No. of leases granted*	%	*No. of houses authorized*	%
1,500 +	165	12.85	189	6.65
1,000–1,499	180	14.02	247	8.69
500–999	468	36.45	944	33.23
0–499	471	36.68	1,461	51.43
Total	1,284	100.00	2,841	100.00

Source: EEO MS., Lease Books I–VIII.

This represented a much wider social spectrum than most contemporaries would have believed actually lived on the Calthorpe estate. The fact that their working-class houses cost at their cheapest £100, or nearly twice as much as the average labourer's dwelling in Birmingham at mid-century, does not fundamentally modify this picture. What had happened to those exclusive aims of the third lord and John Harris? As with many other initially exclusive developments, the preferences of the landlord had melted as the estate had expanded before the irrefutable fact that, even in a town the size of Birmingham, there were simply not enough well-to-do people to fill up so large an estate with villas. Faced, therefore, with the choice of seeing most of their estate remain undeveloped, or lowering the status threshold, the estate managers had unhesitatingly opted for the second alternative.

However, such a policy necessarily obliged them to evolve a system of zoning, so as to keep apart the welcomed wealthy and the tolerated tradesmen (fig. 12). In Edgbaston, segregation meant not only keeping industry out, but keeping tenants of different socio-economic status apart. Fortunately, the wedge-shaped nature of the estate, its links with the town on the northern and eastern sides, and the presence of the Hagley Road on its northern border and the Bristol and Pershore Roads on the south-west side, made it possible to evolve a zoning plan which was simple but effective. Where the estate owned land on the far side of these roads, abutting directly on to the town, the working-class and lower-middle-class houses were tucked discreetly away. Then, acting in conjunction with these three main roads as a buffer against the pressure of the expanding and adjacent town, there was a crescent of middle-middle-class houses. Finally, in the centre of the estate, sheltered from both the cheapest Calthorpe houses and the city as a whole, were those expensive dwellings – fewer in number but much greater in area – which were responsible for the estate's exalted status and reputation.

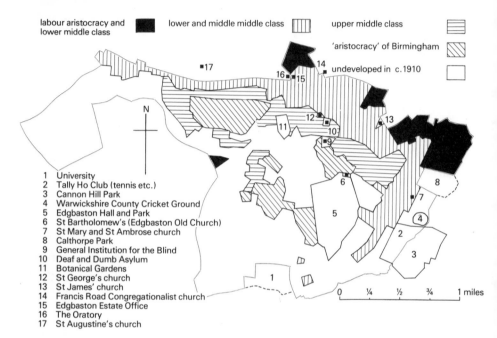

1   University
2   Tally Ho Club (tennis etc.)
3   Cannon Hill Park
4   Warwickshire County Cricket Ground
5   Edgbaston Hall and Park
6   St Bartholomew's (Edgbaston Old Church)
7   St Mary and St Ambrose church
8   Calthorpe Park
9   General Institution for the Blind
10 Deaf and Dumb Asylum
11 Botanical Gardens
12 St George's church
13 St James' church
14 Francis Road Congregationalist church
15 Edgbaston Estate Office
16 The Oratory
17 St Augustine's church

Fig. 12. Edgbaston, *c*.1910: zoning and amenities.

In the same way, the wish to prohibit speculative builders did not hold up inviolate. Certainly, the estate never went to the other extreme of giving them advances or preferential rates. Whoever the lessee, it remained the 'rule to give an allowance of one half the ground rent during the first year of a building lease'.[16] And, as table 8 shows, nearly 90 per cent of the lessees took only one or two leases, built nearly 60 per cent of the houses, spent over 60 per cent of the money in building them, and paid the ground landlord nearly 70 per cent of his ground rent.

But, at the same time, by 1914 nearly 20 per cent of all the houses had been constructed by speculative builders taking ten leases or more. And, relatively small though this aggregate contribution was, they were – predictably – most important in that period when building activity on the estate was at its most extensive (table 9).

The exceptions to this were Winfield, who laid out the artisan area of Duchess and Beaufort Roads in the late 1840s, Whitehouse, who took plots on

Farquhar and Westfields Roads early in the twentieth century, and Thomas, who filled in 17 vacant plots on Princess and Alexandra Roads between 1904 and 1908. Even the Barnsley family, who were active as builders on the estate for three generations, concentrated their activities in the boom years: 17 of their leases were taken between 1863 and 1880. The remainder operated exclusively in that period when the building boom generally was at its peak. Indeed, it was only in this period that large-scale builders' contribution to the making of Edgbaston became really substantial. In 1876, for example, of the 63 leases granted, 17 were to speculative builders, a far higher proportion than for the century as a whole, although even here it was still below one-third.

Table 8. Relative importance of different types of builder, 1786–1914
(percentages in brackets)

Total no. leases taken by individuals	No. of lessees	Total no. leases taken	No. of houses to be built by lessee	Money to be spent by lessee	Ground rent to be paid by lessee
10–49	9	175	518	£243,120	£3,460
	(1.2)	(13.6)	(18.2)	(15.9)	(12.9)
3–9	73	292	682	£339,880	£4,931
	(9.9)	(22.7)	(24.0)	(22.2)	(18.3)
1–2	660	817	1,641	£945,815	£18,519
	(88.9)	(63.7)	(57.8)	(61.9)	(68.8)
Total	742	1,284	2,841	£1,528,815	£26,910
	(100)	(100)	(100)	(100)	(100)

Source: EEO MS., Lease Books I–VIII.

Table 9. Analysis of nine speculative builders operating at Edgbaston 1825–1914

Contractor	No. leases taken	No. houses to be built	Money to be spent	Ground rent to Calthorpe	Period when active on estate
Barnsley	31	82	£71,400	£1,301	1839–1908
Heal	27	54	£34,600	£411	1866–79
Hulston	10	45	£9,870	£141	1863–71
Prosser	14	28	£8,400	£72	1867–76
Rogers	30	153	£51,000	£612	1854–72
Stokes	23	39	£20,800	£245	1869–80(1903)
Thomas	17	48	£14,400	£163	1904–8
Whitehouse	13	17	£15,650	£208	1901–14
Winfield	10	52	£17,000	£307	1825–58
Total	175	518	£243,120	£3,460	

Source: EEO MS., Lease Books I–VIII.
Note: All but one of Stokes' takes were between 1869–80 (the other was 1903).

A

B

C

D

Fig. 13. Edgbaston roads: A. Calthorpe Road, *c.*1910 (by courtesy of Birmingham Reference Library) B. Hagley Road, *c.*1914 (by courtesy of Birmingham Reference Library) C. Charlotte Road, *c.*1890 (by courtesy of Birmingham Reference Library) D. Lee Crescent, 1954 (by courtesy of the City of Birmingham Engineer's Department). Notice the trams on Hagley Road, and the contrast in housing density and foliage between Charlotte Road and Lee Crescent.

It is also noteworthy that the majority of the houses constructed by the speculative builders were at the less expensive end of the scale (see table 10). Apart from some expensive houses constructed by the Barnsleys in Augustus Road – in one of which John Barnsley himself lived – the speculative builders limited their activity to the creation of those relatively low-class, artisan areas to the north of Hagley Road and to the north-east of Calthorpe Park. Both the builders and the tenants who approximated least to the ideal types described by the third lord and John Harris were to be found in the same parts of the estate.

No matter who constructed the houses, the Calthorpes always insisted on the highest possible standards of materials and workmanship. Even the very first lease required that a house of specified value (£400) must be built within two years, and that the materials used should be of good quality.[17] Subsequent alterations in the terms, finally agreed in August 1815, made the requirements even more exacting. For the houses had to be built 'according to a plan and specification to be previously delivered by and at the expense of the lessee to

Table 10. Analysis of houses constructed by nine speculative builders 1825–1914

Contractor	Cost of house				
	£0–499	£500–999	£1,000–1,499	£1,500+	Total
Barnsley	28	18	23	13	82
Heal	20	23	nil	11	54
Hulston	45	nil	nil	nil	45
Prosser	28	nil	nil	nil	28
Rogers	122	31	nil	nil	153
Stokes	24	8	3	4	39
Thomas	48	nil	nil	nil	48
Whitehouse	nil	13	1	3	17
Winfield	46	6	nil	nil	52
Total	361	99	27	31	518

Source: EEO MS., Lease Books I–VIII.

the said lessor, and approved in writing by the said lessor.'[18] Nor was this a formality. Whether the projected house was intended to cost £200 or £2,000, the plans were most carefully vetted, and alterations were often recommended, not so much because the estate constituted itself an arbiter of architectural style, but for strictly practical reasons. For example, it might be that the proposed internal walls were not sufficiently robust, or that neighbouring houses would feel overlooked.[19] As a result of this careful and unceasing vigilance, the houses in Edgbaston were of a quality unrivalled in Birmingham, at least until the very end of the nineteenth century.

3

Because the Edgbaston estate developed so slowly during the course of the nineteenth century, the maintenance of high standards in those areas already built upon went hand-in-hand with the supervision of development in other parts. As one section of the estate was created, others had to be preserved. The first aspect of this policy, mainly confined to those large houses in the centre, concerned the vetting of proposed alterations. The second (and more important) aspect was the enforcement of covenants in those remote parts where the estate bordered on the town as a whole.

Lessees of the larger houses were often eager to extend them and this, like the initial construction, required the written permission of the agent. 'It is necessary', wrote Arthur Davies to one lessee, 'for all plans of alterations and additions to properties to be sent to me for approval.'[20] Again, the plans were carefully inspected, and alterations insisted upon if the standards of construction were inadequate or if neighbours might have grounds for complaint. More important was the problem, late in the century, of greenhouses, which suddenly became fashionable among the suburban rich, for there was always a danger of pollution from the smoke stacks, which would threaten the estate's important reputation for clean and healthy air. Indeed, the covenants in later leases were modified to require that any greenhouse smoke must be discharged through the house chimneys. In the case of the earlier leases, written permission had to be obtained before greenhouses could be erected, and if there was the remotest possibility of a neighbour objecting, then it was withheld.[21]

All this was relatively trivial, however – very much a case of preaching to the converted. None of these offending tenants had any intention of violating the basic tenets on which the estate was run. On the contrary, the desire to make extensions and construct greenhouses were the actions of people who sought to enhance their dwellings rather than abuse them. The real threat to the estate's integrity as a suburban oasis came from those tenants who refused to comply with the covenants prohibiting the carrying on of trade. Ever since the first lease, the use of a house for 'shop or shops, workshop or workshops or other place or places for carrying on any manufacture or manufactures' had been prohibited, and by the 1820s, the restrictions had become even more explicit:

> Any small dwelling house or houses of the description of labourers' or poor persons' houses or which shall be occupied by labourers or poor persons, nor any other small dwelling house or houses, nor any workshop or workshops or other kind of shop or shops, nor any place or places for carrying on any trade or manufacture, nor any brewshop, ale house, tea garden, public strawberry garden, or any other place of public resort or amusement whatsoever . . ., nor any other erection or building whatsoever which shall or may be deemed a nuisance or otherwise injurious to the said Lord Calthorpe.[22]

Ultimately, it was on the vigilance with which this covenant was enforced that Edgbaston's survival as 'the premier suburb' depended, for what was the point in refusing to grant leases for carrying on trade if houses were later converted to that purpose?

For most of the estate, enforcement presented no problem. Within the area bounded by Hagley and Pershore Roads, middle-class exclusiveness prevailed. The real difficulty concerned those houses nearest to the city, extending in an arc from Beaufort Road to Calthorpe Park, where the battle to maintain standards, so lyrically dramatized by Ragg, was long and bitter. Although the houses were well constructed, they were relatively small and converted easily into workshops, a temptation made all the stronger both by the pressure of the adjacent city, and by the fact that it was in this very area that those few Calthorpe leases which *had* allowed trade had been granted. So, from the 1870s, which had seen so much speculative building in the north-eastern corner of the estate, the battle to maintain standards there was well and truly joined.

One instance of 'creeping decay' was treated with delightful humour by a local paper in 1892:

> Edgbaston is degenerating. There is no doubt about it, and unless the inhabitants make a firm stand, they will no longer be able to boast of the aristocratic tendencies of their suburb . . . Edgbaston has a fried fish shop right in its very midst, within sniffing distance of some of its most palatial mansions. It is a fried fish shop of the most flagrant and ostentatious description too, with not a shadow of a doubt about it.[23]

The agent objected, and it was removed. But, by this time, it was not an isolated case. A selection from the estate correspondence in the early 1900s reveals reports of 'transacting business' in Bristol Road, 'carrying on a trade' in Lee Bank Road, advertisements on a house front in Belgrave Road, a dressmaking establishment in Bristol Road, and a moneylender's business in Speedwell Road.[24] Without exception, these infringements took place in those lower-class areas in the north-east corner of the estate which bordered on the city. During the same period, there were no such infringements of covenants to report from the more opulent areas of Edgbaston.

Occasionally, there were more unusual incidents, as in 1874 when an agricultural tenant offered his land, in Pershore Road, to Sangers Circus, in violation of the terms of his lease. This entertainment was billed as including an army of 'War Arabs' and an 'Abyssinian War Hunt with Pack of Hounds'. In addition, it was claimed that 97,000 people had watched this performance at the circus' previous venue in Manchester. Pressure on the tenant proved unsuccessful, and it was not until a court injunction was obtained that the threat was removed.[25] Likewise, in 1870, there was an animated correspondence between the agent and the Birmingham town clerk, on the grounds that bicycling had been allowed in Calthorpe Park, in direct violation of the covenants, and nine years later, there was an even more sensational episode concerning a public urinal which the Corporation had unthinkingly placed nearby, at the corner of Pershore and Speedwell Roads.[26]

4

Insofar as Edgbaston retained its high social tone for so long, and was so successful in avoiding the intrusion of industry, the staff of Lord Calthorpe's estate office deserved much of the credit. But, even though they were legally empowered to inspect twice yearly every building constructed on the estate they could never have maintained a uniformly watchful eye on the 2,500-odd houses which had been constructed on the estate by 1914. Only with the co-operation of the majority of the lessees and tenants – whose preferences were every bit as exclusive as the Calthorpes' – could the enforcement of covenants be made really effective. Indeed, more often than not, it was the residents themselves who drew the agent's attention to infringements. His incoming mail contained letters from tenants reporting breaches; his outgoing correspondence then consisted of gentle reminders to the offending tenants. Very often, the estate office was little more than a mediator between the two groups. In the case of Sangers Circus, or the Calthorpe Park urinal, for example, the estate only acted because other tenants had brought the affair to the agent's notice.

It is clear why the lessees and tenants were so vigilant. Whether they were investors or residents, they did not want the value of their houses to decline. They built at Edgbaston 'without fear of detriment to the value of their property', because they counted on the estate agent to ensure that their neighbours would also respect the covenants.[27] The tenant's agreement not to carry out a trade in his house carried with it a reciprocal undertaking on the part of the landlord not to suffer such action on the part of other residents. Accordingly, the slightest hint that a trade was being carried on next door, the faintest wisp of smoke from a greenhouse chimney, and tenants were only too eager to give the agent a lecture, reminding him where his duty to them lay. Indeed, on occasions pressure from the lessees – on the inevitable grounds that the value of their property was endangered – caused the agent to change his policy, as in 1868, when the ten-year lease on playing fields in Wheeleys Road came up for renewal. A petition was got up by residents demanding that it should not be renewed and the agent, who had been inclined to entertain the possibility, changed his mind as a result.[28] Thus could the tenants' tail on occasions wag the landowner's dog. At the very least, most of the tenants and lessees were the Calthorpes' active and willing allies. For all of them, the preservation of Edgbaston's amenities was self-preservation – and they were all in favour of it.

Such vigilance made Edgbaston not only the most attractive, but incomparably the healthiest suburb in nineteenth-century Birmingham. In the first place, its population density was quite extraordinarily low, partly because the Calthorpes' exacting requirements (however much modified) made it impossible for the majority of Birmingham's inhabitants even to entertain the prospect of living there, and partly because of the vigilance with which they guarded those areas of the estate contiguous with some of the worst areas in the town. In 1911, for example, the population of Edgbaston parish was only one-ninth that of Birmingham parish, while in land area the two parishes were much more closely comparable (2,589 acres as against 2,996).[29] As a result, even though the enforcement of covenants against trade was becoming a more serious battle by the 1900s in the north-east corner of the estate, there were no slums. Even Edgbaston's considerable artisan population was well housed. The *Report of the Committee of Inquiry into Artisans' Dwellings*, published in 1884, offered an interesting comparison between Edgbaston and Saltley – both large parishes with one paramount landlord, but developed very differently. Edgbaston, the committee found, had 'very few houses . . . of the class to which this inquiry is directed'.[30] Saltley, by contrast, was full of inferior, unclean and overcrowded dwellings, thrown up by speculative builders between railway marshalling yards, canals and factories, and completely unsupervised. With an impassioned eloquence rare in official reports, the Committee suggested that such dwellings would make any reasonable man sick and ashamed in approximately equal proportions.[31]

Clearly, the low overall density of housing (still only 1.5 an acre in 1950), the lack of industry, the excellence of house construction and the relative affluence of the inhabitants, allied with the advantages of location and topography, distinguished Edgbaston from all other areas of Birmingham – at least until the great phase of suburban expansion at the very end of the nineteenth century. Within the borough boundaries of 1838, Edgbaston could boast the lowest incidence of deaths from measles, scarlet fever and typhoid fever, as well as having the lowest percentage of back-to-back houses and the highest frequency of water closets.[32] Between 1873 and 1884, the average death rate per 1,000 in Birmingham parish was 21.4; in Edgbaston for the same period, the figure was 11.8.[33]

It was statistics such as these which underlay those many florid, admiring and complacent appraisals of Edgbaston's merits, and which vindicated the estate office's unceasing vigilance. The third Lord Calthorpe and John Harris might have been disappointed that two strands of their initial development policy – the exclusion of all but the most affluent tenants and restrictions on speculative builders – had parted before the reality of economic circumstance. Moreover, the tenants themselves deserved much of the credit for the estate's high standard and tone. Even allowing for that, though, Edgbaston was not an estate which managed itself.[34] The vigilance and rectitude of Calthorpe administration – both with regard to initial development and maintenance of standards thereafter – ensured that Edgbaston was unquestionably the most successful urban estate development in nineteenth-century Birmingham. The middle classes would almost certainly have come to Edgbaston anyway; but without the strong lead given by the ground landlord, its character would never have been so effectively established and preserved for so long.

5

Yet it would be dangerous and slightly misleading to end on too buoyant a note. For the lasting impression is that Edgbaston – splendid and renowned though it still was – had in fact passed the peak of its fame and status by 1910. Admittedly, it remained the 'premier suburb', with the great houses in the centre as grand and splendid as ever, and the majority of inhabitants still anxious that things should stay that way. But at the same time the barriers against industry and commerce were beginning to crumble, at least on the periphery. That delightful piece on the fish shop in Varna Road which began with the words 'Edgbaston is degenerating', was just a little too pointed to be funny. The advent of tramways along Bristol Road in 1876 was an added blow.

Thereafter, no leases were taken of plots along that road for the next 20 years, and some of the houses already built depreciated in value by 50 per cent. In 1872, 47 prominent Birmingham men had claimed Bristol Road addresses; by 1906, there were only four.[35] The next year, Charles Gabriel Beale drew attention to the changed circumstances of the road:

> I know some houses – in my young days the best houses in Edgbaston, where quite the best people lived – that are unlettable practically because this class of property has changed altogether.[36]

Such words only highlighted another problem which was increasingly troublesome by the early twentieth century. By then, those houses built in the region of Five Ways and Calthorpe Road were over 100 years old – out of date, decayed, hard to let, and in some cases unoccupied. And even where the leases still had a few years to run, it was difficult to insist on the enforcement of covenants. So, in one way and another, it was becoming increasingly difficult to maintain standards in those parts of the estate which adjoined the city and boasted some of Edgbaston's oldest houses. If to this was added the new problem of what to do when the leases began to fall in on a large scale – as they were bound to do after 1911 – then it is clear that the early decades of the twentieth century were not without their problems for the ground landlord.

7 Urban revenue and aristocratic aggrandisement, 1810–93

The changes so far described fundamentally transformed the western side of Birmingham, and gave it, during the course of the nineteenth century, a gracious suburb which equalled, if it did not surpass, the West End of Glasgow, Headingley in Leeds, Sefton Park in Liverpool, Victoria Park in Manchester, and North Oxford. And, more than any of these suburbs of similar tone and status, it stood as a powerful monument to the aristocracy's capacity to exploit urban growth, to stamp beauty and refinement on a process all too often sordid and squalid in its results. But at the same time, the making of Edgbaston transformed even more fundamentally the Calthorpes' financial position. If it was an oasis for the town, it was a gold mine for the family; for the beneficent influence which the Calthorpes were able to bring to bear on the process of urban growth was far surpassed by the contribution made by Edgbaston's development to their financial aggrandisement. To an extent unusual if not unique, the new world of the towns supported and succoured the old world of the aristocracy.

1

In the four years after he came of age in 1808, it is clear that George, third Lord Calthorpe, undertook an extensive review of his financial affairs, for the decision to develop Edgbaston was clearly taken within the context of a broader, more general financial analysis. Table 11 details his income for 1810.

It is noteworthy that even in the year when the systematic development of Edgbaston was first considered, it was already the most important single source of revenue. The small estate at Hampton was leased from the Crown, was never of more than trifling financial importance, and disappeared from the family holdings before 1850. Acle, Blakeney, Cockthorpe, Pakenham, Ampton and Elvetham were the historic Calthorpe lands which Barbara had effectively brought with her on her marriage to the first Sir Henry in 1742. They were neither extensive nor consolidated. Pakenham and Acle, in Suffolk and Norfolk respectively, comprised only 2,000 acres together, and although they were the only estates where the agricultural land was even moderately good, Acle was subsequently described as 'arable, pasture, waste and marsh'.[1] Blakeney and Cockthorpe, on the north Norfolk coast, consisted largely of sand dunes and salt marshes, with long grass fit only for cattle grazing.[2] Elvetham was an undrained and inhospitable clay marsh of 1,800 acres.[3] Ampton in Suffolk, the ancestral Calthorpe home, was famed for its beauty, but had only a park, with on estate attached.[4] Hindon and Bramber were the two pocket boroughs, in which the family naturally owned some property. (Bramber, incidentally, should have produced the princely income of £47.[5]) Gray's Inn Road, 23 acres of farmland, and Gough Square, already built on, had been bought by Sir Richard Gough in 1706, and the City Road estate in Clerkenwell had been granted on building leases of 99 years to Lord Shuldham in 1794 at an annual rental of £225.[6] The half share in the New River Company was another Calthorpe heirloom, having been bought by Sir Henry Calthorpe in 1745. Finally, the revenue from canals included dividends from four Birmingham canal companies, and interest received on £17,000 lent out on mortgage to the Duchess of Buccleuch.[7]

Table 11. Lord Calthorpe's income, 1810

Estate	Gross (£)	Net (£)
Edgbaston	5,024	3,566
Hampton-in-Arden	458	271
Acle	1,350	1,051
Blakeney & Cockthorpe	1,251	875
Pakenham & Ampton	1,483	1,033
Elvetham	1,195	659
Hindon	274	63
Gray's Inn Road City Road Gough Square	1,913	1,713
Bramber	nil	nil
New River Co. share	522	522
Canal dividends etc.	2,011	2,011
Total	15,481	11,764

Source: HROCal MS., Box 35, 70-page foolscap MS. 'Rents Received from George Lord Calthorpe from Michaelmas 1809 to Michaelmas 1810'. The figures are rounded to the nearest £.

The properties listed here represented an extraordinary, rag-bag collection of small and scattered estates, the unsystematized holdings of a family still on the make. The Calthorpe lands were as dispersed as the Calthorpe title was recent. Nor did this position fundamentally alter in the nineteenth century. Table 12 (overleaf) gives Bateman's figures.

Admittedly, these ignored the London estates and 2,000 acres at Elvetham which were owned by trustees. And by then there was also a 3,200-acre estate and mansion at Perry Hall in Staffordshire for the heir to the title. On the other hand, the Pakenham estate and the mansion house at Ampton had both been sold by then. In the 1880s as in the 1810s, it was impossible to describe the

Calthorpes as a territorial family of even the second, let alone the front rank. Many country gentlemen could boast acres more broad and holdings more conveniently compact. In the nineteenth century, as well as in the second half of the eighteenth, the Calthorpe estates combined the minimum acreage with the maximum of dispersion.

Table 12. Lord Calthorpe's estates, *c.*1883

County	Estate	Acreage
Warwickshire		2,073
Staffordshire	Edgbaston	197
Worcestershire		16
Hampshire	Elvetham	1,390
	Blakeney	
Norfolk	Acle	2,559
	Cockthorpe	
Suffolk	Newmarket	235
Total		6,470

Source: J. Bateman, *The Great Landowners of Great Britain and Ireland* (1883), 72.

Moreover, in the early decades of the nineteenth century, the income from these scattered holdings was not impressive. Fortunately, there were no mortgages, and the portions to which the third lord's brothers and sisters were entitled were raised by realizing the personal estate of the first lord. But even so, for a peer possessed of shares in two pocket boroughs, a town house in Grosvenor Square, a mansion at Ampton, another country house at Edgbaston, and a shooting lodge at Elvetham, it was not a large income. Moreover, even the net annual income of £12,000 – net meaning after expenses to maintain the estates had been deducted – was not entirely at Lord Calthorpe's disposal. The dowager Lady Calthorpe, the first lord's widow, received a pension of £1,800 a year, the third lord's brother, Frederick, was entitled to £100, and a distant cousin, the Rev. Richard Gough, was allowed £40 per annum.[8] Calthorpe himself was thus left with an income of about £10,000, out of which had to come not only the costs of running his houses, but also those extensive donations to charity which by the mid-1820s were in the region of £500 a year.[9]

As Lord Calthorpe contemplated his financial position in 1810, he must have realized that the scope for improving it was limited. Only Elvetham, Gray's Inn and Edgbaston offered any real prospects, and in the next five years, he and his agent explored them all. In 1814, a private Act was passed which enabled Calthorpe to grant building leases on his Gray's Inn estate, and power was also obtained to set up commissioners to pave, light, cleanse and regulate the streets.[10] The policy adopted for development differed from that at Edgbaston, for the aim was to keep Lord Calthorpe's expenses at a minimum by 'throwing all the expenses for improvement upon the lessees'.[11] Fortunately for the Calthorpes, 'the lessee' turned out to be none other than Thomas Cubitt, then at the beginning of his Olympian career as a master builder. In two 'takes', one in 1815, the other in 1823, he assumed effective responsibility for the estate's development, agreeing not only to construct the houses, but also to fill up and level the land, make the roads and lay the sewers, all at his own expense. Of those three types of builder whom Harris had described to Calthorpe in 1810 when discussing the Edgbaston estate, Cubitt came emphatically within the first category. The Gray's Inn partnership of one speculative builder and one inactive landlord was the exact antithesis of the development scheme evolved for Edgbaston. However, by relieving Calthorpe of these 'great expenses' he saved him some £3,000 in development costs, an amount well worth having considering the other calls on his limited resources.[12]

By the mid-1830s, the Gray's Inn rental had reached its peak of £2,500 a year, at which level it stayed until the leases began to fall in.[13] Indeed, the London revenue as a whole was limited to £3,500 at least until the early 1890s, when the leases at City Road and Gough Square would expire. Nor were the prospects at Elvetham very bright. Between 1821 and 1827, the estate's 1,045 acres were drained, at a cost of £1,200 a year.[14] With agriculture in general so depressed, it was hardly an auspicious time for such an enterprise. In 1822 there was a 25 per cent abatement of rent, and in 1825 the tenants were a further half-year in arrears. Between 1818 and 1826, Calthorpe only drew £500 from Elvetham, while during the same period he had to transfer £2,195 to that estate account from other sources.[15] And in East Anglia the picture was even more gloomy. In 1822, half the arrears were written off at Acle, and in the following year there was a 25 per cent abatement at Cockthorpe.[16] Indeed, in the financial year 1821–2, when agricultural slump was combined with extraordinary expenditure in London, the Norfolk, Suffolk and Elvetham estates between them yielded no net income, while the London account was in debt to the sum of £871. This was, admittedly, exceptional; but for most of the 1820s, Calthorpe's entire net landed income – Edgbaston excepted – was only between £2,000 and £3,000 a year.

Accordingly, the demands on the Edgbaston estate were severe. From its revenues were derived the sums which paid the pensions and gave Calthorpe his disposable income, as well as occasionally financing the improvements at Elvetham and being recycled into the road-making and developments at Edgbaston itself. But the problem was that Edgbaston's early development was so slow that gross revenue did not rise at the same rate as this expenditure. In 1810 it had been £5,000; by 1820 it was only £7,000. In 1822 rebates to the Edgbaston farm tenants were of the order of £1,000 a year, while in 1825 the expenses of road-making were running at £12 per week.[17] Under these trying circumstances, in which Calthorpe found the 'lack of income' to be 'very inconvenient', the only way to make ends meet was to run up an overdraft with

Attwood and Spooner, the estate's Birmingham bankers. As a result, by the end of 1825, the Calthorpes owed them very nearly £6,500.[18]

Then, in late December, following widespread financial panic and collapse throughout the country, Spooners foreclosed on their loan. 'I must beg and beseech you', wrote Spooner to Calthorpe, 'to devise some means by which we can receive this money by Tuesday next at the latest.'[19] The sale of ten shares in the Worcester Canal and of some Edgbaston timber, £1,000 cash contributed by Lord Calthorpe, and a £3,000 loan from Harris, made it possible to meet the bank's demands. But it had been a close call. Calthorpe himself took it as a 'salutary warning' which in future would make him more aware of 'the great difference between nominal and really disposable income'. And at Edgbaston and Elvetham the number of estate workers was dramatically reduced, so that the drainage schemes in Hampshire took a year longer to complete than had originally been intended.[20]

By the late 1820s and early 1830s, the corner was finally turned. Even in 1828, Calthorpe was still expressing 'dissatisfaction as to the amount of expenditure annually on the [Edgbaston] estate', with roads still under construction and farms being extensively repaired;[21] but, by massive economy and a timely ending of the road-building programme, expenses were reduced to £2,889 in 1829. When the next accounts become available for the early 1830s, they show gross rents for Edgbaston 20 per cent higher than they had been in the 1820s, for the early 1830s were good years in Birmingham, with leases being taken up in the boom years, and no need to build any more roads. Indeed, Calthorpe's financial position was so improved that he began to buy land in and about Elvetham in the 1830s, and undertook the rebuilding and extension of the house there.[22] In 1851, the year of his death, he could look back on 20 years of uninterrupted progress and improvement in his financial position. The risks taken and crises weathered in the 1810s and 1820s had been well worth while.

The key to all of this lay in the successful development of Edgbaston, for

Table 13. Lord Calthorpe's income, _c._1850

Estate	Gross (£)	Net (£)
Edgbaston	12,917	7,692
Norfolk and Suffolk	3,823	1,632
Elvetham	_c._ 2,130	_c._ 1,000
London	3,611	2,916
Miscellaneous	1,500	1,500
Total	23,981	14,740

Source: EEO MS., Edgbaston Account Books; HROCal MS., Box 27, Norfolk and Suffolk Account Books; Box 29, London Accounts; Box 18, General Accounts.

without exception, the other estates stagnated, as they were to do for the rest of the century. London's spurt was complete: its revenues would remain unaltered at least until 1892, when the City Road leases expired. The anticipated return on the Elvetham drainage scheme never really materialized: although rental was to rise as the century drew on, it was more as a result of land purchase than land improvement. The Norfolk and Suffolk estates hovered unpromisingly at between £3,800 and £4,800 gross for the whole of the first half of the century. In 1823, Harris examined the Cockthorpe estate, and could not think of any 'circumstances in regard to situation which is likely to increase the future value of the estate'.[23] What was true of Cockthorpe was true of all the East Anglian properties. By mid-century, without Edgbaston, the Calthorpes' financial position would have been extremely uncomfortable. From providing one-third of their gross and net revenue in 1810, its contribution had risen to half 40 years later (see Appendix B). Indeed, as Edgbaston entered its most rapid phase of development, while the other estates continued to stagnate, that proportion was bound to increase.

2

During the lifetime of the next two holders of the title, Frederick, fourth Lord Calthorpe (1851–68) and Frederick Henry William, fifth Lord Calthorpe (1868–93), the mood changed from one of concern, crisis, retrenchment and recovery to one of buoyant and optimistic expansion. There were essentially three reasons for this. To begin with, the problem of current income, which had so pre-occupied the third lord, solved itself. London, Elvetham and East Anglia remained as before, but Edgbaston gave a golden harvest, as gross revenue rose from £12,000 in 1848 to £30,000 in 1892 (graph 2). With estate expenditure levelling out at between £4,000 and £5,000 a year, this meant that net revenue more than tripled. In addition, the restrictive terms of the first lord's will, under which the third lord had laboured, and which had forbidden him to raise loans on the estate for any purpose other than portions, were now removed. In June 1853 the fourth Lord Calthorpe and his son and heir signed a disentailing agreement, thereby becoming joint possessors, with power to raise money on the estates as they wished and when, in 1864, the estates were resettled, only Elvetham and parts of Edgbaston were included. Any new purchases there, as well as the estates in London and East Anglia, were excluded.[24] Finally, in 1844, the Gough family of Perry Hall, the Calthorpes' distant relatives, became extinct in the male line, and their house and estate in Staffordshire passed to the Calthorpes. By a settlement made in 1848, it was agreed that in future the heir to the title should make Perry his home and, in addition to the land and house, there was a trust fund of £157,000 which was to be used to extend the Perry estate when possible, and to be invested soundly in the meantime.[25]

Having thus gained so handsomely on the roundabouts of inheritance, the family were equally fortunate in not losing on the swings of encumbrance, for the raising of portions for the fourth lord's two surviving younger sons (Augustus and Somerset) and six daughters did not present any real difficulty. Augustus was well provided for with the Perry estate, and his remaining brother as well as his six sisters each received portions of £10,000, partly from the residue of the fourth lord's personal estate, partly from the Perry estate, and partly from the personal estate of Lady Frances Gough-Calthorpe, who died unmarried in 1868.[26] So, from 1868 until 1910, there were no more portions to be raised. Moreover, between 1827 and 1910, there was no dowager Lady Calthorpe to maintain. The third and fifth lords never married, and the fourth lord's wife pre-deceased her husband in 1865. Thus for another generation the burden of family encumbrances was kept at bay.

Accordingly, the Calthorpes of mid-century were able to devote themselves, and the income largely derived from Edgbaston, to the creation of a more spacious and authentic aristocratic life style, which earlier financial stringency had denied their predecessors. The theme was now expansion, not survival – accumulation of land, the rebuilding of houses, and the lavish enjoyment of wealth and status. Apart from a few small buys in the Elvetham region, and the purchase of the Curzon estate in 1819 – on which, presumably, the £17,000 previously lent to the Duchess of Buccleuch was spent – the third Lord Calthorpe had not indulged in any grandiose schemes of estate expansion.[27] However, in the 1850s the fourth lord spent £47,000 on the westwards extension of the Edgbaston estate into the parish of Harborne, in confident anticipation of further building development.[28] By so doing, he used up all the residue of the first lord's personal estate which, according to the terms of his will, had to be invested in land once debts and portions had been paid.

In the years which followed, the Calthorpes' financial manoeuvrings became much more elaborate. In the late 1850s, they sold the Pakenham estate for approximately £30,000, and in 1861 parted with Ampton for a sum in the region of £63,000.[29] In addition, between 1854 and 1892, they raised mortgages totalling £164,000, as shown in table 14. In so doing, it is important to stress the use which the fourth and fifth lords made, not only of all the unsettled lands, but also of those newly-acquired parts of the Edgbaston and Elvetham estates, as security for loans. It is equally obvious that only the burgeoning rentals from Edgbaston made it possible to bear interest charges in the region of £5,500 a year in the 1880s.

Since the internal evidence suggests that the first two mortgages were paid off by part of the proceeds of the sales of Pakenham and Ampton, that leaves in total some £234,000 which the Calthorpes spent between 1854 and 1892. An approximate breakdown of their spending is given in table 15. Here, indeed, is an eloquent agenda of aristocratic aggrandisement. The purchase of over 2,000 acres of land at Elvetham represented an attempt to convert their puny holdings there into an estate worthy of the Lord of Edgbaston, and the rebuilding of Elvetham Hall to the designs of Samuel Sebastian Teulon between 1859 and 1862 was the necessary corollary to this.[30] The stud farm at Newmarket was created by the fifth Lord Calthorpe between 1877 – exactly a year before two of the largest mortgages were taken out – and 1887.[31] Finally, in 1870 – another peak year for raising loans – the youngest son of the fourth lord, Somerset, bought himself the 80-acre Woodlands Vale estate in the Isle of Wight, where he built himself a small but comfortable house, once more to the design of S.S.Teulon.[32]

Table 14. Calthorpe mortgages, 1854–92

Estate mortgaged	Date taken	Date repaid	Size of loan (£)	
i Edgbaston	26.12.54	26.1.59	16,000	⎞
ii Edgbaston	23.6.55	26.1.59	7,000	⎬ from Perry
iii Gray's Inn Road	22.8.64	9.11.70	19,000	⎠ trustees
iv Edgbaston	3.7.65	14.9.70	6,000	
v Gough Square	10.10.70	13.5.92	10,000	
vi Gray's Inn Road	10.12.70	13.5.92	25,000	
vii Gray's Inn Road	15.12.70	13.5.92	10,000	
viii Assorted Elvetham farms	14.8.78	1887/8	35,000	
ix Acle	11.10.78	1881/6/9	30,000	
x Elvetham	? 1880	1.1.89	19,000	
xi Newmarket	May 1880	1.1.89	5,000	
xii Eversley Farm, Elvetham	May 1880	1.1.89	3,000	
xiii Readon Farm, Elvetham	May 1880	1.1.89	4,000	
Total			164,000*	

Note: * The actual total here is £189,000. From this should be deducted £25,000, the sum of the third and fourth mortgages, since they were probably paid off by raising the £25,000 mortgage on Gray's Inn Road in 1870.

Source: For the surviving mortgage documents with dates as in the table, see EEO MS., Parcel 6 (i & ii); GLRO MS. E/Cal/25(v); GLRO MS E/Cal/13 (vi); GLRO MS. E/Cal/16 (vii); HROCal MS., Box 18 (ix). For lists of other mortgages see EEO MS. Box 1, Calthorpe *v.* Calthorpe: Bill of Complaint, filed 21 Dec. 1868 (iii & iv); EEO MS., Letter Book 1, 9 June 1888 (viii, x, xii, xiii); HROCal. MS., Box 33 (viii).

Table 15. Calthorpe spending, 1854–92

Expenditure	Amount (£)
Rebuilding Elvetham Hall	70,000
Land purchases at Elvetham etc.	100,000
Newmarket stud farm	44,000
Woodlands Vale, I.O.W.	20,000
Total	234,000

Source: D. Cannadine, 'The aristocracy and the towns in the nineteenth century, a case study of the Calthorpes and Birmingham, 1807–1910' (D.Phil. thesis, University of Oxford, 1975), 140–4.

Fig. 14. Elvetham Hall, Hampshire: an original drawing by the architect, S. S. Teulon (reproduced from *The Builder*, 26 May 1860, by courtesy of Cambridge University Library).

How were all these loans paid off? From the coincidence of dates, it seems a reasonable assumption that the first two were paid off by part of the proceeds of the Ampton and Pakenham sales. Similarly, it seems likely that mortgages (iii) and (iv) were simply converted into mortgage (vi) late in 1870. That then leaves a total of £141,000 to explain. Two minor dents were made in this pile of debt in 1881 and 1885. In the first year, Calthorpe received £2,600 from the Great Eastern Railway Company in exchange for land taken at Acle, of which £1,250 was applied to reducing the mortgage on that estate.[33] Then in 1885 he was paid nearly £20,000 by the Midland Railway Company in final settlement for land which the Birmingham West Suburban Railway had taken in Edgbaston. Of this, £13,750 went in further reduction of the Acle mortgage, while £5,500 went towards the reduction of mortgage (viii) on the assorted Elvetham farms.[34]

However, there still remained £120,500 to be paid off. Between 1885 and 1892, the fifth lord toyed with the idea of selling his Gray's Inn Road estate, partly because the decline in the area – itself the result of covenants in the leases which were much weaker than those at Edgbaston – was beginning to attract comment. But after protracted indecision, he finally decided not to sell in 1892.[35] Meanwhile, in 1888, he had sold his New River Company share, since it was only yielding 3 per cent whereas the interest payments on the remaining mortgages were at 4 per cent. Of the £95,000 thereby raised, £76,500 was used to discharge the mortgages which remained on Acle, the assorted Elvetham farms, and on Newmarket.[36] Finally, in April 1891, the City Road estate was sold for £187,000, of which £45,000 went in the repayment of the two mortgages outstanding on Gray's Inn Road and the one on Gough Square. The residue was then invested in equities.[37]

By early 1893 Frederick Henry William, fifth Lord Calthorpe, was dead; only just in time had he freed his estates from debt. But he had concluded his transactions with great success. The City Road estate had always been a thorn in the Calthorpes' side. It had been extensively sub-leased, and as a result had become notorious for its slum housing. In 1891 it had suffered a further blow when the City & South London Railway put a line through it.[38] In the following year the leases were due to fall in; but the state of the houses meant that no large reversion could realistically be anticipated, for extensive repairs or complete demolition would be necessary, if only because of the pressure of public opinion. As the fifth lord explained: 'I may be bothered by Vestry or County Council to rebuild the rookery parts of the estate, and they will have no mercy on me if I succeed . . . Now all this I get rid of, or ought to, by selling.'[39]

The sale was therefore perfectly timed. In one single manoeuvre, it rid the fifth lord of his most embarrassing estate, enabled him to clear off the remaining mortgages, and still left him with sufficient funds to invest – £135,000 – to ensure that even with a return of 3 per cent, he would enjoy a larger income than he would have had he retained and re-let the City Road estate. Had Edwards been able to secure the Ravenhurst estate adjacent to Edgbaston with some of the money left over from the City Road sale, it would have been an even bigger coup.[40] But as it was, the Calthorpes' only gambler brought the era of expansion to a close in an appropriately flamboyant manner.

3

In 1810 the Calthorpe family could only be described as minor aristocracy. Their title was but a generation old; their town house in Grosvenor Square was a recent acquisition; there was no large mansion in the country; and their estates were small, scattered and unremunerative. By the 1880s, however, they were established, wealthy, socially important aristocrats. At Elvetham there was a large, new mansion and a growing estate; at Perry a separate residence for the heir to the title; at Woodlands Vale a comfortable house for the youngest brother; and at Newmarket a racing stud farm which was patronized and frequented by the Prince of Wales. With an income in excess of £30,000 a year the Calthorpes, if not in the ranks of the aristocratic super-powers, were certainly among the most prosperous and important of second-ranking landowners. If in the eighteenth century the family ascended the ladder of status, in the nineteenth they obtained an income and evolved a style of life fully commensurate with their dignity and title.

Yet in terms of the revenue which made all this possible, the aristocratic façade was a sham. They lived an aristocratic life without aristocratic acres, financing their conspicuous consumption almost entirely out of Edgbaston's

Fig. 15. The Calthorpe family: A. George, third Lord Calthorpe, 1807–51: this picture shows him carrying the Gold Spurs at the coronation of George IV (by courtesy of Cambridge University Library) B. Frederick, fourth Lord Calthorpe, 1851–68 (by courtesy of the Calthorpe Estate Office) C. Frederick Henry William, fifth Lord Calthorpe, 1868–93 (reproduced from *Edgbastonia*, August 1893, by courtesy of Birmingham Reference Library) D. Augustus, sixth Lord Calthorpe, 1893–1910 (by courtesy of the Calthorpe Estate Office).

burgeoning rentals, either directly, in terms of current income, or more obliquely in the form of the interest payments on loans which their ground rents enabled them to make. Of course, by the end of the nineteenth century, many magnates were disproportionately dependent on non-landed income. But the Calthorpes were unusual in that from the 1830s, their aristocratic life-style – which they were increasingly to enjoy in later decades – was already being extensively underpinned by urban rentals. It was urban income which made possible rural extravagance. In the context of Birmingham's evolution, Edgbaston was *important* because it was the town's major high-class suburb; in the context of the Calthorpes' finances, Edgbaston was *vital* because it made them millionaires.

8 Patterns of management and problems of policy, 1810–93

To the middle-class inhabitants of nineteenth-century Birmingham, Edgbaston was a unique and semi-rural retreat – a rustic enclave in an urban environment. To the Calthorpes themselves, however, it was a building estate of prized value – an urban intrusion into their agricultural holdings. What was trees and sunlight to the townsman was bricks and mortar to the landowner. Only the Edgbaston agents saw the estate in both of these paradoxical guises – the sylvan suburb where covenants must be enforced in the interests of the tenants, and the leasehold estate where rentals must be collected on behalf of the landlord. Indeed, their varied activities only reflected this ambiguity. At Edgbaston, they were in charge of day-to-day affairs – letting land, marking out plots, making roads; but by virtue of that estate's large contribution to the family's financial well-being, they also became the Calthorpes' chief financial advisers – suggesting long-term policy and advising on major decisions.

Four Edgbaston agents occupied this niche during the lives of the third, fourth and fifth Lords Calthorpe: John Harris from 1810 to 1843, Charles Yates from 1843 to 1852, Joseph Edwards from 1852 to 1878, and his son George from 1878 to 1894. They in turn were assisted – and on occasions hindered – by two groups of legal advisers: the family solicitors in London, Walters and Co., and the local solicitors in Birmingham, initially the Whateley brothers, who were succeeded by R. H. Milward. Between them, the tenants for life, their Edgbaston agents, and their local and London solicitors superintended day-to-day affairs and also determined long-term policy. The exact distribution of responsibility among them was as much determined by quirks of personality as by the particular nature of the task in hand but, at a more general level, the long-term perspectives were shared and constant. Urban revenue may have been the key to the Calthorpes' aristocratic efflorescence; but it was aristocratic opinion which guided Edgbaston's leasehold development.

1

The first 40 years of Edgbaston's development were presided over by the third Lord Calthorpe in collaboration with John Harris and then Charles Yates. Calthorpe himself was a pious, sober, Evangelical churchman, a friend of Buxton, Macaulay, Gurney and Hannah More, an active supporter of charitable societies in London, and a close friend of William Wilberforce, to whom he was related by marriage.[1] Indeed, when in 1812 the burden of representing Yorkshire became too much for Wilberforce, it was to Calthorpe's pocket borough at Bramber that he gratefully removed.[2] Throughout the 1810s and 1820s, Calthorpe championed liberal causes: the abolition of slavery, Catholic emancipation, moderate parliamentary reform, greater freedom of trade, and enlargement of dissenters' rights. Not only was he the sole nineteenth-century Calthorpe whose political career was of national significance, but he was also, by virtue of the decisions he had reached in the early 1810s, the family's only real entrepreneur – the founder and architect of its fortunes.

In this he was most ably assisted by John Harris, a regrettably mysterious figure. Described in contemporary Birmingham directories as a 'surveyor' or 'land agent', no evidence has survived to suggest where he came from or when indeed he became the third lord's agent;[3] but it cannot have been long before 1810, since never in his letters does he refer to events prior to that date. His own business was in web manufacturing, but, like other agents who began in a different career, he soon found that a proper performance of his new duties 'required a full time concentration on management'.[4] Not only did Harris preside at Edgbaston; he also administered the London estates directly from Birmingham, superintended the stewards at Elvetham and Ampton, personally collected the rentals on all the estates, and drew up elaborate and detailed reports each year on the current condition of his employer's holdings. Indeed, his knowledge of his master's overall financial position was unrivalled.

Moreover, this was allied with a close personal friendship which made his relationship with Calthorpe especially warm. In his letters to Harris, Calthorpe always described himself as 'your sincere friend' or 'your sincere friend and well-wisher', and his concern went far beyond these gracious phrases. When Harris suffered from inflammation of the eyes, Calthorpe's letters expressed genuine concern and sympathy: 'I am sorry that you have had a return of illness, and insist that you certainly should make a trial of the Devonshire air, and trust you will derive benefit from it'.[5] Calthorpe had the highest confidence in Harris's professional abilities: 'I place great reliance upon your integrity and judgment', he wrote to him in February 1814.[6] Indeed, the sacrifices which Harris made on Calthorpe's behalf were heroic. During the difficult period of the 1820s, when ready money was in such short supply, Harris not only made £3,000 of his own funds available to help Calthorpe over the crisis of December 1825, but also went without his salary for six years as Edgbaston agent, and for nine at Elvetham.[7]

With the decisions to develop Edgbaston and Gray's Inn, and to drain Elvetham, this ranks as one of the great partnerships of the nineteenth century between an aristocrat and his adviser. Accordingly, the exact apportioning of responsibility for these decisions is not easy. It seems probable that the third lord, aware of the disadvantages of his scattered holdings, was anxious to take steps to improve his income. Indeed, he may have decided to employ Harris for this very purpose; but, while the great decisions were taken by Calthorpe – as was usual among even the most inattentive of landowners – the schemes

seem to have originated with Harris himself.[8] At Gray's Inn, for example,
Harris later wrote of 'the principle laid down in the letting of which I believe
your lordship fully *approved*' (my italics). And at Edgbaston, those two long
letters from Harris, systematically setting out a programme of development,
leave little doubt as to who originated the scheme. Indeed, Calthorpe's reply –
'I must *approve* of the general principles which you have suggested for the
disposal of the building land' (my italics) – only serves to corroborate this.[9]

In any case, whoever was precisely responsible, there can be no doubt that
the years between 1810 and 1825 were the great entrepreneurial phase in the
development of the Calthorpes' estates. The plans to improve Edgbaston,
Elvetham and Gray's Inn, motivated by the desire for increased revenue, and
financed by short-term savings, involved considerable risk and strain in their
implementation. Moreover, the Edgbaston scheme was particularly uncertain
– not only because Birmingham afforded no precedent for such a development,
but also because, in the early 1820s, with high expenses in road building, but
sluggish rentals, there seemed a real danger that it might collapse. As
Hermione Hobhouse has noted:

> To the twentieth-century mind, the idea that housing speculations . . .
> could fail is ridiculous, but for the great landowners and the builders who
> worked on their land in the eighteenth and nineteenth centuries, this was
> a very real danger.[10]

In finance as in politics, the early years of George, third Lord Calthorpe, were
the family's heroic age.

It was of short duration however. Indeed, if the family had had their way, it
would have been even shorter; for, in the winter of 1823–4, they made a real,
concerted attempt to sell off their non-agricultural estates altogether and to
invest the proceeds in broad acres. In August 1823 Calthorpe learned that the
Culford estate in Suffolk would soon be on the market following the death of
the Marquess Cornwallis.[11] It comprised 11,000 acres of woodland and arable
conveniently bordering on Calthorpe's favourite residence at Ampton. He at
once showed interest in buying it. Harris was sent off to make a report on it
early in September, which he followed up with a detailed valuation in February 1824; a large-scale map of the area was purchased, and a sale catalogue,
announcing the intended auction early in 1824, was acquired.[12] Copies were
made of the will of Henry, first Lord Calthorpe, the terms of which governed
the sale of existing estates and the acquisition of new ones. The advice of
solicitors and chancery lawyers was sought as to its exact meaning, since it
seemed that only the small estates in East Anglia could be sold, while the lands
in London, Birmingham and Elvetham must be retained. Since the lawyers
confirmed this interpretation, it was agreed to seek a private Act to over-ride
these terms, permit the sale of Edgbaston and Gray's Inn, and then to invest
the proceeds in the Culford estate. Harris even went so far as to inquire of the
major leaseholders on the two building estates whether they would like to buy

their freeholds. To his unconcealed delight, he found them 'desirous to purchase . . . at a good price'.[13]

Bearing in mind the amount of time, effort and worry that the Calthorpes had recently lavished on the improvement of Edgbaston and Gray's Inn, this seems an altogether extraordinary plan of campaign. And the fact that Harris himself described the Culford estate as 'composed of land of very inferior quality, and some of it so extremely poor as scarcely to be worth the expense of cultivation' only serves to render their decision even more remarkable.[14] Yet there can be no doubting their firmness of purpose: in September 1823, Harris urged that 'the magnitude of the undertaking requires that no time be lost in laying down a general plan of arrangement', and in November he noted how 'your lordship's whole family are most anxious to have the Culford estate purchased'. Even when the chances seemed to be slipping away early in 1824, Calthorpe himself urged that 'no time should be lost in making the necessary arrangements'.[15]

The key to these plans lay once more in the nature of the estates which the third lord had inherited. Situated in Norfolk, Suffolk, Warwickshire, Hampshire and London, they were too small and too scattered to give their tenant for life any great landed influence. In particular, Ampton, the third lord's favourite home, had no estate attached to it at all. Henry, first Lord Calthorpe, had recognized that some degree of rationalization was called for, and so in his will had made provision for the sale of the Norfolk and Suffolk estates, assuming that the best prospects lay in consolidating a larger holding around Edgbaston or Elvetham. But now, if an Act could be obtained effectively reversing these terms, there was a very real possibility of making the Calthorpes a territorial power of the first rank in East Anglia. The house they had already; the land was on offer. As Harris explained, such a re-grouping of the family estates 'would increase Lord Calthorpe's influence about his residence by bringing his property so much together.' Even though the rental from Culford was less than the combined income from Edgbaston and Gray's Inn, the attraction of the greater social and political influence which would accrue from consolidated holdings gave the Culford estate 'a value beyond a *mere* investment for money'.[16]

In fact, the scheme came to nothing: the difficulties of obtaining an Act in time proved insurmountable; the estate was sold; and the new owner was not interested in putting it on the market again.[17] But the eagerness with which Calthorpe and Harris tried to seize this opportunity shows precisely where their priorities lay. Ideally, the improvement of Edgbaston and Gray's Inn as building estates was but second best. In the short run, such a policy was difficult and risky, and in the long term, even if it turned out well, no building estate would ever be an adequate substitute for broad acres and the social and political influence which – viewed from the standpoint of the early nineteenth century – they might be expected to confer. The Culford estate offered the prospect both of liberation from the financial straitjacket of Edgbaston and of a major, consolidated territorial holding. To an aristocratic title would be added an aristocratic estate worthy of it; there would be real influence to wield in one county rather than little influence in many. Such an opportunity to consolidate the family's aristocratic position might never occur again.

Indeed, if it had, the Calthorpes would no longer have been interested. Those holders of the title who followed the third lord were politically so insignificant that the lack of landed influence cannot have worried them, and by the second half of the nineteenth century it had ceased to be so important in any case. Moreover, by then, the burgeoning rentals from Edgbaston enabled them to enjoy the pleasures of aristocratic existence without the need of an agricultural income: Ampton and Pakenham could be disposed of with impunity. If the Calthorpes failed to become fully-fledged aristocrats by the means that the third lord would have preferred, they were conspicuously successful by another route. It was not agricultural Culford but industrial Birmingham which helped the Calthorpes up the aristocratic ladder. In the short run, the failure to purchase Culford may have seemed painful, disappointing and frustrating; but in the long term, it was an extraordinary piece of good fortune.

Once this scheme had been abandoned, and the crisis of 1825–6 had been weathered, the heroic phase of Calthorpe entrepreneurship came to an end. Like other aristocrats in the 1820s, the Calthorpes came to adopt a lower, managerial profile.[18] No longer was correspondence between Calthorpe and Harris concerned with great decisions, but with routine, day-to-day matters. Indeed, even in the heroic years, this had occupied most of the time. Every month, Harris sent Calthorpe 'full and regular reports' of 'the business at Edgbaston', and letters passed between them at the rate of two a week in each direction.[19] In March 1822, for example, Harris sent Calthorpe a five-page letter about tenants wanting more land, the vacancy of Harrison's farm, the alterations to Edgbaston church and requests for rent rebates.[20] Few landlords can have been as well informed.

From the late 1820s onwards, letters such as this became the norm. The massive reports which Harris sent – that of 1833 was 54 handwritten pages – were simply accounts of the letting of plots for building, the making of roads, and farm improvements.[21] No decisions on Calthorpe's part were required, and even when they were, Harris presented the information in such a manner that the solution he had in mind invariably suggested itself. 'I would do nothing in this way without your lordship's concurrence', he wrote to Calthorpe in 1825, hardly the words of an agent who expected to have his suggestions over-ruled.[22] When Yates replaced Harris in 1843, the system continued as before. The flood of letters and reports flowed undiminished, and Calthorpe's interest remained unabated. Yet the subject-matter was still trivial: the work at Edgbaston church, the theft of trees cut down in Edgbaston park, the construction of a cottage in the Botanical Gardens, and the design of the windows in Mr Iliffe's new house.[23] It was a very staid finale to an era which had opened with such excitement.

2

The early 1850s saw an almost complete change in personnel: the third lord was succeeded by his younger brother Frederick, and Charles Yates, who died in office at the age of 47, was followed by Joseph Edwards. Of this pair, it is regrettably almost impossible to say anything, since no estate papers have survived for the late 1850s or early 1860s, but it seems likely that this period was characterized by the same high standards of administration, and the same lack of entrepreneurial activity, which had been the hallmarks of the later years of the third lord. The fourth Lord Calthorpe had begun to deal with the routine Edgbaston correspondence several years before his elder brother's death, and the continuity of interest and concern therefore remained unbroken. Moreover, there is no evidence from other sources that any large schemes – such as extended speculative development of Edgbaston, or another attempt to rationalize the family holdings – were contemplated at this time.

During the years 1868–93, however, when Frederick Henry William was fifth Lord Calthorpe, matters changed considerably. The other three holders of the title, from George, third lord, to Augustus, sixth lord, were shy and retiring by nature; the fifth lord was extroverted and flamboyant. Although he never married, his will included provision for an annuity of 25,000 francs for a lady in Paris.[24] The other three all had some sense of aristocratic obligation: he did not. As The Times obituarist abruptly noted: 'he took no part in public works'.[25] His chief concern was not with getting money but with spending it. His grandfather had acquired the title; his uncle's schemes had created a large income; his father had rebuilt the mansion: he now proceeded to enjoy the fruits of their collective labours. He was a close friend of the Prince of Wales, a renowned member of the Marlborough House set, and an incorrigible country house visitor. The prime passion of his life was horse racing – hence the creation of the Newmarket establishment, where he also leased several thousand acres of the best partridge shooting in England. In 1888, his horse Sea Breeze won the Oaks and the St Leger, but the really great prizes always eluded him. Nevertheless, on his death, The Times observed that 'the Jockey Club loses one of its senior members, and the turf a very staunch and honourable supporter'.[26]

At the Edgbaston Estate Office, the change was less abrupt. In 1878 George Edwards succeeded his father, having assisted him since 1869. He had begun work at the age of 14 in 1836 as a clerk in Attwood and Spooners Bank in New Street.[27] He rose to become branch manager, and then resigned to move to the Edgbaston office. In addition, he personally administered the estates in London and the former Gough lands at Perry, as well as auditing the accounts for Elvetham and Norfolk. Only the Newmarket property came outside his sphere of influence. He did not die until 1911 and, although he retired in 1894, subsequent agents at the Edgbaston Estate Office often sought his advice.

Indeed, when his immediate successor committed suicide in 1895, he again took over the reins temporarily.[28]

Although the fifth lord was a more harsh employer than his predecessors, his relationship with Edwards was exceedingly cordial. Calthorpe frequently sent him presents of pheasant, and in his will left him £2,000 – twice as much as to his Elvetham agent. 'I am sure you will care more for the feeling which prompted the legacy', wrote Augustus, his successor, 'than for the money itself. He told me to thank you for all you had done for him.' 'I really do not know what to say', Edwards wrote back in gratified amazement, adding that the fifth lord was 'one for whom I had a very great respect and one from whom I have for so many years received so much kindness and considera-tion.'[29] So close a friendship between a low-church Tory and a no-church Liberal, a man of strict morals and a man of self-indulgence, seems unusual, but there can be no doubt that this collaboration witnessed, and was in large part responsible for, the golden age of Calthorpe affairs.

At the same time, the Calthorpes' solicitors became increasingly important: not so much the London solicitors of Walters and Company, who were responsible for such matters as wills and settlements, but the Birmingham firm of John and George Whateley, who looked after day-to-day matters such as leases, conveyances and mortgages. It is not clear when they became the Calthorpes' solicitors. They began practising in Birmingham in 1815, and were certainly acting for the Calthorpes by the time of the Perry estate settlement of 1848. Between them, the Whateley brothers built up the largest practice in the town, including among their clients not only the Calthorpes, but also the governors of King Edward's School, the Great Western Railway, the dukes of Marlborough, and the Inge family.[30] In 1873, John Whateley sold the business to R. H. Milward, who further extended it. He became a J. P., served on the city council, was an active supporter of the Birmingham triennial music festivals, and was well known in Midlands society. Like John Whateley, who was himself a tenant of Edgbaston Hall, Milward lived well: his massive house at Barnt Green was maintained by 13 servants.[31] Indeed, so busy and so grand were the Calthorpes' Birmingham solicitors that they were in large part responsible for two unfortunate episodes during the time of the fifth lord, which temporarily put the Calthorpes' affairs in jeopardy, and permanently soured relations between them and their local legal advisers.

The first of these concerned the Perry settlement of 1848, drawn up four years after the Gough male line had become extinct and their lands had passed to the Calthorpes. The settlement was devised to ensure that, when Frederick succeeded as fourth lord, his son and heir, Frederick Henry William, should enjoy the Perry estates. Then, when he inherited, they should pass to his brother Augustus, and if he in turn ever became Lord Calthorpe, they should then pass on to Somerset, the youngest brother. So, when Frederick Henry William became fifth lord in 1868, Augustus inherited Perry from him. Un-fortunately, it was discovered that the clause shifting Perry from brother to brother had been badly drawn by the Whateleys when they had drafted the settlement, so that its meaning was not clear. If Augustus ever became Lord Calthorpe, there was no guarantee that Somerset was legally entitled to follow him at Perry, as had been intended. John Whateley pleaded that 'this unexpected difficulty has caused me a great deal of anxiety and vexation'; but such excuses were of little comfort,[32] for there was no alternative but to go to Chancery and obtain a decree clarifying matters. This was duly accomplished in April 1869, when a judgment was obtained 'making the shifting clause operate to carry over the estate from brother to brother', as had been intended, but not made sufficiently explicit, in the 1848 settlement.[33]

Although this was an irritating and expensive incident, it was altogether eclipsed in importance by another problem which also arose as a result of the fifth lord's succession. Until 1868, building leases had been granted on the Edgbaston estate in conformity with the terms laid down in the will of Henry, first Lord Calthorpe. In particular, he had stipulated that any such lease 'shall respectively contain proper powers for re-entry on the premises to be demised for non-payment of rent'.[34] But when, on 18 July 1864, the fourth lord and Frederick Henry William re-settled the estates, they changed the terms on which building leases might be granted so that 'powers of distress and entry be reserved for the recovery of rents'.[35] While under the powers granted by Henry Lord Calthorpe's will, the tenant for life could re-enter the land let on a building lease if the rent was not paid, under these new terms he could not only re-enter, but actually obtain the rent owed by confiscating and selling the chattels he found there.

However, the terms of this new settlement, drawn up by the Calthorpes' London solicitors, were never communicated to the Whateley brothers in Birmingham, who drew up the actual lease documents, or to Edwards at Edgbaston, who administered them. Thus blissfully ignorant, they carried on granting leases in conformity with the will of Henry, first Lord Calthorpe. Only on the death of Frederick, the fourth lord, did the terms of the new settlement come to light. The immediate consequence of this was that the leases granted at Edgbaston in the four years since the settlement had been made became invalid, since they contained no powers of distress, and therefore were not consistent with the terms under which the land should now be leased. During that period, 80 leases had been granted, authorizing the expenditure of some £90,000, and the Calthorpes now became liable for the claims of every lessee.[36] In addition, the powers of distress – which in future all Edgbaston leases must contain so as to be consistent with the terms of the re-settlement – were virtually unknown in Birmingham, a preponderantly leasehold town. Edwards contended that if they remained operative, they would seriously injure the estate's future developments prospects, since 'such reservations and restrictions would deter intending lessees from applying for and accepting such leases'.[37] Whatever the attractions of Edgbaston in other ways, Edwards had absolutely no doubt that if the terms of the leases were not agreeable, intending tenants would not hesitate to look elsewhere. Even in the decades before Edgbaston experienced real competition, its success depended on the extent to which it could meet the preferences of potential tenants. They, not the estate, ultimately had the whip hand.

Accordingly, there was a double problem: the leases which had been executed since the new settlement was made were invalid; but the terms under which leases should be granted in future were inappropriate to an estate in Birmingham. The first step which had to be taken was to suspend any further business in Edgbaston: hence the sudden dip in the number of leases granted in 1868–9 (graph 1b). More importantly, a means had to be found of confirming the leases granted since 1864 and over-riding the terms of the 1864 settlement, so that in future new leases might be granted under the same terms as in the past. So, only five months after they had appeared in Chancery over the issue of the Perry settlement, the Calthorpes returned, and obtained the Vice-Chancellor's consent to apply for a private Act.[38] Finally, in July 1869, four months and £1,500 later, 'Lord Calthorpe's Leasing Act' received royal assent.

Although the Whateleys were correct in claiming that 'the mischief created in 1864 . . . did not arise from any fault of the said firm of Whateley and Whateley', these two episodes soured relations between the solicitors and the fifth lord, so much so that his disapproval was visited on their successor.[39] 'There is always delay in your office', Calthorpe wrote in anger to one of Milward's partners in 1879, when the firm had taken three weeks to arrange the conveyancing of a farm at Elvetham. A year earlier, when Milward only managed to borrow £25,000 on the security of the Acle estate, when Calthorpe had wanted £40,000, he was even more outraged, telling Milward on one occasion that 'you do not seem to have managed very well', and on another that 'there is a certain amount of inaccuracy about your business'.[40] Events in the early 1900s, which the fifth lord did not live to witness, were to offer spectacular vindication of his low opinion.

Yet if the relationship between the fifth lord and his Birmingham solicitors only deteriorated, that with George Edwards remained close and confident. It was not, however, in a professional sense, the same as that which the third and fourth lords had enjoyed with their respective Edgbaston agents for, unlike them, but true to his character, Frederick Henry William had not the slightest interest in the day-to-day affairs of any of his estates except Newmarket. He did not even bother to initial the Edgbaston accounts, leaving that job to his younger brother Augustus. Nor was he a frequent visitor to Birmingham. As his *Edgbastonia* obituary noted: 'not one resident upon the estate out of a thousand had any idea of the personal appearance of the late lord of the manor, or had even seen him'.[41] Of his letters to Edwards between 1885 and 1893, not one was concerned with the day-to-day affairs of Edgbaston in the tradition of his forebears. Indeed, on occasion it was difficult to get him to show any interest at all, as he flitted from one country house to another, leaving a paper trail of forwarding addresses. At the height of the troubles over the Edgbaston leases, for example, when a committee on the private bill was being scheduled, Calthorpe's main concern was that his appearance there must be timed so as not to disrupt his social life:

> Would it be possible to get this committee fixed for before one or after four on Tuesday? Lord Calthorpe is particularly anxious to attend the levee (the last of the season), to do which he must be at the palace at two, and he starts for Paris in the same evening.[42]

Likewise in March 1891, when he was toying with the idea of selling the City Road estate, a representative from the firm of auctioneers called 'at Grosvenor Square at four o'clock, but found his lordship had started for Newmarket at three o'clock'.[43]

But if the fifth lord did not share the traditional family sense of aristocratic obligation or concern for the intimate details of estate administration, he had a broad grasp of the overall picture, and an ability to use his estates as pawns in a larger financial chess game, which none of his nineteenth-century relatives could match. His correspondence is that of a man at ease in the world of high finance – of sales, auctions, mortgages, stocks and shares, investments, dividends and so on. The combination of an assured and expanding income from Edgbaston, and of estates in London and the country which were free to be mortgaged, enabled him to devote his life to conspicuous consumption on a scale denied to his predecessors. Nor can there be any doubt that this was *his* policy. 'You had better give notice to all the mortgages that they will be paid off in six months', he wrote imperiously to Edwards in 1888.[44] Likewise, the decision to sell the City Road estate was his alone. 'Lord Calthorpe seems inclined to dispose of the estate', noted Edwards in May 1891. The next month he was told that a decision had been reached.[45]

In all these matters, Edwards was Calthorpe's closest colleague. As Edgbaston agent, Calthorpe had little interest in his work, but as chief financial adviser, Calthorpe's respect for him was of the highest. It was Edwards, rather than the London or Birmingham solicitors, who handled the paying off of the mortgages in 1888 and 1891, and who was consulted most frequently about the wisdom of selling either City Road or Gray's Inn or both. When, in 1888, Calthorpe thought of investing £2,000 in the Sandown Racecourse Company, he asked Edwards 'to go and see the books, and report to me in writing'.[46] After he had invested the residue of the sale of the City Road estate in equities, it was again Edwards whom he asked 'to look over my investments'.[47] The last sentence of a later letter on the same subject only serves to emphasize the confidence the fifth lord had in his judgment:

> I wished you to mark under each investment what you thought of it, whether it was safe, whether it was well bought, or whether it was too

dear, and whether it would be wise to sell at the first opportunity. Nobody shall see your remarks.[48]

Nor did Calthorpe. He died within the month.

3

The fifth lord's imaginative exploitation of the opportunities created by the great increase in Edgbaston's rentals during his tenure of the title marks him out from his two predecessors as much as does his more flamboyant character. And, for his part, George Edwards combined experience, a sound business head and expertise in unsupervised administration with an overview of the Calthorpes' total holdings which none of his successors was to enjoy. At the general level of overall strategy, therefore, this partnership witnessed the high point in the Calthorpes' affairs. Edwards was estate agent, accountant and investment adviser combined, superintending the development of Edgbaston in its phase of greatest expansion and advising Lord Calthorpe on financial affairs of unprecedented complexity. Calthorpe himself combined the pastimes of a playboy with the finesse of a financier. He saw his estates not so much as priceless family heirlooms, but as capital assets which were to be used and exploited to the best possible advantage. He was more interested in their financial utility than in living up to those aristocratic obligations which his predecessors felt their possession implied. His instructions to Edwards concerning the sale of the Ravenshurst estate in June 1892 demonstrate this well: 'I think it ought to be bought at anything less than £150 per acre. Of course, it will pay very bad interest for a long time, but it is better to buy now that land is so much lower in price.'[49] There is not a word here about extending the historic Edgbaston estates: simply concern about the price, the time to buy, and the anticipated return on the investment. If the third lord was the family's only important politician and founder of its wealth, the fifth lord, if the family's only playboy, was also its only real financial expert.

9 The Calthorpes and Birmingham, 1810–68: a 'conservative interest' examined

The successful development of their Edgbaston estate brought the Calthorpes extensive private wealth which made possible considerable aristocratic fulfilment, to an extent, and in a manner, which the purchase of the Culford estate would ultimately have denied them. Yet, consistent with the paradoxical nature of their aristocratic circumstances, the Edgbaston estate also gave them a public face, a social role and a political presence in the affairs of an 'essentially radical' town – whether they wanted it or not. In their day, Attwood, Sturge, Bright and Chamberlain were the idols of Birmingham, but their power was transient and their influence ephemeral. The Calthorpes, by contrast, were part of the public life of the town for as long as they held on to the Edgbaston estate. When Attwood went to his grave, his influence went with him; but when one Lord Calthorpe died, another took his place. At different times, they were admired, respected, envied or disliked; but they could not be ignored, because they were aristocrats, they were wealthy, and they did not go away.

1

The years between 1810 and the introduction of the first Reform Bill in the House of Commons in March 1831 were the most harmonious of the century for the Calthorpes as public figures in Birmingham, a high point after which their eminence and influence were gradually but inexorably eroded. The later battle-lines of the Chamberlain era – middle-class radicals versus idle and opulent aristocrats – had not yet been drawn. Nor was their Edgbaston revenue yet princely enough to make them vulnerable to such attacks – only £10,000 in 1830.[1] Family and town thus did not repel each other as they were to do later. On the contrary, they were drawn together in a co-operative and mutually admiring bond – the result of a transient coincidence of civic need and family interest in the fields of local improvement and national politics.

In Birmingham as elsewhere, the promotion of education, the relief of poverty, or even the making and maintenance of the town fabric itself, were largely matters of private initiative. The Street Commissioners – corrupt, aged and effete – could not solve the problems of social dislocation in a town where population grew from 70,000 in 1811 to 110,000 in 1831 in the ancient parish of Birmingham alone.[2] Middle-class voluntary societies were one response – some devoted to general matters of intellectual and cultural improvement, others specifically for the betterment of working-class conditions. The means by which they were established conformed to a general pattern: a private meeting was held between interested people who then canvassed for local support; a public meeting followed at which a committee was formally appointed; funds were then raised, and the society was established on a permanent basis. Almost from the beginning, those middle-class people who set up such societies sought aristocratic patronage, approval and support – at worst to satisfy their need for reassuring figureheads from the established order, and at best in the hope of money and active support. For this role the third Lord Calthorpe – pious, evangelical and well-informed about Birmingham's affairs and problems – was well fitted.

In the first place, as landlord of Edgbaston, he was both able to assist those local charitable societies whose activities required a healthy environment, and eager to encourage them in the hope of improving the appeal of his estate to those middle-class tenants whom he sought to attract. So in July 1814, he granted land on a generous lease of £100 a year to the Deaf and Dumb Asylum, reduced to £75 in 1822, and agreed to become one of the vice-presidents of the society.[3] Then in July 1829, he was approached by the committee of the Birmingham Botanical and Horticultural Society, who were 'particularly anxious to have the support of those noblemen and gentlemen who have on former occasions evinced an interest in the welfare of this district, and on this account they feel the greater confidence in applying to your lordship'.[4] As a result, not only Calthorpe, but Lords Lyttelton and Howe agreed to become patrons, and Lord Dartmouth was appointed president. With 20 shares each, Calthorpe and Dartmouth were the largest shareholders, and the first list of subscribers also included the Goughs from Perry Hall, John Harris, John Whateley, and three members of the Spooner family, the Calthorpes' Birmingham bankers and cousins by marriage. At a public meeting in September 1829, the society was officially inaugurated, and in the report of the meeting, the names of the noble patrons were prominently displayed.[5]

Nor did Calthorpe's participation in the society's affairs end there. In July 1830 he agreed to lease 12 acres of his Edgbaston estate to the society at the advantageous rent of £100 a year. Harris recommended such a step on the grounds that 'such an establishment will generally promote the interests of the estate',[6] but it was also to the advantage of the society, which was thereby saved the expense of buying a plot of land. A similar society in Leeds, for example, was forced to lay out £3,178 on land alone, an important contributory factor in its financial failure.[7] Not surprisingly, at the annual general meeting of October 1830, the committee unanimously passed a resolution expressing 'their sense of the great liberality with which they have been met by Lord Calthorpe through the agency of Mr. Harris'.[8] The benefits of aristocratic patronage were reciprocal.

Beyond Edgbaston itself, Calthorpe's activities were more varied, but they still followed the same general pattern of benevolent response to the initiative of others. In religious affairs, he accepted invitations to preside at meetings of the Birmingham and Warwickshire Bible Societies and the Church Missionary Association at Stratford. He was kept well informed by Harris of the progress of the Birmingham Society of Arts and the Mechanics Institution.[9] Medicine, too, was well supported. When the Birmingham Fever Hospital was established, Calthorpe sent 'a donation of twenty guineas towards the very useful institution which you have recommended to my attention'. And again, in 1828, he wrote to Harris requesting information on Mr Cox's medical lectures, 'as I am inclined to think from what I see of it in the newspaper that it deserves support'. Two months later, that support was forthcoming.[10]

This pattern of civic initiative and aristocratic cooperation also prevailed in the more controversial field of national politics. When Calthorpe came of age, the situation was rather delicate, for the stable relationship of the 1770s and 1780s, when gentry M.P.s from the area had given parliamentary support to local businessmen like Boulton and Watt, had been severely strained during the Napoleonic Wars. In 1812, for example, Sir Charles Mordaunt, one of the Warwickshire M.P.s, was publicly censured by Attwood at a town's meeting for his 'great inattention upon various occasions when applications have been made to him on subjects of great commercial interest to this town'.[11] As a result, more direct action was resorted to, and in 1820 and 1822, Calthorpe's Tory-Radical cousin, Richard Spooner, attempted to obtain election for Warwickshire as a 'Birmingham' M.P. He was unsuccessful, and although Dugdale and Lawley, the two Warwickshire M.P.s, were normally sympathetic to Birmingham's needs, as Dugdale himself admitted, they felt that 'their knowledge of various subjects connected with the manufactures of the place was defective.'[12]

As a local landowner, and as a peer of markedly liberal views, Calthorpe was well qualified to assist in conveying middle-class political opinion from Birmingham to Westminster. Indeed, between 1820 and 1831, he was asked to present no fewer than 14 petitions:[13]

May 1820	Requesting an inquiry into commercial distress.
May 1821	Requesting revision of the Criminal Law.
May 1823 ⎫ April 1824 ⎭	Requesting gradual abolition of slavery.
April 1825	Requesting revision of the Corn Laws.
April 1825	Requesting restoration of the Combination Laws.
May 1825	In favour of Catholic emancipation.
April 1826	Requesting revision of the Corn Laws.
March 1827	In favour of Catholic emancipation.
June 1827	In favour of the transfer of M.P.s to Birmingham.
February 1828	In support of the repeal of the Test and Corporation Acts.
March 1829	In favour of Catholic emancipation.
May 1829	Against renewing the East India Company's charter.
March 1831	In favour of parliamentary reform generally.

Even when Birmingham petitions were entrusted to others, Calthorpe spoke in the Lords in support of them. In February 1821 he endorsed a petition presented by Grey urging an inquiry into commercial distress; in May 1830 he again supported Grey when he presented a petition protesting against the hostile attitude taken towards Dissenters in the Birmingham Free School Bill; and in February 1831 he backed the local petition presented by Lord Radnor in favour of Parliamentary Reform.[14] Again and again, Calthorpe defended the character of his petitioners, 'men not in the habit of coming to hasty decisions on any subject', 'highly respectable persons who would not come forward with frivolous complaints', and so on.[15] Thanks to Harris's full accounts of affairs in Birmingham, he knew their circumstances well, and as an improving landlord, these middle-class people were the very tenants he sought most enthusiastically for his Edgbaston estate.[16]

Calthorpe's philanthropic and political activities in Birmingham in this decade and a half thus bear witness to a great breadth of interest and activity. Dissenters, Catholics and Anglicans; merchants, tradesmen and the Chamber of Commerce; the poor, the sick and the illiterate: all came within his field of vision and were the objects of his endeavours. The inadequate machinery of local government and parliamentary representation, combined with the great social and economic changes of these years, left needs which the middle classes believed only the aristocracy could fill. Other peers with local, Midlands links, like Dartmouth, Lyttelton and Leigh, were in demand; but it was Calthorpe, more liberal than any of them, and economically more closely linked with the town, whose co-operation was most actively sought. And, as this invitation makes clear, his collaboration was greatly appreciated:

> Associated as you are with the property, the institutions and the charities of this town and neighbourhood, your name and character naturally present themselves on every occasion of a public nature, and I hope will be with your lordship my excuse for the liberty I take in enclosing my invitation to the dinner annually given by the Lower Bailiff for the time being. And should your lordship be in this neighbourhood about the time of the 27th inst., and would condescend to honour me with your company, it will be highly gratifying to my fellow townsmen and myself, who would be happy to mark your presence by every assurance and testimony of respect.[17]

2

The passing of the Great Reform Act, however, shattered irretrievably the political side of that close relationship. To the extent that 'every assurance and testimony of respect' had been prompted by shared political sympathies, it ceased to be manifest. As soon as the first Reform Bill was introduced into the Commons, Calthorpe did not hesitate to condemn it as 'too sweeping, or at all events precipitate.'[18] Assuredly, he had earlier defended the Birmingham Political Union in the Lords, and in the spring of 1832 he was to change his mind, join the Waverers, and vote by proxy for reform.[19] But by then it was too late: damned as a reactionary, he faded into political obscurity as the titans occupied the stage. While the agitation was in full flood, Attwood was the hero of the hour, and when the bill was finally passed, it was Grey, Althorp and Russell who received the town's approbation.[20] Calthorpe had abandoned the middle classes, and they now abandoned him, for with its own M.P.s, Birmingham no longer had need of aristocratic messenger boys to run errands to Westminster. And if it did, there were others, more radical and more eminent, who were willing, such as Lord Brougham, who presented the town's petitions against Church Rate in February 1837, and in favour of the repeal of the Corn Laws in the following year.[21] In politics at least, family interest and civic need no longer coincided as they once had.

So, during the 1830s, the Calthorpes assumed a more conventionally Conservative political posture. When in 1834 the Loyal and Constitutional Association was re-established in Birmingham, it numbered three Calthorpes among its vice-presidents – the third lord himself, his younger brother, Frederick and their cousin John Gough of Perry Hall. In addition, another relative, Richard Spooner, was chairman, and George Whateley, Lord Calthorpe's Birmingham solicitor, was secretary.[22] The Association's declaration of principle, with its emphasis on preservation rather than change, and support of the Established Church rather than Dissent, illustrates emphatically the third Lord Calthorpe's changed political position:

> We hold ourselves pledged to resist all measures by which the connection between church and state may be severed or relaxed; the dignity of the monarchy impaired or its existence endangered; the efficiency of the House of Lords as an integral branch of Parliament fettered or controlled.[23]

It was this body which led the counter-attack in the 1830s and early 1840s to the overwhelmingly popular demand that Church Rate in Birmingham parish should be abolished. Indeed, Calthorpe himself even went so far as to make a rare return to the public stage when, in February 1837, in the company of Lords Bradford and Dartmouth, he presented an address to the king urging that no such action should be taken, since it would weaken the position of the Established Church.[24]

At the same time, between 1838 and 1842, the battle over incorporation raged, in which the Conservative party, revived and led by Calthorpe's relatives and professional advisers, adopted a predictably hostile stance. At a meeting called in January 1838 to get up a petition against incorporation, John Whateley was the chief speaker, and in June 1839 he attacked the council's right to levy a rate to pay for a police force. In the following year, his brother George refused to recognize the right of the borough magistrates to appoint to the Board of the Overseers of the Poor. And Richard Spooner who, like Calthorpe, had abandoned the cause of moderate reform, was even more aggressively reactionary, standing four times as Conservative candidate in Birmingham between 1835 and 1847, only once, in 1844, successfully.[25] In all these frantic and acrimonious battles, however, Calthorpe himself played no part. Old, absentee and still in some ways a liberal at heart (he voted for repeal in 1846), his departure from the scene witnessed the effective end of the political role the Calthorpes had once played in the town. Except for a short and disastrous reappearance in 1880, the Calthorpes were played out in Birmingham as a real force in party politics.

Yet while the shift from left to right of centre lost them support in party politics, it did not seem to damage their standing as aristocrats, for Calthorpe's charitable and improving activities continued unabated in the 1830s, almost as if the change in political allegiance had never happened or did not matter. In response to requests from his tenants, he gave the land and £6,000 towards the building of St George's church, Edgbaston.[26] After the foundation stone was laid in August 1836, the children from the Sunday school repaired to the gardens of the Plough and Harrow, where they enjoyed 'a substantial dinner of roast beef and plum pudding (supplied by the noble founder of the Chapel)'.[27] Two years later, he complained to the Botanical and Horticultural Society that its admissions policy was too exclusive, and persuaded them to admit those members of the public who were not subscribers. In the same year, he became president of the General Hospital. When, simultaneously, the Botanical Society found itself in financial difficulties, he generously agreed to forgo £100 of the £140 he received as rent.[28] Nor was medicine neglected. Even at the height of the reform disturbances in October 1831, he gave a donation to the School of Medicine to enable a library and museum to be constructed.[29] Whatever may have happened on the party-political front, the aristocracy were still indispensable to the successful launching of any middle-class charitable or religious enterprise. When St George's church, Edgbaston, was planned in 1833, Harris told Calthorpe that 'to ensure the success of the measure it is essential your lordship's name should appear at the head of the subscription list'.[30] And what was true for a church in Edgbaston was true for voluntary societies throughout Birmingham.

3

Birmingham's Charter of Incorporation was granted in 1838 and, despite the efforts of the Whateleys, Richard Spooner and other like-minded Conservatives, was ratified in 1842. Then in 1851 the Birmingham Improvement Act was passed, which made the council the sole municipal body, with jurisdiction over the parishes of Birmingham, Edgbaston, Deritend, Bordesley, Duddeston and Nechells, and empowered it to raise altogether £500,000 for street improvements, general purposes, and the purchase of the water supply com-

pany.[31] Such steps might have been expected to threaten the Calthorpes'
position as philanthropists and figureheads – partly because a town council
might be expected to produce its own men of weight and stature, thereby
ending the need to procure aristocratic figureheads to legitimate middle-class
endeavours, and partly because the advent of a powerful local authority, with
large funds at its disposal, might perhaps have undermined the whole system
of voluntary and charitable societies, as the council took over services previously provided by private initiative. As if in confirmation of this trend, the
Calthorpes' subscription lists for this mid-Victorian period were relatively
small: £77 in Birmingham in 1851–2, and £121 for Perry in 1860, and this at a
time when the Edgbaston estate was producing between £16,000 and £20,000
gross per year.[32]

Yet for all that, the years between 1842 and 1868 were an Indian summer for
the Calthorpes in their relationship with Birmingham. In 1851, for instance,
when the fourth lord succeeded, he received this memorial from his Edgbaston
tenantry:

> We the tenants assembled this day at the Plough and Harrow Hotel beg
> leave to congratulate your lordship on your accession to the Edgbaston
> estate, and while we deeply deplore the loss that has been sustained by the
> death of your late brother, we all pray that your life may be long spared for
> the benefit of your tenantry and the town in which we live.[33]

Eleven years later, the fourth lord left Perry Hall, where he had lived since
inheriting the title and while Elvetham was being re-built. On his departure he
received an address, which embodied the warm-hearted thanks of the citizens
of Birmingham:

> We avail ourselves of the occasion to convey to you on our own behalf, and
> in full assurance of the entire concurrence of many others, the expression
> of our sincere respect for your character, and of our high appreciation of
> the great benefits which you have, by your example and your influence,
> conferred upon this neighbourhood.[34]

It went on to extol his charitable activities, his concern for the education of
poor children, his support for the Church of England, his just and firm conduct
as a J.P., and concluded with these words:

> On these grounds, my lord, we venture to address you, and we do so in
> words of deep sincerity, and with a feeling of thankfulness for the example
> which a truly Christian Nobleman has given us, by a continual and
> conscientious discharge of public and private duties.

As well as local aristocrats like Lord Howe, Lyttelton and Leigh, the address
was signed not only by some of the town's foremost Conservative figures like
Richard Spooner and the headmaster of King Edward's School, but also by
representatives of those families responsible, in another generation, for one of

the most famous of the town's 'essentially radical' phases: George Dixon, Samuel Beale, Arthur Ryland, Robert Martineau and John Jaffray. Here is perfectly exemplified that continued respect for rank and title which was so marked a characteristic of urban life in mid-Victorian England.

In part this can be explained by the family's changed political position. While the third lord had ended his life a Conservative, the fourth lord became a Palmerstonian, and his son and heir, Frederick Henry William, was Liberal M.P. for East Worcestershire from 1859 until he succeeded to the title nine years later. From the time of his election, he was committed to the abolition of Church Rate and a widening of the franchise, and in his ensuing parliamentary career, he unequivocally redeemed both of those pledges.[35] But, while this renewed convergence of political opinion was a significant element in this mid-Victorian *rapprochement*, too much should not be made of it. The fourth lord only participated in debates on religious and philanthropic questions. And Frederick Henry William had no more interest in Parliament than he had in Edgbaston. He was an infrequent attender in the Commons, only made one recorded speech, and in no sense may be seen as an aristocratic tribune of the Birmingham people.[36] Although the possibility might have been there for such a role, Frederick Henry William was not interested.

The greater part of the explanation for the Calthorpes' continued celebrity lies in the timidity of the behaviour of the middle classes of Birmingham after the triumphs of reform and incorporation. For these gains were not exploited: at the local as at the national level, the government which governed best was still that which governed least. Between 1845 and 1851, the council was only able to build an asylum, a jail and a public bath. In 1855, Alday and the 'economist' faction defeated an attempt to buy out the water company. Thereafter, the road-building programme and sanitary schemes came to a complete halt, culminating in the dismissal of the borough surveyor.[37] At a time when the majority of town councillors were small-scale businessmen, with neither the experience of handling large sums of money, nor the imagination to know what to do with them, they naturally shied away from any municipal scheme which threatened to be expensive, justifying their timidity by appeals to economy and retrenchment. The potential for municipal aggrandizement made possible by incorporation was not yet realized.[38]

One consequence of this backwardness has long been stressed, namely that much of the vigour of Birmingham's civic renaissance of the 1870s may be explained in terms of the need to make up leeway after a generation's stagnation and missed opportunities.[39] But while these were consequences for the future, there were also important implications at the time. Since the council did so little, voluntary societies remained the principal organ of local, 'improving' endeavour. Moreover, because the reputation of the council was so low, it was still felt necessary by those energetic, middle-class private citizens who operated them to seek aristocratic patronage and support as before. And it was this, combined with a conspicuous easing of the tension between Conservative churchmen and radical Dissenters after the final solution of the Church Rate issue in 1842, which explained why the aristocracy in general and the Calthorpes in particular still loomed large in the public life of Birmingham.[40]

So it was that Edgbaston retained its position as 'patron of the charities of life', with 'buildings dedicate to charity and education', as one local poet put it.[41] When he succeeded in 1851, the fourth lord immediately renewed the arrangement reached in 1844 between his late brother and the Botanical and Horticultural Society, and in 1854 he succeeded Lord Dartmouth as the society's president. Two years before, he had given the land and £6,000 for St James' church, further proof of the growing attractiveness of Edgbaston as a high-class suburb.[42] In 1851, the General Institution for the Blind moved from the centre of Birmingham, out of its congested premises in Broad Street to the sylvan tranquillity of Carpenter Road. More generally, at a time when 70 miles of the town's roads were still without sewers, Lord Calthorpe's generosity in making roads, paving them and providing them with sewers, all at his own expense, was much appreciated by the more progressive members of the town.[43]

It was in Birmingham as a whole, though, that the fourth lord made his greatest impact. When Perry fell to the Calthorpes in 1844, he took up residence there, and remained until 1862. While he did not emulate his elder brother's youthful liking for parliamentary politics, he certainly shared his evangelical earnestness and philanthropic concern and, living so near to Birmingham, he was able to meet demands on his time more easily. In September 1852, he laid the foundation stone of St Mary's church, Ladywood, and in October 1857 that of St Clement's, Nechells. In January 1853 he took the chair at a meeting at which it was resolved to establish an Industrial Institution 'for the care, education, employment and reformation of criminal boys', and when the school was established, he became its first president.[44] A year before he came to Perry, he was elected a governor of the Free Grammar School of King Edward VI, and served as Bailiff, or chairman of the governors, for the year 1849–50. Five years later, he was second president of the Birmingham and Midland Institute, in succession to Lord Lyttelton, and between 1845 and 1861 he sat on the committee of the General Hospital, of which he was president in 1850–1 and again in 1853–4.[45] If to this is added the presidency of the Botanical and Horticultural Society, then it is clear that Calthorpe adorned all the major Birmingham charitable and voluntary societies of the day.

But how active in practice was his association? How influential was Calthorpe when it came to the day-to-day affairs of these organizations? Was he really anything more than an ornamental figurehead? In the case of King Edward's School, the governors held 216 meetings between March 1847 and December 1864. Of these, Calthorpe attended 80, 10 of which were in his year as Bailiff. Although there were others whose records of attendance were worse, Calthorpe was never sufficiently involved to have played a decisive or dominant role. There is no evidence that any changes in policy were sponsored by him, and day-to-day affairs were in the hands of the secretary to the governors and the headmaster of the boys' school.[46] The minute books of the General Hospital tell a similar story. While the fourth Lord was on the committee, there were 67 quarterly meetings, of which he attended but 14. Since he was on these occasions chairman, and since the day-to-day management rested with another committee on which he did not sit, it again seems a fair conclusion that his function was more decorative than efficient.[47] Yet such ornamental impotence was exactly what the citizens of Birmingham wanted and appreciated.

The Calthorpes' reputation in Birmingham reached its apogee in 1857 on the occasion of the opening of the park which bears their name. Three years before, C. B. Adderley, later Lord Norton, had offered the council land for a park in Saltley. The council, ever lethargic, refused, so Adderley ran it himself as a private venture until the council changed its mind in 1862.[48] Calthorpe Park thus had the unique distinction of being the first *public* park in the town. Even here, the first offer, made in 1856, was refused on the grounds of expense, and it was not until a renewed offer in the following year that it was finally accepted. The general conditions on which it was donated reflected the high standards of Calthorpe management in Edgbaston: no smoke, ball games, trade or business. But for the general public, it was Condition One which most attracted them: 'that the working classes shall have free admittance at all hours of the day during the six working days'.[49] Small wonder, therefore, that as Calthorpe and the Duke of Cambridge processed through the town to open the park in June 1857, the fourth Lord was acclaimed as 'the generous donor', and the crowds shouted 'Long life to Lord Calthorpe'.[50]

More than for any decades since, this mid-Victorian honeymoon period saw the Calthorpes at the centre of a 'conservative interest'. They themselves adorned the governing bodies of the town's most important voluntary societies: the Midland Institute, the General Hospital, the Botanical and Horticultural Society, and the School of King Edward VI. Richard Spooner, whose mother Barbara was the first Lord Calthorpe's sister, and who was himself a trustee of the Perry Settlement between 1848 and his death in 1864, served as Conservative M.P. for Birmingham from 1844–7, and for North Warwickshire from 1847–64. In addition, he was governor of King Edward's School from 1851 to 1864, serving as Bailiff for the year 1852–3, vice-president of the General Hospital from 1844 to 1864, and first president of the Birmingham Chamber of Commerce in 1855.[51] His son Isaac succeeded him as governor of King Edward's School from 1864 to 1884, and served as vicar of two of the Edgbaston churches of which the Calthorpes were patrons: St George's from its opening until 1848, and St Bartholomew's from 1848 to 1884. From 1848 to 1864, the vicar at St George's was Edward Lillingston, Richard Spooner's cousin.[52] Another distant relative of the Calthorpes was John Whateley, their Birmingham solicitor, who had married the daughter of one of Richard Spooner's brothers and who lived in Edgbaston Hall from 1852 until his death in 1874. As well as being secretary to the governors of King Edward's School, Whateley and his brother George were solicitors not only to the school, but to the General Hospital and the Vyse and the Inge estates. In 1861, when the Calthorpes opposed certain clauses in the Birmingham Improvement Bill in the Commons, they were supported by King Edward's School and the Inge estate. Whateley's obituarist did not exaggerate when he pointed out that he was a dominant figure in that period of Birmingham's history 'in which politics, institutions and social life were capable of being "managed"'.[53]

4

The evidence here for a 'conservative interest', centred on the Calthorpes, is certainly impressive, but it must not be exaggerated: genealogy should not be mistaken for history.[54] In the first place, the Birmingham landowners as a group, although they shared the same solicitors, only acted self-consciously *as a group* when they felt their interests were being attacked, as in 1861. They neither planned their estates nor dabbled in local politics self-consciously, deliberately, as a group. Moreover, links of family or professional contact were over-ridden by party-political rivalry: Richard Spooner and the Whateleys were Tory while the fourth lord and his son were Whiggish or Liberal. Indeed, the relationship between the Calthorpes and their solicitors was strictly professional. In their correspondence, there is no mention of the voluntary societies and charitable associations with which they were all connected, let alone any attempt to lay down an agreed strategy for committee meetings. And later, with the fifth lord, as we have seen, even their business relations were not of the happiest or closest.

So, although the Calthorpes, their relatives and friends were willing to co-operate with the local middle class, they never provided drive, initiative, or self-conscious, coherent policy or leadership. The initiative lay with the local men. It was the town which went after the Calthorpes, not they who went after the town. At best they provided a historic name, a guarantee of respectability, a little money, and a limited amount of well-intentioned activity, but they were not sufficiently in touch with the day-to-day affairs of any of the institutions with which they were connected to have a powerful say in either the making or implementation of policy. That was done by the men on the spot. Nor was their financial contribution such that they could use the threat of withholding it as a lever, except perhaps in the case of the Botanical Gardens, which would certainly have collapsed without the Calthorpes' generosity: but even there, there is no record of any such attempt.

In short, while the Calthorpes' financial involvement in Birmingham was very large, their 'strategic influence' on the town's charitable societies was much smaller. They needed the town for revenue much more than the town needed them for leadership. Their privileged position in this mid-Victorian period depended entirely on the sufferance of the town's middle-class leadership, and the limited extent of their active civic involvement did not justify the obsequious manner in which they were regarded. All the institutions with which the Calthorpes were connected would have functioned equally well without them. It only required someone to point out that the emperor was wearing no clothes, or for the emperor himself to draw attention to that fact, and the days of Calthorpe celebrity would be over.

During the late 1860s, several events occurred which suggested that the day of exposure was not far off. In 1862, the fourth lord moved from Perry to Elvetham, thereby bringing to an end his career as an active aristocrat in Birmingham. In March 1865, he resigned as a governor of King Edward's School, 'on account of his inability to attend the meetings from having left the neighbourhood of Birmingham', and after his departure he never again attended another meeting of the committee of the General Hospital.[55] Then in 1868, he was succeeded by Frederick Henry William: playboy, financier, socialite, but with no abiding concern for Edgbaston or Birmingham. At the same time, there were the beginnings of momentous changes in the council chamber, too. The era of collaboration was over, and a time of crisis and confrontation was about to begin.

10 Financial problems and managerial difficulties, *c.*1880–1922

In the same way that the continued building at Edgbaston during the 1880s concealed for a decade or so the alarming and long-term collapse in the number of building leases granted, so the exuberantly successful financial dealings of Frederick Henry William, fifth Lord Calthorpe, served to distract attention from a fundamental change which had taken place in his overall financial circumstances. His success in using the unsettled estates as security for loans, the interest payments on which were met by Edgbaston's burgeoning rentals, enabled him to create a more complete aristocratic *ensemble*, which successfully hid the reality of the stagnant or reduced income which prevailed on all his estates by the time of his death. However, his successor, Augustus, sixth Lord Calthorpe, who held the title from 1893 to 1910, could not ignore it. Nor, for a variety of reasons, ranging from the nature of the agricultural depression to the breakdown of the centralized administrative structure which had operated so successfully under his predecessor, was he able to do very much about it. So, on his death in 1910, the twin problems of stagnant income and amateurish management converged, leaving his successor to find the answers.

1

In some senses, Augustus inherited the family holdings in good condition: there were no encumbrances, his brother had doubled the size of the Elvetham estate, and the most embarrassing of the family's possessions, in City Road, had been conveniently disposed of with the minimum of fuss. Indeed, the fifth lord had even timed his death with great skill, sandwiched as it was just after 1892, when the City Road leases had fallen in, and immediately before 1894, when the Liberal government introduced death duties. So, by the time Frederick Henry William's personal estate and the last stages of the City Road sale had been tidied up, and legacies, debts and duties paid, there remained some £50,000 in securities which was passed on, along with the estates, to Augustus. Assuming that they gave a return in the region of 3 per cent, that meant that his income in 1895 was made up as shown in table 16 (overleaf). This is only a rough guide, since the London and Elvetham figures for net income may be over-estimates, and Augustus may have had extensive shareholdings of his own; but the general impression is certainly correct, in particular the almost total dependence of the family on the rentals from their Edgbaston building estate by this time. In 1810 it had provided one-third of Lord Calthorpe's income; by 1850 the figure was one-half; now it was between 75

Table 16. Lord Calthorpe's income, *c*. 1895

Estate	Gross £	Net £
Edgbaston	30,255	25,013
Elvetham	3,931	*c*. 2,000
Norfolk	3,295	1,714
London	2,882	*c*. 2,500
Shares	*c*. 1,500	*c*. 1,500
Total	41,863	32,727

Source: EEO MS., Edgbaston Account Book; EEO MS., Letter Book II, G. Edwards to Calthorpe, 1 Dec. 1893; EEO MS., Letter Book II, 21 July 1894, for half year's London rental, which is doubled for this table.

and 80 per cent of both gross and net revenue. Or, put the other way round, the Calthorpes were, at the most, only receiving 12 per cent of their net income from agricultural rents (see Appendix B). It is hard to imagine a greater degree of aristocratic dependence on non-agricultural resources. Moreover, these proportions remained approximately constant until Augustus' death, as can be seen from table 17.

Table 17. Lord Calthorpe's income, *c*. 1910

Estate	Gross £	Net £
Edgbaston	34,457	27,734
Elvetham	5,130	*c*. 3,000
London	2,905	*c*. 2,500
Norfolk	1,478	*c*. 1,000
Shares	*c*. 1,500	*c*. 1,500
Total	45,470	35,734

Source: EEO MS., Edgbaston Account Book; WVH MS., D/24/11, The Rt Hon. Augustus Lord Calthorpe, deceased, schedule to estate duty account sworn 29 March 1921.

Again, some of the specific estimates may be inaccurate, but as a general picture of the Calthorpes' finances at the end of Augustus' life, it is probably correct, and there can be no doubt that the picture of stagnation presented by comparing these two tables is completely valid. If the first phase of family finance can be viewed in retrospect as one in which an aristocratic income was created, and the second as one in which an aristocratic life-style was evolved commensurate with this income, all that can be said of the third is that it was conspicuous for its uneventfulness, and it was an uneventfulness the more dangerous because accumulated aristocratic wealth and privilege was increasingly coming under attack during Augustus' lifetime.

Predictably, the tone here was set by Edgbaston itself. Just as the expanding Edgbaston revenues had been the foundation stone of the previous era of prosperity, so now it was Edgbaston's stagnation which was the most dominant theme in the period of quiescence. Indeed, the turning point had already been passed a decade before Augustus inherited. But the time-lag in house-building and continued playing of the mortgage game had concealed this. By the mid-1890s, however, there could be no doubt that those halcyon mid-Victorian years, when income doubled every decade or so, were gone. For the next two decades, gross revenue stuck firmly at between £30,000 and £35,000, with net revenue between five and six thousand pounds less (graph 2). Ironically, it was at just this time that the most exaggerated stories begin to circulate about the fabulous wealth of the Calthorpes. Some spoke of their 'enormous income', estimated at between £50,000 and £100,000 a year from Edgbaston alone. And Bateman, in describing the 'gross annual value of the estate' as £112,000, only reinforced this myth, for while he himself took pains to point out that the Calthorpes themselves received no such amount, contemporaries did not read his small print.[1]

If the sky over Edgbaston was murky, it was positively gloomy over the other estates. London remained as before, minus City Road. The leases on Gray's Inn Road did not expire until 1910 onwards, and Gough Square was so small – only 14 houses – that even when re-let, the increased income was negligible. All in all, this source continued to provide about £3,000 a year gross. As far as the agricultural estates were concerned, they had never been financially profitable even in the mid-Victorian decades, and now, at the end of the century, income slumped abruptly. For the ten years 1875–85, Elvetham rents were double what they had been in 1860, but this had resulted from those land purchases of the fifth lord and his father, rather than from any major improvement in productivity. Between 1886 and 1893, however, rentals fell to an average of £3,931, 'being a reduction of £6–6–0 per cent', Edwards calculated.[2] As with Edgbaston, the slump had set in before Frederick Henry William had died, but while he lived, the programme of estate expansion had helped to maintain a buoyant atmosphere. With Augustus, however, that came to an end. Although by 1910, revenue had reached a new peak of £5,000 a year, this was hardly enough to make the estate self-supporting.

However, the situation was worst on the Calthorpes' East Anglian estates. Here, above all, agricultural landownership had become an 'increasingly expensive luxury'.[3] The combined gross rentals of Acle, Blakeney and Cockthorpe dropped by 11 per cent, from an average of £3,703 between 1876–85 to £3,295 between 1886–93, and of this second figure, 48 per cent, or £1,581 a year, went on estate maintenance. As George Edwards put it with considerable understatement, 'the payments here, as they always have been, are very heavy.'[4] And declining current income only reflected reduced capital value. In 1878, the Acle estate, which had been valued, for the purpose of raising mortgages, at £43,225, was described as 'a very desirable freehold estate', and recommended as proper security for a mortgage of up to £32,000; but by 1885, its value was written down to only £28,000, and the fifth lord was asked either to pay off part of the mortgage, or to provide more security.[5]

When Augustus took over, there were no signs of improvement, and the condition of these estates remained depressed well into the new century. As business propositions, they were not worth keeping: indeed, they never had been. Their value had been in their historic associations as the oldest Calthorpe estates, and the façade of broad acres in many counties which they helped to maintain; but that illusion was expensively bought, especially by Augustus. Even the small sum left after estate expenditure was deducted from receipts was not all available for his own personal use. Items such as a £200 donation for the Acle church restoration fund had to be paid, and exceptional demands for estate maintenance, such as the repairing of the Blakeney sea wall between 1905–8, had to be financed from other sources.[6] And 'other sources' meant Edgbaston, as it always had done.

2

In this way, financial affairs lingered on until Augustus' death, with no attempts made to confront, analyse or rectify these problems. Partly this was because of Augustus' character. He succeeded to the title at the age of 64, having been tenant of Perry Hall from 1868. Like his father and his uncle, he was shy, retiring and a poor public speaker, a man with a strong sense of duty, but possessed of no desire to be a public figure. In his funeral oration at Elvetham parish church, the vicar described him thus:

> He . . . preferred the life of a country gentleman which would enable him to take an interest in agriculture and share in the public work of the neighbourhood in which he lived. . . . He never aspired to important positions, preferring in a quiet and unostentatious way to do his best for the welfare of the community, and it was only when he was convinced that he could render useful service that he consented to identify himself with any public movements.[7]

He had no interest in the affairs of the turf or the social whirl of the Marlborough House set, which his late brother had so enjoyed, and the stud farm at Newmarket went immediately under the hammer on his succession.[8] His main pastime was stock breeding, and Elvetham became famous for its Berkshire pigs, Shorthorn cattle, Shire horses, and Southdown sheep. He was a staunch supporter of the local church, and attended divine service twice on Sundays, regardless of who might have been his house guests.[9] The contrast with Frederick Henry William could not have been more marked.

At the agencies, too, it was a time of change. In 1894, George Edwards gave up at Perry and Edgbaston, and in 1900 he resigned from the London agency as well. Perry was subsequently administered by F. P. Lightfoot, and so departed altogether from the main orbit of family estates.[10] At Edgbaston, there was an unfortunate interlude in 1894 when James Pritchatt, a Calthorpe employee for 20 years, succeeded and promptly committed suicide. He was then followed by Arthur Davies who, in 1900, took over the London estates as well. He was the first 'professional' agent the Calthorpes had employed, having previously been the manager of the Corporation Street Improvement scheme on behalf of the council.[11] On his early death in 1902, he was followed by another homegrown product, E. H. Balden, who had been employed in the office as a clerk since 1894. By then, indeed, the centralized administration of the estates, over which George Edwards had presided with such distinction, had almost completely broken down. Balden looked after Edgbaston, but nothing else; Bruce, the Elvetham agent, also administered London; Perry was in the hands of Lightfoot; and the Norfolk estates were farmed out to the firm of Spelman and Co. at Norwich. Only Augustus, old, tired and set in his ways, had any overall view of the financial position. It was a dangerously fragmented and myopic command with which to navigate the stormy waters of the early twentieth century.

Yet, as if unaware of this, the conduct of affairs remained on the same cordial and genteel level as before. With both Davies and Balden, Augustus showed a personal interest in their affairs reminiscent of the third lord's attitude to John Harris. He sent them gifts of pheasant, was most generous to Davies's widow when her husband died, and wrote to Balden a kind and touching letter on the occasion of the death of his father.[12] When he reached his eightieth birthday, Calthorpe told Balden with evident delight and appreciation that their 'association in Edgbaston affairs' had been 'entirely harmonious', and when the sixth lord died in 1910, Balden sent this moving letter to his widow:

> May I for a moment depart from an official tone and offer my most respectful and heartfelt sympathy with your ladyship in the saddest of bereavements which you are called upon to bear by the death of Lord Calthorpe, my revered and noble chief, and one for whom it has been a joy to work.[13]

The stark contrast with the bleak formality of day-to-day estate correspondence is particularly noteworthy.

No such close relationship existed between Augustus and R. H. Milward, his Birmingham solicitor. Indeed, one of the few characteristics which Augustus shared with his late brother was a profound distrust of Milward's professional competence, for he described him disparagingly in 1895 as 'a country solicitor with a badly-organized office'.[14] In March 1902, C. F. Crowder, Milward's son-in-law and (in Calthorpe's opinion) the only competent partner, retired, ostensibly because of failing eyesight. The real reason became apparent three months later, when Milward was found to have defrauded some of his clients of £30,000 which he had used in unwise and dishonest speculations of his own.[15] He was struck off the solicitors' register, and in December 1902 was sentenced to six years' penal servitude on a charge of fraudulent appropriation. By September 1903, however, he was dead.[16] The

'Milward sensation' rocked Birmingham: it was an appropriately spectacular finale to a spectacular career – and entirely vindicated the Calthorpes' judgment of him. As Davies put it, 'I think your lordship had expected something like this to happen for some time.' 'I did not trust him', Augustus replied, 'but always thought his shrewdness would prevent him getting into deep water. Vanity has undone him.'[17] Thereafter, the limited local business which Calthorpe decided to entrust to a Birmingham solicitor was handled by C. F. Crowder who had, it later transpired, left Milward because of 'dissatisfaction at the way in which the financial business of the office was conducted'.[18]

Affairs at Edgbaston were in striking contrast to these sudden and spectacular events in the solicitors' office. In 1893, the tone of letters passing between Elvetham and Edgbaston changed abruptly, from the world of high finance to careful accounts of local events. 'I am glad to have full details of everything concerning the estate', wrote Augustus to Davies when the latter took up his appointment in 1895.[19] That was an understatement, for he had a positive mania for reading and checking everything. While he had been at Perry, he had carefully filed and annotated all the letters he had received. Once he inherited Edgbaston, the same system was applied there. He read, checked and initialled the monthly *resumés* of business, studied and signed the accounts, and did exactly the same with business for the Norfolk estates. While the letters of the fifth lord to George Edwards were hardly ever about Edgbaston affairs, those of Augustus to Davies and Balden were never about anything else. Once a week, every week, Augustus wrote: even when he was in bed with a broken hip, in May and June 1896, or when his only son and heir Walter died in December 1906, the correspondence continued unabated. And it concerned everything, not only great issues like the grants of land to the university, but also the most trivial of problems: Mr Chance's pigeon house, plans of new sewers, the state of the lavatories in the estate office, the fence at Pebble Mill, and so on. When the draft conveyance of land to Birmingham University was sent to him for approval in August 1900, he minuted that the plans were 'carelessly drawn'.[20] One thinks of Philip II's remarks about fleas.

Such care and concern for his estate and his tenants was remarkable – the more so considering that Augustus was an old man by the time he inherited. Indeed, in all ways, he epitomized much that was best in the English aristocratic tradition. On his death, Balden's eloquent letter went on to pay tribute to his master's abiding concern for the humblest of his tenants, 'for whom at all times I have been allowed to make expenditure without regard to its remuneration, if desirable for their humble comfort and convenience'.[21] Despite their unprofitable nature, Augustus gave freely of his money to local causes in Norfolk, and until 1910 the annual audit dinner was a continuing feature of life on his estates there.[22] At his funeral, the pall bearers were the three agents, Balden from Edgbaston, Bruce from Elvetham, and Waters from Spelman and Co., and an Elvetham tenant farmer. The procession included 100 estate workers; among the mourners were the household servants from Elvetham and Grosvenor Square; and the wreaths included one from the Elvetham estate with the inscription 'A token of sorrow for a kind and considerate master'. The vicar of Edgbaston conducted the service, and the lesson was read by the vicar of Elvetham. It was an appropriate farewell to a peer born before the passing of the Great Reform Act.[23]

Unfortunately, admirable though these qualities might be, they were out of date by 1910. Just as Frederick Henry William had the mind of a financier when he was expected to behave like an aristocrat, so Augustus had the outlook of a country gentlemen when he needed the resourcefulness of a businessman. While the vicar was correct in praising Calthorpe's loyalty to and concern for his tenants, he exaggerated excessively when suggesting that as 'a man of business' he had few equals. Although passionately devoted to the administration of his estates, he was unable to visualize them in any broader context. He saw trivial details from close to, but never anything from a more distant perspective. He had too much interest, too little imagination; and, at the very time when it was most needed, there was no all-seeing Edgbaston agent who could fill the gap, for George Edwards had no successor. As a result, no attempt was made to prepare in advance for the death duties which must be met on Augustus' demise, except to empower his successor to raise mortgages on the estates; as she was to learn, this was an inadequate solution.

3

Since Augustus died leaving only four daughters, it was generally assumed that the estates as well as the title would pass to the only surviving son of the fourth lord, Lieutenant-General the Hon. Sir Somerset Gough-Calthorpe of Perry Hall, then in his eightieth year. The Perry settlement of 1848 had implicitly assumed this, and it was generally supposed that Augustus would want to keep estates and title together. But, in 1907, on the death of Walter, his only son, he had re-settled the estates so that they should pass on his death to his eldest daughter Rachel, who married Fitzroy Lloyd-Anstruther in 1908, provided they adopted the additional surnames of Gough-Calthorpe.[24] So, in November 1910, Rachel and her husband removed the 'Lloyd' part of their surname, and tacked the Calthorpe family name on to what was left, thereby becoming Mr and the Hon. Mrs Fitzroy Hamilton Anstruther-Gough-Calthorpe. Meanwhile Somerset, the new and seventh Lord Calthorpe, remained marooned at Perry and Woodlands Vale, Isle of Wight. Two years later he died, and in 1923 and 1928, his successor sold off the Perry estates to Birmingham corporation, thereby ending the family's residential connection with the Midlands.[25]

While, by contrast, Rachel prospered, she also inherited problems commensurate with her wealth. At Edgbaston there was the gloomy picture of 30 years' stagnation in lettings, a suspicion that the status of the suburb was declining, and new and ominous threats posed by the growing demand in Harborne for tramways across the estate. In addition to this, at both Edgbaston and Gray's Inn, the original 99-year leases were about to begin falling in, which was bound to necessitate a major re-appraisal of policy. Then in Norfolk, there were the estates at Acle, Cockthorpe and Blakeney, which had always been a drain on the family's resources. More generally, there was no one in the Calthorpes' employment who could provide the centralized direction and professional expertise necessary to solve these problems. Finally, and with death duties for the first time as well as the reversion duties introduced in the 1909 budget – ironically the very year in which the Edgbaston leases began to fall in in large numbers – the new landlord was faced with unprecedented demands of taxation which could not be met out of current income. Literally as well as metaphorically, the day of reckoning had come.

In other ways, too, the years after Augustus' death were eventful, for to the worries of inheritance were soon added the traumas of war. Captain Fitzroy Anstruther-Gough-Calthorpe was in France on active service between February 1916 and July 1917, and Elvetham Hall was converted into a hospital for wounded officers for the duration of the war.[26] As a result, one event which would otherwise have been an occasion for great celebration – the bicentennial of Sir Richard Gough's purchase of the Edgbaston estate – passed quietly. In April 1917, Balden wrote Rachel a letter of congratulation. 'It is indeed an eventful date', she replied, 'and I only wish it had happened in happier times when we might have celebrated in some way.'[27] But celebrations were little in evidence in these years: there was too much fighting to be done, both at home and abroad.

As far as the impending domestic battles were concerned, Rachel and Fitzroy recognized immediately the need for expert advice 'in all important matters on what we might term questions of policy'. Moreover, they also appreciated the need to put 'the whole administration on a clearly defined and strictly business footing', and so they enlisted the services of Frank Newman, a consulting surveyor. In an attempt to calm any fears he might have that he was being demoted, Fitzroy explained the need for this move in a letter to Balden:

> We have carefully considered the question of the various estates, and having regard to their somewhat exclusive nature and varied location, the conclusion we have come to is that it is absolutely essential we should have the assistance of some expert. This conclusion is all the more heightened on taking into consideration the almost vindictive financial legislation which H.M.G. have thought fit to promulgate in their dealings with real estate.[28]

The decision had not been taken a moment too soon. Together, Newman and the Calthorpes attacked the accumulated problems of Augustus' reign, and attempted to come to terms with the twentieth century. Although they were better placed than many aristocratic families, it was no easy task.

4

The fundamental structural problem with which the new tenant for life was faced in 1910 was that of the falling in of the building leases at Edgbaston and Gray's Inn Road and, more generally, with the deterioration of two estates, parts of which were over 100 years old. Throughout the depressed 1890s and 1900s, the prospect of the gains from the reversions which would soon begin to fall due must have been a great comfort to the Calthorpes. Indeed, it was in anticipation of this reward that it had been decided to hang on to the Gray's Inn Road estate in the early 1890s, and the few leases which fell in at Edgbaston in the 1880s and early 1890s, as those original nine leases expired, certainly augured well for the future. In 1883, for example, Richard Greaves' original lease of one acre between Hagley and Harborne Roads, on which the rental was £10 a year, expired and a new improving lease was granted for 37 years at an annual rental of £90. In the same way, the three-quarters of an acre which had been leased by Thomas Lee in 1787 for £7 10s. a year were re-let for £110.[29]

However, prior to 1910, only 7 such leases had expired: then, between 1910 and 1914, no fewer than 42 fell in. It was almost entirely as a result of these re-lettings that the estate's gross rental in these years grew from £33,000 to £37,200, an increase of 2.5 per cent per annum, a rate unknown since the early 1880s (graph 2).[30] Considering that the number of leases granted in the 1810s was really very small compared with what came after, this meant that the long-term prospects at Edgbaston were excellent. But there were difficulties. On both estates, it proved impossible to re-let some of the houses in the state in which they reverted to the lessor. Moreover, the evolution of that part of the city which bordered on Edgbaston's north-east border meant it was difficult to re-let houses there as private residences, for it was now too near the central business district. And under these circumstances, the 10 per cent reversion duty imposed by Lloyd George in his 'People's Budget' was only an added irritant.

The problem of decay had been recognized for some time. As early as 1897, George Edwards predicted that, at the expiration of the leases, much of the Gray's Inn Road estate would require re-building, 'being old and out of date'.[31] And, of the 68 leases which fell in there between 1910 and 1914, all were described as being 'in a very dilapidated condition'. At Edgbaston, Charles Gabriel Beale put forward the general view when he observed that Hagley Road had 'certainly gone down from what I remember when I was young', partly because of the increased commuter traffic, but mainly because it was 'composed of very old-fashioned houses with no modern conveniences . . . , with no bathroom at all, and really they are quite out of date.'[32] This was even more true of the houses at the north end of Bristol Road, varyingly described, when the leases fell in, as being 'old', 'in a bad state of repair', or 'very dilapidated and untenantable'.[33] Under these circumstances, there were three alternatives. The houses could be demolished, the ground cleared, and new building leases granted. They could be re-let on long-term repairing leases, in which case the tenant would bear the responsibility for repairs. (Naturally, this was the preferred solution, since the rent would be higher than in the case of the old, or a new, building lease.) Finally, the existing houses could be re-let on a short-term tenancy, in which case the freeholder had to undertake all the repairs.

Only 14 Edgbaston houses were re-let on long-term repairing leases between 1910 and 1914, which meant that the majority were re-let on short-term tenancies. Of necessity, this type of re-letting involved the estate in considerable expense. Outgoings at Edgbaston, which had averaged £5,000 in the 1900s, had reached £9,000 a year by 1912–14. And at Gray's Inn Road, where there were those 68 houses in 'a very dilapidated condition', expenses were even higher. It cost £1,076 to render 270 Gray's Inn Road habitable, for example, and £927 had to be spent on 282. Even then, it proved hard to re-let on occasions. No. 282 Gray's Inn Road, for example, was not re-occupied until 1922, although the original lease had expired in 1910.[34]

At Edgbaston, however, a greater problem concerned the long-term redevelopment strategy for that north-eastern corner of the estate where the first leases had been granted. Both as regards the location and value of the land, it was now too near the central business district to make it possible to redevelop as a residential area with any prospect of success, yet to abandon the estate's hitherto exclusively residential policy would cause an outcry from other tenants. In 1914, this issue suddenly came to the fore when the Calthorpes had to decide what to do with the triangle of land at Five Ways bounded by Hagley and Harborne Roads. As early as 1904, Balden suggested that shops should be placed there, and in 1912 a firm of property developers, anxious to get first refusal on the site, sent in plans for a block of flats, four storeys high.[35] This was turned down, but then in April 1914 another company applied to the estate for permission to construct a large and garish cinema on the site. In May the company went so far as to apply for a local licence, and negotiations were all but completed by the estate for a lease of £150, conditional on £10,000 being spent on the building.[36]

When this became known, there was an immediate outcry. A public meeting of Edgbaston residents was held, attended by 200 people, and Rachel was inundated with letters of protest and petitions.[37] For years, they argued, lessees had built houses in Edgbaston confident that the covenants in the leases would be enforced and that the district would thus remain exclusive and residential. Most of the lessees had kept faith with the landlord and maintained their houses voluntarily as the covenants required; but now, they argued, the landlord proposed to break faith with them by allowing to be constructed the very type of building which, at the landlord's express wish, the covenants had hitherto prohibited. 'Such a step', noted one irate correspondent, 'will amount to a break of faith with the lessees who have made the estate what it is.'[38] No less a person than the Bishop of Birmingham weighed in, with a personal letter to Rachel:

> It is considered that it would be a reversal of the Calthorpe estate policy to lower the character of the houses and the inhabitants by allowing such a picture palace to be erected. It would certainly depreciate the surrounding property considerably, and it is felt that if the estate will only wait a little time, the migration on the part of the wealthier people will end, and they will come back from the further afield places to which they have gone.[39]

The last sentence, explicitly stressing the very view of Edgbaston's decline which the Calthorpes did not want to hear, suggests that the bishop was not as competent in tact as he was in theology.

It really was an intractable problem. The decline of the north-east corner of the estate, and its proximity to the rest of Birmingham, made it highly unlikely that anyone would want to become a resident there. Yet, as the tenants constantly stressed, redevelopment on other than residential lines was a breach of faith, and might only serve to accentuate the exodus of high-class tenants from the estate which the Calthorpes were so anxious to reverse. Eventually, a solution was externally imposed. So strident was the local opposition that in June 1914 the local justices refused to grant a licence for a cinema to the company. Because the deal had been so close to completion, the estate was obliged to pay the company £125 to cover their costs.[40] In September, the land was finally sold to the corporation for £3,500, and laid out as a park and recreation ground.[41] In the short term, it was a convenient solution, but it was no long-term answer: the estate could not sell off former building plots indefinitely. The taking of a fundamental policy decision was postponed to another day.

The reversion duties imposed by Lloyd George in 1909 could not be put off so easily, however. Augustus had lived just long enough to see them imposed, and had found it a sorry prospect, believing Lloyd George to be 'quite ignorant of finance, . . . equally obstinate in holding any opinion he has formed, . . . and dishonest too.'[42] In practice, the tax could not be described as iniquitous: the only bill the Calthorpes received for Edgbaston was in May 1912 for £813, and that was subsequently paid back.[43] Nevertheless it was an added irritant at a time when there was so much else to worry about, and it was feared it might be the thin end of the wedge. Moreover, it entailed 'immediate extra work', for the administration involved in calculating the tax on the accrued benefit was considerable. Balden, worried with other problems, found his staff stretched to the limit. In one way and another, it was not an easy time at Edgbaston in the years immediately before the First World War.

5

These issues of decay, reversion and redevelopment were more pressing and difficult than any with which Rachel's predecessors had to deal. Yet, in a very real sense, the problems which the Edgbaston estate threw up in the years after 1910 were the least of her worries. The 1907 settlement had provided a pension for the dowager Lady Calthorpe of £5,000 a year, and required that portions of £10,000 each should be raised for her three other daughters on Augustus's death. And, in addition, there would be the death duties to pay on Augustus's estate. As Balden put it in August 1910: 'the great, and I might add, almost iniquitous duties you have to meet are enough to make one pause and think as to ways and means.'[44]

The fact that Rachel and Fitzroy had appointed Newman as professional adviser suggests that they had paused and thought to good effect: but, to judge from their expenditure between 1910 and 1914, it seems that they did not fully appreciate the magnitude of the financial demands which taxation would impose. In June 1911, they obtained a loan from Hoares, their London bankers, of £25,000 secured on their Norfolk estates, with which to begin paying off the three portions which were due.[45] Augustus's personal estate was wound up without difficulty, and in August 1910 Fitzroy went to visit the Norfolk estates and – a touch of which Augustus would have approved – took tea with the Rector at Acle. Subscriptions to some local charities were reduced, and Fitzroy complained that the revenue was too low, but otherwise there was no change from the days of his father-in-law.[46]

At the same time, between 1910 and 1914, a lavish programme of improvement was undertaken at Elvetham Hall itself – hardly the action of a landowner who believed that her day was done. An entire new wing, consisting of a library and billiards room, was added; new windows were put in; the central hall and staircase were reconstructed; the stables were converted into garages and a fleet of Daimlers was purchased.[47] In addition, more land was bought in the vicinity, but very little money was put aside to meet future death duty bills.

Table 18. Calthorpe spending, 1910–14 *(to nearest £50)*

	£
Portions	25,000
Elvetham repairs	38,000
Elvetham purchases	24,100
For estate duty	12,400
To repay Hoares' loan	14,350
Miscellaneous (fees, etc.)	4,500
Balance	12,700
Total	131,050

Source: WVH MS. D/80/8, Trustees Capital Account, 1910–36, 36.

Very nearly one-half of total expenditure went on 'conspicuous consumption' in a manner of which Frederick Henry William would have approved; but England was a very different place in which to be an aristocrat in the 1910s compared with what it had been even in the 1880s. Such expenditure was a brave gesture of confidence in the future of landed society; but it was not a very perceptive response to a situation already worrying, and soon to cause anxiety.

Apart from Hoares' loan, most of the money spent had been raised by selling land, as table 19 shows. At Edgbaston, a site was sold to the Blue Coat

Table 19. Calthorpe revenue, 1910–14 *(to nearest £50)*

	£
Elvetham sales	21,250
Edgbaston sales	8,000
London sales	20,500
Norfolk sales	⎧ 25,650
	⎩ 27,800
Hoares' loan	25,000
Miscellaneous	2,850
Total	131,050

Source: WVH MS. D/80/8, Trustees Capital Account, 1910–36, 35.

School, which was anxious to leave the city centre for the suburbs, and the Corporation bought that plot of land at the Five Ways which had given so much trouble. On the Gray's Inn estate, the Royal Free Hospital was sold its freehold, and at Elvetham, some land was also sold as part of a policy of rationalization.

Most striking, however, was the disposal of the Acle, Blakeney and Cock-thorpe estates in their entirety, at an auction in Norwich in July 1911 for, by bringing the oldest Calthorpe lands under the hammer, the link between the Calthorpe family and East Anglia which had lasted since the Middle Ages was finally severed. Frank Newman, in explaining the decision to sell to Waters, the partner of Spelman and Co. who was responsible for them, stressed that the need to provide 'the necessary funds for payment of death duties and other charges' made it 'imperatively necessary to realise a good portion' of the family's estates. He went on to stress with what 'considerable regret' Fitzroy and Rachel had reached this decision, 'for as you know, it really was their wish to take a real interest in these particular properties'.[48] But, although this letter was a masterpiece of tact, the evidence of expenditure belies the argument. In common with many other families in the years immediately before the First World War, the Liberal legislation finally persuaded the Calthorpes to part with estates which for nearly a generation had lost their limited social and political appeal and which now, viewed coldly as investments, made little sense.[49] More particularly, since they were now well established as landowners and aristocrats at Elvetham, the pretence of aristocratic grandeur in East Anglia – understandable in more spacious, less threatened days – was no longer worth maintaining.

So, by the time war was declared, the first phase of adjustment following the death of Augustus was completed. The capital account was as good as squared, half of Hoares' loan had been repaid, and there was a sufficient surplus left (over £12,700) to repay the rest. But during the next two years, the valuation of Augustus's estates was completed, and assessments for death duties were finalized (table 20).

Table 20. Death duties charged on sixth Lord Calthorpe's estate

Estate	£	Capital value £	Duty (rate per cent charged) £	%
Edgbaston		1,143,900	171,600	15
Miscellaneous ⟨	500			
	4,000			
Elvetham (part)	14,750	72,700	10,900	15
Norfolk	25,650			
Acle	27,800			
Gough Square		9,400	1,400	15
Elvetham		157,700	15,750	10
Gray's Inn Road	175,450			
Norfolk (part)	1,300	178,500	26,700	15
Miscellaneous	1,750			
Total		1,562,200	226,350	

Source: WVH MS. D/24/11, Lord Calthorpe (deceased), Schedule to Estate Duty Account, 7 March 1921.

Since all the outlying estates had already been sold, there was no more land which could reasonably be realized. The only solution was to raise loans on the remaining estates, a strategy consistent with the terms of the 1907 settlement, which had allowed mortgages for the purpose of paying off death duties to be raised as an encumbrance on the estates (table 21).[50] But even this was not enough.

In June 1918, the final sacrifice was made: some of the Edgbaston estate was put up for sale to raise the money necessary for the last two instalments of death duty payments due on that estate. 'I can only hope that every lot may sell well and that the net result will be of much benefit to the family finances', wrote Balden. 'It is hard to sell for the purpose of paying state duties after a two hundred-year ownership.'[51] Not surprisingly, the area sold consisted of those working-class districts between the Worcester Canal and Bristol Road where covenant enforcement had become most difficult in recent years, and where

Table 21. Money raised by the Calthorpes, 1915–22 *(to nearest £50)*

		£
	Balance from 1910–14 Account	12,700
July 1915	Edgbaston mortgage (4½–5%)	30,000
July 1915	Edgbaston mortgage (4½%)	100,000
August 1915	Elvetham mortgage (8%)	4,500
December 1917	Gray's Inn Road mortgage (6½%)	50,000
December 1917	Edgbaston mortgage (6½%)	47,650
June 1918	Edgbaston sales	48,150
	Miscellaneous	7,000
Total		300,000

Source: WVH MS. D/80/8, Trustee Capital Account, 1910–36, 37–9.

prospects of reversion were not good.[52] In all probability, the Calthorpes were glad to be rid of them.

By these means, sufficient money was raised to meet all outstanding obligations (table 22). Death duty payments were higher than the original assessments, because they were paid over six years and therefore included additional payments of interest. Miscellaneous expenditure covered succession duty, fees for lawyers, solicitors, surveyors and auctioneers, and a small amount of re-investment in equities. But there was not much room in which to manoeuvre: the Edgbaston sale brought in £48,150, and the last two instalments of death duties on Edgbaston which the auction was designed to pay were £45,250.

Table 22. Calthorpe payments, 1915–22 *(to nearest £50)*

	£
Edgbaston death duties (1916–18)	196,000
Norfolk death duties (1915)	11,250
Gough Square death duties (1915–18)	1,600
Elvetham death duties (1921)	19,150
Gray's Inn Road death duties (1918)	31,950
Repayment of Elvetham mortgage	4,500
Balance of £25,000 Hoares' loan	10,650
Balance of three portions	4,500
Miscellaneous	15,100
Balance left in account	5,300
Total	300,000

Source: WVH MS. D/80/8, Trustees Capital Account, 1910–36, 37–9.

6

So by 1922 the Calthorpes had rendered unto Caesar the tribute which he required. In addition they had paid off the portions due to Rachel's younger sisters, and lavished another small fortune on the modernization of Elvetham; but taxation and embellishment had cost them dear. The family's most historic holdings in Norfolk had been liquidated; parts of the three remaining estates had been lopped off; Edgbaston was still mortgaged for £177,650 and Gray's Inn for £50,000. Hence Fitzroy's plaintive cry to Balden in March 1922: 'Please keep down estate expenses to the lowest minimum compatible with efficiency. Although the uninitiated would not believe it, it is difficult for us to make ends meet.'[53] Thus was acknowledged the passing of half a century in which it had become increasingly difficult to sustain an aristocratic life-style. Agricultural depression, a democratic franchise, higher taxation, war and a revolution in landholding: all this and more lay behind these words, as the aristocracy in general and the Calthorpes in particular struggled to survive in a world ever more hostile and unsympathetic.

This is a one-sided picture, however, for the Calthorpes were much better equipped to survive than many in these testing and difficult years. Like all landowners, their agricultural estates had been depressed in the 1880s and 1890s, and Edgbaston's performance was disappointing compared with the mid-Victorian period. Put another way, however, a guaranteed income of £30,000 a year from Edgbaston at a time of falling prices effectively insulated them from the vicissitudes of agriculture. Just as Edgbaston had made possible the achievement of an aristocratic life-style in the middle of the nineteenth century, despite a lack of aristocratic acreage, so it made it possible to sustain it in the early decades of the twentieth century at a time when it became increasingly difficult for those whose revenue was largely derived from land. Once more, the failure to buy Culford had proved to be providential. The sale of the East Anglian estates was simply a recognition of this, the logical conclusion of a policy of rationalization begun by the fourth lord in the late 1850s when he parted with Pakenham and Ampton. Unlike many aristocratic families, the Calthorpes did not face a fundamental crisis between 1910 and 1922, and they knew it. Times were difficult, but the problems were not insurmountable, for while selling land was a sign of worry, restoring Elvetham was a gesture of confidence, and it was the Edgbaston estate which made that possible. By 1923, its gross rent was up to £45,000.[54] So, when the war was over, the Calthorpes' life continued vey much as before. The day of reckoning was postponed again.

11 External threats and internal weaknesses, *c.*1870–1914

In the long run, the combination of a large and valuable building estate and small and scattered agricultural holdings enabled the Calthorpes to weather the agricultural depression more easily than many other aristocrats. The lack of broader acres might have been a cause for sorrow in the 1820s; but by the 1890s it was a positive blessing. Yet even so, in the short run the 1880s were not without their problems: the age of Augustus was most decidedly the age of anxiety, and this was as true of Edgbaston itself as of their estates in general. It was not only the decline in status, the threats of competition from other new suburbs, the departure of some of its most illustrious residents, and the stagnation in building leases and rentals, which caused concern, worrying enough though all this was; it was also that the rise of a new ring of suburbs on the estate's south and western borders generated so much commuter traffic that demands for mass transport across the estate became increasingly difficult to resist and worrying to contemplate, occurring as they did at a time when aristocratic privilege in general was under conspicuous attack.

1

Until the 1860s, the Edgbaston estate was relatively immune from threats presented by public utilities. The Worcester Canal had been hedged around with so many restrictions where it crossed the estate that it had become an amenity rather than a threat and, during the railway mania, no line was laid across Edgbaston at all. Indeed, although the estate was the largest single landholding near the town centre, the fact that it was on the south-western side of Birmingham once more worked to its advantage (fig. 16), for the major industrial regions to which the town aspired to be linked did not lie in that direction. The Black Country, Lancashire and the Potteries lay to the north-west, Derby and the Trent Valley to the north-east, and London to the south-east. To all of these areas went canals in the last quarter of the eighteenth century and railways in the second quarter of the nineteenth; but to the south and west lay the Severn Valley, mid-Wales and the Cotswolds, none of them thriving industrial centres. So the Calthorpes' estate survived well into the second half of the nineteenth century with only the Worcester Canal penetrating its borders. Even the south-westerly rail link with Gloucester, built in 1840, was happily routed to the east of the estate.[1]

However, in 1815 a scheme was mooted to put a steam railway along the Bristol Road, which pertinently anticipated future problems in this direction. The third lord recognized that it might 'materially affect my individual advantage', and Harris immediately grasped the central issue of private versus public interest which was to become so intractable for the estate later in the century.[2] As he noted, the question was 'whether such advantage in the aggregate will be of such public benefit' as to outweigh 'the inconveniences and injuries which must be inflicted on many individuals through whose property the road will pass',[3] and Calthorpe himself took the same view. 'I have no wish whatever', he declared, 'that the proposed Bristol or any other rail road should pass through the estate.' But on the other hand, he admitted that if the plan appeared 'to be conducive to the advantage of the public, I should not be inclined to make any opposition to it.'[4] In fact, the scheme came to nothing, but the problems already diagnosed then were to recur with increasing frequency in the second half of the century.

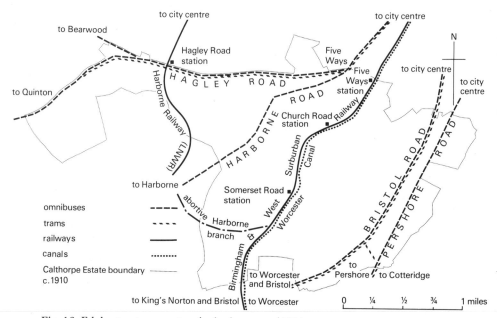

Fig. 16. Edgbaston transport: principal routes, *c.*1914.

Unfortunately, in seeking to keep railways and trams at bay, the Calthorpes were less well armed than in their skirmishes with industry. There they were at least legally omnipotent: no one could deny them the right to grant or withhold leases on such terms as they chose; but in dealing with public utilities, their powers were much more circumscribed. They had no legal right to debar commuters from using the roads which crossed the estate; public utilities had powers of compulsory purchase; and local authorities in an expansionist frame of mind could always mobilize the ratepayers – the majority of whom did *not* live on the Calthorpe estate – in their own support. These were strong, wealthy, determined and immortal opponents, fortified on most occasions with the argument that 'the public interest' required that they should prevail and that the estate should give way. Nor was this easily refuted, since the Calthorpes were vulnerable to the accusation that at worst they only represented themselves, and at best that they only represented their tenants. Moreover, by the end of the nineteenth century, such opposition was expensive, and less likely to succeed in a world in which the climate of opinion was increasingly hostile to any form of aristocratic privilege. Whereas, by comparison, as Joseph Edwards explained to R. H. Milward, 'corporate bodies have no soul to be damned and no body to be killed'.[5]

From the estate's viewpoint, the problem was compounded by the fact that the issue was rarely this clear-cut. Although opposition to factories, wharves, sidings, and warehouses along canals and railways was absolute, the size and location of the estate meant it could never be completely hostile to mass transport, for it was so big – three miles from east to west and two miles from north to south – that the areas remotest from the centre of town, such as Metchley, Beech Lanes and Chad Valley, could only be developed successfully if some form of public transport was available. Unlike the Devonshires at Eastbourne, where railways were vital if the resort was to have any chance of success, or the Bedfords in Bloomsbury, where the estate was so small and intimate that they must be resisted at all costs, the Calthorpes' attitude to public transport was of necessity ambivalent. Although the steam train and the tram were in many ways abhorrent, once their sights were set on the full-scale development of Edgbaston, the Calthorpes really could not do without them.

In the 1860s, however, these problems still lay in the future. Early in 1866, the Harborne Railway was promoted, a suburban line only three miles long, which left the main L.N.W.R. line north of Rotton Park Road, and curved gently southwards beneath Hagley Road and across the Edgbaston estate to Harborne. 'There can be no doubt about the policy of opposing the proposed line of railway through Edgbaston', observed the future fifth lord – not so much outright, but because the proposed line of the scheme, between Westfield and Norfolk Roads, might threaten the development of that area as a high-class region.[6] Accordingly, the Calthorpes, with the support of 17 of their tenants, persuaded the promoters of the company to place their line further westward, on land unlikely to be built on in the foreseeable future, beyond Westfield and Hermitage Roads. In addition, where the land fell sharply away to the south of Hagley Road, the company undertook to erect earthworks rather than unsightly viaducts, and agreed that there should be no station built on the Calthorpes' land without their written consent and approval.[7] This agreement was subsequently embodied in the Act incorporating the company, which was passed in June 1866. For the six acres of land taken by the company, Calthorpe received a perpetual rent-charge of £250 a year. In 1870 the Harborne Company was taken over by the L.N.W.R., and only in 1874 was the line finally opened.[8]

By then, however, the full complexity of the problems which public transport might create had become apparent. In 1870, a company was formed called the Birmingham & West Suburban Railway, which sought to build a single line from a station at Granville Street in the town centre to Kings Norton, with a westerly branch line from Pritchatts Road to Harborne. The main line, where it crossed the Calthorpe estate, was to be laid adjacent to the Worcester Canal, and stations were proposed at Five Ways, Church Road and Somerset Road. In the two reports which Edwards made on the scheme, he concluded enthusiastically in its favour. He did not believe that the line would require much land, nor did he think that its presence would deter intending lessees. More important, he felt that the branch line to Harborne, which would run across Metchley Farm, would bring 'the furthest part of the estate . . . into immediate proximity with the centre of the town', thereby holding out the prospect of 'opening lands and making new roads on that part of your lordship's estate.' Accordingly, *provided* the Harborne branch was built, Edwards concluded that the railway 'will ultimately prove beneficial of Lord Calthorpe's estate'.[9]

By the end of January 1871, a draft agreement had almost been completed. The company agreed to build bridges according to Calthorpe's wishes, so that roads at Metchley could be made at a later date; there would be no level crossings; an additional station would be provided at Metchley Lane; the plans of all stations on the estate must be approved by Calthorpe's agent; the embankments of the Harborne branch must be planted with evergreens; and Calthorpe's costs would be paid by the company.[10] Then in February the company decided to abandon the Harborne branch, which 'materially altered' the estate's views, for with that line gone, the scheme's attractiveness was much diminished. Yet by now the bill was already in the Lords, awaiting a committee. The Calthorpes therefore gave notice of their intention to petition against the scheme, on the grounds that it would affect the estate 'in a most objectionable and injurious manner', while behind the scenes the respective solicitors of landowner and company hammered out an agreement.[11] On 6 March 1871, ten days before the Lord's Committee was due to meet, a compromise was reached, which contained essentially the same terms as the draft agreement, with the added restriction that the company was to construct no buildings of any kind except stations and station houses along the line. In addition, clause 35 of the bill recognized that the company would not carry heavy goods traffic, as that remained the monopoly of the Worcester Canal.[12]

In 1873, a further Act was passed which slightly altered the nature of the line at the north end, but since it was not on Calthorpe land, the estate was unaffected. Two years later, the B.W.S.R. was taken over by the Midland Railway, and the new company agreed to fulfil all the obligations of the old.[13] Finally, a single line was opened in 1876, the estate having previously approved the stations to be built and the fencing to be used. In October 1875, when the line was nearing completion, there was a minor scare when it was rumoured that once the single track was opened the Midland Railway would immediately seek powers enabling them to double the line. Calthorpe was determined to petition so as to ensure that the estate was adequately safeguarded, but in February 1876 the company abandoned the scheme.[14]

Early in 1879, the Midland gave notice that it intended to obtain another Additional Powers Act to enable it to reconstruct the line and make it double track. Clause 4 of the new bill proposed to release the Midland from the obligations of the B.W.S.R., which included the agreement reached with the Calthorpes for the protection of Edgbaston. In addition, the Midland had bought out the Worcester Canal Company's monopoly on goods traffic.[15] Accordingly, if the bill became law as it stood, the Midland would be able both to carry whatever goods it wished on the line, and to use the land at Edgbaston in any way it chose. Calthorpe himself was livid when he heard how he had been out-played. In two withering letters, he castigated Milward for not having ensured that he had been better protected initially. 'My interest was not sufficient guarded', he complained, adding pointedly, 'I have just received your enormous bill.'[16]

A petition was hurriedly put together and presented in committee at the end of February 1879, along with a separate one from 36 lessees. It argued that, since 'a considerable portion of the estate has been let on building leases for the erection of private villa residences of a very high class', if the bill was passed unamended, it would 'destroy the character of these residences' and 'greatly deteriorate their value'.[17] While this public battle was being fought, negotiations were once more in progress behind the scenes. By the beginning of April, an agreement was reached and embodied in the bill as a clause 'for the protection of the Edgbaston estate'. It contained ten sub-sections, of which the most important were agreements that there would be no goods station or sidings at Edgbaston, nor any buildings other than those necessary for the working of the railway. No buildings could be put up without the consent of Lord Calthorpe's agent, and no goods of any kind could be stored by the company in the parish of Edgbaston.[18] But the restriction of goods traffic was gone for ever. All the Calthorpes succeeded in salvaging was a guarantee that there would be no shunting of goods trains in sidings. Indeed, some lessees were so annoyed at what they regarded as negligence on the part of the estate that they continued the fight alone,[19] but eventually they, too, acquiesced. It had not been a happy episode, and the fact that the estate had obtained 'every protection that can be given consistently with the working of a railway' was small comfort.

In 1881, the last battle was fought, when the Midland sought to link up the suburban line to their main station in New Street, thereby obtaining a more direct line between the main line to Bristol – which the B.W.S.R. joined at Kings Norton – and the centre of the town. In addition, it empowered them to carry out the construction authorized, but not yet begun, by the 1879 Act. This time, the Calthorpes acted more speedily, and managed to extend the provisions of the 1879 Act 'for the protection of Lord Calthorpe' into the new bill as well.[20] But it was an untidy conclusion to an unsatisfactory episode. The branch to Harborne, of which so much was hoped, had never materialized, and instead of a single-track suburban line alongside the Worcester Canal, the estate had been forced to concede a double track line, which was part of the main route to Bristol, on which there were in effect no traffic restrictions. But at least the adjacent lands had been preserved from the risk of factories and other industrial buildings, which offered some crumbs of comfort.

2

Despite the retirement of the railway from the fray, the later years of the century saw renewed threats to Edgbaston's green acres. In the 1880s, telephone lines began to make their appearance, and an unsightly web was woven over Edgbaston without the Calthorpes' consent. Well into the new century, there was a perpetual battle, as poles were put up in Bristol, Wellington, Hagley and Farquhar Roads, and the estate sent increasingly heated letters of protest, culminating in 1900 in the threat of legal action.[21] Although many of the offending poles were removed as a result, the estate was not entirely successful. Despite hopes to the contrary, it failed completely in its attempt in 1894 to persuade the National Telephone Company to remove the poles it had placed along the line of the Midland Railway, and in 1913 the *Birmingham Daily Mail* published a picture headed 'the telephone eyesore', showing a veritable forest of wires and poles in Balsall Heath Road.[22]

However, the greatest challenge of all came from the tram. Indeed, as early as 1876, a horse tramway was constructed along the Bristol Road as far as Bourne Brook, which was run by a private company. It was converted to steam power in 1885, which was replaced by electric cars in 1890, and by overhead cables in 1890.[23] The Calthorpes themselves offered no opposition to this, in part because it was not at the time realized what the consequences of trams would be, in part because the residents of Bristol Road were themselves undecided, and in part because the road was practically on the estate boundary. Occasional private schemes were also proposed in the 1880s for the laying of trams along Harborne and Hagley Roads, but they never materialized because the council, itself eager to secure control of the tramway network, opposed them. But in November 1900, a new tramway committee was set up by the corporation, with the influential Charles Gabriel Beale – thrice chosen lord mayor, vice-chancellor-elect of the new university, and architect of the Elan Valley water scheme – as chairman. And, as Davies explained to Calthorpe, 'their principal duty is to consider the question of a large extension of the tramway system, including links along the Pershore Road, Hagley Road and Harborne Road, to be worked by the City Council direct'.[24] Clearly, battle was about to be joined.

The ensuing conflict raged intermittently until 1914, posing the issue of private property versus public interest in its starkest form. Should the limited interest of Edgbaston's wealthy landlord and tenants be allowed to prevail, or the demands of the working-class communities farther east, as yet unincorporated in the city, but soon to be brought under the sway of the Council House? With an anti-aristocratic Liberal Government in power from December 1905, how much weight would the opposition of a peer carry? How far did he dare – or even want – to oppose? For again, the tram was as much a boon as a curse. Edwards believed the tramways 'may/will be of great advantage to the estate, especially to the distant parts of it.'[25] But the fifth lord took the opposite view, stressing how 'tramways would injure the quiet and therefore the value of property wherever they were allowed to be, except in the lowest neighbourhoods'.[26] If he was correct, then the added threat to the status of parts of Hagley and Harborne Roads, already declining due to their age, would be most unwelcome.

The early months of 1901 thus found Arthur Davies on his guard. In March the corporation asked the estate for land so that it could widen the Pershore and Hagley Roads. Normally the Calthorpes were most co-operative in such matters but, since such a move was felt to be 'a preliminary to the application to Parliament for powers to lay down tram lines', the request was turned down.[27] Three months later, the city council gave notice of its intention to apply for powers to lay tramlines along Hagley Road. Calthorpe, aware that 'there is a strong feeling abroad in favour of quick and cheap measures out of town', doubted whether opposition would succeed, and made it plain that he would not oppose alone. If the tenants wanted to fight, then they must pay too.[28] An *ad hoc* tenants' committee was formed, which took a poll. Only 46 were in favour while 383 were hostile. A general meeting was held at the Edgbaston Assembly Rooms, at which Davies was urged to state Calthorpe's views unequivocally; but this he refused to do, for Calthorpe himself, although aware of the residents' opposition, doubted whether a Lords' Committee would throw out the bill. By November, however, he had decided to oppose the bill, independently of, but in collaboration with, his tenants.[29]

Then, at the end of the year, the General Powers Bill in which the tramway scheme figured was defeated by a poll of ratepayers for entirely different reasons, so that the whole bill, tramways and all, was dropped.[30] The next attempt was equally unsuccessful. Early in 1904, the residents of Harborne petitioned the council for a tramway, which resulted in a line to Harborne being included in a new comprehensive scheme announced in June that year. By December, however, this scheme, too, had fallen through, and Balden, who had now replaced Davies, was able to express the hope that 'Harborne will enjoy freedom from tramways for some time to come.'[31]

It was a rash prediction. By 1,738 votes to 368, the inhabitants of Harborne again declared for a tramway in October 1906, and the city council agreed to go to Parliament early in the new year to obtain the necessary powers.[32] Again the Edgbaston committee clamoured for Calthorpe's support, and again he equivocated. For, although he declared in public that he 'must support the tenants in opposition', in private it was clear that it was only the pressure from the tenants which tempted him 'to thwart the City Council in their proposals as to the trams.' As Balden explained, 'the House of Commons as now constituted with a large radical majority may not give ear to the grievances of landowners generally, and more especially to those of a member of the House of Lords.' Added to which was the realization that the cost of opposition – if the battle was hard and long – would 'run into some hundreds of pounds.'[33] Once more, however, Calthorpe finally made up his mind to oppose, but only 'if it is made clear that the leaseholders do so also, and do not leave me in the lurch.'[34] The evidence of the decline in the will to resist was most marked. Against the Midland Railway, it was the tenants who had followed their landlord's lead; but now the situation was reversed.

Later in December 1906 the bill was published and approved by the majority of ratepayers. Again, at Calthorpe's request, Balden made it clear to the chairman of the residents' committee that Calthorpe's 'opposition to the bill is only in support of the lessees', and that they could not expect him to go on alone if the tenants withdrew.[35] In March 1907, the bill reached committee, where Calthorpe presented one petition and 625 residents presented another. Essentially their cases were the same: that the introduction of trams would seriously depreciate the value of their property; that those living in the houses adjacent to the tramways would leave; that the houses would prove to be impossible to re-let so that the whole district would decline; and that the case for trams to Harborne was not overwhelming.[36] The Corporation's representatives were unable to shake this case, so the committee ruled that 'it is not expedient to proceed with that part of the bill which relates to tramways'.[37]

Once more the enemy had been routed; but Calthorpe had been obliged to meet a bill of £616 in solicitors' fees, and this for supporting a course of action with which he did not entirely agree.[38] Moreover, there was no doubt that there had only been a postponement of the conflict for the summing-up by the counsel for the City made it clear that they would not give up: 'Nobody, my lord, I think for one instant, will say that Edgbaston can for all time resist a tramway passing through if it is the desire of Harborne to have the tramway.'[39] Nor, indeed, did they do so, for in 1909 a new tramway bill was prepared as part of a larger package of municipal imperialism which also included the Greater Birmingham bill and a town planning scheme. This latter measure, covering some 2,320 acres of Harborne and Quinton, itself gave the Calthorpes some difficult moments, for it included not only the whole of those Harborne acres which had been bought in the 1850s, but also a strip of land on the eastern side of Metchley Lane. The estate objected – with little success – to this further erosion of autonomy; but the coming of war postponed the implementation of the scheme.[40]

In the case of the tramways, however, the threat was much more real. In April 1910, the residents of Harborne sent in a new petition to the Corporation, 13,026 of whom were in favour of the trams, and only 802 of whom were against.[41] A year later, the city tramway committee recommended that application should again be made to Parliament for powers to make tramways along both Hagley and Harborne Roads. As before, the Edgbaston residents were determined to fight. By 149 votes to 19, they condemned the scheme, and so began the by now familiar round of meetings, protests, petitions and letters to the local papers. 'Every residential road along which trams have been run has deteriorated', wrote one Edgbastonian. 'The Corporation will never be able to make or maintain a suburb such as Edgbaston is. Yet they wish to destroy it.' 'Why should a district and road admitted to be beautiful be damaged by the unsightly posts and annoyance?' asked another. If trams were allowed, argued a third, then 'the grandest suburban road in England' would be destroyed. When the opposition committee was re-convened, it instantly re-affirmed the familiar theme of 'the heavy depreciation that would follow the construction of a tramway along Hagley Road.'[42]

Although their tenants were prepared once more to man the barricades with their accustomed vigour, the Calthorpes – worried by death duties and other problems – were less belligerently disposed than they had been even in 1906–7. While Balden thought 'it only right that dissenting lessees should be backed by the estate in some way', he made it clear to the committee that this time the Calthorpes would not set up in opposition on their own. On the contrary, their contribution was confined to a cheque for £100 and Rachel's signature on the petition, although Balden himself did consent to join the committee.[43] But even he was not sanguine. As he explained to Augustus shortly before he died: 'Trams must come sooner or later is a point which I'm afraid must be conceded, and Edgbaston cannot always hope to hold out between Birmingham and the districts beyond Edgbaston.'[44]

For if the case in favour of tramways had been sufficiently strong even for Augustus to recognize its force in 1907, by 1912, when the suburban communities had been fully integrated into Greater Birmingham, it was overwhelming. In the first place, the balance of numbers was on their side, as the *Birmingham Daily Post* explained in an editorial:

> There are and must be many living on or near to the Harborne or Hagley Roads who still believe that tramways will destroy the amenities of Birmingham's best suburb. Nonetheless, we think the time has arrived when the manifest interests of districts which have grown up beyond the Edgbaston boundary, and the admitted needs of the tramway system as a whole, should have greater weight than those personal objections.[45]

The *Birmingham Daily Mail* was no more sympathetic to the Edgbaston residents' arguments:

> They have not got the right to say that, in order that their privacy shall be preserved, the large and rapidly increasing community which has sprung

up on the outer fringe shall remain for ever cut off from communication with the city . . . The wealthy residents of Edgbaston must make the same sacrifices in the interests of the general community as have been made by residents in other quarters of the city.[46]

The argument about 'the public interest' could not have been more forcibly put. Indeed, it may well be that the Calthorpes recognized it, and deliberately chose to adopt a lower profile on this occasion in the hope that their tenants, rather than themselves, would be the object of attack.

Moreover, Hagley and Harborne Roads were by now so busy with commuter traffic that it was difficult to argue that trams would make matters much worse: for, as Henry Clarke explained:

As a quiet and seclusive residential quarter, Hagley Road is 'done for'. It is a main arterial road. Its chief purpose is now to convey a growing population to the roads which issue from Hagley Road and to the important and well-populated districts all round the Bearwood and Lightwoods area.[47]

The result, as A. W. Langham pointed out, was that Hagley Road was no longer the place it had once been:

The property on Hagley Road, in accordance with the property market in general, is surely at the lowest ebb already. Houses are being continually offered for sale and can be procured at absurdly low prices. As the leading residential road in Birmingham, Hagley Road has had its day: the houses are not the demand of today. They are not modern, or so suitable to the present requirements, and some of them are a continual source of expense in the way of repairs.[48]

This was hardly a glowing appraisal of the city's 'premier suburb'. Time and circumstances seemed emphatically on the side of the trams.

By April 1912, the bill had reached the House of Commons Committee. Once more, the petitioners trotted out all their old arguments: Edgbaston was primarily a residential suburb; tramways would therefore ruin it; their property would be depreciated; the scheme would never pay; the objections of 1907 which had been upheld then were still valid now.[49] But all these points carried much less weight than before. On the council's side, massive evidence was produced showing that 'Hagley Road was one of the main thoroughfares of the city', so much so that the addition of tramways could not possibly depreciate the neighbouring property any more than it had been already. One witness pointed out that there was a five-minute service of omnibuses along the road, and another claimed to have counted between 15 and 20 heavy motor lorries in half an hour, making it 'an exceedingly noisy road'. J. B. Whitehouse, who had actually built houses on the Calthorpe estate, claimed that no one would any longer think of buying a house on Hagley Road 'for quiet residential purposes', and added that houses there would continue to depreciate, trams or no trams, simply because they were too old.[50] Equally unanswerable was the evidence marshalled by the corporation to show that the western suburbs beyond Edgbaston were growing rapidly. The population of Oldbury had tripled between 1901 and 1911; that part of Smethwick adjacent to Hagley Road had grown from 730 to 9,630 between 1886 and 1912; and 1,300 houses had been built in Harborne since 1901. By comparison, the population of Edgbaston had remained virtually stagnant, 'because there has been a migration further out'.[51]

For the Calthorpes, this was a most depressing spectacle, as their dirty linen was washed so blatantly in public. Nor was this the last time for, the Commons Committee having surprised everyone by allowing the Hagley Road line but refusing the Harborne Road scheme, the fight moved on in July 1912 to the Lords' Committee, where all the old arguments and counter-arguments were brought out again.[52] This time the Edgbaston petitioners played what they believed to be their trump card by calling on Balden as a witness, but it was to no avail. Once more, the Hagley Road tramway was approved. In a letter to Rachel, Balden described the decision as 'very unfortunate', and felt sure that 'property will suffer in value'.[53] But Fitzroy resorted to an old and familiar argument in an attempt to look on the bright side: 'Perhaps good will come out of evil after all. The tramway will no doubt give access to the outlying portions of the estate, and may result in development of some sort or other.'[54]

Some of the Edgbaston opposition committee, fearful that the decision would lead to an 'exodus' of residents, and that Hagley Road would become 'a wilderness of empty houses', began a rearguard action to get the trams postponed and an experiment conducted with buses instead. Although a stay of execution was won in October 1912, work began on the tramlines in March 1913, and the scheme came into operation in the following September.[55] As such, it represented the triumph of numbers and civic initiative over wealth and aristocratic ownership. And, as the *Birmingham Daily Post* put it, in an editorial which precisely summarized Edgbaston's changed circumstances, it was the correct decision:

> The fact . . . is that Edgbaston has long ceased to be the western limit of Birmingham. Harborne and Bearwood have been rapidly closing round it, while Warley has become populous and is sufficiently ripe for development as to be the area for a town-planning scheme . . . Hagley Road, long and spacious, has thus become not mainly a residential route, but the chief route to a rapidly expanding district, greatly needing quick and convenient means of access to the centre of the city.[56]

In a 'democratic' age, burdened with other worries, and with an unconvincing case, there was little an aristocratic landowner could have accomplished by way of opposition – except, wisely, to oppose as discreetly as possible, and to accept defeat with resignation rather than defiance.

3

This picture of a middle-class estate, outflanked by speculative developments of an inferior quality, penetrated and congested by commuters, raked by tramways, and interlarded with lower-middle- and working-class housing, is typical of the experience of many middle-class suburbs in the period from the 1880s to the First World War. In particular, the threats to the quietude and social exclusiveness posed by the trams – those 'gondolas of the people', with their loud and vociferous working-class passengers – were resisted with as much vigour but no more success in Hampstead, Kelvinside, Victoria Park and elsewhere.[57] The middle classes felt themselves to be under attack and, as at Edgbaston, once their *cordon supérieur* was breached, they retreated to establish new bastions of exclusiveness farther out. It is important to stress, however, that the enemy was also within the gates for, in Birmingham as elsewhere, the drive to put tramways through exclusive suburbia came from town councils still essentially middle class in composition. Indeed, over the issue of the Edgbaston tramways, opinion among the Calthorpes' tenants themselves was sharply divided. Most of the councillors responsible for the scheme lived at Edgbaston, and Charles Gabriel Beale, whose brainchild it was, was one of the estate's foremost residents. For some of Edgbaston's tenants at least, the loss of exclusiveness was a price worth paying for the enhancement of municipal grandeur.

Where Edgbaston differed from these other bastions of middle-class suburbia was that it was owned by an aristocrat, and the picture of declining landed energy and confidence which the episode of the trams reveals is illuminating. The fifth lord was exceedingly belligerent against the railways: where he led, the lessees followed, and defence on the grounds of self-interest was both possible and successful. Augustus, by contrast, although probably more fond of his estate, was less belligerent in its protection when it came to fighting off the trams. The climate of opinion was against him; it would be expensive; the evidence of new suburban expansion beyond Edgbaston was plain to see – and yet his sense of duty obliged him to support his tenants and run his own campaign, although only after the fullest assurances that he would not be left in the lurch. Finally, with Rachel, the tenants almost entirely superseded the estate as the guardian of the amenities. Worried about death duties, absorbed in improvements to Elvetham, arranging the sale of the Norfolk estates, and anxious to avoid criticism in Birmingham itself as the incarnation of exclusive privilege, it was strategically more prudent to bow out of the last battle and retain a low profile. For a family as wealthy as Birmingham had made the Calthorpes, it was too dangerous to make an enemy of the corporation.

12 The Calthorpes and Birmingham, 1868–1914: a 'conservative interest' in decline

By the late 1860s, the Calthorpes' public links with Birmingham had passed through three phases: the pre-Reform Act era of collaboration and shared liberal opinions; the period of confrontation and conflict in the 1830s and early 1840s, as the family took up a more Conservative position; and then the mid-Victorian *rapprochement*, the product of shared Whiggish and Liberal views, continued middle-class diffidence and obsequiousness, and renewed local interest and activity on the part of the Calthorpes themselves. But during the late 1860s, it became increasingly apparent that the renown and prestige which the family had enjoyed for a generation could not be expected to last much longer. On the town's side, the Anglican-Dissenter consensus was once more breaking down, and a revived and radical nonconformity was again beginning to confront a decayed and conservative Established Church. So the 'rude noises' began to make themselves heard, as in the *Town Crier*, a local satirical magazine, whose declared objective was that of 'putting incompetent and pretentious people out of the way', be they lethargic councillors or bloated aristocrats.[1]

This heightened middle-class self-awareness coincided with a change in the Calthorpes' local public image from concerned and committed philanthropists to idle and opulent absentees. The fourth Lord Calthorpe had left the town in 1862 and died in 1868, and his successor, Frederick Henry William, was not temperamentally equipped to play the part in local affairs which his father had. The pleasures of the turf and of high finance took precedence over any sense of aristocratic obligation. Edgbaston he regarded as a source of revenue and little else, and philanthropy as an activity not be indulged in generously or personally. 'You may give Mr Thos. Tutin £5 or what you think proper', he wrote angrily to his agent in 1885, 'though he has no claim but that of poverty and I have daily applications.' 'I know they think I ought to subscribe more, but I will not, as I think the congregation ought to do this kind of work', he replied to an appeal for funds from St James' church.[2] Augustus, too, who now succeeded to the Perry estates, played a far less conspicuous part in public affairs than the third or fourth lords had done. He occupied the essentially honorific post of High Sheriff of Staffordshire in 1881, and was president of the General Hospital in 1873–4, but to the town in general, he was completely unknown. At the same time, Edgbaston was entering its most rapid phase of development, and grossly exaggerated rumours were beginning to circulate about its supposedly fabulous rental. Yet in return, this new generation of Calthorpes seemed more reluctant than ever to perform those acts of patronage and philanthropy customarily expected of aristocrats. From the family's viewpoint, it was a situation fraught with danger.

1

The first major decision Frederick Henry William took exemplified both his ignorance of that danger and the ease with which a crisis might be provoked. When his father had made the arrangements concerning Calthorpe Park, he had been unenthusiastic and unco-operative.[3] Now, as a tenant for life, he could indulge such feelings more openly. So, in May 1870, and at his request, Whateley and Company sent a letter to the town council asking that part of the park be returned. As if this was not tactless enough, it later transpired that Calthorpe wanted to let the land on building leases and, to add insult to injury, he offered in exchange a piece of very poor quality land between the park and the River Rea, which was so located that it was clear the Calthorpes would never be able to develop it.[4] Tact, graciousness and any sense of aristocratic obligation faded before the desire for money.

In fact, the fifth lord had every *legal* right to behave in this way; because that part of the Edgbaston estate was settled, the fourth lord, as tenant for life, had only been able to *lend* the land to the town: he could not actually *give* it in fee simple. But understandably, this apparent disregard by the fifth lord of the spirit of his father's wishes caused 'considerable feeling'.[5] His past record of Liberal voting, even on two issues so appealing as church rate and parliamentary reform, gave him no immunity from attack when he ceased to behave in the manner generally felt to be appropriate to an aristocrat. At a council meeting in September 1870, he was severely attacked by Alderman Avery.[6] He recalled how, at the opening of the park, the fourth lord had been gracious enough to concede that those possessing rank and wealth should give something back in return:

> Lord Calthorpe said on that occasion that . . . his property had been much increased in value by the trade and manufacturers of Birmingham, and he thought he could not make a better return to the people of Birmingham (than) by affording them a means of healthful recreation.

But now, Avery went on, his son – apparently contemptuous of that ideal – chose to ignore his father's wishes – and at a time when the Calthorpes' debt to Birmingham was greater than ever:

> The Edgbaston estates were now magnificent estates with princely revenues . . . Now what has created this vast wealth, and surrounded this family with vast opulence? . . . It was the industry, the untiring labours, the ingenuity, the sagacity, energy and judgment of the people of Birmingham.

He finished by giving the fifth lord an unequivocal lesson in aristocratic obligation:

> No one grudged English noblemen their high position or their vast possessions, but they still had duties in connection with their position and possessions. These duties were clearly recognized by the *late* Lord Calthorpe.

The innuendo could hardly have been plainer. From the radical press, who *did* grudge English noblemen their high position, Calthorpe received an even more savage beating. The September issue of the *Town Crier* included an item entitled 'A Letter to a Lord', in which the anonymous author explained, 'As you do not often visit Birmingham, being doubtless more agreeably engaged, I am obliged to address you by letter.'[7] He went on, in a similarly vitriolic vein, to accuse Calthorpe of disloyalty to his father's wishes, of 'looking only to the "rights" and not the "duties" of property', and claimed that the land he intended to give in exchange was little more than 'a piece of delightful swamp'. His conclusion left no doubt as to the conditional nature of approval for the aristocracy in Birmingham:

> I think, my Lord, that if I were in your place, . . . the good opinion of three or four hundred thousand people from whom I derived a large proportion of my revenue would be to me a matter of importance.

In short, if the Calthorpes, who took so much from Birmingham in the form of rents, behaved graciously and generously in return, then they were tolerated in some quarters and even appreciated in others; but if they tried to flaunt their rank unthinkingly and selfishly, they would receive no mercy.

Eventually in 1871 a compromise was reached. The land was exchanged as the fifth lord wanted, and with the consent of his two brothers he granted the new plot to the council rent-free.[8] This was not the end of the matter, however, for with the advent of Joseph Chamberlain – who was, ironically, until 1880, Edgbaston's most illustrious tenant – the whole system of voluntary self-help and private charity, which had been an indispensable part of the Calthorpes' continued celebrity, was superseded by an altogether more lavish style of 'improvement'. The Chamberlain revolution brought to the council chamber men experienced in the methods of big business, opposed to economy and retrenchment, captivated by efficiency and the prospect of making local government work, and eager to exploit and extend the statutory powers under which they operated.[9] The result was spending on 'improvement' on an unprecedented scale. The purchase of the gas companies involved raising the borough debt from half a million to two and a half million pounds. The land for the Corporation Street scheme cost £1,310,000, and the Elan Valley water project swallowed up £5 million.[10]

Almost overnight, the status of the voluntary societies, and with them the aristocrats who had once been their guarantee of respectability, declined. As Chamberlain explained to the council in 1875, 'all private effort, all individual philanthropy, sinks into insignificance compared with the organized power of a great representative assembly like this.'[11] This was certainly true as far as the financial contribution of Lord Calthorpe was concerned: his regular subscription list to Birmingham charities was only £312.[12] For a man who was drawing £25,000 annually from the town, that was small; by comparison with the funds which the town itself could mobilize via the council, it was trivial. Ten years after his Birmingham speech, when he launched his 'unauthorized programme', Chamberlain repeated his municipal arguments in a national setting. Having listed the evils of working-class life – poverty, bad housing, under-nourishment – he went on:

> Private charity is powerless, religious organizations can do nothing, to remedy the evils which are so deep-seated in our system. . . . I venture to say that it is only the community acting as a whole that can possibly deal with evils so deep-seated as those to which I have referred.[13]

So the voluntary societies were overtaken as the prime medium of middle-class improvement by municipal benevolence, and in that process the local aristocracy was inevitably devalued. Where there had once been exaggerated gratitude for limited generosity at a time of private self-help, there was now anger that, by comparison with the resources which the town could mobilise, they had done so little.

Nor was this the only way in which Chamberlain's revolution affected and weakened the aristocracy's position: for by stressing the innate value and nobility of local, civic government, he loosened the psychological ties of middle-class dependence. Anti-monarchist and anti-aristocrat as he was at this time, Chamberlain stressed that civic activity was quite adequate and legitimate *by itself*. It needed no props from an alien world, no grandees as a guarantee of respectability. The whole ethic of civic gospel, of a crusade, of an 'earnest and hearty desire to promote the welfare of the town', of 'the nobility of the duty we perform', was not only a direct attack on the squalor and inefficiency of the town's government in the 1850s and 1860s, but also on those timid middle-class figures whose confidence in the value of their endeavours was so limited that they sought anachronistic and comforting patronage from those who neither toiled nor spun.[14] If patrons were needed, they should be home-grown products, who had established their right to be esteemed by virtue of their civic careers, not grandees whose only claim to respect was an inherited position.

2

Under these changed circumstances, it was rash in the extreme for Augustus Calthorpe, the fifth lord's brother and heir, to stand against Joseph Chamberlain at the 1880 general election. For the local party, the electoral campaign of that year was the climax of a Conservative revival begun in the 1870s under the auspices of J. B. Stone, and a supreme effort was made to crown these endeavours by toppling Chamberlain himself, whose hold on the town was still not fully established.[15] For this purpose, the Conservative committee obtained as a candidate Colonel Burnaby, a man who had become famous by riding to Khiva in central Russia and back. It was an inspired choice. Described by his biographer as 'perspicacious, determined, resourceful, tenacious, amazingly daring', he was the very antithesis of Chamberlain in all except courage.[16] His politics were exuberantly and flamboyantly imperialist, and he was an impressive performer on the public platform. If anyone could unseat 'Joe', it was he.

Another candidate was needed, however, and so Augustus was persuaded, with great reluctance, to stand as his running mate. In all ways, this was a bad choice. Although he lived nearby at Perry, he was little known in Birmingham, having 'taken a comparatively small part in Birmingham's public work.'[17] Few people in the town even knew his name, and his fitness for public life was unproven. To put up such an innocent against Bright, Muntz and Chamberlain, three men well used to the rough-and-tumble of the hustings, was very unwise. Following the Calthorpe Park *débacle*, it was all too easy to picture his candicacy as an insult to the town, and he himself as a member of a family who had taken much from Birmingham, given little back, and now wanted more. In the *Town Crier*, 'Jacob' wrote a withering attack:

> What are your claims upon Birmingham? . . . You have no claims whatever. . . . For years you have lived close to us, in possession of abundant means and ample leisure. You have never been amongst us, never lifted a finger to help us, never given us, so far as the public knows, one single moment of your time. Your family derives a large income from Birmingham; an income which might satisfy a prince. What, may I ask, does your family do in return for the town? We look at the lists of those who conduct our great educational, charitable, and social movements; those who give time and labour and money towards improving the condition of the town, enhancing its reputation, promoting, strengthening, purifying its public life. But in these lists the name of Calthorpe is conspicuous by its absence. . . . You are glad to get our money; and you keep it, close and hard, when you have got it. Our enterprise and industry have converted your land into a veritable gold mine, but all the increase goes to you. We do not benefit by it, for you escape even rates and taxes: these are paid by your tenants. . . . We never hear of you but when you want something. One Calthorpe comes twice a year for his rents; another Calthorpe comes once – it will only be once – and asks us to give him a seat in Parliament.[18]

The 'rude noises from Birmingham' were making themselves heard emphatically. How different was such an attitude to that which had prevailed only one generation before, when townsmen 'of all political opinions' could speak, with reference to the Calthorpes and themselves, of 'that cordial union which is happily manifested in this neighbourhood in the promotion of those objects which affect the well-being of large classes of its inhabitants'.[19]

As if Augustus was not vulnerable enough, he was also a notoriously poor public speaker, and was lampooned mercilessly in satirical magazines such as *The Dart*, *The Owl* and *The Gridiron*. In December 1879, *The Dart* published a cartoon entitled 'The Modern Sphinx', savagely attacking Calthorpe's known taciturnity and assumed wealth:[20] it showed Augustus caricatured as the Sphinx, surrounded by crowds begging him to speak. Beneath was the caption: 'The Calthorpe Motto: "Silence is Golden"'. Seven months earlier, when

Fig. 17. Cartoon of Augustus Calthorpe from the General Election of 1880 (reproduced from *The Dart*, 6 December 1879, by courtesy of Birmingham Reference Library).

his candidacy was already known, the *Town Crier* had run a questionnaire on him, which asked these questions among others:

 1. Where is the Hon. Mr Calthorpe?
 6. Can he make a speech at all?
16. What are his political opinions?[21]

Matters were only made worse when Augustus did open his mouth, for he was prone to self-deprecation which, although engaging among friends, was a great liability in the public arena as it only served to provide his opponents with more ammunition. As he observed on becoming a candidate: 'Hitherto, gentlemen, I have taken but a small part in public life, and I must confess to having felt very considerable reluctance to plunge into its troubled waters.'[22]

Despite these shortcomings, he persevered, and survived the most vitriolic and acrimonious election campaign since Richard Spooner was unseated in 1847. The Conservatives threw everything into the attempt to defeat Chamberlain, depicting him as a money-grabbing capitalist, 'a vile abuser of his fellow-townsmen, whose ambition is power'.[23] Even Augustus, descending from the heights of patrician Olympus, joined in, describing Corporation Street as a 'crooked abortion', and the Chamberlain Monument as an 'architectural abomination'.[24] He accused the Liberals of benefitting their party, rather than the town, condemned their extravagant and self-interested spending, and was reported as saying that they had paid over £100 to disrupt Conservative meetings. Chamberlain, himself no novice at the hustings, was amazed by the extent of the campaign against him. In one letter to Collings, he said it had made him feel five years older, and in another he wrote that 'nothing can exceed the virulence with which the Tories have attacked me. No slander has been too gross, no calumny too improbable.' In the long run, the turn of the tide against Liberalism in Birmingham had already begun.[25]

In the short run, however, the outcome was different. Although newspapers such as the *Birmingham Gazette* backed the Conservative candidates and confidently predicted victory for them both, the combination of Bright, depicted as the great statesman, Muntz, the colleague of Attwood, and Chamberlain, the maker of modern Birmingham, proved invincible. Burnaby's bombastic histrionics were no match for Bright's set-piece orations, and Calthorpe was at some disadvantage when he kept admitting 'I am no orator; it is not my nature to be so'.[26] At a meeting in St Martin's ward, he was shouted down, and at Deritend five days later 'concluded his speech amid some confusion'.[27] Chamberlain, knowing his position was at risk, hammered away at the disparity between Calthorpe's oft-repeated desire to serve Birmingham and his conspicuous failure to have done so thus far, and suggested that although he lived near the town, he was as much a stranger to it as was Burnaby.[28] The radical press, too, kept up its stream of invective. As polling day drew near, *The Owl*, for instance, offered this marvel of wit:

> Why is Mr Calthorpe likely to withdraw?
> Because he has been such a retiring man all his life.[29]

At the final Conservative meeting on 30 March, Burnaby made a rousing speech. Augustus – characteristically – managed a bow.[30]

Although the *Gazette* maintained until polling day itself that 'the return of both the Conservative candidates is beyond any question', the outcome represented a depressing rebuff for Augustus:[31]

Muntz	22,969
Bright	22,079
Chamberlain	19,544
Burnaby	15,735
Calthorpe	14,308

The party itself could draw comfort from these figures: Chamberlain was bottom among the Liberals, and the Conservative vote was higher than it had ever been before; but for Augustus there was no such consolation. The fact that he had polled only 1,000 votes less than Burnaby was a tribute, not so much to his own popularity, as to the efficiency of the Conservatives' organization and the appeal of Burnaby himself, to whose large coat tails he had been so reluctantly attached.

Although Augustus's politics were conventionally Disraelian, he had been attacked not as a Conservative but as an aristocrat, not because of what he stood for, but because of what he was. Whereas once his family had been admired and respected as aristocrats, that was now a positive liability. Emphatically, this episode was the Calthorpes' swan song in Birmingham party politics. Their absenteeism, the trivial nature of their philanthropy compared with Chamberlain's grand designs, and their large Edgbaston rental, made them too vulnerable. Augustus retained his membership of the Birmingham Conservative Association, put in occasional appearances at meetings, and was considered for the Lord Lieutenancy of Staffordshire in 1888 on the grounds that he was 'a thorough Conservative'.[32] Finally, in 1897, his younger brother Somerset briefly considered standing in Birmingham.[33] But beyond that, there was nothing. Ironically, Augustus's last political act was grudgingly to donate ten guineas to Joseph Chamberlain's seventieth birthday present from the town.[34]

3

Although the 'unathorized programme' and Chamberlain's most radical out-bursts were still to come, the 1880 general election marked the climax of hostile relations between the town and the Calthorpes which had progressively worsened from the time the fifth lord succeeded and Joseph Chamberlain entered the council chamber. For the 1890s saw yet another *rapprochement*. Chamberlain crossed the floor, held office in Conservative administrations, and became the friend and colleague of some of the greatest aristocrats in the land, and the town itself became a bastion of Unionism essentially unbreached until 1945.[35] On the family's side, too, matters improved when Augustus succeeded his brother in 1893. In the following year, he and his son conveyed Calthorpe Park in fee simple to the corporation, finally settling that episode.[36] Three years later, he was president of the Birmingham Music Festival Committee, and among his more permanent posts were the presidencies of the Deaf and Dumb Asylum and the Botanical and Horticultural Society.[37] Like his pre-decessor, he gave land for churches – for St Mary and St Ambrose on the Pershore Road – and in 1905 contributed £500 towards the fund to purchase Warley Woods and Lightwoods Park. He increased his late brother's subscription list from £313 to £546, and the objects of his benevolence included six hospitals, the Deaf and Dumb Asylum, the Botanical Gardens and three church schools.[38]

So, with a return to type in Augustus, a calmer time set in, but it was in no sense a return to the balmy days of the 1850s. Admittedly Augustus took on more jobs, was more tactful, and genuinely possessed a stronger sense of aristocratic obligation than did his late brother. However, he was 64 when he inherited, and after he moved to Elvetham only visited Birmingham twice a year. As his obituarist noted, 'from that time, his active connection with Birmingham ceased, for although he sometimes visited Perry Hall, it was only at rare intervals that he attended any public function in the city.'[39] His younger brother Somerset, who followed him at Perry, was himself 62, and preferred to spend his time at Woodlands Vale in the Isle of Wight.[40] Rarely, in fact, did he stay as much as four months of the year at Perry. Old, absentee, and worried about agricultural depression and the advent of death duties, such men could not be expected to stand in the forefront of local affairs.

Meanwhile, even the closed corporations and voluntary societies were taken over by the Chamberlain group and were suitably moulded to fit the creed of the new 'civic gospel'. At the Birmingham and Midland Institute, the local aristocracy were swept from the field, and were replaced as presidents by men of real intellectual distinction or political ability.[41] The governing body of the Schools of King Edward VI was similarly transformed. Gone were the Calthorpes, Spooners and Whateleys. In their place, presiding over the Foundation's golden age of expansion and revival, were to be found members of all the great Birmingham nonconformist families: R. W. Dale, J. T. Bunce, William Kenrick, Jesse Collings, Thomas Martineau, Richard Chamberlain and George Dixon.[42] The same was true of the General Hospital, and by 1910 even the Botanical and Horticultural Society included among its vice-presidents Joseph Chamberlain, Jesse Collings, G. H. Kenrick and Charles Gabriel Beale.[43] Since Calthorpe himself was president, here was further evidence of that Unionist-Conservative *rapprochement* which had taken place since the acrimonious days of the early 1880s.

Indeed, the establishment of the University of Birmingham illustrates this even more eloquently. Built on Calthorpe land, with Joseph Chamberlain as its first chancellor, it did embody on a larger scale some real collaboration between the two: but the Calthorpes, like other aristocrats, were very much the junior partner. While Chamberlain took care to associate the local aristocracy with the venture for the purpose of window-dressing, the idea and the initiative were his, and the planning and finance ensured that it became a monument to his own nonconformist oligarchy. No peer sat on any of the crucial sub-committees: Dartmouth, Cobham and Windsor declined their invitations.[44] Nor could any peer rival the sums donated by local businessmen. One of Chamberlain's relatives, Charles Gabriel Beale, was vice-chancellor; another, G. H. Kenrick, was chairman of the vital canvassing sub-committee. Even among the life governors, the businessmen outnumbered the aristocrats, and Lord Windsor was the only peer on the council.[45] Most significant of all, however, was the fact that with the exception of Bristol – where the university was again a monument to the initiative of another non-conformist, business elite –

Birmingham University was unique in not importing a peer of great local standing to be chancellor.[46] The balance of power between town and aristocrats had shifted more markedly away from the aristocracy in Birmingham than in many other large cities.

However, the need for a new site outside the centre of the city made it possible for the Calthorpes to be associated with the venture in a manner more spectacular than was originally intended. As with the Deaf and Dumb Asylum and the Botanical Gardens early in the nineteenth century so, at the end, Edgbaston was the only suburb which could provide land in large quantities at once near to the town centre but in rural surroundings. Twice Chamberlain approached the Calthorpes, and on both occasions they gave land: 25 acres in 1900 and a further 20 in 1907.[47] Although the Calthorpes had in part been attracted to this in the hope that the university's presence on their estate might stimulate demand for housing close by, the local press did not stint itself in praise of their generosity. The *Daily Post* congratulated 'his lordship on the form in which he has chosen to associate himself with the greatest Birmingham and Midland enterprise of the present generation', and the *Gazette* took the opportunity to recall earlier gifts of the family.[48] The University Council recorded its 'high appreciation' of the gift, and Chamberlain himself expressed his 'deep sense of the liberality' of the donation. Indeed, at a time when the town council was taking an increasingly predatory attitude towards Edgbaston on the subject of tramways, such benevolence was remarkable.

4

In this as in so much else, the death of Augustus in 1910 was a major watershed. Rachel and her husband, assisted by Frank Newman, not only instituted a thorough review of the family's finances, but also reconsidered their public and political position with regard to Birmingham in particular. For, although Augustus had himself long since abandoned any personal role in Conservative party politics in the town, the estate had continued to identify itself with the party by subscribing five guineas annually to the local association. In the era of the 'People's Budget', Limehouse and Lloyd George, to say nothing of the problems of tramways and death duties, even this token partisan political act was thought to be unwise. An early letter from Rachel's husband to the local agent spelt out the final act of political surrender:

I see that a subscription of £5–5–0 is paid in January every year to the Conservative Association. Will you please cancel this subscription in future. I should like to know the address of the Association so that we can pay it direct, and *not* through the Estate Office. Our feeling on the matter is that an estate like the Edgbaston estate should not identify itself with any particular party. In other words, the estate as such should have *no* politics.[49]

Nor was this the only subscription to go from the Edgbaston account books. In an economy drive surely more token than real, 14 of the 47 estate subscriptions which had been paid to Birmingham charities during the lifetime of Augustus were cancelled in 1910, and a further six were crossed off the list five years later.[50] In philanthropy as in politics, the Calthorpes' 'conservative interest' had passed from impotence to oblivion.

13 The 'Belgravia' of Birmingham

Many of those Birmingham families who freed themselves from their psychological dependence on the local aristocracy in the late 1860s and 1870s were in fact residents of Edgbaston. While, in this period, their *public* relationship with the Calthorpes was one of hostility and antagonism – between radical, nonconformist businessmen on the one side who claimed to speak for the town, and Anglican aristocrats on the other who spoke for no-one but themselves – in *private* the same people filled the very different roles of suburban tenants and ground landlord. So those nonconformist families who undermined the Calthorpes' position as figureheads in the local community by their constant stress on the autonomy and innate nobility of local, municipal government, also raised both their status and their revenue as urban landlords to unprecedented heights by taking up residence in Edgbaston. However anti-aristocratic their rhetoric, the local elite demonstrated its tacit acceptance of aristocratic cultural hegemony by choosing a suburban life-style which was in many ways but a scaled-down version of the country-house world they affected to despise.

Even in the era of antagonism, then, there was already extensive common ground which belied the sharply articulated differences in religion and politics; and from the late 1880s these public areas of disagreement tended to lessen. Many of the civic elite who had previously been Liberal became Unionists, and many who had hitherto retained some of the social attitudes of players increasingly came to behave like gentlemen. By the 1890s, families like the Kenricks and Chamberlains were happy to send their children to public school and Oxbridge, and early in the new century, Joseph Chamberlain lent his support to attempts to establish a bishopric in Birmingham at a crucial moment.[1] So, while Edgbaston in the 1870s had been the fountainhead of those 'rude noises' directed against the local aristocracy, within two decades it had become – and has since remained – the safest Unionist and then Conservative seat in Birmingham. If the Calthorpes' relationship with Birmingham was multi-faceted and ambiguous, then their tenants' relationship with them – as revealed by their life style as much as by their politics – was equally paradoxical. In more ways than one, a suburb often seen as a bastion of middle-class values was also an outwork of aristocratic supremacy.

1

The pre-eminence of the citizens of Edgbaston in the life of late nineteenth-century Birmingham is eloquently revealed by the remarkable concentration

Table 23. Members of Birmingham Town Council resident in Edgbaston, 1866–1902

Year	Aldermen/Total	Councillors/Total
1866–7	10/16	17/46
1877–8	11/15	18/47
1881–2	11/16	22/48
1891–2	11/18	19/55
1901–2	10/18	15/53

Source: *Kelley's Directories of Birmingham*: 1868, 436; 1878, 585–6; 1882, 673–4; 1892, 732–3; 1902, 974–6.

of the civic elite within one district (see table 23). Having successfully established its reputation during the first 50 years of slow development, by the end of the century the Edgbaston estate housed the majority of that 'small knot of non-conformist families, who knew each other well, frequently inter-married, and continued until the middle of the twentieth century to dominate local social life'.[2] Beales, Chamberlains, Kenricks, Nettlefolds, Crosskeys and Martineaus were united in the past by common ancestors as in the present by corporate activity. What, then, could be more natural than that they should live in close proximity? And who could be surprised that they should constantly intermarry?[3] Here was the epicentre of that 'great village' which R. W. Dale rightly believed Birmingham to be.[4] Indeed, the history of the town in its most heroic and famous phase was very largely the history of the public lives and corporate activity of the Calthorpe's most illustrious tenants.

Indeed, the fact that these families lived self-consciously as a group, in close proximity to the town centre, rather than dispersed about the circumference, was only possible because of the manner in which the Calthorpes had developed and maintained Edgbaston. This, at least, was the view of contemporaries like Walter Barrow:

> No town in the country possesses a suburb which is so truly a garden suburb as Edgbaston. One result has been that the Birmingham middle classes have contined to reside in the city and within a mile or two of its centre. They have therefore continued in close touch with the public life and charitable institutions of the town; the result has been wholly beneficial, and I believe that much of the public spirit on which Birmingham prides itself is due to the fact that the wealthier inhabitants do not cut themselves off from the city by residing at a distance.[5]

Of this group, the outstanding members of four of its greatest families – all of whom lived at Edgbaston for much of their lives – may be taken as representative: George Cadbury, Quaker, chocolate maker and philanthropist, pioneer in town planning and factory reform, Liberal politician and proprietor of the *News Chronicle*; Joseph Chamberlain, Unitarian, screw manufacturer, three

times mayor, originator of the schemes to take over the gas and water supply
and to build Corporation Street, M.P. for the town from 1876 to 1914; his
relative, Charles Gabriel Beale, solicitor, three times lord mayor, architect of
the Elan Valley waterworks scheme, father of the tramway system, and vice
chancellor of the new university; and another relative, Sir George Kenrick,
lord mayor in 1909, and chairman of the Educational Committee from 1903 to
1921. And these were only the most outstanding of the 345 figures who had
been included in the series 'Edgbastonians Past and Present' between 1881
and 1910.

So, while topography and location predisposed Edgbaston towards
middle-class occupation, and while the preferences and plans of the landowner exploited this, it was the civic elite itself which set the final seal on its
development by investing it with a specific set of cultural values which the
landlord's policy made possible but could not itself provide. Like the Boston
brahmins on Beacon Hill, the civic elite of Birmingham gave Edgbaston a set
of sentimental and symbolic values by virtue of their presence there which
further enhanced its attractiveness. In both areas, among the residents, there
was the same self-conscious group identity, the same 'complex network of
blood relationships', the same civic zeal, and the same pride in having been
born or lived in one area of the town.[6] Here, for example, is Walter Firey's
description of Beacon Hill:

> Located some five minutes' walking distance from the retail centre of
> Boston. This neighbourhood has for fully a century and a half maintained
> its character as a preferred upper class residential district, despite con-
> tiguity to a low rent, tenement area . . . During its long history, Beacon
> Hill has become the symbol for a number of sentimental associations
> which constitute a genuinely attractive force to certain old families of
> Boston.[7]

If Birmingham is substituted for Boston, and Edgbaston for Beacon Hill, the
description remains valid. In each area, 'a wide range of sentiments – aesthetic, historical, familial – . . . acquired a spatial articulation.'[8] Why, otherwise, did the civic elite of Birmingham at the end of the century continue to
reside where their predecessors had?

While this was what Edgbaston came to stand for, however, the majority of
its inhabitants did not conform to this stereotyped ideal. If they had done, the
exclusive preferences of John Harris and the third Lord Calthorpe would not
have been undermined so markedly. But in fact the majority of the suburb's
inhabitants, spread around the periphery in houses of only middling size and
value, did not share the ancestors, wealth, religion, cultural values or group
solidarity of the nonconformist elite to be found in the centre. Varna Road was
not Farquhar Road, Duchess Road not Ampton Road. But, by sharing the
same Edgbaston address, it was possible for those of lower status to enjoy the
reflected glory of the suburb's more wealthy and famous residents. Lower-

income groups naturally sought to get as close as possible to that part of the town occupied by the civic elite and, clustered on the periphery of Edgbaston, they were able to satisfy their craving for suburban respectability without intruding on their betters' wishes for suburban exclusiveness. Like most middle-class suburbs of nineteenth-century England, Edgbaston was an 'ecological marvel', combining high social status with a broad social spectrum.[9]

At one extreme came the great hardware princes – brewers, chocolate makers, screw manufacturers – who owned houses in the centre of the estate, set in grounds of several acres, often costing in excess of £2,000, complete with stables and servants' quarters, containing perhaps six large bedrooms, a dining room, a drawing room, a ballroom, a billiard room and a greenhouse, and needing a butler, gardeners, a housekeeper and perhaps five domestic servants to maintain them. Such houses included 'Whetstone' in Farquhar Road, where a branch of the Kenrick family lived, 'Westbourne' in the road of the same name, where Neville Chamberlain settled down after his marriage, and 'Mariemont' in the same road, where Sir Oliver Lodge, first principal of the new University, lived with his wife and 12 children. At the other extreme were those small houses, costing £500 or less, to be found on the periphery of the estate, merging into the urban sprawl beyond. There lived the clerks, small businessmen, shopkeepers and skilled labourers. If they could afford a house in Duchess or Alexandra Road, they might also boast one general domestic. But in the area between the Worcester Canal and Lee Bank – the least prepossessing on the estate – even that would be asking too much. Between these two extremes was the broad crescent of middle-middle-class houses along the Hagley and Bristol Roads, prosperous and comfortable, belonging to successful professionals – doctors, lawyers, solicitors and accountants – with large gardens, three servants and perhaps even a cook or a nanny.

As well as being socially a more diverse community than its exclusive reputation suggested, Edgbaston was also a more mobile and dynamic society than its public image of stability and solidarity implied. Two-thirds of the households with three or more servants in 1841 had departed within ten years, and the same was true of the households established there in 1851. Even as late as 1861, two-thirds of the adults in Edgbaston had been born, not only outside the suburb, but outside Birmingham itself.[10] And, although this might be explained by the fact that until the late 1870s, most of the suburb had been recently created, the same held good thereafter. Only three of the 40 heads of household in Duchess Road in 1881 were still there 20 years later, and only five of the 44 in Alexandra Road in 1892 remained in 1911. Among the higher echelons of Edgbaston society, the same picture presents itself: of the ten names recorded for Westbourne Road in the directories of 1871, only one was left in 1892, and in Arthur Road only four out of 18 stayed over the same period.[11]

Fig. 18. Edgbaston houses: A. Whetstone, Farquhar Road, home of Sir George Kenrick.

B. 51 Calthorpe Road, home of John Cadbury.

c. Longworth, Priory Road, home of J. T. Bunce.

D. Winterslow, Bristol Road, home of Dr R. W. Dale (by courtesy of Birmingham Reference Library).

2

In general terms, then, Edgbaston may be described as a neighbourhood in two of the senses in which that word has meaning for sociologists. If the nonconformist elite is taken in isolation, then it was, as Dale saw, a 'great village', a face-to-face community, where the residents enjoyed close contact – social, familial, personal, religious, cultural and political.[12] For those within this charmed circle, the rules of 'society' – of leaving cards, 'at homes', teas, dinner parties and the like – were every bit as strict as in London. There was, for example, both a 'right' side (on the Calthorpe estate) and a 'wrong' side (on the Gillott estate) of Hagley Road, and even residence on the Calthorpe side did not automatically guarantee entry into Edgbaston's highest society. One of Brett Young's characters, Clare Wilburn, although married to a prosperous solicitor who lives in 'Halesby' (Hagley) Road, is unable, in the early 1900s, to gain access to the nonconformist elite.[13] If the second definition of neighbour-hood is taken – a statistical aggregate within a recognized physical area, in which the inhabitants share certain characteristics but impersonally – then this is equally valid for Edgbaston as a whole.[14] All wanted to be thought of as the elite of Birmingham, with servants and an Edgbaston address, and the possession of the second might at least be thought of as implying the possibility of the first. Indeed, for the great majority of inhabitants dwelling on the periphery of Edgbaston, their ambition was to break into that exclusive world in the centre.[15] For those who were not only socially ambitious but materially successful, the move from Varna Road to Westbourne Road – while only a short distance physically – was a massive leap socially, from peripheral obscurity to recognition.

In Francis Brett Young's novels, Owen Lucton makes such a journey.[16] He begins his married life in the early 1900s in Kings Road, 'Alvaston', which was probably in the Duchess or Princess Road area. He is a clerk in his father's firm of accountants, and he and his wife can just afford a cook/general servant. Their house has three ground floor rooms, and a small garden with lilacs in front: it could be any of those lower middle-class areas on the periphery of Edgbaston. Reality afforded many similar examples. Between 1908 and 1911, for instance, the young, orphaned J. R. R. Tolkien lodged with Mrs Faulkner at 37 Duchess Road.[17] She was known for her occasional musical evenings, and was happy to take in lodgers. In Tolkien's time, the *ménage* included Mr Faulkner, a wine merchant who was excessively fond of his own products, their daughter Helen, Annie the maid, Tolkien himself, and Edith, another orphaned lodger. And in this 'gloomy, creeper-covered house, hung with lace curtains', Tolkien lived for the three years before he went up to Oxford, in classic Midlands Pooterland, on the very frontiers of suburban gentility. For many residents on the Calthorpe estate, that was what life in Edgbaston was like.

Tolkien escaped to Oxford; Owen Lucton to the greater respectability of central Edgbaston. During the years after the First World War, the prosperity of the family accountancy business – which by now Owen has inherited from his father – enables his wife to entertain more lavishly, to hire a parlour maid and a nurse, and to hold 'At Homes' on second Thursdays. Finally, the small house is sold, and 'Alvaston Grange' is purchased – complete with six bathrooms, a squash court, five gardeners, a butler and half a dozen servants.[18] For the majority of professional people, however, such grandeur would be exceptional. The household of Granville Bantock, Principal of the School of Music at the Birmingham and Midland Institute, and Professor of Music at the new University of Birmingham, would be more typical.[19] In the years before the First World War, they lived at 'Ferndell', in Elvetham Road – a comfortable, but not extravagant, early Victorian house. As well as the Bantock parents, there were four children, a lodger, two maids, a nurse and a gardener. The ground floor contained the school room, the dining room and a sitting room, and extensive kitchen quarters. On the first floor was Bantock's study, the lodger's room, and the Bantock parents' bedroom, bathroom and dressing room, and above were located the rooms of the maids and children. The extensive garden boasted two lawns, a greenhouse, a vegetable garden, a stable and a rockery. Although the Bantocks' extroverted and Bohemian way of life served to cut them off from the society of respectable Edgbaston, their house was typical of those many professional people who lived in the region of Hagley and Bristol Roads. Dudley Wilburn's house, for instance, at 197 'Halesby' Road, with its cook/housekeeper, its maid and its gardener, its six bedrooms and a tennis court, is almost identical.[20]

Yet the social summit of Edgbaston was on an altogether higher plane of existence, beyond the imaginings even of Mr Lucton in fiction, of Granville Bantock in fact. In *Dr Bradley Remembers*, Francis Brett Young captured beautifully the elite of Edgbaston when he created the Lacey family. Martin Lacey is a medical student at 'North Bromwich' Medical School in the 1880s, where he meets the uncouth John Bradley, who has fought this way there from an obscure village and orphaned upbringing in Shropshire. They become firm friends, and Bradley begins to learn about Lacey's family:

> He was an only child of one of the great families of Liberal Unitarians, who, together with the Quakers, had made fortunes in industry; who had used their wealth well, and now constituted an intellectual enclave in the civic life of North Bromwich. Unlike most of their wealthy neighbours, these people had not been satisfied with the mere making of money . . . They bought pictures, built music rooms, amassed libraries, of which they were proud, and maintained an eager and vivid interest in the latest developments in the arts and sciences; . . . they were, in short, the fine flower of the new industrial aristocracy.[21]

Martin Lacey's father is a manufacturer of optical glass, and numbers among his friends Gladstone, Burne Jones, Cobden and Matthew Arnold, Not surprisingly, when he goes to visit the Lacey house in 'Alvaston', John Bradley is overwhelmed:

> The house he remembered vividly – not only because it was the most imposing he had ever entered, but also for its quietness. It was a low, stuccoed Regency building, with a square porch supported by fluted pillars. When one opened the front door, one looked down the length of a wide corridor, to an expanse of green lawn bordered by brilliant beds of geraniums edged with lobelias, and the corridor was so thickly carpeted that even hob-nailed boots made no sound. Its walls were hung with pre-Raphaelite drawings and pictures, and one room at the right at the end of it, overlooking the lawn, was even quieter than the rest. This was Mr Lacey's library, which his friend William Morris had furnished for him with tapestries, hangings and curtains printed in madder and indigo. There was only one picture here: a painting by Rosetti of a girl . . . The walls were lined from floor to ceiling with bookshelves . . . It was, John Bradley thought then, and still thought as he remembered it, the most beautiful, the most tender room, he had set eyes on.[22]

Brett Young was not always as kind to the Edgbaston elite. In *White Ladies*, he created the Fladburns, another Unitarian family – important in the public life of the city, once more resident in 'Alvaston', but so obsessed with doing good and avoiding evil that their lives are completely joyless.[23] But here, in the Lacey household, he caught the quintessence of 'Alvaston' life at its most privileged and civilized.

Nor was it a fanciful picture: Joseph Gillott, the pen maker, who lived at 9 Westbourne Road, surpassed in wealth and refinement even Brett Young's fictional characters. He was born in Sheffield in 1799, and moved to Birmingham in 1821, where he soon became pre-eminent in the making of steel pens by new, mass production methods.[24] At first he had lived in Newhall Street, in the centre of town, close to his works, but growing prosperity enabled him to move to the Calthorpe estate. Even by contemporary Edgbaston standards, his house was lavish – six bedrooms, a library, extensive wine cellars, two picture galleries, stables, an aviary, a greenhouse and a carpenter's shop. He bought land in many parts of Birmingham, including the 500-acre Noel estate to the north of Hagley Road for £90,000 in 1851, and a house and estate at Stanmore near Harrow.[25] But he remained a suburban rather than a country gentleman, for it was at his Edgbaston house that he built up his collections of stringed instruments and paintings. His 140 musical instruments included seven Stradivarius violins, and his paintings were described, without exaggeration, as 'one of the most extensive and choicest collections in England'. Although old masters were not well represented, he had an outstandingly comprehensive collection of works of the English school, including 13 Gainsboroughs, 9 Constables, 25 Turners, 7 by Landseer, and 3 by Reynolds. At his death in 1872, the stringed instruments were auctioned for £4,194, the domestic contents of the house fetched £6,832, and the 500 paintings were sold at a six-day auction at Christies for £164,501, a dispersal described as 'grevious to all lovers of art', and 'disappointing to the town which knew and prized it.'[26] Assuredly, it was a very different world to that which the young Tolkien was to know, even on the same estate, 40 years later.

3

In its late-Victorian heyday, then, Edgbaston was a more diverse and dynamic society than its high social tone and its comforting appearance of rustic permanency would have suggested. In part this may be explained by the unity of planning and control exercised by the Calthorpes, and the strong sense of corporate consciousness which characterized its nonconformist elite. However, from the 1880s, this was further enhanced by the appearance of the periodical, *Edgbastonia*, which is at once the best expression of, and guide to, the suburb's sense of corporate self-consciousness. It was founded in May 1881 by Eliza Edwards, and some 3,000 copies of it were distributed monthly, free of charge, to houses in Edgbaston. Edwards' aim was to produce a 'high-class periodical, free from political or sectarian bias', which would appeal equally to 'the educated and the unlettered' – a tacit admission of the broad social spectrum which existed in Edgbaston at the time.[27] Revenue came from advertising for, as Edwards pointed out, *Edgbastonia* was 'THE medium for advertisements of high class wares of all kinds, schools or colleges, seaside and country hotels, hydros and boarding houses.' The first issue set the tone as far as future contents were concerned, with articles on R. T. Cadbury (the first in the 'Edgbastonians Past and Present' series), Parisian sketches by an Edgbastonian, synonyms, words and phrases, anachronisms and geographical errors, a song for the piano, and a review of *Sungleams and Shadows* by E. Capern (author of *Wayside Warbles* and other classics).[28] Subsequent issues boasted articles on how to make a cup of tea, preserve cut flowers, cook green peas in a new way, and cure indigestion, stammering and backache. In short, its tone was quintessentially suburban.

It also included articles on the history and objectives of local voluntary societies of which, by the turn of the century, there were a considerable number. In the first place, Edgbaston was the educational Mecca of the town. Within its borders was housed the University, which brought with it a new academic elite to add to the professions already well represented. Life as an Edgbaston professor is well recalled in the memoirs of Sir Oliver Lodge for the 1900s and E. R. Dodds for the 1920s.[29] In addition, Edgbaston High School for Girls was established on the initiative of George Dixon and with the collaboration of a predictable smattering of Beales, Kenricks and Chamberlains, to offer non-sectarian education to middle-class girls. And – as if as a counterblast – the Edgbaston Church of England College was set up ten years later. The one took over two houses on Hagley Road near the Five Ways, the other was

Fig. 19. Edgbaston educational establishments: A. Edgbaston Church of England College, 1897 (by courtesy of Birmingham Reference Library); B. Birmingham University, 1909 (reproduced from *The Builders' Journal*, 7 July 1909, by courtesy of Birmingham Reference Library).

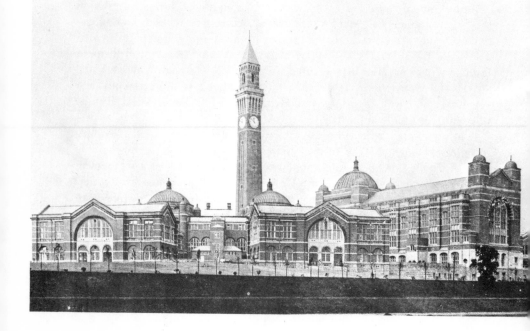

Fig. 20. Edgbaston institutions: A. The Deaf and Dumb Asylum, *c*. 1880 (reproduced from *Edgbastonia*, September 1888, by courtesy of Birmingham Reference Library); B. The Plough and Harrow Inn, *c*. 1850: half a century later, this hostelry was the scene of the meetings at which the Edgbastonian anti-tram lobby tried to whip up support (by courtesy of Birmingham Reference Library).

established at 31 Calthorpe Road, 'in the best part of Edgbaston'.[30] Most of the local boys went either to King Edward's School in New Street (which removed to Edgbaston shortly before the Second World War) or to the Edgbaston Proprietary School which had again been set up by the local nonconformist elite in 1838 and was situated on the northern side of Hagley Road at the Five Ways, just beyond the estate boundary. Finally, at the bottom of this educational pyramid were those expensive private preparatory schools for boys and girls, whose ethos is well evoked by Francis Brett Young in 'Alvaston Manor' and 'St Monica's'. For, as he pointed out, 'Alvaston' people were 'deeply anxious that their children should not perpetuate the stigma of provincialism on which they affected to pride themselves'.[31] In addition, there was the Deaf and Dumb Asylum, which had 15 inmates in 1815 when it moved to Edgbaston, but 154 by 1888, and the General Institution for the Blind, which had only 7 places in 1847 but 50 years later had 518.[32] The maintenance and support of such institutions – as Brett Young made clear when he created the Fladburns – was an important part of life in Edgbaston, for its inhabitants liked to be thought of as being 'serious sober and orderly'.[33]

Recreational facilities also thrived. As early as 1825, Lord Calthorpe's agent had laid out half an acre for bowling and quoits, and the club was 'supported by a select body of subscribers'. Although it waned through lack of support, a new Edgbaston Quoit Club was in being in the early 1870s, once more described as 'consisting mainly of the well-to-do inhabitants of that pleasant suburb'. By that time, it had been joined by the rowing club, which used Rotton Park Reservoir to the north of Hagley Road, and the Archery and Lawn Tennis Club, which occupied land adjacent to the Botanical Gardens. Both had a limited membership, and annual subscriptions in excess of 30s. a year. In addition, the first game of tennis ever played in England is reputed to have taken place in Edgbaston; Warwickshire County Cricket Club took up a permanent home there in 1885; and in the 1890s, both riding and cycling became popular among the inhabitants. Also, of course, as Sir Oliver Lodge recalled, in the gardens of the great houses, tennis, cricket, hockey and croquet could all be played.[34] It was a leisured and comfortable life these Edgbastonians lived, more akin to the aristocracy whom many at some stages claimed to dislike, than to the working classes of Birmingham in whose interest they said they governed the town.

On occasions, recreation could be more cerebral – as befitted a suburb where libraries were a necessary part of any house's equipment. Sir Oliver Lodge, for instance, recalls the Shakespeare Reading Society, already 20 years old by the time he joined in 1900, and supported by the omnipresent Kenricks, Beales and Dixons. Every fortnight, during the winter, it met in the evening in the house of a member, and part of a play was read and then discussed. 'The members of this reading circle', Lodge noted, 'were very friendly, and formed a sort of brotherhood.'[35] Even more renowned was the Birmingham and Edgbaston Debating Society, founded in 1846, for men only, although lady visitors were tolerated. In the second half of the century, its membership fluctuated between 250 and 350, and it usually managed ten meetings a year, for which an annual subscription of five shillings was paid. Its objects were 'the discussion of any subjects, literary, political, historical, social or otherwise', and the highlight of the year was the annual dinner at the Grand Hotel, where the outgoing president delivered his address. In 1896, it was Joseph Chamberlain, himself a leading light in the society between his arrival in Birmingham in 1854 and 1863, who spoke on 'the art of public speaking'. Many Kenricks, Beales, Martineaus and others from the nonconformist elite served as presidents or committee members, and the society rightly prided itself on being the forcing house of local – and in some cases national – political talent.[36]

Other forms of entertainment were easily available and less demanding. In the early 1880s, the Botanical Gardens was extended and, in an effort to recoup the costs, a programme of concerts and theatricals was arranged, which soon became a permanent feature. Between June and August, on Monday, Wednesday and Saturday afternoons, concerts, military bands, itinerant players, flower shows, fairs and fêtes were all to be found.[37] Then, in 1884, on the northern side of Hagley Road, the Edgbaston Assembly Rooms were built, containing 'suites of rooms for assemblies, balls, public meetings, evening parties, wedding breakfasts, dramatic entertainments, concerts, etc.', which soon established themselves as *the* social centre of the suburb.[38] The Priory Lawn Tennis Club held its annual ball there, and every year in April or May the Birmingham Amateur Operatic Society put on a production of a Gilbert and Sullivan opera. Dances, balls, orchestral concerts and recitals all took place, sometimes for local and charitable purposes, as in April 1890 when there was 'an entertainment' on behalf of the British and Foreign Sailors Society, featuring 'dramatic recitals', 'vocal and instrumental music', 'the band of the Edgbaston philharmonic society', and 'tableaux vivants by Edgbaston ladies.'[39] On a more serious note, it was at meetings held in either the Assembly Rooms or at the Plough and Harrow a little further along Hagley Road, that opposition to the tramways was mobilized.

Such recreation was genteel, exclusive and expensive: by no means available to the majority of Edgbaston residents. Again, however, it served to create the picture of Edgbaston as a homogenous society, a bastion of middle-class values, a highly moral, orthodox and conformist society, believing, like Mr Lucton, in 'the sanctity of family life . . . , the stability of the Crown . . . , the Bank of England or the M.C.C.'[40] Nowhere was this more fully displayed than in the extraordinary vivacity of its religious life. Despite the fame of its nonconformist elite, it was preponderantly an Anglican community and, since the Calthorpes would not offer accommodation to Dissenters, they had to attend churches elsewhere in the city, such as the Oratory on the northern side of Hagley Road, where lived that highly unorthodox Edgbastonian, Cardinal Newman, or the Congregationalist Church in Francis Road, or the Unitarian

A

Fig. 21. Edgbaston amenities: A. The Botanical Gardens, c.1890 (by courtesy of Birmingham Reference Library); B Edgbaston Assembly Rooms, c. 1910 (by courtesy of Birmingham Reference Library).

B

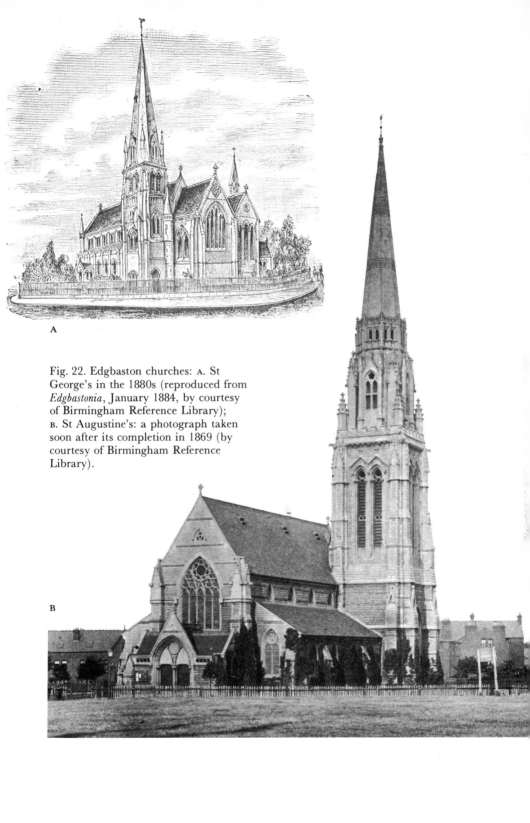

A

Fig. 22. Edgbaston churches: A. St
George's in the 1880s (reproduced from
Edgbastonia, January 1884, by courtesy
of Birmingham Reference Library);
B. St Augustine's: a photograph taken
soon after its completion in 1869 (by
courtesy of Birmingham Reference
Library).

B

Church of the Messiah in nearby Broad Street, which the Chamberlains, Kenricks and Martineaus habitually attended.

As an Anglican community, Edgbaston was extremely well provided for. It could boast four churches on Calthorpe land – St Bartholomew's, St George's, St James' and St Ambrose – and St Augustine's to the north of the Hagley Road built on Gillott land in 1869. At each of these churches, in the late nineteenth century, there were three services on Sunday, and morning and evening prayers daily, as well as innumerable other activities, including bible reading, amateur theatricals, children's associations and prayer meetings. No part of Birmingham was as well equipped with churches as Edgbaston and, as the St Ambrose magazine noted smugly in 1904, 'we are thankful to say that church life has never been so vigorous, or social relationships so healthy and hearty, as at present.'[41]

Such was Edgbaston at the turn of the century, when still at its zenith: complacent, assured and exclusive, seeking in its leisured existence that aristocratic world which was just beyond the horizon, yet at the same time a broadly-based, mobile community, home of a civic elite of unique probity, rectitude and social compassion, and of a suburban population of more humble status and limited aspirations. Nowhere is the abiding impression of superiority better caught than in this description of Sunday morning church at St Augustine's in 1892 – admittedly on the 'wrong' side of Hagley Road, but in fact the local church for many of Lord Calthorpe's tenants as well:

Edgbastonians are usually careful to eschew the name of Birmingham for reasons which, no doubt, are satisfactory to themselves. The inhabitants of Edgbaston – Edgbasston they call it – are IN EVERY WAY SUPERIOR to other people of the neighbourhood. They are better bred, more highly educated, more fastidious in their eating. Vulgarity and pride of purse are totally unknown, and are all legibly stamped with the caste of Vere de Vere. They live in an atmosphere of Liberty silks and blush roses. They speak in voices of exquisite sweetness. The Edgbaston 'tone' is recognised and valued in every debating society worthy of the name. The atmosphere of Edgbaston has a powerfully elevating influence on the neighbouring city, which is proud of its juxtaposition to so much culture and thankful for the privilege . . . So in visiting an Edgbaston church I may be excused a little trepidation, a kind of nervousness, a sort of diffidence arising from a sense of personal unworthiness. Years had elapsed since I last gazed upon the splendours of the Hagley Road. Living in a comparatively low quarter affected by artists, authors, editors and other members of the dangerous classes, I was quite out of training, and the aristocratic air of Edgbaston proved almost overpowering. Everybody seemed to be going to church. Crowds of well-fed, well-dressed people moved briskly in every direction, with the decided step and serious air of people having a definite object. Richly-robed ladies hung on the sleeves of elegant coats. Sprightly old gentlemen chatted merrily with pretty young girls. White-haired women walked quietly with the niece, daughter or 'ladies' companion'. Two by two the pupils of a Ladies School passed demurely by, with the regulation downcast look, which, however, did not prevent each individual member of the procession from keenly inspecting the passing throng through the tail of her eye. . . . Everybody is prosperous, happy and content. The worshippers move in an atmosphere of beauty. The church itself, its music, its officers, its surroundings, are agreeable, delightful, satisfactory, verging on perfection.[42]

Enough evidence has been adduced in this chapter to indicate where the impression contained here is misleading. But as a picture of the *haute bourgeoisie* in late-Victorian Edgbaston, it is a memorable and perceptive portrait.

4

During the years before the First World War, this exclusive splendour was increasingly coming under attack. The weakened resolve of the landlord, the decline in standards in the north-west corner of the estate, the advent of the trams along Hagley Road, the tendency of the wealthy to move farther out, and the actual sale of some of the estate: all this suggested that the great days of aristocratic landlordism and middle-class pre-eminence were gone. Moreover, the advent of those new, competing suburbs, such as Moseley, Erdington, Handsworth and Handsworth Wood, which appealed to the middle-classes in a way which only Edgbaston had done before, robbed the 'great village' of its dominance in the Council House. At the same time, the Greater Birmingham Act so increased the physical size of the city and enlarged the membership of the council that it only accentuated this trend (table 24).

Table 24. Members of Birmingham Town Council resident in Edgbaston, 1902–22

Year	Aldermen/Total	Councillors/Total
1901–2	10/18	15/53
1909–10	8/16	18/53
1911–12	8/29	18/90
1921–2	6/29	10/90

Source: *Kelley's Directories of Birmingham*: 1902, 974–6; 1910, 1119–20; 1912, 1135–6; 1922, 1286–7.

By the inter-war years, the extraordinary monopoly which Edgbaston boasted of the elite of Birmingham had disappeared. *Edgbastonia* abandoned its survey of local worthies temporarily in 1910 and permanently in 1917.[43] After the war it never really recovered, and in the late 1920s, this most visible expression of Edgbaston's corporate solidarity and pride ceased publication.

Nor, from the landlord's standpoint, was the reign of Rachel any more creative than the age of Augustus. The policy of adding to the estate, which was maintained inviolate until the end of the fifth lord's time, was put smartly into reverse. The extensive sales for death duty purposes in 1918 were only a beginning. During the inter-war years, it became a matter of policy to sell off land on the south side, adjacent to the University site – either to the University itself, to the School of King Edward VI, or to the local hospital board. Again the motives were mixed: to block off the best part of the estate from the encroachment of Harborne and Selly Oak; to raise money to pay off mortgages; to offer accommodation to the most important institutions in the city; and to throw the responsibility of developing some of Edgbaston's still virgin acres on to other shoulders. Yet in reality, little new building took place in these years. Six groups of flats were put up on Hagley Road where some old houses were demolished when their leases expired; shops were built along Islington Row; and 800 houses were constructed, in the area of Lordswood Road, Fitzroy and Hamilton Avenues.[44]

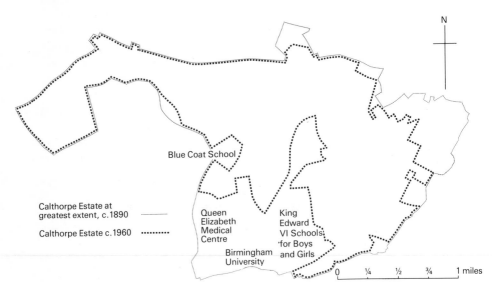

Fig. 23. Edgbaston: landownership pattern, *c.*1960.

In the main, though, Edgbaston remained remarkably unchanged during the inter-war years. The 'Alvaston' of Owen Lucton in the 1930s, differed little in its essentials from the 'Alvaston' of John Bradley in the 1880s. The great houses remained, with their servants, croquet lawns and all the accoutrements of graceful living. The western lands continued undeveloped, and in the 1930s even the tramways were removed from Hagley and Bristol Roads. Commuter traffic continued to increase, and the pre-eminent exclusiveness of the late nineteenth century was irrecoverable; but the threats in the years before the First World War proved less than expected. In this, as in so much else, it was the Second World War which was the vital watershed. The death of Neville Chamberlain in 1940, and the massive gains made by the Labour party in 1945 in Birmingham, symbolized the eclipse of the great Unionist families who had continued to dominate the town until the outbreak of the Second World War.[45] Although their descendants still remain in Birmingham, they no longer dominate the corridors of power: their collective identity, their religious zeal and their residential propinquity have all gone. The spatially-referred cultural values which Edgbaston itself symbolized have vanished too, along with their great houses which, in the straitened post-war conditions, have become too big, too old and too expensive to maintain.

Simultaneously, the landlord's view had altered. Further sales of land in the 1950s and 1960s mean that the estate, now reduced to 1,625 acres, has retreated almost entirely into an enclave bounded by the Hagley and Bristol Roads (fig. 23). In the 1950s, a development plan was commissioned, which finally and systematically accepted that Edgbaston could not survive entirely as a low-density residential area so close to the town centre.[46] Since then, the north-east corner has been fully integrated – as Balden and Augustus had foreseen in the 1900s – into the central business district, with the construction of shops and office blocks. At the same time, the middle-middle-class houses along the Hagley and Bristol Roads, where generations of Dudley Wilburns lived, have been adapted for use as offices, consulting rooms and hotels. In the centre of the estate, where once the great houses stood, there are now schools, colleges, and higher-density, integrated developments for young and servantless middle-class families. 'Whetstone' has been replaced by one such unit; 'Westbourne' is now the site of a preparatory school; and 'Mariemont' has been replaced by a hall of residence for the neighbouring college of education. Only the trees, walls and commemorative plaques speak of a vanished and more spacious age.

Yet the tantalizing ambiguities remain for, whatever the extent of the post-war transformation, the continued predominance of one single landowning authority has meant that Edgbaston has retained its character much more successfully than those other high-status suburbs like Handsworth, Moseley, Erdington and Handsworth Wood, whose competition was so persistent a feature of the period from the 1890s to the 1930s.[47] Since the Second World War, they have declined from being high-class, well-servanted areas into immigrant ghettoes and red light districts, and the original character of the development has been completely lost. Edgbaston, however, has retained its reputation as the most sought-after address in the town, 'the graceful suburb', a 'bastion of middle-class values', home of 'the most intelligent professional people in Birmingham'.[48] John Harris and the third Lord Calthorpe would assuredly have been delighted.

14 Conclusion: 'The same way, but by different steps'

During the course of the nineteenth century, the Calthorpes' extensive and continuous involvement in the affairs of Birmingham took four different but related forms. In the first place, the creation of Edgbaston embodied to a high degree an element of collaboration between the aristocracy and the towns: between the Calthorpes who administered the estate, and the citizens of Birmingham who built and lived in the houses. Secondly, as a suburban development, Edgbaston was a bastion of middle-class values which, although attached on occasions to a radical local elite, were also in emulation of the aristocracy themselves. Thirdly, the Edgbaston estate was financially the most important and administratively the most demanding piece of land which the Calthorpes owned. And finally, whether they liked it or not, the possession of the Edgbaston estate, combined with a peerage, placed them in an exposed public position in the town which, depending on the circumstances, could be a peak of privilege and favour, or a sore thumb of attack and ridicule.

1

In the creation and development of nineteenth-century building estates, the preferences of aristocratic landowners and middle-class town dwellers were – at least in theory – very similar. The aristocracy preferred to cater for tenants of the highest social class which the town could provide – because such an estate would enhance rather than debase the family's standing in the eyes of the world; because aristocratic landlords were not interested in short-term profit; and because the prospects of reversion 99 years hence were better the higher the standard of initial development.[1] In the same way, the middle classes' increased loathing for the polluted towns which their factories had brought into being, their fear of the working class, and their desire for privacy and seclusion in which to practise the domestic virtues of Victorian family life, predisposed them to similarly exclusive views.[2]

Of course, it did not always work out as easily as this. In some cases, the middle classes failed to appear or, having appeared, moved on almost at once, as the Bedfords found to their cost in Bloomsbury.[3] In others, the landowner's estate was too disadvantageously situated to attract the middle classes, as was the case with the Norfolks in Sheffield, or too large to fill up with middle-class residents, as was the case with the Butes in Cardiff; and in some towns, like Leeds and Manchester, there were no great urban estates at all. Under these circumstances, alternative arrangements were made for the middle classes. Several middle-class people might form a company, buy up plots of land advantageously situated, and administer them along the same restricted lines that were so often the hallmark of aristocratic ownership, as at Victoria Park near Manchester or in parts of Glasgow's Kelvinside.[4] Or, as at Hampstead, speculative builders might themselves provide the tone of elegant uniformity by constructing houses of a similar style and standard to those already standing close by.[5]

At Edgbaston, however, the preferences of the landlord and the middle classes converged, and remained thus fused for nearly a century. The great houses in the centre of the estate, with their large gardens, greenhouses, libraries, picture galleries and all the appurtenances of suburban gentility, were exactly what the third Lord Calthorpe and John Harris had wanted and, for their part, the Calthorpes and their tenants were prepared to see the estate administered very much according to the canons of aristocratic landownership. With the possible and transient exception of Frederick Henry William, fifth Lord Calthorpe, they were not concerned to maximize their profits, and would no doubt have expressed incomprehension or dismay had they been asked if that was their policy. In terms of the return on their land, the Calthorpes utilized their Edgbaston acres extraordinarily inefficiently and irrationally: the great houses with even bigger gardens; the willingness to turn down applicants prepared to pay more if thought inappropriate tenants; the steadfast refusal, even in the depressed years at the end of the nineteenth century, to woo speculative builders: these are not the actions of ruthless, profit-maximizing capitalists. On the contrary, they embodied the policy of administrators of extraordinary rectitude, seemingly more concerned – provided, of course, that revenue was *adequate* – to run Edgbaston as a public utility than as a business venture.

At the same time, although Edgbaston may have been seen by its owners as an estate beyond or above the sordid mechanisms of market forces, it was, nevertheless, very much subordinate to them. Although it was a considerable financial success, and although it embodied to some extent the preferences of the third lord and John Harris, their original proposals had been extensively modified. For there were simply not enough of the respectable middle classes, even in a town with an economic structure as favourable as Birmingham, to fill up the whole estate with villas. So the working classes, speculative builders, and even a few workshops were let in and far out-numbered those gracious houses in the centre which gave the suburb its high reputation. Moreover, as the Calthorpes recognized at the height of the Leasing Act crisis, they could not compel their preferred tenants to come to Edgbaston. If the terms were wrong, prospective tenants would stay away. In the 1820s, Harris had feared that Aston might be a competitor in high-class villa accommodation.[6] That threat proved to be groundless; but when, at the end of the nineteenth century, new suburban developments began to take place, in conscious emulation of, but nevertheless in competition with, Edgbaston itself, the Calthorpes were not in a position to resist. In the last analysis, the Calthorpes were as vulnerable to the forces of supply and demand as any businessman, and they knew it.

Nor was this their only weakness. For as the nineteenth century advanced, the circumstances under which the third lord and his agent had been able to think in terms of a hundred years or so ceased to prevail. Internally, it became increasingly hard to enforce the covenants on the oldest buildings, and the rapid rate of technological advance in high-class housing – unthinkable at the beginning of the century – made these old homes obsolete and unattractive. Externally, too, there were changes which the Calthorpes were powerless to resist: as Edgbaston was surrounded by new suburbs, the demand for trains, trams and telephones across the estate were cries against which the Calthorpes could not stand for ever. Indeed, as J. R. Kellett has noted, 'the whole idea behind the great estate was, in fact, to deny that the lower orders, retail trades, or public transport existed', and yet inevitably, such a denial could not be sustained indefinitely.[7] Whatever the advantages of topography and location which predisposed Edgbaston to high-class development, and which the Calthorpes did their best to exploit, they might mould, divert or influence the process of urban growth, but in the event they were never able to dominate it.

2

However, the Calthorpes' relationship with the process of urban growth was no more ambiguous than were the attitudes of the middle classes of Birmingham towards them. Throughout the nineteenth century, the English middle class 'faced both ways' politically, and its suburban location reflected this spatially.[8] On the one hand, the aristocracy could be the embodiment of hostile privilege, and collaboration with the working classes might be entertained to attack them. On the other, they might stand for success, order and property in the face of hostile working-class opposition. After all, to a member of the late nineteenth-century working class of Birmingham, there was little difference between Lord Calthorpe and his most opulent tenants: both had 'ample means and ample leisure', while he had neither.

So, in one sense, suburban Edgbaston represented a renunciation of aristocratic values. It opposed a middle-class, urban, earnestly religious nuclear family to the rural, Anglican, landowning, latitudinarian extended family of the aristocracy. The one would be dominated by a stout, crusty, cheerful country gentleman, waiting at the stable for a last ride with a son about to depart for a boarding school. The other, by contrast, would be under the watchful eye of a tall, solemn gentleman, attired in a black frock coat, standing in the drawing room, bible in hand, awaiting family prayers. He would certainly disapprove of the wayward and licentious morals of the aristocracy, and regard his private, secure, suburban existence as its very antithesis.[9] And in the Fladburns of 'Alvaston' Brett Young caught this ethos beautifully:

Liberal, abstemious, hard-working, thrifty, highminded, motivated by a strong bourgeois sense of civic duty, and of civic pride.

From this cultural nexus of suburban values as the antithesis of the country house it was but a short step to the anti-aristocratic tone which so often was the hallmark of Birmingham's politics. For Attwood, Bright and Chamberlain, the essence of their political rhetoric was a union between the middle and working classes in an attack on aristocratic privilege. In Chamberlain's case, at least in the first phase of his career, that anti-aristocratic stance had a specifically local contextual articulation, for it was a hostility directed strongly and specifically at his own ground landlord – Lord Calthorpe. And if this was the negative side of his creed, its positive aspect was a real commitment – unique both in its force and its longevity – to better the town in which he lived, either out of genuine compassion or for motives of civic aggrandizement. Whatever the reason, the elite of Birmingham retained its commitment *to the town*: that was where the action was. They were no absentee figures, living on their country estates. On the contrary – and how ironic – it was the very existence of Lord Calthorpe's Edgbaston which gave them all that the country could offer but in an urban location.

Indeed, it is at this point that qualifications have to be entered, for the obverse of civic zeal and urban involvement remained suburban existence. The great attraction of Edgbaston was that it *seemed* to be in the country, and indeed until the last decade or so of the nineteenth century, it did in fact border on it. However nonconformist or radical or concerned about the welfare and greatness of Birmingham they might be, the elite of the town were as much enslaved by the cultural values of the aristocracy as any other middle-class group. Their great houses, with their tennis courts and croquet lawns and stables and billiard rooms, their delight in employing servants who had actually been in service with the real aristocracy; their enjoyment of leisured, expensive, exclusive recreations like tennis and riding: all this marked them as a suburban elite which defined personal, social success in terms of aristocratic emulation. If the Fladburns were one aspect of the 'Alvaston' suburban experience, then the Luctons – socially ambitious, adoring title and hating squalor – were the other half. When Rachel Anstruther-Gough-Calthorpe bought her fleet of Daimlers in the early 1910s, her most illustrious Edgbaston tenants were doing the same thing. Political differences did not preclude the possibility of a cultural consensus.

Nor, indeed, were political differences always so severe. Three times in the nineteenth century – before the first Reform Act, in the 1850s and early 1860s, and at the end of the century – the Calthorpes were in accord with Birmingham political opinion, first as Tory-radicals, then as Whig-Liberals, and finally as Unionist-Conservatives. Indeed, by the end of the nineteenth century, Edgbaston itself, home of the nonconformist, radical elite, had become the foremost Unionist stronghold in the town. And, for the whole of the century, with the exception of the 1860s and 1870s, there was a strong streak of obsequiousness in many Birmingham citizens which meant that they still loved lords, and felt that their patronage was the necessary precondition for the success of any of their local endeavours. Even when the middle classes differed from the Calthorpes on political grounds, they could still, at the same time, look up to them as members of the established order. For all their local patriotism, the middle classes' sense of social insecurity, in Birmingham as elsewhere, was profound.

3

Of course, the Calthorpes themselves had once been bourgeois, *parvenu, nouveau riche*, in the time of Sir Richard Gough. Indeed, their eighteenth-century ascent up the ladder of status – 'trade, a fortune, the acquisition of a landed estate, a baronetcy, membership of Parliament, and finally a peerage' – conforms to the classic recipe for social advancement in pre-industrial England.[10] However, while the manner by which they rose was far from unusual, the means by which they were able to live up to their title and status in the nineteenth century most decidedly was. For it was the rising curve of rentals from Edgbaston which underpinned the re-building of Elvetham, the extension of the estate there and the creation of the stud farm at Newmarket: in short, the whole façade of aristocratic life. The fact that between 1810 and 1910 their gross income more than tripled was almost entirely due to the revenue which they drew from Sir Richard Gough's initial purchase, and that figure – spectacular though it is – only gives the increase in *money* terms. In *real* terms, with prices falling by half throughout the century, there must have been something approaching a six-fold increase in real income. Since the average rise in real incomes throughout the nineteenth century was probably no more than 100 per cent at the very most, then it is clear that, at least in the Calthorpes' case, the rich were definitely getting richer.[11]

  If the Calthorpes had been successful in their attempts to buy Culford, they would have been denied such financial fulfilment and salvation, in part because the income from an arable estate in East Anglia could never have increased in the manner which Edgbaston's did, and in part because they would not have been insulated from the chill blast of agricultural depression in the way that they were. Between 1810 and 1888, some £47,000 was spent by the estate on the making of roads. During the same period, rents at Edgbaston rose from £5,233 to £28,882.[12] The figures speak for themselves, and do so even more eloquently when it is recalled how much other families were investing in agricultural improvements in these years, and how little they were getting back.[13] Most striking of all, however, is the fact that their ground rents were paid by men who made their money in industry or the professions. As radicals were quick to point out, the Calthorpes' wealth ultimately derived from the prosperity of Birmingham manufacturers: indeed, at the opening of Calthorpe Park in 1857 the fourth Lord Calthorpe had admitted as much. How ironic that the town of Attwood and Bright and Chamberlain should in part be responsible for turning a minor landed family into millionaires!

Yet, for all that, it is important to stress just how slow the development of Edgbaston was. Indeed, spectacular though its rentals were by the end of the century, they did not rise at an impressive rate compared with other aristocratic estates. Between 1863 and 1885 the ground rental of the estate of the governors of the School of King Edward VI in Birmingham, who owned a much smaller area of the town than did the Calthorpes, grew from £11,000 to £27,000. Between 1800 and 1837, the value of the rents which the Derby family drew from Liverpool and Bury quadrupled. The development of the Bishop of London's estate in Paddington was even more spectacular. In 1833, ground rents stood at £5,797; by 1843 the figure was £18,637; ten years later it was £27,703.[14] Moreover, at least until the building leases began to fall in at Edgbaston the expiry of the 99-year term, the middleman who owned the house (and on occasions sub-let it) was drawing much greater revenue than the ground landlord. Number 3 Ampton Road, for example, carried with it a ground rent due to Lord Calthorpe of £23 a year. But the rent for the house itself which the occupant paid the owner was £175 a year.[15] Indeed, it was on the basis of house rental rather than the ground rental that Bateman's misleading valuation was arrived at.

Of course, an income of £35,000 a year by the end of the nineteenth century did not by any means put the Calthorpes in the super-power league. Families like the Bedfords and Westminsters and Butes were enjoying gross incomes of eight to ten times that amount. Nevertheless, having enabled the Calthorpes to enjoy an aristocratic life style during the first three-quarters of the nineteenth century, the revenue from Edgbaston also enabled them to survive the following 70 years more easily than they would have done otherwise: compared with many other families, the assured income from Edgbaston allowed them to weather the vicissitudes of the period from the 1870s to the Second World War relatively easily. Not until 1953 did they part with Elvetham Hall, and in the inter-war years the régime there had continued very much as before. While other families with only agricultural acres felt the pinch, the Calthorpes – thanks to Edgbaston – were able to soldier on.

4

However, while the Calthorpes were happy to enjoy the revenue which Edgbaston's expansion brought them, they were less at ease in playing the public role which their title and economic interest obliged them to fill in Birmingham. Of course, they were not expected to play so large a part in the affairs of the town as did, for example, the Norfolks in Sheffield. To begin with, Birmingham was larger, and its civic life was more energetic; and, as a newly-risen family, the Calthorpes lacked both the established lineage and high status which made the Norfolks so significant. Moreover, they were not a major political power in a highly urbanized country, as the Derbys were in Lancashire. Nor were they actually responsible for having brought the town into being, as were the Butes at Cardiff, and they were not major political figures in their own right, like the Fitzwilliams. Thus their 'conservative interest' was of necessity weaker than those of other greater grandees in smaller towns.

In addition to this, the Calthorpes did not make the most of their opportunities. All his life, the third lord was an absentee, as was the fourth lord after 1862. The fifth lord just did not care. Despite the fact that in the 1860s he lived near Birmingham, and was a Liberal in politics, he had no wish to use his influence and his wealth to build up a political power base in Birmingham, although it seems possible that he might have succeeded had he so wished; but he really was not interested in such activity. Finally, both the sixth lord and his brother were, after 1893, not only absentees but old and tired absentees. Accordingly, although their part in the public, political life of Birmingham was not entirely insignificant, it is the history of a weak 'conservative interest' rather than a powerful one. At the end of the day, the Calthorpes needed Birmingham more than it needed them.

So, although their general relationship with Birmingham followed the pattern outlined earlier, their profile was always low. The third lord was not only less influential in Birmingham in the 1820s than the Butes in Cardiff and the Donegalls in Belfast, but even less so than the Fitzwilliams in Sheffield. During the passage of the Great Reform Act and the controversies of the late 1830s, the Calthorpes themselves were so insignificant that they were not worth attacking. Even in the mid-Victorian period, their renewed position as figureheads was shared with men like Harrowby, Lyttelton and Norton, whose public fame far exceeded theirs. Only in the 1870s and early 1880s did the Calthorpes come to the forefront, partly in consequence of the Calthorpe Park *débacle*, and partly because the ensuing era of conflict and confrontation was personified in the clash between Augustus Calthorpe and Joseph Chamberlain in the general election of 1880. After this, however, during the subsequent *rapprochement*, the Calthorpes once more assumed a low profile.

That is not to say that during this last phase Birmingham did not share in the heightened awareness of civic dignity and love of ritual and ceremonial which characterized other industrial towns. On the contrary, the building of the Council House and the Corporation Street scheme may be seen as initiating this new phase of civic glamour. In the ensuing years, too, the opening of the law courts by Queen Victoria, the installation of Charles Gore as Bishop, the seventieth birthday celebrations of Joseph Chamberlain, and the inauguration of the new university buildings by Edward VII, were all occasions in which the splendour of the city was ritualistically re-affirmed. But, unlike other towns, these ceremonies were not centred on the local aristocracy: there were no titled mayors, and there was no aristocratic chancellor. On the contrary, if anachronistic dignity was needed, it was provided by the royal family itself; and in some cases, even this was ignored.

By the end of the century – however much his grip in the 1870s and 1880s may have been weak – the control of Birmingham by Chamberlain and his Unionist allies was virtually unbreakable. And, unlike in other towns, it was they, the middle-class leaders, who were at the centre of civic ritual and ceremonial, rather than the aristocracy. Even in his seventieth birthday speech, Chamberlain was still stressing the importance and innate nobility of local government.[16] So, while in Birmingham as elsewhere, there was a real *rapprochement* between a unionist leadership and the local aristocracy, the Calthorpes were very much the junior partners. Compared with other late nineteenth-century industrial towns, Birmingham was parodoxically both more conservative and less aristocratic, and the power of Chamberlain on the one hand, and the weakness of the Calthorpes on the other, in part explains why.

5

Two over-riding impressions remain. The development of Edgbaston in the nineteenth century transformed both the western side of Birmingham and the Calthorpes' financial position. In a way that was very different from the making of Kelvinside in Glasgow or Hampstead in London or Headingley in Leeds or Victoria Park in Manchester, Birmingham obtained its high-class suburb. And, in a similarly unusual manner, the Calthorpes were able to enjoy an aristocratic lifestyle on the proceeds of urban, not agricultural, income. The town obtained its suburb under aristocratic auspices, and the landed family drew its income largely from urban revenue. To both, in different ways, the Calthorpe motto was equally applicable: 'The same way, but by different steps'.

Part Three
The Devonshires
and Eastbourne

15 Introduction: the landowners and the land, 1782–1849

Spring comes to Beachbourne as it comes to no other city on earth, however fair; say those of her children who after long sojourning in other lands come home in the evenings of their days to sleep. The many-treed town that lies between the swell of the hills and the sparkle of the sea, sluicing deliciously the roan length of Pevensey Bay, unveils her rounded blossom in the dawn of the year to the kind clear gaze of heaven and of those who today pass and repass along its windy ways. Birds thrill and twitter in her streets. There earlier than elsewhere the arabis calls the bee, and the hedge sparrow raises his thin sweet pipe to bid the hearts of men lift up: for winter is passed. Chestnut and laburnum unfold a myriad lovely bannerets on slopes peopled with gardens and gay with crocuses and the laughter of children. The elms in Saffrons Croft, the beeches in Paradise, stir in their sleep and wrap themselves about in dreamy rainment of mauve and emerald. The air is like white wine, the sky of diamonds; and the sea winds come blowing over banks of tamarisk to purge and exhilarate.[1]

The similarity between this description, by Alfred Ollivant, of the exclusive, refined and fictional seaside resort of 'Beachbourne' and Brett Young's evocation of suburban 'Alvaston' is remarkable, not only in terms of what they described, but also of how they described it. Once more, in luxuriant, purple prose, the reader is regaled with descriptions of the lushness of the trees, the vitality of the birds, and the cleanliness of the air. 'Beachbourne', at the height of its renown in the Edwardian era, was in many ways but 'Alvaston' by the sea: a town beautifully planned and laid out, with wide, tree-lined streets, elegant squares and terraces, palatial villas set in extensive grounds, and serious, wealthy and high-minded residents, who frequented assiduously the many local churches, patronized concerts and other entertainments, and lived a life of secluded, leisured ease, in a town largely free from industry, squalor or poverty.

As with 'Alvaston', 'Beachbourne' was no invention. On the contrary, it was but a very thinly disguised version of Eastbourne, where Ollivant himself was resident between 1901 and 1911, and to whose inhabitants he dedicated *Two Men*, another of his local novels. For 20 years before Ollivant moved to Eastbourne, and throughout the Edwardian era, guide book after guide book extolled the town's manifold virtues. Here is one account for 1897:

The inhabitants of Eastbourne claim for their town – the favoured child of down and sea – the proud title of 'The Empress of Watering Places'. And, assuredly, it possesses many claims to that distinction. The peculiar charm of Eastbourne is that, despite the constant building operations, it has preserved a certain air of rusticity. Old trees have been left standing at the side of, or even in the middle of, new thoroughfares; thousands of new trees have been planted. The houses and mansions in the principal suburbs are intended for persons of means, and everything in the town proclaims the fact that it attracts, and deserves to attract, visitors of the better class.[2]

Seven years later, nothing had changed:

It seems to stand apart from all ordinary seaside health resorts with a distinctiveness which is one of its most engaging characteristics. Refinement and retirement are written on every hand . . . The cleanliness of the town, the uniformity and breadth of its roads, the taste displayed in its architecture, and the variety of its attractions and amusements arrest attention, combined with the elegant residences abounding on every hand, the palatial hotels, noble and well-built boarding houses, the numerous handsome shops, and the brightness of the place, and its remarkable salubrity.[3]

Indeed, at the end of the nineteenth century, such luxuriant eloquence was commonplace: a score of guide books vied with each other to do justice to Eastbourne's charms. One more, which did so in a comparative framework, must suffice:

Brighton is democratic; Hastings is salubrious (and, it must be confessed, a trifle dull); but Eastbourne, with its wide tree-lined streets, its miles of cultivated sea front with shaven lawns and prim *par terres*, is distinctly and decidedly elegant. He who sets himself to write in praise of Eastbourne would seem to have a never-ending task.[4]

In the same way that Edgbaston was hailed and acclaimed as the Calthorpes' creation, so Eastbourne was held up as exemplifying all the benefits which accrued when a dukedom connected itself with a watering place. The seventh duke of Devonshire was described as 'Eastbourne's patron saint', 'the principal landowner' and 'a patron of commanding influence and great sagacity'.[5] Nor was this limited to local publications whose opinions might be expected to be somewhat biased. The *Christian World* spoke of 'the hand of the Duke of Devonshire, who is the ground landlord and ruling spirit of the place'; the *Whitehall Review* noted that 'you cannot be in Eastbourne ten minutes without seeing that there is some beneficent controlling influence at work'; and the *Saturday Review* described the seventh duke as 'an enterprising and wealthy promoter, with authority practically unlimited . . . who has been the good genius, the tutelary deity, of Eastbourne.'[6]

Twentieth-century observers have endorsed this view, seeing in the resort a model of early planning which 'should be recognised by town planners as . . . a masterpiece of its genre', a classic example of controlled, zoned and high-class development.[7] Indeed, of the three major forays into urban development which the Devonshires undertook in the eighteenth and nineteenth centuries, it was arguably the most successful: larger and more famous than Buxton, better planned and more stable than Barrow. Moreover, the Devonshires were the grandest and greatest family to be involved in the creation of a large seaside town – surpassing the Radnors, Palks and de la Warrs in the splendour of their titles, the breadth of their acres, and the size of their income. Whereas the Calthorpes were made by the development of Edgbaston, Eastbourne was made by the development of the Devonshires. Birmingham raised up the Calthorpes; the Devonshires raised up Eastbourne. But how did they come to hold their lands in Sussex, and when did they decide to develop them in this way?

1

'Sprung from the loins of a fourteenth-century lawyer, rising to wealth on the devastation of the monasteries, earls by grace of the first James, dukes for their part in dethroning the second', the Devonshires were already, by the middle of the eighteenth century, among the greatest of the Crown's subjects, and have since so remained. Indeed, their rise to the forefront of the aristocracy, combining quite extraordinary success in heiress-hunting with political acumen and good fortune, and lasting over three centuries and more, reads like an epic version of what the Calthorpes – beginning more humbly and rising by marriage, but less spectacularly – achieved on a smaller scale during the eighteenth century.[8]

The family originated in the Suffolk village of Cavendish from which it took its surname and were, by the early decades of the sixteenth century, established at the periphery of London court life. In 1547, Sir William Cavendish, who had established his reputation as one of Cromwell's assistants at the time of the dissolution of the monasteries, married Bess of Hardwick, his third wife, who brought into the marriage considerable lands in Derbyshire. She it was who completed the building of Chatsworth after the death of Sir William and constructed Hardwick Hall nearby. Her second son by this marriage finally inherited all her estates, and was created Lord Cavendish in 1605 and Earl of Devonshire in 1618. His great grandson, the fourth earl of Devonshire, was made duke of Devonshire and marquess of Hartington as a reward for his support of William III. At the same time, he was installed as a Knight of the Garter, an honour which every subsequent duke – with the exception of the present one – has enjoyed, in itself an achievement unequalled by any other English ducal family. During the last 20 years of his life, the first duke devoted his energies to the reconstruction of Chatsworth and – although altered and extended by the sixth duke in the early nineteenth century – it is his house which stands today.

His grandson, William, third duke of Devonshire, had four sons – William, fourth duke, George Augustus, Frederick and John (see genealogical table, Appendix C). Lord George Augustus Cavendish, the second son, inherited an estate at Holker in Lancashire from his cousin, Sir William Lowther of Marske, third and last baronet, but this was a relatively minor gain compared with the matrimonial *coup* accomplished by his elder brother. In 1748, while still Marquess of Hartington, he married Charlotte Boyle, only child of the third earl of Burlington. As a result, the Devonshires acquired estates at Bolton Abbey – where there was a house – and Londesborough in Yorkshire, Lismore Castle and lands in Waterford, as well as both Chiswick and Burlington Houses in London. Already grandees of the first rank in England, the Devonshires now became landowners of prime importance in Ireland as well. Indeed, by the middle of the eighteenth century, their houses, acres and wealth were such as to excite envy, wonder and admiration.

Their success at the marriage market did not desert them in the next generation either. The fourth duke's eldest son, William, fifth duke, married the fabulous Georgiana, whose charm and radicalism placed Devonshire House firmly at the centre of Whig society at the end of the eighteenth century. Their son, William, the sixth and bachelor duke, was the patron of Paxton, whose extravagant re-buildings at Chatsworth, Bolton, Devonshire House and Lismore were to leave his descendants with an extensive legacy of debt. Meanwhile, the fourth duke's second son, Lord George Augustus Henry Cavendish, inherited the Holker estate when his namesake died unmarried in 1794; but by then he himself had already married (in 1782) Lady Elizabeth Compton, daughter and heiress to the Marquess of Northampton. And by this means he also acquired, to add to his Holker lands, a 7,000-acre estate in Sussex including the mansion house of Compton Place.[9]

Although a younger son, Lord George Augustus Henry Cavendish was in consequence a landed magnate of importance in his own right and, from the time of his marriage until his death in 1834, he lost no opportunity to add to his lands, especially those in Sussex. Between 1782 and 1805, evidence exists for no less than 27 purchases of houses, farms and malt-houses. For the period 1783 to 1827 there have survived conveyances to him of land in Sussex totalling £57,500, and this is obviously only a small part of his total purchases.[10] Even as early as 1821, Robert Simpson, his local agent, computed the size of the Sussex estate at 8,577 acres, with a rental of £9,028, and it is clear that Cavendish continued to extend it further until his death.[11] In 1831, in the midst of the Reform Bill crisis, he was raised to the peerage as Earl of Burlington, thereby reviving the title which had become extinct on the death of the fourth duke's father-in-law. Three years later he died and because his son, William, had died in 1812, the title passed to the first earl of Burlington's grandson, another William, then a young man of 26.

His expansive inheritance included lands in Somerset and Lincolnshire, as well as the more extensive estates in Lancashire and Sussex, each with its own mansion house. Even the subsidiary branch of the Devonshire line, thanks to fortunate inheritance and opportune marriage, could rival many more ancient and well-established families. Meanwhile, the sixth duke of Devonshire, the second earl of Burlington's second cousin, was still unmarried, and it seemed likely that young Burlington would one day inherit the larger ducal holdings as well. On the sixth duke's death in 1858, this is exactly what happened, so that all the Cavendish estates which had been accumulating since the time of Bess of Hardwick were brought together under the stewardship of William Cavendish, second earl of Burlington and now seventh duke of Devonshire. (Throughout this part of the book, the seventh duke will be referred to as Burlington until 1858, and Devonshire thereafter.) It was an extraordinary inheritance, indeed so fabulous that on one occasion the seventh duke admitted that he had more houses than he knew what to do with: Compton Place in Sussex, Holker Hall in Lancashire, Lismore Castle in Ireland, Burlington, Chiswick and Devonshire Houses in London, Beaufort House at Newmarket, Bolton Abbey in Yorkshire, and Hardwick and Chatsworth in Derbyshire. It is in this Olympian context that the Sussex estates in general, and the lands at Eastbourne in particular, must be set.

2

By the 1880s the Sussex estates which the Cavendishes had acquired by yet another of their advantageous marriages totalled some 11,000 acres, making them one of the four greatest landowners in the county – the others being the dukes of Richmond at Goodwood, the dukes of Norfolk at Arundel, and the earls of Egremont at Petworth. Indeed, the history of the county's politics may largely be written in terms of the interaction between these families.[12] Of their Sussex estate, some 2,600 acres came within the parish of Eastbourne, where the mansion house, Compton Place, was also located. Sheltered at the foot of the South Downs, with undulating, well-wooded countryside sweeping down to the sea, and with a south-easterly prospect, it was an agreeable site. To the north-east was the low-lying land of the Crumbles, marshy, only ten feet above sea level, and liable to flooding: but towards the south-west, the land rose gently, reaching nearly 500 ft at Beachy Head, where the Downs plunged spectacularly into the sea. And between the cliffs at one end and the marshes at the other was a two-mile stretch of sandy beach.

Within the parish, the concentration of landownership was almost as remarkable as at Edgbaston (table 25). Over 98 per cent of the landowners – mainly smallholders, fishermen and agricultural labourers – held less than one-fifteenth of the land, and of the three estates which held land in excess of 100 acres, the Cavendish estate was easily the largest. Their holdings amounted to 2,625 acres, or very nearly two-thirds of the parish, and included – strategically – most of the coast line (fig. 25). A comparison with Blackpool, where two-thirds of the land was held by owners each with less than 100 acres, places Eastbourne right at the other end of the spectrum as far as the pattern of landownership in seaside towns is concerned. Indeed, the land was concentrated in the hands of one owner to a greater extent than in any other resort town with the exception of Skegness where, in 1849, the earls of Scarbrough held 75 per cent of the acreage.[13]

Of the other two owners with estates in excess of 100 acres, 178 acres were rectorial glebe land, and the other estate, amounting to 956 acres or just under one-quarter of the total, belonged to the Gilbert family, who were always in the

Fig. 24. Compton Place, Eastbourne, in the inter-war years (by courtesy of Eastbourne Public Library).

Table 25. The structure of landownership in Eastbourne, 1841 *(to the nearest acre)*

Size of estates (acres)	Landowners		Area occupied	
	nos.	%	(acres)	%
Erratum Table 25. The column under the heading 'Size of estates' should read: Under 1 1 and under 5 5 and under 10 10 and under 25 25 and under 100 Over 100				
Totals	168	100.00	3,999	100.00

Source: PRO IR. 29/35/87, Eastbourne Tithe Award, 1841.

Cavendishes' shadow. In the first place, their land was scattered in three holdings, did not include any of the coast, and was dwarfed by the Cavendishes' more spacious accumulations (fig. 25). Moreover, they were not themselves a particularly wealthy or famous family. In 1883, their entire holdings were put at 3,526 acres in Sussex, and 2,895 in Cornwall, the gross annual value of which was only £8,734 – or less even than the relatively modest income which the Calthorpes had enjoyed as long ago as 1810.[14] The founder of the family, Davies Giddy, was the son of a Cornish clergyman, a patron of Richard Trevithick and Humphry Davy, M.P. for Totnes and then Bodmin, and President of the Royal Society in 1827, who bought his way into land in Cornwall. In 1807 he married Mary Anne Gilbert of Eastbourne, whose estates he inherited and name he took on the death of her uncle in 1816. He himself died in 1845, and the estates in both Cornwall and Sussex then passed to his grandson, Carew Davies Gilbert, who held them until his death in 1913.[15] Like his grandfather, he was first and foremost a Cornishman, where he was a J.P. and Deputy Lieutenant, and served as High Sheriff in 1908–9. It was the West Country, rather than the Sussex Downs, which had first claim upon his affections.

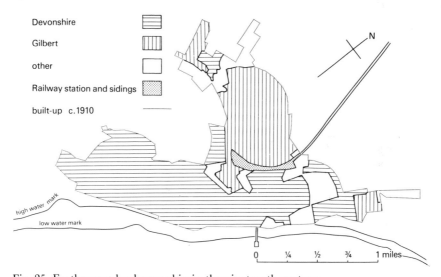

Fig. 25. Eastbourne: landownership in the nineteenth century.

Of limited wealth, and with their lands less advantageously placed, the Gilberts offered no real threat to the Cavendishes' dominant territorial position in Eastbourne. Moreover, relations between the two families were uniformly cordial – with the temporary exception of the early 1850s, when they fell out over the question of the water supply. In 1873, for example, when Nicholas Whitley was preparing plans to make more of the Gilberts' land available for building, he wrote of 'the great improvements done by the Duke of Devonshire especially at the sea frontage', which had 'reacted beneficially on this estate'. Even in the early 1880s, when Carew Davies Gilbert was President of the local Conservative Association while Lord Edward Cavendish was President of the Liberals, political differences in no sense affected the close co-operation between the two estates: they were, in this context, landowners and developers first, and party politicians a long way afterwards.[16] And after Home Rule, even this difference disappeared. 'It must be in your interest to keep in with the duke', Gilbert's solicitor wrote to him in 1894. 'The Duke of Devonshire has worked so cordially with us in every respect to the mutual advantage of the two estates', his agent noted in the following year. And when, in 1913, the duke lowered the price at which his Eastbourne freeholds were sold from 30 to 25 years' purchase, the Gilberts followed suit immediately. 'If you are, I shall do the same', their solicitor wrote to the duke's agent.[17]

3

However, this is to anticipate, for during the early decades of the nineteenth century the acres of both the Gilberts and the Cavendishes at Eastbourne remained undeveloped. While Brighton attracted the sustained patronage of royalty, and Southend played host to day trippers from among the London working class, Eastbourne stagnated. In 1801, there were a mere 1,600 inhabitants, and 50 years later the figure was only twice as great. At the end of the eighteenth century, Eastbourne had enjoyed limited but fruitless royal patronage from Prince Edward and the Princesses Elizabeth and Sophia, and been described as 'one of the favourite summer retreats for sickness, indolence and dissipation.' In 1803, it boasted two circulating libraries, a theatre and a ballroom, and one visitor claimed that 'the bathing may be equalled, but cannot be surpassed'.[18] But few bothered to test his verdict. William Wilberforce, who went there in 1809, noted that 'here we seem to enjoy more quiet than almost any place we were ever at': hardly a description of a rising, let alone a thriving resort.[19] In 1830, the population of 3,000 could boast only one lawyer, one brewer, one wine and spirit merchant and five inns. Even in 1842, there were only 600 recorded houses, spread out in four distinct villages: Eastbourne proper, Meads, Southbourne and Sea Houses, three of which were inland, and all of which were separated from each other by distances of two to three miles.[20] Meanwhile, by the middle of the nineteenth century, Brighton's population had passed the 65,000 mark, and Southend had reached 30,000.

By this time, though, schemes for improvement of their Eastbourne acres had already been entertained by successive owners of Compton Place. Local legend – for which no documentary corroboration exists – has it that in 1833 Decimus Burton approached Lord Burlington with a proposal to create a new town on the coast to be called Burlington; but the earl, reluctant to spoil his rural quietude, was unenthusiastic.[21] Three years later, however, his grandson, the second earl of Burlington, was again in contact with Burton, as building plans were made, draft leases prepared, and estimates calculated for yet another development.[22] At first, it was planned to open up some 60 acres for building by the construction of roads, sewers and sea walls at a cost of £2,200, with further developments envisaged at a later date which would bring the whole cost up to £7,500. By January 1838, Burton's plan was fully drawn up, and in 1840 he produced another scheme for the development of Meads.

Between 1837 and 1839, Trinity Chapel was built – as usual the church being the first large-scale piece of construction. In January 1838, Burlington conferred with Burton and Benjamin Currey, his solicitor, and 'decided to offer land on building leases near the new chapel at Eastbourne, but on a small scale at first.'[23] Three months later, however, Burton was still 'very anxious to make a beginning at Eastbourne', and shortly afterwards abandoned the still-born enterprise altogether for the more promising venture he was already involved in at St Leonards.[24] Why exactly Burlington lost interest in the scheme in the late 1830s is not clear, but certainly the death in the early 1840s of Blanche, his adored wife, his increasing seclusion at Holker, and his almost total preoccupation with the early stages of development at Barrow-in-Furness, meant that he was largely indifferent to the fate of his south coast estate.[25] Indeed, between 1840 and 1842, he actually considered selling it altogether and, on a visit in June 1844, noted in his diary: 'It is two years since I have been here'.[26]

In the second half of the decade, however, his interest began to revive. In 1846, the London, Brighton & South Coast Railway opened its branch to Hastings, which passed through Polegate, only six miles from Eastbourne itself. Three years later, he succeeded, by a combination of threats and cajolery, in persuading the company to build an extension to Eastbourne itself, and the line was duly opened on 14 May 1849, to the strains of the band playing 'Behold the Conquering Hero Comes'. The programme of celebrations lasted from dawn until dusk, and included a formal luncheon with toasts and speeches, attempts by amateur acrobats to climb a greasy pole for the sake of a leg of mutton at the top, and a firework display in the evening; but above all, 'the excitement amongst the natives was very great, for many of them had never travelled by train, or even seen a locomotive engine'.[27]

Two years before, Burlington had commissioned James Berry, the County Surveyor, 'to set out and survey the first portion of Eastbourne'. During the summer, the earl stayed at Compton Place, and spent 'a good while at the seaside considering plans for building, which seems probable owing to the railway'; but, he added, 'the sea has made great inroads lately, and a sea wall will be necessary if buildings go on'.[28] June 1849, a month after the railway had arrived, he again visited Eastbourne to discuss matters with William Simpson, his local agent. His diary for 15 June contains this – retrospectively – momentous entry:

I had a good deal of talk today with William Simpson about building plans here. He evidently wishes me to make a beginning myself. But I hesitate. The railway has certainly improved the prospects of the place considerably.[29]

4

From this moment may be dated the decision to create a seaside town which, within 30 years, was to become the fastest growing in Sussex, and earn the title of 'The Empress of Watering Places'. Nevertheless, as with the first phase of Edgbaston's development, the early years were far from easy.

16 The making of a high-class resort, 1849–1914

The documentation of the growth of Eastbourne is, if anything, even more complete than in the case of Edgbaston. Again, the best indications of both short- and long-term fluctuations are the numbers of building agreements reached each year with the Devonshires and the Gilberts. Those for the Devonshires are the records of the actual agreements: the year in which the contract was signed, but not necessarily the year in which the houses were built. Those for the Gilberts are a record of permission to build according to a specified and agreed plan so, as graph 3 shows, there was a time-lag of three to four years between the Devonshire estate cycle and that on the Gilbert lands, not because builders moved from one estate to another, but because the two sets of figures represent different stages of the building process. Three distinct long-term cycles suggest themselves: from the mid-1850s to the late 1860s, the early 1870s to the late 1880s, and from the early 1890s until the outbreak of the First World War. In addition, graph 4, combining cumulative Devonshire agreements with the population figures for Eastbourne, gives some idea of the overall pace of growth.

1

The first complete cycle lasted from the original planning stage of Burlington and his advisers until the prolonged slump in building agreements between 1868 and 1872. As with the development of Edgbaston in the 1810s and 1820s, initial optimism and confidence was soon replaced by doubt, worry and uncertainty. Berry's plan was finally perfected in 1851, and envisaged the development of that part of the sea front which today runs from the pier westward to Devonshire Place, with a promenade, and houses arranged in squares behind. With no less than 70 building agreements snapped up in the years 1850–3, the scheme began favourably. 'Fifteen large houses are nearly complete, and the thing seems to promise well', Burlington recorded optimistically in his diary for December 1851.[1] 'The new buildings are going on well, and the scheme seems likely to prosper', he predicted five months later.[2] As the parade was finished and the houses neared completion, his optimism further increased 'Much appears to have been done since I was last there'; 'several houses are now approaching completion'; 'on the whole things are doing pretty well': these are the entries in his diary for 1854–5.[3]

However, as the downturn in graph 3 shows, this confidence was misplaced. By the mid-1850s, old buildings were still being completed, but new agreements had come to a virtual standstill. The early contractors who had under-

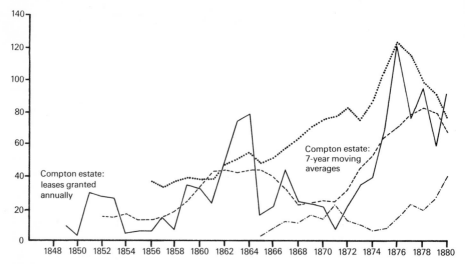

Graph 3. Building leases granted at Eastbourne, 1849–1914 (CEO MS, Agreement
Books, 0-XIII; ESRO Gilb.MS 147–50, 'Registers of House Plans Approved in
Eastbourne'; J. Parry Lewis, *Building Cycles and Britain's Growth*, 1965, 316–17).
Note: Figures for the Compton estate are for leases granted; those for the Gilbert
estate are for permission actually to build. Hence the lag effect.

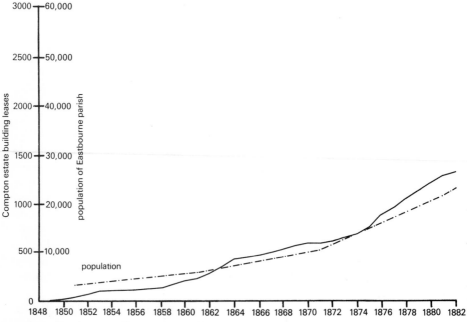

Graph 4. Eastbourne leases and population growth, 1849–1914 (CEO MS,
Agreement Books, 0–XIII; J. C. Wright, *Byegone Eastbourne*, 1898, 180).

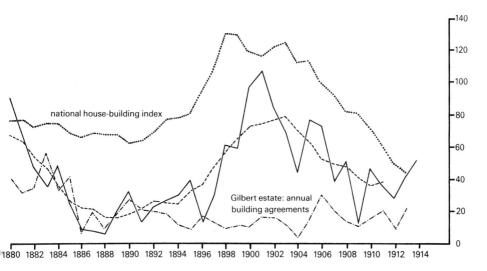

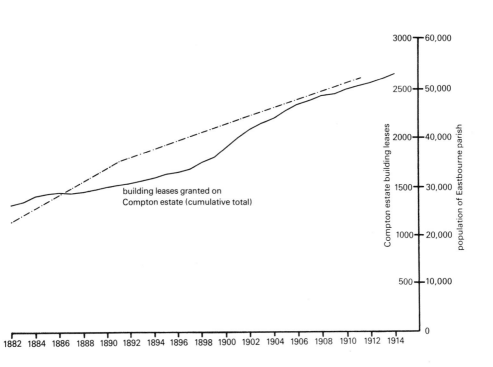

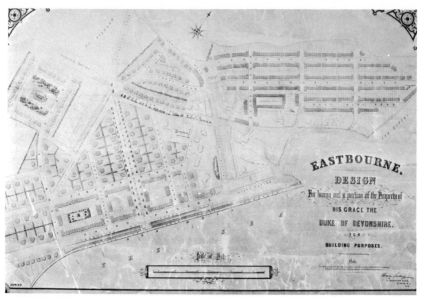

Fig. 26. Henry Currey's plan for Eastbourne, 1859 (reproduced from a copy made two years later, by courtesy of the Trustees of the Chatsworth Settlement).

taken to build the houses and construct the sea wall ran out of money, and were unable to recoup their losses by selling or letting their houses. Burlington, faced with the choice between abandoning the whole venture almost before it was begun, or intervening to support the builders financially, chose the second alternative, and advanced £37,000 between 1850 and 1855.[4] Eventually, all these early houses were auctioned at Brighton in 1859 but, as one long-lived local recalled: 'None but those who had to assist in starting the town can have any idea of the trouble, anxiety and serious losses sustained by them in doing so . . . Speculation too often spelt bankruptcy to the builders and serious losses to the tradesmen.'[5] To make matters worse, Devonshire, now burdened with the added and weighty responsibilities of the ducal estates from 1858, fell out with Berry, whom he sacked in 1859 and replaced with Henry Currey, a relative of his solicitor, and it was Currey who drew up his first development plan in 1859 (fig. 26).[6] At the same time, Devonshire quarrelled with Mrs Gilbert over the question of water supply for the new town. Still, by the end of the year, Currey's plan had been completed, a local board had been established, and gas and water companies set up.[7]

Fig. 27. Eastbourne sea front in 1866 (reproduced from the *Eastbourne Gazette*, 5 December 1866, by permission of the British Library).

By the early 1860s, then, it looked as if the corner had at last been turned. Population had increased from 3,105 in 1841 to 5,795 in 1861 (graph 4), and a local directory was able to report on 'the very rapid advance which Eastbourne has made in the last twenty years.' In 1862, 50 building agreements were negotiated, and two years later a new peak of 78 was attained. The *Eastbourne Gazette* noted 'the rapid strides which have been and are now being made in the improvement of our fashionable watering place. New buildings meet the eye on every side.'[8] 'Fields are turned into streets, squares and other buildings', it added in the following year.[9] Devonshire's diary was once more filled with confidence:

> A great deal has been done since I was last here. The sea wall is finished to the west end of Devonshire Place, and the walls and terraces connected with it are also completed and really look extremely well. Many houses are in progress, and sites for many more are disposed of. We have also a great number of applicants for others, and altogether the place seems likely to expand rapidly.[10]

The trustees of the Gilbert estate were of a similar opinion. Already, in 1858, they had obtained power to grant building leases for 99 years, and in 1862 their surveyor Nicholas Whitley drew up a plan for the development of the Upperton area, at a provisional cost of £3,817, on the grounds that

> The town of Eastbourne has largely increased of late years and is still increasing, and there is a great demand for land for building purposes in, and in the immediate vicinity of, such town. Parts of the Gilbert estate are so situated as to be admirably adapted for the extension and improvement of such town.[11]

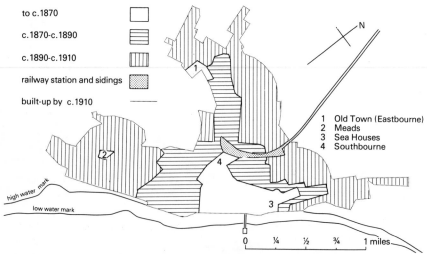

to c.1870	
c.1870-c.1890	
c.1890-c.1910	
railway station and sidings	
built-up by c.1910	

1 Old Town (Eastbourne)
2 Meads
3 Sea Houses
4 Southbourne

high water mark
low water mark

0   ¼   ½   ¾   1 miles

Fig. 28. Eastbourne: chronology of development, *c.*1850 – *c.*1910.

So another plan with roads and sewers and building plots was drawn up which, in conjunction with that of the Devonshires, effectively opened the whole of Eastbourne to speculative builders.

As in the 1850s, however, the confidence engendered during the first half of the decade was not borne out by events in the second. The combination of an inadequate water supply and no arterial drainage made the town especially vulnerable to an epidemic of scarlet fever which broke out late in 1863, resulting in 'great injury inflicted on our trade and lodging-house keepers'.[12] The local board tried to remedy matters by embarking on a new drainage scheme, but when it became more elaborate than they had anticipated and the contractor went bankrupt, they were unable to continue the work, so that only a timely intervention with financial support by Devonshire enabled the scheme to be completed.[13] Other undertakings were equally uncertain. Eastbourne College, founded in 1867 as a place of education for 'gentlemen', stagnated until 1870, when the foundation stone of the college buildings was finally laid. The Pier Company, established in 1863, was so divided by internal squabbles that by 1870 the pier itself was still only half completed. The Gas Company also went through troubled times, and the regatta and flower show collapsed completely. So, as graph 3 shows, did the number of building leases. 'Building has not advanced rapidly for the last year', recorded Devonshire in March 1866.[14] Yet, by 1871, the population had passed the 10,000 mark, and there were nearly 1,800 inhabited houses. Although contemporaries had no way of telling, the corner had very definitely been turned by the early 1870s.

2

The long and nationally uniform building boom of the late 1870s and early 1880s not only witnessed the creation of modern Edgbaston but, at Eastbourne, saw the development of a seaside resort on the basis of the infrastructure which had been established with such uncertainty during the previous cycle. Population mushroomed from 10,361 in 1871 to 34,278 20 years later, making Eastbourne the fastest-growing town in Sussex, surpassing all its rivals in size with the exception of Brighton (graph 4). The number of building agreements on the Devonshire estate rose from 583 to 1,500 over the same period, and contemporaries spoke of the 'gigantic strides', the 'methodical and extraordinarily rapid progress', which the town was making.[15] Guide books, the local press, and the seventh duke's diary present a unanimous record of progress and chorus of delight. 'A good many buildings are going on or will shortly begin', Devonshire observed in April 1873 at the beginning of the upturn. 'There seems every prospect of the place continuing to prosper', he added three years later. Thereafter, entries noting 'a good deal of building', 'a great many new houses', 'every sign of prosperity', 'the rapid increase of the town', and 'every thing here seems to go well', appear and reappear with almost monotonous regularity.[16] The local press, such as the *Gazette* in

1875, was even more unrestrained in its enthusiasm: 'Brilliant as has been the last ten years of Eastbourne's existence, its sun of success has only just dawned, and will rise higher and higher as years move on, bathing its enterprising inhabitants in floods of golden light.'[17] Although the prose was rarely this florid, the sentiments were invariably as excited. 'Cornfields and barns have given place to substantial shops and dwelling houses, almost from one end of the parish to the other', noted one authority in 1883. 'Looking at the immense number of new houses, it is surprising that there are so few void of tenants', observed another.[18]

On all sides, the town expanded (fig. 28). In 1870, Nicholas Whitley drew up the first fully comprehensive development plan for the Gilberts' land. A decade later, roads were laid out in Hartfield Square and in the area known as Upperton, which 'until so recently open country has now become a well-tenanted suburb', full of high-class terraces and squares.[19] To the north-east of the pier, the local board spent £50,000 between 1880 and 1884 on the construction of the Royal Parade, behind which a large but well-planned artisan quarter began to take shape. To the west of the Wish Tower, the Duke financed the extension of the parades towards Holywell – 'a work of considerable magnitude' – as well as the making of scenic roads to Beachy Head.[20] As the *Gazette* noted in 1884: 'The west of the town is increasing with marvellous rapidity, and the magnificent series of terraces reaching to Holywell furnishes a choice of promenades unrivalled for beauty and extent in England.[21] In 1872, Henry Currey drew up a plan for the duke which envisaged the development of the west end of the town, sheltered by the new parades, as the 'Belgravia' of Eastbourne, with wide, tree-lined streets and large villas set in extensive grounds.[22] By the end of the 1880s, great progress had been made: from the sea front to the walls of Crompton Place itself, gracious villas were now to be found.

Again, and with more immediate confidence and success, the amenities were improved. The 1870s saw the establishment of Eastbourne's most famous hotels – the Grand, the Queen's and the Cavendish – as well as the foundation of the Devonshire Club in 1872 for the town's most important residents and visitors. In 1873, the Devonshire Parks and Baths Company was set up to provide high-class recreation on a grand scale. The baths and floral hall were opened in the following year, concerts were begun in the Pavilion in 1876, and a theatre was built in 1884. Early in 1877, the pier was partly destroyed in a storm of unprecedented ferocity, but it was successfully rebuilt on a more lavish scale in time for the following season. The flower show and the regatta were both resuscitated in 1874; the waterworks was enlarged in 1881; electric light was provided on the sea front in the following year; and the drainage system was extended in 1881–4.[23] Finally, in 1883, the town was incorporated, and the duke's agent became, fittingly, the first mayor. Three years later, a grand and splendid town hall was opened.[24] In 1884, agitation was begun to obtain direct parliamentary representation:

There are scores of boroughs of far less importance than Eastbourne which enjoy the right of selecting their special representative in Parliament, and it seems cruel that we should still be left out in the cold. When the question comes forward for consideration, we trust the claims of Eastbourne will not be forgotten.[25]

In fact, they were; but even so, the civic aggrandizement of the early 1880s was a fitting climax to two decades of uninterrupted progress and prosperity.

Fig. 29. Eastbourne town hall, *c*.1910 (by courtesy of Eastbourne Public Library).

By the late 1880s, the orgy of building had spent itself. Indeed, the years 1886–8 were among the worst of the century, for the slump was longer and more damaging than that of the early 1870s had been. As the seventh duke noted in one of his last diary entries on the town: 'there is certainly much less prosperity than there was until recently. The place has for the present been rather overbuilt.'[26] Indeed, as the *Gazette* had noted one year before, this was something of an understatement:

The fact must be faced that Eastbourne has been very much overbuilt . . . It is no secret . . . that a very large number of houses are unoccupied . . . about eight hundred: eight hundred houses in a borough of thirty thousand inhabitants! And it must be remembered that since last October comparatively little building has been carried on. It was in the years 1880–4 that the activity occurred. Then fortunate builders turned property into cash very rapidly. Now many builders are in liquidation and those who own houses find them a drag on the market.[27]

And this was no exaggeration. Ruben Climpson, one of the foremost builders in the town, went bankrupt in 1888 with debts of £20,000, and he was only the most spectacular example. James Peerless, who was an even larger contractor, and employed more labour than any other business in the town, died in the same year. 'We hear', noted the *Gazette*, 'of builders one after another becoming bankrupt, of others who are expected to call their creditors together any day, and of others who cannot sell their property.'[28] Unemployment soared as a result with 'large numbers' of 'carpenters, bricklayers, labourers, masons and others' out of work. Relief Committees were set up by the mayor and the local churches, but they only succeeded in alleviating some of the symptoms, rather than the cause, of distress.[29] And the queen's Golden Jubilee of 1887 only served to shorten further a season which had never really taken off to begin with:

> Large numbers of honest, able-bodied men seek in vain week after week for work out of town. As a consequence our industrial population is being gradually decreased by removals, and scores of empty houses tell the sad tale of domestic sufferings and want of means.[30]

To make matters worse, this savage cyclical downturn coincided with a crisis in the town's civic and municipal affairs. In 1891 the seventh duke of Devonshire died, followed by George Ambrose Wallis, his agent and first mayor, four years later, and the deaths of the town's two founding fathers severed the most important links with Eastbourne's prosperous and Devonshire-dominated past. At the same time, excursionists, previously a nagging rather than significant problem, came increasingly to threaten its much-cherished seclusion and quietude, and in 1891 there was a protracted crisis when the council tried – unsuccessfully – to restrain the Salvation Army from playing music on Sunday afternoons.[31] Finally, in the middle of the decade, there was a severe public clash between the council – emancipated from the control of George Wallis and eager to indulge in schemes of municipal aggrandizement to proclaim its newly-won autonomy – and the eighth duke of Devonshire, proprietor of the profitable and important waterworks company. Dissatisfied with the supply, the town council promoted a bill in Parliament to buy the company out. Devonshire resisted, and promoted his own rival bill to extend the size and scope of his company.[32] In this he succeeded, but for the second time in only five years, conflict and crisis in Eastbourne was national news.

Not surprisingly, the local papers constantly urged the duke, the Gilberts and the council to take steps to provide more work. In September 1886, in an article entitled 'A Programme of Improvements', the *Gazette* advocated the provision of a steamboat service, an art gallery and a public library, as well as an improvement to the facilities on the pier. Two months later, it added a harbour and a yachting marina to its list of suggestions.[33] In response to such pressure, some action was indeed forthcoming. The council undertook road improvements at Willingdon, and the Queen's Hotel was extended. But, although the council was constantly urged to do more, it was not until the slack in housing had been taken up, and the two landowners began to consider further schemes of expansion, that conditions really began to improve. In 1886, the seventh duke sanctioned the making of a zig-zag road from Cliff Road to the summit of Beachy Head, to be called Duke's Drive, which served to give employment to a large number of those at present unemployed.[34] Four years later, 'considerable activity' was reported in 'road making and paving at Meads', and at the same time, work was begun on the development of the Redoubt Estate. 'Everything seems going on satisfactorily', recorded the duke, 'and a good many buildings have made their appearance since I was here last year.' Finally, in 1893, the Gilberts began to open up 'an extensive tract of building land' to the north of St Anne's Well and Carew Road.[35]

3

On the basis of this extensive preparation, the next upswing, when it occurred, was spectacular (graph 3, fig. 28). Not for Eastbourne a generation of stagnation while other resorts boomed. Indeed, as early as 1890, George Wallis reported that 'there are not now many private houses to let and', he wrote to a speculative builder, 'I believe that if you were to cover the land with suitable buildings, they would soon be taken up.'[36] In this he was quite correct for, as a local paper noted five years later, 'buildings are occupied almost before they are completed'. The Devonshires opened up the Redoubt Estate in the east, where there was 'an enormous growth of the population',[37] and further extended their developments towards Beachy Head, in the direction of Buxton, Chesterfield and Staveley Roads. The Gilberts were equally active, and the area around Upperton Road, Victoria Drive, Prideaux Road and Green Street was soon covered with houses, all of which found eager buyers. In 1900 the *Chronicle* noted enthusiastically the 'largely increased accommodation resulting from the prodigious activities of speculative builders'.[38] And, for once, this self-congratulatory hyperbole was merited: the 1891 census recorded 5,064 houses; by 1907 there were 8,617. In the same period, population rose from 34,278 to 51,554. On the Compton Estate alone, the number of building agreements grew from 1,500 in 1891 to 2,513 20 years later (graph 4).

The expansion of amenities kept pace with this burgeoning growth. The train service was improved, so that through expresses ran to Eastbourne from the Midlands and the North. The facilities of Devonshire Park were extended, and a full-time orchestra was established in answer to the competition from Bournemouth and Brighton. Pleasure gardens were laid out on the Redoubt Estate, and a Technical Institute was opened in 1907. Between 1899 and 1901,

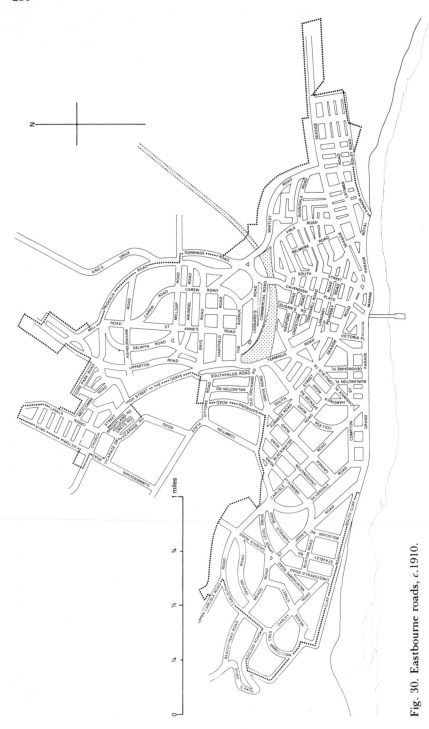

Fig. 30. Eastbourne roads, c.1910.

the council acquired Hampden Park near Willingdon, and built a new, triumphal road to link it with the town. In 1903, a municipal bus service was begun, the first of its kind in the country.[39] In 1897, at the conclusion to the wrangle over the water supply, a new waterworks was opened at Friston, and in 1909 the local gas company extended its powers to Hailsham. The powers of the council were augmented and, in 1911, Eastbourne became a county borough.[40] As a friend of the eighth duke, Edward VII patronized the town both before and after he became king, and the ninth duke and George V were also good friends, with results equally beneficial to the town. Most important of all, the agreement of the eighth duke to serve as mayor in 1897, and his successor's decision to follow suit in 1909, set the final seal of success and respectability on the town. 'The Empress of Watering Places' had secured as its first citizen one of the Crown's greatest subjects, a distinction which no other seaside resort could claim.

4

So, despite its uncertain and belated start, Eastbourne was by 1914 among the largest, most exclusive and most successful holiday resorts in the country – home of a duke and host to his king. Of course, it could rival neither the raffish cosmopolitanism nor the size of Brighton, its near neighbour. By 1911, 'old ocean's bauble' could boast a population in excess of 150,000; but in second place, all with populations of between 50,000 and 60,000, came Blackpool, Scarborough, Southport, Bournemouth and Eastbourne, with Hastings, Torquay, Folkestone and the Welsh and East Anglian resorts all a long way behind. So, in terms of its size, its status and its facilities, Eastbourne was in the very front rank of holiday resorts by the turn of the twentieth century and, when compared with the Devonshires' other forays into urban development, the results were equally outstanding. The new town once projected for Ireland had never even been begun. Buxton, despite its elegant late-eighteenth-century crescent, had never rivalled Bath, and never revived spectacularly in the nineteenth century, however much money the seventh duke lavished on it. Barrow, having expanded prodigiously in the 1860s and early 1870s, collapsed almost as suddenly thereafter. By contrast, and even allowing for the cyclical ups and downs, Eastbourne's growth was cumulative and impressive. In 1875, before its greatest phases of expansion had begun, one local paper had made this prediction:

Eastbourne, important, strong and powerful as she may appear to be, is really but in the infancy of a maturity the degree of vigour of which it is almost impossible to conceive, but assuredly which will one day place her – if not at the head of English watering places – at least in the position to hold her own against the most powerful rival. If within the last ten years

Fig. 31. The development of the Western Parades: A. The early 1870s, before building had begun (by courtesy of Eastbourne Public Library). B. The same view *c*.1910 (by courtesy of Eastbourne Public Library).

she has more than doubled her population, what may now be expected in a decade or two more? How strange . . . all these changes . . . must seem to the student of history.[41]

A copy of this article was sent by the local agent to the seventh duke at Chatsworth. By the time of his death, let alone that of his successor, this prophecy had been triumphantly vindicated: Eastbourne could indeed 'hold her own against the most powerful rival'. But the extent and nature of these changes was more strange than any contemporary – to say nothing of 'the student of history' – would have imagined.

17 The superintendence of development, 1849–1914

The 'unity of management and control' to which George Edwards had drawn attention when explaining the coherent manner in which development had occurred at Edgbaston was even more in evidence at Eastbourne. For, although the Devonshires did not own as much of Eastbourne as the Calthorpes did of Edgbaston, their uniquely powerful role in the creation of amenities, and their near-monopoly of the sea front, compared with the relative insignificance of the Gilberts' holdings and resources, ensured that the initiative in matters of development lay firmly with them. Where the Devonshires led, both in decision-making and planning, the Gilberts meekly followed; and, while it was their extensive investment in amenities which gave the Devonshires their leverage over the affairs of the town, it was the manner in which they supervised development, and then preserved and maintained standards, which was the most immediately visible monument to their power and influence.

1

In the first place, the overall planning of their estate was careful and coherent, as noteworthy for the exclusion of industry as it was for the encouragement of a rural atmosphere and a strict and careful policy of zoning. As at Edgbaston, the most important strand of their policy was keeping industry out – a policy which the Devonshires enforced with as much vigour as the Calthorpes, but with the added advantage that there was no big city adjacent which had to be held at bay. Since they were starting a new town from nothing, the Devonshires were in a position to keep out any industry other than that which they judged appropriate for the making and servicing of a high-class holiday resort, such as building, laundries and expensive shops. Telephone lines were put underground, and applications for the construction of unsightly advertising hoardings were turned down.[1] In 1907 a commercial pier was projected on the Crumbles, to the north-east of the town. 'It will be necessary', observed the eighth duke's agent, 'to offer the strongest opposition', so as to keep out the pier's 'unavoidable adjuncts – stacks of coal and timber, warehouses and merchandise in general.' So the scheme was opposed and subsequently abandoned.[2] Indeed, this description of Eastbourne in 1863 held good for the whole of the century:

Eastbourne may claim a purer atmosphere than generally falls to the share of larger towns, on account of the almost total absence of manufacturing operations, absolutely free from noxious vapours which impregnate the atmosphere of all larger towns, to an extent proportionate to the nature and multiplicity of their products.[3]

If the exclusion of heavy industry was the negative aspect of the Devonshires' policy, the creation of a rural atmosphere represented the positive side. The roads made by the Compton estate, as well as being wide, sewered and laid far apart, were planted with trees before any building was allowed, so as to 'keep up the rural and ornamental aspects in the streets'.[4] For this inimitable umbrella of green, Eastbourne became famous. 'The streets are boulevards', noted one guide book in 1886, 'the highways wooded avenues . . . almost as green and leafy as country lanes.' 'The principal streets are skirted with magnificent trees', observed another four years later, 'which add immeasurably to the charm of the place.' Brochure after brochure extolled the 'boulevard-like character of Eastbourne's streets' and the 'prodigious use made of trees'.[5] Indeed, in both the Devonshires' and Gilberts' leases, the trees in any garden or meadow were specifically protected: pruning and felling could only be carried out with the consent of the estate office. Thus fostered, the vegetation by 1913 had become so lush that some locals even began to fear 'the injury done to the health and brightness of the town by the overflowing foliage in our roads'![6]

These provisions, so similar to those adopted by the Calthorpes at Edgbaston, imply that the Devonshires at Eastbourne entertained initial expectations as exclusive and exalted as John Harris and the third lord Calthorpe had done in the early 1810s and, although there is no systematic statement of the Earl of Burlington's original intentions comparable to Harris's 'Observations for Lord Calthorpe's Correction', the early policy pursued would certainly seem to confirm this. Henry Currey's plan of 1859, the layout of Meads and the West End from 1871, and also schemes drawn up by Whitley for the Gilberts in the same decade, were all conspicuous for their lack of working-class accommodation. Apart from a few houses costing £300 or thereabouts constructed in the region of Pevensey Road in the 1860s, the working classes were all but ignored. The first great building boom of the late 1870s and early 1880s was almost entirely confined to the construction of large and spacious houses, so much so as to excite comment in the local press:

No houses of moderate rent are built – at least, not in the proportion to the size and progress of the place . . . I see long streets, noble frontages, ample squares and beautiful terraces, all on a grand scale, equal to that of any great and wealthy city . . . But nowhere do I see comfortable houses for people of moderate means . . . a certain class of house and of inhabitant have been completely forgotten. There are in fact scarcely any comfortable houses suitable to ratepayers of moderate income . . . At present building is entirely in the shape of palaces and villas, or rows of five-storeyed dwellings, expressly intended for visitors of the higher class.[7]

Indeed, agitation for 'small houses, at a cheap rental, for the working man' continued well into the late 1880s.[8] Only with the belated construction of the eastern sea wall (over a decade after the western parades), and the opening up of the Redoubt Estate in 1890, was the need met. The second great building boom, at the turn of the century, included many more small houses than had its predecessor.

Accordingly, by 1914 the distribution of houses on the Devonshires' Eastbourne estate was as shown in table 26.

Table 26. Value of houses built on Eastbourne estate, 1851–1914

Value of house (£)	No. of leases granted	%	No. of houses authorized	%
1,500+	565	22.99	601	18.40
1,000–1,499	218	8.89	251	7.69
500–999	290	11.80	362	11.09
0–499	1,384	56.32	2,059	62.82
Total	2,457	100.00	3,273	100.00

Source: CEO MS., Agreement Books, 0–XIII.
Note: The total for the number of leases granted does not agree with the figure given on p. 249, since that refers to *all* building leases, whereas this table is confined to houses, and excludes workshops, etc.

As at Edgbaston, the overwhelming preponderance of working-class and artisan housing is once more apparent – in this case, indeed, an even greater proportion. Again, the high social tone and reputation of the building estate was belied by the breadth of the social spectrum of tenants. In both cases, the high reputation of the developments represented a triumph for the status of the few over the condition of the many. Unlike Edgbaston, however, the social structure revealed in this table is not so much a pyramid but an hour-glass – albeit one with a larger lower section. Instead of tapering neatly the higher up the social scale it went, the Eastbourne estate contained many of the urban rich as well as the urban workers, but fewer of those middle-middle-class people who were so conspicuous at Edgbaston. Relatively speaking, there were far more great suburban houses at Eastbourne, but fewer of the more humble middle-class abodes.

Although, therefore, the Devonshires were free of the major problem which beset the Calthorpes in later years – that of trying to keep the ever-expanding and adjacent town at bay – they too were obliged to accommodate a broad social spectrum beneath their umbrella of green: broader, indeed, than they had originally intended, and broader than that at Edgbaston. In part, this was because the rich of Eastbourne were richer and lived more ostentatiously than the rich of Birmingham; but it was also because, in creating an entire new town, the Devonshires were obliged to accept the economic and structural logic of this, and recognize that accommodation must be provided for those members of the working class who initially built the town and thereafter serviced it. While Edgbaston could be parasitic on Birmingham for many of its services, Eastbourne had to provide them for itself. Builders, carpenters, plumbers, glaziers and labourers were necessary to put up the houses and make the roads and sea walls, just as laundries, shops and entertainments were vital to the successful functioning of a leisure town 70 miles from London. So, while Eastbourne was spared the pressures of an adjacent industrial town, the corollary of this was that it had to provide facilities for itself which the Calthorpes at Edgbaston did not need to concern themselves with. Once more, initially exclusive preferences had to be modified in the face of the realities of economic circumstance. As a result, at Eastbourne there was more to zone and it had to be done more carefully (fig. 32). There was less need to resist pressure from without, but greater need to reconcile diversity within. The key to this policy was, as the *Gazette* noted as early as 1868, 'the enforcement of buildings of a class suited to each locality'.[9] When, for example, a would-be shopkeeper asked permission of the Devonshire estate to take a plot of land in Longstone Road, he was told firmly that 'permission cannot be given to build a shop in this road'.[10] For, owning as they did the majority of the coastline and much of the back land, the Devonshires – once they had recognized the need to provide extensive working-class accommodation – were able to plan with almost unlimited authority. Here is George Wallis's description of planning strategy as it had been evolved by 1888:

> Although our building area is represented at the present time by six hundred acres, these . . . have not been laid out without a very careful

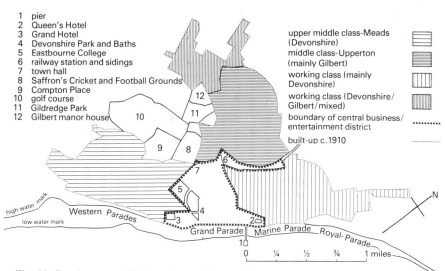

Fig. 32. Eastbourne, *c.*1910: zoning and amenities.

examination of the adjoining land, so as to develop it in connection with the present building estate, so that there would be the extension of good, large houses in one direction, and there would be the extension of smaller houses in another direction; and they are not mixed up. We have what we call our artisan town; and we have our high-class villa town; and we have our terrace houses; and they are all quite separate.[11]

A guide book of 1919 made exactly the same distinctions between the central commercial area, the working-class houses to the north-east, and the high-class, residential suburbs to the south-west.[12] Here, evolved with a completeness rivalled only by Folkestone, is the classic, ideal form of nineteenth-century resort zoning.[13]

Indeed, so perfect was it that it deserves elaboration. To the south-west, ascending the wooded, undulating slopes towards Beachy Head, and basking in the reflected glory of proximity to Compton Place, were to be found those opulent houses, costing between two and ten thousand pounds, which belonged to Eastbourne's wealthiest inhabitants – those rentiers, retired professionals and local big businessmen who made up the town's elite. The cliffs and western parades protected them from the beach, and the grounds of Eastbourne College and the Parks and Baths Company effectively insulated them from the noise and bustle of the central entertainments area. That in its turn was located between the railway station and the shore, and included the promenades, the bandstand, the pier, hotels and winter gardens. Finally, beyond the pier, on relatively low-lying ground, were located those few service industries – laundries, builders' yards and so on – and the artisan quarter itself, which consisted of houses of less than £500, built by speculative builders. Here was to be found a considerable working-class population of servants, builders, labourers and artisans. Yet, as contemporaries noted, these communities were 'all quite separate'. The central entertainment area was rigidly defined. Its western extremity, the Grand Hotel, marked the transition to high-class residential housing. And at the eastern end, the massive Queen's Hotel served to block any possible encroachment of working-class housing. (For their part, the Gilberts developed their land to the west of the station as a high-class villa town and, later in the century, both the Gilberts and the Devonshires provided further space for working-class housing at the western extremity of the town towards Willingdon.)

Of course, in planning their estate in this manner, the Devonshires assisted nature rather than overturned it. Their power to zone was, statutorily, enormous because they owned so much land; but their ability to zone was of necessity constrained by the topography of their estate. Just as it seems likely that Edgbaston would have attracted middle-class residents regardless of the landownership pattern because of its advantages of location and topography, so it seems probable that Eastbourne might have evolved according to a similar spatial pattern regardless of ownership. The zoning might have been

Fig. 33. Eastbourne roads: A. Blackwater Road, *c.*1890: a typical 'west end' thoroughfare (by courtesy of Eastbourne Public Library)
B. Cavendish Place, *c.*1910: part of the central entertainments district, with its shops, hotels and bars (by courtesy of Eastbourne Public Library).

less distinct and less coherent, but the south-west – undulating, elevated and well wooded – would surely have attracted high-class housing; the central area – flat and adjacent to the beach – must have become the location of entertainments, and the east end – low, marshy and liable to flooding – would inevitably have attracted the working classes and whatever industry there was. As the *Gazette* noted in 1883:

> It is a singular fact that in many towns including watering places, the east end is found to obtain the opposite to an aristocratic character. No doubt the physical conformation has much to do with the fact, and Eastbourne is no exception to the rule, simply because the West End is more umbrageous and picturesque than the East.[14]

In short, it was the combination of topography and unified ownership which together were responsible for the coherent and segregated planning of Eastbourne, in which the principles of Victorian seaside planning reached their highest level of perfection.

2

In many ways the successful transference of these schemes from plans in the estate office to the land itself was all the more remarkable since Eastbourne was – to a much greater extent than Edgbaston – the creation of the speculative builder (see table 27).

Table 27. Relative importance of different types of builder, 1851–1914
(percentages in brackets)

Total no. of leases taken by builders	No. of lessees	Total no. of leases taken	No. of houses to be built by lessee	Money to be spent by lessee
50+	8	603	782	£624,855
	(2.19)	(24.55)	(23.9)	(26.35)
10–49	56	1,119	1,469	£915,160
	(15.34)	(45.54)	(44.9)	(38.57)
3–9	99	480	622	£486,150
	(27.13)	(19.54)	(19.0)	(20.49)
1–2	202	255	400	£346,200
	(55.34)	(10.37)	(12.2)	(14.59)
Total	365	2,457	3,273	£2,372,365
	(100.00)	(100.00)	(100.00)	(100.00)

Source: CEO MS., Agreement Books, 0–XIII.

Whereas at Edgbaston by 1914, some 20 per cent of the houses had been built by speculative builders taking ten leases or more, at Eastbourne, by that time, almost 70 per cent of the houses had been so constructed. While the area around Carlisle Road was opened up 'to people who desire to build houses for their own occupation' – those very similar to many Calthorpe tenants – in the main, Eastbourne was the creation of speculative builders.[15]

Nor should this come as any surprise. At Edgbaston, the resident population moved in from elsewhere in Birmingham, acquired a plot of land, found their own local builder, and had one or two houses constructed, with the intention of taking up residence as soon as possible. Edgbaston was parasitic on Birmingham for builders and tenants as much as for most other services. Yet, because Eastbourne was created out of nothing, the houses – like other amenities – had to be built ahead of demand. Would-be inhabitants had to be attracted by the sight of completed houses, rather than left to make their own arrangements as regards construction. Hence the preponderance both of speculative builders in general, and of eight firms in particular, who operated on a scale altogether beyond the most important contractors in Edgbaston. Table 28 gives the details of their operations.

Table 28. Analysis of eight speculative builders operating at Eastbourne, 1851–1914

Contractor	No. of leases taken	No. of houses authorized	Money to be spent £	Period in which leases taken
Cornwell	52	75	40,005	1875–1906
Harding	56	57	83,000	1864–90
Miller	93	99	32,300	1899–1914
Peerless	105	170	163,550	1851–84
Stevens	93	129	126,800	1884–1911
Vine	84	84	37,450	1893–1911
Wallis & Wallis	50	80	94,900	1868–1913
Wood	70	88	46,850	1875–1903
Total	603	782	624,855	

Source: CEO MS., Agreement Books, 0–XIII.

As well as operating on a greater scale and being active over a longer period of time, these major contractors built houses across a broader social spectrum (table 29) than did their opposite numbers at Edgbaston. Some contractors, like Cornwall, Miller, Vine and Wood, restricted their activity almost entirely to the bottom end of the scale. Others, like Harding, specialized almost exclusively at the top end. And the rest – Peerless, Stevens and Wallis & Wallis – were active at both ends of the spectrum. Indeed, the profile of houses constructed by these contractors appropriately resembles the overall picture: an hour-glass with a larger lower section. Among the great builders as among the lesser, it was houses for the very rich or the poor which were attractive. But dwellings in the £1,000–1,499 bracket – which were so prevalent at Edgbaston – were decidedly unpopular.

Table 29. Analysis of houses constructed by eight speculative builders, 1851–1914

| Contractor | Cost of house | | | | |
	£0–499	£500–999	£1,000–1,499	£1,500+	Total
Cornwell	61	5	0	9	75
Harding	4	7	7	39	57
Miller	95	4	0	0	99
Peerless	77	27	15	51	170
Stevens	20	62	17	30	129
Vine	71	10	3	0	84
Wallis & Wallis	30	5	5	40	80
Wood	73	2	5	8	88
Total	431	122	52	177	782

Source: CEO MS., Agreement Books, 0–XIII.

Since so many houses, both for the rich – whom the Devonshires wanted to attract – and the working class – whom they were forced also to accept – were built for speculation in the first instance, it was more than ever necessary to superintend their construction diligently. For no plan, however carefully evolved, could be implemented successfully if the houses were jerry-built. Indeed, one stage before this, it was vital to ensure that the sea walls and roads were well constructed. George Ambrose Wallis, the local agent to the duke from 1864–95, ceaselessly pursued builders, and bombarded them with letters, to make sure they did the job properly, to use the correct cement when constructing the sea wall, to lay drains of better quality, and so on. 'I am somewhat astonished to see. . . '; 'I must ask you for the future to take more care . . .'; 'Please press on . . .'; 'I must order you to stop this at once . . .'; 'I hope you will give the matter your attention . . .'; 'I shall be obliged by . . .': these were the phrases and commands which flowed from his pen as he exhorted, cajoled and bullied the building contractors into action.[16] But the results were worthwhile. The fame of Eastbourne's roads derived not just from the care with which they were planned, but the thoroughness with which they were made.

This applied equally to the construction and alteration of houses. 'It is contrary to the regulations of the estate for houses to be commenced before the plans are approved', Wallis wrote to one unfortunate building tenant who had had the mistaken temerity to begin building before he had secured the necessary consent.[17] And, as at Edgbaston, the plans were carefully vetted, and alterations were frequently recommended. In the same way, tenants could not 'alter or add to any house without the consent in writing of the duke or his agent', and this held good whoever the applicant might be.[18] Tenants wanting to add a bedroom or a billiard room, the local croquet club seeking to add a lavatory to the club house, the Grand Hotel wishing to erect a garage: all such requests were carefully vetted and examined, and approval was by no means automatic. Here, for example, is a letter from the files of 1892:

> The building you propose to erect at Meads for a Fire Station is much more formidable than I was led to suppose. The plan drawn blocks the view from the farmhouse, and is much in advance of the Building Estate building line. I must ask you therefore to be good enough to very considerably modify the plan.[19]

If the tenant was foolish enough to modify his plans after they had been approved by the estate office, the rebuke was even more damning:

> I hereby give you notice to stop all buildings now in the course of erection in the garden at the rear of your house in the Terminus Road, the same not being in accordance with the plans approved.[20]

Wallis missed nothing, and the high standards of constructional excellence manifested by the streets, the sea walls and the houses of Eastbourne owed much to his untiring vigilance. While Eastbourne was in a very real sense the creation of a few, large-scale speculative builders, it was almost entirely free from the difficulties usually associated with them. Wallis was neither exaggerating nor being conceited when, in 1888, he claimed that 'the place is remarkably free from jerry-building' – a verdict in striking contrast to that of the town clerk of Southport, who admitted that even his own house was jerry-built.[21] Later observers, like this one of 1904, took the same view:

> The speculative builder has had a wise, restraining hand laid upon him, and there are no purlieus, no slums to contend with . . . The houses of our new Eastbourne are not of a papier mâché type, set up quickly by the strong to be sold to the weak . . . It is . . . gratifying to find that the speculative builder wears a mask, and whatever is built is built on well considered plans, with a little lime in the mortar.[22]

So, although the manner in which the houses were constructed was very different, the end product was very like suburban Edgbaston.

In addition – again, like Edgbaston – the exclusion of industry and the vigilant superintendence of development was accompanied by stringent covenants restricting the uses to which property could be put. Indeed, by the end of the nineteenth century, the restrictions were even more strict than those contained in the Calthorpes leases':

> And will not use the said premises, or any part thereof, as a public house,

or beershop, or for carrying on any trade or business whatsoever nor otherwise than as a private dwelling house, without the consent in writing of the Duke of Devonshire . . . And will not do or permit to be done upon the premises any act or thing whatsoever which may be or become a nuisance, annoyance or injury to any land of the duke . . . or any act or anything which may tend to deteriorate the value of such land.[23]

The terms in the Gilberts' leases were almost identical, and in both cases the general ban on industry was followed by an explicit enumeration of trades thought to be particularly offensive.[24] Of course, in the central entertainments area and in the working-class district, it was necessary to allow those trades vital to the successful functioning of a high-class resort: schools, hotels, laundries, builders' yards, and so on; but, as at Edgbaston, the covenants were specifically for one type of industry or trade, and no other. Likewise, when land was given for a church, or to the council (as in the case of the parades), the restrictive covenants were inserted in the conveyance.[25]

As at Edgbaston, these covenants were vigorously enforced. Normally, this took the form of a sharply-worded reminder: that business should not be carried on; that washing should not be hung out on Sundays; that a house needed painting or a garden fence wanted attention; or that a tree should not be pruned by the tenants. Indeed, the managers of the estate were anxious 'to avoid litigation as far as possible'.[26] It was expensive; it was time-consuming; there was the possibility of defeat; and the publicity, whoever won, would not be good. But in the last resort, they were prepared to call in the letter of the law against the most recalcitrant tenants – as in 1899, when they obtained a court injunction to prevent Mr Brookshaw from using his premises as a fish-shop, and in 1900 when Mr Vincent tried to convert his house into a blacksmith's forge.[27] All this the Calthorpes' agents would have recognized and envied: recognized because the tenets of estate policy were so similar to their own, and envied because the lack of pressure from a neighbouring, industrial town meant that their chances of success were that much the greater.

But the converse also applied. If the Calthorpes had to cope with the pressure of decay on the periphery, they were at least free from problems of how to re-zone within their estate. Industry was kept out, and that was that; but at Eastbourne, as the new community, self-contained and self-sufficient as it was, expanded, it became necessary to allow for the conversion of premises from one user to another. As the central entertainments area grew, for instance, permission was granted to convert houses into shops or hotels. Terminus Road, by the end of the century the main shopping street, had begun as a high-class residential area, and many of the hotels on the front, like the Burlington and the Cavendish, had started life as expensive villas or terrace houses.[28] In the same way, as Eastbourne became a centre of education, some of the large villas in Meads were converted to boarding houses for the college, or into private preparatory schools.[29] Such changes were only allowed after scrupulous investigations had been made. The consent of the neighbours to the proposed change had to be obtained before a licence authorizing the change of user was granted, and it was only for the particular tenant, not for the building.[30] So, when the tenant left, the building reverted to its former use, or a new licence was granted.

One example will illustrate this. In 1899, Mrs Browne, who ran a boarding school in the west part of the town, tried to secure from the eighth duke a licence for the building, having already obtained a personal one. To this the duke's advisers were strongly opposed. 'It has been, and rightly so', one of them argued, 'the rule of the estate that school licences are granted to a certain person to use certain premises for educational purposes, and it does not allow that the premises only are licensed.'[31] The danger would be that such a step would have momentous consequences:

In granting Mrs Browne's request, the estate would be creating a most undesirable precedent which I am most anxious to avoid. The fact of her being granted an unlimited licence would soon become known amongst the confraternity, and would in my opinion lead to endless trouble.[32]

The refusal to grant more than a personal licence was one of the 'clearly defined rules . . . laid down by the estate, the outcome of long experience and necessity' and, in this particular case, despite constant pressure from Mrs Browne, the estate refused to budge.

Of course, as at Edgbaston, matters were made easier because the estate had the majority of the tenants on its side. At the seaside even more than in suburbia, the middle classes of the nineteenth century were determined to enjoy privacy and quietude. Thus, as at Edgbaston, the enforcement of covenants was not so much an enterprise undertaken on the initiative of the estate office, but very often was in response to complaints by tenants. Time and again, the estate office received complaints and petitions, concerning a neighbour hanging out washing on Sunday, a house nearby being used as a nursing home, the need to improve the quality of a road, or the fear – Heaven forbid! – that lower-class houses would be constructed nearby.[33] On such occasions, those who complained predicted disaster for the estate unless steps were taken, and feared that the value of their own property would be depreciated – a fear which haunted insecure middle-class homeowners throughout the nineteenth century. It was the realization of such rampant middle-class exclusiveness, as much as of the restrictive policies of the landlord, which caused one observer to make this analysis of the town in 1904:

The general character of Eastbourne is such that nothing in the shape of a menace can arise without raising immediate and loud complaints, and matters which in many places are accepted as necessary evils, arising out of trade processes or other cause, would not be tolerated in Eastbourne.[34]

3

The combined effect of this careful planning, supervision and control was that, once the crisis of 1867 had been surmounted, Eastbourne rapidly became one of the healthiest towns in England. Even as early as 1863, the death rate had been only 17 per 1,000, compared with 22 per 1,000 at Brighton,[35] and by the 1880s, the town was congratulating itself on enjoying 'the lowest death rate in the United Kingdom'[36] – a piece of self-congratulatory rhetoric for which there was, for once, statistical verification (table 30).

Table 30. Death rate (per thousand) in selected English resorts

Resort	1899	1904
Eastbourne	10.8	10.2
Hastings	14.5	13.2
Southport	16.1	14.7
Bath	18.2	15.4
Great Yarmouth	18.7	17.5
Brighton	19.0	16.6
Scarborough	19.3	14.8

Source: *Eastbourne Gazette*, 11 April 1900, 3 May 1905.

Compared with the great provincial towns, the figures were even more impressive. In 1899, the death rate of 33 great towns averaged 20.2 per thousand, and four years later, the figures for Liverpool, Manchester and Birmingham were 22.6, 21.3 and 19.9 respectively.

Nor were the reasons far to seek: 'the entire absence of manufactories, and the consequent freedom from smoke nuisance, the great width of almost every public thoroughfare, which permits the free fresh air to blow "where it listeth", and the luxuriant foliage which everywhere abounds'.[37] And this, contemporaries had no doubt, in its turn resulted from the control which the Devonshires themselves had exercised. Power, wielded by one authority in a responsible manner, produced wide, tree-lined roads and well-built houses, which in their turn made for a healthy environment. To contemporaries, at least, the causal connection was as simple as that:

> Thou has no over crowded dwelling places,
> Where, vainly, health may seek for open spaces;
> No builders' brick and mortar speculation.
> But, builded by elaborate cogitation
> The will and working of one master mind
> Guided by wisdom and a taste refined.[38]

Or, as the *Saturday Review* put it, more prosaically: 'It is certain that, had the works been undertaken piecemeal by small local proprietors and speculators with conflicting interests, there would have been a decided increase in the death rate.'[39] However, as a result of the control exercised by the Devonshires, Eastbourne was able to experience a massive rise in population and a spectacular fall in the death rate simultaneously. By 1890, it did indeed seem to be 'a resort capable of any amount of expansion without degenerating.'[40]

4

Therefore, unlike Edgbaston, Eastbourne experienced no decline in the years before the First World War. It expanded spectacularly in both of the two great national, late nineteenth-century building booms, so that the depressed and worried tone which characterized correspondence at the Edgbaston Estate Office from the 1880s was entirely absent. Bexhill and Folkestone might aspire to rival its pre-eminence during those long, hot Edwardian summers; but their chances of success were limited. Indeed, in terms of its growth and its management, the superintendence of Eastbourne's development was remarkably trouble-free. Once it was clear that it would 'go' as a resort, and that the Gilberts' development schemes would be of a similar standard, the Devonshires were happily emancipated from the two greatest fears which beset aristocratic developers of urban estates: that no-one would take the houses once built, and that decay would creep in from neighbouring lower-class areas. From both of these threats Eastbourne was exempt by the last decades of the nineteenth century. For all its large working- and lower-middle-class population, it was as 'The Empress of Watering Places' that it was known and established in the popular imagination.

18 The provision of amenities, 1849–1914

In creating their suburban building estate at Edgbaston, the Calthorpes were not obliged to lavish money extensively on the provision of amenities – which, considering their relatively limited financial resources during the first half of the nineteenth century, was perhaps as well. The granting of sites for churches, charities, parks, botanical gardens and the university, and the £47,000 they spent on roads between 1810 and 1888 were the sum total of their endeavours in this field. The wealth, initiative and energy of the citizens of Birmingham meant that, once the Calthorpes had launched their estate and established the correct and elevated 'tone', they could safely leave such matters in the hands of the residents. Yet for a town started almost from nothing, and some 70 miles from a great metropolis, the provision of amenities by the developing land-owner must necessarily be on a larger and more extensive scale, in anticipation of demand, and therefore without immediate expectation of profit. By definition, there was no indigenous elite which could afford or undertake such ventures: only the local landowner would have the resources, the contacts, and the long-term priorities which would allow him to bear short-term expense and loss in the hope of long-term gains. While Edgbaston was parasitic on Birmingham, Eastbourne was parasitic on the Devonshires.

Until the early 1860s, however, it was a miserable resort, with a short sea wall, an indifferent water supply, a primitive and unsatisfactory drainage system, and possessed only of the limited recreational facilities afforded by cricket, croquet and archery.[1] There was no pier, no library, theatre or winter garden worthy of the name. If anything, it could boast fewer facilities than suburban Edgbaston. Indeed, one visiting rhymester – more perceptive than poetic – drew emphatic attention to the fact:

> 'Eastbourne with all thy faults' – thou has a few.
> I'll name them now I'm in a scribbling cue.
> Thou hast no spacious baths, thou hast no pier,
> But these, I joy to find, shall soon appear;
> And we may safely trust nobility
> To make both beautiful and worthy thee.[2]

His diagnosis was as correct as the remedy he suggested, for while the local press constantly urged residents to 'put their own shoulders to the wheel and provide facilities for the same social and intellectual enjoyments which are found in other watering places', it was always frustrated in this wish.[3] The enthusiasm to found and manage such undertakings far outran the town's capacity to provide either sufficient initial finance or adequate local patronage. So, time and time again, such enterprises, founded amid absurdly euphoric expectations, floundered and failed. And, on each occasion, the disappointed, indebted directors went to Compton Place, cap in hand, to ask Devonshire for his support.

By this means, the seventh duke was drawn inexorably into providing amenities for the town on a far larger scale than he could ever have envisaged at the outset. Once he had set his mind on the creation of a high-class resort town, he could not afford to see collapse those very attractions which must be promoted if the venture was to succeed. Accordingly, appeals to him for funds, for land, or even for a public declaration of support, were rarely in vain. He was as much the 'Fairy Godfather' of Eastbourne as the Earl of Scarbrough was later to be of Skegness. 'What', inquired the *Gazette*, 'would Eastbourne have been without the generous liberality of the Duke? He has expended thousands upon thousands in making the place what it is.'[4] And, since the act of 'calling on Providence in the shape of a Duke' never seemed to fail, the population was increasingly indifferent – at least until the mid-1890s – to any efforts at self-help.[5] Not for them the energetic promotion of amenities which characterized the councils of Blackpool or Bournemouth or Southport, where 'Fairy Godfathers' were less in evidence. As the *Gazette* put it: 'Every trades-man and lodging house proprietor quibbles . . . yet appears to expect that all efforts to improve matters in this respect shall be undertaken by others, without the slightest trouble or sacrifice to himself.'[6] There was no doubt as to whom was meant by 'others'. This chapter is an account of what, precisely, 'others' did.

1

The necessary pre-condition for the successful establishment of any seaside resort was that it should be accessible, which meant that it must be connected with a railway. For all holiday resorts begun in the Victorian period, from Bournemouth to Blackpool, Southport to Skegness, population surged dramatically in the decade following the arrival of the railway.[7] Even Brighton, which had grown so spectacularly in the 1820s and 1830s, enjoyed another spurt of impressive expansion after the railway arrived in 1850 and, in this as in much else, Eastbourne was no exception. Where, however, it was unusual was that it possessed, in the person of the seventh duke, a particularly powerful figure who could lobby the local railway company on its behalf. Indeed, from the foundation of the town until the 1880s, it was the duke who was the most important figure in any matter to do with Eastbourne railways – not only because of the support he could give, but also because of what he might and – on occasions did – oppose.

In 1846, the London Brighton & South Coast Railway, whose main line to Brighton had been opened in 1841, built a branch from Lewes to St Leonards, the town on which Decimus Burton had chosen to lavish his talents after the development schemes entertained by Burlington at Eastbourne between 1836 and 1838 had come to nothing. The closest the line came to Eastbourne was Polegate, six miles away, and an omnibus service was available to take visitors on from there to Eastbourne itself. But Burlington was aware that only a direct line would suffice if there was to be any possibility of developing the town as a seaside resort and so, in 1849, by which time he had again turned his attention to the Compton estate, he persuaded the company to build the extension to Eastbourne, which was opened with such celebrations in May that year.[8] Thereafter, the station was extended in 1866, 1872 and 1886, as the increased traffic required.

However, the trains thus provided did not live up to expectations. They were slow and infrequent; the service was less good than to Brighton or Hastings; it was necessary to change at Polegate; and under these circumstances it was difficult to attract those wealthy commuters and residents whose patronage the resort so much desired. In 1869, there were only seven trains in each direction, the fastest of which did the journey in 2 hours and 5 minutes, the slowest in 2 hours and 40 minutes. By comparison, the journey from Brighton to London, which was only 15 miles shorter, took but 1 hour 25 minutes by the fastest train of the day, and 1 hour 45 by the slowest.[9] The company argued that it was impossible to provide a better through service as long as the junction at Polegate remained unreconstructed – and then resolutely refused to rebuild it. Finally, after much outcry in the local press, they agreed to rebuild the junction, but it was not until August 1871 that the work was completed, and through trains ran direct from London to Eastbourne for the first time.[10]

At a more fundamental level, the problem was that Eastbourne was not served by a railway company which regarded the line to that town as its first priority. The London Brighton & South Coast Company was pre-occupied with its Brighton line, and regarded the spur from Lewes to Eastbourne and St Leonards as of secondary importance and, in the same way, the South Eastern's chief interest lay in its direct route to St Leonards. Because Brighton and Hastings were already in existence at the time of the railway mania, they secured direct lines from the beginning; but Eastbourne, which only began to grow later, enjoyed no such direct line.[11] Accordingly, throughout the 1860s and 1870s, many inhabitants of Eastbourne, supported by the seventh duke, sought to persuade one or other of the companies – and they really did not mind which – to provide a better line. At the same time, the two companies themselves were in competiton to see which could secure as their exclusive territory that particular part of Sussex. Meanwhile, ever more exasperated, other citizens of Eastbourne, including George Ambrose Wallis, the duke's agent, toyed with the idea of promoting their own, direct and rival line to London. The result was a long saga of railway politics of quite extraordinary complexity and tedium.

In 1864, the South Eastern, much to the delight of Eastbourne's inhabitants, projected a spur off its London to Hastings line, from Battle to East-bourne. Alarmed by this threat, the London Brighton & South Coast pro-posed a new, direct line from Croydon to Eastbourne via Turnbridge Wells, which would significantly shorten the journey from Victoria.[12] But the finan-cial panic of 1866–7 was not the most auspicious time in which to raise money for new railway schemes and so, to the great annoyance of the town, both lines were abandoned.[13] In 1874, the seventh duke himself intervened, and met Sir Edward Watkin, the chairman of the South Eastern, and personally appealed to him to construct 'a new line of railway connecting Eastbourne with the South Eastern system'.[14] But the Brighton Company bought the South East-ern off and – once more in response to Devonshire's prodding – in 1877 promoted a direct line of their own to Eastbourne via Tunbridge Wells. The duke hoped that such an arrangement would mean that 'we shall not have much ground for complaint'. Indeed, when the line was opened in 1880, the *Gazette* was convinced that 'the line will doubtless prove very advantageous to Eastbourne, as it will be rendered more accessible to visitors'.[15]

Again, however the hope was vain. The line had originally been privately projected as a narrow gauge railway, before the Brighton Company took it over. As a result, it suffered from excessively steep gradients and sharp curves, and the earthworks were unsafe and liable to subsidence,[16] so the hoped-for direct service did not materialize. Ever since 1877, Devonshire had been aware that if this scheme failed, 'we shall find it necessary to promote a new line' and, in 1883, this is exactly what happened.[17] Wallis, assisted by other prominent citizens of Eastbourne, proposed a direct route and persuaded the duke – much against his will – to give the venture his grudging support.[18] In the summer of 1883, the town was gripped by railway fever, as the bill reached committee in London and Lord Edward Cavendish gave evidence on behalf of his father; but it was all to no avail. Both the Brighton Company and the South Eastern opposed, and it was clear that a line which went through sparsely populated country in Kent and Sussex was unlikely to pay. So the scheme was thrown out, and the town returned to its old battles with the established companies. Not until the 1890s was the town's sense of grievance and ill-treatment eradicated.

2

By comparison, the provision of basic amenities was similar to that on any large building estate. To begin with, during the crisis years of the late 1850s, Burlington advanced some £37,000 to speculative builders to ensure that they were able to finish the houses they had begun. This, like the assistance the Duke of Bedford gave Thomas Cubitt in the late 1820s, was an extraordinary and unique occurrence. The builders later paid the money back, and there-after, no more loans were ever made. 'Monetary advances are not undertaken by the estate', noted George Wallis in 1878, a maxim of which his opposite number at Edgbaston would wholeheartedly have approved.[19] Then there was the donation of pieces of land for religious and philanthropic purposes, whereby it was possible to give effect both to genuine evangelical zeal and the desire to establish a high social tone. Between 1859 and 1914, the Devonshires gave land for nine churches, four church schools, a technical institute, and a library, and in each case they invariably gave handsome donations as well. In this, as in their landholding, they far outclassed the Gilberts. When, in 1855, St Saviour's church was built, Devonshire gave the land and £5,000. The Gilberts' contribution was £100.[20]

These activities were the necessary pre-conditions for the successful promotion of any high-class building estate, whether in the town or by the seaside; but, in making a resort town, it was necessary to go much further. Drainage in particular was a matter of prime importance – both because it had to be started from nothing, and because a watering place must not be suspected of being unclean. In the early 1860s, therefore, the local board considered the installation of a cheap system, the outfall from which would have been just below where the pier is today. On the advice of McLean, who had been responsible for much civil engineering in Barrow, Devonshire urged the board to site the outfall three miles away at Pevensey, so as to ensure that the sea was not polluted. The board was persuaded, and James Hayward agreed to undertake the work at a cost of £10,000, of which Devonshire provided £1,000, the Gilberts £500, with the rest being obtained in the form of a loan to the board itself.[21] However, the cost of laying pipes across the two marshy miles of the Crumbles to Pevensey was as prohibitive as the exercise was difficult, and in the middle of 1865 the contractor went bankrupt and work was necessarily suspended. 'I fear I shall in consequence be put to considerable additional expense', Devonshire noted laconically in his diary,[22] and he was right: if he did not come to the rescue of the local board, there was no-one else who could.

Indeed, by the time the major part of the scheme had been completed in 1867, Devonshire, who had undertaken to bear all the additional cost himself, had laid out some £38,000, to which was added a further £5,000 during the next five years. Here, more than anywhere, was the key to Devonshire's position in the town, as the *Eastbourne Gazette* recognized shortly before the scheme was officially inaugurated:

> There is one gentleman to whom the town will be for ever indebted for the successful carrying-out of this project – we refer to His Grace the Duke of Devonshire – although we need scarce have mentioned his name; and we have little hesitation in saying that, but for the munificence displayed by His Grace, the above-named scheme would never have been accomplished, at least not in our day.[23]

Singlehandedly, Devonshire had financed a venture which had proved to be too great for the limited resources of the local board. 'Had it been left to our local authorities, or had a less monied person taken it in hand', then the scheme would have foundered, or been completed in a much more shoddy manner.[24] Devonshire's advice, and subsequent financial assistance, ensured the completion of the project to the highest possible standards of sanitary excellence. In the long run, this was to be important in establishing the town's much-prized reputation for health and cleanliness. As the *Saturday Review* noted:

> The drainage of Eastbourne offers an example of excellence in design and execution well deserving of study and imitation by other seaside places which desire to compete with it for public favour. This work may be truly described as the first great effort that has been made to remove even the suspicion of the presence of sewerage from waters in which visitors are intended to bathe.[25]

In addition to the excellence of its drainage, Eastbourne was also renowned for the splendour of its parades and promenades. In *The Builder* it was observed that an esplanade was 'an indispensable requirement at all seaside localities', and in this respect, again as a result of the Devonshires' activity, Eastbourne was second to none.[26] In the 1850s and 1860s, the Grand Parade was constructed, and in the 1870s and 1880s it was extended two miles further west to Holywell. Finally, from 1890 onwards, the Redoubt sea wall was constructed. All this was financed by Devonshire, who subsequently conveyed the parades to the town: the Grand Parade in 1861 and 1874, the Western Parades in 1902, and the Redoubt and Royal Parade in 1906.[27] By comparison, the local board and corporation were only able to build the Marine Parade, and the Gilberts, owning no land on the sea front at all, made no contribution. As the *Gazette* put it in 1882, 'it is a vast advantage to a pleasure resort like Eastbourne to have so great an improvement carried out free of any cost to the town, and it adds one more splendid link to the chains which bind the inhabitants to the Duke of Devonshire in the bonds of gratitude'.[28]

3

If the first requirement of any aspiring high-class watering place was that it should be well-drained and have no sewerage problems, the second was that it should have an uninterrupted supply of pure water. In 1844, it was reported that 'the want of a good water supply has driven from the place many good families, and prevented many more from coming to it'.[29] Subsequently, the Eastbourne Water Works Company was founded, the first of many local undertakings into whose affairs the seventh duke found himself inexorably drawn. As with others, his interest and involvement was marginal at first, and it was only when disaster threatened the company – and by implication the development of Eastbourne as a whole – that he intervened. Like the drainage scheme, intervention was invariably accompanied by a massive financial contribution, which automatically made the duke the most influential figure in the affairs of the company. But the water works was unique in that, unlike the other companies with which the Devonshires became connected, it was a highly profitable and successful enterprise.

By 1854 the old supply from a pump was inadequate, and a company was formed with £1,500 worth of capital. Burlington, who had been asked for his support 'in obtaining a regular and ample supply of water to meet the increased demand', subscribed £500 and Mrs Gilbert £100. Of the original six directors, two – Robert Insoll and William Simpson – were employed by him. In 1857 a further £3,700 worth of share capital was raised, to enable the company to extract water from a spring which flowed into Motcombe Pond. On this occasion, Burlington took no more shares.[30] However, Mrs Gilbert opposed this scheme on the grounds that it violated the customary rights of some of her tenants downstream from the pond, whose water supply would now be threatened.[31] She took legal action, and appealed to Devonshire to use his influence to persuade the company to adopt an alternative plan. But as he pointed out, his power was minimal: 'I cannot take upon myself to represent the waterworks company, in which I am only one among a very considerable number of shareholders, whose aggregate amount of shares much exceeds my stake in the company.'[32]

This was soon to change, however, for by now the company was in difficulties. If they persevered with the Motcombe scheme, which they could afford, it seemed certain that extensive litigation with Mrs Gilbert would ensue; if they abandoned it, they would have to obtain their supply elsewhere, and the costs would be prohibitive. Finally, and under pressure from Devonshire, the company decided to abandon the Motcombe scheme, and take water from Bedford Well instead. In order to finance this, Devonshire bought out all the shareholders of the old company, and a new firm was established by Act of Parliament in 1859, expressly empowered to take water from Bedford Well and prohibited from using Motcombe Pond. In saving the water company, Devonshire had effectively taken it over. In December 1858, the directors of the old company expressed their appreciation of

> the liberal and equitable manner in which His Grace the Duke of Devonshire proposes to bear the expense of the Act, and to advance the capital for the new works, thus releasing the company from the difficult position in which they found themselves placed.[33]

In July 1859, Devonshire visited 'the new works', which he found to be 'nearly finished'. 'The supply will, I believe, be excellent,' he added.[34]

It was and, with the exception of the years 1895–7, it remained so. Unlike the other local companies with which Devonshire became associated, the water works flourished. Further Acts of Parliament were obtained in 1875, 1881, 1889, 1896 and 1897 to increase the company's capital and enable it to find new sources of supply at Wannock, Holywell and Friston. In 1860 it had 423 customers and its gross revenue was £842; 30 years later the same figures were 5,100 and £14,500.[35] The seventh duke's diary reflected this. In July 1876, for instance, he recorded that 'the water works are doing well, and the demand is so great that a new engine is wanted . . . The supply continues to be abundant.' Four years later, he observed how 'the rapid increase of the town makes it necessary to be thinking of enlarging the supply.' And in 1883, after a further round of extensions had been completed and opened by the Prince of Wales, he observed with evident glee that 'they seem to be working famously.'[36]

As this 'very substantial and profitable undertaking' expanded, and new issues of capital were authorized, the Devonshires' grip on the company remained strong.[37] By 1893, the total authorized capital was £304,680, of which £202,580 had been subscribed. In all, Devonshire himself held £117,390, or over half of the shares, and the remainder were taken up by his business associates, in a manner similar to his investments in Barrow.[38] The Currey family, his London solicitors, and George Wallis and Robert Insoll, the Sussex agents, held between them all the remaining shares, and did so on the assumption that, should they wish to part with them, Devonshire was to be given the first refusal.[39] As Wallis noted in 1889, 'The present capital has been subscribed by the duke and those immediately connected with his Sussex estates, and it has *always* been considered that it would be prejudicial to His Grace's interest to offer the capital to the public.'[40] Not until a new issue of capital in 1890 did it become necessary for the Company to offer its shares publicly and to the highest bidder, and even then, 'nobody attended the sale except present shareholders'.[41] Indeed, it was only in 1898, when 3,000 shares were offered for sale, than an outsider at last bought his way in;[42] and even then, he only obtained 55 shares, while Devonshire bought 2,945. As much as the Furness Railway in Barrow, the Eastbourne Water Works Company was a Cavendish organism.

4

By comparison, the pier company was a much-troubled enterprise. The first notice of the project came at the end of 1863, when a structure 1,000 ft long and costing £12,000 was suggested. The duke was reported to be 'highly favourable' towards it,[43] but progress was delayed, and he refused to allow the company to site the pier opposite Devonshire Place. Only in October 1864 was this 'agreed satisfactorily', when a site at the junction of the Marine and Grand Parades was settled upon.[44] Five London directors were appointed in March 1865, and the local prospectus took pains to stress that 'the undertaking has also met with the sanction and approval of the Duke of Devonshire, and His Grace has moreover consented to render material assistance towards its execution.'[45] The first pile was driven in April 1866 by Lord Frederick Cavendish and it was he who, four years later, opened the first stage of the completed pier.[46] By 1872, the entire structure was finished; but on New Year's Day 1877 the whole shoreward section was swept away in a storm of unprecedented ferocity.[47] Reconstruction was rapid, however, and growing revenue towards the end of the century enabled the management to construct a theatre, a bar, a café, a landing stage and a games saloon between 1893 and 1903.

Fig. 34. Eastbourne pier, 1903: a photograph taken soon after the completion of the extensions, looking from the entrance out to sea (by courtesy of Eastbourne Public Library).

Unfortunately, throughout its early years the company was hampered by a severe lack of funds, difficulties with the contractors, and internal squabbles among the directors. By July 1865, only 214 £10 shares had been applied for – a completely inadequate base on which to award a contract of £13,400. By November 1867, £5,000 was still needed, and the contractor showed understandable reluctance to be paid in shares in a company whose commercial future was distinctly uncertain. A year later, in an attempt to make the enterprise more attractive to local investors, the London directors were ousted and replaced by men from Eastbourne,[48] but this did not end the early difficulties. In March 1869 the company came close to being wound up, an extraordinary general meeting actually being summoned for that purpose, and early in the following year, the contractor died.[49] By March 1872, £6,000 was still needed to complete the pier, and further expenditure on strengthening the structure in the early 1870s cost an additional £2,500. Finally, the calamity of January 1877 obliged the directors to find another £20,000 in debentures.

As each new difficulty arose, and as each new appeal for shares failed to evoke the hoped-for response, the directors scurried to Compton Place in search of ducal support. In January 1867, the company secretary was 'directed to communicate with His Grace the Duke of Devonshire with a view of obtaining some financial assistance.'[50] Two years later, the company inquired 'as to the additional number of new shares which His Grace the Duke of Devonshire will take in the company so as to complete the pier.'[51] Then in August 1870 he was again asked to 'take further shares in the company', and in April 1872 the directors were hopeful that he would provide the whole of the £6,000 which was needed so as to complete the pier.[52] Again in November 1875 and February 1876, when it was necessary to raise further sums to meet the costs of strengthening the pier, Devonshire was asked 'how far he will assist the directors in raising the amount necessary'.[53]

In response to such requests, Devonshire's policy was that of reluctant support – never as wholehearted as the directors wished, and only on condition that others must back the venture as well. He would lend support to an ailing – if promising – enterprise; but he would never carry the burden alone. The *Gazette's* claim in 1864 that 'the whole affair is got up by the duke' greatly overestimated both his financial hold and his entrepreneurial connection,[54] for while he was the major, he was never the majority shareholder. Of the 214 shares that had been applied for by July 1865, he took 50 and Mrs Gilbert took 20.[55] In late 1867, he agreed to 'take an additional large number of shares', but only on the condition that 'the inhabitants of the town show their appreciation of the undertaking'. If they subscribed £4,000 he would contribute £1,000. In fact, the £4,000 was not forthcoming, but Devonshire took up his allotted number nevertheless, and in October 1870 he accepted a further 100 shares. By 1875, after which he made no more investment, his total holdings were £3,250 in ordinary shares, and £3,000 in debentures.[56]

In a company which by 1875 had £20,000 in ordinary paid-up shares and £7,000 in debentures, Devonshire was not, by definition, the controlling voice. He himself was not a director, and in 1869 his local agent, Robert Insoll, refused to join the board.[57] Even so, by lending the immense prestige of his name to the company, and by coming publicly to its assistance in its most uncertain days, Devonshire's support was of a strategic importance out of all proportion to his actual investment. Only because he did not give up were others tempted to invest. Accordingly, at the opening ceremony, the toast to 'the health, happiness and prosperity, and every good wish and thanks, to the Duke of Devonshire', provoked the loudest cheering of the day,[58] and thereafter his influence as the largest single shareholder remained powerful. In the summer of 1873, for instance, a band began to play daily on the pier, including a performance of sacred music between eight and nine o'clock in the evening on Sundays. Local opinion was outraged by this gross violation of the Sabbath, and the directors were petitioned to withdraw the band on Sundays. They refused, whereupon the opposition appealed to the duke. He made it clear to the directors that he felt 'it would be wise to discontinue the performance' and so, 'in accordance with His Grace's advice', the band was indeed withdrawn.[59]

5

The troubled history of Eastbourne College bears a striking similarity to that of the pier company. In June 1865 a public meeting at Eastbourne endorsed the suggestion of Dr C. C. Hayman and J. H. C. Coles that a proprietary college should be established. Predictably, a petition was sent to the duke inviting his support on the grounds that 'with the most strenuous endeavours on our part, we cannot without the counsel and assistance of Your Grace accomplish the undertaking' – an opinion which was to be verified time and

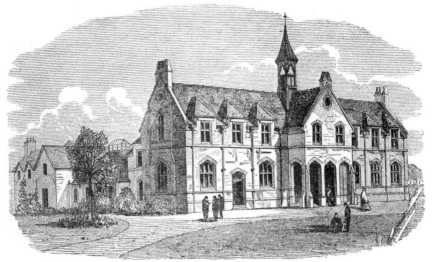

Fig. 35. Eastbourne College: Henry Currey's original design, *c*.1870 (reproduced from the *Illustrated London News*, 11 March 1871, by courtesy of Cambridge University Library).

again during the next two decades.[60] Devonshire received a deputation at Compton Place, concluded that the venture 'would probably be of use to the place', and offered his support.[61] In September the prospectus was issued, which squeezed every drop of advantage out of ducal patronage:

> We believe we are justified in saying that not only is His Grace the Duke of Devonshire fully aware of the importance of the movement but that, as in other things of public merit, he has become a large promoter of the scheme.[62]

The school opened for business in temporary accommodation in August 1867, with a headmaster, two full- and two part-time masters, and 15 pupils. In July 1870, Lady Edward Cavendish laid the foundation stone of the school buildings, and in the following year, Devonshire reported that 'the new college . . . seems to be going on satisfactorily, and has now about sixty boys.'[63] Shortly afterwards, a gymnasium and chapel were completed, and by 1874 there were 100 boys in the school. Further new buildings were added in 1877, and the presence of Princess Alice at speech day in 1878 seemed to set the seal on the school's success.[64] A further round of extensions followed in the late 1880s and early 1890s, when the chapel was enlarged, and a library and more classrooms were added. 'The numbers,' Devonshire observed, 'have largely increased, and there seems now a prospect of it becoming prosperous.'[65] By the time of his death, there were over 200 boys in the school, and early in the 1900s, another round of extensions was undertaken.

In the short run, however, progress had been anything but smooth. As with the pier, excessively high initial expectations, internal squabbles, shortage of capital and customers, and problems with the buildings, blighted its early years. 'With what confident hopes', trumpeted the *Gazette* unrealistically in January 1867, 'we may look forward to the realization of this important project.'[66] Devonshire himself, well-versed in the problems of educational institutions, was much less sanguine. 'They contemplate', he recorded in his diary ten months later, 'a college to contain five hundred boys with large playgrounds altogether requiring nearly thirty acres. I have little belief in the college ever attaining such large dimensions.'[67] And he was quite correct: not until the early 1970s was that number finally reached. The vicious cycle of the college's early years was simply diagnosed but broken only with difficulty: without pupils, there would be no fees, no subscriptions and no building; but until the buildings were constructed, no parents would wish to send their children to a school which had no physical existence, and no insurance company would advance a loan, for there was no adequate security.[68]

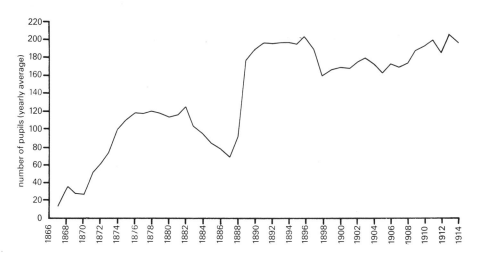

Graph 5. Pupils at Eastbourne College, 1867–1914 (V. M. Allom, *'Ex Oriente Salus': A Centenary History of Eastbourne College*, 1967, 156).

Thus in the early years, the school tottered from crisis to crisis. Indeed, the first came before the permanent buildings had even been begun. It proved to be impossible to obtain a mortgage to finance the buildings; in 1868 there was an epidemic of scarlet fever; and the headmaster fell out with the school council, and resigned in 1869, taking most of the boys with him. In the summer of 1868, there had been 43 pupils; a year later, only 9 remained. A general meeting of shareholders was called at which it was proposed to close the school down.[69] Under a new headmaster, there was a further period of expansion, but then again in the early 1880s, there was another time of trouble. In 1882, two of the housemasters quarrelled, and the affair became the talk of the town; a third was sacked in 1883; and scarlet fever returned in 1885. The headmaster resigned in the following year, and his successor only lasted 12 months. The number of boys fell from a peak of 130 in 1882 to 60 in 1888, and Devonshire felt 'rather doubtful whether the college was worth keeping alive'.[70] But under Crowden, the fourth headmaster, who brought with him 90 boys from his previous school at Cranbrook, an entirely new régime was effectively begun, and it was largely as a result of his energetic efforts that the school made such marked and rapid progress in the 1890s.

However, at a more fundamental level, it was to the seventh duke that the school was indebted for its survival. The land was provided by the Compton estate at a rental well below the market rate, and even this was forgone in times of real crisis, as in the early 1880s. Even more important was his intervention in May 1869, when those at the extraordinary general meeting called to close the school down were persuaded to stay their hand by a message from the duke stating that 'if the shareholders thought the difficulties could be overcome, he thought it better not to wind up the company', which was correctly construed to mean that if the shareholders wanted to keep the company going, Devonshire was prepared to support them.[71] And support them he did. In 1869, he 'decided on laying out from £4,000 to £5,000 on buildings', the construction of which made possible the expansion of the early 1870s.[72] Then again in the late 1880s, Devonshire's own inclination was to let the college collapse; but he allowed himself to be argued out of it. 'I fear', he noted in his diary in an entry reminiscent of that concerning the drainage 20 years before, 'I shall have to find a good deal of money for various improvements.'[73] Once more, as in the 1870s, the school's second burst of expansion ultimately depended on the construction of new buildings at the seventh duke's expense.

By the end of his life, he was not only the majority shareholder with holdings of £5,580, but he had also lavished an additional £12,468 on buildings, and endowed two entrance scholarships of £90 each. Indeed, it was only his constant willingness to allow his name to be associated with the venture, and to provide the necessary funds, which kept the school going at all. Without his much-publicized support at the beginning, and his crucial interventions in 1869–70 and again in 1886–9, there can be no doubt that the venture would have foundered. Devonshire's 'characteristic liberality', which in this context meant his willingness to persevere with the school on occasions against his own better judgment, was the indispensable pre-condition for the school's successful establishment.[74] As its historian notes, Devonshire

> is rightly honoured as the school's founder: for, although the idea of starting it belonged to others, without his active co-operation and continued support, it could neither have started nor survived the innumerable crises of its early years[75]

What was true of the school was also true of the drainage, the water works, the pier and the Parks and Baths Company.

6

Although the pier and the college came close to failure, and were only saved by last-minute infusions of Devonshire capital and support, the Parks and Baths Company, later to be described as 'the sheet-anchor of Eastbourne's prosperity', actually collapsed completely, and had to be restarted from nothing. In 1867 the Royal Marine Baths and Laundry Company was formed, with a nominal capital of £10,000 'for the purpose of establishing baths' in Eastbourne 'on a scale commensurate with its requirements'. It was enthusiastically supported by the local press, and was backed by some of the town's most important worthies.[76] J. H. C. Coles, who had initiated the college, was secretary, and George Wallis and Robert Insoll were two of the original directors. Unlike the pier company, the Compton estate was associated with the venture from the outset. Freehold premises on the Pevensey Road, which had previously housed on a steam laundry, were acquired for £3,500, and a further £3,000 was spent in converting them to baths. At a later date, it was hoped to add a billiard room, a library and a reading room.

Yet the venture suffered from two chronic drawbacks. In the first place, the site at the corner of Pevensey Road was unappealing – too near the artisan quarter, and too remote from the central entertainments district. Secondly, the company was short of funds. It was the same story as with the college: until the baths were built and operating profitably, no one would subscribe; but unless there were subscriptions in advance, it was impossible to build anything of sufficient magnitude to attract either shareholders or customers. At first, only 317 of the 1,000 shares offered were taken up, and of these, 152 went to the directors. By 1872, no dividends had been paid, and new loans had to be raised to pay the interest on those already existing. So, in December that year, the company was wound up, with a mortgage debt of £3,200, and a paid-up capital of £4,540, of which the directors themselves had finally subscribed £3,200.[77]

Significantly, although two of the directors were Devonshire's close associates, they had tried to run the company without recourse to his financial assistance: but, when the venture failed, involving them personally in considerable loss unless something was salvaged from the wreckage, they too took the road to Compton Place to ask for help. Nor did they ask in vain. In May 1873, the Eastbourne Baths Company Limited was established, with a nominal share capital of £15,000.[78] Devonshire himself was prepared to take shares to the value of £1,000, and to offer a piece of land much better situated at the westerly end of the town for a nominal sum of £250, when its value was in excess of £2,000. His reasons were predictable:

> Considering that it would be very injurious to the town generally to be without public baths, and having regard to the fact that the directors of the dissolved company have been large losers, both in time and money, by their endeavours to keep the company going.[79]

Yet support was still unforthcoming from the town, and so Devonshire was obliged to dig further into his pocket, for he

> expressed himself willing in the most liberal manner possible not only materially to benefit the property of the company, but also to provide for the town of Eastbourne a want which has long been felt to be greatly needed, viz. that of a good assembly room, suitable for first class concerts, baths, etc., and by which, under proper management, the length of the present season would be increased, and also a great inducement held out to winter visitors.[80]

As well as the construction of the baths, the plan involved 'a building of the same kind as the Pavilion in Buxton Gardens', which would have a frontage of 350 ft, and contain 'a large assembly room, skating rink, winter gardens and accommodation for a public library'.[81] More elaborate schemes for 'an aquarium for the reception, collection and exhibition of Fishes and Marine and Fresh Water Animals, Plants and Products' were envisaged for the future.[82] The nominal capital of the company was increased from £15,000 to £50,000, and Devonshire was given shares in the company in exchange for financing these new schemes at an estimated cost of £16,000. As a result, the venture was re-named the Devonshire Parks and Baths Company. By July 1874 the Floral Hall and Baths were, in Devonshire's words, 'now finished, and appear to be most successful', and in July 1876 the Pavilion was completed as well, the event being celebrated with a lavish inaugural concert.[83]

However, that concert, like all entertainments held there, neither attracted much support nor covered its costs. 'Perhaps', Devonshire noted perceptively in July 1876, 'it may just at present be beyond the requirements of the place.' Or, as the *Gazette* put it more strongly: 'the directors of the Devonshire Park have not met with the encouragement that their enterprising spirit merits.'[84] Lack of support was thought to mean that the facilities were inadequate. So, at Devonshire's expense, they were again extended, but business did not improve, and the whole cycle began again. In the 1880s, expenditure was particular heavy, as tennis courts, a cricket ground and a theatre were all provided. 'I have unfortunately a good deal of money to find', observed the duke in 1888, in words reminiscent of those he had written of the college and – on a much larger scale – of faraway Barrow.[85] So, by the early 1890s, Devonshire held £45,170 of the £72,330 worth of capital that had been subscribed. Like the water works, it was, literally, his company.

Fig. 36. Devonshire Park, Eastbourne, 1881 (reproduced from the *Illustrated London News*, 23 July 1871, by courtesy of Cambridge University Library).

The last contribution which the Cavendishes made to the company which bore their name was to establish in 1907 the Duke of Devonshire's (Private) Eastbourne Orchestra, intended not only to play in the park, but also to tour the provinces, in response to the challenge of the Bournemouth Symphony Orchestra under Dan Godfrey. In the early twentieth century, orchestras were as much an affirmation of a resort's wealth and progressiveness as winter gardens had been in the 1870s, and Eastbourne was determined not to be outdone. Once more, 'providence in the shape of a Duke' intervened, and provided Eastbourne with what was described locally – and somewhat extravagantly – as 'an orchestra of such commanding size and proficiency as will serve the double object of making a powerful addition to the list of high class attractions and of assisting to advertise the town';[86] but it was, for the eighth duke, an expensive undertaking. The wages bill averaged £150 a week, and between 1908 and 1910 Devonshire spent no less than £17,000 on it.[87]

Table 31. Devonshire investment in Eastbourne companies, 1893

Company	Total paid-up share capital (£)	Total Devonshire holdings (£)
Water Works	202,580	117,390
Pier	37,500	6,250
College	c. 7,000	5,580
Parks and Baths	72,330	45,170

Source: CEO MS. Report by Mr C. H. Currey and Mr Henry Currey on His Grace the Duke of Devonshire's Sussex Estates, 28 March 1895, Appendix VII.

7

Shortly after the seventh duke's death, the Devonshires' holdings in their Eastbourne companies were precisely calculated (table 31). Of course, this is by no means an exhaustive list of the town's companies. There was the Gas Company, set up in 1859, in which the duke held £3,350 worth of shares which he sold in 1881 for £4,293. And there were other ventures such as the Electric Light Company, the Artisans Dwellings Company, and the large hotels like the Queen's and the Grand, in which he never invested at all.

But even allowing for this, the Devonshires' contribution to the creation of Eastbourne's amenities was massive, dominant, unrivalled and strategically crucial. Without the promenades, the sea walls and the drainage, there could have been no healthy seaside resort at all. And as far as the development schemes of both the Devonshires and the Gilberts were concerned, neither could have proceeded but for the water supply afforded by the duke's company. In the same way, the pier was a vital attraction, and the college was important in establishing the town's high social tone, but in each case, without the duke's support, they would have foundered. The Parks and Baths Company, too, for all its limited support and profitability, provided nearly all of those genteel and exclusive recreational facilities which were of first importance in establishing the resort.

Neither the Gilberts nor the local board could rival this extensive provision of amenities. As one guide noted in 1871, at the height of the Devonshires' involvement:

> The Duke of Devonshire, who is the principal landowner here, has taken a deep interest in the growth and well-being of Eastbourne. To him we are indebted for our beautiful parades, drives and lounges, along the sea coast. The waterworks are his, and he nobly relieved the parish of the onerous duty of carrying out our drainage.[88]

The duke's role was long remembered, as another publication made clear 40 years later.

> Modern Eastbourne is indeed largely a monument of the far-seeing judgment and lavish generosity of its noble founder, for without the duke's bold initiative and fostering care, the governing authorities could never have pursued the high ideals which have produced the magnificent results now visible.[89]

More than anything else, it was this predominant role in the provision of amenities which explains why, for so long, Eastbourne was not only 'The Empress of Watering Places', but 'The Duke's Town' as well.[90]

19 The making of a new town: outlay and income, 1849–91

During the lifetime of the seventh duke, the financial dominance of the Devonshires in the town's affairs was at its greatest. As the *Gazette* put it in 1875, echoing a widely-held opinion, 'in this town we owe much to the Cavendish family – Eastbourne is its creation'.[1] But if the Devonshires loomed large in the town's finances, how important was Eastbourne in theirs? Was it, as contemporaries assumed, a 'mine of wealth', a 'beneficent speculation', which 'proved amply remunerative'? If the growth of Edgbaston enabled the Calthorpes to achieve fulfilment as aristocrats, how far did Eastbourne contribute to the improvement of the Devonshires' financial position, popularly supposed to have taken place during the lifetime of the seventh duke?[2] Why, indeed, had he decided to create a seaside resort in the first place?

1

In 1834, William Cavendish had become second earl of Burlington on the death of his grandfather, and succeeded to lands which made him a far more weighty patrician than the third Lord Calthorpe had become on his inheritance in 1807, since he succeeded to estates in Lancashire, Sussex, Somerset and Lincolnshire with a gross rent roll of £31,000, and a net income of £25,000 – twice that of Lord Calthorpe.[3] With country houses at Holker and Compton Place, and an assured position in the county politics of Sussex, he was a territorial magnate of some distinction. Unlike the third Lord Calthorpe, however, the encumbrances which Burlington inherited were on a scale commensurate with his resources: secured on his estates were mortgages totalling £200,000, which absorbed some £8,000 of his disposable income – a heavy, if not crippling burden.[4] In part the debt arose from family portions; but the majority was the result of the extensive purchases of land which his grandfather had made, especially in Sussex. Burlington was sufficiently impressed by his inherited indebtedness to set up a sinking fund into which he proposed to pay £5,000 a year. But the development of Barrow, in which he had invested over £100,000 by 1858, prevented any successful attempts at debt-reduction. On the contrary, by that year, the total encumbrances secured on the Burlington estates had risen to £250,000.

In 1858, the still grander inheritance of the dukes of Devonshire was combined with the Burlington lands. Altogether, he was now possessed of estates in 11 English and three Irish counties, computed by Bateman in 1883 as shown in table 32.

In the early 1860s, he enjoyed from these broad-acred sources a current income of nearly £110,000 a year. (Current income is here defined as gross agricultural rent plus dividents, less arrears, tithes, taxes and costs of improvement. The statistical evidence relating to income and expenditure for the period covered by this and chapter 21 has been gathered together in Appendix D.) If he had been a grandee of substance before, he was now one of the great subjects of the crown, with an acreage only surpassed by Scottish magnates like the dukes of Buccleuch and Sutherland.

Table 32. Duke of Devonshire's estates, *c.*1883

County	Acres
Derbyshire	89,462
Yorkshire, West Riding	19,239
Lancashire	12,681
Sussex	11,062
Somerset	3,014
Lincolnshire	1,392
Cumberland	983
Middlesex	524
Nottinghamshire	125
Staffordshire	26
Cheshire	28
Co. Cork	32,550
Co. Waterford	27,483
Co. Tipperary	3
Total	198,572

Source: J. Bateman, *The Great Landowners of Great Britain and Ireland* (1883), 130.

Yet, once again, it was a tarnished inheritance, for Devonshire had succeeded his second cousin, the sixth duke, whose sense of financial responsibility had never been even dimly developed. Largely as a result of his extravagance – including the extensions to Chatsworth, the rebuilding of Bolton Abbey, Lismore Castle and Devonshire House, to say nothing of his mania for collecting – he bequeathed the ducal estates to his successor encumbered to the extent of £750,000.[5] Accordingly, the total debt secured on the combined Devonshire-Burlington estates in 1858 was slightly in excess of £1,000,000 and, as a result, no less than £38,390 of the duke's princely income was earmarked in charges to service the debt (see Appendix D). As the seventh duke confided to his diary, it was hardly an encouraging prospect:

The income is large, but by far the greater part of it is absorbed by the payment of interest, annuities, and the expense of Chatsworth, leaving but a comparatively insignificant surplus, and much of this will at present be required for legacy and succession duties. This is a worse condition of matters than I had expected, although from knowing the duke's ignorance of business, I did not expect to find them very flourishing.[6]

Between the years 1834 and 1858, then, Burlington was preoccupied with his indebtedness – so much so, indeed, that he toyed with the idea of selling his Sussex estate in 1840, and his Irish lands in 1858, as the best way of effecting a large reduction.[7] But such spectacular measures would have reduced the territorial standing of the family as well as its encumbrances, so they were not proceeded with.[8] On the other hand, the development of Barrow – and, to a lesser extent, Eastbourne – held out the prospect of increased income. There seems little doubt that this was one of the main considerations in Burlington's mind when he began seriously to consider the development of Eastbourne in 1848. 'We do not imagine that the duke was activated by pure philanthropy' noted the *Gazette* in 1881.[9] And when, seven years later, the duke's agent was asked: 'The duke has spent a great deal of money, but you hold, I think, that he has spent it all upon a commercial basis?', he replied: 'Certainly, I do not think that the duke has done it for philanthropic purposes.'[10] Indeed, at the very beginning of the venture, in 1851, Burlington himself had noted this entry in his diary: 'Building is likely to go on at Eastbourne. It at present entails expense, *but no doubt will pay.*'[11]

Two qualifications must be made before Burlington is neatly pigeonholed as a 'debt-driven developer'.[12] In the first place, if the evidence in his diary is any guide, Burlington was far more concerned with how much he was spending than with the anticipated return, for there is only one other entry where he referred to the return on his outlay, when he wrote that 'the expenses from the beginning have been very heavy, and the results hitherto only uncertain'.[13] That apart, the main items in his diary apropos of the finances of the Eastbourne venture concern 'a good deal of expense', 'a considerable expense', and so on.[14] His hopes for future, long-term gain, to say nothing of what he actually understood by the venture 'paying', were never precisely formulated, worked out or written down. Perhaps, too, it is unwise to set Burlington's decision solely within the limited – if important – context of financial consideration. He was, after all, an intelligent man, with a taste for risk and adventure, as the beginnings of the Barrow enterprise showed. Moreover, he possessed a high, evangelical sense of duty towards his estates. What, then, could be more natural than that he should consider developing Eastbourne to its fullest potential as he had with Barrow? After all, in the 1840s and 1850s, it was quite the fashion for enterprising landowners to call in experts like Decimus Burton to plan resort towns, as at Fleetwood and Bournemouth. Even if he had not been indebted, therefore, it seems highly likely that Burlington would have been anxious to develop and exploit his Eastbourne acres in this way, if only because for a man in his position, 'it was the sensible thing to do'.[15]

2

Even if indebtedness is not an altogether satisfactory explanation as to why the seventh duke became involved in the development of Eastbourne, it was certainly important in influencing the actual way in which the venture was financed. Most landowners beginning to develop seaside towns had recourse to external funds, raising mortgages so as to finance the large initial outlay on roads, sewers, sea walls and other indispensable amenities. This practice was followed by the Palks at Torquay, the Scarbroughs at Skegness, the Radnors at Folkestone, the Tapps-Gervis-Meyricks at Bournemouth, and the Fellows of Sidney Sussex College at Cleethorpes; and, in legal terms at least, it would have been easy for the seventh duke to have followed suit. He was unusual among the great landowners of nineteenth-century England in possessing the whole of his estates in fee simple, as his predecessor did, and as his successor was to do also.[16] Although this meant that there were no legal obstacles to mortgaging the estates to the maximum amount they would bear, he was naturally anxious to reduce, rather than increase, the pile of debt. Only at the very beginning, in the 1850s when he advanced £37,000 to help out the first speculative builders, did he have recourse to external funds, and all this was subsequently paid back.

That apart, Burlington was determined that the development of Eastbourne should not increase his overall indebtedness. Accordingly, its evolution as a seaside town was designed to be both self-contained in its accounting and self-sufficient in its financing. Again, it was the ownership of the land in fee simple which made this possible, for as a result, the Earl's advisers were able to evolve a scheme whereby during the first ten years of the 90-year building lease, the lessee was allowed the option to purchase the freehold, initially at the rate of 30 years' purchase, but reduced to 25 in 1913.[17] If Burlington had not owned the estate outright, such a scheme would have been impossible; but as it was, from selling off land at written-up, development value, Devonshire derived the majority of the income which he used to finance the building of the sea walls and roads, and those companies whose activities were so important in establishing Eastbourne as a high-class seaside resort. It was not from mortgages or income syphoned off from other estates that the development of Eastbourne was financed, but from income obtained from the realization of the land itself.

However, the necessary consequence of this was that the ground rents themselves – the second largest item of income – did not rise as spectacularly as they did on other building estates, developed more conventionally without giving the lessee the option to purchase the freehold. Unless a sudden upsurge in the sale of ground rents was accompanied by an increase in the number of new building leases negotiated, then the actual income from rentals would not necessarily increase at all, but might even decline. So, as graph 6 shows, the line for income rises much less purposefully than was the case for the Calthorpes at

Edgbaston. Between 1850 and 1876, ground rents only rose from £166 to £3,000 – a much less spectacular increase than one might have expected, given the rapid rate at which the resort expanded in these years, but easily explained when the high level of redemptions between 1859 and 1876 is considered. The great glut of building agreements in the late 1870s and early 1880s then pushed rentals up rapidly to a peak of £10,000 in 1883–4, but thereafter, more freeholds were bought than new leases were taken up in the slump of the late 1880s and early 1890s, so that income from ground rents actually fell to £7,500 a year by 1895. Altogether, between 1850 and 1893, income from this source only totalled £160,000. As more freeholds were sold off, short-term income might be increased; but the prospects of long-term revenue on current account actually diminished. Indeed, in the very long term, the necessary consequence of the estate being self-financing in this way was that it was also self-liquidating. When all the ground rents were sold off, there would be nothing left.

The last major item of income consisted of the dividents paid by these companies in which the Devonshires – either voluntarily or unwillingly – became major schareholders during the life of the seventh duke (see table 33).

Table 33. Devonshires' income from Eastbourne dividends, 1850–93

Company	Dividends (£)
Water Works, 1858–93	88,441
Pier, 1872–93	5,353
Devonshire Club, 1881–93	197
Parks and Baths, 1874–93	4,294
College, 1865–93	nil
Gas Works, 1854–81	2,939
Total	101,224

Source: CEO MS., Account Books, 1850–93.

Of the six companies with which which the Devonshires were financially connected, the water works stands out as the most consistently prosperous. Rarely were dividends below 6 per cent, so that by the late 1880s, the income from this source was averaging between £5,000 and £6,000 a year.[18] The gas works, too, were a highly profitable undertaking, declaring dividends of 7 per cent by the late 1870s, and even 12 per cent by the middle of the following decade.[19] But by then, the Devonshires had liquidated their holdings, making a slight capital gain in the process: shares bought for £3,350 were sold for £4,293. Finally, after an early period of uncertainty, the pier began to pay a regular dividend of 6 or 7 per cent, providing £350 a year by the early 1880s.[20]

Between them, these three companies provided the majority of the income which the seventh duke derived from Eastbourne in the form of dividends. Devonshire expected these investments to yield a handsome return, and they

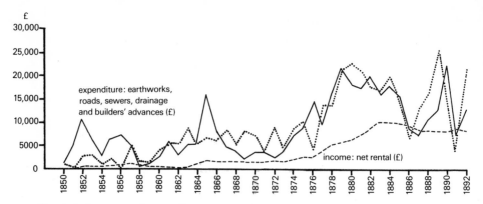

Graph 6. Income and expenditure on the Compton building estate, 1850–1914 (CEO MS Accounts).

did not disappoint him; but the other two enterprises – as their troubled histories imply – fared much less well. The college, for example, never paid a dividend at any time during the seventh duke's life. As Herbert Currey noted in 1895, 'until Dr. Crowden's appointment as Headmaster a few years ago, it was more or less in a chronic state of bankruptcy.'[21] Yet, although Devonshire himself thought on more than one occasion of letting it die, he 'preferred to lay out large sums of money upon the buildings, for which only a small return is obtained in an annual rent of £500.' The same was true of the Parks and Baths Company, which 'did not show a very satisfactory return for the large outlay which has been made.' However, as Currey explained to Hartington in 1890,

> although the Devonshire Park has not been financially successful, as would have been wished, there is no doubt that it has had a great effect in expediting the development of His Grace's building estate, as it is an attraction which induces a large number of visitors to go to Eastbourne.[22]

Like the college, the strategic importance of the company gave it a value which was not necessarily expressed in terms of high dividends for, as with the drainage scheme, which Devonshire recognized would put him to 'considerable additional expense', when completed, it would be 'of great benefit to the place'.[23]

As table 34 shows, the realization of ground rents, rentals themselves, and dividend income from the local companies, were the three major items of revenue for the estate between 1850 and 1893. To these should be added the repayment of most of the builders' advances (with interest), sales of land and gas company shares, and other miscellaneous items. All in all, then, during the lifetime of the seventh duke and the first two years of his successor, the Compton building estate yielded gross income a little short of threequarters of a million pounds.

Such a bizarre conflation of current and capital account would hardly win

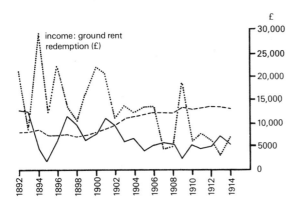

the approval of an economist; but that was how the estate's accounts were drawn up, and it was on the basis of the information thus presented that decisions about spending were taken. And, although aggregate accounts are not easily drawn up, it is possible to give a summary of the general picture on the other side of the ledger. Most striking is the small size of the surplus – a mere £36,968 – which averages out at less than £1,000 a year. However the estate may have developed in later times, during the lifetime of the seventh duke it is impossible to depict the income derived from it as being of major importance as far as the family's overall financial position was concerned. Insofar as historians have suggested that Eastbourne was an important element in the supposed rehabilitation of the Devonshire finances undertaken by the seventh duke, they have been mistaken.

Table 34. Income and expenditure on the Compton building estate, 1850–93

Income		*Expenditure*	
Source	*Amount (£)*	*Type*	*Amount (£)*
Freeholds sold	396,149	Earthworks, roads and sewers	335,532
Ground rents received	161,538	Drainage	29,266
Dividends	101,224	Company investments	176,240
Repaid advances	39,660	Land transferred from	
Land sales	41,880	agricultural estate	77,801
Gas Company shares sale	4,293	Builders' advances	37,023
Miscellaneous	3,597	Other advances	10,396
		Grand Redoubt	8,342
		Eastbourne College buildings	12,468
		Salaries etc.	10,707
		Miscellaneous	13,598
		Surplus	36,968
Total	748,341	*Total*	748,341

Source: CEO MS., Account Books, 1850–93.

Apart from this small surplus, all the Devonshires themselves had to show for their outlay were the shares in the local companies, which they might realize if they chose, as indeed they did in the case of the gas company. But the most striking item on this side of the balance sheet is the sum of nearly £400,000 which was spent on earthworks, roads, sewers, drainage, the Redoubt Estate and the buildings of Eastbourne College. In effect, the money which the duke received from the inhabitants of Eastbourne, either in the form of ground rents, water rates or the redemption of freeholds, far from being put towards the reduction of the ducal debt, was effectively re-cycled in the form of new, local expenditure. Those many inhabitants of Eastbourne, who constantly praised the duke for his unstinted generosity, who hailed the development of Eastbourne as an example of what could be done 'when unlimited money is available', and who no doubt thought that it was from other sources that such funds were derived, were in fact themselves providing the necessary money. The Compton estate effectively acted as an intermediary, channelling revenue derived from the local middle- and working-class residents back for the creation of further items of 'lumpy', urban capital. Other aristocrats pursued the same policy by borrowing from insurance companies, who in turn derived most of their loanable funds from the savings of the urban middle and working class.[24] Devonshire simply followed this policy more directly.

The strategic importance of Devonshire's role in the making of Eastbourne was that he chose to spend the income he derived from the estate in this manner rather than more self-indulgently or in the reduction of the ducal debt; but the fact remains that the source of this income was the pockets of the residents of Eastbourne themselves. It was they, rather than Devonshire himself, who actually provided the money. He did not dig into his own pocket, as he did at Barrow; he dug into theirs. Of course, at some future date, when it was no longer necessary to lavish money on earthworks, roads, sewers and drainage, the income obtained from the sale of freeholds, the ground rents themselves, and the dividends from the companies, might be used for more self-indulgent purposes, as long as the estate was still in being, and before it had entirely liquidated itself. By 1893, the value of agricultural land brought into the building estate was £77,801. Yet, although £365,922 had been realized by the sale of freeholds by 1891, the building estate was still valued, for death duty purposes, at £238,061. If this land could be realized in the form of sales, and the revenue not be diverted back into further development, then no doubt, as the seventh duke had hoped, the venture would 'pay'; but that was not to be during his lifetime: long before he could begin to see an adequate return, he himself was dead.

3

The self-financing, self-sufficient nature of the development of the Eastbourne estate served to set it apart from the rest of the seventh duke's lands and financial affairs. Moreover, while the potential from capital appreciation augured well for the future, during his lifetime the Eastbourne venture made no appreciable impact on his overall financial position: for a surplus averaging out at less than £1,000 a year was trivial when compared with the income he enjoyed from other sources. As table 35 shows, it was the steady and growing income from his agricultural acres, combined with the spectacular dividend revenue derived from the Barrow-in-Furness venture, on which he relied for his current income.

Table 35. Income and expenditure on current account of seventh duke of Devonshire, 1863–88

| | *Income (£)* | | |
	1863	*1874*	*1888*
Net estate rental	94,456	141,716	106,888
Dividends	14,483	169,361	25,084
Miscellaneous	224	233	nil
Total	109,163	311,310	131,972

	Expenditure (£)		
Debt interest	38,390	50,102	81,353
Annuities	7,940	5,655	2,645
Insurance	6,791	7,223	7,168
Family allowances	3,900	4,710	6,300
Subscriptions	5,407	15,640	4,135
Legal and administrative fees	3,591	2,954	3,011
Elections	664	10,182	408
Holker rebuilding	nil	9,088	nil
Household	12,867	23,340	17,727
Miscellaneous	2,310	653	736
Surplus to capital a/c	27,303	181,763	8,489
Total	109,163	311,310	131,972

Source: Currey MS., Seventh Duke's Accounts, 1858–88.

Indeed, at the peak of the Barrow boom, 90 per cent of total investment revenue – equivalent to nearly half current income – came from Barrow, while Eastbourne dividends provided a mere 1.6 per cent (table 36). Even in the late 1880s, when the Barrow boom burst while the Eastbourne dividends continued to increase, revenue from that second source was still less than 20 per cent of total dividend income. This fact was well reflected in the overall structure of the seventh Duke's investment portfolio (table 37).

By 1858 he had already invested £100,000 in Barrow enterprises, compared with only £500 in the water works and £200 in the gas company at Eastbourne.

Table 36. Composition of dividend income of seventh duke of Devonshire, 1858–88

(1) Year	(2) Total dividend income (£)	(3) Barrow dividend income (£)	(4) Eastbourne dividend income (£)	(3) as % of (2)	(4) as % of (2)
1858	8,987	6,470	27	71.9	0.3
1860	8,945	6,139	553	68.6	6.2
1862	14,991	7,795	669	52.0	4.5
1864	16,894	12,065	1,019	71.14	6.0
1866	24,016	19,996	859	83.3	3.6
1868	37,656	32,029	1,230	85.0	3.3
1870	43,202	38,298	1,650	88.6	3.8
1872	72,236	65,822	2,139	91.1	3.0
1874	169,361	151,820	2,751	89.6	1.6
1876	91,005	64,645	4,470	71.0	4.9
1878	80,113	62,206	2,894	77.6	3.6
1880	113,139	89,972	3,791	79.5	3.4
1882	112,541	91,090	4,018	80.9	3.6
1884	50,951	16,742	4,972	32.8	9.8
1886	24,974	7,623	4,733	30.5	19.0
1888	25,084	8,487		33.8	

Source: Currey MS., Seventh Duke's Accounts, 1858–88.
Note: There is here an element of double counting, since the Eastbourne Estate was self-contained, and its dividends should not have appeared – as in fact they did – in the overall, consolidated accounts, and they should not have been available for general spending; but the Devonshires' accounting system, whereby each estate kept separate accounts, and then aggregate balance sheets were also drawn up independently, makes this unavoidable. In any case, the general point being made – namely the relative smallness of the dividend income derived from Eastbourne compared with that from Barrow – is beyond question, at least during the life of the seventh duke.

Even at Buxton, investments were nearly seven times that amount and, although the seventh duke subsequently became more involved in the affairs of Eastbourne companies, this was completely eclipsed by his investment activities elsewhere. By the mid-1880s he had lavished over £200,000 on Irish railways in a vain attempt to improve the prosperity of the south-eastern corner of the country, where his extensive estates lay.[25] Even more spectacular was the £2,000,000 – over 80 per cent of his total investments – which he had poured into Barrow. In investments, then, both in terms of outlay and income, the Eastbourne venture was relatively insignificant.

Accordingly, it seems fair to argue that during the lifetime of the seventh duke, the Eastbourne venture made no major contribution to the rehabilitation of his finances both because the scale of operations there was relatively small, and the return on them miniscule; but in addition, it is important to stress that there was actually no major financial recovery at all. For while the Barrow venture flourished and boomed during the first 15 years when

Table 37. Composition of investments of seventh duke of Devonshire, 1858–85
(percentages in brackets)

	1858	1873	1885
Barrow	£102,945 (67.9)	£948,896 (81.8)	£2,144,306 (83.9)
Buxton	£4,748 (3.1)	£23,229 (2.0)	£26,800 (1.0)
Eastbourne	£700 (0.4)	£41,589 (3.5)	£115,235 (4.5)
Irish railways	nil (0.0)	£117,810 (10.1)	£202,343 (7.9)
Other	£43,135 (28.6)	£28,919 (2.6)	£67,659 (2.7)
Total	£151,528	£1,160,443	£2,556,343

Source: Currey MS., Seventh Duke's Accounts, 1858–88.

the seventh duke held the Devonshire estates, during the remainder of his life spectacular collapse was followed by stagnation. By 1888, the dividend income derived from that source was less than one-sixth of what it had been in the halcyon days of the mid-1870s, as the world depression in prices of iron ore hit Barrow with particular severity. And so, whereas in times of boom Devonshire had been able to finance the expansion of Barrow companies largely by ploughing back their spectacular dividends, in times of slump he was obliged to support them still further by extensive borrowing. As a result, by 1888 the total mortgage debt secured on his estates – which it had been his strongest ambition to reduce – stood at an unprecedented £2,000,000. The Barrow enterprise, which had seemed set fair in the mid-1870s to be the harbinger of financial salvation, was grotesquely transformed so as to undermine Devonshire's affairs still further.[26]

During the last 15 years of his life, therefore, the seventh duke was an exceedingly worried man, as his income was squeezed on all sides. (see Appendix D). Dividends were reduced to £25,000 a year, and continued to fall, while the cost of servicing the huge debt had risen from £40,000 a year in the mid-1860s to £80,000. And, at the same time, landed income declined from £140,000 to £106,000, with rent rebates of from 10 per cent to 30 per cent being given throughout his estates. 'Agricultural affairs have a very gloomy appearance', he noted in May 1885.[27] Three years later, he admitted that 'the position of my affairs' was 'far from comfortable, owing to the general depression which has largely reduced my income in all its sources.'[28] Indeed, by then, while current income was £20,000 greater than it had been in the late 1850s and early 1860s, outgoings made necessary by the need to service the enlarged debt had increased by twice that amount. Between them, the rise and fall of the Barrow meteor, the massive and worrying increase in indebtedness, and the decline in disposable income which resulted, were the dominant themes in the duke's financial affairs. Because it was self-financing, Eastbourne did not add to these difficulties; but because it was also a relatively minor enterprise when seen within the context of the Devonshire estates as a whole, it did not serve to alleviate them, either.

4

However, if the perspective is shifted and the affairs of the Compton estate are set in the context of Eastbourne's municipal finances, rather than of the Devonshire estates as a whole, then a very different picture emerges. While the Devonshires' income from Eastbourne was of very little use at Chatsworth, their expenditure was of major significance in the town itself – far surpassing, in this period, the spending of the local board or council. In 1862, a rate of one shilling in the pound raised the princely sum of £884. Under these circumstances, the decision in 1864 to raise a loan of £7,000 with interest charges amounting to £472 a year for the financing of the new drainage system, was a great adventure. A year later, the local board attempted to borrow a further £2,500, but could find no one prepared to advance the money on such flimsy security.[29] Indeed, as the crisis over the drainage in the late 1860s demonstrated, the local board was in practice as dependent on the financial resources of the seventh duke as were the local companies. Even as late as 1879, a shilling rate produced an income only slightly in excess of £4,000, and the Eastbourne Improvement Act of that year sanctioned spending by the local board of £40,000 – a relatively trivial sum compared with that which was passing through the seventh duke's hands.[30]

By the late 1880s, increased income, incorporation, and two Improvement Acts had gone some way to increasing the scale of operations of the local municipal body: but in 1882, for instance, total borough spending, from both loans and rates, was only £15,641, while £26,691 was spent on the town by the duke. Indeed, even as late as 1882, accumulated borough indebtedness only stood at £176,505, made up as shown in table 38.

The generally trivial nature of this list is immediately apparent. Indeed, it includes only three large items of expenditure, all of which served – paradoxically – only to emphasize the greater financial might of the Devonshires. The money spent on the making of the Royal Parade and the sea walls in the early 1880s was insignificant compared with the seventh duke's spending on the Grand Parade, the Western Parades and the Marine Parade, which was four times as much. Moreover, as with the drainage in 1867, the contractor employed by the local board went bankrupt, work was temporarily suspended, and acrimonious litigation ensued.[31] In the same way, the purchase of a site for the town hall, and the actual construction of the building, dragged on from 1874 to 1886, as successive schemes proposed in 1864 and 1880 were vetoed on

Table 38. Expenditure by Eastbourne local board and financed by council loans, 1864–88

Item	*Cost (£)*
Sea wall	48,961
Town hall	38,628
Drainage	45,071
Paving	6,076
Street improvements	10,299
Parade protection	3,500
Lighting	1,100
Pavilions	1,249
Steam roller	400
Recreation ground	753
Stables	3,400
Beachy Head Road	850
Groynes	5,990
Urinals	250
Improvement Bill expenses	4,178
Ash yard	300
Sanatorium	5,500
Total	176,505

Erratum

Table 38. Caption should read: Expenditure of Eastbourne local board and council financed by loans, 1864-88.

Source: R. J. Graham, *Eastbourne Recollections* (1888), 78–9.
Note: By 1888, £19,131 of the borough debt had been paid off, so that the actual debt in that year stood at £157,375.

the grounds of expense, and the scheme which was finally adopted was delayed by doubts about the suitability of the design. And, even when this 'signal narrative of controversy, mishaps, bickerings and recriminations was over', the finished product still cost less than the seventh duke had spent on the Parks and Baths Company alone.[32] Finally, the £45,000 spent by the local board on drainage in the early 1880s only served to emphasize the extraordinary generosity and forbearance of the seventh duke who had spent so lavishly on the town's drainage two decades before.

In short, although the seventh duke and the local municipal body were engaged in the same enterprise – namely the mobilization of local funds so as to create a holiday resort – the Devonshires were, during this first, formative period, the more powerful. Much more money passed through the Compton Estate Office on its way to make a holiday town than was mobilized by the local board or the council. The board was hesitant, timid, unwilling – and often unable – to spend, and was always happy to call on 'Providence in the shape of a Duke'. Devonshire, on the other hand, was always prepared – after a show of sincere but unavailing reluctance – to respond by making money available for what he believed to be a worthy local venture. But, it must be stressed once more, the money which he made available had in fact been derived from the town. The upper limit on Devonshire's capacity to spend in Eastbourne – given his wish that the enterprise should be self-financing – was the size of the income he derived from the Compton building estate. And, in the same way, the major constraint on the municipal body's capacity to spend – given that they had to have enough income to pay interest on loans – was the amount that they could raise from the local inhabitants in the form of rates. In a very real sense, then, the key to the Devonshire's prominence in Eastbourne during the time of the seventh duke was that they were able to mobilize a greater proportion of local wealth for the creation of a seaside resort than were the council or the local board.

5

Accordingly, for the lifetime of the seventh duke, his financial involvement in Eastbourne may be easily summarized. The building estate was almost entirely self-contained and self-financing, and from it he himself drew barely any income. As a result, the large sums which he allowed to be recycled meant that the amount spent in the town by the Devonshires far surpassed the funds which the local municipal body could mobilize. The very fact that the seventh duke chose not to enjoy personally the income derived from the estate but preferred to let it be ploughed back in the form of additional investment, meant that what they lost in income at Chatsworth they gained in financial power at Eastbourne. As the *Eastbourne Gazette* noted in 1878: 'The Duke can do without Eastbourne, but Eastbourne cannot do without the Duke.'[33]

20 Influence and control: the local oligarchy, 1849–91

The high status and national standing of the Devonshires, combined with their local position as predominant landowners and chief provider of amenities, gave them great influence not only on the physical shaping of the town, but also in the running of its day-to-day affairs. Whereas the Calthorpes in Birmingham were an *arriviste* family who owned land on the edge of a large city, the Devonshires at Eastbourne were a great dynasty who had themselves largely created the town. By deliberately choosing to forgo the income generated by the Compton building estate, and allowing it instead to be recycled in the creation and extension of the town's amenities, the seventh duke effectively exchanged income for power. He himself did not, personally, control the affairs of the town. But the oligarchy which came into being to administer his interests there necessarily dominated the town as well, for his position there was so preponderant that he could have said – although he would never have dreamed of doing so – *la ville c'est moi*.

1

As the ducal sun around which these lesser and dependent luminaries revolved, Devonshire himself ranked as Eastbourne's most august figure.[1] First Smith's Prizeman at Trinity, Cambridge, where he also took a First in Classics and Maths, he brought to a fabulous inheritance a first-rate mind, an unshakeable evangelical earnestness, and a strong sense of duty towards his vast possessions. For three centuries before he inherited, his ancestors had played the aristocratic marriage market with unflagging skill and success and this, combined with the bachelor existence of the sixth duke, meant that his successor presided over an accumulation of Devonshire lands which none of his predecessors had rivalled and none of his descendants was to equal. Burdened more than exhilarated by his broad acres and numerous houses, he was a recluse for whom the glittering prizes of public life held no allure; but as an educationalist and benefactor, he left an indelible mark. Chancellor of London and then of Cambridge University; founder and benefactor of the Cavendish Laboratory; chairman of the Royal Commission on Scientific Instruction and the Advancement of Science, first president of the Iron and Steel Institute, Fellow of the Royal Society: Devonshire held a uniquely esteemed position among the Victorian aristocracy, rivalled only by that of the first duke of Westminster. As one contemporary noted of him: 'Had he not been a duke, he would have been a worthy professor of mathematics . . . The

Duke has nothing left to wish for until some new order of knighthood superior to the Garter shall be invented.'[2]

Such ducal grandeur, combined with his own strategically crucial role in bringing the town into being, meant that throughout his life he was accorded unique respect by the inhabitants of Eastbourne. His agreement to open or inaugurate a new undertaking in the town was the supreme accolade, and was invariably accompanied by fervent expressions of appreciation by the locals of all the duke had done for the town. In 1867, for example, he opened the town's new sewerage and drainage system, which he himself had done so much to promote.[3] It was a day of general rejoicing in the town. All shops closed at one o'clock, 'in order that all classes might be enabled to participate in the enjoyments of the day'. The streets were highly decorated, and the weather fine. At three o'clock, a large procession drew up outside Wallis's offices in Pevensey Road, ready to make the eight-mile journey to the outfall. The members of the local board took the lead, followed by 60 or 70 other carriages, accompanied by a crowd on foot, with the band of the Sussex 19th Rifle Corps. The procession reached Compton Place, where it was joined by the Duke, Lord Edward Cavendish, Mr and Mrs Howard and their children, and then continued on its triumphant way to Langney Point. There, the works were inspected, the drainage scheme duly opened, and the duke took a bottle of wine and christened it the Devonshire Outfall. An illuminated address was then presented to him:

> We, on the part of the middle classes, tradesmen and inhabitants gener-
> ally of Eastbourne, approach your Grace with feelings of the most pro-
> found respect and gratitude, to express our sincere admiration of those
> noble qualities which so pre-eminently distinguish Your Grace. It would
> be difficult to estimate the values of all the benefits conferred upon this
> town by the munificent liberality of Your Grace; but we would wish on
> this occasion to allude particularly to the grand scheme of drainage,
> which has been so auspiciously inaugurated this day, and which, but for
> the generous and spontaneous action on the part of Your Grace, would
> never have been so rapidly and effectually carried out so as to render the
> town one of, if not the best drained, in the kingdom.

The address went on to refer to Devonshire's great academic distinction and his 'courage and patriotism' in continuing to reside in Ireland despite the 'recent troubles' there. The memorial was read amid deafening cheers and in replying, Devonshire was clearly surprised by the warmth of his reception. 'It had', he told the crowd, 'quite taken him by surprise.' Nevertheless, he was able to express his satisfaction at receiving such 'gratifying proof' of the 'entire approval of the scheme by the middle classes and other inhabitants', and to make a platitudinous reply:

> I thank you for the address – I accept it with pleasure as a most gratifying

proof of having received the approval of my neighbours at Eastbourne, in whom I am interested, and with whom I am so closely identified; but I feel I have so inadequately expressed my thanks, as had I expected such a reception, I should have been better able to express the feelings I entertain towards you all [loud and prolonged cheering].

The procession thereupon reformed and made its way back to the town, 'in a broken line, each party looking to their own particular destination'.

However, the proceedings were not yet finished, for that night there was a sumptuous dinner held in the Anchor Hotel, presided over by the Rev. T. Pitman, Vicar of Eastbourne, and chairman of the local board, at which – predictably – Devonshire was the guest of honour. Seventy people sat down to dinner; the catering 'gave most general satisfaction'; and the wines 'were first rate, and called forth especial remarks'. At nine o'clock the proceedings began, with toasts to the queen, the bishop and clergy of the diocese, and the army, navy and volunteers. The chairman then urged everyone to 'fill their glasses, as the toast he was now about to give was one in which he felt sure they would all heartily join'. He then proceeded to extol, for half a column or more, the virtues of the seventh duke, embellishing the words of the address presented earlier even more fulsomely. Most particularly, he drew emphatic attention to the disparity between the financial resources of the local board and of the duke:

> Though the local authority have a great deal of power and can do a great deal of work, they could not have done the work we have today inaugurated [cheers]. I will tell you plainly why they could not because they never could [loud cheers and laughter]. They never could have found money to accomplish an undertaking as great, and nothing but the personal liberality of our friend the Duke of Devonshire [tremendous cheering] – nothing, I say, but His Grace's liberality could have placed us in the position we occupy today [cheers].

Accordingly, his toast could have only one object, and in proposing it, he nearly raised the roof:

> The toast I have to propose has reference to all our great works, embodied in the toast of our excellent patron, our genial saint of Eastbourne, our right honourable friend and guest on my right, His Grace the Duke of Devonshire [tremendous cheering], who has taught us so well to love him that he must not be surprised when our lips give utterance to the feelings of our hearts, in the desire that health and happiness, in every one of its shapes, and in every one of its conditions, may attend him [loud applause]. Gentlemen, let us drink to 'the health of the Duke of Devonshire' [enthusiastic applause].

Thereafter, it was all anticlimax. Devonshire replied, again being received 'with deafening applause', expressed his interest in the town, his admiration for the contractor and engineer, and proposed the health of the chairman of the local board. Further toasts followed, including that of Lord Edward Cavendish '(drank with three times three)', the visitors, the drainage committee and the press. Between the toasts, the Brighton Glee Union 'added greatly to the pleasure of the evening', and the proceedings terminated at 'a late hour'.

During the lifetime of the seventh duke, events such as this were commonplace, and he himself, or some other member of his family, was invariably to be found as the centre of attention and attraction. When a new life-boat was launched in December 1863, the health of the duke was drunk 'with deafening cheers'.[4] Seven years later, when the first half of the pier was opened, the mention of the name Devonshire caused such loud applause that the crowd almost became delirious with appreciation.[5] In August 1870, the foundation stone of Eastbourne College was laid by Lord and Lady Edward Cavendish, when the duke himself was again acclaimed for displaying 'generosity and consideration for others which the most generous would admit [applause]'.[6] When the town was incorporated in 1883, the duke presented the mayoral chain, thereby adding 'one other to the many debts of gratitude which this town owes to His Grace, who seems never tired of doing things for the town, which owes its very existence to his liberality and good spirit'.[7] The laying of the foundation stone of the town hall by Lord Edward Cavendish in 1884, and its opening three years later, were occasions for more fulsome praise. Accounts of the duke as an Irish landlord or as the benefactor of Buxton appeared in the local press, and the comings and goings of the great at Devonshire House in London appeared in the *Eastbourne Gazette* as 'local news'.[8] In July 1888, the duke entertained the Sunday School children to tea at Compton Place, and the local press described the event in terms of such hushed and awestruck admiration that he might have been a deity from Olympus:

> Another highly interesting incident was the taking of photographs of the aged Duke of Devonshire . . . The Duke was very simply dressed and wore a soft felt hat. He seemed thoroughly to enjoy the occasion, and to enter fully into the gaiety of the young folk.[9]

Of course, by this time, the Devonshires' national political position had begun to change fundamentally as the consequences of Gladstone's conversion to Home Rule became apparent. But the tortuous and convoluted manoeuvrings in which Hartington in particular was involved at Westminster, to say nothing of his ambitions for the highest office, were unknown to the inhabitants of Eastbourne, who continued to look on the family as the embodiment of probity and rectitude rather than as partisan politicians.[10] Indeed, as the split with Gladstone deepened, the very independence of the Cavendishes was seen as a virtue. So, in July 1886 for instance, the *Gazette* observed that Hartington 'occupies an honourable position. Everyone admits that throughout this bitter conflict he has conducted himself in a manner that cannot fail to win our admiration.'[11] And three years later, surveying the political events of 1888, the praise was even more fulsome:

> The secession of the Liberal Unionists, which first seemed temporary, is now complete . . . We do not regard this disaffection in the light in which too many Liberals are apt to regard it. We regret the change, but we cannot brand men such as Lord Hartington and Mr. John Bright with infamy simply because they hold different opinions to ourselves. They have a right to their opinions, and their defection only illustrates the intrinsic firmness of Englishmen, and raises their character far higher than if they blindly followed a party in a course which was contrary to what appeared to them to be right.[12]

In short, whatever political position the Devonshires took up, and for whatever motive, as far as the town was concerned, they could do no wrong.

Not surprisingly, ducal tragedies were felt by the inhabitants of the town with a sense of personal loss. The assassination of Lord Frederick Cavendish in 1882, for example, evoked the full outpouring of Victorian grief. Newspapers were black-edged; shops were closed on the afternoon of the funeral; meetings were cancelled; and messages of condolence were sent by the local board to Chatsworth. As the *Gazette* put it:

> On every side, whatever political views might be, the greatest sympathy has been expressed with the Duke of Devonshire and his family on the unparallelled bereavement which has befallen them. The first thought that went out from the mind of Eastbourne was for their generous benefactor, whose grey hairs were rendered greyer, and whose heart was smitten with sorrow . . . The calamity is so great and appalling that it must completely subdue all differences of opinion, whether political or otherwise.[13]

Four years later, the duke's sister, Lady Fanny Howard, died at Compton Place, and was eulogized as a 'lady who has for so long a time displayed an unselfish regard for the institutions of Eastbourne and the welfare of the townspeople'.[14] Finally, at Christmas 1891, the seventh duke himself met his Maker, and the town abandoned its Yuletide celebrations and braced itself for the orgy of grief. Full-page obituaries were carried in all the local papers. His long and useful life, his lack of ostentation and display, his great intellectual accomplishments, his importance as an educationalist, and his generosity and concern for his tenants – all this was described. And, in Eastbourne itself, where he was 'known to many', it was confidently asserted by one editor that 'I never heard a single ill word spoken of him'.[15] The town council immediately passed a resolution

> expressing their deep sense of the great loss sustained through the death of the Most Noble William Seventh Duke of Devonshire, K.G., to whose

liberality and forethought Eastbourne owes its present providential position amongst the seaside resorts of the kingdom, and whose unfailing
generosity, public spirit and warm interest in the welfare of his tenants
and Eastbourne's prosperity, will long be remembered by the inhabitants.[16]

The mayor himself prepresented the corporation at the funeral at Chatsworth,
and simultaneously memorial services were held in Eastbourne at the parish
church – which was attended by the council – and St Saviour's. 'At most of the
churches a funeral knell was rung for about an hour. In the town, not only were
all the business houses closed, but in several instances black shutters were put
up to the windows.'[17]

The Devonshires, then, were seen as being grand and splendid in life, and
heroically tragic in death. But it was respect for rank and appreciation of
benevolence, rather than affection for a neighbour; for while Lady Fanny
Howard and her husband were resident full-time at Compton Place, the duke
himself, endlessly processing from one of his many residences to another,
preoccupied with committees in London and affairs at Barrow, was never
more than a short-term visitor. As the *Gazette* put it, greatly daring, in 1872,
'the requirements of his position prevented His Grace coming to Eastbourne
too much'.[18] Indeed, it was partly because his visits were such a rarity that
they provoked such paroxysms of joy when they took place, usually in July,
and then only for three weeks or so. Indeed, in September 1880, the *Gazette*
went even further in its comments:

> It would be too much to even hint that His Grace the Duke of Devonshire
> is guilty of absenteeism [by which they meant, of course, that in fact he
> was] . . ., but could not somebody prevail on the duke just to favour
> us a little more with his presence during a portion, at least, of the
> Season?[19]

This was not to be, however. Old, ailing and infirm, shattered by the death of
Lord Frederick, his favourite son, the duke became more of a recluse than ever,
more comfortable at Holker than in any other of his houses.

Accordingly, his real grip on day to day affairs in Eastbourne was negligible.
Like most grandees, he himself took all the fundamental policy decisions, but it
was on the basis of the (carefully-selected) information which his local agents
chose to let him see.[20] They, and other local figures, would visit him at
Compton Place, and solicit his approval for this scheme, and his financial
support for that; and, however much the duke may have been constrained –
either by doubts as to the viability of the venture, or by unwillingness to spend
money when his affairs in general were becoming increasingly bothersome –
they rarely appealed in vain. When in Eastbourne, he would drive around the
town, stop and inspect the sea wall or the water works, consult with his agents,
and get some overall picture of affairs; but his day-to-day involvement with the

town was non-existent. Dr Marshall's words describing his relationship with Barrow apply equally to his links with Eastbourne:

> He had as little and as much direct responsibility for the growth and development of Eastbourne or Buxton as for the growth of Barrow; he listened, encouraged, made money available, and allowed extremely capable underlings to get on with their work. On the positive side, he was a good enough judge of men to be able to appoint and keep these assistants, and his personal influence and great social standing carried some weight . . . He was very much more than a figurehead, and his attitude . . . was that of a well-informed and observant 'improving' landlord.[21]

But who were these 'extremely capable underlings' in the case of Eastbourne? And what was their work which he 'allowed them to get on with'?

2

The central figures in the business affairs of the dukes of Devonshire throughout the nineteenth century were their London solicitors, the Currey family. Benjamin Currey became solicitor to the sixth duke of Devonshire in 1827, and subsequently began to deal with the affairs of Lord George Augustus Cavendish as well.[22] On his death in 1848, he was followed by his son William, who was solicitor and adviser to both the sixth and seventh dukes until 1886. He in his turn was succeeded by his eldest son, Francis Alfred Currey, who was responsible for the overall direction of the Devonshires affairs until 1916. Another relative, Francis Edmond Currey, cousin of William Currey, was agent for the ducal estates in Ireland from 1839 until 1881, and again from 1883 to 1885. For three generations, therefore, the Curreys audited the ducal accounts, offered advice on ventures such as the Barrow companies and the Furness Railway, and mediated between the duke himself and the local agents.[23] Successive generations provided the secretaries of the Barrow Haematite Company, whose registered headquarters were located at the Curreys' office, and the family invested extensively in Barrow enterprises.

The same was true for Eastbourne. Again the Curreys provided successive secretaries to the Water Works and the Parks and Baths Companies, whose registered headquarters were at their own London office. Indeed, there were often directors' meetings of the Barrow and Eastbourne companies on the same day, with the same Cavendishes and Curreys participating in both. In addition, William Currey, besides his overall responsibility for the duke's affairs, was agent for the duke's Sussex estates from 1864 until 1886, and this post was then passed on to his younger son, Charles Herbert Currey, until 1896. As at Barrow, so at Eastbourne; the family invested heavily in those enterprises with which the Devonshires were involved, and had extensive shareholdings in the Water Works Company in particular. Finally, there was

Henry Currey, brother of William, and uncle of Francis Alfred and Charles Herbert.[24] Trained as an architect under Decimus Burton, Currey executed a variety of commissions for the seventh duke, including the Palace Hotel at Buxton and St Paul's church at Chiswick; but it was at Eastbourne that his influence was most marked, for he was employed as the chief architectural consultant from the dismissal of James Berry in 1859 until his death in 1900. He was responsible for the overall plans drawn up in 1859 and 1872, for the vetting of all the designs of houses submitted by lessees, and for many of the major buildings on the estate, including the theatre and pavilions of the Parks and Baths Company, the College and the Queen's Hotel. Moreover, in 1883, he was appointed the final authority in the dispute which was then raging about the design of the town hall. In a very real sense, he was the single most important aesthetic influence on the making of Eastbourne in the nineteenth century.[25]

Both as regards their estates in general, and particularly concerning Sussex, therefore, the affairs of the Devonshires may be seen in part as the interaction between the Cavendish and the Currey families. At Eastbourne itself, though, the most dominant figure during the first 20 years of development was Robert Insoll.[26] Born in 1811, he started in business as a coach builder in Lewes, but in 1858 was appointed local agent for the duke's Sussex estates. In this capacity, he soon came to be connected with all those aspects of the town's affairs with which Devonshire himself was linked. He was a member of the board of guardians, a J.P., and one of the original members of the local board, on which he sat until 1880. He was a founder and director of the Water Works Company, in which he held shares, chairman of the Parks and Baths Company until his death in 1898, a member of the council of Eastbourne College, and an enthusiastic supporter of the local hunt, which habitually met at his home. His important role in encouraging and persuading the duke to invest in Eastbourne was widely recognized, and his death in 1898 occasioned 'general and sincere sorrow'.

However, Insoll, powerful, experienced, and well-connected though he was, was gradually superseded as Eastbourne's Pooh Bah by George Ambrose Wallis who, between the 1860s and 1880s, created for himself a position of power reminiscent of that occupied by James Ramsden in Barrow and E. W. Wilmott in Buxton.[27] Born in Sussex in 1840, he trained as a civil engineer, moved to Eastbourne in 1860, and immediately became associated with the development schemes of the seventh duke. In 1864 he became local agent of the Sussex building estate, and thereafter superintended the making of roads and sea walls, as well as the construction of the houses themselves. In 1884, on Insoll's retirement, he took over the administration of the Sussex agricultural estates as well. In addition, he was a founder and director of the Parks and Baths Company, and chief engineer, and then general manager of the water works, which on one occasion he was grand enough to refer to as 'my company'.[28] Like the Curreys, he was a shareholder in both undertakings and, from 1880, was the most powerful single figure on the council of Eastbourne College. In one way and another, therefore, almost all the Devonshire enterprises in Eastbourne were handled or run on the spot by Wallis himself.

Yet even this was only part of Wallis's multi-faceted activity; he was also, in his own right, in partnership with his brother William Lumb Wallis, one of the foremost speculative builders in the town. In this capacity we have already met his firm, which took 50 leases authorizing the construction of 80 houses worth £94,000 over the years 1868 to 1913: however, this was only a limited part of his activity. His offices, at 14 Sea Side Road, were not only his headquarters, but also those of the Compton Estate, as well as being the local office of the Water Works Company. In practice, these three theoretically separate undertakings were controlled by Wallis himself: employees and headed notepaper were interchangeable. So it was that Wallis the agent was able to award the major ducal contracts in the town to Wallis the builder. Accordingly, his firm was responsible for the completion of the drainage scheme in 1865–7 when the original contractor appointed by the local board went bankrupt; for the Western Parades and Duke's Drive; for the theatre and pavilion of the Parks and Baths Company; and for the offices and pumps of the Water Works Company. If Devonshire provided the money, and Henry

Fig. 37. 14 Sea Side Road, as decorated for the coronation of George V, 1911; by this time, the Devonshire Estate Office had been moved, at the insistence of the eighth duke, to the grounds of Compton Place (by courtesy of the Eastbourne Water Works Company).

Currey was responsible for the overall plan, it was Wallis himself who actually brought much of the town into being.

3

So it was that while the many threads which wove the pattern of Eastbourne's nineteenth-century development emanated from the seventh duke at Chatsworth or Holker, they were all – sooner or later – gathered into Wallis's hands in Eastbourne itself. Yet even this was not the sum total of his empire. His unique position of dominance in the town derived not only from his influence as the foremost local representative of the duke, but also from his power and authority on the local board and town council, which his presence effectively made an extension of the Cavendish-centred oligarchy. Of course, neither the local board established in 1858 nor the council which replaced it in 1883 represented, during the life of the seventh duke, any real threat to his prominent position. The board might be responsible for the lighting and policing of the town; but it was the larger financial manipulations of the Devonshires which had brought the town into being. Indeed, most of the decisions fundamental to the town's affairs – when and how to develop, and in what particular way – were not taken in Eastbourne at all, or if they were, were reached within the walls of Compton Place, rather than at the local board. Timid, possessed of small financial resources and even less imagination, and always more eager to ask the duke for assistance than to act creatively or energetically themselves, the local board was little more than the scene of petty, trivial, and highly disorganized squabbles. On the eve of its transformation into a council, for instance, the *Gazette* pleaded that the new municipal body should not perpetuate the bad conduct of its predecessor, where there was no order in debates, and where it was customary for two or three people to speak together, at interminable length. Indeed, as the *Gazette* explained in defending itself from complaints that its reports of local board debates were inaccurate, this was hardly surprising, since sometimes it was impossible to hear or see what was going on.[29]

Nevertheless, the local board and its successor did consist, from the earliest, of the 'social leaders' of the town, and insofar as its composition altered during the lifetime of the seventh duke, it was because the 'social leaders' of an obscure Sussex fishing village in the 1850s were very different from the 'social leaders' of the thriving, high-class holiday resort which Eastbourne had become 30 years later. As table 39 shows, from the 1850s onwards, the farmers and tenants of the duke's rural Sussex estates were gradually superseded by the speculative builders and representatives of the entertainments and service industries. As early as 1882, the 'plethora of builders on the Board' began to attract attention in the local press, and they were soon joined (predictably) – by those tradesmen who catered for the needs of a high-class resort – booksellers, tailors, upholsterers and auctioneers.[30]

Table 39. Composition of Eastbourne local board and council, 1858–90

Year	Farmer	Builder	Doctor	Legal	Clergy	Drink/ hotelier	Tradesman	Rentier/ gent.	Misc.
1858	6	2	2	0	2	4	2	2	4
1860	4	2	2	0	2	4	2	3	5
1865	3	2	4	0	1	4	2	3	5
1870	3	3	2	0	1	4	3	4	4
1875	2	7	2	1	1	3	4	3	1
1880	1	8	3	1	1	3	3	3	1
1883	0	6	3	3	0	3	5	3	1
1885	1	9	2	3	0	3	9	3	2
1890	1	8	3	3	0	2	9	3	3

Source: Nominations printed in the local press, returns of members in local board and council Minute Books; and street and commercial directories.
Note: The local board consisted of 24 members, the council of 32.

But in the same way that the great companies in the town were financially indebted to, and psychologically dependent on, the power and wealth of the seventh duke, so the local government organism was itself in effect an extension of the ducal oligarchy. Robert Insoll, whom we have already met, was a member of the local board – and is here classified as 'gentleman' – from its inception in 1859 until its disappearance in 1883. He was supported by F. J. Howard – another 'gentleman' – who was the duke's brother-in-law, the tenant of Compton Place, a J.P., a member of the Board of Guardians, a member of Eastbourne College Council, and again on the local board from the beginning. And in the same category came another relative, Lieutenant F. W. H. Cavendish, formerly of the Foreign Office, but resident in Eastbourne from 1850, once more a J.P., a member of the board of guardians and the College council, and a long-serving representative on the local board.[31] So, while there were, significantly, no direct representatives of the Gilbert family on the local board, these three gentlemen, of impeccable and unrivalled local status, ensured that the duke's interests were well safeguarded. As the *Gazette* had the temerity to put it in 1863, criticizing the 'duke's influence over parish affairs' as being already 'too preponderating', 'it has been said that Paris is France and France is the Emperor. May we not with equal plausibility say that the local board is Eastbourne and the Duke is the local board?'[32]

This comment was occasioned by the appointment of George Ambrose Wallis as the surveyor to the local board, thereby strengthening the ducal party still further.[33] Three years later, he resigned this post, and was elected a member of the board itself. Immediately he was put on the Highways Committee, on which Insoll already sat, and – despite local objections that 'although they had a very generous duke' they 'did not want all duke's men on the committee' – there he stayed.[34] As a result, he wrote to the board in his capacity as ducal agent, asking them to take over roads he had often built as a contractor, which he as a member of the Highways Committee of the board would then approve;[35] and when, in 1881, there was the faintest suggestion that the board might consider bidding for the duke's water company, Wallis was able to ensure that there were enough abstentions at the meeting to prevent the matter even being discussed.[36] The local board was as much part of the Devonshire-Wallis oligarchy as any of the town's great companies were.

By the early 1880s, Insoll, Cavendish and Howard were beginning to feel 'the weight of years', and took the change from local board to council as an opportunity to withdraw from municipal life.[37] Wallis, however, was by now in so commanding a position that this in no way undermined his dominance; for, in April 1883, on the very eve of incorporation, he had become chairman of the local board, and this, combined with his unrivalled and diverse activities elsewhere in the town, meant that there was 'no doubt' he would become first mayor.[38] To the *Gazette*, at least, it seemed that having defined the qualities necessary in a mayor, they pointed inexorably – and appropriately – to one man alone:

> He must be kind, courteous, liberal, ready with his tongue and pen, acquainted with all the requirements of the town, and be willing to assist to the utmost to aid in all measures of public good. He must be tolerably wealthy . . . The choice of the town points instinctively to one man who possesses, in great degree, all the requirements we have pointed out. We need scarcely say that we allude to Mr. George Ambrose Wallis . . . To be the first Mayor of this Borough would be a proud distinction for any gentleman, and we shall be very pleased – and in saying this we feel we are expressing the general wish of the town – to see this distinction conferred on our well-known and esteemed townsman, Mr. George Ambrose Wallis.[39]

Having topped the poll in the first municipal elections, he was unanimously elected mayor.[40] The seventh duke presented the mayoral chain, and there was a lavish mayoral banquet in the Devonshire Park. In October 1884 he was unanimously re-elected for a second year, and received an illuminated address, embodying the thanks of the council for

> his constant endeavour to promote, during his year of office, the welfare of the Borough generally, and for the due performance of his public duties under many circumstances of delicacy inseparable from the transfer of power from a Local Board to a Municipal Corporation.[41]

So in the mid-1880s, both municipal affairs – centred on the town hall – and ducal business – conducted from 14 Sea Side Road – were dominated by Wallis. As the *Eastbourne Chronicle* put it on his death, 'Not only no other man, but no combination of men, have played anything approaching the close and active part in relation to the development of Eastbourne' that he had.[42] And his power in each separate but complementary sphere only served to increase his influence in the other. At Chatsworth and Compton Place, he was not only a subordinate, ducal agent, but could speak with the authority of the town's first mayor, while in the council chamber his municipal prestige was uniquely enhanced by being the local representative of the House of Cavendish as well. He was both the biggest decision-maker in the town, and the man responsible for providing the evidence on which the biggest decision-maker outside the town reached his conclusions as well. Accordingly, while in other seaside towns incorporation might be the result or symbol of municipal emancipation from aristocratic tutelage, at Eastbourne – so long as Wallis continued to straddle both worlds so effectively – the town and its council remained subordinate to ducal control.

As the foremost townsman, Wallis's position was thus as unrivalled as it was impregnable. But for a man of his boundless energy, consuming ambition and breadth of outlook, even all this was not enough. An Improvement Act, passed in 1879, had made it possible for the local board to borrow £30,000 so as to begin work on the sea wall to the east of Grand Parade (the only major part of the foreshore which the Devonshires did not own), and to construct a town hall;[43] but both of these ventures were delayed, the first because the contractor went bankrupt, the second because a design could not be agreed upon. So Wallis's first act as mayor was to obtain a second Improvement Act, which made possible the raising of further funds so as to complete these schemes.[44] Even then his ambition was not satisfied. He tried to become a contractor on an epic, heroic scale, by promoting a new and direct railway link between Eastbourne and London, and he aspired to national fame and celebrity by seeking election to the House of Commons for the newly-created Eastbourne constituency of Sussex in 1885. Because these episodes reveal much about Wallis's position in Eastbourne and his relationship with the seventh duke, they are best examined in turn.

4

By the early 1880s, both Devonshire in particular and the inhabitants of Eastbourne in general were increasingly dissatisfied with the lamentable service which they felt was being provided between Eastbourne and the capital by the London, Brighton & South Coast Railway. In July 1882, while he was visiting Compton Place, Devonshire discussed the matter with C. H. Currey, Wallis and Insoll. 'We have been endeavouring to get the Brighton Company to make some improvements', he later recorded. 'They do not absolutely refuse, but give very unsatisfactory answers.'[45] To Laing, the managing director, he wrote imperiously:

The prospects of obtaining an improved service to Eastbourne appear to be very unsatisfactory . . . I am unwilling to abandon hopes of such improvements being speedily effected, but if such should prove not to be the case, I shall hold myself at liberty to endeavour by other means to obtain such railway facilities as the size and importance of Eastbourne now require.[46]

By this threat, Devonshire did not mean the taking of independent action, but rather that 'our wants' must be 'supplied by some other company', preferably the Midland; but the men on the spot had other ideas.

In August 1882, the very same month in which Devonshire had sent off his withering letter to the London Brighton & South Coast, Wallis and some local colleagues elaborated a scheme for a direct line from London to Eastbourne, passing between the main lines of the London Brighton & South Coast and the South Eastern, via Uckfield and Westerham to Beckenham, where it would join up with, and have running rights over, the London, Chatham & Dover Railway, all the way to Victoria. Predictably, the trump card which Wallis hoped to be able to play was to obtain the support of the duke and the services of his solicitors. After all, he had been able to persuade the duke to give money for many local ventures, and a direct railway, although on a larger scale, was essentially the same type of undertaking. William Currey showed immediate enthusiasm, and wrote a tactful letter to the duke, in which he recognized his 'reluctance to associate yourself with any scheme which might involve you in any liability to provide funds', but at the same time asked him if he would be prepared to contribute £5,000 towards the cost of promotion.[47] Indeed, throughout September 1882, Wallis and Currey bombarded Devonshire with letters and memoranda, arguing that without such a direct line, the town's future prospects might be irredeemably harmed, and that 'such an opportunity as now exists . . . may not occur again for a very long period.'[48]

Devonshire was not convinced. Still dazed by the assassination of Lord Frederick, concerned about the gloomy state of affairs at Barrow, and worried by the general reduction in income which the account books had shown over the last few years, he was far from eager to become involved with another large, costly and potentially unprofitable enterprise. Moreover, as he took pains to point out, he had never at any time indicated his willingness to support an independent venture. Assuredly, he shared to the full the feelings of hostility to the London Brighton & South Coast which were harboured by the local inhabitants. But, as he explained in a letter, his idea of finding 'other means' to solve the problem had meant supporting a scheme emanating from another major company – a fact of which Currey and Wallis had been made well aware at the July meeting at Compton Place:

I am extremely sorry not to be able to agree with you and Wallis on this question, but I cannot at any rate reproach myself for having on any occasion caused you to supppose that I should be in favour of a direct line. The subject was certainly alluded to when I saw your son Herbert and Wallis in July at Compton Place, but it was alluded to in connection with an idea that the Midland Railway Company might possibly be disposed to take up the scheme. If I had had the slightest idea that it was in contemplation to undertake it as an independent scheme, I should have expressed myself unhesitatingly against it.[49]

Thus chastised, the Curreys, bowing to the duke's 'decision not to encourage the line', ceased to act as solicitors to the promoters.[50]

However, Wallis's 'ambition to pose as a railway promoter and engineer' was not to be thwarted so easily.[51] He obtained the support of other major landowners along the route such as Lords Chichester, de la Warr and Stanhope, and induced 'about a score of the wealthiest and most influential townsmen' in Eastbourne to 'put their names down as a guarantee for the preliminary expenses of promoting the bill in Parliament'.[52] Assailed by Wallis with such news, Devonshire felt obliged 'to some extent . . . to reconsider his decision'. He still believed it unlikely that a parliamentary committee would be convinced, and would himself have preferred 'to make another attempt to induce the London and Brighton Company to give better accommodation to Eastbourne'. Yet in the light of all this evidence of local support, he was prepared, grudgingly, to change his views. However, he made it emphatically plain that he would not 'undertake to take any shares in the company should the bill be obtained' and, in a letter to Currey of November 1882, he made his position unequivocally clear:

As the proposed direct Eastbourne railway has received so much support at Eastbourne, and as the promoters make such a point of your acting as London solicitors, I do not think it would be right for me to refuse my assent, provided you can make it clearly understood that I am not thereby committed to any active support of the undertaking. I am still unable to promise it any active assistance, as I continue to think that it is in the power of the Brighton Company to give Eastbourne a much improved service, and that being obviously their interest to do so, they cannot permanently withhold it.[53]

And, he added ominously, if the bill did appear before a parliamentary committee, 'I shall certainly not disguise my real opinion. I fear it is quite possible my evidence would do more harm than good.'

The bill was finally deposited late in December 1882, and the directors included Robert Insoll and the Wallis brothers, who were also named as the company's engineers.[54] In the early months of 1883, excitement in Eastbourne ran high. It was confidently asserted that 'there would be such a procession of landowners to the committee rooms of the House of Commons who would give such favourable evidence, that success is certain'.[55] One of the last major acts of the local board was to pass a resolution unanimously supporting the venture, and in April the *Gazette* reported triumphantly that 'thousands of the inhabitants of Eastbourne have signed the petition in favour of the new line';[56]

but Devonshire remained unconvinced. He gave £1,000 towards the fund to pay the parliamentary costs, and grudgingly agreed that if the bill was passed he would take up shares to the value of £20,000 or £30,000.[57] Even if this was going farther than he would have wished, it was far less lavish support than Wallis had hoped for.

Moreover, the proceedings in London vindicated his scepticism for, despite the support of the landowners through whose estates the projected line might pass, the opposition, including as it did the London, Brighton & South Coast, the South Eastern Railway and the London, Chatham & Dover, over whose metals the proposed line was intended to run for part of its length, was overwhelmingly strong, and its case formidable. Was it really likely, their counsel inquired, that the £3,000,000 needed to finance the venture could be raised locally, as the promoters claimed, when so far only £250,000 had been promised? If the present service to Eastbourne was so utterly unsatisfactory, why was it that the town had grown with such spectacular rapidity in the last 20 years? And was it really plausible to maintain that a line which did not pass through a single large town between Eastbourne and London could be made to pay purely on the basis of holiday and commuter traffic? Nor was Lord Edward Cavendish, appearing on behalf of his father, exactly ideal witness material as far as the promoters were concerned:

> He did not take the initiative in the commencement: he wished to wait and see what the feeling of the inhabitants of Eastbourne was . . . He was prepared to give it his support . . . The duke is rather backing up the people of Eastbourne than taking any initiative himself.[58]

Not surprisingly, the bill did not pass.

Angry and bruised, the local promoters were determined to recover some of their parliamentary costs from the L.B.S.C.R., and – predictably – sought the assistance of the duke in this endeavour. But, while he himself reluctantly subscribed a further thousand pounds towards paying off their debts, he would not be drawn into this new battle. 'I am sorry that the undertaking has turned out so unfortunately for the professional men concerned', he wrote to Currey after it was all over, 'but they must surely have been aware that they were incurring a serious risk.' 'I strongly disapproved of the direct London and Eastbourne railway', he added, 'and I thought it a great mistake.'[59]

Wallis's second grand design did not meet with any greater success. The re-distribution Act which had been passed in 1885 after the Third Reform Act created the 'south' or 'Eastbourne' constituency of Sussex, its name an apt reflection of the fact that nearly one half of the population in this otherwise rural region lived in Eastbourne itself. Although Wallis had taken care to avoid party politics on the council during his time as mayor, and although his own political views were largely unknown, it was rumoured during the spring of 1885, as the second year of his mayoralty drew on, that he might contest the constituency in the Liberal interest.[60] In May 1855, he was formally chosen, and the local papers at once threw their weight behind him. The *Gazette* claimed that, despite the area's reputation for being highly Conservative, Wallis's 'success at the poll is almost assured', and contrasted his high 'personal status and popularity' with the 'fallacies' and 'sophistries' of the 'Conservative candidate and satellites', Captain Field, previously M.P. for Croydon. The latter retaliated by claiming that the Eastbourne press dealt with his campaign 'unfairly', and argued that Eastbourne was a pocket borough of the Duke of Devonshire.[61]

Wallis, for his part, had taken the greatest care not to tread on the toes of the Cavendishes. Indeed, he had ensured that none of them wished to stand for the constituency before allowing his own name to go forward. Moreover, in May 1885, Lord Edward Cavendish wrote to Wallis from Chatsworth on behalf of his father, announcing that he had heard 'with much satisfaction' of Wallis's candidacy, and sending 'best wishes' for his success.[62] As the campaign hotted up in the summer of 1885, the *Gazette* hammered away at the disparity between the claims of Wallis, the local worthy, and Field, the complete outsider. On the one hand, it argued, the mayor was of proven 'sagacity, judgment, tact and indomitable energy', and his claims were 'founded upon personal fitness, a community of interests and a political intelligence before which those of Captain Field sink into insignificance'.[63] Field, by contrast, was depicted as an outsider in terms remarkably similar to those which had been used by the radical press of Birmingham to describe Augustus Calthorpe in 1880:

> A perfect stranger in the town and neighbourhood. So far as we know, he has never contributed a shilling of money to promote our interest; he owns not a sod of earth, a blade of grass, or a brick in a building throughout the whole constituency.

For the editor of the *Gazette*, at least, the choice was therefore simple, between

> A man who has nothing in common with you, of whom you know nothing, who knows nothing of you, and cares as much, beyond obtaining your suffrage; or your neighbour, the owner of so much of your rateable property; the Chairman and Director of many of your Companies, the man whom you have delighted to honour with the highest position of your Corporation for two successive years.

Certainly, throughout the summer months, Wallis's meetings in the town itself were a triumphant success, and the *Gazette* was anxious to make the most of them. 'Seldom if ever has so large and enthusiastic a political meeting been held at Eastbourne', it noted after the large Liberal gathering, chaired by Lord Edward Cavendish, held in June.[64] By contrast, the press argued, Field's meetings in the town – to which it gave less than half the space it lavished on Wallis's – were unenthusiastically attended, so much so that there could be 'little doubt' of the Liberal majority in the town.[65] And yet, as even the *Gazette* hinted on occasions, Wallis fared less well in the rural villages whose combined voting population equalled, if it did not actually surpass, that of Eastbourne itself. There, on occasions, Wallis was shouted down, while Field, knowing that Eastbourne itself was as good as lost, shrewdly concentrated his efforts on the rival parts of the constituency.

He did so to good effect. For even though the Liberals brought down Harcourt to speak for Wallis at a monster meeting in the town held in early December, the town did not prevail over the country, as the final results showed:

> Captain Field 3,561
> G. A. Wallis 3,497

In consequence, the champagne supper which Wallis had had prepared at the town hall in celebration of his momentous victory was never eaten, but so narrow was his defeat that the townsmen looked upon it as a 'moral victory', and eagerly dragged Wallis's carriage in torchlit procession through the streets, before carrying him shoulder high to his home.[66]

5

Although Wallis had been defeated only by a whisker, and although the growth of Eastbourne might have been expected to shift the balance of voting in that constituency in his favour, Wallis in fact never again stood for Parliament. For Wallis and Eastbourne, like the Devonshires, moved to the Unionist side as a result of Home Rule, and the constituency became that bastion of Conservatism which it has since remained: it was Captain Field, not Wallis, who was the chief beneficiary of this charge. But this setback, and his failure as a railway promoter, while they marked the end of his attempts to break out from the confines of Eastbourne on to a larger stage, in no sense diminished Wallis's standing or his influence in the town. A year after he retired as mayor, his portrait was hung in the newly-completed town hall, to the enthusiastic endorsement of the local paper:

> The first Mayor of the Borough always has a difficult task. He has no precedent to guide him, and he has to lay down precedents for his successors. Mr Wallis was an admirable chief magistrate . . . 'Best Mayor we are ever likely to have', was a common remark during the two years Mr Wallis held office.[67]

In October 1886, his name was canvassed as a worthy Jubilee Mayor, and two years later, he was once more suggested: 'Everyone would hail Alderman G. A. Wallis as Mayor again with delight and, provided he would stand again, no better President of the Council could be desired.'[68] Again, nothing came of it. But as an alderman, the architect of incorporation, the local representative of the duke, and a major building contractor in his own right, he remained the most dominant figure in the town and on the council. His grandiose house,

Fig. 38. George Ambrose Wallis as first mayor of Eastbourne, 1883–5 (by courtesy of Eastbourne Borough Council).

Holywell Mount, built in 1879, at a cost of £10,000, was the largest dwelling in the town, with the exception of Compton Place, and was the centre of local society.[69] Ten years later, he moved to an even more sumptuous house, Fairfield Court. He and his brother were both J.P.s, and leading lights in the Eastbourne Hunt. Wallis himself was a patron of the Flower Show and Cycle Club, a member of the local branch of Freemasons, a Life Governor of Princess Alice Hospital and a Director of the Queen's Hotel. Even today, he is remembered in the town as the man who could 'fix' anything.

Fig. 39. Fairfield Court, home of George Ambrose Wallis, 1889–95 (by courtesy of Eastbourne Public Library).

As long as Wallis continued to straddle the two worlds of the estate office and the council chamber, there was no real possibility of any major clash between the council and the resident landowner, as had already occurred in other resorts like Southport or Torquay. The combination of sustained and lavish ducal spending and Wallis's immense local stature delayed the emancipation of the council in Eastbourne longer than in any other major resort. In 1892, however, shortly after the succession of the eighth duke, he resigned from the council, on the grounds of pressure of work. His decision was greeted with 'unfeigned regret' by the inhabitants of the town, and he was unanimously urged to reconsider;[70] But he could not be persuaded. His absence from the local governing body was ever after lamented, for, as the *Gazette* explained in August 1894, 'his retirement from the Council is still a frequent source of regret to those who have at heart the interests of the town, and favour a policy of enterprise and progress'.[71] A month later, his daughter married, and the rival paper took the opportunity to summarize Wallis's unique contribution to the town:

> The primary and dominating factor was undoubtedly the high and widespread esteem entertained for the bride's father, whose long, prominent and honourable association with the best interests of the town is generally and appreciatively recognized by all the townspeople. No man knows Eastbourne better; no man has laboured more diligently and with results more practical and lasting to build the enviable reputation which distinguishes it; no man has identified himself more heartily with its local institutions and recreative engagements, and the election of Mr Wallis as first Mayor represented an honour no less deserved than exalted. Few public men have enjoyed a larger measure of popularity and regard among their former citizens, and fewer still have more steadfastly maintained the respect due to their services and character.[72]

Only a year later, he died, suddenly and unexpectedly. Like France on the death of General de Gaulle, Eastbourne was widowed by his passing. He, more than any other man, had created and dominated the town, and it was quite impossible to imagine the place without him. The morbid eloquence of the local press was unbounded:

> Words utterly fail to express any adequate sense of the mingled stupefaction and sorrow which the sad event has produced, from one end of the town to the other . . . The deplorable occurrence is not simply a misfortune. It is a calamity . . . The news yesterday that he had actually succumbed, produced an almost appalling sensation throughout the town, and became the sorrowful and sole topic of discussion amongst all classes. It was difficult to recognize the stern and awful fact that Eastbourne's foremost townsman, whom all creeds and social classes have so often delighted to honour, had been taken away, never again to figure amid the scenes and the community to which he was so strongly attached.[73]

His funeral, attended by all the members of the town council, every local J.P., and the entire staff from the offices of 14 Sea Side Road, was the greatest public spectacle in nineteenth-century Eastbourne. Six coaches of family mourners were followed by another 50 carriages in an endless cortège, and there were over 100 wreaths. Predictably, but appropriately, the headmaster of Eastbourne College, who delivered the funeral oration, observed that 'It may be said that of George Wallis, all Eastbourne is the tomb. *Si monumentum requiris, circumspice*.'[74] Monuments were subsequently placed in St Saviour's church, of which Wallis was a first churchwarden and where he regularly worshipped, and in Eastbourne College, where a scholarship was also endowed in his memory. His will was later proved at £85,000: Wallis and Eastbourne had benefitted reciprocally from their association.[75]

6

The early 1890s were accordingly a turning-point in Eastbourne's history, and in the Devonshires' contribution to it. The death of the seventh duke, so strikingly lamented in 1891, and the departure of Wallis from the town council in the following year, brought to an end the first phase in the town's history. During that period, Wallis has provided the ideas, and the duke had made the money available. A weak and psychologically dependent local board and town council could no more match the resources of the duke than it could, or wished to, threaten his power. Occasional words might be said against the influence of 'the duke's party', and in the 1885 general election, the Devonshires were briefly toppled from their Olympian position above the party-political battle; but these were temporary, and soon-forgotten, aberrations. The combination of a grand aristocratic owner and his energetic local representative meant that during the lifetime of the seventh duke, Eastbourne was the scene of the strongest aristocratic influence, and the home of the least assertive, most dependent municipal body of any major seaside resort. In this period, it was truly 'The Duke's Town' – even though it was 'Wallis's town yet more.

21 Changed policy and improved fortunes, 1891–1914

Four years before Wallis's death, the seventh duke had been succeeded by his eldest and only surviving son, Spencer Compton. Until very recently, it has been assumed that he played an insignificant part in his family's financial history. Here, for example, is Bickley's account:

> He loved his lands, but the fact that his father's life overlapped with his by so many years relieved him, during the greater part of his career, of the responsibilities of the management of his broad acres. When at last his property came to him from the capable hands of the seventh duke, it was in a very different condition from that to which it had been reduced by the sixth duke's lavishness.[1]

And Holland, in his mammoth biography, complemented this picture with an account of the eighth duke as an idle and feeble man of business:

> His innate slowness, or lethargic habit of mind made it increasingly difficult for him to keep in touch with the movements of other minds. His own mind worked slowly . . . His duties as chairman of companies in which he was by far the largest shareholder were rather irksome to him. He distrusted his knowledge of business matters, consequently he did not, as a rule, attempt to force his views as chairman on his colleagues . . . His business mind worked slowly . . . I have heard him say 'It may be all right and clear, but I don't understand it in the least'.

Indeed, Charles Hamilton, his personal secretary and adviser, to whom Holland was indebted for this information, went even further, and claimed that on one occasion the duke had told him that his motto should have been, 'Never do today what you can put off till tomorrow'.[2]

Under these circumstances, so the traditional argument runs, it was perhaps as well that the eighth duke was free to enjoy his estates: at East-bourne, for instance, he was no innovator, but a 'worthy upholder of the Cavendish traditions'.[3] Yet, in the same way that recent research has replaced the traditional picture of the eighth duke as an indolent and slow-witted politician by a more realistic portrait which sees him as cunning, shrewd and ambitious, so the evidence which will be advanced here forces a similarly different interpretation on his activities as a landlord and man of business, both with regard to his estates in general, and to Eastbourne in particular.[4] For it was in large part as a result of the policy decisions taken by the eighth duke in the years immediately after he inherited that relations between the family and the town were fundamentally altered.

1

The overall financial situation in 1891 was – *pace* Bickley – far from encouraging. The debt secured on the ducal estates was twice that which his father had inherited; it was mopping up an unprecendented £80,000 a year in service charges; and at the same time the slump at Barrow combined with the agricultural depression had severely reduced current income (see Appendix D). Early in 1894, by which time his father's affairs had been wound up, the eighth duke finally took stock of the situation, and was overwhelmed by what he found. 'It vexed me to see you so worried and bothered about affairs', his sister wrote to him after a meeting at which the sale of Devonshire House had been discussed. Urging him to reconsider, she suggested the disposal of lands in Derbyshire and Ireland,[5] but her suggestions brought him little comfort. 'I am sorry to say', he wrote back 'that financial prospects do not improve on examination.'[6] He went on to explain why:

> I do not think they were ever so bad, even in the time of the old duke . . .
> An immense amount of capital, in the shape of coal and iron royalties, has
> been used up and sunk in unproductive Barrow investments, and there is
> now no surplus income over the fixed charges except that from such
> dividends as remain, and are liable to still further reduction. I can't say
> that at present I can see anything to be done except to shut up Chatsworth
> and Hardwick, and make large reductions there.

Indeed, as he investigated the accounts more deeply, his anxiety only increased. 'Money cannot be shorter anywhere than it is here', he noted; a not unreasonable comment at a time when estate revenue had plummeted to £65,000, when dividend income was sliding to a trough of £15,000, and when more than half his current income was appropriated to service the debt.[7] Finally, the very same year in which the eighth duke came to terms with the problems of his inheritance was that in which the Liberal government introduced their death duties. At a rate of 10 per cent on estates of over £1,000,000, they were hardly crippling, but to a landowner as encumbered as the eighth duke, they represented a severe burden: so much so that he actually wrote to Harcourt, pointing out the difficulties which his successor at Chatsworth would face in meeting such demands, with heavy mortgages and a depleted income. However, Harcourt was unsympathetic.[8]

Once the shock of discovery was past, the duke took immediate and purposeful action. The two chief themes of his father's policy – the exploitation of estate resources to their fullest extent, and the increase in encumbrances so as to finance the necessary business ventures to make this possible – were both put smartly into reverse. At Barrow, the large Devonshire holdings in the Steel Company, the Shipbuilding Company and the Naval Construction and Armaments Company were gradually liquidated. Only in the Furness Railway did the family retain a controlling interest, and this vanished in 1923 when the company was absorbed into the L.M.S. In Ireland the seventh duke's holdings in the Waterford, Dungarvan & Lismore Railway were sold off, and at Buxton the majority holding in the Baths Company was also liquidated.[9] At the same time, the systematic sale of land enabled the eighth duke and his successor to begin reducing the massive pile of encumbrances. By 1899, the debt had been cut to the level at which it stood in 1858, and by the time of the eighth duke's death in 1909, it was down to less than £500,000 (see Appendix D). The need to pay death duties on his estate meant that reduction was temporarily halted, but by 1933 the last of the outstanding mortgages had been paid off. By then, indeed, the sale of land and of Devonshire House in London had given the family sufficient surplus capital for them to invest extensively in home and foreign shares, so that from the 1920s some two-thirds of their current income was derived from equities rather than agricultural rentals. In many ways, therefore, the decisions of the eighth duke brought the Devonshires into a new financial world, the practices and presuppositions of which would have been alien to the seventh duke's way of thinking.[10]

2

Nowhere was this more true than at Eastbourne. For there, even more than at Barrow, Devonshire was convinced that his father's affairs had been mismanaged, and that revenue which should have been made available for the family had in fact been frittered extravagantly away by the irresponsibility of Wallis and the Curreys, whom on one occasion – reminiscent of the fifth Lord Calthorpe's appraisal of R. H. Milward – he described as being 'enough to ruin anybody'.[11] Indeed, he had entertained such suspicions even before he inherited. In 1890, perhaps aware that his father would not live much longer, and that new responsibilities would soon be his, he asked Herbert Currey for a statement 'showing the receipts and expenditure on the building estate at Eastbourne', as well as a 'description of the working of' the estate.[12] The reply has, alas, not survived, and Hartington himself – as he then was – never committed his doubts to paper, so that they must be inferred from subsequent reports and correspondence. Yet he was clearly worried that Wallis had become more interested in making money for himself than for the duke, and that so closely-knit an oligarchy could not be relied upon always to take decisions in the best interests of the landowner.

Nothing the eighth duke discovered on inheriting served to allay his doubts and suspicions and so, undeterred by the embarrassments and pain which his actions might cause, he commissioned two independent inquiries into the administration of the Eastbourne building estate since 1859, one from Price Waterhouse, the accountants, the other from Mr Farrant, a surveyor.[13] As he explained in a letter to Francis Alfred Currey, it was a decision which he regretted, but from which he would not be dissuaded:

I am afraid that the course of action which I have taken may indicate some want of confidence in your brother's management of the Eastbourne building estate. But I wish to state that although I may have doubts as to his experience and professional knowledge of the management of a building estate, I entirely disclaim any want of confidence beyond this . . . I have for some years past heard from more than one source criticisms of Mr Wallis' position in regard to the Eastbourne estate. They have been so indefinite that I have taken no notice of them; but it appears to me that his position is in some respects so peculiar that an independent examination would be satisfactory to all concerned.[14]

Indeed, in another letter to Charles Herbert Currey, he was even more direct, arguing that 'the results which have hitherto been obtained from the development of the building estate are inadequate, and that a change of policy . . . is necessary if any proper return is to be realized for the large expenditure which has been incurred.'[15] Accordingly, both Charles Herbert Currey and his cousin Henry, as well as Wallis himself, were instructed to give Price Waterhouse and Mr Farrant every facility they might require for their investigation.

Their conclusions appeared to vindicate fully the eighth duke's suspicions. Indeed, on the basis of Farrant's first report, drawn up by July 1894, and which concluded that 'it would be possible to obtain a large income from the Eastbourne estate . . . by getting a better price for the land or by a reduction of the expenditure on works, etc.', Devonshire gave instructions that, until the final reports were completed, 'the sales or lettings now in progress' should be 'suspended as far as possible'.[16] Price Waterhouse's report, running to 35 pages of foolscap, finally appeared in November, and drew attention to the curious manner in which the estate accounts were kept, whereby no distinction was made between capital and current account, and pointed out how remarkable it was that during the last three years, all the work which had been undertaken by the estate 'passed through Messrs Wallis & Wallis' hands'. They further stressed that the costs of managing the estate had only been £250 a year in the 1850s, whereas by the early 1890s, they had increased to £950.[17] This was followed in January 1895 by Farrant's report, which noted that since development had been begun, the expenses of Eastbourne's development had absorbed all the income – on both capital and current account – which had been produced; and he went on to suggest that as well as expenses being too high, rents were too low.[18] Altogether the reports – which Devonshire read and annotated carefully in his own hand – added up to an extensive criticism of the management of the estate under the eighth duke's predecessor, and did much to confirm his suspicions.

Clearly, this was a challenge to their professional integrity, and perhaps to their livelihood, which neither the Curreys nor Wallis could afford to ignore. Under these circumstances, it is hardly surprising that Wallis retired from the town council in the autumn of 1892, for by then it was probably already clear that the new duke would be a more alert and critical taskmaster than his predecessor. Accordingly, in the first three months of 1895, Charles Herbert Currey (who was, of course, as agent directly in charge of the estate and the man to whom Wallis was theoretically responsible) and Henry Currey (who had been in charge of the overall planning) produced a reply which amounted to 125 handwritten sides of foolscap. It was, Herbert Currey, admitted, 'a work of great magnitude, and has imposed on immense amount of labour upon myself and four of my assistants'. Moreover, he went on to express the hope that its contents would 'satisfy Your Grace that the development of the building estate has not, as Your Grace has been advised, been unsatisfactory, but on the contrary decidedly successful'.[19]

In the first place, Herbert Currey argued, while it was true that the sea walls and parades had been expensive, 'if this money had not been expended, Eastbourne would not have developed into the place which it now is'.[20] Moreover, insofar as contracts had been carried out by Wallis & Wallis, they had always been at cost price, with only the materials and labour charges being billed to the estate.[21] Above all, he stressed that 'no new work or any fresh developments were ever undertaken without full particulars, and the estimates of cost being previously submitted to the late duke and approved by him', and that 'no new works have been begun since the late duke's death.' Henry Currey's defence followed similar lines. As far as the contracts undertaken by Wallis & Wallis were concerned, he reiterated the view that 'they have been treated as ordinary customers. No favour or advantage whatever has been allowed to them.'[22] As to the accusation that the scheme of sea walls and broad, tree-lined roads was too extravagant, he contended that 'the liberality of treatment of roads and open spaces has made Eastbourne a favourite residential property, and tended very much to its success'.[23] Accordingly he, like his cousin, ended with a conclusion which combined defiance and wounded outrage in equal proportions:

> I cannot but feel some concern that, after thirty-five years work upon this estate, my professional capacity should be criticised in a somewhat hostile spirit by a gentleman who, I venture to think, has not the same experience in developing building estates as I have had. It is disappointing to find that an estate which has hitherto been considered a success should by an unusual manipulation of figures be represented as one of little financial value.[24]

Eighty years on, it is difficult to be sure who had the better of the argument. Whether the Curreys and Wallis had indeed been excessively extravagant, and had looked on each year's income as theirs to spend, rather than as a potential remittance to be sent to Chatsworth for the benefit of the duke, is not clear. The fact that expenditure in the years up to 1891 so nearly balanced income, combined with their awareness that if income was spent in Eastbourne, it would make them greater figures in the town, whereas if it was sent to Chatsworth, it would not, may have weighed heavily with the Curreys, and especially with Wallis. Moreover, as the episode over the direct railway to London showed, the Curreys and Wallis were on occasions all too eager to confront the duke with schemes which they had themselves evolved, which it was then difficult for him not to support, however reluctantly.

For what was true of the railway was also true of the Parks and Baths Company (whose facilities Devonshire had been convinced were too large), the College and the Parades.[25] While the Curreys were no doubt correct in asserting that not one penny had been spent on the estate without the duke's sanction, that still left open the possibility – and this was no doubt the eighth duke's main suspicion – that the constant requests for money to which the seventh duke had felt himself obliged to agree, were motivated more by delight in grand schemes for their own sake than for any real concern about what was best for the duke's affairs. A stray comment by Wallis in a letter to Currey – 'I do not think we should have much difficulty in getting the duke to accept our views of this matter' – certainly supports the eighth duke's suspicions, as does an earlier entry in the seventh duke's diary, where Wallis 'strongly recommended' the further extension of the sea wall, but Devonshire was 'not altogether satisfied that it is wanted at present'.[26] As the *Gazette* had noted as early as 1883, it was Wallis, the man on the spot, who 'induced the duke to spend so many thousands of pounds'.[27]

On the other hand, as the Curreys stressed in their report, unless a strong lead had been given by the duke – which meant the spending of considerable sums of money – the development would probably never have been successful at all. Of course it was true that the outlay on the sea walls, the Parks and Baths Company and the College had been large, and that there was no literal return on any of these investments; but such amenities were vital if a resort town was to be established: their strategic importance was far greater than any mere monetary return. Moreover, it is possible to argue, as the Curreys themselves did, that coincidental with the death of the seventh duke, the great phase of spending had come to a halt. The Parades were completed, the companies all as fully expanded as was necessary, the roads now such as would not be filled up with houses for several decades. As Herbert Currey put it:

> This heavy expenditure . . . has now been completed, and should Your Grace decide to continue the development, the expenditure would as far as I can foresee be limited to such outlay as must ordinarily be incurred in the development of any property for building.[28]

And it was certainly the case that between 1895 and 1908, expenditure on the estate was a mere £7,000 a year – only half of what it had been in the years 1880–94 (graph 6). But whether (as the Curreys insisted) the progress of development would have made this reduction inevitable anyway, or whether (as the eighth duke feared) expenditure, if unchecked by him, would have continued at its previous high level, it is impossible to say. In fairness to the

Curreys, however, it should be said that as far as the Barrow ventures were concerned, there is documentary proof that they had urged the seventh duke to pull out when things began to go wrong, and – at least as far as the College was concerned – Charles Herbert Currey claimed that he had 'on more than one occasion' urged the duke not to commit any more capital to the venture.[29] Moreover, at Eastbourne itself, in 1885, the seventh duke actually recorded in his diary that 'Wallis thinks a good deal of improvement, and also reduction of expenditure, may be brought about'.[30]

The most that could be said for the duke's suspicions, then, was that some evidence did suggest that on occasions Wallis and the Curreys had become more interested in extending Eastbourne and aggrandizing themselves than was altogether consistent with their professional obligations to the duke. The best that could be said in their defence was that without heavy expenditure in the short term (from 1858 to 1890), there was no real long-term prospect that the venture would be a financial success. What is not in doubt is that there were – no doubt as a consequence of this episode – fundamental changes in the management of the estate. Wallis himself died in 1895, and in the following year Charles Herbert Currey ceased to act as agent for the Sussex estate. Five years later, Henry Currey died – and for the previous decade or so, he had excercised no real control over aesthetic matters. Accordingly, in 1896, the eighth duke himself appointed as resident agent James Cockerell, a man who took over all the functions once exercised, with regard to the Sussex estates, by the two Curreys and Wallis.[31] He, like his successor Roland Burke, was first and foremost a professional agent; and above all he was the duke's man. Finally, in 1901, the estate office was removed from 14 Sea Side Road, and new buildings were constructed within the grounds of Compton Place itself.[32] The unified power of the old Currey-Wallis elite, of which the buildings at 14 Sea Side Road had been the apt symbol, was broken for good.

3

The result was a system of administration which, although in many ways outwardly similar to that which had prevailed in the days of the seventh duke, was in fact much more efficient and responsible. Every year in late January or February, estimates were sent to the duke of the anticipated income and expenditure for the year.[33] The filling of important local jobs, such as the engineer to the Water Works Company in 1907, was only undertaken by Currey and Cockerell after they had 'ascertained the duke's wishes' relative to the appointment.[34] Occasional letters survive from Cockerell direct to the duke, with accounts of routine business such as the state of cottages on the agricultural estate, and the need to extend land for building purposes.[35] Devonshire was unfailingly the supreme authority in decisions as to whether the estate should go to court to enforce covenants, and whether it should allow the granting of a licence to turn a residential house into a shop or preparatory school. 'His Grace does not think that the use of no. 49 Blackwater Road as a nursing home will prove a nuisance to the neighbours or diminish the value of the adjoining property', Cockerell informed Currey after Devonshire had waded through an interminable amount of correspondence, petitions and complaints on the subject.[36] The licence was accordingly granted.

Early in the new century, one further embarrassing episode occurred between the Curreys and the duke, reminiscent of the problems that the Calthorpes had with R. H. Milward, and further proof of Devonshire's sound judgment and intuitive insight. In 1901, he decided that the overall accounts concerning his affairs which were drawn up by the Curreys in their office at 14 Great George Street should be externally audited, and Price Waterhouse was again called in.[37] Almost immediately, they discovered that the Curreys' chief cashier had defrauded the duke of £12,100 and the partners themselves of nearly £10,000 over a ten-year period.[38] F.A. Currey grovelled once more, abjectly offering to repay the duke the amount he had lost from his own resources,[39] but Devonshire would hear nothing of it, and declared his intention 'to bear the loss myself', adding in consolation, 'I regret to learn that your private loss is considerable'.[40] Late in July, Noble, the cashier, was sentenced to five years' penal servitude.[41] As with the report on the Eastbourne estate, it is not easy to infer exactly what was going on in Devonshire's mind. But there can be no doubt that the audit which revealed the fraud 'was made at his request and on his initiative', and tradition has it that the duke's suspicion had first been aroused by seeing Noble at Ascot.

For whatever precise reason, there can be no doubt that the years 1891–1914 saw a fundamental change in the financial position of the Devonshires in Eastbourne, just as they saw a more general change in their overall circumstances. To begin with, the same policy was adopted with regard to the Eastbourne companies as had been pursued with reference to Barrow, Buxton and Ireland. Appeals for further funds from the College and the Pier Company in the mid-1890s which, had the seventh duke still been alive, would surely have been looked upon favourably, were refused.[42] In 1897, and again in 1913 and 1914, unsuccessful but determined attempts were made to sell off the entire Parks and Baths Company to the council.[43] Although the dukes were prepared to finance – for the benefit of the town as a whole – a private orchestra, this expenditure was of very short duration.[44] At Eastbourne as elsewhere, the policy of the seventh duke was rapidly reversed.

In the same way, there was no more extensive spending under the heading of 'earthworks, roads and sewers'. The Western Parades and Duke's Drive – the road from the town to Beachy Head – were both completed, and no further large projects were undertaken. The result was exceedingly beneficial as far as revenue was concerned.[45] Once more, it is not possible to strike an exact balance sheet, and the new system of accounting introduced by the eighth duke meant that the figures and categories are not directly comparable with those from the seventh duke's time. In particular, income from dividends, and further investment in the water company, were now treated as part of the aggregate accounts, so that it did not appear on the Eastbourne estate accounts. Nevertheless, the change in circumstances which these accounts reveal is most marked, and is clearly the result of changed policy rather than a statistical illusion created by a different method of accounting (graph 5).

Most spectacularly, the expenditure on earthworks, roads and sewers was reduced. According to Francis Alfred Currey, between 1850 and 1893, some £343,875 had been spent on earthworks, roads, and sewers, and a further £42,966 on drainage: an average of £8,791 a year. But between 1893 and 1908, expenditure had only totalled £109,400 and averaged £6,837 a year. Even more important, the great building boom which began in the mid-1890s meant that rents once more began to rise, from £8,000 a year in 1890 to over £13,000 a year by 1914, and income from the redemptions of freeholds rose equally impressively, from £3,919 in 1891 to a peak of £22,000 in 1900. Accordingly, a very simple balance sheet is given in table 40.

Table 40. Income and expenditure on the Compton building estate, 1895–1914

		£
Income	Redemptions of freeholds	241,057
	Ground rents	214,241
	Total	455,298
Expenditure		218,380
Surplus		236,918

Source: CEO MS., Account Books.

Averaged out, this represents an annual net income from the Eastbourne building estate of over £11,000 a year – a marked improvement on the figure of less than £1,000 which was the average during the lifetime of the seventh duke. The harvest for which he had occasionally dared to hope, and which his son was determined to gather in, was finally garnered.

Even so, the figures are still far from spectacular. Certainly, as far as current income is concerned, they were insufficient to justify contemporary opinion concerning the 'supposed gigantic revenues of the ducal estate'. As with the rentals of the Calthorpes, the local inhabitants clearly believed that the ground rents ran into the region of hundreds of thousands of pounds annually;[46] but even the averaged figure is probably misleadingly high, for on several occasions much of the building estate surplus was ploughed back to finance further agricultural improvements on the neighbouring broad acres in Sussex. So, at a time when the current ducal income was in the region of £120,000 a year, it is probable that the remittances to Chatsworth from Eastbourne were never more than 10 per cent of that figure. Even in this second and more lucrative phase of their financial affairs, therefore, the revenue from Eastbourne was neither as large nor as important as contemporaries then or historians now have, perhaps, supposed.

4

Nevertheless, as far as Eastbourne itself was concerned, this change in the nature of the Devonshires' financial involvement with the town was of the greatest significance. During the time of the seventh duke, the Cavendishes were the most important local financial intermediaries, raising more from the inhabitants in the form of rents and redemptions than the local board or the council did in the form of rates. And, because the seventh duke felt that he did not need the revenue, the fact that it was ploughed back into the making of Eastbourne gave the Devonshires a position of unrivalled power and strategic influence. But their decision, in the early 1890s, to change their priorities, and to use the local revenue to buttress Chatsworth rather than extend the amenities at Eastbourne, of necessity lessened their local influence. Moreover, at the very same time, the corporation – previously unable to compete with the Devonshires, and psychologically as well as financially dependent on them as a result – now began to extend its ambitions, to compete with, and ultimately surpass, the influence which the Devonshires had wielded consequent upon their financial dominance.

Indeed, during the 1890s, the council began to spend much more lavishly and adventurously, emulating the large-scale ventures which Chamberlain had pioneered in Birmingham some 20 years before. Between 1894 and 1898, a new storm-water drainage scheme was built, which cost the council over £70,000.[47] In 1898, it bought out the local Electric Light Company, for a sum in excess of £80,000, and was able to raise the loan without the slightest difficulty: a conspicuous reversal of the penny-pinching ineptness which had characterized earlier attempts to raise money for the town hall and the eastern sea wall in the 1870s.[48] Indeed, by 1907, total capital outlay on the electricity supply – including the purchase price of the company – was over £180,000.[49] Predictably, the borough debt soared as a result, trebling in 20 years to reach £434,000 by 1905. At the same time, annual expenditure necessarily rose, so that by the 1900s it was averaging £80,000: a greater sum than the Devonshires had spent even in the most expansive days of the seventh duke.[50]

Therefore as the Devonshires' financial dominance began to wane, and as the council began to flex its own muscles, the balance of power between the two necessarily altered. Between 1911 and 1913, for example, a new sewer was constructed at the initiative of the council at a cost of £15,000. The majority of the expense was borne by the council, but the ninth duke – at the council's request – contributed £2,000: a conspicuous and revealing reversal of the events of the 1860s, when the seventh duke had come to the rescue of an impecunious local board.[51] In the same way, while it was the seventh duke who, as Earl of Burlington, had first brought the railway to the town in 1849, and had consistently lobbied the London, Brighton & South Coast Railway to provide better services until the 1880s, it was the council which, in 1906, entertained the directors of the railway to a local banquet, and obtained their agreement to run through trains from Liverpool, Manchester and Birmingham to Eastbourne.[52]

Contemporaries were well aware that this shift in the balance of power was taking place. In 1883, for instance, the *Gazette* took the occasion of incorporation to thank the seventh duke for his 'profuse liberality' but went on to urge that 'Eastbourne should now be old enough and, let us hope, rich enough, to run alone.'[53] Although such developments were to be delayed by a further decade, by the 1890s the prediction had been vindicated. As the *Chronicle* noted as early as 1895, the family's 'direct influence' necessarily lessened as many of the freeholds were purchased; in addition, as the *Gazette* observed four years later, it was no longer to the duke, but to the 'well-directed efforts of the local authorities' that the townsmen should look for efforts 'to enhance the attractiveness' of the town.[54] But the most eloquent recognition of these changed circumstances came from the Devonshires themselves: at his inaugural banquet as mayor in 1909, the ninth duke pointed out that the relationship between his family and the town was that of parent to children, and that 'one must expect and anticipate that as one's children grow older, they grow stronger and more vigorous, and they wish to assume greater responsibilities.'[55]

5

Accordingly, as the willingness of the Devonshires to spend in the town the revenue they derived from it declined, the desire of the council to assume a more vigorous financial role correspondingly increased. Slowly but inexorably, the balance of power shifted, as the council came to replace the Cavendishes as the largest single financial force in the town. At Chatsworth, where the eighth duke remained worried about his financial affairs, the results were satisfactory. Instead of absorbing all of the revenue, the Eastbourne building estate was beginning to yield some income which might be directly applied to buttressing the ducal régime. Whereas before, it was the town which had needed the Devonshires more than they needed it, now the family needed Eastbourne more than it needed them.

In the inter-war years, this trend was only intensified. In 1919–20, agreement was provisionally reached between the council and the duke for the sale of the Water Works Company, and when the scheme fell through, it was because some members of the council, not the duke, objected. Two years later, another provisional agreement was reached between the same parties, this time in a further attempt to convey the Parks and Baths Company to the council but, as in 1913 and 1914, the ratepayers defeated the proposal. As a result, the Devonshires began selling it off piecemeal instead. The baths went to the council for £16,000 in 1924, and the floral hall, winter gardens and grounds followed in 1930 for £55,000, the very same year in which the Devonshires also liquidated their remaining holdings in the Pier Company. The council, meanwhile, ever more expansionist, had bought out the Gas Company, and also acquired the Downs for £91,000, including 1,748 acres from the duke.[56] The financial preponderance of the corporation, already great before 1914, had by 1939 become overwhelming.

22 Political conflict and social celebrity, 1891–1914

Wallis's funeral in 1895 was also a requiem for a style of local politics which were by then already a thing of the past, for while the years between 1850 and 1891 saw the local elite, centred on the seventh duke, at the height of its power, the decade which followed witnessed its disintegration. On the one hand, the new duke chose to spend less in the town; on the other, Wallis had no successor. For the seventh duke, the price of power had been high: income which might have gone to Chatsworth was instead recycled at Eastbourne. The eighth duke, by contrast, exchanged power for income. He was prepared to hand on to the council the responsibility of financing new amenities, and to use the revenue from the building estate which was thereby made available for more personal ends. At the same time, there was added to increased income greater social prominence within the town. The seventh duke had been a recluse, hardly a man to capture the popular imagination in Eastbourne; but his two successors were both more flamboyant public figures, behaving with a grandeur and gusto still expected of aristocrats, and their decorative role in the social and municipal life of Eastbourne greatly surpassed that of the seventh duke. If real power was slipping from their grasp in the closing years of the nineteenth century, the Devonshires nevertheless became the object of unprecedented displays of civic obsequiousness. However, before the relationship between the family and the town was re-established on this new and changed basis, there was a major period of conflict, crisis and confrontation.

1

As long as Wallis remained a member of the town council, and as long as most citizens were prepared to look to 'Providence in the shape of a Duke' whenever they wanted anything, rather than provide it for themselves, there was no real likelihood of an aggressive or acquisitive town council coming into being which would threaten the Devonshires' dominant pecuniary position in the town. After 1885, Wallis might no longer be the chief magistrate, but his unrivalled prestige on the council ensured the continuation of its psychological dependence longer than was the case in most 'aristocratic' resorts. In 1884, though, Wallis himself had been responsible for piloting through a second Eastbourne Improvement Act, which had served to enlarge the powers of the council by taking over the powers of the Pevensey Levels Commissioners and other local and antiquated bodies. Under Wallis's auspices, this relatively small increase in municipal jurisdiction was hardly a threat to the Devonshires, but there was always the possibility that at some future date, when the council no longer looked so respectfully towards Compton Place or 14 Sea Side Road, their powers might be further augmented, and this time in a manner which did imply a threat to the duke. After all, such conflicts had occurred in other resorts, and as early as 1874–5, the first (and ineffectual) demands had been made for the municipalization of the local water supply.[1] It was only a matter of time before they were raised again.

Wallis's resignation from the council in 1892 severed for ever the direct link between the estate and the local municipal body. After Wallis, there were no ducal agents who sat on the council, both J.P. Cockerell and Roland Burke refusing to stand, although asked.[2] So, although the ducal agent remained a person of great local prestige – patron and president of many societies and activities – the town council was no longer his to command as it had been in the days of Wallis. Ominously, it was at the very same meeting, in October 1892, at which the council accepted Wallis's resignation 'with regret' that Councillor Sturge proposed 'that in the opinion of this Council the time has now arrived for the acquisition by the council of the Water Works of the town.'[3] Indeed, it may have been in part because he had an inkling of the new attitude beginning to manifest itself on the council that Wallis – reluctant to be caught in the crossfire – decided to withdraw. For this, combined with the coincidental challenge to his position from the interfering eighth duke, well armed with the damaging Price Waterhouse report on estate affairs, meant that Wallis's position with the duke needed more careful protection.

In the summer of 1893, the council approached the Water Works Company to inquire if they were prepared to sell to the council, and if so, on what terms. The company refused to budge, and there the issue rested.[4] Then in the following year, a problem arose in another quarter. In March 1894, the corporation called in a civil engineer, Mr Law, to advise them on the need for a new storm-water drainage system.[5] In October, he produced his report, which outlined the extensions necessary. The council adopted it without hesitation, and decided to approach both the duke and Mr Gilbert for some contribution towards the cost, on the grounds that it would be the value of their lands which would ultimately be augmented.[6] Devonshire, however, refused to make any contribution until he had made a separate inquiry into the scheme.[7] Accordingly, he called in Sir Benjamin Baker, builder of the first Aswan Dam and the Forth Bridge, the most outstanding civil engineer of his time, who concluded that Law's scheme was 'ruinously expensive', and that it would cost £117,000 to complete, rather than the £84,000 which Law himself had estimated.[8] Although Devonshire made this report available to the council, they decided in April 1895, by a majority of 14 to 10, to proceed with the original scheme, and subsequently obtained the necessary sanction from the local government board to apply for a loan.[9]

This free-spending independence was hardly the way in which the council would have behaved towards the House of Cavendish in the days of the seventh duke. Clearly, the council was beginning to find its feet, and the innate importance of civic work was beginning to be stressed in Eastbourne with an anti-aristocratic twist reminiscent of Birmingham in the 1870s. In December 1895, for example, when the issue of the drains was still a source of controversy, the *Gazette* took the occasion of the appointment of Alderman Skinner as mayor to attack those excessively deferential municipalities who took titled first citizens:

> The great cities of the north may obsequiously elect as their chief magistrates 'a marquess' or 'a duke', but Eastbourne is well content to secure once more the services of Alderman J. Skinner, a native of the town, whose honourable career has won for him the goodwill and regard of all who knew him.[10]

As opinion in the town hardened against the duke, Wallis, making what turned out to be his last speech (at Alderman Skinner's inaugural banquet) urged that 'the unity which had existed between the Corporation and the Duke of Devonshire and Mr Davies Gilbert' should 'continue in the future' – a clear indication that he feared it might not.[11]

By that time, however, another and more important problem had arisen.[12] In the summer of 1895, complaints were made that the local supply of water, for which the duke's company was responsible, was becoming increasingly salty and unfit to drink. At the same time, an inspection of the springs at Bedford Well from which the company drew the majority of its supply revealed that one was greatly charged with chlorine. The company, however, seemed to be lethargic in taking steps to deal with the problem, and the council in particular, and local opinion in general, became increasingly outraged both at the delay and at the way in which the resort's reputation was being 'seriously damaged' as a result. The Eastbourne Medical Society passed a unanimous resolution condemning the local water as undrinkable; the Eastbourne Schoolmasters Association also complained; and the *Gazette* thundered that 'the inhabitants will not tolerate the least delay in regard to the provision of an improved supply'.[13] Finally, in November 1895, the council, tired of waiting, resolved by 21 votes to 4 to promote a parliamentary bill to take over the company, and asked the duke to receive a deputation so that negotiations might be begun.[14] The company, on the other hand, took the view that the whole campaign against the water works was an elaborate ruse to drive down its value so that the council could then obtain it at a lower cost to the ratepayers, and so the duke refused to receive a deputation. Opinion was outraged at this rebuff by what was described as a 'vested interest and monopoly', and at a stormy town meeting in early December, Wallis was shouted down.[15] Two weeks later, at the height of the controversy, he died, his end almost certainly hastened by the pressure on his position which had been increasing, from the council on the one side and the duke on the other, since 1891.[16]

The orgy of public and municipal grief which accompanied Wallis's passing temporarily stilled the battle, but in the new year it was renewed with full vigour. A poll among the ratepayers, which was necessary before the council could proceed to Parliament for legislation, resulted in defeat by 3,752 votes to 3,527.[17] Accordingly, the corporation dropped their bill, and the duke finally agreed to receive a deputation. The outcome was that the company agreed to go to Parliament for a bill which would enable them to obtain new supplies from Wannock and Holywell and the council – although not entirely happy with the provisions of the scheme – agreed to withdraw its opposition so that the bill could be passed, and work begun, as soon as possible.[18] During the summer of 1896, however, it became necessary to lay pipes throughout the town to bring water from Holywell. Even then the supply was insufficient. Some residents had to carry water in buckets through the town. One took it illegally from the Bourne Stream, and contracted typhoid as a result. More generally, the town enjoyed its worst summer season for years.[19] Annoyed once more by what they believed to be lethargic progress, the council urged the company to greater action.

In the end, the council were so dissatisfied with the company's efforts that in October 1896 they revived their scheme to buy out the company, and decided to seek further powers to take water from Friston – a course of action which they had been urging on the company for the whole of the summer, but to no good effect. This time, the bill was sanctioned by a substantial majority of the ratepayers, 4,309 as against 3,135.[20] Opinion had indeed markedly sharpened against the duke and his interest. At the same time, the company promoted its own rival bill, which also sought to take water from Friston. The clash between the duke and his company on one side, and the town and its council on the other, could have hardly been more direct. In November 1896, the town clerk had written to the duke arguing that the ratepayers 'desire that the water supply of the town should be in the hands of the Corporation'. The duke's reply to this invitation to surrender was defiant, claiming that the corporation's object was that of discrediting the management of the affairs of the company and depreciating the value of their property. And, in view of the impending parliamentary contest between the two sides, he went on: 'No such conflict need, however, arise unless it is provoked by the action of the Corporation, and the responsibility for the consequences will rest entirely with them.'[21]

With the two sides so firmly and defiantly entrenched, there was no hope of any compromise, so that in May 1897, the duke and his company and the mayor and his council, each seeking parliamentary sanction for their mutually-exclusive bills, battled it out in public. The corporation's bill was considered first. Its advocates argued that the company's management was incompetent and inefficient; that they should have gone to Friston for a new supply as early as the summer of 1895; that the council would run the company more efficiently; that municipalization was fashionable and in the interests of the town; and that it had been markedly successful elsewhere. For their part, the duke's counsel, supported by the Gilberts, retorted that the corporation's business acumen was unproven; that they would not be able to raise the £600,000 or so necessary to buy out the company; that the scheme would not be financially viable; and that the company had done all it could in the most trying and difficult of circumstances to ensure a constant and pure supply. Even the duke himself gave evidence, and the proceedings of the committees were front-page news in the town.[22]

Although the outcome was uncertain, it represented, in the short run, a great triumph for the duke and his party, for the corporation's bill was defeated, and the company was allowed to proceed with its scheme to take water from Friston.[23] But the very fact that the council, now freed from the influence of Wallis, had had the temerity to go to such lengths publicly to challenge the position and property of the duke, signalled a fundamental change, not only in attitudes, but also in the balance of power: a change which was coincidentally to be accentuated as a result of the new policy which the eighth duke had just initiated as regards spending. While the council failed in this particular endeavour, it succeeded elsewhere – as in the case of the electricity company – and the balance of financial power between the mayor and the duke began to shift fundamentally and irrevocably. Instead of the town leaning on the duke, the duke came more and more to lean on the town. Whereas the family had once supported the ailing institutions of the town, it was increasingly the town which was to rescue the ailing companies of the duke.

At the same time, the ferocity of the clash of 1895–7 was not easily forgotten and, embarrassed and perhaps a little worried by it, both sides resolved to live at peace with one another thereafter. The duke already had enough worries of his own, and was anxious not to annoy the town any further at the very time when he was looking to his estate there to provide him with a badly-needed increase in income. For its part, the corporation, having asserted its independence of mind and vigour of policy, was anxious that the town should not acquire a reputation for faction and conflict. Accordingly, a great festival of reconciliation was staged on 6 August 1897, when the duke himself formally turned on the new water supply at Friston, and the mayor and corporation took the opportunity to present him with a petition:

> We avail ourselves of the present auspicious occasion to testify our heartfelt appreciation of the great advantages ever derived by Eastbourne from its connection with Your Grace's family. Its beautiful parades and wide boulevards, constructed at very great expense, demonstrate the forethought and care displayed by Your Grace and Your Grace's noble father for the health and pleasure of its inhabitants, and Your Grace's presence today is but another proof of your great interest in the welfare and prosperity of the borough which, as its municipal authority, we heartily recognize and trust may continue.[24]

A municipal lunch followed, at which Devonshire responded with a speech of equal graciousness, in which he expressed the hope that 'the presentation of this address marks the final conclusion of all subjects of difference that have arisen between the Company, the Corporation, and the inhabitants of Eastbourne'. Once more, he asserted that the occasion marked 'a final end of any differences which have existed between us', and concluded by proposing the health of the mayor and corporation.

Fig. 40. The eighth duke of Devonshire inaugurating the new Friston water supply, August 1897 (by courtesy of the Eastbourne Water Works Company).

Although, superficially, the memorial presented to the eighth duke on this occasion resembled closely that which had been presented to his father 30 years before when the drainage scheme was inaugurated, the actual circumstances had fundamentally altered. The first was an expression of real gratitude, untainted by any threat to the ties of dependence which bound the town to the duke. The second was more a display of civic good manners as the council, aware now of its own power and independence, was prepared to acknowledge the generosity of past dukes. Nor did matters end there; at the very same lunch, Devonshire agreed to become mayor for the ensuing municipal year. Once he had ceased to wield real power on the council, its members were happy to invite him back as an ornamental mayor. For all the blustering hostility which had been expressed to aristocratic mayors in that *Gazette* editorial of 1895, when the opportunity presented itself for Eastbourne to follow suit, it proved to be irresistible. But it was an opportunity only taken when the real power of the Devonshires over the council had been broken for good.

2

And so, within 12 crowded and tumultuous months, the fury of hostility was replaced by warm affection and delight. Indeed, when it was first rumoured that the eighth duke might possibly occupy the mayoral chair, the local press was positively a-twitter with excitement:

> The possibility of His Grace the Duke of Devonshire consenting to fill the Mayoralty next year has evoked lively feelings of satisfaction throughout our town. It seems almost too much to hope that a nobleman whose time is more or less engrossed with affairs of state, and who already holds many responsible public positions, will yield to the popular wish in this matter.[25]

But the miracle happened, and he agreed, a decision which sent

> a thrill of delight and satisfaction through the borough. All classes have joined in the fervent hope that His Grace might see his way to responding favourably to the appeal, which was backed up, not only by the unanimous voice of the Town Council, but by one of the largest and most influential requisitions that have every been promoted in the town. A few months since, and suggestions that the Duke of Devonshire might become the next Mayor of Eastbourne would have been scouted as absurd. In the interim, fortunately, much has happened to compose the differences and restore the relations of the contending factions, the most notable change of attitude being that furnished by the municipal body itself, whose warlike spirit has given way to serener counsels. The Duke's consent to act as Chief Magistrate puts the seal, as it were, to the new unwritten bond of unity and mutual trust between the inhabitants of Eastbourne and its chief landlord and patron.[26]

The bitterness of the preceding three years was thus forgotten, as the duke and the council kissed and made up, and Devonshire was 'carried into office upon a wave of popular enthusiasm'.[27]

Nor did his year as mayor disappoint, for the eighth duke, even if worried by the state of his finances, gave no public hint of it in Eastbourne. Much more so than his cleverer but retiring father, he possessed that attribute of aristocracy spotted by Bagehot: 'visibility'. He behaved, as he was expected to do, *heroically*. His inaugural banquet, held at the Queen's Hotel, was of unprecedented grandeur and magnificence, and was followed by a garden party at Compton Place, to which the elite of the town were invited. In January 1898, the old folk of Eastbourne were entertained to dinner in the town hall, where they feasted off beef, mutton, pork, pudding and jelly: 'The clatter of the knives and forks, the hum of conversation, and the rapid movements of the waiters bearing the steaming viands, rendered the scene one of great animation.'[28] A month later, the duke's mayoralty reached its apogee with a ball in the Devonshire Park Pavilion. The duke, wearing the Garter and mayoral chain, and the duchess, clad in 'a green and white satin gown, embroidered with showers of seed pearls', and wearing 'her diamond coronet with all the dignity of one born to the purple', greeted their guests, who took supper and then danced in the pavilion, especially decorated for the evening by Maple and Company, with 'oriental fabrics and hangings, the choicest products of India, China and Japan'. As with the Countess of Chell's ball at 'Bursley', Eastbourne was thrilled. 'It may be said without the slightest fear of contradiction', observed the *Gazette* triumphantly, 'that it was the most costly and splendid entertainment that has ever been given in Eastbourne.'[29]

Fig. 41. The eighth duke of Devonshire as mayor of Eastbourne, 1898 (by courtesy of the Trustees of the Chatsworth Settlement).

In commemoration of his mayoralty, the duke gave a plot of land as the site for a proposed Technical Institute, and grandly and splendidly donated his salary to local charities.[30] By this time, the council was practically purring with pleasure, as the unanimous resolution, passed at the end of his year of office, showed:

> That the grateful thanks of this Corporation be accorded to His Grace the Mayor for accepting the office of Mayor of this borough, and for the great honour His Grace conferred upon the town by so doing, and by the generous manner in which he has filled the duties of the office during the past year.[31]

Finally, as if setting the seal on the newly-established *rapprochement* between family and town, Their Graces were generous enough to appear at the inaugural banquet of the new mayor. The point was not lost on the local press:

> It clearly betokened on their part a warm and growing attachment to a town of which it was feared at one time they were not greatly enamoured. The noble duke in his speeches has been careful not to leave any mistaken impression as to the cordiality of his sympathy with the interests and aspirations of the borough. All of which again points to the fine tact and wisdom of those who last year prevailed upon His Grace to accept the office of Mayor.[32]

Yet beneath this glittering social and ceremonial façade there lay very little, for Devonshire's role as mayor was almost entirely ornamental. As the *Gazette* recalled a decade later, 'the principal events of his term of office' were 'the banquet at the Queen's Hotel and the Mayoral ball given at the Devonshire Park'.[33] Indeed, on the news of his election in November 1897, even the most favourable newspaper reported that for a man as busy as he was, 'any supposition that His Grace could devote himself systematically to the mayoral responsibilites would be unreasonable'.[34] In the same way, J.P. Cockerell, when explaining to Devonshire what would be required of him, pointed out that he was not expected to attend all the council meetings, but that 'a garden party at Compton Place and perhaps a ball at the Town Hall would be very much appreciated by the inhabitants'. He went on to explain that, if Devonshire chose to appoint Mr Skinner as Deputy Mayor, 'he will do everything in his own power to make your year of office as light as possible'.[35]

Devonshire himself was only too pleased to fall in with this scheme. 'I do not suppose for one moment', he said on the news of his election, 'that in electing me to this office you have done so with the expectation of receiving from me any valuable or special service in the discharge of those duties.'[36] He certainly did not give any, and with extraordinary candour freely admitted on one occasion – in words very reminiscent of those used by the Marquess of Bute in describing his role as Chief Magistrate of Cardiff – that he was 'one who could not give constant or personal and active attention to the duties of the position'.[37] And, in the same speech, he went on to describe himself as an 'ornamental mayor', an appropriate description for one who only attended 3 out of 14 council meetings, and who had to leave one of these early so as to catch a train to London.[38] In the same way, the letter book specially maintained by the Compton agent during the year of the duke's mayoralty contained 235 items, not one of which referred to any matter of substantive, municipal importance. Instead, they dealt with trivia such as the arrangement of chairs at the inaugural banquet.

Indeed, although most of the inhabitants were dazzled by such ducal condescension, a few criticisms of this sham mayoralty were voiced. 'Is it policy', inquired 'A Large Ratepayer' in a letter to the *Chronicle*, to continue the practice of appointing to the chief office men who are not active participants in the general work of the Council, and therefore very imperfectly acquainted with the inner workings of the local government body? I incline to the opinion that we should revert to the old order of things, and that an active 'working bee' be selected as Mayor for the ensuing year.[39]

His advice was not heeded, for the coporation unanimously agreed to ask the duke to serve for a second term; but for his part, the duke agreed whole-heartedly with the criticism, as he made plain in his speech at a presentation to Alderman Skinner, who had served as deputy mayor with such tact and skill during his year of office:

It might be all very well for once in a way to have an ornamental Mayor, but as a rule, an office of this importance – at all events in a town of this character – ought to be held by someone who was prepared to give constant and assiduous attention to the duties.[40]

However, at least as far as the majority of the inhabitants were concerned, this 'ornamental' discharge of mayoral duties more than sufficed. Indeed, for the rest of his life, the eighth duke basked in the reflected glory of his momentous year as mayor. In 1900, his name was once more canvassed, but this was admitted to be 'rather hoped for than expected'.[41] Unable to serve in this capacity, he became instead the town's first freeman, and the ceremony at which he received it was yet another occasion for long, emollient speeches, as the duke and the council behaved like a mutual admiration society.[42] Two years earlier, a statue of the seventh duke had been unveiled on the promenade (fig. 42), and, once more, the town was reminded of the 'grand and imperish-able part' which the seventh duke had played in its creation. Indeed, the statue was explicitly seen as 'a lasting monument of friendliness and co-operation between the town of Eastbourne and the House of Cavendish, which the present duke and duchess have done so much to foster and enhance'.[43] The eighth duke's decision to be present, in August 1904, at the opening of the Technical Institute which had been built on that plot of land he had donated at the close of his mayoralty, was an added bonus. 'By their presence,' noted the *Chronicle*, 'the Duke and Duchess of Devonshire added a lustre that is never wanting in any event with which Their Graces may be associated.'[44]

As with his father, the eighth duke was seen, not as a party politician, but as a man of national stature: 'a statesman first and a partisan afterwards'.[45] As the *Gazette* took pains to explain in 1906:

He has never taken a very active part in local politics . . . Only once during the last sixteen years has he addressed a political meeting here. The duke's pronouncements on political questions are received with respect in Eastbourne as elsewhere; and what makes them specially worthy of consideration is the fact that His Grace is known to be disinterested. Indeed, the fact that he has not been eager to secure the Premiership has been a source of deep regret to many.[46]

As well as being above the political battle, he was a personal friend of the Prince of Wales, later Edward VII, who was a frequent guest at Compton Place, along with other members of high society. On occasions, indeed, the duke was able to persuade the Prince of Wales to perform some small public function in the town, as in July 1899, when he opened an agricultural show. Here was splendour and grandeur which surpassed even that of the House of Cavendish – and, as the *Chronicle* was quick to spot, besides vanity being satisfied, there was a real commercial pay-off as well:

> Thanks to the duke, Eastbourne has been honoured by the patronage of Royalty on various occasions. Apart from the pleasurable interest attaching to the presence here of members of the Queen's family, it is patent that Eastbourne has derived therefrom a very substantial advertisement with results highly stimulative of its growth and prosperity.[47]

Yet at the same time, as well as being seen as grand and remote, a pillar of state and friend of the king, the eighth duke was also looked upon with a mixture of affection and loyalty as a 'neighbour', a member of the local community.[48] When his final illness began, the council sent a unanimous resolution wishing him well, and on his death a resolution of condolence was conveyed to the duchess.[49] In its editorial, the *Chronicle* caught the prevailing tone well:

> The hand of death has robbed England of one of her noblest sons, and Eastbourne of a great citizen and landlord, as well as a very staunch friend . . . [Eastborne] is weighed down by the mournful reflections that he is no more who, for many years, has been honourably and usefully identified with the town, and has given conspicuous and enduring proofs of his attachment and goodwill.[50]

Once more, the mayor and town Clerk represented the town at the funeral at Chatsworth, two local memorial services were held, and Eastbourne came to a standstill.[51] Two years later, a statue (fig. 43) was unveiled as 'a lasting tribute of affection' to 'Eastbourne's best friend'.[52]

3

The new ninth duke, formerly Mr Victor Cavendish, was the son of Lord Edward Cavendish, for although the eighth duke had finally married, the union had been childless. Since Mr Cavendish had spent most of his adult life at Holker, he was not intimately acquainted with Eastbourne, where the newspapers described him as being 'entirely unknown by the majority of inhabitants', a man who had never 'appeared at any public function in the town'. However, after a decent interval, interest in the town's newest and greatest landowner began to grow. As the *Chronicle* put it: 'Natural curiosity is felt in Eastbourne to make the acquaintance of the new duke, and also as to the effect which the change in the dukedom is likely to have on the town.'[53] Within a year, that curiosity was amply satisfied, for in June 1909, 'in response to a hearty and unanimous invitation from the Council', he consented to follow his illustrious uncle and serve as mayor.[54]

Once more, opinion was as delighted as it was flattered. 'In entering upon his duties', the *Gazette* noted, 'as Chief Magistrate, the present duke will be assured of the loyal and hearty co-operation, not only of the members and officials of the Corporation, but of the inhabitants generally.'[55] Moreover, unlike his predecessor, who had carried absenteeism and the purely 'ornamental' functions of the office to the limit, there seemed a very real possibility that the ninth duke – whose public and political commitments were more modest – would play a larger, more active part in the community:

> We understand the duke has no idea of merely passing as the titular head of the municipality, his intention being, as far as his private and other public duties will allow, to enter heartily into the work of the Council, and into the general public affairs of the Borough. There is good reason to believe, also, that the duchess will appear frequently at local functions, and otherwise do her best to render the duke's term of office a happy and successful one.[56]

So, while the previous Devonshire mayoralty had been seen as a public gesture of reconciliation between the town and the family, this repeat performance was viewed as a welcome re-affirmation of the new *status quo*.

As in the time of his late uncle, the social side of the ninth duke's mayoralty was splendid. His inaugural banquet, at the Grand Hotel, was the most magnificent that had ever been held, deliberately intended, Devonshire explained, 'to cement and strengthen the ties of mutual affection and regard which have long existed between Eastbourne and members of my family.'[57] After he had proposed the loyal toast, the health of the bishop and clergy, Her Majesty's judges and the imperial forces were proposed, in speeches of quite interminable tedium, and then Dr Crowden, former headmaster of Eastbourne College, the man who had delivered the eulogy of Wallis, rose to propose the health of the duke:

> And now, my Lord Duke, it is with gratitude and pride that we see you occupy the Mayoral Chair which twelve years ago the distinguished duke, your uncle, occupied. Like him, you bring into our municipal life the inspiring traditions of your noble house, rare gifts of statesmanship, a keen interest in art and science, in education, in religion and philanthropic work; in brief, you bring us that great heritage of honour and duty which is summed up in that word of noble meaning and infinite suggestiveness – the word 'aristocracy', the rule of the best [loud applause].

Fig. 42 Statue of the seventh duke of
Devonshire, Grand Parade, Eastbourne.

Fig. 43. Statue of the eighth duke of
Devonshire, Western Parades,
Eastbourne.

Before he finished, Crowden also suggested that Eastbourne in all probability
bore a strong resemblance to the City of God in Heaven. Other toasts followed,
to the town and its trade, to the visitors, the aldermen, town councillors and
officials. Not until after midnight did the party break up.

In the following March, the duke and duchess gave a ball for 900 at
Compton Place.[58] Once more, like that of his uncle in 1898, it exhausted the
superlatives of the local press: 'We shall not be chargeable with any approach
to exaggeration when we say that the gathering, pleasurable, brilliant and
successful from every point of view, was worthy of the best traditions of the
princely and hospitable House of Cavendish, and that it was, moreover, a
triumph of of organisational skill and foresight.' The ballroom, the dresses, the
food, even the fire precautions and electric light, were described in loving

and awe-struck detail, and the conclusion was as hyperbolic as it was predictable:

> That the ball given by the Duke and Duchess of Devonshire eclipsed in
> point of numbers as well as in splendour, any social entertainment of the
> kind previously given may be affirmed without any qualification what-
> ever; and, locally, the gathering will be looked back upon as an historic
> one.

Once more, we are in that world of municipal obsequiousness which Arnold
Bennett caught so beautifully when describing the grandeur of the Countess of
Chell as mayoress of Bursley.

In other ways, too, the ninth duke followed the pattern established with
such success by his predecessor. The gift of Motcombe Gardens and his
decision to donate his salary to local charities were further and welcome signs
of heroic behaviour, generosity and benevolence. In addition, the duke chaired
a ratepayers' meeting in the town hall in August 1910, at which a bill designed
to raise Eastbourne to the rank of a county borough was discussed. Once more,
as in 1898, his mayoralty was marked with the passing of a unanimous vote of
thanks, and a request from the town clerk that he should continue in office for
another year:

> 'I am sure it is quite unnecessary for me to attempt to say how deeply the
> Council have appreciated your acceptance of the office during the present
> year, nor to say that it would afford them the greatest pleasure to hear that
> you were willing to accept the office again.'[59]

Like his predecessor, however, he felt graciously obliged to decline. Even then,
the town would not let him go without a complimentary dinner at the Grand
Hotel, attended by 200 well-wishers, where the oratory and the wine once
more flowed.[60]

But as in the case of the eighth duke's mayoralty, there was little real involvement by his successor in the day-to-day affairs of the town or of the council. His
name and status may have been of marginal help in securing the passing of the
Eastbourne Corporation Act but, that apart, his services were no more substantial than those of his illustrious predecessor. Once again, it was the
combination of emollient speeches, grand social occasions, and a generous gift,
which got him through. As he honestly admitted at his own inaugural banquet, he had 'no qualifications for the duty which you have placed on me.'[61]
And, at his farewell dinner, he reiterated the same point, even more emphatically:

> I knew I had no experience, no knowledge of the work required of me.
> There were many details, many intricate matters, which had to come
> before us, and which, as I had served no apprenticeship, it was obvious I
> should be ignorant of.[62]

Indeed, the duke's attendance was no better than his syntax. Most councillors were normally present for between 80 and 100 meetings of the council itself and their appropriate sub-committees in the course of the municipal year. The duke attended but 12.[63] His mayoral letter book was as full of trivia as the eighth duke's had been. The correspondence included such items as the amount of wine to be provided for the orchestra, and the vexed question of whether invitations from Devonshire for the inaugural banquet should, or should not, bear the ducal coronet. The contrast between these two splendid but impotent ducal figureheads, and the real power which Wallis had wielded on the council for 20 years, is most marked.

Like the eighth duke again, the ninth duke, although a prominent figure in the Conservative party hierarchy and president of the Eastbourne Conservative Association, was seen in the town as an essentially non-political being. 'Eastbourne people', observed the *Gazette* in 1909, 'prefer to regard the Duke of Devonshire as a friend rather than as a politician; and his affection for the town is the best passport to their favour.'[64] And when, in 1913, he reached the age of 45, the same paper re-stated the theme even more emphatically:

> From the position he occupies, the Duke is able to render important service to the whole town of Eastbourne, and we take this opportunity of pointing out the fact that, whilst conflicting opinions on political matters must always exist, no one in Eastbourne who possesses a single spark of generous feeling can fail to reciprocate the really friendly interest which His Grace has manifested in the town.[65]

In a largely Conservative constituency, where the Labour movement was weak (there were only two Labour councillors as late as 1913), the non-partisan appeal of an established grandee was bound to be considerable. Even in the midst of the 1910 December General Election, it was possible for both the Liberal and Conservative prospective candidates to be present at the farewell dinner given for the duke, at which 'all political differences were

Fig. 44. Cartoon of the ninth duke of Devonshire, 1913: the caption beneath reads:
'The Duke of Devonshire's birthday: Eastbourne's sincere and hearty congratulations' (reproduced from the *Eastbourne Gazette*, 4 June 1913, by permission of the British Library).

merged in the spirit of social harmony and . . .municipal good fellowship that prevailed.'[66] Although the local press denied it, there was a very real sense in which the inhabitants regarded the Devonshires with 'awe struck and reverential admiration'.[67] Or, as the *Gazette* put it on another occasion: 'It is apparent to everyone that the Dukes of Devonshire have done infinitely more for Eastbourne than other ground landlords have done for the health resorts of which they have been ground landlords.'[68]

4

Although to the citizens at large, the two Devonshire mayoralties were an affirmation of the continuing close links between family and town, they also demonstrated the extent to which the balance of power had indeed shifted between the council and the Devonshires since the death of the seventh duke. 'Only when aristocratic influence had become a spent force would the prestige of the peerage be exploited to further civic dignity' might be stating the matter a little too emphatically in the case of the Devonshires and Eastbourne,[69] but the fact that the balance of power had fundamentally shifted certainly could not be denied. Indeed, events between the close of the ninth duke's mayoralty and the outbreak of the First World War only accentuated this trend. The need to meet death duties levied on the estate of the eighth duke not only slowed down, temporarily, the policy of financial rehabilitation which he had so successfully begun, but also necessitated the implementation of further economy measures. On the estates as a whole, encumbrances were once more increased, and at Chatsworth, some heirlooms such as Caxton prints and a Shakespeare folio were sold off. At Eastbourne, the ninth duke gave up his mastership of the local hunt, let the stud farm at Polegate which his predecessor had created, and leased out Compton Place itself in the summer of 1913.[70] Most importantly of all, he also tried to sell off the Devonshire Parks and Baths Company to the corporation.[71]

Although it was rightly described as 'the sheet anchor of Eastbourne's prosperity', providing as it did the majority of high-class recreational facilities in the town, the Parks and Baths Company had never been a financial success.[72] The extensions of the 1880s and 1900s, which it had been hoped would attract more support and increase profitability, had proved unsuccessful, and the orchestra begun by the eighth duke in 1907 cost £30,000 during the next three years, again with no appreciable return for such an extensive outlay.[73] Indeed, since 1894, the company had only twice paid a dividend, at the princely rate of 1 per cent in 1895 and 2 per cent in 1909. During the course of his mayoralty, the ninth duke made it plain to the council that he was not prepared to shoulder the burden indefinitely. Unlike his grandfather, if an investment in Eastbourne did not pay, he was eager and anxious to be rid of it, preferably to the local authority whose financial resources and vested local interest were now so much greater than his. Eventually, at the end of 1910, the

Parks and Baths Company agreed to relieve the duke of the burden of directly financing the orchestra although, since he himself owned the company, it was no long-term solution to the problem. Nevertheless, the decision was recognized by the local press for what it was: an admission on the part of the ninth duke that he could no longer come to the rescue of the town in the way in which his grandfather had:

> The upkeep of this large force of instrumentalists has entailed a very heavy personal outlay, and His Grace feels the time has come when the town as a whole should realise the indispensability of such an attraction and be prepared to maintain it.[74]

The days of 'Providence in the shape of a Duke' were definitely over.

Yet the problem was that the Parks and Baths Company could no more afford the cost of the orchestra than could the duke. In the first year in which they were responsible for its maintenance, it cost £7,000 in all.[75] Accordingly, in 1912, the duke made a determined attempt to sell the company off to the council, orchestra and all. By then, the property included the baths, floral hall, theatre, racquets court, public bar, manager's house, pavilion, eight shops in Carlisle Road, and eight acres of grounds.[76] Altogether, the company had spent £152,209, but if offered to sell its assets to the corporation for £100,665. The duke himself took the biggest loss, for he agreed to accept £23,085 for his £46,170 worth of shares, and of that half sum, he agreed to return £10,000 to the corporation.[77] In March 1912, a sub-committee of the corporation recommended the purchase of the company on these terms, and suggested that in future it should be run by a committee of seven, five of whom were to be appointed by the council, and two by the duke. On 15 November 1912, the corporation agreed by 24 votes to 11 to seek the approval of the ratepayers to promote a bill in Parliament to buy out the company on these terms.[78] Agreement was as good as reached.

However, although the local press acclaimed the ninth duke's princely generosity in forgoing £33,085, opposition in the town was soon forthcoming: not, as in the case of the water works, against the duke, but against the council.[79] In November 1912 a meeting was held in the town hall under the auspices of the Eastbourne United Temperance Council, which opposed the scheme because it would result in the council holding an intoxicating liquor licence. More generally, it was argued that the Park would be a drain on the council's resources. In addition, criticism was voiced of the corporation owning shops, or continuing to maintain the Sunday concerts which the company had recently inaugurated.[80] Then in January 1913, at a public meeting of ratepayers in the town hall, objection was taken to the continuing influence of the duke in the Park's affairs, by being able to nominate two of the committee of management. The council, abashed by the extent of the hostility, made a determined effort to come up with more favourable terms. Accordingly, the duke was persuaded to surrender his rights of nomination to the proposed committee of management, and further agreed to return the interest on the £12,585 he was to receive from the council, so that it might be used to help maintain the orchestra.[81] Even these changes did not suffice, though, for when a poll was taken in February, the council was defeated by 2,965 to 2,542.[82]

Although there is a superficial similarity between this episode and the crisis over the water works in the mid-1890s, it is the contrast which is even more revealing. On this occasion, it was not the council and the ratepayers in outraged alliance against the duke, as had been the case in 1896–7, but the council and the duke in alliance against the ratepayers. The duke was anxious to sell the company, and the council was eager to acquire it: it was the ratepayers who prevented them. Indeed, for his part, the duke was prepared to make almost any concession of power or money to rid himself of this irksome and embarrassing incubus. And for their part, the council pressed the duke to make these further concessions, not out of any spirit of malice or hostility towards him, but because they were anxious to produce a scheme which would be acceptable to the ratepayers. As the town clerk explained to the Compton agent, there was 'no wish on the part of the Council to disturb the amicable co-operation between the duke and the Council.'[83] Indeed, when it became known that the ratepayers had rejected the scheme, the council passed a motion expressing to the duke

> their sincere appreciation of the generous contribution he proposed to make towards the purchase by the Corporation of the property of the Devonshire Park and Baths Company, and to regret that a majority of the electorate rejected the Council's recommendation to accept the same.[84]

While the council was prepared to take over the Park, the ratepayers themselves were still retrenchment- and economy-minded. For them, the venture was too expensive and would not pay: therefore others must continue to shoulder the burden.

In the autumn of 1913, however, the management of the company announced that their financial position was so precarious that they would be obliged to close the Devonshire Park in November, and abandon the winter season which was regarded as the most important single contribution to attempts to make Eastbourne an all-year-round resort. Immediately, the council received a petition with 3,485 signatures urging that the company be taken over; but ominously, there was also an opposition petition with 3,152 signatures.[85] Once more, the matter was referred to a special committee, which again recommended purchase, a decision endorsed by the council in October by 21 votes to 9.[86] At the same time, the duke agreed to waive his last condition, and allowed the interest on the £12,585 he received from the council to be used for any purpose, and not necessarily for the maintenance of the orchestra. Once more, agreement seemed so close that Arthur Battock in the Curreys' office felt able to congratulate Roland Burke 'on the acceptance of your scheme by the Corporation'.[87] But again, they had not reckoned with the recalcitrance of the ratepayers for, in February 1914, they once more rejected the scheme, this time by 3,468 votes to 2,773.[88]

Of necessity, there had been a public meeting in the town hall shortly before the poll, which was particularly noteworthy for an attack made on the ninth duke by Mr Reginald Smith:

> He was heartily sick of the cant and humbug that they had heard with reference to the Duke of Devonshire. They were always being told of the generosity of the duke, who had an income of £180,000 a year. What proportion did he get from Eastbourne? [A voice: 'Nearly all of it.'] His predecessors had been gracious and had been good to Eastbourne, but had the present duke? [Cries of 'No'.] He said, advisedly, that the present duke had not taken the same attitude with regard to Eastbourne as his predecessors had done. [Cries of dissent.] First he sold his farm, then he did away with his stud [interruptions, and cries of 'Keep to the point'], then he disbanded the orchestra, then he let Compton Place instead of coming to live there, and lastly he wanted to thrust the Devonshire Park on them [A voice: 'We won't have it']. They were there to look the facts in the face, not humbug. If the duke had done what his predecessors had done, had kept Compton Place and invited the King to come amongst them [cheers], he would have brought more visitors to the town than all the Devonshire Parks in the United Kingdom [applause].[89]

Apart from being in error about the duke's overall financial position, as well as over-rating the importance of Eastbourne revenue to the ducal exchequer, this speech is noteworthy because the duke was not being criticized, in the manner of Lloyd George at Limehouse, because he was rich or because he was a duke, but because as a duke *he was not doing enough*. Even a generation after such hopes had ceased to be realistic, many in the town still looked first and foremost to 'Providence in the shape of a Duke' rather than to 'Providence in the shape of the ratepayers'. For many, even as late as 1914, the aristocracy were still expected to be heroic, and to shoulder local responsibilities uncomplainingly. Vociferous ratepayers such as Mr Smith felt the change in the balance of power since 1891 had not been a change for the better.

5

Whereas the fierce battle over the water works was itself an expression of the changing balance of power in the town between the duke and the council, the negotiations concerning the sale of the Devonshire Park were but confirmation of the great change which had taken place. The institution was ailing, and the duke preferred to hand it over – even at the cost of some short-term financial sacrifice – to the council rather than succour it further himself, as the seventh duke would surely have done. During the inter-war years this policy was continued, as the ninth duke, in continuation of the eighth duke's policy, sought to sell off more of the companies which the Devonshires had created so as to facilitate the development of their estates.

Yet despite the gradual and progressive financial liquidation of the Devonshires' interests in Eastbourne, all did not change. The era of decorative and ornamental splendour was remarkably long-lasting. In 1916, the ninth duke was made a freeman, like his uncle before him, 'in recognition of his many services to and generous interest in the Borough, and of his appointment as Governor General of Canada, and of his having held office of Mayor of Eastbourne during the year 1909–10'.[90] Compton Place was re-opened after the First World War, and the ninth duke became a frequent visitor, bringing down King George V and Queen Mary, most notably for the king's long convalescence in 1935.[91] The resident agents, Roland Burke and Charles Alix, continued to be important figures in the town and in 1933, on the occasion of the golden jubilee of incorporation, a splendid municipal banquet was held at the Grand Hotel, where the duke himself proposed the health of the borough.[92] On his death in 1938, a memorial service was held in the town, attended by the mayor and corporation, at which 'Eastbourne's sincere friend' was eulogized. When the tenth duke died only 12 years later, wreaths and flowers were sent to Chatsworth from ten local organizations with which he had been connected.[93]

In this as in so much else, the Second World War was a far more important turning-point than the First. The need to meet death duties twice within 12 years once more put the Devonshires financially on the defensive, and brought to an end the prosperous inter-war period, which owed so much to the policy changes instituted by the eighth duke. Hardwick Hall was given to the National Trust, and the family now no longer resides at Compton Place. As more and more freeholds have been realized, the proprietary link with the town has lessened; so much so that since the Second World War, there has no longer been a resident agent at Compton Place. Between 1946 and 1957, the last remaining sections of the Devonshire Park Company, the theatre and the racquets court, were finally sold off to the corporation, some 60 years after the Devonshires had begun their attempts to rid themselves of that strategically important but financially burdensome asset.[94]

Yet even so, the paradoxes remain. The family retains its links with the College, and is still a major shareholder in the Water Works Company. As late as 1955, the town clerk could describe the Dowager Duchess of Devonshire, in whose name the majority of the shares in the Parks and Baths Company were vested, as 'the principal shareholder' who 'dictates the policy of the company'.[95] In 1973, a £1,000,000 warehouse scheme at Hampden Park was launched by the Trustees of the Chatsworth Settlement, and was described in terms which would have been familiar to Wallis. 'The Duke', a spokesman noted, 'has taken a personal interest in the scheme. He is not so much interested in maximum profits as he is in the high standards that have always been maintained as the guiding principle of the Chatsworth Settlement.'[96] Two years later, an acrimonious debate took place in Parliament when the

Chatsworth Trustees sought permission to develop the 400-acre Crumbles site, their last remaining piece of virgin land, as an integrated housing scheme and leisure centre. The protagonists in that debate, although referring to the Devonshires' historic role in the town, were somewhat lacking in specific information.[97] But even so, the fact that in 1975 the power of an aristocrat in a town could still be a subject of warm debate serves as an eloquent reminder, not only of the first phase of real power and influence, but also of the long-lasting era of decorative importance and social celebrity which followed.

23 The 'Empress of Watering Places'

The components in the making of nineteenth-century Eastbourne might be summarized thus: the reflected glory of ducal ownership and aristocratic patronage; the careful supervision by the landowners and their agents of planning, development and zoning; the massive recycling of estate revenue on the creation of amenities; and the extensive control by a local oligarchy – initially ducal, subsequently municipal – of the town thus created. In trying to explain the 'social tone' of Victorian seaside resorts, H. J. Perkin has argued that the most important determinant was the nature of the landownership pattern (was it unified or fragmented?), and the outlook of the elite which came to dominate the town. 'In general', he suggests:

> the most important factor in determining the social tone was the competition for the domination of the resort by large wealthy residents, hotel keepers and providers of genteel entertainments such as concert halls and bathing establishments; by small property owners, boarding house keepers, and purveyors of cheap amusements; and, later in the century, by large, capitalist enterprises, usually financed from outside, providing cheap, spectacular entertainment for a mass public.[1]

In the pattern of landownership as in the outlook of the local elite, Eastbourne exemplifies to perfection the first of Perkin's types. Although there was friction between the ducal and municipal parties in the 1890s, and although thereafter the duke's advisers were never again to be so powerful, the quarrel had been about means not ends, about power, not policy. The issue between them was not what *kind* of town Eastbourne should be, but who should *run* it. Accordingly, as the corporation replaced the Devonshires as the most powerful single force, Eastbourne's high social tone remained unaltered.

1

The original impetus towards high-class development came from the Devonshires themselves, whose power and preferences ensured that Eastbourne 'was especially planned for the accommodation of the wealthy'.[2] Expensive houses, wide roads, ample open space, strict supervision of building and enforcement of covenants all dictated that the town should evolve as an Edgbaston by the sea, with the added advantage that there was no neighbouring industrial town to threaten its pristine purity. From these initial decisions, all else followed. If the estate was only prepared to allow large, well-constructed houses, those contractors whose stock-in-trade was jerry-building for the working classes would – and did – stay away. For them, Eastbourne offered no attraction and, since it was policy to create and protect a rustic atmosphere and appearance, there was little point for those involved in noisy, smelly or unattractive trades seeking to set up in business there.

In the same way, the amenities which the seventh duke fostered were of an exclusive nature. Eastbourne College was explicitly founded for 'sons of noblemen and gentlemen', and on occasions resentment was caused in the town because it refused to offer accommodation to the sons of local trades-men.[3] Similarly, the pier, with its bands and its theatre, only offered the highest class of entertainment. But above all, it was Devonshire Park, with its theatre, concert hall, tennis, croquet, baths and gardens which set the tone, for it provided no cheap thrills or amusements so beloved of working-class trip-pers and excursionists. Its entertainment was staid, refined and respectable. Indeed, insofar as provision *was* made for the working-class population it was of an earnest, morally improving kind, such as Leaf Hall, opened in 1864 'to promote the scientific, moral and spiritual welfare of the working classes of Eastbourne', complete with a reading room, recreation room, library and lecture hall.[4]

As long as they continued to dominate the resort, the Devonshires them-selves were the major agents in the making and preservation of its unspoilt, exclusive appearance. The absence of shops along the sea front, for example, for which Eastbourne was (and is) famous, was a direct result of the Devon-shires' planning. And when the estate conveyed land to the town, the coven-ants were strict, and the corporation agreed to take 'all reasonable steps' to enforce them. In 1902, for example, when the Western Parades were donated, the conveyance explicitly prohibited the foreshore from being used for

> cricket, lawn tennis, football, kite-flying, or any games whatsoever, nor as licensed premises, nor for any roundabouts, steam organs, or con-veyances for hire, nor as standing places for any roundabouts, steam organs or conveyances for hire, or for any stalls, booths, barrows or other conveyances, or stabling or movable stands used for the sale of refresh-ments or any other goods or articles whatsoever.[5]

Moreover, the council was not allowed to tolerate

> hawking, peddling, or offering for sale of any goods or articles whatsoever by itinerant vendors, nor any performances by musicians or bands of music except performances by musicians or bands of music in the em-ployment or under the control of the corporation, nor any performances of any kind, nor any meetings or public speaking or preaching of any kind.

In this way, the exclusive provisions originated by the Devonshires were passed on to the council, which solemnly – and eagerly – undertook to maintain them. As the mayor noted in 1894: 'We have a grand town handed over to us, and it behoves us all in authority to see that proper laws are carried out, so that we may carry this town on in the manner it has been carried on before'.[6]

So it was that as the balance of power shifted, the social tone did not change. As early as 1885, when Wallis had steered through the second Eastbourne Improvement Act, many of its provisions were concerned with applying the standards of the Compton Estate Office to the field of municipal affairs. Clauses 62–99, for example, regulated the construction of housing, and imposed the standards already enforced by Wallis and Henry Currey on the duke's land. Clauses 100 and 122 were equally comprehensive with regard to sanitary matters. A further section of the Act empowered the council to make bye-laws so as to ensure 'order and good conduct among persons frequenting the parades, foreshore and sands'. In the same way, the council prevented the owners of hackney carriages from the 'blowing of horns or other noisy instruments or the beating of drums', and by clause 177, 'any householder' who was offended by the noise of a nearby entertainment could request the local police to remove it. Finally, clause 169 explicitly prohibited processions with music on Sundays.

Nor, once Wallis had departed and the Council had emancipated itself from its dependence on the duke, did matters alter, for it remained quintessentially middle-class, still dominated by the 'social leaders' of the town – builders, retired business and professional people, and those involved in trades catering for high-class clients, such as drapers, upholsterers and booksellers (see table 41).

Table 41. Composition of Eastbourne council, 1885–1910

Year	Farmer	Builder	Doctor	Legal	Clergy	Drink/ hotelier	Tradesman	Rentier/ gent.	Misc.
1885	1	9	2	3	0	3	9	3	2
1890	1	8	3	3	0	2	9	3	3
1895	1	5	3	2	0	2	13	3	3
1900	1	7	1	2	0	1	10	5	5
1905	1	6	1	1	0	1	11	5	6
1910	1	6	1	0	0	1	10	6	7

Source: Nominations printed in the local press, returns of members in council Minute Books, and street and commercial directories.

So, as it had always done, the council continued to stand for order and the defence of property. Not until 1913 did two Labour representatives join the town council, and the *Gazette's* condescending – and slightly worried – comment echoed that of the majority of citizens:

> That the results of the elections held here on Saturday last were an unwelcome surprise to many cannot be denied. But we live in times when comparatively rapid changes are inevitable; and the only sensible course

is to make the best of them . . . Honest and straightforward Labour men, men who make sure of their facts before they speak, may do good service not only to those of their own rank in life, but to the community as a whole.[7]

Accordingly, as further local Acts were passed and bye-laws made, they continued to embody the same exalted, exclusive preferences. In 1891–2, for example, the council mounted a concerted assault on the 'niggers, blind men and others, . . . beach performers, and itinerant vendors of fruit, sweetmeats and ice cream', on the foreshore. They were particularly anxious to remove one blind man who played 'discordant music with a fiddle' and another who was in the habit of 'reading stories from the bible'.[8] The Corporation Act of 1902 gave them further power to make bye-laws concerning hawking on the parade.[9] Then in 1910, another Corporation Act prohibited the distribution of handbills, banned the use of vehicles for advertising, empowered the corporation to grant licences for street traders, and to set up a register of peddlers. Anyone found peddling without being on the register was liable to a 50s. fine in the first instance, and £5 thereafter.[10]

Just as the majority of the tenants of the Compton building estate were anxious to see the covenants enforced, so the newspapers kept up a constant campaign against the infringement of local bye-laws. In 1886, for example, the *Gazette* attacked 'costermongers and other itinerant vendors of fish, fruit and vegetables', who were allowed 'by the police to shout and bawl through the streets at the top of their voices, much to the annoyance of quiet-living residents and visitors.'[11] Four years later it criticized the hawking of newspapers on the front: 'They must keep Eastbourne select. It was considerably lowering the tone of the place.'[12] No doubt it was in response to such pressure that steps were taken in the following year. In 1907, a new threat had arisen: 'Unless drastic methods are adopted to check it, the handbill plague will cause serious mischief at Eastbourne, by robbing the town of one of its greatest merits – its orderly, well-kept and scrupulously neat appearance.'[13] Again, in the Act of 1910, action was soon taken. Finally, in the same edition, the *Gazette* took issue with 'barking dogs, loud talking in the streets, midnight motors and other things', which prevented both residents and visitors 'taking the rest to which they are entitled.'

For the inhabitants at large, such regulations seemed appropriate; to outsiders they seemed merely bizarre. In 1913 one correspondent in the *Daily News and Leader* satirized them delightfully.

I know of no popular seaside town where the authorities forbid the people to do so many things . . . Occasionally, I am told, a graceless visitor will write a grumbling letter to the local paper, but on the whole the people drag their chains with the utmost politeness . . . They prohibit, by bye-law 1006, the hawking of all commodities on the beach. If we want to buy a chocolate fruit, we must deserve it by getting up and going far afield . . .

Evening newspapers afford some of us a pleasant recreation as we sit idly by the sea, but the boys who sell them are (by bye-law 601) not allowed to approach within a certain prescribed distance from the pier . . . By bye-law 2085, dogs are prohibited from barking on the beach. This particular prohibition was the subject of much vulgar ridicule in some of the London newspapers at the time of its first publication, but our authorities are not the kind of men to be deflected from their course by newspaper criticism. After all, there is something derisive about a dog's bark: a robust mockery, a suggestion of profane laughter, and one can understand that such a sound uttered on land owned by a duke must strike the shocked authorities as something closely akin to sacrilege, like laughing in church.[14]

The Eastbourne *Chronicle*, which published the report in full, was not at all amused. 'A Churlish Critic's Resentment of Reasonable Regulations: Ill-Mannered Attack upon The Duke of Devonshire', were the headlines beneath which it ran the story.

In essence, the point of the article was valid. The limits on behaviour imposed by the council were as comprehensive as were the restrictions placed on building by the Devonshires and the Gilberts, and it was this very complementariness of attitudes which explained why Alderman Simmons could say with pride that 'This town is primarily and essentially one that appeals to the best social grades.' Indeed it did, as another tongue-in-cheek account made plain:

> What it does not do is to encourage trippers. There is not an odd corner in the place where the tripper can be accommodated. This is the most miserable place on the south coast for the half-day tripper – no picture palaces on the front, no whelk stalls in the street, no sixpenny dinners or ham and beef teas, no crowds of yelling bathers, no barking dogs and no ventriloquists, phrenologists, cheap-jacks, fortune-tellers, niggers or pierrots anywhere in sight. To the tripper who wants a kaleidoscope of joys in three hours for half a crown, Eastbourne, it must be admitted, is a dismal failure. Eastbourne is not a philanthropic or charitable institution. It does not desire that its magnificent parades and beautiful streets shall be receptacles for orange peel and ginger beer bottles of the half-day invader. Its policy is to preserve itself from the jolly greeting of cloth-capped thousands – and until now it has succeeded very well.[15]

Moreover, there can be little doubt that the majority of the inhabitants hoped that such would long continue to be the case.

2

A town which was created under such rigid and exclusive auspices – whether ducal or municipal – was bound to evolve a somewhat eccentric economic and social structure. As early as 1877, *Beckett's Eastbourne Directory* gave a graphic impression of the skewed occupational distribution in its listing of the principal trades and industries under only seven headings (table 42).

Table 42. Occupational structure of Eastbourne, 1877

Professional		*Clothes, etc.*	
Architects	4	Boot and shoe makers	16
Dentists	1	Drapers	18
Doctors	12	Dressmakers	13
Music teachers	7	Hatters	5
Resident J.P.s	6	Hosiers	13
Solicitors	8	Outfitters	8
Vets	2	Tailors	12

Hotels, etc.		*Building, etc.*	
Beer houses	16	Bricklayers	4
Dining rooms	3	Builders	24
Hotels	36	Carpenters	14
		Gas fitters	7
Educational		House decorators	4
		Plumbers	9
Schools (gentlemen)	13		
Schools (ladies)	13	*Miscellaneous tradesmen, etc.*	

Food		Auctioneers	3
		Booksellers and newsagents	12
Bakers	21	Cabinet makers and upholsterers	9
Butchers	18	Chemists	10
Dairymen	7	China warehouses	9
Fishmongers	6	Confectioners	17
Greengrocers	21	Fancy repositories	9
Grocers	32	Florists	4
		Fly proprietors	6
		Hairdressers	4
		House agents	6
		Ironmongers	6
		Laundries	13
		Photographers	5
		Printers	5
		Tobacconists	5
		Watch and clockmakers	6

Source: *Eastbourne Gazette*, 28 March 1877.

The impression conveyed by these figures is exactly as expected: concentration on high-class, consumer goods, trades and leisure activities. Doctors, music teachers and expensive shops proliferated, but industry was represented only by building and its allied trades, whose economic importance was aptly reflected in their strong representation on the council. Nor had this picture altered fundamentally by the early twentieth century, as a more selective glance at the occupational structure in 1911 will demonstrate (table 43).

Table 43. Occupational structure of Eastbourne, 1911: most significant professions

Professional		*Clothes, etc.*	
Doctors	61	Bootmakers	67
Insurance agents	31	Drapers	33
Music teachers	29	Dressmakers	51
		Hairdressers	39
Hotels, etc.		Hosiers	22
		Milliners	23
Boarding establishments	52	Tailors	47
Hotels	29		
Licensed victuallers	31	*Building*	
Educational		Builders	46
		Carpenters	23
Ladies' schools	37	Gas fitters	25
Public schools	22	House decorators	38
Schools and colleges	23	Plumbers	32
Food		*Miscellaneous, tradesmen, etc.*	
Bakers	40	Chemists	23
Butchers	39	Coal merchants	20
Confectioners	41	Laundries	32
Dairymen	27	Newsagents	26
Fishmongers	20	Stationers	23
Greengrocers	44	Tobacconists	27
Grocers	60	Upholsterers	29

Source: *Gowland's Eastbourne Directory* (1911), *passim*.

Although only those professions which were represented by 20 or more practitioners are listed here, the overall picture remains unchanged: a leisured, exclusive town, with industry kept firmly and successfully in check.

The census abstracts for 1901 confirm this impression, and also demonstrate the close similarity between the occupational structure of Eastbourne and other high-class holiday resorts. In all cases, as the *Gazette* noted of Eastbourne, there was 'a very large preponderance of females'[16] – not only delicate middle-class ladies, maiden aunts and widows of substance, but also the retinues of servants, washerwomen and schoolmistresses (table 44). Indeed, the high percentage of the female population employed in the service industries meant that there was actually a lower proportion of retired or unoccupied women in Eastbourne and similar resorts than overall throughout England and Wales.

Particularly noteworthy is the high proportion of women involved in teaching, in most cases running preparatory schools patronized by the aristocracy and professional classes, especially colonial and Indian civil servants. In his novel *Rossenal*, for example, Ernest Raymond created the Eastbourne prep school of Glendammery, 'where they incubate about seventy boys for Osborne and the tip-top public schools'.[17] Indeed, many of the great houses in Meads were adapted for such use, like Kent House, founded in 1887, 'very much for the sons of gentry', attended by 30 pupils. Among its most famous alumni was William Beveridge, who attended between 1890 and 1892, and whose parents had recently returned from India, where his father had been a civil servant, and settled in the town.[18] Another pupil was E. M. Forster, who boarded there from 1890 to 1893. His father was an architect, who was related to many of the great nineteenth-century evangelical families, and it was from a distant relative, Marianne Thornton, that in 1887 he inherited £8,000, the interest from which paid for his education. Like Beveridge, Forster was intellectually precocious, but unhappy and bullied, and his early sexual experiences on the Downs near Beachy Head would certainly have ruffled the feathers of the Eastbourne matriarchs and matrons.[19]

The selected occupations for men give a complementary view (table 45). Whereas there were more women employed than nationally, there were fewer men: emphatic evidence of Eastbourne's attraction for the old, the leisured and the retired. At the same time, building and food, drink and lodging were overwhelmingly the most important industries in the town, and this was reflected in their preponderant representation on the council. Once more, as with female occupations, the similarity between the figures for Eastbourne and other high-class resorts is remarkable.

3

For all its aristocratic pretensions, then, Eastbourne was a quintessentially middle-class town, and that was as true of the solid, comfortable bourgeois residents of Meads as of its summer visitors. R.N. Wilson may have described it in his guide book of 1904 as 'the home of the aristocratic section'; but it was 'aristocratic' only in terms of the major ground landlord and the guests he brought down to Compton Place.[20] While its residents and its visitors were unquestionably respectable, the town never acquired that reputation for raffish grandeur which Brighton kept until the twentieth century. As Ollivant pointed out in another of his novels, 'Beachbourne' boasted 'hotels with *aristocratic* names and a *middle class* clientele'.[21] And here, admittedly from 1920, but appropriate for pre-war years, is a fuller description of hotel life:

There were the usual clergyman and his family, the usual landowner with his invalid wife, there were the Anglo-Indians and the Scottish ladies by the window. There were beards and bald heads, there was the painted

Table 44. Selected female occupations in high-class resorts, 1901 (women over 10) *(percentages in brackets)*

Resort	Total	Retired or unoccupied [xxiii]*	Teaching [iii]	Domestic servants [iv.i]
Eastbourne	21,422	12,579 (58.8)	452 (2.1)	3,771 (17.6)
Bexhill	5,808	3,800 (65.4)	137 (2.4)	892 (15.4)
Folkestone	14,794	9,143 (61.8)	252 (1.7)	2,608 (17.6)
Hastings	32,848	20,625 (62.8)	551 (1.7)	4,912 (15.0)
Southport	24,037	15,067 (62.7)	359 (1.5)	3,616 (15.0)
Torquay	17,640	10,539 (59.7)	206 (1.2)	3,259 (18.5)
Worthing	10,222	6,262 (61.3)	153 (1.5)	1,872 (18.3)
National Aggregate	13,189,585	9,017,834 (68.3)	172,873 (1.3)	1,330,783 (10.0)

Source: *Parliamentary Papers*: 1902, CXIX, 382–3, CXVIII, 594–5, CXXI, 382–3; 1903, LXXXIV, 230–1.
* Census classification.

Table 45. Selected male occupations in high-class resorts, 1901 (men over 10) *(percentages in brackets)*

Resort	Total	Retired or unoccupied [xxiii]*	Commercial or business clerks [v.2]	Conveyance of men, goods and messages [vi]
Eastbourne	14,134	3,425 (24.2)	260 (1.8)	1,440 (10.1)
Bexhill	3,955	947 (23.9)	56 (1.4)	329 (8.3)
Folkestone	10,249	2,052 (20.0)	174 (1.7)	1,589 (15.5)
Hastings	21,068	4,763 (22.6)	405 (1.9)	2,402 (11.4)
Southport	15,710	3,366 (21.4)	413 (2.6)	1,811 (11.5)
Torquay	10,683	2,229 (20.9)	156 (1.5)	1,178 (11.0)
Worthing	6,362	1,505 (23.6)	85 (1.3)	539 (8.5)
National Aggregate	12,134,259	1,977,283 (16.2)	307,889 (2.5)	1,094,301 (9.0)

Source: *Parliamentary Papers*: 1902, CXIX, 382–3, CXVIII, 594–5, CXXI, 382–3; 1903, LXXXIV, 230–1.
* Census classification.

widow and the stout widow and the determined spinster who found the ham less good than at Sidmouth, there were two compact and pleasant families of athletic girls and big schoolboys, who thought of nothing but

Charwomen [iv.3]	Laundry and washing [iv.3]	Clothing [xix]	Food [xx]
110 (0.5)	672 (3.1)	885 (4.1)	737 (3.4)
27 (0.5)	110 (1.9)	132 (2.3)	228 (3.9)
101 (0.7)	288 (1.9)	538 (3.6)	522 (3.5)
248 (0.7)	942 (2.9)	1,207 (3.7)	1,367 (4.2)
231 (1.0)	495 (2.0)	1,130 (4.7)	1,316 (5.4)
130 (0.7)	673 (3.8)	999 (5.7)	522 (3.0)
85 (0.8)	237 (2.3)	432 (4.2)	411 (4.0)
111,841 (0.8)	196,141 (1.4)	691,701 (5.2)	300,798 (2.2)

Building [xii]	Food, drink and lodging [xx]
2,152 (15.2)	1,473 (10.4)
709 (17.9)	367 (9.3)
1,615 (15.7)	1,048 (10.2)
2,625 (12.5)	2,569 (12.2)
2,052 (13.1)	1,375 (8.7)
1,393 (13.0)	1,008 (9.4)
987 (15.5)	674 (10.6)
1,042,864 (8.6)	774,291 (6.4)

golf and swimming, a honeymoon couple, a stockbroker, some Jews, and the usual horrible fill ups.[22]

Twenty years earlier, the situation had been identical. The 'Fashionable Visitors List' in the *Gazette* of 20 August 1902, at the height of the Season, extended for one whole page, but only 12 of the visitors were titled.[23]

The leisured of Eastbourne fell into three distinct categories. The first were 'those who came to settle down in Eastbourne, after having spent the earlier part of their lives in business' or administration, to die comfortably, quietly and unostentatiously.[24] One such figure was T. H. Huxley, who retired from London to Eastbourne in 1890, and settled in Staveley Road, 'where my wife and I may go down hill quietly together, . . . solaced by an occasional visit from children and grandchildren.' After the bustle and controversy of his life, he evolved a calm, tranquil routine:

> The day began . . . early; he never relaxed from the rule of an eight o'clock breakfast. Then a pipe and an hour and a half letter writing or working at a short essay. Then a short expedition around the garden, to inspect the creepers, tend the saxifrages, or see how the more exposed shrubs could best be sheltered from the shrivelling winds.
>
> Then would follow another spell of work till near one o'clock; the weather would tempt him out again before lunch; but afterwards he was certain to be out for an hour or two from half past two. However hard it blew, and Eastbourne is seldom still, the tiled walk along the sea wall always offered the possibility of a constitutional. But the high expanse of the Downs was his favourite walk. The air of Beachy Head, 560 feet up, was an unfailing tonic . . .
>
> After his walk, a cup of tea was followed by more reading or writing till seven; after dinner another pipe, and then he would return to my mother in the drawing room and settle down in his particular arm chair, with some tough volume on history or theology to read . . . At ten he would migrate to the study for a final smoke, before going to bed.
>
> Such was his routine, broken only by occasional visits to town on business. Old friends came occasionally to stay for a few days, and teatime would often bring one or two of the small circle of friends whom he had made in Eastbourne. These he also occasionally visited, but he scarcely ever dined out. The talking was too tiring.[25]

For five years, that was Huxley's life: doubtless more cerebral and intellectual than most of his neighbours would have appreciated or understood. Nevertheless, in its limited, comfortable way, it epitomized much that was common among the less ostentatious of the Eastbourne middle-class community.

Yet this life was a world away from the active, snobbish, socially ambitious activities of many of the *haute bourgeoisie* – those rentiers, businessmen, and local entrepreneurs who made up local society. R. N. Wilson caught their tone well:

> Inhabiting the numerous villas in terrace and square is a large population of the leisured classes, whose gentility is founded upon family connection or sufficient private means. From these sources are chiefly drawn the members of that 'smart' society which is of leading merit in the matter of fashionable affairs and vivacity of manners.[26]

On a slightly larger-than-life scale, the best example was George Ambrose Wallis himself. In 1879, he constructed Holywell Mount at a cost of £10,000, making it the most expensive private building in the town, with the exception of Compton Place. In January 1884, at the zenith of his term as mayor, he gave a ball there, splendidly described in the local press:

> The mansion was built in 1879, and the style of architecture is the domestic Gothic, which is admirably adapted for cosy residences in which English gentlemen so much delight. The interior is decorated throughout in the Jacobean style, a great improvement on the Queen Anne style, now so commonly prevalent. On entering from the carriage drive, we mount a flight of steps from which most interesting views of Beachy Head are obtained . . . Passing from the small outer hall, we enter the inner hall, a handsome apartment, 30 feet by 20 feet, with an oak parquet floor . . . The dining room is a most commodious room, fitted with an old fashioned chimney sunk in the wall, after the style of the chimney corners in Haddon Hall . . . There are altogether forty rooms in the house, contained in the ground, first, second and third floors. The domestic offices are almost entirely detached from the main building, and are communicated with by a separate staircase. Each floor is fitted with a separate hot and cold water service. . . The billiard room is formed in the high-pitched roof . . . Connecting with this room is the octagon room, fitted as a smoking room, the views of which are of the most extensive and varied character. On the land side can be seen the Downs, stretching away to Willingdon, while on the sea side can be seen . . . the magnificent heights of Beachy Head. The billiard room was last night used as a supper room, and was sufficiently capacious to seat 100 guests. The furniture and fittings of the mansion generally partake of the Oriental and the Antique; everything is arranged in the most artistic manner, thus harmonising with the style of architecture . . . We have not space this week to describe the charming paintings and beautiful works of art, with which the rooms are studied – everything which a refined taste could require or suggest is provided, and last night, when the rooms overflowed with fair ladies in the most brilliant costumes, . . . the whole formed a spectacle of beauty and loveliness which it has been the lot of few to witness.[27]

During the Season, which began in May but reached its peak in August and

September, the indigenous *haute bourgeoisie* were joined by their metropolitan cousins, either as holidaymakers in the great hotels, or as semi-permanent residents, renting a house in Meads for three months, with the father occasionally going up to town on business. For such figures, the allure of Devonshire Park would be irresistible. As one guide noted, 'in Devonshire Park throughout the season, the elite of Eastbourne society may be seen.'[28] In addition, the most important local men, and the most well-connected visitors, would be members of the Devonshire Club, an institution proudly described as being 'of somewhat exclusive and limited membership, but . . . an important focus of men's society, and particularly those gentlemen of leisure who, with their families, form the first circle of Eastbourne's social life.'[29] While the men enjoyed themselves in this equivalent of a London club, their ladies might patronize the high-class local shops, listen to the band which played every day (except Sundays) on the Promenades, or even avail themselves of a bathing machine and sample the waters – suitably distanced from male bathers. All was elegant, genteel and refined.

The same was true of the winter months. The Devonshire Park continued its concerts, theatrical productions and other entertainments. Local society became more private, and concentrated itself in homes, where afternoon teas, dinner parties and dances flourished as at Edgbaston. As in the summer, many residents would go to church, and some might even be involved in local temperance or philanthropic work; but the central focus of male society was the Eastbourne Hunt, founded in the 1870s, which afforded 'sport and recreation to numerous influential residents and visitors', and was active between November and March.[30] All the most influential local figures were connected with it: the Wallis brothers, Roland Burke and J. P. Cockerell, C. D. Gilbert, the ninth duke of Devonshire, and Freeman Freeman-Thomas, later Lord Willingdon. Between 70 and 120 turned out regularly, and the day's sport was enthusiastically reported in the local press. Hunting dinners were frequent and the annual ball, in the Queen's Hotel, held 'a foremost position in the list of winter festivities'.[31] Indeed, it was probably only equalled by the mayoral banquet itself, the high point of corporate, bourgeois, municipal solidarity and self-esteem. Only when there was a ducal mayor, with a ball at Devonshire Park and a garden party at Compton Place would this be upstaged. Predictably, it was the summit of local, bourgeois ambition to be invited to such grand, heroic gatherings.

As at Edgbaston, the social gradations were more minute and subtle than are quantifiably recoverable today. Just as Edgbastonians found a 'right' and a 'wrong' side of Hagley Road, so there was at Eastbourne a 'right' and 'wrong' side of Terminus Road, the main shopping street. Even the parades were, by some unwritten rule, carefully segregated and, although at some parts of the front there were three, and at others five, the general principle was the lower the parade, the lower the social tone. Here, for example, is an account of the three-level part:

The Upper Parade is almost entirely relegated to the 'Upper Ten' ... The promenaders of the Upper Parade look down with the severe and ineffable contempt of true born hidalgos on the motley crowd of nondescripts who saunter lazily along the lower walk, while the latter seldom think of ascending to the fashionable Olympus above them, and are generally satisfied with the space allotted to them below.[32]

From a slightly later date, Sylvia Lynd's account of five-fold segregation gives a very similar picture.[33]

Such was Eastbourne at the turn of the century – physically distanced from the great, polluted towns, catering successfully for the wealthy, leisured middle-class rich, with the working class only represented in its most conservative guise of shopkeepers and domestic servants, whose very livelihood gave them a vested interest in the continuation of such a régime. Crime was limited to petty pilfering for, like Edgbaston, Eastbourne was 'well-ordered', with its inhabitants 'usually a law-abiding race'.[34] In 1876, for example, the Eastbourne magistrates had only 140 cases to deal with, the majority being larceny, drunk and disorderly or offences against the bye-laws. Only five were committed to the assizes.[35] As the *Gazette* noted with evident pleasure in 1893, 'roughs and criminals are comparatively absent'.[36] The Labour party was weak, and trades unions and strikes were unheard of. Insofar as there was any problem for the comfortable middle classes it was that of the servant question. In 1902, the *Gazette* complained that 'far too many' were becoming 'increasingly exacting and unreliable', and five years later, it pointed out that 'the difficulty of obtaining trustworthy and industrious domestic servants is enhanced in the present day by the fact that various employments are open to young women'.[37] But this was the only cloud in the sky: for the *haute bourgeoisie* of Eastbourne, life seemed cosy, comfortable and assured.

4

Three quotations may serve as a summary of the 'Empress of Watering Places' at its most splendid. The first, from the files of the *Gazette*, captures delightfully the Church Parade during Sunday mornings in high summer, when the elite of the town disported themselves upon the promenade:

To see the Church Parade in all its glory, one must visit Eastbourne during the height of the Season, namely during the months of August and September. On Sunday last, for instance, the spectacle presented on the Promenades between the hours of twelve and one was in every respect a brilliant one. An excellent bird's eye view of the spectacle may be had on any Sunday from the top of the green slope leading to the Wish Tower. From this point we see what seems to be a moving mass of colour stretching as far as the Pier. No disagreeable sounds mar the enjoyment of

Fig. 45. Church parade at Eastbourne, *c.*1910; the large, château-like building to the right is the Grand Hotel (by courtesy of Eastbourne Central Library).

the scene. We hear the pleasant buzz of conversation proceeding from the hundreds of promenaders walking to and fro, but beyond this and the soft, idle lapping of the waves on the shore, there is no sound of any kind. Not even a band disturbs the general air of quietness and peace. . .
By descending the path from the Wish Tower, we can at once mix with the throng . . . Coming along the middle terrace – where the crowd is usually most dense and difficult to penetrate – the rich variety of the costumes of the ladies either promenading or sitting on the rows of chairs is particu-larly noticeable . . . All the ladies carry sunshades whose varied tints impart additional colour to the scene. Dresses there are of such bewilder-ing colours and styles that the attempt to describe them would be ridicu-lous. Even the children in the Church Parade look smart.[38]

More pithily, the prevailing flavour of piety and prosperity, smugness and hypocrisy, prudishness and uprightness, is delightfully caught in William Neil's recollection of the same event:

A friend of mine, who spent his boyhood in Eastbourne (in Victorian or Edwardian England) recalls that it was the done thing from twelve to one o'clock to parade in front of the Grand Hotel with a prayer book under the arm. This showed that you were the kind of person who went to church (whether you had been there or not) and, equally important, that you were the kind of person who did not need to cook his own dinner.[39]

Or, as T. H. S. Escott put it, even more succinctly: 'No earthly spot could perhaps be so virtuous as Eastbourne looks.'[40]

24 Internal difficulties and external threats, *c.* 1890–1914

Such was Eastbourne during those never-ending Edwardian summers before the First World War, an exclusive resort in which the principle of residential segregation was carried to its most extreme form of development: internally, in that the working classes and the *haute bourgeoisie* of the town were kept far apart, and externally because there was no major industrial town adjacent or even close by. The residents of Edgbaston, worried by the encroachment of the city, and the growth in commuter traffic across the Calthorpe estate, would have been envious. Indeed, when they read advertisements in *Edgbastonia* for high-class hotels in Eastbourne, the town must have seemed attractive as the epitome of all Edgbaston's virtues, while suffering none of its disadvantages. Yet, to the natives themselves, this would have seemed an unrealistically rosy picture: for just as *fin-de-siècle* Edgbaston had its problems, so too did Eastbourne.

1

Internally, the economic and social structure of such a seaside resort necessarily brought with it its own troubles, for although the relatively large working-class population was mostly employed in occupations of a conservative hue, the corollary of this was that they were those most prone to seasonal unemployment.[1] All of those members of the working-class involved in industries dependent largely on visitors – servants, waiters and waitresses, cab drivers, high-class shop assistants – experienced a severe fall-off in trade and work between October and April. And, because the only other principal industry in the town was building, there was nowhere they could transfer to, since building itself, and all the subsidiary trades connected with it, also experienced its slackest period at the time of short days and bad weather. As the *Gazette* explained in 1884:

> Pleasure resorts like Eastbourne have to contend with many disadvantages, not the least of which is that they possess no staple industry to fall back on in the winter, and the result is that a bad season, or an unusually short period of summer weather, causes an immense amount of genuine distress.[2]

Moreover, this perennial problem was accentuated when the effects of long-term cyclical downturns were superimposed. Between 1885 and 1896, for example, a substantial downturn in the building cycle, a series of bad winters and the row over the water supply, combined to bring unprecedented misery upon the town. In 1886 the *Gazette* was able to predict trouble as early as September:

> Eastbourne has been living on building operations for twenty years. Now the town is overbuilt, scores if not hundreds of houses are empty, and it is supposed that if all the builders rested, after completing their present contracts, it would be at least two years before the growth of the town justified any further operations . . . But if they can afford to stop building, and employ their capital in other directions, their workmen, or many of them, cannot afford to migrate to places where the building trade still thrives; and the prospect of hundreds of men out of work in Eastbourne throughout next winter must be faced . . . In five or six or seven weeks, loaves of bread will be hard to get in many a household, and goods will commence a pilgrimage to the pawnbroker.[3]

This prophecy proved to be all too accurate. In January and February 1887, the *Gazette* ran a series entitled 'Winter Distress in Eastbourne', drawing attention to the plight of workers, and the ineffective attempts by council, churches and private charity to cope with the problem. In late January over 70 men paraded in the streets, demonstrating in request of more action against unemployment. But the *Gazette* felt able to report, with evident relief, that 'the great body was more sensible than to resort to anything like riot or disturbance . . . No banners were displayed, and no disturbance resulted from these unusual proceedings.'[4]

For all its wishes to be thought to be 'almost without poor', the problem of working-class poverty in Eastbourne was therefore very real.[5] In the period immediately before the First World War, when the second great nationwide building boom had spent itself, it returned. As the *Gazette* pointed out, 'In the face of so many outward and visible signs of growing wealth and luxury in Eastbourne, one is almost tempted to forget that some of the problems of poverty exist here in our town.'[6] But as it made clear two years later, 'There is in our midst, whether we like to see and confess it or not, a great deal of poverty which it will tax all our energies to deal with intelligently.'[7] Once more, the mayor set up a relief fund, and the council and the Devonshire and Gilbert estates began programmes of public works. Again, however reluctantly, it was necessary to admit that even in the 'Empress of Watering Places', there 'were hundreds of our fellows face to face with awful conditions of suffering', not only 'every winter', but especially when bad weather and cyclical downturns coincided.

Pockets of poverty, cyclically intensified, necessarily implied bad conditions of housing for some inhabitants, even though brochure after brochure proudly claimed that 'anything approaching a slum is not to be found in this town.'[8] Assuredly, on the Devonshire and Gilbert estates, there was much substance in this claim, but in those small areas of land which they did not own, and which escaped the vigilance of local inspectors, slums and bad housing conditions did indeed proliferate. In 1911, for example, the *Gazette* ran a series on the 'Eastbourne underworld'. A lady reporter, suitably disguised, was asked to 'investigate the conditions in which the inhabitants of the underworld life' by spending three nights in a common lodging house.[9] Although she gave up after the first night, she left a memorably eloquent peroration to her final report:

> I have shown *Gazette* readers a home where the very air is so foul, so polluted, that any knife might be blunted in a vain effort to cut through its fetid impurity; a home where a bed means just anything on which may be piled a heap of malodorous rags; where every room at night becomes a resting place for people – abject, dejected beings of both sexes and all ages, herding together indiscriminately; where it is an impossibility to observe any of the most elementary decencies of life.[10]

She concluded:

> all this in beautiful, palatial Eastbourne! It is within easy reach of the refined appointments, the luxurious equipment, of the residences of the elect. Would they, could they, go on day by day, leading their own sweet, wholesome lives, dreaming their own pure dreams, enjoying their healthful sports and pleasures, if once they could be transported to these dens, and realize that the same sun that shines so brightly on their homesteads, serving to sweeten still further already ideal conditions, is in these pestiferous places . . . ripening dirt and disease . . . accentuating squalor and filth?

2

This was heady stuff, which can hardly have made palatable reading for the matrons of Meads, elegantly sipping their afternoon tea. Yet, just as the town was blighted with real, apparently ineradicable poverty, so there was always the fear of working-class solidarity and hostility over the horizon. Most working men in the 1870s and 1880s prided themselves on being 'Advanced Liberals', and it was not until 1913 that two Labour councillors were elected. Moreover, despite the very real spatial segregation, the nature of the employment meant that in the main the bonds of deference and respect remained strong. However, by the 1890s, there was a growing realization in certain working-class areas that the town was not being run in their interests.

In 1901, for example, it seemed possible that the London, Brighton & South Coast Railway might site its new engine works in the town, and there were discussions between the mayor and the company chairman. The working classes were in favour, because this alternative form of employment would make them less dependent on the transient and fickle cycles of the Season and the building industry; but the Chamber of Commerce, representing the town's largest businessmen, was 'horrified at the thought of a colony of artisans', and roundly condemned the scheme. And, at a public meeting, their class interest was mercilessly ridiculed by one of the more eloquent champions of artisan opinion. 'One would imagine', he observed, 'by the hysterical wail that went up from the sacred precincts of the Chamber of Commerce, that the Corporation had invited a colony of convicts, and that the whole of the inmates of Dartmoor were about to be let loose in the town.'[11]

In the end, the scheme was dropped, but the arguments which were made were played out again, more eloquently, acrimoniously and lengthily, over the issue of trams. Just as the 'gondolas of the people' threatened the exclusive middle-class suburbia of Glasgow's West End, Manchester's Victoria Park, London's Hampstead and Birmingham's Edgbaston, so they represented an equal threat to those seaside bastions of middle-class exclusiveness, Torquay, Worthing, Hastings, Bexhill, Bournemouth and Folkestone. In part, this was because, as with the suburbs, there was a danger that trams would enable the working classes to penetrate what had previously been exclusive middle-class areas. But in addition, there was the added danger that tramlines, with their noise and ugly apparatus, would deter those very high-class visitors which these resorts had been created to attract. As a result, in all such holiday towns between the 1880s and the early 1900s, there were protracted, acrimonious debates as to the best course of action to adopt. Bournemouth, Brighton, Bexhill, Hastings and Torquay all finally constructed tramways; Folkestone, true to its especially 'superior' image, held aloof.[12]

At Eastbourne the first serious proposal came in July 1896, when 'an Eastbourne gentleman' suggested a tramway from Seaside along the front as far as Beachy Head. Nothing came of it, and the paper in which it was published noted that 'we should be very chary of proposing anything that would in any way tend to lower the high tone of which the town is so justly proud.'[13] A year later, another scheme was mooted, and the duke's endorsement solicited, but his agent replied that 'His Grace is not at present inclined to give the scheme his support.'[14] At the same time, however, there was a growing demand from the citizens of the east end for some form of cheap, rapid mass transport. As the *Gazette* noted in May 1899, 'very clear and unmistakable are the tones in which the East Enders demand electric tramways'.[15] Indeed, so strong was the pressure that in the same month, the Electric Lighting Committee of the council recommended that a tramway should be constructed from Seaside, via Sea Side Road, to the town hall itself. At that same meeting, a petition against the tramways was presented, containing 1,370 signatures, from residents of the western part of the town, and another in favour was deposited, most of whose signatories came from the east end.[16]

Thus were the two opposing sides drawn up, and the battle raged all the summer. The Electric Lighting Committee argued that trams were 'a delightful mode of locomotion', being 'speedy, smooth and noiseless', and that they would be financially viable. The opponents argued that if trams were built, then Eastbourne would 'say goodbye to the better class of visitor'. Such an 'abominable system', it was asserted, would 'ruin the town', by which, in fact, was meant that the council 'could not sacrifice the interests of the west end for the interests of the east'. As with the debate over the railway works, the concept of the 'best interests' of the town differed markedly from one end of Eastbourne to the other. Once more, it was the west end which won. There was insufficient support for the committee's recommendation, and the scheme was dropped. It was revived briefly at the end of the year, when yet another deputation from the east end urged the need to be linked with the centre. Once more, at a council meeting in November, it was rejected.[17]

There the matter rested until January 1902, when the Electric Lighting Committee recommended the adoption of a scheme to link the east end with the centre of the town. Again, the protagonists claimed that the trams were 'an elegant, rapid and comfortable means of transit', now being adopted so generally that if Eastbourne did not follow suit quickly, it would be 'absolutely the last town of any importance in the United Kingdom' to adopt them.[18] Moreover, as Alderman Wenham, one of the few councillors who consistently supported the interests of the working classes, pointed out, 'the people of the East Ward are emphatically in favour of trams'. Ominously, in February, a petition 47ft long was presented, containing 1,049 signatures from the east end, urging the 'great and increasing need' for the trams to be built.[19] It was, indeed, the most assertive display of working-class solidarity in Eastbourne before the First World War.

Predictably, outraged middle-class hostility was severe. When the new scheme was first mooted, the *Gazette* noted that 'the majority of the members [of the council] will not countenance any scheme for constructing tramways in those districts in which the inhabitants consider that the lines would be detrimental to their interests'. It was quite correct: there was never any possibility of trams being allowed to the west of the town hall. Even to the east, the middle-class interpretation of what was in the best interests of the town held sway. 'For my own part', noted one columist in the *Gazette*, 'I have always recognised . . . the imperative necessity of paying the utmost deference to the wishes of those well-to-do residents and visitors who are the mainstay of the town'.[20] There was no doubting what their views were. As he put it even more stridently a little later:

> The construction of tram lines in the western districts or in Terminus Road is utterly out of the question . . . As commonsense business men, the members of the committee are bound to countenance nothing that would injure the position of Eastbourne as a first class watering place. The wishes of the moneyed classes must be studied.[21]

Once again, although the Committee recommended the scheme, the council as a whole threw it out.[22]

Instead, the council decided to adopt a fleet of omnibuses, thereby becoming the first municipality in the country to do so: a piece of local initiative which eloquently demonstrated the high priority they placed on cleanliness and quiet.[23] At first the scheme was a great success, but in September 1903 an unfortunate series of breakdowns and accidents led to a revival of the demand for trams. At a meeting in the east end, 1,500 inhabitants urged the council to introduce trams and do away with the buses,[24] but again, the interests of the rich triumphed. As the *Chronicle* put it, it was 'the wishes of the inhabitants generally' (by which they meant the residents of Meads) rather than 'a section of persons quartered at one particular end of the town' which must be considered.[25] Or, as the *Gazette* argued, even more emphatically, trams 'would destroy some of the amenities of Eastbourne, and render the town less popular to those upon which it largely depends – visitors and residents of the wealthier classes.' Once again, the council threw the scheme out.[26] Finally, in the autumn of 1906, continuing objection to the noise, smells and unreliability of the buses led to a last attempt to have them replaced with trams.[27] The arguments were by now so familiar that they need not be repeated here. And, once more, the outcome was defeat for the trams. The forces of exclusiveness had triumphed over working-class demands.

3

These threats from within, although occasionally worrying, did not in fact amount to much. Although there was poverty, it was of limited incidence, and working-class consciousness was hardly developed at all. Eastbourne was, in Victor Bailey's words, a town where 'the pattern of social relationships retained a deferential character.'[28] But while problems from within could be contained if not eradicated, it was less easy to cope with those threats mounted by excursionists. Preferring stalls and catch-penny amusements to concerts and grand hotels, they were a real threat to a town whose best shops aspired to rival those of the West End of London. Moreover, since Eastbourne provided none of the amusements which such trippers required, there was little for them to do, except to roam the streets or drink, thereby confirming the residents' worst fears.

Early in the town's development, the threat became apparent. In 1872, for example, the *Gazette* attacked the London Brighton & South Coast Railway for allowing excursion fares, which resulted in 'shoals of artisan excursionists' who caused 'annoyance and discomfort to our usual visitors'.[29] Five years later, a 'very objectionable class of excursionist' visited Pevensey Castle in force on a Sunday, where they were so impertinent as to interrupt Divine Service by their ribald behaviour. Indeed, on one occasion, a 'scene, not only of disorder, but of absolute indecency' took place, when a trap driven by two drunken women overturned in a ditch. 'One of the women was shortly afterwards found there, still sitting in the trap, but so intoxicated as to be completely oblivious of her situation.' By order of the owner, the Duke of Devonshire, the castle was closed.[30]

Thereafter, even the slightest suggestion of plebeian intrusion drove the local press into paroxysms of rage and hysteria. In 1880, it was that 'dangerous specimen of depraved humanity – the London rough', who 'infested' the town, which was the object of the *Gazette's* wrath.[31] In 1907, it attacked 'bibulous and noisy trippers' who did 'far more harm than good to any town on which they thrust their unwelcome presence.' And, two years later, it had another go at the 'bibulous bands of beefeaters and trippers', who contrasted so markedly with the choir and Sunday school outings.[32] In part, this hostility was because it was felt that Eastbourne, as a 'fashionable resort' had 'nothing to gain and everything to lose' by allowing trippers to defile its exclusive parades and promenades. The town relied on the patronage of middle-class visitors, which would surely be withdrawn if its peace and quiet could not be guaranteed. In addition, it was not just that excursionists were objectionable, but that 'they create a demand for trashy entertainments, for costermongers' wares, and other objectionable concomitants of second-class resorts', which the council, as much as the Compton estate, was determined to avoid.[33]

Perhaps the worst episode concerning the excursionists took place in the summer of 1894, when the match girls from the London factory of Bryant and May went to Eastbourne for the day, and 'danced about in the middle of the road, and generally comported themselves in a reprehensible manner.' Significantly, the newspaper in which the episode was reported added: 'the effect of such conduct may be to drive our best visitors away.'[34] Indeed, in that year, and again in 1898, attempts were made to persuade the London Brighton & South Coast Railway either to stop issuing excursion tickets to Eastbourne altogether, or to build a separate station in the east end of the town, so that it would not be necessary for the excursionists to parade through the main shopping streets and entertainment area on their way to the front. However, nothing came of either scheme, so that the excursionists remained, in the revealing words of one councillor, 'a necessary evil'.[35]

4

This problem was faced on an enlarged scale between 1890 and 1893, when Eastbourne became the scene of violent and well-publicized clashes between the residents and the Salvation Army.[36] In this, of course, the town was by no means unique. From its inception in 1878 until the mid-1890s, the Army sought to obtain publicity by parading in towns – especially in the south and home counties – where local feeling was known to be hostile and the means of law enforcement were strictly limited.[37] Indeed, there was so much disturbance at Hastings and Worthing in 1884 that a conference of Sussex municipalities was held at Brighton, the upshot of which was that there was inserted in the Eastbourne Improvement Act of 1885 clause 169, which explicitly prohibited processions in the town on Sundays if accompanied by music: a deliberate attempt to prevent the Salvationists' loud and strident processions.

For the Army and all its works were anathema to the majority of citizens, both middle- and working-class. T. H. Huxley, for example, who wrote a series of letters from Eastbourne to *The Times* criticizing the army even before the local difficulty had arisen, found the combination of fanaticism and despotism particularly disconcerting.[38] The Army was loud, vulgar, emotional, evangelical, anti-intellectual, well-disciplined and authoritarian, working-class in composition, stridently announcing its appearance with bands, processions and music.[39] Moreover, by claiming a special mission to save the multitudes of depraved members of the working classes, it was a constant and irritating reminder of the presence in Eastbourne of those very people whom the middle-classes tried to pretend did not exist. As early as 1883, the *Gazette* eloquently and critically articulated local hostility:

> The Salvation Army is commendable for its earnestness, its energy and enthusiasm; but as to its methods and creed (what there is of it), they are objectionable and repulsive. Marching the streets, singing absurd songs, making noisy, foolish and irrelevant prayers, shouting out subjective delusions, and calling upon others to share them, is not my idea of what constitutes a good and true religion.[40]

For the Salvationists, however, the restrictive clause in the local Act was a challenge to their rights which they could not ignore, and an opportunity for publicity which they could not resist. In 1888, they had been successful in overturning a similar clause in the Torquay local Act and, encouraged by that success, they turned their attention to Eastbourne. Having paraded and evangelized in the town during the late 1880s, they were sufficiently well represented to construct their own local citadel in Langney Road in 1890. 'The Salvationists, whose advent was a source of disquietude to many, have evidently come to Eastbourne to stay', noted the *Gazette* with reluctance.[41] By May, they could boast a trained band, 250 adherents and growing self-confidence and assertiveness. So much so, indeed, that they applied for permission to hold open-air services and to stage musical processions through the streets on Sundays. Both requests were refused, and clause 169 was given as the justification. In August, however, the Army processed with its band playing in deliberate violation of the council's ruling, and it became clear that there would be trouble during the next season.

In April 1891, the Army again gave notice of its intention to march, which the *Gazette*, rightly, saw as an ominous development: 'the Salvationists, as everyone knows, live to a great extent on opposition. A series of disturbances and prosecutions here would be a Godsend to General Booth.' But, at the same time, it warned that 'any attempt to inflame the public mind over a miserable squabble of this kind' could not in any way be 'of advantage to the town.'[42] In May, the Salvationists modified their request, and merely sought permission to process in those parts of the town which the high-class visitors did not frequent; but, once more invoking clause 169, the council refused the request by 17 votes to 5. In explaining the decision, the mayor, Alderman Morrison, made his own position unequivocally clear: 'I cannot imagine anything more calculated to endanger the residential claims of this town than for it to be infested with noisy bands promenading the streets.'[43]

Thereafter, from May until November, the Salvationists, accompanied by their band, processed in Eastbourne almost every Sunday, in deliberate and calculated violation of clause 169; but, as happened in other towns, local opposition, in the shape of the Skeleton Army, was powerful, well-supported and violent. On May 24, for instance, 'unruly lads' pushed and hustled the bandsmen, and there were scenes of 'disgraceful rowdyism.'[44] At other times, the Salvationists' instruments were damaged or stolen, they themselves were assaulted, pelted with rotten eggs, cabbage stalks and apple peel, bullocks were driven in among the procession, and once, after a meeting on the shore, the pressure from the Skelton Army was so strong that several Salvationists were forced into the sea. For a quiet, peaceful town, it was a most disturbing spectacle: the Salvationists, with their supporters specially drafted from London, numbered 1,500 or more, and estimates of their opponents ranged from 2,000 to 5,000. The violence was reported in all the national newspapers and, as the *Gazette* remarked, that could only 'injure the trade of the town.'[45]

In theory, the corporation should have been as hostile to the Skeleton Army, which was disturbing the peace, as to the Salvationists who were defying the local Act. Indeed, at Brighton, when there had been a similar problem, a firm policy towards the violence of the Salvationists' opponents was the major reason why the matter was settled. At Eastbourne, though, as in many other small south coast towns similarly invaded, the authorities, while claiming to be administering justice impartially, were in fact indignantly opposed to the Army, and gave every encouragement to its local opponents in the hope of persuading the Army to 'take its religious excesses out of the borough'.[46] In April 1891, at a meeting of the Watch Committee, of which the mayor was chairman, it was agreed to withdraw police protection from the Salvation Army. 'That', commented another member, 'would be handing over the members of the Salvation Army to the mob to be smashed up.' 'That', replied the mayor, 'is what I should like to see.'[47] Subsequently, he was reputed to have described the Salvationists as 'animals with two legs', who were 'infamous, degrading and atrocious'. Nine local clergymen also chipped in, urging the Salvationists to leave town. Undaunted, the Army gave as good as it got. One supporter described the mayor as an agent of the devil and a reptile, while Mrs Booth visited the town and prayed with him.[48]

More importantly, the magistrates and police were far more eager to arrest and convict Salvationists than members of the Skeleton Army. In June 1891, five Salvationists were sent to prison for one month each, after having refused to pay the £5 fine, for having taken part in an illegal procession on 17 May.

Then on 7 June, 30 Salvationists were arrested, whereas only two members of the public were detained for attacking the army.[49] The *Brighton Herald* cited this as 'another melancholy illustration of how "justice" can be distorted', and criticized the council for punishing the Army while allowing the 'anarchists' to go free.[50] The Salvationists' own magazine, the *War Cry*, was even more adamant:

> The rod is given unsparingly to the Salvationists who break the local act, but the rioter gets the very mildest of reprimands . . . The Salvationists get fined £5 or a month in Lewes Jail, . . . while of the roughs whom the police had caught red-handed, so many have been dismissed, and the remainder have been bound over.[51]

In retaliation, Herbert Booth threatened to bring down 200,000 men and 100 'dossers' from London. Finally, in late July, on the explicit orders of the mayor, the nine musicians of the Camberwell band were arrested.[52]

Although the parades continued, violent and disconcerting, for the rest of the summer, the real scene of action shifted to the courts and ultimately to Parliament itself. The members of the Camberwell band were duly sent for trial by the local magistrates at Lewes Quarter Sessions. There it was suggested that the council might allow the Salvationists to process in particular parts of the town, not frequented by high-class visitors. As before, however, this scheme was rejected, and the council's decision was overwhelmingly endorsed by the majority of residents in the area proposed, by 224 votes to 47.[53] Meanwhile, the case had been transferred to the Central Criminal Court, where the defendants were acquitted of contravening the local Act, but convicted of unlawful assembly, for which they were each sentenced to three months' imprisonment. For the town, this was enough. When he returned from London with the news, the mayor received an enthusiastic welcome. The horses were taken out of his carriage, and he was pulled by his admirers in torchlit procession to his house. Yet the judge's summing up had been full of ominous implications. The law, he argued, should be obeyed, but only so long as it was the law; and, he went on, the mob who had harrassed the Salvationists should have been punished.[54] Finally, in January 1892, the Camberwell band convictions were quashed.

Ever since the summer of 1891, the Salvationists had made it clear that they had intended to follow the same tactic they had used with such success at Torquay in 1888, and try to get the offending clause in the local Act repealed, by promoting their own bill in Parliament. In January 1892, the council decided to oppose this move by 23 votes to 3, and their decision was supported by the ratepayers by 3,257 votes to 470.[55] For the *Gazette*, as for many inhabitants, the issue was simple: 'Are the people of Eastbourne to have Sunday bands thrust on them at the dictation of General Booth? The recent plebiscite showed plainly what the opinion of the bulk of the population is.'[56] But others disagreed: when the second reading of the bill was debated in the

Commons, Louis Jennings, the Liberal M.P. for Southport, castigated clause 169 as 'a local law under the cover of which a turbulent and brutal mob work their will every Sunday on a small band of defenceless men and women.' Despite a strong speech by Admiral Field against the bill, its second reading was passed by a majority of 147.[57] Jubilation in Eastbourne turned to sorrow, as the bill sailed calmly through Commons and then Lords Committees, received the royal assent in June, and came into force in September. Clause 169 was dead. 'The whole dispute', concluded the *Gazette*, 'has been a most unhappy and unfortunate one for Eastbourne, and it now behoves all sober and law-abiding citizens to make the best of a bad business.'[58]

As if to add insult to injury, the council's attempt to circumvent these limits on its power by framing bye-laws which would effectively have replaced clause 169 was vetoed by the Home Office. Thereafter, the Salvationists could parade, process and play their instruments with impunity. Altogether it had been a sorry episode. Unequivocal evidence had been advanced to show that justice had not been meted out fairly; that Eastbourne had been more eager to rid itself of the Salvationists than to prosecute the Skeleton Army which attacked them; and that clause 169 of the local bill was contrary to the general law of the land concerning processions. Yet it is easy to sympathize with the viewpoint – but not the methods – of the mayor. Eastbourne was a small town, with a police force of only 38 men, which owed its livelihood to its reputation for peace and quiet. The Army was a powerful, dictatorial, publicity-seeking organization, of national dimensions, with little respect for the law, which had made a habit of invading small southern towns.[59] Middle and working classes – soon to be split on the question of trams – were at one in resenting the intrusion and regretting defeat. As the *Gazette* noted: 'The Salvationists have incurred the lasting resentment of the people here. Years must elapse before the feeling of bitterness that has arisen entirely dies away.'[60]

5

In fact, the episode was soon forgotten, and this, combined with the triumphant vindication of the council's gamble of backing buses in preference to trams, meant that by the decade before the First World War, the threats to Eastbourne's exclusiveness which had seemed so powerful in the 1890s and early 1900s had been successfully surmounted. Like bourgeois suburbia, the middle-class seaside survived the impact of the First World War largely unscathed. In 1926, bands, buses and bathing were finally allowed on Sunday,[61] but that was the only major change in the inter-war years. In all other respects, Eastbourne of the 1920s and 1930s would have been as familiar to Wallis as to the seventh duke. The town described by Clunn and Ward Lock differs hardly at all from that depicted in the pre-war guide books.[62] Servants remained plentiful; entertainments were exclusive; educational establishments continued to flourish; the duke was still resident at Compton Place. As the town's most recent history notes, 'the years between the wars saw no great development or fundamental changes . . . Eastbourne remained, as it had done for so long, the "Empress of Watering Places".'[63]

As at Edgbaston, the Second World War was the major turning point. The town was evacuated and the schools closed down, many never to re-open. This time, it was indeed impossible to return to the leisured, exclusive, middle-class world of the inter-war years. Extensive house-building has taken place, and the town has established itself as a conference centre. Control of the pier passed to a London consortium, and the eleventh duke sold off the last assets of the Parks and Baths Company. In the pavilion, where once the local inhabitants danced at ducal balls and feasted at ducal banquets, wrestling matches take place each week during the summer season. And yet, even now, all has not changed. The formal gardens in front of the Burlington Hotel bloom each year as of old. The band still plays upon the promenade. The elderly and leisured remain disproportionately represented. As in the 1900s, the statues of the seventh and eighth dukes adorn the sea front and parades which were their creation, and behind them remains a town whose elegant plan and sylvan appearance stands as a monument to their initiative and enterprise.

25 Conclusion: 'The Duke's town'[1]

No aristocratic family in nineteenth-century England could boast so diverse and multi-faceted a connection with the urbanization process as could the Devonshires in the century from the 1780s. In Derbyshire, the fifth duke created and the seventh duke enlarged Buxton, the most outstanding example of controlled development in spa towns. In London, Lord George Augustus Henry Cavendish built the Burlington Arcade in what had once been the grounds of Burlington House, thereby creating a new fashion in shops and shopping which was to be emulated for a century and more. In Cambridge, both the seventh and eighth dukes were chancellors of their University, and the seventh duke, by endowing the laboratory which to this day bears his family name, established a research institution of unrivalled fame and renown. At Barrow, the seventh duke provided the money and support for an episode of urban growth which – although ultimately costly and unsuccessful – was in the short run as spectacular an example of urban expansion as could be found anywhere in England. And in Chiswick, Keighley and Carlisle, the fabulous inheritances and acquisitions of the Devonshires through generations of marriage enabled them to develop a variety of building estates in which they are still commemorated in the names of the roads.

Although this catalogue of diverse urban activity constitutes a list which no other nineteenth-century aristocratic family could rival, it is arguable that in Eastbourne the Devonshires created their most successful single town. Assuredly, it was less ancient than Buxton, less fashionable than the Burlington Arcade, less renowned than their connections with Cambridge, and less spectacularly successful and lucrative than Barrow in its years of boom. Yet, while it could not compete with these other towns in some senses, in other ways its success was greater and more enduring. Buxton was developed too late and on too small scale ever to be really successful as a spa, and the seventh duke's attempts to revive it in the middle of the nineteenth century were only marginally successful. Barrow, for all the fabulous bonanza of the golden years of the early 1870s, became within a decade a worrying and embarrassing failure, from which the eighth duke withdrew in despair. Moreover, although the Devonshires had been of crucial importance financially, they had never taken any close interest in the evolution of the urban fabric, which may go some way to explain why the town was a renowned health hazard, why the density of housing was dangerously high, and why overcrowding was rife.[2] And with London, Cambridge, Chiswick and Carlisle, their links were of a relatively limited nature. Eastbourne, by comparison, in terms of its size, its success and its long-term expansion, ranks as the greatest and most outstanding example of the Devonshires' involvement in the urbanization process. Of all the towns with which they were connected, it was the one which succeeded most completely in realizing the hopes which had initially been entertained of its development, and was more successful as a seaside resort than Buxton was as a rival to Bath, or Barrow was in becoming a second Liverpool.

1

In part, this was because it embodied more successfully than did either of these two towns a greater degree of collaboration with middle-class needs and aspirations. Buxton was developed too late as a spa: by the 1780s the fashion was beginning to change; and in any case Bath's dominance was too well established to be broken. In the same way, although the founding fathers of Barrow aspired to rival Liverpool and Glasgow, the town was founded too late, its economic base was too narrow, and its hinterland too small, to make such hopes realistic. Eastbourne, by contrast, was begun at exactly the right time, catered for middle-class demands of seaside exclusiveness which grew rather than diminished as the century advanced, and had, by the end of the century, obtained a place in the front ranks of resort towns. The conclusion is inescapable that at Eastbourne the Devonshires were providing something which large numbers of middle-class people wanted and were prepared to pay for.

This was true in at least three senses, socially, administratively, and entrepreneurially. Socially, the town exemplified to perfection the degree to which middle-class aspirations were in many ways a scaled-down version of aristocratic cultural values. As at Edgbaston, the great houses at Meads, with their retinues of servants, were attenuated country mansions. Many were the homes of retired colonial civil servants, those middle-class people whose public-school education and mandarin, patrician administrative careers enabled them to obtain the status of gentlemen. Many participated in the Eastbourne 'season' – a scaled-down version of London society – and were proud to think that the town's shops could rival those of the West End. Like their aristocratic betters, the boundary between the town and the country was effectively non-existent; and for all of them, the social summit of the town was not the great houses of the residents – as was the case of Edgbaston – but Compton Place itself: the real presence of the aristocratic ethos. Eastbourne was a middle-class leisure town; but its activities and aspirations were quintessentially aristocratic.

Administratively, too, there was great collaboration. The making of Eastbourne increased the Devonshires' power over the urban world, at least in the short run. There were new livings to which they were able to present, new companies whose boards they chaired, and a whole variety of new offices which they were to fill. However, while their power was only *extended*, that of middle-class figures like Wallis was actually *created*. Wallis, more than any other, was carried to fame and fortune in his local community on the coat-tails of the seventh duke in the same way that Ramsden and Wilmott were in Barrow and Buxton. At this level, even in mid-Victorian England, the entrepreneurial ideal was not necessarily opposed to the aristocratic. Landowners wanted their land exploited; entrepreneurs were prepared to develop it. The alliance could be reciprocally beneficial.

What was valid on an epic sale in the case of Wallis was more generally true of the smaller men. To begin with, by his initial advances, the Earl of Burlington tempted builders to come to Eastbourne to construct their houses. Subsequently, as the resort expanded, they needed no such encouragement. At the same time, while it was the seventh duke and his associates who provided the overall plans and drive, the money which they used was largely derived from the residents of the town themselves. The Devonshires were re-cycling – with aristocratic flair and panache – local funds in the making of an urban community. The middle classes and the workers provided the resources, the labour and the entrepreneurship, but it was the Devonshires and their advisers who supplied the overall guidance, vision and power of direction. Collaboration between the classes in turning the country into the town could not be more perfectly illustrated.

Yet, while Eastbourne was smaller and more conservative than Birmingham, the clash between the town and the landowners when it finally took place, although within this shared nexus of cultural values, was sharper and more brutal. In large part, this is explained by the fact that in Eastbourne the battle was about real power – who should run the town? – whereas in Birmingham that was never so. The Calthorpes had never dominated the city as a whole; they had merely decorated some of its more important voluntary societies. But in Eastbourne, however much the balance of power shifted in the last decade of the nineteenth century, it remained exclusive, genteel and peer-loving. Even if it was more in charge of its own affairs than it had been in the days of Wallis and the seventh duke, it was culturally still enslaved to aristocratic values, as the battles over the Salvation Army and the trams demonstrate.

2

Partially, then, the success of Eastbourne may be explained by saying that it provided in the nineteenth century a quasi-aristocratic mode of life and leisure which an increasing number of middle-class people were eager and willing to enjoy. In that sense, Eastbourne is merely one example of a general social trend, which may be equally well illustrated with reference to Folkestone, Southport, Torquay or any other high-class resort. In addition, Eastbourne exemplifies, in the most extreme possible form, the role and power of the aristocracy in that part of the urbanization process concerned with the making of the seaside town. In a very real sense, it was the ideal form of one-man, or at least one-family, resort. As the *Gazette* rightly observed: 'It is apparent to everyone that the Dukes of Devonshire have done infinitely more for East-bourne than other ground landlords have done for the health resorts of which they have been ground landlords.'[3]

In part, this was because the Devonshires were the most outstandingly grand, powerful, wealthy and famous family to be associated with the making of a premier seaside town in the nineteenth century. The figures in table 46, culled from Bateman, and suitably revised in certain cases, help to explain why.

Table 46. Income and acreage of aristocrats who developed resort towns, *c.***1883**

Town	Family	Acreage	Gross annual value (£)
Folkestone	Radnor	24,870	42,900
Bournemouth	Tapps-Gervis-Meyrick	21,204	16,641
Torquay	Haldon	10,109	37,500
Skegness	Scarbrough	21,698	31,597
Bexhill	de la Warr	23,366	21,606
	Brassey	3,617	4,417
Southport	Fleetwood	4,128	24,909
	Scarisbrick	3,505	34,811
		3,133	33,960
Eastbourne	Devonshire	198,572	180,750

Source: J. Bateman, *The Great Landowners of Great Britain and Ireland* (1883), *passim*; Lord Haldon's Estate Act (1885), 25.

As always, they should be treated with caution. But even so, there can be little doubting the general impression which they convey. Clearly, the Devon-shires were unique among those aristocrats who developed resort towns in the nineteenth century in being a family of the first rank. Neither the Scarisbricks nor the Fleetwoods had hereditary titles. The Tapps-Gervis-Meyricks were but baronets. The peerages of the Haldons and the Brasseys were created in the second half of the nineteenth century. And neither the Scarbroughs, the de la Warrs nor the Radnors could compete with the Cavendishes in lineage or title. Moreover, the entire acreage of all these families combined did not equal that of the Devonshires. Nor did any one of them produce a single figure of major political importance in the nineteenth century. And, even allowing for the Devonshires' financial difficulties, their income, to say nothing of their capital assets, was incomparably greater. Insofar as aristocratic families involved themselves in resort creation in the nineteenth century, therefore, the Devonshires were a whale among minnows.

Accordingly, there seems no doubt that they were prepared to commit far greater financial resources to the making of their resort town than were any other landed family. Only the Haldons at Torquay came close to the Devon-shires' role in supporting so many of the local amenities on so large a scale.

Unlike the Devonshires, however, they lacked the resources to undertake such a venture. By 1885, their relatively narrow estates were burdened with mortgages in excess of £400,000, one-quarter of which had been incurred by developing the harbour and resort at Torquay.[4] As a result, some 90 per cent of Lord Haldon's income was spent in servicing his debt, and in 1885 a start was made in selling off his estates so as to satisfy his creditors. In consequence, the 1900s, which were for the Devonshires a decade of social fame and splendour in Eastbourne, witnessed the entire disappearance of the Haldons from the town which they had created.

In the years before the 1880s, the Haldons at Torquay came closest to rivalling the influence which the Devonshires wielded at Eastbourne, for there, as in all resorts, those who financed the amenities wielded the power. But in other resorts, which arose on landed estates, the landowners were less important in the creation of amenities. If Eastbourne and Torquay come at one end of the spectrum, then Bournemouth and Southport come at the other, where relatively minor local families were overhauled by aggressive and acquisitive councils as the dominant financial power in the town. So, while the 'conservative interests' of families such as these were necessarily weak, and while that of the Haldons in Torquay – although stronger – was transient, the Devonshires were alone among the aristocratic creators of resorts in wielding great influence over a lengthy span of time. The first phase of control and dominance was longer than for any other resort. Even incorporation made no difference at first, for the council was dominated by the local agent, and ducal spending still far exceeded municipal. Accordingly, the battle for emancipation was long delayed and, once successfully won, was soon forgotten, for the Indian summer which followed it was as sweet as it was long-lasting, surpassing in splendour and status anything which the lesser nobles in their resorts could rival in ostentation and grandeur.

3

The Devonshires' creation of Eastbourne was, therefore, not only the most successful single episode of urban involvement of which the family could boast, but also the grandest single example of aristocratic connection with seaside towns. They were a more splendid, more wealthy, more broad-acred family; they spent more on the making of amenities; and they wielded greater power, both directly and indirectly, for a longer period of time, than did any other family in similar circumstances. No other resort was so big or so successful as a result of the efforts of one single family.

Here indeed, a comparison with the Calthorpes may be instructive, for while the Devonshires were the most powerful of those families who created resorts in the nineteenth century, the Calthorpes were the smallest and least important of those involved with the great industrial centres. A glance at the relevant figures (table 47) will confirm this.

Table 47. Income and acreage of aristocrats linked with great industrial towns

Town	Family	Acreage	Gross annual value (£)
Belfast	Shaftesbury	21,785	16,083
	Donegall	22,996	41,649
Cardiff	Bute	116,668	151,135
	Windsor	37,454	63,778
Liverpool	Derby	68,942	163,273
	Sefton	20,250	43,000
	Salisbury	20,202	33,413
Sheffield	Norfolk	49,866	75,596
	Fitzwilliam	115,743	138,801
Huddersfield	Ramsden	150,048	*c.* 70,000
Potteries	Sutherland	1,358,545	141,667
Black Country	Dartmouth	19,518	58,657
	Dudley	25,554	123,176
Birmingham	Calthorpe	6,470	*c.* 40,000

Source: J. Bateman, *The Great Landowners of Great Britain and Ireland* (1883), *passim*;
C. Stephenson, *The Ramsdens and their Estate in Huddersfield* (1972), 21.

For all the problems with Bateman's figures, the overall impression is inescapable. The Calthorpes were as small in this league as the Devonshires were large in theirs. Every family except the Ramsdens had a title of higher status and greater antiquity; all had more land; and the two whose income was less – the Salisburys and the Shaftesburys – were incomparably more important politically. Here, indeed, in terms of acres, wealth, lineage and influence, is a list of many of the greatest families in the land – a list, indeed, in which the Devonshires could be quite properly placed with no incongruity, apart from the different nature of their urban involvement. And, reciprocally, in terms of acreage, income and unimportance, the Calthorpes could be placed more happily in the list of seaside aristocrats.

4

In a sense, then, these two families are ill chosen. The Calthorpes are out of place among the great industrial grandees, just as the Devonshires were more splendid than their colleagues beside the seaside; but their value lies in the way in which they illuminate the diverse nature of aristocratic involvement with urban growth in the nineteenth century. At one extreme, the Calthorpes were relatively poor and *parvenu*, wielding little influence in a great town, yet successfully establishing themselves as aristocrats on the basis of a preponderantly urban income. The Devonshires, at the other, were already grand, rich and powerful, and wielded great influence in a smaller town whose development never made more than a marginal contribution to their financial well-being. While the Calthorpes needed Birmingham more than the town needed them, Eastbourne needed the Devonshires more than they needed it. Birmingham made the Calthorpes; the Devonshires made Eastbourne.

Part Four
Interpretations and Perspectives

26 The impact of the aristocracy on Victorian cities

The hundred years from the 1780s witnessed the high point of aristocratic involvement in the process of urban growth in Britain. Before then, although aristocrats had long been able to exploit non-agricultural resources on their estates, the slow rate at which towns expanded physically had restricted their role as urban landlords to Dublin, London and some spas. And, in the last 100 years, the weakened position of the aristocracy – politically, socially and as owners of land – has necessarily lessened their influence on the making of the urban environment. During the century between, however, the rise of population, the increase in wealth, and the growth of leisure activities all expressed themselves – at least in part – in demands for more and better housing, especially for the middle classes, in London, the great provincial towns, and at the seaside. Yet these changes took place in a country where the land remained concentrated in the hands of that same few who, despite constant forebodings, continued to provide 'the great governing families of England'. As the towns and cities expanded, bricks and mortar replaced wheat and barley as the most profitable crops which fields might grow. How far, then, did this enable the aristocracy to play a major role in moulding and creating the evolving urban environment?

1

In general, the importance of landowners seems well established. Asa Briggs, for example, pointed out long ago that 'the fundamental study of property relations is of major significance in understanding the workings and individuality of Victorian cities.' C. W. Chalklin has drawn attention to the 'extent to which the physical patterns of landownership of the potential building land affected the way in which the landlord or developer laid out the streets and building plots.'[1] More emphatically, J. R. Kellett, while ostensibly examining *The Impact of Railways on Victorian Cities*, in fact concluded that 'it was the ground plan formed by property titles' which was the key to explaining 'the whole course of development of certain types of urban area, and the emergence of characteristic residential and industrial zones'.[2] And Professor Perkin has noted how, in nineteenth-century England, 'someone had to plan the new streets and thoroughfares of all the new and expanding towns, and sell or lease off the building plots to the builders and contractors, and who could do this but the local large landowners?'[3]

Moreover, in recent years some urban geographers have come to share this view. David Ward, for example, having investigated the pattern of landownership in Leeds, found 'a significant coincidence of the present pattern of building and the earlier pattern of ownership', which led him to reject the 'theoretical patterns' of the Chicago school in explaining urban evolution, and to stress instead 'the more amorphous and complex character of the city as it really existed'.[4] M. J. Mortimore, having examined nineteenth-century Bradford, reached a similar conclusion.[5] Even more specifically, George Rowley has attacked Jeremy Whitehand's approach, which takes an abstract and theoretical stance, because 'it fails to take sufficient account of the role of landownership, . . . despite the fact that his ideas applied to a period when landlords had more influence in controlling development than at present.' And, having himself looked at the Fitzwilliams' estate in Sheffield, he concluded emphatically that 'landownership in Britain has been, and still continues to be, a matter of fundamental importance in urban development.'[6]

As the last example suggests, recent investigation has been primarily concerned with those who might best be described as aristocratic landowners. In large part, this refers to those many gentry and aristocratic families whose doings – both in general and in particular – have been studied in this book but, in addition, it also includes the Crown, corporate bodies such as the Ecclesiastical Commissioners, Oxbridge colleges, public schools and the great London companies.[7] Equally diverse was the size of their holdings. In central London, they might be very small. The Bedfords, for instance, held only 119 acres in Bloomsbury and Covent Garden combined, and the Westminsters' estates in Belgravia and Mayfair only totalled 500 acres.[8] Even these were monsters compared with the puny 23-acre Calthorpe estate in Gray's Inn Road. At the seaside, they might be much larger, as at Eastbourne, where the Devonshires held 2,600 acres, or at Skegness, where the earls of Scarbrough held 2,200. And in the provincial towns, they might be even greater. The Ramsdens' Huddersfield estate, for instance, was 4,300 acres at its greatest extent, and the Norfolks' Sheffield holdings were, in 1910, only slightly smaller.[9]

Under these circumstances, the easiest way to define such aristocratic landowners is not so much in terms of the size or location of their holdings, but rather in terms of how they actually managed them. Almost without exception, their land was held under elaborate statute or settlement (although, of course, this was not true of the Devonshires' lands at Eastbourne), either by 'families concerned to preserve and enhance their long-term social and financial position, or by corporations equally concerned about the future.'[10] Neither the desire to maximize profits, nor immediate financial concerns, was their major preoccupation: how could it be, as statutes and settlements almost invariably prohibited sale? So the long-term value of their estates and the maximization of prestige were more important considerations. As a result, leasehold development was preferred: it gave the owners an opportunity to draw up and implement a coherent estate plan; it meant that some of the costs of development could be shovelled off on to the contractors; and it enabled the landlord, at the expiration of the 99-year lease, to assume possession both of the land and of the buildings which had been erected at the expense of the lessee.

The need to retain ownership – although not necessarily the use – of the land, and preparedness to think in the very long term, were pronounced presuppositions on the basis of which aristocratic estates were managed. Such attitudes were rarely written down, and often have to be inferred more than transcribed from estate correspondence, but there can be little doubt that this was the world-view within which agents and owners operated. Moreover, the desire to maximize prestige throughout the duration of the lease, and the wish to enjoy a succulent reversion at the end of it, meant that high-class development was usually preferred to industry or working-class accommodation. As one witness before the Select Committee on Town Holdings put it: there was 'a great tendency on the part of the people who have building estates rather to seek to develop them for dwellings for the middle classes, and not to develop them in the first instance for dwellings for the labouring class.'[11]

These were the aristocratic landowners whose policies, unaltered in their essentials for a century, were as much the object of radical attack in the 1880s as they are the subject of scholarly investigation today. Indeed, those academic authorities quoted earlier merely echo in more restrained and scholarly language the polemics of such hostile contemporaries. Here is one typical outburst:

> If we suppose that one individual is the owner of an entire parish, or an entire town . . . , he can, by means of the covenants he inserts in the leases, cause the inhabitants either to emigrate *en masse*, or to carry on their trade according to his pleasure for, say one hundred years, so that there shall be just as many and just as few butchers' and grocers' and publicans' shops, and in just such quarters of the town, as he and his successors may dictate.[12]

Even more emphatically, Frank Banfield depicted *The Great Landlords of London* as resembling 'Old Rhine Barons of the Dark Ages', the 'Pharaohs of Egypt', and 'Oriental monarchs of the past'. 'No Mogul, No Persian Satrap, was ever harder on a conquered people', he argued, than was Lord Portman when the time came for the leases to be renewed on his estate. Indeed, even the agents of these urban grandees described their régimes as resembling 'enlightened despotisms'.[13]

Very recently, however, the fashion of argument among urban historians has begun to change once more, as they have come to refine their earlier claims about the power of 'aristocratic' landowners to mould the urban environment. Increasingly, they have become aware – at a *general* level of explanation – of the many ways in which these great estates were constrained by the forces of the market, however much they might resemble 'putative planning authorities' in other respects.[14] 'Landowners . . . ', observes M. J. Daunton in his study of Cardiff, 'could only modify a particular market situation', a view corroborated by F. M. L. Thompson in his study of Hampstead.[15] Even more revealing is the intellectual odyssey of D. J. Olsen. He began by believing that the key to London's idiosyncratic nineteenth-century development lay in 'the concentration of landownership in the hands of a few families', who were able to 'exert an immense control over the fortunes of the metropolis.' Further research and reflection, however, persuaded him that 'the ground landlord . . . was only one element in the complex pattern of varied and conflicting actions that made the metropolis what it is.' And most recently, he has come to feel that 'the great landlord proprietors theoretically had vast powers for shaping and reshaping their estates, but in practice were only able to achieve what ends they did by co-operating with the realities of the market.'[16]

This scholarly argument, like the one which stresses landowners' power, may also be found in the polemics of the 1880s. The reply of the representatives of the landowners to the argument that they behaved despotically was to assert that this was not so, that the landowners themselves were constrained by the market, and were unable to force tenants to live on their land or to compel them to stay.[17] To that extent, the differing reflections of scholars today almost perfectly reflect the arguments of the late nineteenth-century polemicists. But there is more to resolve than this relatively simple antithesis: for, at least so far as the protagonists of the 1880s were concerned, there were not only areas of disagreement between the two arguments that were made, but also contradictions within the positions adopted on each side. As far as those hostile to landlords were concerned, part of their argument stressed the great – indeed excessive – power wielded by aristocratic landowners. At the same time, many also argued that aristocratic estates were so badly administered, their owners so impotent, that leasehold housing decayed more rapidly than freehold. Reciprocally, those defenders of landed estates argued – in reply to the first line of the radical attack – that urban landowners were not all-powerful; in response to the second argument, they claimed that the power of the aristocratic landlord enabled him to ensure that the quality of his housing was better.[18] In short, at differnt times and for different purposes, both sides argued that aristocratic landlords were powerful or were impotent.

This chapter seeks to evaluate these two conflicting interpretations – in both their original and more recent, scholarly form – in the light of the evidence presented in this and other recent studies, for the century from the 1780s when the power of aristocratic landowners was at its greatest. The problem will be examined both at the level of individual estates and the specific decisions made with regard to them, and at the more general level of the overall evolutionary pattern of the nineteenth-century towns. Moreover, it will be investigated with reference to London, the great provincial cities and the seaside towns.

2

Of all nineteenth-century British towns, London itself illustrates most emphatically the importance of aristocratic landownership. At least, that is what historians have argued until very recently. In his path-breaking study, *London: The Unique City*, S. E. Rasmussen devoted an entire chapter to the great aristocratic landlords, and in the same way, Sir John Summerson drew constant and emphatic attention to 'that system of speculation by hereditary landlords who brought half of London into being'.[19] Likewise, Asa Briggs has noted how 'the history of the West End of London was determined by the building plans and leasing arrangements of great aristocratic estates, either entailed in a family or held in trust by a corporation', and H. C. Prince has pointed out 'the innumerable local differences in the direction, width and density of streets, in the style of houses, in the provision of amenities' which 'mark unmistakably the differences between adjoining estates'.[20] The development of the squares, from Covent Garden in the 1630s to Belgrave Square in the 1820s, has often been described.[21] In the suburbs too, the presence of 'aristocratic' landowners like Eton and Dulwich Colleges in Hampstead and Camberwell respectively, means that a map of landownership patterns is as much an indispensable starting point on the outskirts as for the city centre.[22]

At the level of the particular, all this is quite correct. If the object of the exercise is to try to find out why a certain part of London was developed at a specific time, or why the roads went this way rather than that, or why a particular type of housing was characteristic of a locality, or why the streets were named exactly as they were, then the number, background, intentions, decisions and policies of the local landowners are central to any such explanation. At this level, George Rowley's argument for Sheffield applies with equal force for London, namely that 'decision-making by the large local landowner . . . remained an essential element of urban growth.'[23] The reason, for example, why the third Lord Calthorpe began to develop Gray's Inn Road in 1812, to say nothing of his motives for deciding to employ Thomas Cubitt, are clearly of major significance if the intention is to understand why a certain type of housing came into existence on these 23 acres of land adjacent to Gray's Inn Road at the time it did. And what was true of the decisions reached by Lord Calthorpe was valid also in the case of the Westminsters and Belgravia, the Bedfords and Bloomsbury, the Governors of Eton College and Chalcots, and so on. At that level of inquiry, then, the impact which aristocratic landowners had on the evolution of parts of London is of major significance.

Yet while the precise timing and boundaries of development, the exact contours and width of a road, or the specific plan adopted might all stand as eloquent and lasting tribute to the aristocratic landowner who combined 'the will to plan with the power to do so', it is not altogether clear how important are the policies of these grandees at a more general level of explanation, which would be concerned with the overall pattern of spatial evolution, rather than the particular, precise outline of development of any one estate.[24] Assuredly, it can be argued that the lands to the north and west of the metropolis were preponderantly aristocratic in ownership, and almost exclusively well-to-do and residential in occupation. Reciprocally, the area to the south and east was in the main one of fragmented landholdings: the home of industry, the docks, the City and working-class communities. The coincidence of a high-status West End, located on large, aristocratic estates, and a low-status East End, situated on small landholdings, seems exact enough to attribute to the land-owner a major role in this evolutionary process:

> The larger the estate, the richer the landlord, the more likely it was to be comprehensively planned at the outset, and to have its character main-tained thereafter by the enforcement of covenants and by well-considered re-building projects at the expiration of leases; such estates were more likely to have middle-class residents. Working-class neighbourhoods were more likely to grow up in districts characterized by fragmentation of ownership.[25]

Yet such a pattern may be explained equally convincingly without recourse to the question of landownership at all. On the contrary, it might well be argued that the key influences on London's spatial evolution were in fact history and topography – history because, from Tudor times onwards, the metropolis began to be divided between one area increasingly attractive to the court, the government and – as a consequence – the aristocracy, and another where industry, trade, the docks and – again as a consequence – the working classes were predominant;[26] and topography because the one remained static in the low-lying lands of the east, while the other showed an increasing propensity to migrate westwards in search of better-drained land, higher ground and purer air. As early as 1662, for instance, Petty noticed that people who could afford it were leaving the City for the west to escape 'the fumes, steams and stinks of the whole easterly pile', and a century later, Defoe made the same point even more emphatically:

> The City does not increase, but only the situation of it is a going to be removed, and the Inhabitants are quitting the Old, Noble Streets and Squares where they used to live, and are removing into the Fields for fear of infection; so that as the People are run away into the Country, the Houses seem to be running away too.[27]

From the sixteenth to the twentieth centuries, this 'drang nach Westen' has been a constant feature of London's spatial evolution: 'the inexorable move-ment of fashion westwards' in search of space, light and air.[28]

Some landowners benefited from this process; some were defeated by it: none was powerful enough to influence it profoundly. The development of the Grosvenors' London lands illustrates this to perfection. Building began on their Mayfair estate in the 1720s, but it was badly superintended: the coven-ants in the leases were weak; trade was not forbidden; taverns and coffee houses proliferated; there was no overall aesthetic control; and the estate administration was then, and remained throughout the nineteenth century, much less efficient and vigilant than that of the Bedfords.[29] Likewise, when Cubitt developed Belgravia from the 1820s, the estate itself took a relatively passive role. The first marquess of Westminster was not a careful man of business; agreements were mislaid or never written down at all; covenants were only enforced at Cubitt's insistence; and his power to make roads, footpaths and sewers was unusually large.[30] Yet, despite these inauspicious beginnings, these two areas became, and remained, the most glamorous in London: the quintessence of elegance, opulence and exclusiveness. J. R. Kellett has argued that these developments show 'as clearly as anywhere in England . . . the tangible signs of the landed aristocracy's importance in moulding urban growth'.[31] However, volume xxxix of the *Survey of London*, after a detailed investigation of Mayfair, offers a very different interpretation:

> From the time of its development in the eighteenth century, it has always enjoyed immense advantages of topographical position. At first it was a natural refuge of the *beau monde* in westward retreat from the once fashionable but soon crowded and declining streets of Covent Garden and Soho. Then the proximity of Hyde Park came to be regarded as an added attraction – as was not the case in the early eighteenth century. Still more important, the existence of the Park on the western boundary of the estate dammed up further migration westward. Thus Mayfair is one of the few areas of London to benefit from the outward movement of the well-to-do without later suffering from it. No surface railway or railway constructed on the cut and cover principle has ever been built either on or near the Grosvenor estate there, nor has it ever had undesirable neighbours of lesser social distinction whose mere existence on adjacent streets might have detracted in the course of time from its own *bon ton*.[32]

In short, Mayfair – and Belgravia too – had everything going for it; the surging forces of the market transmogrified indifferent management into outstanding success.

Pimlico illustrates, by contrast, the importance of other market forces which again the aristocratic landowner was unable to control. In the first place, it was developed for a lower class of clientèle than either Mayfair or Belgravia, yet still took over 50 years to complete: eloquent proof that high-class tenants were in distinctly short supply, even if the landowner was a Grosvenor and the lessee a Cubitt. Moreover, Cubitt's energetic role as developer of Pimlico meant that the local landowners – even the Grosvenors – faded into relative insignificance. The overall unity of Pimlico derives not at all from the initial pattern of landholding, but from the coherent vision and strong control of the developer, for he acquired land of different sizes, levels, conditions and prospects, from five owners – the Grosvenors, the Crown, Sloane, Wise and Johnson – and superimposed on it a coherent and comprehensive plan.[33] Far from reflecting the structure of aristocratic landownership, therefore, the elaborate grid-like road plan, with its emphatic diagonals superimposed, is a negation of the landlord's autonomy. As Hermione Hobhouse has noted:

> The particular interest and importance of the Neathouses area is that he (i.e. Cubitt) was paramount; the Wise and Sloane Smith estates were too small for their owners to dictate to Cubitt, and the Neathouses area was relatively unimportant for the Grosvenors in comparison with Mayfair and Belgravia, and his commanding position in the area made all his landlords disinclined to argue with him.[34]

If the Grosvenors' developments in Mayfair, Belgravia and Pimlico show what could be achieved despite lethargic management if market forces, topography and vigorous entrepreneurship were on the landlords' side, the Bedfords' experience with their Covent Garden and Bloomsbury estates shows the exact opposite: namely how little even a well-organized and determined aristocratic landowner could accomplish if these forces worked against him. At first, in the seventeenth century, Covent Garden had been developed as *the* high-class area outside the city. But as the tide of fashion began to move inexorably westwards in the early years of the eighteenth century, it began to decline, so that by the 1820s it was full of decayed mansions housing poor persons mostly employed in the Market itself.[35] Under these circumstances, all the Bedfords could do was to capitulate, and promote it as a mercantile neighbourhood, but it was always an embarrassment to them, and their decision to part with it before the First World War was proof of their inability to manage it successfully.[36] The physical structure of the Piazza might remain as a monument to the initial decision which the Earl of Bedford had taken, yet its changed use showed emphatically the limits of the landlord's capacity to keep as tenants those for whom the Piazza had originally been constructed.

In Bloomsbury, too, while the estate office's vigorous management made it possible, once more, to maintain the outward physical appearance of the estate, it was again powerless to keep these high-class tenants who had temporarily stayed there in the course of their inexorable march to the west. The building of Euston Station, just to the north of Bloomsbury, brought with it an unwelcome increase in through traffic, and only accentuated the problem.[37] In short, neither at Covent Garden in the eighteenth century, nor at Bloomsbury in the nineteenth, could the forces of aristocratic landownership prevail against the power of the market. As D. J. Olsen has noted:

> The Grosvenor estate had all the advantages of location, the Bloomsbury estate none. It was one thing to build a street of mansions with Belgrave Square immediately to the rear and the grounds of Buckingham Palace to the front; quite another to maintain the character of an enclave of first-class houses surrounded on every side by socially inferior districts . . . The Grosvenor estate took every advantage of its magnificent geographical situation, while the Bloomsbury estate did everything that could reasonably be expected of it to counteract the drawbacks of its own location.[38]

Yet, as Olsen himself earlier admitted, for all the Bedfords' efforts, Bloomsbury was nothing but a 'magnificent failure'.[39] And while it was the Bedfords
who decreed that it should be magnificent, it was the market which declared it
a failure.

One of the greatest problems for the Bedfords was that the estates which
bordered Bloomsbury to the north and the east, although of aristocratic
ownership, were of a distinctly unsavoury appearance. The entire ring of
properties, from Somers Town to Figs Mead to Clerkenwell, most of which
were developed in the 1800s and 1810s, and which numbered among their
owners Lords Southampton, Camden, Calthorpe and Northampton, as well
as the Brewers Company and the Ecclesiastical Commissioners, have enjoyed
a uniformly bad press.[40] The owners were rarely bothered about the status of
the initial development; plans and superintendence were often lacking; third-
rate houses, factories and tenements were sanctioned. Indeed, the lack of
care in these arrangements is reminiscent of the Grosvenors' first ventures
in Mayfair, but the results were very different. For the tide of fashion
debased these early aspirations still further, rather than exalted them to
unprecedented heights. Fashionable residents never came; industrial neighbours abounded; the three stations of Euston, King's Cross and St Pancras
intruded. Above all, the estates were too far east and too far north. So, while it
may seem correct at the individual level to stress the inadequacy of management, it is difficult to avoid the conclusion that, with the most powerful,
status-conscious estate office in London, the ultimate appearance of this area
would not have been much different. Large estates were not necessarily
well-managed nor middle-class, for the forces of the market were no respecters
of titles.[41]

If the estate was well located, if fashion and taste were loyal, and if the
railways were kept out then, even though the property in question was
lethargically managed, its development would be successful, as the Grosvenors, Portlands and Portmans all found out with certain parts of their land;[42]
but if the location was bad, if fashion was fickle, and if railways and industry
were conspicuous neighbours then, even with the most energetic management,
success was unlikely. Indeed, a glance at that 'undeserved success', the lands
of Eton College at Chalcots, suggests that the argument may be pushed one
stage further,[43] for that estate, while topographically advantaged, boasted a
management even less energetic than that of the Grosvenors in eighteenth-
century Mayfair. Sir John Summerson, for instance, has described its
development as 'a process which comes as near as possible to complete
anonymity in its results, for it can truthfully be said that not one solitary soul
was ever really interested in what the physical, visible results would be.'[44] The
Provost and Fellows probably never saw the land; they gave no financial
assistance to the builders; they did not even make the roads and sewers; and
their administration has been described as 'inefficient and lackadaisical.'[45]
Insofar as anyone was responsible for the creation of the suburb, it was the

speculative builders who, of their own volition, developed it as an upper middle-class area, with a high and uniform social tone, and the middle-class house buyers who were eager to bask in the reflected glory of Regents Park and St John's Wood. As D. J. Olsen observes, 'what generations of architects, surveyors, solicitors and stewards strove vainly to achieve on the Bloomsbury estate, Eton Chalcots seems to have managed without really trying.' The implication is clear: the experience of Eton suggests that, 'given sufficient size and a favourable location, a Victorian suburban estate planned and managed itself.'[46]

What was true of Chalcots in particular also held good for the development of Hampstead in general. While paying due regard to the pattern and structure of landownership, F. M. L. Thompson is in no doubt that the landowners' role in the creation of the suburb was minimal. While Hampstead provides 'as near perfect a working model of single class residential zoning as one can expect to encounter over such a large area as 2,500 acres', this was achieved despite the fact that 'these acres have never been in single ownership or control'.[47] Even those relatively large, aristocratic estates which made up the parish, such as the Ecclesiastical Commissioners' 240-acre Belsize estate, were developed piecemeal, in plots of 30 acres or so, by different speculative builders. 'No one planned this transformation', Thompson notes, 'no one intended it, no one controlled it. It was a response to the external forces of urban expansion.'[48] Landowners' covenants were never anything more than a safety net: the lower limit below which standards of development could not sink. In fact the higher, socially homongeneous level at which housing was actually constructed resulted from the spontaneous decisions of a multitude of speculative builders. It was they, rather than the landowners, who imposed on the multiplicity of holdings a coherent, elevated social tone.[49]

Why did they do so? The answer, F. M. L. Thompson suggests, is that

> from the side of a housing demand, there was a very powerful urge for people of like condition to want to live in the same neighbourhood with their kind, to decline to be mixed up with their social inferiors. These were strong tides making for segregation.[50]

At once we are transported into the world of suburban Boston which Sam Bass Warner, Jr, has done so much to uncover; for there, to an extent much greater than in Hampstead, land was held in 'thousands of parcels' by a 'mass of people, each with but one small house and lot'.[51] Yet again, the overall tone was socially homogeneous, despite the lack of any single planning authority: 'The presence of houses of a similar cost and style encouraged a man to build his own house in keeping with existing ones. No plans, however, prevented him from building something different.'[52] Just as large holdings were normally, but not necessarily, associated with zones of high status, so a multitude of smaller holdings were usually, but not always, connected with zones of lower status. Warner's 'streetcar suburbs' were a more fragmented, but no less homogeneous, Hampstead, and there was not an aristocratic landowner in sight. This transatlantic comparison is as important as it is informative.

Accordingly, as far as London is concerned, it seems fair to conclude that, while the *specific* features and delights of its West End may owe their existence to the precise decisions of aristocratic landowners, the *general* way in which the town's spatial pattern evolved owed more to forces like topography, fashion, the desire of the upper classes to get out of the city, and the wish of the middle classes to emulate them, than to any master plan imposed from above by aristocratic landowners. When they collaborated with these general market forces, they triumphed; when they opposed them, they failed. Indeed, it seems fair to hazard the suggestion that – all other things being equal – if the landowning pattern in the metropolis had been completely reversed, with great estates to the south and east, and small landholdings to the west and north, the overall spatial pattern would still have evolved in largely the same way. The planning of the West End would have been less coherent, but its status would still have been high. And even if control had been more in evidence in the east and south, it is doubtful if the land utilization pattern would have been fundamentally altered.

3

In the same way that the aristocracy did not own all of the land on to which nineteenth-century London expanded, they were by no means preponderant landowners in all the great provincial towns. This self-evident fact would not merit attention, were it not that, in the provinces as in London, historians have concentrated on the study of leasehold estates, thereby perhaps giving the impression that they were a more ubiquitous element in the urbanization process than was in fact the case. In evidence given to the Select Committee on Town Holdings in 1886, for instance, a solicitor who had circularized 261 provincial towns in England and Wales, asking whether any considerable part of their land was owned by large, aristocratic landlords, found that half the towns replied emphatically in the negative.[53] In 1914, the report of the Liberal Land Enquiry Committee concluded that

> substantially more than half of the urban population of England and Wales is living under ordinary freehold tenure; about one twentieth under freehold subject to some form of perpetual annual payment; somewhere about one tenth under long leasehold; and rather under one third under short leasehold.[54]

These figures, and the definitions also, should be treated with caution, but they do serve to emphasize the most important fact about the impact of the aristocracy on the evolution of English provincial towns, namely that the number of towns where it occurred was strictly limited.

With that very important qualification borne in mind, there were four great

provincial cities where entire suburbs were developed by aristocratic landowners along successful and relatively exclusive lines: north Oxford, 'the most
quintessentially Victorian of all England's suburbs', administered by St
John's College; Sefton Park in Liverpool, owned by the Earl of Sefton; The
Park in Nottingham, developed by the Duke of Newcastle; and the Calthorpes'
Edgbaston estate in Birmingham. Each of these estates, resulting as they did from
the convergence of landowners' exclusive and exalted preferences on the one
hand, and the desire of the new middle classes for social segregation on the
other, formed the 'West End' of their respective towns, regardless of their exact
location. Each witnessed a high degree of control by an aristocratic landlord,
both in terms of overall layout and enforcement of covenants. And all illustrate
to perfection that oft-assumed link between large, single areas of ownership,
and high-status housing. Here, in the provinces as much as in London, is
emphatic assertion of the importance of aristocratic landowners in influencing
the urbanization process.

Now again – as in London – at the level of the particular estate and suburb,
this is all quite correct. If the object of the exercise (as in part has been the
case in this book) is to find out why, in Edgbaston or Sefton Park or north
Oxford or The Park, land was made available for building at a certain date, or
why the roads were laid at a specific time and given the exact names they were,
or why a particular type of housing was allowed, then the activities, presuppositions, decisions and policies of the local, aristocratic landowners are crucial to
any explanation. In the provinces as in London, 'decision making by the large
local landowner . . . remained an essential element of urban growth.'[55] As this
study of Edgbaston has shown, the decision to begin systematic development
in 1810, the sudden collapse in the number of leases granted in 1866–7 because
of the Leasing Act affair, and the decision to sell off certain 'outlying parts' of
the Edgbaston Estate in 1914 – to take but the most obvious examples – cannot
be understood or adequately explained without reference to the landowners
themselves. And what was true of the Calthorpes in Birmingham was equally
valid for the Seftons in Liverpool, the Newcastles in Nottingham, and St John's
College in Oxford. At that level of inquiry, the impact which the decisions of
local aristocratic landowners had on the towns with which they were territorially connected was crucial.

Yet, as with the great estates in western London, it seems clear that at a
more general level of explanation, the connection between large units of
aristocratic landownership and high-class housing was more coincidental
than causal, and that here, too, success only came to those families who were
able – like the Grosvenors in Mayfair and Belgravia – to co-operate with
benevolent market forces or exploit topographical advantages. Both Edgbaston and The Park, for example, were on the western side of the town, thereby
avoiding smoke and pollution. Both were well drained and wooded, with
undulating, south-facing slopes – the ideal location and topography for exclusive, middle-class residents. None of these important attractive features owed

anything to the aristocratic landowner: he may have benefited from them, but he certainly did not create them. Moreover, while The Park, being only 150 acres in extent, was soon completely filled up with these preferred middle-class residents, Edgbaston was so large that, regardless of the initially exclusive preferences of the third Lord Calthorpe and his agent, it proved impossible in practice to develop all the land on such exclusive lines.[56] Much of Edgbaston was given over to the lower middle classes and the more prosperous members of the working class, and as late as 1914, large parts of it were left entirely undeveloped. Just as, in London, it proved impossible to fill all of the West-minsters' extensive holdings with houses for the super-rich, so in Edgbaston it had to be accepted that there were simply not enough wealthy people in the town to fill the estate entirely with high-class development. So, while the laying, naming and specifications of, for example, Farquhar Road could only be understood with reference to the family circumstances of the landowner and the plans and hopes of his agent, the fact that it remained unfilled for several decades can only be understood with reference to these more general consider-ations.

Moreover, as the figures on aristocratic landownership suggest, while most large, nineteenth-century provincial cities had their Edgbastons, they did not all have their Lord Calthorpe. High-class suburbs could be created under very different patterns of landownership. In the first place, while there could be unified landownership, it did not necessarily have to be aristocratic. In Man-chester, for example, a company was set up in 1836 to buy 10 acres two miles south of the town, there to establish an exclusive, middle-class suburb, which was to be planned and supervised with all the care which Lord Calthorpe's agents lavished upon Edgbaston. By the Victoria Park Act of 1837, the company was empowered to lay out some of the land as a park, to construct roads, squares and crescents, to build houses with a minimum annual value of £40 a year, to prevent trade, and to set up gates and levy tolls to deter outsiders. Despite a period of financial difficulty at the end of the decade, the undertaking as it emerged in 1845, in the form of the Victoria Park Trust Committee, carried out this policy essentially unaltered. Tolls and rates were levied; roads were maintained; the building tie was enforced; the public was allowed a right of way only if on foot. Here, undertaken by a private, middle-class company, was a scheme of management every bit as exclusive, not only in intention, but also in accomplishment, as that to which the Calthorpes aspired less successfully at Edgbaston.[57]

However, all of these provincial developments, whether aristocratic or not, were unusual in that the pattern of landownership was so coherent and unified. In other towns, however, similar developments could result, as at Hampstead, from a very different structure of landownership. At Roundhay and Headingley, for example, the suburban elite of Leeds chose to make their homes from the early decades of the nineteenth century; but the land was developed piecemeal, the original aristocratic owners having sold it off to speculators early in the nineteenth century.[58] In the same way, the West End of Glasgow rivalled both Edgbaston and The Park as a bastion of middle-class exclusiveness. Yet it was created on the basis of a landownership structure which had more in common with suburban Boston than with Birmingham. Altogether, there were some 23 estates, covering 1,250 acres, owned by a variety of merchants, lawyers and country gentlemen, the same people who leased parts of the Belsize Estate in Hampstead from the Church Commissioners in the days before development was begun. And, although most of these estates changed hands between 1840 and 1867, and were developed independently of each other, the result was a middle-class suburb which surpassed Edgbaston and rivalled Hampstead in uniformity and exclusiveness. As its historian notes: 'The district has a harmony which might be the work of a single authority of voluntary co-operation. It is difficult to tell where the estates meet, and yet there seems to have been no co-operation between the developers to harmonise their plans.'[59] What, then was the answer? As at Hampstead, it was in part contagion. Just as St John's Wood and Regents Park set the tone for Chalcots, so Blythswood, the first, inner middle-class suburb of Glasgow, set the tone for adjacent Kelvinside. And, again as in Hampstead, topography was crucial: wooded drumlins rising to 200 ft, cleansed by the west wind and commanding views of the Clyde, were no more appropriate for working-class homes than they were for industry; but they were ideal for those middle-class grandees aspiring to health, seclusion and gentility.[60] Like Hampstead, Glasgow's West End was an Edgbaston, but one without its Lord Calthorpe.

One tentative conclusion which may be drawn from this is that there was no necessary reason why towns without a preponderantly aristocratic pattern of landownership should lack a high-class aristocratic suburb, even though in other towns these were associated with aristocratic landownership and management. Because of their location and topography, it seems likely that Edgbaston and The Park would have become well-to-do in any case. It is the *specific* details of development which must take account of the plans and intentions of Lord Calthorpe and the Duke of Newcastle. As in London, if aristocrats owned land in the right place in a provincial town, they would prosper. But, again as in London, if they owned land which was disadvantageously situated, however grand their original aspirations might be, there was little likelihood of their being successful. Birmingham, for example, was ringed by aristocratic estates, and was especially noteworthy for the prevalence of the leasehold system.[61] Yet if the Calthorpes, with all the coincident advantages of topography and location, were unable to fill up their broad acres with tenants of the preferred social group, then what were the prospects for those who owned land much less favourably situated? Lord Norton, for instance, held large estates on the eastern side of the town at Saltley. Like the third Lord Calthorpe, he was a generous, high-minded philanthropist, but the area was low-lying, criss-crossed by 30 acres of railway sidings, and full of bad housing and slums which were described in 1884 as the worst in Birmingham.[62] It was the antithesis of Edgbaston in every sense except one: aristocratic landownership was common to both. Yet such similarity was powerless to prevail against other, more deeply-rooted differences.

Sheffield offers an even more interesting example. The greatest landowner in the town, whose estates, lineage, wealth and title far surpassed those of little Lord Norton in Saltley, was the Duke of Norfolk, premier duke and hereditary Earl Marshal of England. It has recently been argued that successive dukes exercised 'an important influence on the pattern of residential development' in the town;[63] but it is difficult to see how in practice it was any greater or any more successful than the part played by Lord Norton in Birmingham. Despite the unified pattern of landownership, the development of the Norfolks' Sheffield estates resulted in as great a shambles as Saltley: cheap buildings, densely crowded houses, steel mills and working-class communities proliferated.[64] While it is true that this coincided with 'mismanagement and ducal indifference', which meant an 'absence of planning and controls over building', the history of the Grosvenors' London estates shows that, even under these circumstances, it did not automatically follow that development would be shoddy, industrial, and of low status.[65] However, unlike the Grosvenors, the Norfolks' acres in Sheffield were low-lying, on the eastern side of the town, and criss-crossed with railway lines, very much like Lord Norton's lands in Saltley.[66] Under these disadvantageous circumstances, the estate was hardly likely to evolve as Sheffield's Belgravia however energetic (or lethargic) the management was. Once more, aristocratic landownershop was powerless to prevail against topography, fashion and the market. As D. J. Olsen has noted: 'Nothing the dukes of Norfolk could have done would have made Sheffield attractive to the already suburbanized middle-classes of the town.'[67] There was nothing intrinsic to the nature of unified aristocratic holdings, whether well or indifferently managed, which meant that they should automatically become high-status areas.

Indeed, in Sheffield, not only did the unified, aristocratic landholding fail to attract the town's civic elite, but the area of the town which did become Sheffield's Belgravia displayed very similar characteristics to the West End of Glasgow. The gracious, exclusive, elegant middle-class suburbs of Broom Hall, Endcliffe and Kenwood Park were developed to the west of the town. Again, the land immediately prior to development had been held in relatively small plots, yet the overall tone after building was one of prosperous uniformity. Once more, topography offers the best explanation: in this case the prevailing wind, the proximity of the Peak district, and the rolling, wooded, south-facing slopes.[68] So, while unified holdings in the town housed industry and the workers, fragmented holdings were the location of segregated, middle-class suburbia. The relationship between landholding and status in nineteenth-century Sheffield was the exact opposite to that in London. On the other hand, the relationship between status, topography and location was exactly the same. Identical patterns of urban zoning existed despite diametrically opposed patterns of landownership.

Aristocrats who owned part of the ground onto which towns expanded were therefore constrained by two major factors: the first was the location and topography of the land they owned; the second the number and nature of the local population. If the land was unsatisfactorily located, or insufficiently attractive, then the middle-classes would rarely colonize it. And even if it was agreeable and they did settle, they probably did not exist in sufficiently large numbers to fill all the houses built for them, or to adorn all the estates which aspired to attract them.[69] 'The simple, unchecked competition of rival estates sent into the market to hustle against each other' was as much a reality in the provinces as in the metropolis, and in all cases, there were more losers than winners.[70] In eighteenth-century Dublin, for example, both the Fitzwilliam and Gardiner estates had been developed as high-class areas. However, during the nineteenth century the Fitzwilliam estate – now passed to the earls of Pembroke – continued to prosper, while the Gardiner estate went inexorably downhill. The explanation is the same as for the success of Belgravia and the failure of Bloomsbury: 'After the Union Dublin could not afford such a vast acreage of "good" property: the "good" tenants simply were not there to live in it all.'[71]

This survey suggests some tentative generalizations. If an aristocratic estate was both small and well-situated, like The Park in Nottingham, then it would succeed completely; if it was large and well-located, like Edgbaston in Birmingham, then it would be a partial success; but if it was badly located then whether it was small, as at Saltley, or large, like the Norfolks' lands in Sheffield, it would not succeed. And so, to extend the argument one stage further, if it was very large, encompassing almost the whole area of the town, it would – paradoxically – have almost no influence on the way in which the town evolved. Almost the whole of Huddersfield, for example, was owned by the Ramsden family but, for all their tight legal control, the zoning pattern remained primarily influenced by topography and numbers. The poor lived close to industry on low-lying land, and the rich lived at a distance on the north-west side,'classically located on the rising ground away from the river and factories'.[72] The same was true of Belfast where, at least until the 1820s, the Donegalls were pre-eminent territorially. There too, it was matters such as sentiment and topography which took the middle classes to the heights of Malone Ridge, to the south of the town, by mid-century. Neither the leasing policy of the Donegalls while they owned the land, nor their decision to sell it all off in the late 1820s, had any fundamental effect on the way in which the town evolved.[73]

The same was true of Cardiff where, by the inter-war years, the Butes owned over one-third of all the building land.[74] In a very real sense – much more so than any other great industrial provincial town – Cardiff was the creation of an aristocratic family, for it was the decision of the second marquess to build the docks which actually brought it into being. Yet such an industrial base necessarily brought with it a certain social structure which, when translated into demands for housing, proved irresistible, even by the landowner who had created the town. Its heavy industrial base meant that there were insufficient middling capitalists for the Butes to create many Edgbastons in its midst. On the contrary, they were unable to preserve Bute-town as an exclusive area 'in the face of forces of change much stronger than the wishes of the Bute estate'. And all they could do in the case of working-class housing – for which there was an overwhelming demand – was to ensure that it was better built than it might otherwise have been. At the very most, though, that merely modified, but did not in any sense overturn, a particular market situation.[75]

In other words, as in London, so in the provinces; topography and location on the one hand, and numbers and social structure on the other, were in effect 'given' as far as aristocratic landowners, anxious to develop their estates, were concerned. While there was a considerable area of decision-making within which landowners had autonomous power, they could not alter the location or physical features of their estates any more than they could influence the size or social structure of the town. Whoever owned the land, and in whatever sized holdings, the fact remained that in the nineteenth century it was usually more rational to place industry on low-lying land near lines of communication, to house workers with limited incomes close by, and to place these with large incomes and more time on higher ground and at a distance. Under most circumstances, the size of the units of landownership was subordinate to that essential element of topographic determinism.[76] And, in the same way, it was also subordinate to the logic inherent in the economic and social structure of the town. The extent of middle- and working-class housing, for instance, was not so much influenced by the decisions made and restrictions imposed by landowners, but by the amount which the inhabitants of the town could afford to spend, and the relative numbers of middle- and working-class people. This in turn depended on the nature of the town's economic sub-structure. As one witness before the Select Committee on Town Holdings put it: 'It is not the landowner that enforces his covenants or his schemes upon the building public, but that the building public forces the landowner to comply with their demand.'[77]

Accordingly, the question of leasehold versus freehold, of aristocratic estates versus small plots – the issue with which that Committee allowed itself to become so obsessed – was in fact of only secondary importance in understanding why some housing was bad and some good in the great nineteenth-century provincial towns, and why the overall spatial pattern took the form it did. Indeed, two witnesses before that Committee who – unlike the majority – had no vested interest either in freeholds or in leaseholds, actually made this point. The first, the Town Clerk of Nottingham, stressed the greater importance of topography over ownership:

It is only fair to the committee to say that there is no distinction whatever between the residential portions of Nottingham, whether it is the Alexandra Park, which is freehold, or the Nottingham Park, which is a leasehold estate. There is no difference between the class of houses put up or the class of people who live there. The character of the building is not governed by the tenure? – That is not governed by whether it is leasehold or not; it is governed by other considerations. You say there is no preference? – There is no preference for the one or the other. A man would prefer to go to Nottingham Park if he wished to have a sandy soil to live on, and a warm neighbourhood; and if he wished to live a little higher, where the air was a little keener and a little more bracing, he would go to the Alexandra Park. That is the only question to determine where he would go, and not whether it is freehold or leasehold.[78]

And the second, William Matthews, a land agent and surveyor in Birmingham, not only corroborated these general conclusions, but stressed also the importance of the economic sub-structure:

Comparing the buildings of one town under one system with the buildings of other towns under the other system, which do you consider are the best? – I do not think it has anything to do with the system; what I say is that the buildings in Birmingham which are on the leasehold system are, as a rule, better than the buildings in adjoining towns, which are on the freehold system; that I think, is solely due to the wealth of the community, and has nothing whatever to do with the tenure.[79]

Within the limits imposed on one side by topography and location and on the other by numbers and social structure, the landowner still retained power to manoeuvre, as the study of Lord Calthorpe which has formed part of this book demonstrates: but the limits remained, all the same.

4

In general terms, then, the picture of aristocratic influence on the spatial development of the great provincial towns corroborates the argument made for London. Those many authorities who have stressed the importance of the individual decisions made by particular landowners are quite correct, provided they are placed within the context of numbers and topography, which necessarily served to restrict landowners' freedom of action. But what of aristocratic involvement in the creation and control of seaside towns? Here again, an impressive battery of authorities may be found who stress the importance of landownership, of whom the most emphatic and systematic is J. A. Barrett. Resorts like Eastbourne, Llandudno, Torquay, Folkestone and Bexhill could, he argued, 'be called "one man towns", in that most of their development, especially before 1914, was the work of one landowner – or rather one landowning family.' More than anything else, he suggested, the origin and survival of such towns was due to the landowners' stringent and select control.[80]

More recently, Harold Carter and H. J. Perkin have endorsed this view. The former, in explaining the evolutionary pattern and chronology of Llandudno, argued that the key to its development lay in the 'degree of concentration of decision-making', in the hands of the second Baron Mostyn and his agents, who controlled over 90 per cent of the land. So, Carter concluded, 'the more the power of making decisions is concentrated . . ., the clearer and more unequivocal will be the consequences and the more uniform the plan, for it is a consequence of one voice and not a multitude.'[81] More generally, in seeking to explain the different 'social tone' to be found in neighbouring north-western resorts, H. J. Perkin, having dismissed possible explanations such as proximity to great industrial centres or relative isolation, finally settled for 'the original pattern of land distribution, the type and size of the landowners, and the policies they pursued in selling or leasing land for development'. Accordingly, he contrasted Southport, where there were only two major aristocratic landowners, with its 'large hotels, residential villas, genteel public and large private gardens' with Blackpool, where there was a mass of 'ill-planned and small properties' with their 'boarding houses, small shops, working-class terraces, and so on'.[82] So he echoes D. J. Olsen's generalization, made for the great metropolis itself, but now applied to the seaside: the greater the unification of landownership, the higher the social tone of the development; the more fragmented, the more likely it is that the tone will be lower.[83]

Yet, as John Myerscough has argued, 'seaside towns provide urban historians so minded with a rich hunting ground for exceptions to general historical rules;'[84] and, in the main, the exceptions in the case of seaside towns follow a similar pattern to those of London and the great provincial cities. Most predictably, high hopes did not necessarily produce a high-status resort, even when they were entertained by an aristocratic landowner. Fleetwood provinces a classic example. In the 1840s Sir Peter Hesketh Fleetwood sought to develop his coastal estate as a high-class holiday town, with a fishing port alongside. Accordingly, the esplanade was laid out by Decimus Burton in the grand manner, 'in the style of Brighton and St. Leonards'; Zemin Vantimir was imported from the Euston and Victoria Hotels in London to attract 'gentlemen and noblemen' by the magnificence and renown of his catering; and 'handsomely furnished dwelling houses' were built on Queen's Terrace; but all to no avail. After a few years of success and prosperity in the early 1840s, the greater attraction of other new resorts, and the financial embarrassment of the Fleetwood family, meant that the scheme dwindled and faded. Lower-class houses were constructed along the once-grand avenues, and the town increasingly concentrated on its other activity of fishing. Finally, the Fleetwoods themselves sold off their land.[85]

Another, equally familiar variation on the theme was the aristocratic owner whose initial aspirations were not as high or exclusive as was usually the case.

Ironically, one instance of this is the Earl of Scarbrough's development of Skegness at the end of the nineteenth century, usually hailed as 'the finest example of comprehensive resort planning',[86] for while the Earl invested extensively in the local amenities, he never intended development to be select. On the contrary, he sought the patronage of those very excursionists from the great industrial centres of the Midlands with the same single-minded enthusiasm that the creators of other resorts sought to keep them out. The Great Northern Railway was lobbied to increase the number of excursion trains; an energetic policy of national advertisement was undertaken; holders of excursion tickets were allowed into the public parks and gardens of the town free of charge; complaints from local residents that Sunday excursions ruined the Sabbath with 'dissipation and vice' were brushed aside. Although the initial plan had only been drawn up as late as the 1870s, by 1882 some 230,000 excursionists were recorded as visiting. In 1890, the town was described as 'one of the most crowded and popular seaside resorts in England for day excursionists from the Midland counties', and by 1913 there were over 750,000 excursionist visitors annually. Here was a popular resort, not because of fragmented landownership or because the first high expectations had not been realized, but because that was how it had been planned from the beginning.[87]

Reciprocally, it is possible to cite examples of resorts with a high 'social tone' where there was no unitary aristocratic pattern of landownership: the seaside equivalents of Hampstead or Kelvinside. Indeed, Brighton – the greatest of them all – is the most notable. Even in the 1900s, when its halcyon days had been passed for over three-quarters of a century, it could still boast more members of the nobility among both its residents and visitors than could 'the Empress of Watering Places'. Yet it has accurately been described as 'a large, leasehold town, with a fragmented pattern of landownership', in which there was no controlling, aristocratic authority.[88] High-class enclaves like Kemp Town or the West Hove Estate were developed with no regard to the overall planning of the town.[89] And later in the century, neighbouring Worthing was developed, without any single aristocratic landowner behind the scheme, yet attained as high a 'social tone' as any exclusive, aristocratic resort.[90] Even more noteworthy was Grange-over-Sands, 'the smallest and most select of the north-west resorts of note', where again development was completely un-planned, but which has continued until this day to merit the description first given it in 1867: 'not gay, not fast, not boisterous nor overcrowded'; the very characteristics more usually associated with aristocratic resorts.[91]

Between these two familiar extremes of aristocratic control (which might or might not result in exclusive resorts) and fragmented ownership (in which high-class development could still be possible) comes a curious half-way stage to which there is no exact metropolitan or provincial equivalent, namely, collaboration between an aristocratic landowner and a local railway company. At Cleethorpes, for example, the aristocratic landowner was Sidney Sussex College, Cambridge, which was possessed altogether of nearly 60 per cent of the township. Like the Fleetwoods at the resort which bears their name, the College's first aspirations for development were high in the late 1850s, but the slow pace of growth forced them to lower their sights towards the end of the 1880s, and only then were building plots taken in any considerable numbers. At the very same time, a further and complementary stimulus was given to development by the decision of the Manchester, Sheffield & Lincolnshire Railway to pour money into the resort and promote new amenities. In the 1880s, the sea defences, the pier, the gardens and the swimming pool were all taken over by the company: enterprises which, in other aristocratic seaside towns, were founded and succoured by the local landowner.[92]

By contrast, the resorts of Essex take us back to a world more familiar, for there could be found 'company' towns, where the requisite authority, although a private business, behaved very much like an aristocratic landowner, as was the case in London with Cubitt at Pimlico, and in the provinces with the Victoria Park syndicate at Manchester. Clacton, for example, was created and dominated by the London Steam Boat Company, which set up a subsidiary in 1877 entitled the Clacton-on-Sea Land, Building and Investment Company. By 1882, it had accumulated 285 acres of land, and had acquired a controlling interest in the local hotel, pier, gas, water and library companies. In 1889, both the parent and subsidiary companies were reorganized into the Coast Development Company, which dominated the town until 1914. In terms both of planning the control, the trustees of the Victoria Park Company would have recognized a kindred enterprise. From the beginning, in 1877, the company resolved to lay out the 285-acre estate in such a way as to ensure that Clacton became 'a fashionable residential area'. Covenants were put in the leases strictly limiting users; there was a minimum price for houses; the town was carefully zoned between commercial and residential areas; and there was a deliberate restriction and control of the siting of railway sidings. The entertainments district was kept away from the sea front and (like Eastbourne) no shops or bazaars were allowed there.[93]

Most of the exceptions to the general rule concerning seaside towns and aristocratic landowners come in the same categories as those described for the great metropolis and the provincial towns: aristocrats whose initially-exclusive aspirations went wrong, or who were never exclusive to begin with; large landowners behaving in an aristocratic way, but who were commercial or entrepreneurial; and high-class resorts which evolved despite a fragmented pattern of landownership. It is also important to recognize that in aristocratic resort towns as much as in London or the provinces, landowners worked within the constraints imposed by topography, numbers and social structure. High, wooded, well-drained hills tended to attract the most wealthy local residents, while the working classes and those few necessary industries tended to congregate on the lower-lying land. Eastbourne illustrates this to perfection in the contrast between the high-class Meads district and the area below the pier; but the same was also true of Folkestone, Torquay and Llandudno.[94]

Again, however exclusive even the aspirations of the Devonshires or the Radnors were, a high-class seaside resort carried with it its own inexorable economic logic, which dictated that there must be a large working-class population of builders, servants and entertainers, who had to be housed somewhere.

5

However, while this argument which has stressed the limits to the landowner's power is by now familiar, the fact remains that the observed coincidence between high-class resorts and unified landownership does indeed seem more common than the link between aristocratic ownership and high-class development in London or the great provincial towns. The resorts which prove the rule – Eastbourne, Folkestone, Torquay, Bournemouth, Bexhill, Southport – are both more numerous and on the whole larger than those which are the exceptions – Brighton, Hastings, Worthing, Clacton, Grange-over-Sands. In other words, it does indeed seem to be true that 'in resort towns, large-scale estate development is probably better represented than in any other type of town'.[95] Why should that be the case? What, if anything, was intrinsic to the process of resort development which enabled the aristocracy to play a more important role than in London or the great industrial towns? Is the link here not only coincidental but causal as well?

In a very general sense, of course, the process by which a resort town was created was similar to that by which new suburbs were added on to the great metropolis or large provincial towns. The land had to be surveyed, the roads made, the plots marked out, the builders attracted, and the tenants encouraged. Indeed, as the history of Belgravia or Edgbaston or Eastbourne shows, such speculation and development had its risks, problems and uncertainties whether it took place in the largest city in western Europe at one extreme or an obscure Sussex fishing village at the other. Hermione Hobhouse's words on urban estate development in the great metropolis apply to other towns as well: 'To the twentieth-century mind, the idea that housing speculations in London could fail is ridiculous, but for the great landowners and the builders who worked on their land in the eighteenth and nineteenth centuries, this was a very real danger.'[96]

But for all that, the creation of an extension to an established town was a less uncertain or demanding enterprise than the making of a resort, out of nothing, in the middle of nowhere. Initial spending on roads and drainage would be greater. Sea walls and promenades would have to be constructed. New companies would have to be established to provide gas, water, electricity, entertainments and amenities, for unlike a suburb, there would be no adjacent town on which the resort could be parasitic. Whereas in the provinces or in London the builders could simply enlarge the built-up area by extending their own sphere of operations out into the country, at the seaside they would actually have to be brought there *de novo*. In the same way, while it was reasonable to expect the middle classes to move out of their polluted towns to the suburbs, and to build houses speculatively on the basis of that assumption, it was a much greater risk to construct them in a new, distant, unknown resort, in the hope of a similar exodus.

So the creation of a seaside town could not be left initially to those market forces – topography and location, numbers and social structure – which, mediated by speculative builders, seem to have been most important in creating suburban appendages to London and the great provincial towns. Of necessity, during the first 10 or 20 years in the life of a resort town, investment had to be greater, the return was smaller, and the threat of failure was more omnipresent than in the case of suburban development. Accordingly, the 'initial aspirations' of developers in seaside towns had to be far stronger if the venture was to succeed than they did in the making of suburban communities.[97] Railway or steamship or specially-established companies might on occasions be set up to initiate such development – the seaside equivalent of the Victoria Park Company – but in the main, it was aristocrats, who already held the land in large parcels, whose high status and credit-worthiness gave them access to the London money market, and whose lack of concern for immediate income made them particularly well suited to investments which were slow to give a return, who were the most frequent initiators of seaside town development. In London and the great provincial cities, aristocratic landowners were subordinate to the market: one agent of urban expansion among many, responding to a dynamic process whose origins lay elsewhere. But in the seaside towns, it was the aristocratic landowners themselves who actually had to initiate the process, attract the people, and create the market. So, while a Victorian surburban estate might 'plan and manage itself', a Victorian seaside estate – at least at first – could not.[98]

This may be illustrated by comparing the initial investment which was required in metropolitan, provincial and seaside development. In London, home of the money market, with a massively expanding population, and possessed of the largest-scale speculative builders in the country, aristocratic investment was relatively small. The Fellows of Eton at Chalcots, the Bedfords at Bloomsbury, the Grosvenors at Belgravia and Pimlico, and the Calthorpes at Gray's Inn, could leave not only the making of the houses, but also the construction of the roads, sewers and footpaths to the speculative builder. As John Harris explained in his letter to Lord Calthorpe, the great advantage of allowing a man like Cubitt to undertake development was that it was possible to 'throw all the expenses for improvement upon the lessee.'[99] Under these circumstances, the balance of power between the landowner and builder was tilted strongly in favour of the latter. In bad times, the landlord might occasionally lend money, and he might even think it was important to make a donation of a piece of land for a church, but beyond that, he could act as the sleeping partner, and leave the investment and the risk-taking to others.

In the provincial towns, however, the contribution of the landowner was slightly more positive. The middle classes were fewer in numbers, the builders operated on a much smaller scale, and money was less easily available, so the 'initial aspirations' of the landowner – both in terms of his financial contribution and the consequent risks he was prepared to bear – had to be larger. The Calthorpes, for example, paid for all the roads and sewers, and spent £47,000 between 1810 and 1888, as well as donating land and money for churches and other charitable associations. In Cardiff, the Windsors lavished £36,000 on the making of their Grangetown suburb between 1858–67. And at Huddersfield, which in some ways was almost a new town, the Ramsdens had spent over £125,000 by the 1880s.[100] Thus, in the provinces, the landowner who was prepared to go to these greater lengths in financing building estate development effectively compensated for the lack of those large-scale speculative builders who in London performed the same functions.

In the resort towns, by comparison, the landowners' outlay – both relatively and absolutely – was very large indeed (table 48).

Table 48. Outlay on initial investment in aristocratic resort towns

Resort	Family	Duration of investment	Amount (£)
Bexhill	de la Warr	1885–1900	50,000
Bournemouth	Tapps-Gervis	1834–50	40,000
Cleethorpes	Sidney Sussex	1853–1907	30–40,000
Eastbourne	Devonshire	1850–93	711,000
Skegness	Scarbrough	1878–90	53,000
Torquay	Haldon	1850–85	100,000

Source: Earl de la Warr's Estate Act (1885), clause 4; J.V.N. Soane, 'The general significance of the development of the urban and social structure of Bournemouth, 1840–1940' (Ph.D. thesis, University of Surrey, 1975), 100; P. J. Aspinall, 'Speculative builders and the development of Cleethorpes, 1850–1900', *Lincolnshire History & Archaeology*, XI (1976), 46; table 34 above; T. W. Beastall, *A North Country Estate: The Lumleys and Saundersons as Landowners, 1600–1900* (1975), 186; Lord Haldon's Estate Act (1885), 25.

As has already been argued, most of these landowners who invested in the seaside were – with the conspicuous exception of the Devonshires – not among the front rank of the aristocracy in terms of wealth. Most aristocrats who created seaside resorts were not rich, but spent relatively handsomely. Yet, by contrast, most of the grandees who were involved in estate development in London and the great provincial towns were – with the exception of the Calthorpes – decidedly wealthy, but did not need to spend so much.

The same contrast emerges when returns on the outlay are considered. In London, where those who owned land were already often rich, not only was outlay low, but revenue was high. As early as 1844, for example, the Duke of Portland was taking £50,000 in ground rents from his Marylebone estate – a sum far in excess of any income derived by either the Devonshires or the

Calthorpes from their estates which have been studied in this book.[101] Yet by the end of the century, even this figure was looking paltry, for by the 1880s the Bedfords were drawing over £100,000 from their combined London estates, and by the next decade, the first duke of Westminster was receiving £135,000 from Mayfair alone.[102]

In the provinces, by comparison, outlay was somewhat larger, income rather lower. At Huddersfield, for example, the Ramsdens' income was a paltry £3,654 in 1769: but by 1869 it had grown to £42,331, and by 1919 reached £63,810 – a level at which it was beginning to rival the great estates of London.[103] The Calthorpes' Edgbaston income, by contrast, rose more slowly, from £10,000 in 1810 to £20,000 by 1850, to £30,000 by 1880, at which level it remained until the 1910s. Finally, the income which the Butes derived from their building estate in Cardiff rose from £3,487 in 1850 to £28,348 by 1894.[104] In all cases, these were solid, respectable totals, but they were less spectacular than the London giants, and were a lower return on a higher initial outlay.

However at the seaside, outlay – for these minor families – was relatively much greater and the return was decidedly miserable (table 49).

Table 49. Ground rents from seaside building estates

Resort	Family	Date	Rental (£)
Cleethorpes	Sidney Sussex	1909	7,000
Eastbourne	Devonshires	1885	10,000
	Gilberts	1913	10,272
Folkestone	Radnor	1900	14,739
Skegness	Scarbrough	1896	2,961
Torquay	Haldon	1885	16,000

Source: P. J. Aspinall, 'Speculative builders and the development of Cleethorpes, 1850–1900', *Lincolnshire History and Archaeology*, XI (1976), 47; ESRO Gilb. MS 132, Schedule of Rents; Kent County Record Office, Radnor Papers, Estate Accounts; T. W. Beastall, *A North Country Estate: The Lumleys and Saundersons as Landowners, 1600–1900* (1975), 199; Haldon Estate Act, 26.

These figures are not spectacular, even by the yardstick of provincial building estates, let alone London. Moreover, interest charges on the mortgages raised were consuming a considerable amount of these rents: £2,000 to finance initial development at Cleethorpes, slightly more at Skegness (which left the Scarbroughs with almost no surplus), and £4,000 a year at Torquay.[105]

In other words, investment in making seaside resorts in the nineteenth century required a relatively high outlay and gave a relatively low return. The reasons for the high outlay are clear: but why was the rental so low? In part, it was because seaside estates were the last to be developed. The great estates in London came first, then the provincial towns, and the seaside resorts were a long way behind. Skegness in 1896, for example, had only been developing for 20 years. So, necessarily, the income was lower than from those estates with reversions, repairing leases and all the mouthwatering increases in income 100 years on, which were still in the distant future in the resort towns. Moreover, as development spread out from London, the intensity lessened. In London, houses were tightly packed in squares and terraces. In the provincial suburbs, villas in large grounds and space-consuming amenities were more prevalent, and in resorts, leisure towns *par excellence,* much space was given over to parades, winter gardens, schools and bandstands, so that the average rental per acre was even lower.

6

Urban estate management was, as Hermione Hobhouse has argued, essentially 'the art of the possible'. [106] And, in London and the great provincial towns, what was possible depended primarily on fashion, topography, location, numbers and social structure. Together these formed those 'social and economic realities' which D. J. Olsen has come to see as being 'so much more powerful than either private or public planning agencies'.[107] Accordingly, while at the level of the particular the impact of these great aristocratic families on urban evolution may have been large, at a more general level it should not be overstated. All the evidence advanced here suggests that London and the great provincial cities would probably have developed essentially as they did, whether they boasted aristocratic owners or not, because identical patterns of urban zoning can be seen to exist when there are diametrically opposite structures of landownership. That is not to ignore the particular circumstances of urban evolution, nor to forget the aristocracy's political or social role in the towns, nor to deny the towns' contribution to the aristocracy's financial survival. What it *is* to say is that in regard to the general issue of urban evolution, their importance has, perhaps, been overestimated.

Except, that is, in the case of the seaside towns, where the venture was more difficult, more risky and more expensive, and the return lower. There, if anywhere, did the aristocracy play a fundamentally creative role in the process of urbanization, initiating development where it might never have begun, and sustaining it when it might otherwise have faltered. And since, if we exclude Lord Calthorpe from the one category and the Devonshires from the other, most aristocratic landowners in London and the great provincial towns were super-powers, while those involved in resort creation were less grand, one paradoxical conclusion of this chapter is that these relatively insignificant families who owned land at the seaside and turned it into resort towns may have wielded more real power over the process of urban growth in nineteenth-century England than did the grandees in the great towns and in London.

27 The aristocracy and the towns in the twentieth century

However one may view the involvement of the aristocracy in the urbanization process in the century prior to the 1880s, there can be little doubt that it has changed fundamentally during the last 100 years. Before then, towns expanded most rapidly in terms of population and unprecedentedly in terms of size, thereby allowing the landowning aristocracy a greater part in the urbanization process than they had played previously. But since the 1870s, while the rate at which town *populations* have grown has been less impressive, expansion in *size* has been on an altogether larger scale, facilitated first by the suburban railway and the tram, and in the inter-war years by the bus and the car. Yet paradoxically, the extent to which the aristocracy has been involved in this second phase has been much less than before. Why, at the very time when more land than ever was being eaten up by the ever-advancing urban frontier, did the territorial grandees play a diminished part? What does this imply about the changed circumstances of the aristocracy during the last 100 years or so?

1

By the end of the nineteenth century, the management of the great aristocratic urban estates – whether in London, the provinces or the seaside – was entering a new phase. Estates which 100 years before were on the edge of towns were now surrounded by houses, crossed by heavy commuter traffic, and raked with tramways, and so needed redeveloping in a manner which recognized these fundamentally changed circumstances. In the great metropolis, the last vacant plots in Belgravia, Bloomsbury and Pimlico, which Cubitt had taken half a century before, were finally filled up by his descendants. Elsewhere on these estates, leases were about to fall in in large numbers for the first time, 99 years after the first great building boom of the 1770s. In Birmingham, the Calthorpes faced similar difficulties – partly because, though not fully covered, Edgbaston's development had slowed to a snail's pace, and partly because, with the expiry of these early leases of the 1780s, re-development was a problem which would soon be demanding expert attention. And even though building was still buoyant in the seaside towns, there also the balance of power was beginning to shift – more rapidly in some towns than in others – as the local authority's role increased, and the influence of the landowner began to fade. As Professor Ashworth has noted, 'from the later nineteenth century, the plans of individual landowners were far less dominant in determining the appearance of the towns'.[1]

As if these problems were not challenging enough for the great urban landowners, the 1880s proved to be a distinctly disagreeable decade for the aristocracy in general. From Conservative as well as Liberal Governments came legislation and proposals which, when set in the context of continued agricultural depression, made sorry contemplation. Gladstone's Settled Land Act, his third Reform Act and his Irish Legislation – both implemented and unsuccessful – to say nothing of Lord Salisbury's reform of county and London government, combined with those investigations into the working of the great urban estates embodied in the Select Committee on Town Holdings and the Royal Commission on the Housing of the Working Classes, and the more general outbursts against the peerage, amounted to a more concerted attack on the landed interest than in any decades since the 1830s and 1840s. While the 1890s brought some reprieve, the 1900s saw the clouds of gloom gather once more, with Lloyd George's 'People's Budget', and the attack on the House of Lords. Collectively, these threats and measures, strung out over three decades and more, served greatly to increase the corporate anguish and doubt which had been ushered in for the aristocracy by the agricultural depression, and which was never fully to be dissipated.

Moreover, the effects were fundamental, long-lasting and irreversible, first halting, and then overturning these presuppositions on the basis of which landowners had held, administered, developed and augmented their estates, in some cases for over 400 years. The belief that the ownership of broad acres conferred on its possessor sufficient social prestige and political influence to outweigh its low financial return; the conviction that estates should be developed and extended to their full potential, largely free from outside, governmental interference or regulation; the confidence that decisions could be made on the assumption that circumstances would not be fundamentally altered a hundred years hence: all these beliefs which lay at the centre of the existence of landed society were one by one eroded.[2] Instead of seeing their landed estates as family heirlooms to be cherished and passed on, landowners came increasingly to regard them as unremunerative and vulnerable assets, which should be exchanged for investments which were less risky, more remunerative, and demanded less by way of aristocratic obligation. The Settled Land Act of 1882, which gave tenants for life greater powers to sell, made such a policy possible for many landowners for the first time. And, although the depressed land market from the 1870s to the 1890s meant that few – except those who held estates in Wales – were able to avail themselves of its provisions until the years immediately before and after the First World War, the change in attitude had come about many years before. As the Duke of Marlborough put it in 1885: 'Were there any effective demand for the purchase of land, half the land of England would be in the market tomorrow.'[3]

More especially, the increased powers given to the local authorities in these years undermined both the confidence and the autonomy of aristocrats with urban estates. Although, for example, such measures as the Health of Towns

Act and the Artisans Dwelling Act were essentially enabling rather than mandatory, although few local authorities initially adopted them with the vigour of Chamberlain in Birmingham, and although well-run aristocratic estates had nothing to fear from such legislation, they nevertheless betokened an increase in the willingness of the state to interfere in the affairs of urban landowners. Subsequently, during the years before the First World War, these powers were increased and made mandatory, and the Town Planning Act of 1909 gave local authorities the right to appropriate undeveloped land, to impose a plan on it and – on completion of the scheme – to exact a betterment levy from the increased revenue accruing to the original landowner.[4] As the solicitor to the second duke of Westminster observed in 1905: 'legislation is constantly curtailing the rights of the landowner and extending the power of the Public Authorities over all new buildings'.[5]

So, in the towns as in the countryside, the unfavourable climate of opinion, coinciding as it did with specific problems of administration, policy and re-development, obliged many aristocrats to reconsider the wisdom of holding onto their estates in a manner which before had been axiomatic. In the towns, as in the countryside, the old policies of accumulation and long-term thinking went into reverse. As with agricultural holdings, the timing of the about-turn varied, depending on such idiosyncratic matters as the age and outlook of the tenant for life, the shrewdness of his advisers (if he had any), and the value, location and prospects of his lands. So decisions could be taken quickly or slowly, and might even appear to be contradictory. In the 1880s, for example, the fifth Lord Calthorpe was already thinking of selling off both his London building estates, because of the low return on Gray's Inn and the bad state of the buildings at City Road. Yet, in the early 1890s, he was still eager to add to his more extensive and lucrative urban estate at Edgbaston in the tradition of his ancestors. In general, however, it is fair to say that between the late 1880s and the First World War, many major aristocratic landowners with ground rents contemplated or authorized sales of urban land which would have been unthinkable 30 years before.

The sale by the Duke of Bedford of his Covent Garden estate illustrates this sudden change of outlook in its most abrupt and spectacular form. As late as 1897, the duke's London steward reiterated the traditional policy in advising his master strongly to hold on to his Covent Garden estate:

> I am fully persuaded that the wisest policy is (as far as possible) to avoid selling any part of the Covent Garden Estate which I regard as the choicest and most valuable portion of His Grace's property. I would go even further and urge that, when opportunity offers, this part of the estate should be added to.[6]

And yet, within a decade, the same duke approved a complete reversal of the policy pursued by generations of his ancestors, who had steadily enlarged the family's landed estates – both rural and urban – throughout the previous four centuries. In October 1913, the duke's principal adviser noted that there were now 'profound misgivings as to the future of real property, especially in towns', and strongly advocated selling. And when, shortly after, the news broke that the duke intended to part with that urban estate on which the first integrated development had been constructed by Inigo Jones, it caused a sensation.[7]

Of course, it was not the first such sale: Lord Calthorpe's decision to part with his City Road estate had been reached 20 years before. Yet the stature of the vendor, the wealth of his family, and the fame of his estate, all ensured that it was this particular transaction more than any other which really signified the beginning of the end for the great urban holdings of the aristocracy. Parts of Mayfair were sold by the Westminsters before the First World War, and further sales took place in the late 1920s, including the entire Millbank estate for over £900,000.[8] In 1919, the Duke of Bedford, Lord Portman, Lord Camden, Lord Cadogan and Lord Northampton all sold off parts of their London lands, and the entire Berkeley London estate, including the most famous of all London's squares, home of the nightingale, was sold to a property company for £2,000,000. Then in 1925, Lord Howard de Walden, who had inherited the Duke of Portland's London estate, sold off Great Portland Street to Sir John Ellerman.[9] Although the disposal of metropolitan land had not gone as far as the sales of agricultural estates, nevertheless the tide appeared to be flowing strongly in the same direction.

Even more spectacular in the great metropolis was the demise of many aristocratic town houses which had stood as the proudest and most assured assertion of the landed elite's claim to be also the governing elite. Early in 1919, the Marquess of Salisbury sold his town house in Arlington Street, which initiated the same process with regard to the great town palaces that the sale of Covent Garden had begun for urban estates. Thereafter, Devonshire, Grosvenor, Lansdowne and Dorchester Houses disappeared as private residences, as Mayfair was increasingly turned over to apartment houses, shops, showrooms and offices.[10] And, as the example of Devonshire House well demonstrates, the reversal of policy was as abrupt here as in the case of urban estates. In 1893, and throughout his tenure of the title, the eighth duke had resolutely refused to sanction the sale of Devonshire House, but by 1922 it had gone under the hammer. Writing in 1937, the Duke of Portland drew attention to a major revolution which had taken place in the metropolis. In the old days, he noted, the great town houses 'were thrown open every season for large social gatherings', and he mentioned Hertford, Grosvenor, Dorchester, Londonderry, Lansdowne, Devonshire, Spencer, Chesterfield, Stafford, Bridgewater, Apsley, Montague and Holland Houses. 'At present', he noted, 'only Londonderry, Apsley, Bridgewater and Holland Houses remain as private residences.'[11]

In the provincial and seaside towns, there is evidence of a similar abdication, the first signs of which, again, may be seen in the years before the First World War. In 1885, the Haldons began to sell off their holdings in Torquay in a belated effort to restore their finances, so that by 1914 they had ceased to have any territorial link with the town at all.[12] In 1894, the Huddersfield Corporation began to negotiate with the Ramsdens for the sale of their urban estate, but in this case, no arrangement was made.[13] By 1912, the Sutherlands' great house at Trentham was a ruin, the grounds were donated to the new City of Stoke on Trent, and the family abandoned completely any part in the public life of the Potteries. In the same way, the Earl of Radnor ceased to be resident at Folkestone, and Earl de la Warr leased out his manor house at Bexhill.[14] Finally, in 1918, the Calthorpes reluctantly consented to the sale of the 'outlying parts' of their Edgbaston estate.

However, as in London, it was only during the years immediately after the First World War that sales really gathered momentum. At the seaside, the great families were especially quick off the mark. Lord Radnor began systematic sales at Folkestone in 1920, and the Gilberts sold off their old manor house to Eastbourne Corporation three years later.[15] In 1921 and again in 1924, Sir George Tapps-Gervis-Meyrick disposed of his ground rents in the centre of Bournemouth, and in 1923, the Earl of Malmesbury sold off his 600-acre building estate in the town, an event rightly described in the local press as 'another epoch in the history of the town.'[16] Finally, in 1926-7, the Scarisbricks and the Heskeths systematically auctioned off their holdings in Southport.[17]

In the great provincial towns, the picture was very similar. At Huddersfield, the entire Ramsden estate was sold to the corporation for £1,300,000 in 1920, and Lord Derby began to dispose of his Liverpool ground rents soon after.[18] In Cardiff, the Butes sold off the docks to the Great Western Railway in 1922, and liquidated their building estate – over one-third of the built-up land in the town – in 1937.[19] Further north, the Dudleys began a systematic disposal of their Black Country lands, including not only their large agricultural estate at Witley Court in 1920, but also 4,385 acres in the traditional mineral and industrial areas of Dudley, Sedgley, Tipton and Brierley Hill for £854,301 between 1926 and 1944.[20] Finally, in Belfast, Lord Shaftesbury abandoned his personal links with the town in 1927, preferring to play the role of resident grandee in Dorset, and in 1934 presented Belfast Castle and grounds to the town.[21] In the provinces as much as in London, the grandees were in retreat.

Nor was this the full extent of their abdication; for it was also true that, in an increasingly hostile climate, those aristocrats who continued to own land which might be developed as a building estate were less eager to consider such activity than they once might have been. The future seemed so uncertain that to think in terms of a century or so seemed not just unwise but positively foolhardy. Instead of looking to some doubtful reversion a century ahead, it seemed preferable to sell off agricultural land, at written up, development value, and to leave to someone else the risk and responsibility of development. Again, the change in attitudes is fundamental. Gone was the old, traditional policy of assuming possession of the estate to be permanent and development of it, over a long period of time, a sacred duty. Now, if it could be disposed of quickly and profitably at written-up value, sentiment was ignored. Ironically, much of the evidence given to the Select Committee on Town Holdings, in which agents laid bare the essence of their policy, and stressed matters of family pride and long-term perspective, was a requiem for policy from the last century, rather than a manifesto of policy for the next.

The development of Bexhill and Skegness tend to be the exceptions that prove the rule. No other ambitious projects of resort creation were initiated by aristocrats thereafter, and the suburban expansion of the provincial towns in the inter-war years tended to be on land which was either freehold or, if leasehold, was owned by development companies rather than aristocrats. At Bradford, for example, the Rolle family sold off their entire estates – undeveloped but mouthwateringly adjacent to the city – in 1912.[22] In Birmingham, the manors of Solihull and Moseley were sold to developers, whereas they would certainly have been developed leasehold by the owner a generation earlier.[23] At Edgbaston, after the First World War, the Calthorpes conveyed land undeveloped to the Governors of King Edward's School and the local hospital board. And at Perry, the eighth Lord Calthorpe sold off the entire house, park and estate in two lots in the 1920s. The mansion was demolished, the grounds were converted into a park and – ironically – the farmland was developed as a building estate by the local corporation.[24]

Yet it is the Sheffield estates of the Fitzwilliams which provide the fullest evidence of a change in policy. During the third quarter of the nineteenth century, they had begun to develop their Eccleshall estate on the traditional leasehold pattern, laying out roads and letting plots to speculative builders. But by the early 1900s such a policy seemed to the seventh earl's advisers to be increasingly anachronistic and inflexible, and they felt that a change in policy was called for: 'In view of recent legislation, it would be advisable to give facilities for selling sites on the Eccleshall Estate. Things have completely changed since the original scheme was drawn up fifty years ago.'[25] In short, the presuppositions on which leasehold development had been based had themselves been overtaken by events: it now appeared preferable to sell to developers, thereby making an immediate gain, than to develop by leases and lavish hopes on an uncertain future reversion. So sales duly began, although at first only slowly. By the mid-1920s, however, they were in full swing. In Sheffield as in other towns, at the very time of unprecedented suburban expansion, the aristocracy, frightened by the risks more than they were entranced by the prospects, opted for sale rather than leasing.

2

So, in the towns as in the countryside, the period from the 1870s until the outbreak of the Second World War saw the aristocracy under attack and in retreat. Redevelopment of building estates already in being was rendered increasingly unattractive financially, and local authorities seemed ominously poised to interfere further. At the same time, the making of new building estates seemed too much of a risk, and the future too uncertain to embark on schemes which would only mature in a century or so. Accordingly, the temptation to sell, whether the estate was already built over or not, was very strong; but as a result, the aristocracy's power to influence the evolution of the urban environment was further diminished. So, whereas during the first three-quarters of the nineteenth century it had been the planning of the landowners which had often been acclaimed, in the period which followed, model villages, municipal housing and speculation by private companies came to the fore as the most discussed and glamorous agents of urban transformation.

However, this argument should not be allowed to prevail without some qualifications. At a general level, the aristocracy may have been less important in influencing patterns of urban evolution in the century from the 1780s than is sometimes supposed. It is also true, though, that in the subsequent period of apparent decline and eclipse, they not only survived and adapted with more skill than they are often given credit for, but also wielded influence on urban redevelopment which has, perhaps, been under-rated. Assuredly, the facts of territorial decline are inescapable, but the degree to which the aristocratic presence in towns survived and flourished also needs to be stressed.

To begin with, the extent to which the legislation at the turn of the century really undermined the autonomy of landowners with urban estates must seriously be questioned. Leasehold enfranchisement did not come, for all the sound and fury of the campaign. The reversion and other duties levied by Lloyd George's 'People's Budget', despite the furore they had created at the time, were abolished in 1920. His more general campaign against land, which he had hoped would be the centrepiece of the expected 1915 general election campaign, was thrown out by moderate opinion in the Liberal party even before the war intervened.[26] And in practice, the power of local authorities to interfere in areas where development had already taken place remained small. In retrospect, at least, it seems that the aristocracy over-reacted to the threats of the time, and began assiduously to cultivate that persecuted pose which has become more plausible only in recent times.

Certainly, this is the impression conveyed by contemporary archives, if not by contemporary aristocrats; and it is especially true of estate papers, where the evidence of continuity from the nineteenth to the twentieth century is striking. The rows of letter and account books, most still meticulously written in copper plate; the carefully-kept rent books and extensively audited accounts; the hand-written letters from agents to the head of the family: as far as all these matters were concerned, the First World War might never have happened. This was particularly so for urban estates. At Edgbaston, Balden's letters to Dame Rachel Anstruther-Gough-Calthorpe continued in the same style as those he had written to her predecessor. At Eastbourne, Roland Burke was succeeded by Charles Alix, and the local régime continued very much as before. In fact, this description of the administration of the Mayfair estate of the second duke of Westminster in the inter-war years has a much wider applicability:

> These were the final years in which great urban landlords could still treat their urban estates much as their forbears who had laid them out had been accustomed to, as their own private property, broadly subject only to the landord's covenants contained in their own leases, to the limitations of their own family settlements, and to the statutory building regulations administered by the local authority and the district surveyors. Public overlordship by planning had hardly started . . . The zoning of land use, the re-development of outworn buildings, the style and aesthetics of architectural design, and the preservation and destruction of the historic fabric – all these were still, as they had always hitherto been, private matters for decision by the ground landlord and his advisers.[27]

Indeed, the generous act of the second duke, who remitted rents to his urban estate tenants whose houses were damaged by enemy action during the Second World War, showed that the mentality of the *ancien régime* survived even into the age of the rocket.

This paradoxical amalgam of continuity in a time of change, adaptability in an era of adversity, which is particularly well demonstrated with reference to the urban estates of the aristocracy in the inter-war years, was but a reflection of their more general circumstances. While many owners of urban estates were indebted (the Ramsdens, for instance, owed their bankers £800,000), the Haldons seem to be the only family who were excessively burdened.[28] Nor at this time were death duties as severe as they were later to become. So, for the majority of families discussed here, sales of estates, both rural and urban, as well as of London town houses, were not the despairing last resort of a group with their backs to the wall, but a conscious decision to re-structure and rationalize their assets. The Bedfords, for example, invested the proceeds from the sale of Covent Garden not, as legend has it, in Russian bonds which later became worthless, but in colonial and overseas shares. The Ramsdens, Sutherlands, Devonshire, Westminsters, Butes and Dudleys all followed a similar course of action.[29]

So, in many cases, by the late 1920s, these super-rich families had cleared off their debts (if they had any), disposed of their least attractive agricultural estates and most embarrassing urban properties, and were enjoying an income from equities probably as large as that which they had previously derived from land.[30] Just as a family like the Devonshires traded power for prestige in Eastbourne, so more generally in the inter-war years, the super-rich among the landed aristocracy – which by definition included those able to hold on to their urban estates – traded acres for higher income. Their mode of life remained *landed* in *expenditure*, but became increasingly *plutocratic* in its source of *income*.

The behaviour of the great families in the inter-war years was therefore a curious and often contradictory amalgam. At one level, they behaved as if there would be no tomorrow; at another as if tomorrow would be the same as yesterday. So, while the Calthorpes protested about Lloyd George and his taxes, and Balden wondered how the death duties on the estate of the sixth lord would ever be paid, the family re-equipped and extended Elvetham – hardly the action of landowners who felt that oblivion was nigh. The Berkeleys may have sold off the square which bore their name, but the proceeds were used to restore their ancestral home in Gloucestershire.[31] And the itinerant régime of the ninth duke of Devonshire – from Chatsworth to Hardwick to London to Eastbourne to Lismore – accompanied by retinues of servants, to say nothing of the splendours of a family Christmas in the ducal household recalled by Harold Macmillan, may have been financed more by dividends than rentals, but it certainly belied the pessimistic appraisal of affairs which the eighth duke had made on inheriting.[32]

3

The decline of the aristocracy was, then, a gradual affair. In the towns, they had traded power for prestige from the 1880s, and in the country they had exchanged broad acres for larger, non-agricultural revenue from the 1910s. In politics, though, the continued electoral prominence of the Conservative party helped to conceal their gradual disappearance from Westminster and Whitehall, and in society they still remained exciting, glamorous and heroic, even if increasingly challenged in this regard by the film stars of Hollywood. The threats which had been perceived in the period from the 1880s to the First World War had by no means been idle; but they had still been less than expected.[33] In this as in so much else, it was the Second, not the First World War which was the great watershed. The supply of servants disappeared for good this time.[34] Country houses were demolished. Taxes and death duties rose to unprecedented heights. Once more, the land market was very active. Evelyn Waugh wrote *Brideshead Revisited* as a panegyric for a defunct class, and as a nostalgic memoir of the vanished splendours of country-house life.

As in the inter-war years, this was reflected in a further aristocratic withdrawal from the towns. In London, for example, the war effectively brought high society to an end. Indeed, as early as November 1939, Henry Channon had recognized that the writing was on the wall: 'They have shut up Hampden House, Londonderry House too has been shut, and also Holland House, where there will surely never be another ball . . . It is sad that the houses of the great will never again open their hospitable doors': and he was right. In October 1940, Holland House was bombed, and Spencer and Londonderry Houses later suffered similar fates.[35] At the end of the Second World War, unlike the First, the lights of London society were not re-lit. In 1939, 109 peers had Mayfair addresses, but by 1965 there were only 34, and none of these could boast large town houses as of old. 'Aristocracy', noted Nancy Mitford in 1956, 'no longer keep up any state in London, where family houses hardly exist now.'[36]

Yet this was only the most ostentatious evidence of decline, for the sale of many of those urban estates which had survived the inter-war period now proceeded apace – not, as in the 1920s and 1930s, as a result of a voluntary and deliberate policy of financial rehabilitation, but in response to demands for death duty payments of unprecedented magnitude. This time the landowners' backs were more firmly against the wall. In 1947 Lord Sefton sold off his Kirkby estate to Liverpool Corporation, and parted with Aintree Race Course two years later. The fourth marquess of Bute presented Cardiff Castle and Park to the city, thereby severing completely his family's link with the coal metropolis.[37] And, again in 1947, the Dudleys sold off Himley Hall to the Coal Board, so that, apart from the Garden of Remembrance and other small plots of sentimental significance in the Black Country, they now own not an acre there.[38] At Eastbourne, the Devonshires did not return to Compton Place after the Second World War, and at Skegness, the death of the eighth earl in 1945 and the ninth in 1969 compelled the Scarbrough family to sell off many of their ground rents.[39]

In London, the picture was identical. The death of Dame Rachel Anstruther-Gough-Calthorpe in 1951 obliged the Calthorpes to sell their entire Gray's Inn Road estate, and the Westminsters, faced with a death duty bill in excess of £10 million on the death of the second duke in 1953, sold all of Pimlico. In the same way, on the Portman, Bedford and Cadogan estates, extensive sales, all for death duty purposes, took place in the late '1940s and early 1950s'.[40] As a result, the territorial holdings of the great families in London have been considerably reduced (see table 50).

Under these circumstances, where the great London estates were but a shadow of their former selves, it was not surprising that, in the late 1940s and early 1950s, when the question of leasehold enfranchisement was once more

Table 50. London estates of major aristocratic landlords

Family	Acreage c. 1880	Acreage c. 1967
Westminster	500	300
Howard de Walden (Portland)	c. 200	100
Cadogan	c. 200	90
Portman	258	100
Bedford	119	30

Sources: Roy Perrott, *The Aristocrats* (1967), 156; F. Sheppard (ed.), *The Survey of London*, vol. XXXIX, *The Grosvenor Estate in Mayfair*, Part I, *General Survey* (1977), 1; O. Marriott, *The Property Room* (1969), 103; private information.
Note: The Howard de Walden estate was previously the property of the Dukes of Portland, but passed to the Howard de Walden family in 1879.

raised, the thrust of the attack had markedly changed since the days of Lloyd George. For no longer were the aristocracy criticized for their landed monopoly. On the contrary, when they were mentioned, more often than not it was to receive praise and applause for embodying sound principles of management. The real villains were now seen to be property companies and small speculators who had bought their way in as the grandees sold out. As Lord Salisbury explained in a debate in 1951, on the subject of leasehold enfranchisement, the days of aristocratic domination were long since over: 'there still seems to be an impression in Labour circles that all the land of England is owned by a small number of immensely rich and almost Medieval territorial magnates . . . But, my Lords, that conception, of course, is really long out of date.'[41]

But was it? For how tantalizing is the attempt to find a date at which the demise of the aristocracy may most plausibly be pinpointed! If the 1920s and 1930s were one Indian summer, the 1950s were another. The Macmillan government was a cousinhood unrivalled since the days of the great Lord Salisbury.[42] Evelyn Waugh, in his preface to the second edition of *Brideshead Revisited*, published in 1960, admitted that when he wrote the novel in 1944, it was 'impossible to foresee . . . the present cult of the English country house . . . The English aristocracy had maintained its identity to a degree that then seemed impossible.'[43] Much of his book, he concluded, was 'a panegyric preached over an empty coffin.' Even among the remaining owners of urban estates, there was some revival, as they began to think and plan again on a long-term time scale. The Calthorpe estate redevelopment plan for Edgbaston, published in 1958, confidently looked forward 'to the year 2,000 A.D.', and George Ridley, the senior trustee of the Grosvenor Estates, could bravely affirm that 'Our ability is to look far far ahead. Fifty years is nothing to us, and one hundred years is normal.'[44] The death of the fourth duke in 1967 hit the Westminsters far less hard than had that of the second duke in 1953. 'The management of the estates', it was noted, 'will go on as before, and nothing is likely to cause any disintegration or fragmentation of the estates.' So the Grosvenors, too, commissioned a redevelopment plan, and their *Strategy for Mayfair and Belgravia* was published in 1971.[45]

Such resilience was remarkable. Indeed, while the role of a much more powerful aristocracy in moulding the urban environment may have been over-rated for the nineteenth century, the power of their enfeebled descendants to re-plan it in the twentieth has been constantly understressed; their 'initial aspirations' may have received too much emphasis, their 'defensive resolves' not enough.[46] While Edgbaston might have been middle-class and Belgravia upper-class in the nineteenth century without Lord Calthorpe or the Duke of Westminster, it is doubtful if these areas would have *remained* so refined and exclusive in the post-war years of the twentieth century had there been no single ground landlord. After the Westminsters sold Pimlico, it went inexorably downhill, and in Birmingham, areas like Moseley and

Handsworth, which had once aspired to rival Edgbaston, have suffered the same fate. Of course, the great estates, as ever, have had to bow to social forces emanating from outside their own boundaries, and recognize that there is no longer a wealthy, servant-consuming aristocracy or middle class in need of great houses or town palaces.[47] Even so, the power of the aristocratic landlord to modify a particular market situation, to preserve the old tastefully or plan the new coherently, remains impressive.

Of course, to act in this way now requires professional expertise of a type and to an extent undreamed of in the days of George Ambrose Wallis or John Harris and, as a result, the management of those few remaining aristocratic estates has changed out of all recognition. No longer does the final authority rest with a single aristocrat, the head of the family, assisted and advised by a single agent and solicitor. Elaborate trusts and settlements have been devised under which the old tenant for life is but one beneficiary, and which place estate administration and broad policy decisions in the hands of trustees. As one such beneficiary explained recently, 'for some years now, the . . . estate in London has been run by Trustees. I am, therefore, myself rather out of touch.'[48] Indeed, this description of the change in the administration of the Westminster estates after the death of the second duke applies broadly to the others which remain:

> The days when the reigning duke, as tenant for life, was pretty much the director of the whole of the family fortunes, were, in fact, ended, and in order to preserve the totality of the estate . . . , the management of the whole vast concern was now handed over to very able professional trustees acting for all the beneficiaries.[49]

The need to avoid death duties, and the increasing complexity of administering, maintaining and redeveloping the remaining urban estates, means that the style of estate management which had survived, however modified, until the Second World War, has vanished.

At the same time, the late 1960s and 1970s have once more seen a change in the climate of opinion, which has led to further restrictions and controls on those few remaining aristocratic estates. In 1967, the very year in which the Westminster estates commissioned their comprehensive redevelopment plan, the Labour Government passed the Leasehold Reform Act, which, 80 years after the leasehold enfranchisement campaign had begun, finally enabled tenants to buy their freeholds. As in the 1950s, it was the property companies, rather than the aristocratic landowners, who were the object of this legislation. And, in certain circumstances, it was (and is) possible for estates to retain powers of management and planning for the general benefit of the area. Nevertheless, such a measure strikes at the heart of the remaining estates, by threatening their territorial integrity. At Edgbaston, for example, although the Calthorpe estate has acquired a Certificate of Good Management, the Leasehold Reform Act has 'substantially weakened the estate's confidence in its ability to carry through' its development scheme.[50] Or, as another estate agent pessimistically put it, 'It's the beginning of the end.'

4

So for the few remaining estates today, the outlook is decidedly uncertain. Attempts to replan are hedged with legal restrictions, threats to their territorial integrity, and a hostile climate of public opinion. The second earl of Burlington could take the decision to develop an entire resort town at Eastbourne without needing the sanction of any government department. How different were circumstances by 1975, when the eleventh duke of Devonshire sought to obtain parliamentary approval for the development of the Crumbles. In the same way, the Westminsters were placed under pressure by the local authority to modify aspects of their redevelopment proposals for Mayfair and Belgravia: restrictions undreamed of in the lifetime of the second duke. And at Edgbaston, the Calthorpes' redevelopment schemes have been criticized by councillors, because the proposed density was too low; by tenants, who felt that their interests had not been consulted; and by the conservationists, who feared the threat to Edgbaston's historic past. One wonders what the third Lord Calthorpe and John Harris would have made of all this.

Yet how odd it is that, despite these ever-growing limitations and restrictions, the redevelopment of parts of some of the greatest towns in England remains bound up with families of distinctly aristocratic lineage. The tercentenary of the Grosvenors' links with Mayfair was recently celebrated; the Calthorpes have been connected with Edgbaston for 250 years; and parts of Bloomsbury have belonged to the Bedfords since the days before they were dukes. Indeed, even in those many towns where the original aristocratic owners have departed, the proud street names, the gently curving roads and elegant squares stand as a memorable reminder of an episode of urban and aristocratic history, when a declining but resilient ruling class stamped its mark on an evolving urban society, and in so doing both hastened and postponed its own demise.

Appendix A

Genealogical table of the Calthorpe family (simplified)

Note: underlined names indicate branch of family connected with Edgbaston estate.

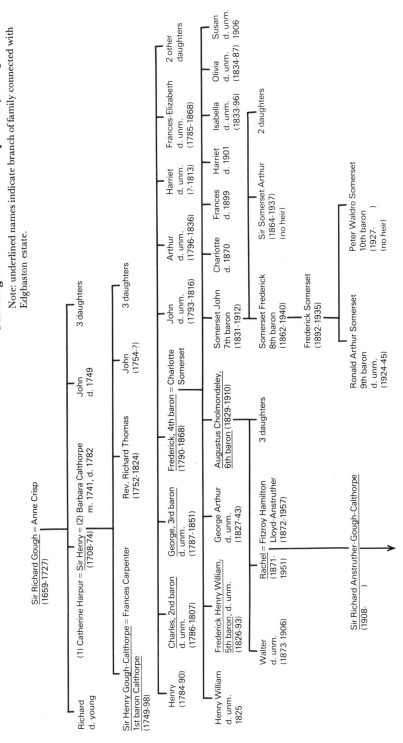

Appendix B

Composition of Lord Calthorpe's income, 1810–1910

Note: Figures in brackets indicate percentage of total

1. Gross income

Year	Edgbaston (£)	London (£)	Norfolk and Suffolk (£)	Elvetham (£)	Other (£)	Total (£)
1810	5,024 (32.4)	1,913 (12.4)	4,084 (26.4)	1,195 (7.7)	3,265 (21.1)	15,481 (100)
c. 1850	12,917 (53.9)	3,611 (15.0)	3,823 (15.9)	c. 2,130 (8.9)	c. 1,500 (6.3)	23,981 (100)
c. 1893	30,255 (72.3)	2,882 (6.9)	3,295 (7.9)	3,931 (9.4)	c. 1,500 (3.5)	41,863 (100)
1910	34,457 (75.8)	2,905 (6.4)	1,478 (3.2)	5,130 (11.3)	1,500 (3.3)	45,470 (100)

2. Net income

Year	Edgbaston (£)	London (£)	Norfolk and Suffolk (£)	Elvetham (£)	Other (£)	Total (£)
1810	3,566 (30.3)	1,713 (14.5)	2,959 (25.2)	659 (5.6)	2,867 (24.4)	11,764 (100)
c. 1850	7,692 (52.2)	2,916 (19.8)	1,632 (11.1)	c. 1,000 (6.8)	c. 1,500 (10.1)	14,740 (100)
c. 1893	25,013 (76.4)	c. 2,500 (7.7)	1,714 (5.2)	c. 2,000 (6.1)	c. 1,500 (4.6)	32,727 (100)
1910	27,734 (77.6)	c. 2,500 (7.0)	c. 1,000 (2.8)	c. 3,000 (8.4)	c. 1,500 (4.2)	35,734 (100)

Source: EEO MS., Account Books.

Appendix C

Genealogical table of the Devonshire family (simplified)

Note: underlined names indicate holders of ducal estates.

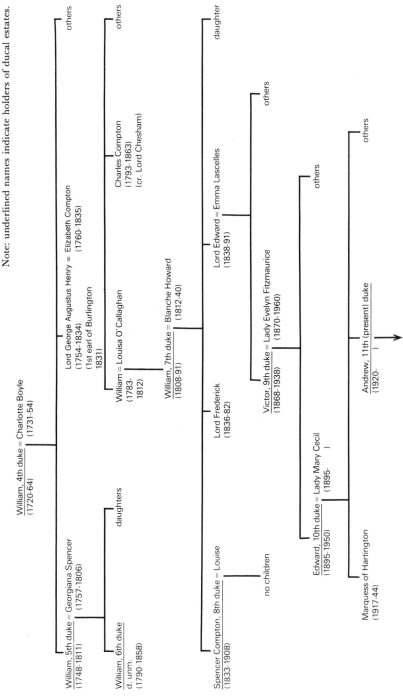

Appendix D

The finances of the dukes of Devonshire, 1858–1931
(Source: Currey MS, seventh, eighth and ninth dukes' Accounts, 1858–1931.)

a Size and composition of Devonshires' current income, 1858–1926
b Dividend income as percentage of total current income, 1858–1926
c Devonshires' current income and expenditure on interest, 1858–1931
d Percentage of current income spent on interest, 1858–1926
e Mortgage and bond debts secured on Devonshire estates, 1859–1931

Note: broken lines indicate no data available

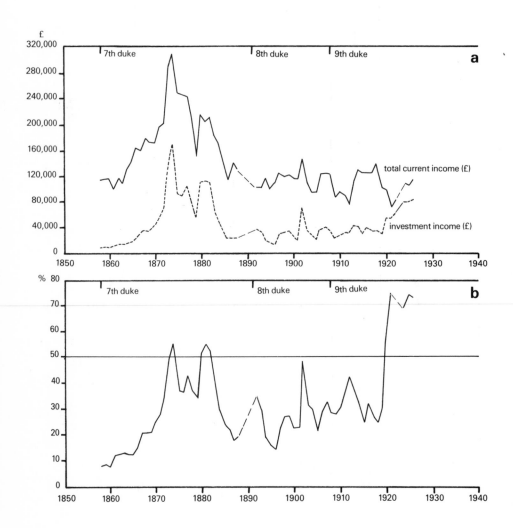

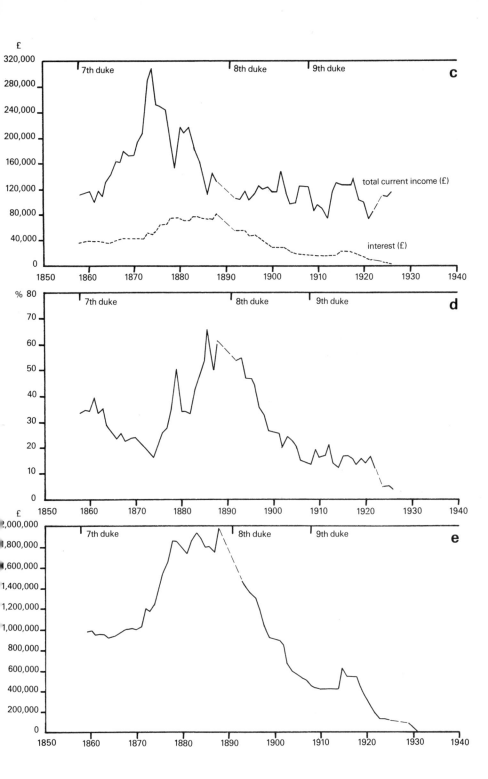

Note on sources

In the course of preparing this book, I have used the following collections of unpublished material:

Birmingham Botanical and Horticultural Society: minute books; general correspondence; lists of officers.

Birmingham General Hospital: minute books; general correspondence; lists of officers.

Birmingham and Midland Institute: minute books; lists of officers.

Birmingham Reference Library: Local Collection: deeds; newspaper cuttings; pamphlets; sale catalogues; Edgbaston tithe award.

Birmingham University Library: Joseph Chamberlain Papers: correspondence concerning 1880 general election and foundation of university; *University Collection:* committee and sub committee minute books; correspondence.

Chatsworth House, Derbyshire: correspondence of fifth, sixth, seventh and eighth dukes of Devonshire; estate and business correspondence and accounts deposited by Currey and Co.; diary of seventh duke of Devonshire; deeds and correspondence concerning Devonshire Parks and Baths Co.

Compton Estate Office, Eastbourne: estate correspondence and accounts; newspaper cuttings.

Currey and Co., London: accounts of seventh, eighth and ninth dukes of Devonshire.

East Sussex County Record Office: Gilbert Papers: estate accounts and correspondence.

Eastbourne College: minute books.

Eastbourne Corporation: minute books; correspondence.

Eastbourne Pier Company: minute books; registers of shares.

Eastbourne Public Library: Gilbert Papers: correspondence.

Eastbourne Water Works Company: minute books.

Edgbaston Estate Office, Birmingham: estate correspondence and accounts; financial papers of fifth and sixth lords Calthorpe, deposited by Walters, Vandercom and Hart.

Foundation Office of Schools of King Edward VI, Birmingham: governors' order books; register of meetings attended.

Mr N. Gillott, Birmingham: Gillott Papers: deeds and correspondence.

Greater London County Record Office: Calthorpe London Estate Papers: deeds.

Hampshire County Record Office: Calthorpe Papers: personal papers of George, third Lord Calthorpe; estate papers and accounts for London and East Anglia.

House of Lords Record Office: minutes of Lords and Commons Select Committees.

Kent County Record Office: Radnor Papers: estate accounts and correspondence.

Public Record Office: minute books of London Brighton & South Coast Railway; tithe awards; wills.

Sydney Mitchell and Co., Birmingham: Gillott Papers: deeds and correspondence.

I have omitted a comprehensive list of dissertations and printed sources used, as the references are themselves a running bibliography. All books are published in the United Kingdom unless otherwise stated and references to printed sources are given when first cited in each chapter.

Abbreviations

AAAG	*Annals of the Association of American Geographers*
AgHR	*Agricultural History Review*
AmHR	*American Historical Review*
BBHS	Birmingham Botanical and Horticultural Society
BGH	Birmingham General Hospital
BRL MS.	Birmingham Reference Library, Manuscripts
BUC	Birmingham University Collection
CW. MS.	Devonshire Papers, Chatsworth
CW. (Currey) MS.	Estate papers and correspondence deposited by Currey and Co., at Chatsworth
CW. (DP & B) MS.	Devonshire Park and Baths Papers, Chatsworth
CEO MS.	Compton Estate Office Papers
Currey MS.	Papers at Currey and Co., London
EBC	*Eastbourne Chronicle*
EBG	*Eastbourne Gazette*
EBLB	Eastbourne Local Board
EBPC	Eastbourne Pier Company
EBTC	Eastbourne Town Council
EBWWCo	Eastbourne Water Works Company
EcHR	*Economic History Review*
EEO MS.	Edgbaston Estate Office Papers
EHR	*English Historical Review*
ESRO	East Sussex Record Office
FGSKE	Free Grammar School of King Edward VI, Birmingham
Gilb. MS.	Gilbert Papers
GLRO	Greater London County Record Office
HJ	*Historical Journal*
Min. HC(HL)SC	Minutes of Evidence from House of Commons (House of Lords) Select Committees
HROCal. MS.	Calthorpe Papers, Hampshire County Record Office
JC MS.	Joseph Chamberlain Papers
JHG	*Journal of Historical Geography*
PP	*Parliamentary Papers*
PRO	Public Record Office
7 DD	Diary of Seventh Duke of Devonshire
SCTH	Select Committee on Town Holdings
TRHS	*Transactions of the Royal Historical Society*
VCH VII	W. B. Stephens (ed.), *A History of the County of Warwick*, VII, *The City of Birmingham* (1964) (*Victoria County History*)
VS	*Victorian Studies*
WVH MS.	Walters, Vandercom and Hart Papers

Notes

1. THE ARISTOCRACY AND THE TOWNS: AMBIVALENCE AND AMBIGUITY

1. J. D. Chambers, review of David Spring, *The English Landed Estate in the Nineteenth Century: Its administration* (1963), *EHR*, LXXX (1965), 634.
2. F. M. L. Thompson, *English Landed Society in the Nineteenth Century* (1963), 1.
3. R. E. Pumphrey, 'The introduction of industrialists into the British peerage: a study in adaption of a social institution', *AmHR*, LXV (1959), 15; Thompson, *op. cit.*, 16, 118; L. Stone, *The Crisis of the Aristocracy, 1558–1641* (1965), 15.
4. T.H.S. Escott, *England: Its People, Polity and Pursuits* (1885), 26.
5. Lord E. Hamilton, *Forty Years On* (1922), 131–2, 136.
6. S. Churchill, *Lord Derby: 'King' of Lancashire* (1959), 104; Lord Birkenhead, *'F.E.': The Life of F. E. Smith, First Earl of Birkenhead* (1965), 176; M. Girouard, *The Victorian Country House* (1971), 2.
7. D. Sutherland, *The Landowners* (1968), 43.
8. Girouard, *op. cit.*, 1; H. A. Taine, *Notes on England, 1860–70* (New Jersey, 1958), 151; R. R. James (ed.), *'Chips': The Diaries of Sir Henry Channon* (1967), 477; M. Harrison, *Lord of London: A biography of the second duke of Westminster* (1968), 74, 78–97, 106–19.
9. O. F. Christie, *The Transition to Democracy, 1867–1914* (1934), 248–9; V. Bonham Carter, *Winston Churchill as I Knew Him* (1967), 137.
10. *The Result of the General Election* (1830), 21.
11. Quoted in A. Briggs, *Victorian People* (1965), 205.
12. W. L. Guttsman, 'The changing structure of the British political elite, 1886–1935', *British Journal of Sociology*, II (1951); D. C. M. Platt, *Finance, Trade and Politics in British Foreign Policy, 1815–1914* (1968), xxv–xxx; R. T. Nightingale, 'The personnel of the British Foreign Office and Diplomatic Service, 1811–1929', *American Political Science Review*, XXIV (1930); D. A. Hartman, 'British and American ambassadors, 1893–1930', *Economica*, XI (1931); H. C. G. Matthew, R. I. McKibbin and J. A. Kay, 'The franchise factor in the rise of the Labour Party', *EHR*, XCI (1976) 724–5.
13. D. E. D. Beales, *From Castlereagh to Gladstone, 1815–1885* (1969), 251–2.
14. J. P. D. Dunbabin, 'The politics of the establishment of county councils', *HJ*, VI (1963); *idem*, 'Expectations of the new county councils and their realisation', *HJ*, VIII (1965).
15. Taine, *op. cit.*, 181.
16. A. C. Ewald, *The Crown and its Advisers* (1870), 129.
17. J. L. Sandford and M. E. Townsend, *The Great Governing Families of England* (2 vols., 1865), I, 112.
18. Girouard, *op. cit.*, 1.
19. W. D. Rubinstein, 'Wealth, elites and the class structure of modern Britain', *Past and Present*, LXXVI (1977), 103–4.
20. J. Bateman, *The Great Landowners of Great Britain and Ireland* (1883), 34, 63, 69, 129, 130, 140, 168, 334, 337, 431. I have deliberately omitted those

landowners whose revenues appeared Olympian simply because of misleading urban estate valuations. For a fuller account of the aristocratic super-rich, see: D. Cannadine, 'The landowner as millionaire: the finances of the dukes of Devonshire, c1800–c1926', *AgHR*, xxv (1977), 77–9, 92–3.

21. Churchill, *op. cit.*, 95; R. Colby, *Mayfair: A Town Within London* (1966), 46. The most comprehensive analysis of the Westminsters' finances is to be found in: F. H. W. Sheppard (ed.), *The Survey of London*, XXXIX, *The Grosvenor Estate in Mayfair*, Part I: *General History* (1977).

22. R. E. Pumphrey, 'The creation of peerages in England, 1837–1911' (Ph.D. thesis, Yale University, 1934), 39.

23. D. Spring, 'The role of the aristocracy in the late nineteenth century', *VS*, IV (1960), 62–3.

24. Stone, *op. cit.*, 7.

25. B. Moore, jr, *Social Origins of Dictatorship and Democracy: Lord and peasant in the making of the modern world* (1969), 32.

26. R. Nevill, *English Country House Life* (1925), 38–9.

27. F. Bédarida, 'Population and the urban explosion', in A. Briggs (ed.), *The Nineteenth Century: The contradictions of progress* (1970), 122; G. Best, *Mid-Victorian Britain, 1851–75* (1971), 6.

28. R. Vaughan, *The Age of Great Cities* (1843), i; A. F. Weber, *The Growth of Cities in the Nineteenth Century: A study in statistics* (New York, 1899), 1.

29. Vaughan, *op. cit.*, 92.

30. A. Briggs, *Victorian Cities* (1968), 59, 86; Best, *op. cit.*, 6–7, 11.

31. H. J. Dyos, 'The slums of Victorian London', *VS*, XI (1967–8), 10–24.

32. J. Knox, *The Masses Without! A Pamphlet for the Times* (1857), 30.

33. Best, *op. cit.*, 6.

34. *Bentley's Miscellany*, VII (1840).

35. Quoted in Briggs, *Victorian Cities*, 67.

36. H. Perkin, *The Origins of Modern English Society, 1780–1880* (1969), 162.

37. Vaughan, *op. cit.*, 2–3, D. Fraser, *Urban Politics in Victorian England* (1976) 22, 186.

38. Vaughan, *op. cit.*, 149.

39. Briggs, *Victorian Cities*, 66–8.

40. Quoted in *ibid.*, 71.

41. D. A. Reeder, 'The politics of urban leaseholds in late Victorian England', *International Review of Social History*, VI (1961); B. Gilbert, 'David Lloyd George, land, the budget and social reform', *AmHR.*, LCCCI (1976); *idem*, 'David Lloyd George: the reform of British landholding and the budget of 1914', *HJ*, XXI (1978).

42. N. McCord, 'Some difficulties of Parliamentary Reform', *HJ*, X (1967), 381.

43. D. Spring, 'Earl Fitzwilliam and the corn laws', *AmHR*, LIX (1954), 287.

44. W. L. Burn, *The Age of Equipoise: A study of the mid-Victorian generation* (1968), 316.

45. J. T. Ward, 'West riding landowners and the corn laws', *EHR*, LXXXI (1966); W. O. Aydelotte, 'The Country Gentleman and the repeal of the corn laws', *EHR*, LXXXII (1967).

46. D. Cannadine, 'The theory and practice of the English leisure classes', *HJ*, XXI (1978), 457.

47. Perkin, *op. cit.*, 315; F. M. L. Thompson, 'Whig and Liberals in the West Riding, 1830–1860', *EHR*, LXXIV (1959), 216.

48. L. Namier, *England in the Age of the American Revolution* (2nd edn., 1974), 16; Perkin, *op. cit.*, 42.

49. E. Percy, *Some Memories* (1958), 12–18.

50. Thompson, 'Whigs and Liberals', 26.
51. D. Spring, 'Landed elites compared,' in D. Spring (ed.), *European Landed Elites in the Nineteenth Century* (1977), 10–12; M. Girouard, *Life in the English Country House: A social and architectural history* (1978), 5–7.
52. Stone, *op. cit.*, ch. vii; H. J. Habakkuk, 'Economic functions of English landowners in the seventeenth and eighteenth centuries', *Explorations in Entrepreneurial History*, vi (1953); G. E. Mingay, *English Landed Society in the Eighteenth Century* (1963), ch. viii; D. Spring, 'English landowners and nineteenth-century industrialism', in J. T. Ward and R. G. Wilson (eds.), *Land and Industry: The landed estate and the Industrial Revolution* (1971).
53. Perkin, *op. cit.*, 60–2.
54. D. M. Joslin, 'London private bankers, 1720–85', *EcHR*, 2nd ser., vii (1954); P. G. M. Dickson, *The Sun Insurance Office, 1710–1960: The history of two and a half centuries of British insurance* (1960), 250; B. E. Supple, *The Royal Exchange Assurance: A history of British insurance, 1720–1970* (1970), 319.
55. D. Cannadine, 'Aristocratic indebtedness in the nineteenth century: the case re-opened', *EcHR*, 2nd ser., xxx (1977), 633–44.
56. N. T. Burke, 'An early modern Dublin suburb: the estate of Francis Augier, Earl of Longford', *Irish Geography*, vi (1972); J. Summerson, *Georgian London* (1970), ch. vii.
57. *Ibid.*, 39, 111; G. Rudé, *Hanoverian London, 1714–1808* (1971), 12–13.
58. M. D. George, *London Life in the Eighteenth Century* (1966), 86; Summerson, *op. cit.*, 164.
59. Rudé, *op. cit.*, 13–15; Summerson, *op. cit.*, chs. xii, xiv, xx; D. J. Olsen, *The Growth of Victorian London* (1976), ch. iv.
60. S. J. Darroch, *Ottoline: The life of Lady Ottoline Morrell* (1976), 118.
61. The fullest list of aristocratic landowners with urban estates in the provinces is in Spring, 'English landowners and nineteenth-century industrialism', 42–3.
62. A. C. Ellis, *An Historical Survey of Torquay* (1930), 351; C. H. Bishop, *Folkestone: The story of a town* (1973), 80.
63. W. H. Marshall, *On the Landed Property of England* (1804), 135.
64. T. H. S. Escott, *Social Transformations of the Victorian Age* (1897), 113; J. E. Williams, 'Paternalism in local government in the nineteenth century', *Public Administration*, xxxiii (1955).
65. N. Gash, *Politics in the Age of Peel: A study in the technique of parliamentary representation, 1830–1850* (1953), ch. ix and appendix D; H. J. Hanham, *Elections and Party Management: Politics in the time of Gladstone and Disraeli* (1959), ch. iii and appendix III.
66. T. J. Nossiter, *Influence, Opinion and Political Idiom in Reformed England: Case-studies from the north east, 1832–1874* (1975), 29, 118–23; C. E. Whiting, *The University of Durham, 1832–1932* (1932), 223–9.
67. Williams, *op. cit.*, 440–2.
68. A. Armstrong, *Stability and Change in an English County Town: A social study of York, 1801–1851* (1974), 10.
69. F. Hill, *Victorian Lincoln* (1974), 63; R. Newton, *Victorian Exeter, 1830–1910* (1968), 36, 293; Perkin, *op. cit.*, 179–80.
70. P. Joyce, 'The factory politics of Lancashire in the later nineteenth century', *HJ*, xviii (1975), 552; M. Anderson, *Family Structure in Nineteenth-Century Lancashire* (1971), 37–8; Best., *op. cit.*, 14–16; N. McKendrick, 'Josiah Wedgwood and factory discipline', *HJ*, iv (1961); D. A. Reid, 'The decline of "St. Monday", 1766–1876', *Past and Present*, lxxi (1976), 81–3.
71. T. M. McBride, *The Domestic Revolution: The modernisation of household service in England and France, 1820–1920* (1976), 37.

72. Best, *op. cit.*, 10; Olsen, *op. cit.*, 204.
73. G. Best, 'The making of the English working class', *HJ*, VIII (1965), 278; *idem*, *Mid-Victorian Britain*, 244.
74. Burn, *op. cit.*, 309
75. *The Times*, 23 Dec. 1899; W. Vamplew, *The Turf: A Social History of Horse Racing* (1976), 226.
76. H. J. Dyos, *Victorian Suburb: A study of the growth of Camberwell* (1961), 170.
77. Thompson, *English Landed Society*, 37–40; S. T. Coleridge, *On the Constitution of Church and State* (1839), 25.
78. Perkin, *op. cit.*, 38.
79. Namier, *op. cit.*, 16, 19; Best, *Mid-Victorian Britain*, 16.
80. J. F. C. Harrison, *The Early Victorians, 1832–51* (1971), 109–10; H. Pelling, *Social Geography of British Elections, 1885–1910* (1967), 22–3.
81. D. C. Itzkowitz, *Peculiar Privilege: A social history of English fox-hunting, 1735–1885* (1977), 58–9.
82. N. McKendrick, 'Home demand and economic growth: a new view of the role of women and children in the industrial revolution', in N. McKendrick (ed.), *Historical Perspectives: Studies in English thought and society in honour of J. H. Plumb* (1974), 191–8.
83. D. C. Coleman, 'Gentlemen and players', *EcHR*, 2nd ser., XXVI (1973), 106.
84. Fraser, *op. cit.*, chs. vi and x; G. B. A. M. Finlayson, 'The politics of municipal reform 1835', *EHR*, LXXXII (1967).
85. Perkin, *op. cit.*, 375–6; Best, *Mid-Victorian Britain*, xvi; J. Vincent, *The Formation of the Liberal Party, 1859–68* (1968), 97–8, 105–8.
86. Joyce, *op. cit.*, 526.
87. W. D. Rubinstein, 'Men of property: some aspects of occupation, inheritance and power among top British wealth-holders', in P. Stanworth and A. Giddens (eds), *Elites and Power in British Society* (1974), 168.
88. Olsen, *op. cit.*, 37, 42; Briggs, *Victorian Cities*, 72; R. Blythe, *Akenfield: Portrait of an English village* (1972), 16.
89. J. Burnett, *A Social History of Housing, 1815–1970* (1978), 102–3, 107.

2. THE GREAT PROVINCIAL TOWNS: CONFRONTATION AND COMPROMISE

1. J. Davies, 'Glamorgan and the Bute Estate, 1776–1947' (Ph.D. thesis, University of Wales, 1969), 193–250; M. J. Daunton, *Coal Metropolis: Cardiff, 1870–1914* (1977), 198.
2. J. M. Crook, 'Patron extraordinary: John, third marquess of Bute (1847–1900)', in *Victorian South Wales – Architecture, Industry and Society* (seventh conference report, The Victorian Society, 1969); M. Girouard, *The Victorian Country House* (1971), 125–30; *Western Mail*, 10 October 1900.
3. D. J. Owen, *History of Belfast* (1921), 187–92; R. W. M. Strain, *Belfast and its Charitable Society* (1961), 212–37.
4. W. A. Maguire, 'The 1822 settlement of the Donegall Estates', *Irish Economic and Social History*, III (1976), *idem*, 'Lord Donegall and the sale of Belfast: a case study from the Encumbered Estates Court', *EcHR*, 2nd ser., XXIV (1976).
5. *Belfast Telegraph*, 28 March 1961.
6. D. Whomsley, 'A landed estate and the railway: Huddersfield, 1844–54', *Journal of Transport History*, new ser., II (1974).
7. N. Gash, *Politics in the Age of Peel: A Study in the technique of parliamentary*

representation 1830–1850 (1953), xi; D. Fraser, 'Voluntaryism and West Riding politics in the mid nineteenth century', *Northern History*, XIII (1977).

8. R. Brook, *The Story of Huddersfield* (1968), 187.
9. J. R. Kellett, *The Impact of Railways on Victorian Cities* (1969), 176.
10. E. Richards, *The 'Leviathan of Wealth': The Sutherland Fortune in the Industrial Revolution* (1973), 61; D. Fraser, *Urban Politics in Victorian England* (1976), 13.
11. *Liverpool Echo*, 15 June 1908.
12. R. S. Churchill, *Lord Derby: 'King' of Lancashire* (1959), 129–30; *Liverpool Echo*, 4 February 1948.
13. D. Spring, 'Earl Fitzwilliam and the Corn Laws', *AmHR*, LIX (1954), 293–6; E. A. Smith, *Whig Principles and Party Politics: Earl Fitzwilliam and the Whig Party, 1748–1833* (1975), 363–7.
14. F. M. L. Thompson, 'Whigs and Liberals in the West Riding, 1830–1860', *EHR*, LXXIV (1959), 231–9.
15. G. Rowley, 'Landownership in the spatial growth of towns: a Sheffield example', *East Midland Geographer*, VI (1975).
16. H. J. Perkin, 'The development of modern Glossop', in A. H. Birch (ed.), *Small Town Politics* (1959); D. J. Olsen, 'House upon house', in H. J. Dyos and M. Wolff (eds), *The Victorian City: Images and realities* (2 vols., 1973), I, 340–5.
17. H. K. Hawson, *Sheffield: The growth of a city* (1968), 45, 135, 204, 216, 340; S. Pollard, *A. History of Labour in Sheffield* (1959), 101–2, 111, 183; A. W. Chapman, *The Story of a Modern University: The history of the University of Sheffield* (1955), 99–102, 174, 195, 277; *Sheffield Daily Telegraph*, 12 February 1917.
18. E. Richards, 'The industrial face of a great estate: Trentham and Lilleshall, 1780–1860', *EcHR*, 2nd ser., XXVII (1974); *idem*, 'The social and electoral influence of the Trentham interest, 1800–1860', *Midland History*, III (1975); F. Bealey, 'Municipal politics in Newcastle-under-Lyme, 1835–1872', *North Staffordshire Journal of Field Studies*, III (1963), 68.
19. E. J. D. Warrillow, *A Sociological History of Stoke-on-Trent* (1960), 157, 216, 351.
20. A. Bennett, *The Card* (1956 edn), 9, 97, 101–5, 113–18, 130; M. Drabble, *Arnold Bennett, a Biography* (1975), 159, 184; The Duke of Sutherland, *Looking Back: The autobiography of the Duke of Sutherland*, (1957), 45, 47; Millicent, Duchess of Sutherland, 'On the dangerous processes in the potting industry', in H. Owen (ed.), *The Staffordshire Potter* (1901).
21. T. J. Raybould, 'The Dudley estate: its rise and decline between 1774 and 1947' (Ph.D. thesis, University of Kent, 1970), 379–88.
22. G. Rickword and W. Gaskell, *Staffordshire Leaders: Social and political* (1907), 151–2.
23. C. Gill and A. Briggs, *The History of Birmingham* (2 vols., 1952), II, 190, F. W. H. Hackwood, *A History of West Bromwich* (1895), 60.
24. C. Sykes, *Nancy: The life of Lady Astor* (1972), 107–9, 187–200, 226, 307, 473; M. Collis, *Nancy Astor: An informal biography* (1960), 57, 127, 229–31.
25. A. Briggs, *Victorian Cities* (1958), 38.
26. Davies, *op. cit.*, 220; Owen, *History of Belfast*, 255–9.
27. F. M. L. Thompson, 'Land and politics in England in the nineteenth century', *TRHS*, fifth ser., XV (1965), 36–9; D. Martin, 'Land Reform', in P. Hollis (ed.), *Pressure From Without in Early Victorian England* (1974); Fraser, *Urban Politics*, 21–2, 122.
28. Richards, 'Social and electoral influence of the Trentham interest', 131–41.
29. Strain, *op. cit.*, 212–37; Thompson, 'Whigs and Liberals', 231–7.
30. T. J. Raybould, *The Economic Emergence of the Black Country: A study of the*

Dudley estate (1973), 118–20; A. Redford, *The History of Local Government in Manchester* (3 vols., 1939–40), I, 192–6, 223–4, II, 12, 92–4; R. Skidelsky, *Mosley* (1975), 30; Davies, *op. cit.*, 295; R. W. Sturgess, 'Landowners and mining and urban development in nineteenth-century Staffordshire', in J. T. Ward and R. G. Wilson (eds), *Land and Industry: The landed estate and the Industrial Revolution* (1971), 184, 188.

31. *Staffordshire Advertiser*, 2, 9, and 16 March, 1861.
32. *South Wales Daily News*, 10 October 1900.
33. G. Best, *Mid-Victorian Britain 1851–75* (1971), 239–53.
34. CW. MS. 7 D. D., 15 December 1863, 20 May 1868, 6 October 1873.
35. Quoted in W. L. Burn, *The Age of Equipoise: A study of the mid-Victorian generation* (1968), 309–10.
36. A. Arnold, *Free Land* (1880), 41.
37. Best, *op. cit.*, 242.
38. *PP*, 1888, XXII, SCTH, QQ. 3, 513, 7, 819.
39. Warrillow, *op. cit.*, 186; Bealey, *op. cit.*, 69; W. S. Childe Pemberton, *The Life of Lord Norton, 1814–1905* (1909), 248–9; Briggs, *Victorian Cities*, 65.
40. Daunton, *op. cit.*, 198; Brooke, *op. cit.*, 181; Hawson, *op. cit.*, 1–2.
41. *Western Mail*, 11 October 1900; *South Wales Daily News*, 15 October 1900; *Sheffield Telegraph*, 16 February 1943.
42. Kellet, *op. cit.* 150; D. Ward, 'The pre-urban cadester and the urban pattern in Leeds', *AAAG*, LII (1962).
43. T. H. S. Escott, *Social Transformations of the Victorian Age* (1897) 113; Anon., 'The citizenship of the British nobility', *Quarterly Review*, CLXXXIV (1896) 283–7. The first historian to notice this trend was Elie Halévy, *A History of the English People in the Nineteenth Century*, V, *Imperialism and the Rise of Labour 1895–1905* (1961), 22–3: 'It was significant that a very large number of municipal bodies had lately made a custom of choosing as their honorary president the bearer of some great name.'
44. C. Chamberlain, 'The growth of support for the Labour party in Britain', *British Journal of Sociology*, XXIV (1973), 481–6; Perkin, *op. cit.*, ch. x.
45. J. P. Cornford, 'The transformation of conservatism in the late nineteenth century', *VS*, VII (1963).
46. Briggs, *Victorian Cities*, 32; R. S. Ferguson, 'On the dignity of a mayor, or municipal insignia of office', *Transactions of the Lancashire and Cheshire Antiquarian Society*, XI (1894); A. C. Fox-Davies, *The Book of Public Arms: A complete encyclopaedia of all royal territorial, municipal, corporate, official and impersonal arms* (1894); H. R. H. Southam, *A Short Account of the Insignia and Plate of the Staffordshire Corporations* (1899); J. W. Tonks, 'Borough seals and civic maces', *Journal of the British Archaelogical Association*, new ser., II (1896); A. Service, *Edwardian Architecture: A handbook to building design in Britain, 1890–1914* (1977), 143–7.
47. A. L. Lowell, *The Government of England* (2 vols, 1908), II, 15; G. W. Jones, *Borough Politics: A study of the Wolverhampton town council, 1888–1964* (1969), 251.
48. Bennett, *The Card*, 9, 25.
49. For this paragraph, see *The Herald and Wednesbury Borough News*, 14 January 1899.
50. Thompson, 'Whigs and Liberals', 218.
51. Burn, *op. cit.*, 310
52. *Sheffield Daily Telegraph*, 6 and 7 October 1857; 21 and 26 February 1902.
53. *Ibid.*, 27 November and 7 December 1860; 12, 14, 15 and 16 February 1917.
54. *Staffordshire Advertiser*, 2, 9 and 16 June 1861; 24 September, 1 October 1892; *Liverpool Echo*, 22 April 1893; 15 and 17 June 1908.

55. Daunton, *op. cit.*, 198; Davies, *op. cit.*, vii–viii, 347.
56. Warillow, *op. cit.*, 217, 277; Churchill, *op. cit.*, 131; *Belfast Telegraph*, 28 June 1961; *Dudley Herald*, 23 May 1885; *Western Mail*, 10 October 1900.
57. Marquess of Bute to Miss Skene, 23 January 1891. Quoted in D. Hunter Blair, *John Patrick, third Marquess of Bute, K. T., A memoir* (1921), 174.
58. Anon, 'The citizenship of the British nobility', *Quarterly Review*, clxxxiv (1896), 288.
59. A. N. Shimmin, *The University of Leeds: The first half century* (1954), 17, 30, 36, 62, 67; S. Dumbell, *The University of Liverpool, 1903–53* (1953), 7, 36–7; H. B. Charlton, *Portrait of a University, 1851–1951* (1951), 139–40; Chapman, *op. cit.*, 99, 195; T. W. Moody and J. C. Beckett, *Queen's Belfast, 1845–1949: The History of a University* (2 vols., 1959), II, 482.
60. H. J. Hanham, *Elections and Party Management: Politics in the time of Gladstone and Disraeli* (1959), 80.
61. H. E. Meller, *Leisure and the Changing City, 1870–1914* (1976), 91–5; M. Sanderson, *The Universities and British Industry, 1850–1970* (1972), 71–3; J. L. Garvin and J. A. Amery, *The Life of Joseph Chamberlain* (6 vols., 1932–69), IV, ch. lxxxxiv; Briggs, *History of Birmingham*, 109–10.
62. Moody and Beckett, *op. cit.*, ii, 482, 536; Chapman, *op. cit.*, 277.
63. Sanderson, *op. cit.*, 81.
64. H. Perkin *The Origins of Modern English Society, 1780–1880* (1969), 436.
65. *Liverpool Echo*, 4 February 1948.
66. Jones, *op. cit.*, 252–4; J. M. Lee, *Social Leaders and Public Persons: A study of county government in Cheshire since 1888* (1963), 5–6.
67. Sykes, *op. cit.*, 415, 472.
68. Davies, *op. cit.*, 193–230.
69. Churchill, *op. cit.*, 137, 600–5; P. F. Clarke, *Lancashire and the New Liberalism* (1971), 75; *Liverpool Echo*, 4 February 1948.

3. THE HOLIDAY RESORTS: NEW TOWNS, NEW OPPORTUNITIES

1. T. H. S. Escott, *Society in the English Country House* (1907), 52.
2. H. Perkin, *The Age of the Railway* (1970), 224–6.
3. C. W. Chalklin, *The Provincial Towns of Georgian England: A study of the building process, 1740–1820* (1974), 76–7, 80.
4. R. G. Heape, *Buxton Under the Dukes of Devonshire* (1948), 28–30, 35; T. Marchington, 'The development of Buxton and Matlock since 1800' (M.A. thesis, University of London, 1961), 97–130; A. Savidge, *Royal Tunbridge Wells* (1975), 25–30, 53, 97, 114–15.
5. J. Lowerson and J. Myerscough, *Time to Spare in Victorian England* (1977), 41.
6. C. H. Bishop, *Folkestone: The story of a town* (1973), 80–4.
7. *Ibid.*, 118–20, 146.
8. A. C. Ellis, *A Historical Survey of Torquay* (1930), 272–9, 285–9, 361–5.
9. *Torquay Times*, 31 March 1883.
10. Ellis, *op. cit.*, 287–8.
11. D. S. Young, *A History of Bournemouth* (1970), 50–1, 60.
12. *Ibid.*, 73, 136–7, 142; H. Clunn, *Famous South Coast Pleasure Resorts* (1929), 172.
13. M. Russell-Cotes, *Home and Abroad: An autobiography of a Victorian* (2 vols., 1921), I, 130.
14. *Bournemouth Daily Echo*, 14 May 1928.
15. F. A. Bailey, *A History of Southport* (1955), 91–2, 131.

16. *Southport Guardian*, 1 December 1886; *Southport Visitor*, 7 September 1886; E. Bland, *Annals of Southport* (1888), 208–11, 218.
17. J. E. Jarratt, *Municipal Recollections: Southport, 1900–1930* (1932), 90–1.
18. R. Gurnham, 'The creation of Skegness as a resort town by the ninth earl of Scarbrough', *Lincolnshire History and Archaeology*, vii (1972), 63; J. A. Barrett, 'The seaside resort towns of England and Wales' (Ph.D. thesis, University of London, 1958), 50.
19. T. W. Beastall, *A North-Country Estate: The Lumleys and Saundersons as landowners, 1600–1900* (1975), 187, 189, 195.
20. W. Kime, *Skeggy! The Story of an East Coast Town* (1969), 73–4.
21. *Skegness Standard*, 7 March 1945.
22. L. J. Bartley, *The Story of Bexhill* (1971), 18–21.
23. *Ibid.*, 109, 122.
24. *Bexhill-on-Sea Observer*, 12 September 1907.
25. *Ibid.*, 18 December 1915.
26. H. Pelling, *Social Geography of British Elections, 1885–1910* (1967), 133, 167–8, 169–70, 278–9.
27. Clunn, *op. cit.*, 307; P. J. Aspinall, 'Speculative builders and the development of Cleethorpes, 1850–1900', *Lincolnshire History and Archaeology*, xi (1976), 43, 46.
28. Kime, *op. cit.*, 50.
29. A. L. Lowell, *The Government of England* (2 vols., 1908), ii, 145.
30. *Torquay Times*, 2 February 1883.
31. Bartley, *op. cit.*, 123.
32. *PP*, 1888, xxii, SCTH, QQ. 8,615, 8,639.
33. Jarratt, *op. cit.*, 90–1.
34. *North Wales Pioneer*, 20 September 1934.
35. Pelling, *op. cit.*, 136.
36. *The Times*, 15 May 1908.
37. *Ibid.*, 20 July 1948.
38. J. K. Walton, 'The social development of Blackpool, 1788–1914' (Ph.D. thesis, University of Lancaster, 1974), 22; H. J. Gayler, 'The coastal resorts of Essex: their growth and present-day function' (M.A. thesis, University of London, 1965), 124.
39. For a full list of mayors of Bournemouth between 1890 and 1955 see Young, *op. cit.*, 245–6.
40. Russell-Cotes, *op. cit.*, I, 87–8.
41. *Bexhill-on-Sea Observer*, 21 March 1908.
42. *Ibid.*, 12 November 1932.
43. Russell-Cotes, *op. cit.*, II, 67, 81–3.
44. *Ibid.*, ii, 113.
45. *Bexhill-on-Sea Observer*, 28 September 1907, 31 October 1908.
46. *Ibid.*, 16 November 1935.
47. Lowell, *op. cit.*, II, 15.
48. *North Wales Pioneer*, 20 September 1934.
49. Jarratt, *op. cit.*, 90.
50. *Bexhill-on-Sea Observer*, 10 October 1903.
51. *Southport Guardian*, 17 January 1923.
52. *Ibid.*, 20 May 1933.
53. *Folkestone Express*, 18 December 1901, 12 July 1902, 15 November 1902.
54. Bartley, *op. cit.*, 22.
55. *Bexhill-on-Sea Observer*, 4 July 1908, 8 August 1908.
56. *Ibid.*, 9 November 1935.
57. *Ibid.*, 12 December 1903.

58. The account in this and the subsequent paragraph is taken from the *Bexhill-on-Sea Observer*, 16 November 1907.
59. *Bexhill-on-Sea Observer*, 2 March 1918; *Skegness Standard*, 7 March 1945; *Folkestone Express*, 30 June 1968; Bartley, *op. cit.*, xvii.
60. *Folkestone Express*, 16 November 1901.
61. *Southport Guardian*, 20 January 1923.
62. *Bexhill-on-Sea Observer*, 12 September 1907, 5 September 1908.
63. *Ibid.*, 31 October 1908, 7 November 1908, 21 November 1908.
64. Ellis, *op. cit.*, 287–8.
65. Bartley, *op. cit.*, 23.
66. Bailey, *op. cit.*, 23, 217, 219.
67. *Skegness Standard*, 7 March 1945, 2 July 1969.
68. *Bexhill-on-Sea Observer*, 2 March 1918.
69. *Folkestone Express*, 16 November 1901.

4. INTRODUCTION: THE LANDOWNERS AND THE LAND, 1717–1810

1. F. Brett Young, *White Ladies* (1935), 216.
2. R. K. Dent, *Old and New Birmingham* (1880), 619; T. Anderton, *A Tale of One City* (1900), ch. viii.
3. *Edgbastonia*, May 1881, 1.
4. *Edgbaston Directory and Guide for 1853* (1853), 3.
5. *The Builder*, 27 November 1897, 440.
6. *T. P.'s Weekly*, 29 January 1904.
7. W. Barrow, 'The town and its industries', in J. H. Muirhead (ed.), *Birmingham Institutions* (1911), 47.
8. *Edgbaston Directory Guide for 1853*, 3.
9. Anderton, *op. cit.*, 90.
10. EEO MS., Release of the Manor of Edgbaston in the County of Warwick, 16 April 1717; BRL MS., 252,037, conveyance deed, 10 July 1717.
11. BRL MS., 252,058, partition deed, 23 December 1700; EEO MS., Release of the Manor, 16 April 1717.
12. For a fuller account of Sir Richard's ancestry, see S. Shaw, *The History and Antiquities of Staffordshire* (2 vols., 1798–1801), II, 188–90.
13. R. Sedgwick, *The History of Parliament: The House of Commons, 1715–1754* (2 vols., 1970), II, 73.
14. Shaw, *op. cit.*, II, 190.
15. Sedgwick, *op. cit.*, II, 73.
16. L. Namier and J. Brooke, *The History of Parliament: The House of Commons, 1754–1790* (3 vols., 1964), II, 522.
17. For the Calthorpe family, see C. W. C. Calthrop, *Notes on the Families of Calthorpe and Calthrop in the Counties of Norfolk and Lincolnshire* (1905), *passim*.
18. PRO, will of Henry, Lord Calthorpe, drawn up 29 July 1790, codicil 22 June 1797, proved 5 May 1798, 20.
19. EEO MS., John Snape, A Plan and Survey of the Parish of Edgbaston in the County of Warwickshire, belonging to Sir Henry Gough, Bart., and others, surveyed in the year 1787.
20. HROCal. MS., Box 35, John Harris, Observations for Lord Calthorpe's Correction, 1811.
21. EEO MS., Parcel 7, Harris to Calthorpe, 14 July 1819.
22. EEO MS., Parcel 7, Pearce to Harris, 26 September 1819; Harris to Calthorpe, 28 July 1819.

23. F. M. L. Thompson, *Hampstead: Building a borough, 1650–1964* (1974), 75–6; H. J. Dyos, *Victorian Suburb: A study of the growth of Camberwell* (1961), 40–1; M. A. Simpson, 'The West End of Glasgow, 1830–1914', in M. A. Simpson and T. H. Lloyd (eds.), *Middle-Class Housing in Britain* (1977), 47.
24. Gillott MS., will of Joseph Gillott, dated 6 February 1865, codicils, 10 October 1867, 9 May 1870.
25. EEO MS., Box 2, Thompson and Debenham to J. W. Whateley, 29 July 1872.
26. EEO MS., Box 7, Lord Calthorpe to G. Edwards, 24 June 1892.
27. 'Berm', 'Edgbaston Hall and Park', *Edgbastonia*, June 1883, 84.
28. F. M. L. Thompson, 'Hampstead, 1830–1914', in Simpson and Lloyd, *op. cit.*, 88.
29. J. R. Kellett, *The Impact of Railways on Victorian Cities* (1969), 349–50.
30. EEO MS., Box 6, Sir Henry Gough to Thomas Willetts, building lease, 28 January 1786.
31. Qutoed in Lord Calthorpe's Leasing Act (1869), 3–5.
32. R. A. Pelham, 'The Worcester and Birmingham canal', *University of Birmingham Historical Journal*, v (1955).
33. BRL MS., list of Proprietors of the Worcester and Birmingham Canal Navigation, 1 June 1798, 4; The Birmingham and Worcester Canal Act (1791), clauses 4, 5, 13.
34. C. W. Chalklin, *The Provincial Towns of Georgian England: A study of the building process, 1740–1820* (1974), 287.
35. HROCal. MS., Box 35, John Harris, Observations for Lord Calthorpe's Correction, 1811.
36. HROCal. MS. F/C/157, Harris to Calthorpe, 14 June 1813.

5. THE MAKING OF AN 'ARISTOCRATIC' SUBURB, 1810–1914

1. BBHS Annual Report, 1885.
2. *VCH* VII, 14.
3. *Wrightson and Webb's Directory of Birmingham* (1846), 185.
4. HROCal. MS., Box 35, Harris to Calthorpe, December 1823.
5. EEO MS., Box 1, Harris to the Hon. F. G. Calthorpe, May 1818.
6. C. Pye, *Description of Modern Birmingham* (1819), 190.
7. HROCal. MS. F/C/161, Harris to Calthorpe, 4 July 1814; BBHS MS., Committee Minute Book, 17 July 1829 to 20 June 1836, 29–30; EEO MS., Box 1, Harris to Calthorpe, 4 January 1833; *Kelly's Directory of Birmingham* (1894), 13.
8. HROCal. MS. F/C/161, Harris to Calthorpe, 4 July 1814.
9. HROCal. MS. F/C/1217, Harris to Calthorpe, 9 September 1830; T. Ragg, *Scenes and Sketches from Life and Nature* (1847), 130.
10. *Gentleman's Magazine*, xcv pt 1 (1825), 393.
11. J. Drake, *The Picture of Birmingham* (1831), 116.
12. J. R. Kellett, *The Impact of Railways on Victorian Cities* (1969), 132.
13. Pye, *op. cit.*, 191; W. Hutton, *History of Birmingham* (1806), 457–8.
14. Quoted in C. Gill and A. Briggs, *The History of Birmingham* (2 vols., 1952), I, 125.
15. HROCal. MS., Box 35, Harris to Calthorpe, 23 October 1812; EEO MS., Box 5, Calthorpe to Harris, 3 July 1828; EEO MS. Box 4, Calthorpe to Harris, 13 June 1831.
16. *VCH* VII, 14, 126, 128, 173.
17. A. Briggs, *Victorian Cities* (1968), 184.
18. *VCH* VII, 14.

19. EEO MS., Box 8, tenders for new Edgbaston Estate Office, 1864.
20. *VCH* VII, 13.
21. W. Southall, *Popular Guide to the Botanical Gardens, Edgbaston* (1886), 2.
22. *Edgbastonia*, May 1881, 14–15.
23. 'Berm', in *Edgbastonia*, June 1883, 84.
24. EEO MS., Box 12, plan of Lord Calthorpe's Estate, referred to in the agreement of 20 December 1872; WVH MS. Edgbaston Estate Vesting Deed, 24 February 1926, map; EEO MS. Box 8, map dated 29 July 1880.
25. J. Parry Lewis, *Building Cycles and Britain's Growth* (1965), 85–6, 91–4, 136–7.
26. Gill and Briggs, *op. cit.*, II, 25–6, 29; Briggs, *Victorian Cities*, 229–30.
27. EEO MS., Letter Book I, G. Edwards to Calthorpe, 8 May 1886.
28. EEO MS., Box 7, Calthorpe to Davies, 16 February 1899.
29. EEO MS., File K/5, Davies to the Hon. Walter G.-Calthorpe, 16 July 1900.
30. *PP*, 1888, XXII, SCTH Q. 1,766.
31. C. A. Vince, *The History of Birmingham Corporation*, III (1902), 61.
32. *VCH* VII, 14.
33. EEO MS., Letter Book III, Davies to Calthorpe, 10 August 1895, 1 November 1895, 16 March 1896, 30 July 1898.
34. EEO MS., File K/5, Davies to Calthorpe, 1 June 1901; Letter Book IV, Balden to Calthorpe, 22 September 1905.
35. HROCal. MS., Box 30, Davies to Calthorpe, 27 April 1898.
36. Kellett, *op. cit.*, 363.
37. *VCH* VII 18; Gill and Briggs, *op. cit.*, II, 139–48.
38. *Birmingham Daily Post*, Greater Birmingham Supplement, 22 May 1911, 2.
39. EEO MS., Letter Book I, G. EDWARDS TO CALTHORPE, 24 NOVEMBER, 1883.
40. *Birmingham Daily Post*, Greater Birmingham Supplement, 22 May 1911, 2.
41. Min. HCSC on Harborne Railway Bill, 14 May 1866, 6.
42. *Birmingham Daily Mail*, 26 November 1903. Quoted in Gill and Briggs, *op. cit.*, II, 140.
43. EEO MS., Birmingham Corporation Bill, Evidence, 13 March 1907, 61.
44. EEO MS., Letter Book IV, Balden to Calthorpe, 10 December 1904.
45. EEO MS., Birmingham Corporation Bill, Evidence, 7 March 1907, 28.

6. THE SUPERINTENDENCE OF DEVELOPMENT, 1810–1914

1. EEO MS., Box 1, G. Edwards, SCTH draft evidence, 1888, 5.
2. T. Ragg, *Scenes and Sketches from Life and Nature* (1847), 153.
3. *Edgbastonia Directory for 1883* (1883), 41.
4. W. Barrow, 'The town and its industries', in J. H. Muirhead (ed.), *Birmingham Institutions* (1911), 47.
5. D. J. Olsen, *Town Planning in London in the Eighteenth and Nineteenth Centuries* (1964), 214–15.
6. C. W. Chalklin, *The Provincial Towns of Georgian England: A study of the building process, 1740–1820* (1974), 83.
7. Ragg, *op. cit.*, 110, 154.
8. C. Gill and A. Briggs, *The History of Birmingham* (2 vols., 1952) I, 122–3; Chalklin, *op. cit.*, 82–9.
9. BRL MS., 270,065, agreement between Sir Thomas Gooch and the proprietors of the Birmingham and Warwick Canal, 29 July 1795.
10. Gill and Briggs, *op. cit.*, I, 123–4.
11. BRL MS., 414,908, valuation of the Colmore Estate, 1826, 1, 2, 13, 20.

12. EEO MS., Box 1, G. Edwards, SCTH draft evidence, 1888, 2.
13. EEO MS., Box 1, J. Edwards to Town Clerk, 15 March 1856; Lease Book VII, précis of conveyance, 1 October, 1900; Lease Book VIII, précis of conveyance, 7 January 1908.
14. D. Cannadine, 'The aristocracy and the towns in the nineteenth century: A case study of the Calthorpes and Birmingham, 1807–1910' (D.Phil. thesis, University of Oxford, 1975), 249.
15. Ragg, *op. cit.*, 129; *Birmingham Weekly Post*, 6 June 1891.
16. EEO MS., Letter Book IV, Davies to A. G. Latham, 23 April 1901.
17. EEO MS., Box 6, building lease granted to Thomas Willetts, 28 January 1786.
18. EEO MS., Box 6, copy of building lease to Miss Minors 'agreed by Lord Calthorpe as the standard form from which the building leases are to be in future prepared', 3 August 1815.
19. EEO MS., Minute Book VI, 8 February 1899, 5 April 1901.
20. EEO MS., Letter Book, 1899–1902, Davies to G. Townsend, 25 April 1902.
21. EEO MS., Letter Book, 1899–1902, Davies to R. Cartwright, 9 May 1901; Davies to F. W. Amphlet, 2 January 1902.
22. EEO MS., Box 6, building lease granted to Thomas Clowes, 25 March 1828.
23. EEO MS., Minute Book V, unnamed newspaper cutting, 6 October 1892.
24. Cannadine, *op. cit.*, 265.
25. *Birmingham Gazette*, 20 June 1874; EEO MS., Box 5, Whateley, Milward and Co. to J. Edwards, 6 June 1874.
26. EEO MS., Box 6, J. Edwards to Chairman of Parks Committee, 2 April 1870; Box 2, G. Edwards to Whateley, Milward and Co., 24 February 1879.
27. *Edgbastonia Directory for 1883*, 41.
28. EEO MS., Box 8, J. Edwards to W. Rodgers, 8 February 1869.
29. *VCH*, VII, 13–14.
30. Borough of Birmingham, *Report of Artisan's Dwellings Inquiry Committee* (1884), 40.
31. *Ibid.*, 48; J. R. Kellett, *The Impact of Railways on Victorian Cities* (1969), 133.
32. R. Woods, 'Mortality and sanitary conditions in the "Best-governed city in the world" – Birmingham, 1870–1910', *JHG*, IV (1978), 49–55.
33. J. T. Bunce, *The History of the Corporation of Birmingham*, II (1885), 118.
34. D. J. Olsen, *The Growth of Victorian London* (1976), 248.
35. EEO MS., Birmingham Corporation Bill, Evidence, 8 March 1907, 77; 11 March 1907, 117.
36. *Ibid.*, 7 March 1907, 13.

7. URBAN REVENUE AND ARISTOCRATIC AGGRANDISEMENT, 1810–93

1. HROCal. MS., Box 25, Acle marsh lettings, 1905.
2. EEO MS., Box 2, Blakeney sale catalogue, 1911.
3. HROCal. MS., Box 30, Harris' report on Elvetham, 6 April 1825.
4. HROCal. MS. F/C/733, Harris to Calthorpe, 6 September 1823.
5. HROCal. MS., Box 35, rents received 1809–10.
6. F. H. W. Sheppard (ed.), *The Survey of London*, XXIV (1952), 57.
7. HROCal. MS., Box 35, New River Company to Calthorpe, 2 June 1874.
8. HROCal. MS., Box 35, rents received 1809–10, list of expenditure, September 1810 to March 1812.
9. HROCal. MS. F/C/1207, Lord Calthorpe's subscriptions, February to June 1829.

10. Lord Calthorpe's Building Act (1814); Gray's Inn Paving Act (1814).
11. HROCal. MS. F/C/690, Harris to Calthorpe, 19 June 1823.
12. HROCal. MS., Box 29, T. Cubitt's proposals and comments by James Spiller, 13 August 1822; H. Hobhouse, *Thomas Cubitt: Master builder* (1971), 20–35.
13. HROCal. MS., Box 29, London Estate Accounts.
14. HROCal. MS., Box 30, Harris's report, 6 April 1825.
15. Elvetham Rental Book, 1819–36, in personal possession of Sir Richard A.-G.-Calthorpe.
16. HROCal. MS., Box 35, report on Lord Calthorpe's estates, August to October 1823, 10–11.
17. EEO MS., Box 5, summary of Edgbaston accounts to 31 December 1822.
18. HROCal. MS., Box 32, Calthorpe to Harris, 21 December 1821; EEO MS., File 41/5, account of Lord Calthorpe's business, September 1825.
19. EEO MS., Box 4, I, Spooner to Calthorpe, December 1825.
20. HRO Cal. MS., Box 30, Edgbaston accounts, 1826; EEO MS., Box 4, Calthorpe to Harris, 20 December 1825.
21. EEO MS., Box 5, J. Whorral to Harris, 18 April 1828.
22. HROCal. MS., Box 35, Harris to Calthorpe, 30 July 1832.
23. HROCal. MS., Box 35, report on Lord Calthorpe's estates, August-October 1823, 11.
24. EEO MS., Parcel 6, disentailing agreement, 1 July 1853; WVH MS. D/25/6, settlement of estates of Lord Calthorpe, 18 July 1864.
25. EEO MS., Box 11, Perry Hall Estates deed of settlement, 25 April 1848.
26. EEO MS., Box 11, Chancery Papers, 30 April 1870.
27. EEO MS., Parcel 7, Harris to Pearce, 9 October 1819.
28. EEO MS., Box 2, Thompson and Debenham to J. W. Whateley, 29 July 1872.
29. HROCal. MS., Box 27, C. Spooner to Calthorpe, 10 May 1859.
30. EEO MS., File 43/2, Lord Calthorpe's Hampshire Estate: schedule of purchases, 1868–93.
31. EEO MS., Minute Book v, records of sale of Newmarket stud farm, 11 and 12 October 1893.
32. N. Pevsner and D. Lloyd, *The Buildings of England: Hampshire and the Isle of Wight* (1967), 51, 210–11, 766; M. Girouard, *The Victorian Country House* (1971), 201; *idem*, 'Acrobatic Gothic', *Country Life*, cxlvii (1970).
33. EEO MS., Letter Book i, G. Edwards to Calthorpe, 16 June 1882.
34. EEO MS., Letter Book i, G. Edwards to Calthorpe, 30 June 1885; File K/3, G. Edwards to the Hon. Augustus G.-Calthorpe, 23 January 1888.
35. J. R. Kellett, *The Impact of Railways on Victorian Cities* (1969), 249–50; *Pall Mall Gazette*, 10 October 1888, EEO MS., Letter Book ii, G. Edwards to Chinnock and Co., 3 October 1892.
36. EEO MS., Letter Book i, notice to pay off mortgages, 25 June 1888.
37. EEO MS., Letter Book ii, G. Edwards to Calthorpe, 14 May 1892. For other examples of aristocratic investment in equities at this time, see F. M. L. Thompson, *English Landed Society in the Nineteenth Century* (1963), 306–8.
38. EEO MS., Box 2, correspondence between Calthorpe, G. Edwards and Milward, January to March 1891.
39. EEO MS., Box 7, Calthorpe to G. Edwards, 22 May 1891.
40. EEO MS., Box 7, Calthorpe to G. Edwards, 24 June 1892.

8. PATTERNS OF MANAGEMENT AND PROBLEMS OF POLICY, 1810–93

1. For a fuller account of the public life of the third Lord Calthorpe see D. Cannadine, 'The aristocracy and the towns in the nineteenth century: a case study of the Calthorpes and Birmingham, 1807–1910' (D.Phil. thesis, University of Oxford, 1975), ch. i.
2. R. Coupland, *Wilberforce: A narrative* (1923), 374.
3. *Wrightson's Triennial Directory of Birmingham* (1823), 63; *Wrightson's Triennial Directory of Birmingham* (1825), 66.
4. EEO MS., Box 1, Harris to Calthorpe, 6 April 1822; F. M. L. Thompson, *English Landed Society in the Nineteenth Century* (1963), 157.
5. EEO MS., Box 4, Calthorpe to Harris, 27 November 1813.
6. EEO MS., Box 4, Calthorpe to Harris, 3 February 1814.
7. HROCal. MS., Box 36, Lord Calthorpe's indebtedness to John Harris, 21 July 1828.
8. Thompson, *op. cit.*, 175.
9. HROCal. MS. F/C/690, Harris to Calthorpe, 19 June 1823; EEO MS., Box 4, Calthorpe to Harris, 19 August 1811.
10. H. Hobhouse, *Thomas Cubitt: Master builder* (1971), 73.
11. HROCal. MS. F/C/720, Reed to Calthorpe, 22 August 1823.
12. EEO MS., Box 1, Harris to Calthorpe, 17 September 1823.
13. HROCal. MS. F/C/777, Harris to Calthorpe, 10 November 1823.
14. HROCal. MS. F/C/733, Harris, report on Culford, 6 September 1823.
15. EEO MS., Box 5, Harris to Calthorpe, 17 September 1823; HROCal. MS. F/C/778, Harris to Calthorpe, 13 November 1823; EEO MS., Box 4, Calthorpe to Harris, 27 February 1824.
16. HROCal. MS. F/C/784, Harris to Hall and Thompson, 2 December 1823; EEO MS., Box 4, Harris, rough report, 15 February 1824.
17. HROCal. MS. F/C/807, R. de Beauvoir to Calthorpe, 5 March 1824.
18. E. Richards, 'The industrial face of a great estate: Trentham and Lilleshall, 1780–1860', *EcHR*, 2nd ser., xxvii (1974), 414, 425–9.
19. EEO MS., Box 4, Calthorpe to Harris, 1 August 1825.
20. EEO MS., Box 1, Harris to Calthorpe, 1 March 1822.
21. EEO MS., File 41/15, Edgbaston business reports, 1830–3.
22. HROCal. MS., Box 35, Harris to Calthorpe, 21 December 1825.
23. EEO MS., Box 5, Calthorpe to Yates, 25 September 1843, 4 July 1846.
24. PRO, will of fifth Lord Calthorpe, proved 24 August 1893, 2.
25. *The Times*, 27 June 1893.
26. *Edgbastonia*, August 1893, 116; *The Times*, 27 June 1893.
27. *Birmingham Daily Mail*, 14 February 1911, obituary notice.
28. EEO MS., File K/3, G. Edwards to Calthorpe, 25 January 1895.
29. EEO MS., Box 7, Calthorpe to G. Edwards, 25 November 1893; HROCal. MS., Box 30, G. Edwards to Calthorpe, 27 November 1893.
30. *Birmingham Daily Post*, 19 December 1874.
31. *Birmingham Daily Mail*, 18 September 1903.
32. EEO MS., Box 2, J. W. Whateley to the Hon. Augustus G.-Calthorpe, 18 August 1868.
33. EEO MS., Box 2, transcript of hearing in Court of Chancery, 22 April 1869, Vice Chancellor James' judgment.
34. Quoted in Lord Calthorpe's Leasing Act (1869), 5.
35. *Ibid.*, 23.
36. EEO MS., Box 11, draft affidavit of Mr Whateley, 2–3.

37. EEO MS., Box 11, draft affidavit of Mr J. Edwards, 2–3.
38. EEO MS., Box 11, Vice Chancellor Malins, order on petition, 24 March 1869, 2–3.
39. EEO MS., Box 11, draft affidavit of Mr Whateley, 2.
40. HROCal. MS., Box 33, Calthorpe to Soden, 19 September 1879; EEO MS., Box 2, Calthorpe to Soden, 19 September 1878; Calthorpe to Milward, 21 September 1878.
41. *Edgbastonia*, August 1893, 113.
42. EEO MS., Box 11, G. Whateley to Dorrington and Co., 26 May 1869.
43. EEO MS., Box 2, Chinnock to Milward, 13 March 1891.
44. EEO MS., Box 7, Calthorpe to G. Edwards, 19 June 1888.
45. EEO MS., Letter Book I, G. Edwards to C. G. Wray, 11 May 1891.
46. EEO MS., Box 7, Calthorpe to G. Edwards, 21 November 1888.
47. EEO MS., Box 7, Calthorpe to G. Edwards, 9 May 1893.
48. EEO MS., File 43/2, Calthorpe to G. Edwards, 31 May 1893.
49. EEO MS., Box 7, Calthorpe to G. Edwards, 24 June 1892.

9. THE CALTHORPES AND BIRMINGHAM, 1810–68: A 'CONSERVATIVE INTEREST' EXAMINED

1. EEO MS., account books.
2. C. Gill and A. Briggs, *The History of Birmingham* (2 vols., 1952), I, 157–99; *VCH* VII 9.
3. HROCal. MS. F/C/161, Harris to Calthorpe, 4 July 1814; R. K. Dent, *Old and New Birmingham* (1880), 366.
4. HROCal. MS. F/C/1202, F. Darwall to Calthorpe, 24 July 1829.
5. BBHS MS. Committee Minute Book, 17 July 1829 to 20 June 1836, 8–9; J. A. Langford, *A Century of Birmingham Life* (2 vols., 1868), II, 481, 189–90.
6. HROCal. MS. F/C/1217, Harris to Calthorpe, 9 September 1830.
7. R. J. Morris, 'The organization and aims of the principal secular voluntary societies of the Leeds middle class, 1830–1851' (D.Phil. thesis, University of Oxford, 1970), 393–4.
8. BBHS MS. Committee Minute Book, 17 July 1829 to 20 June 1836, 30.
9. EEO MS., Parcel 5, E. Burn to Calthorpe, 13 July 1822; HROCal. MS. F/C/330, W. Spooner to Calthorpe, 26 September 1821; EEO MS., Box 1, Harris to Calthorpe, 3 December 1827.
10. EEO MS., Box 5, Calthorpe to Dr Davies, 24 August 1828; Calthorpe to Harris, 18 November 1828.
11. A. Briggs, 'The background of the parliamentary reform movement in three English cities (1830–2)', *Cambridge Historical Journal*, x (1951), 295, n. 8; *VCH* VII, 290.
12. Langford, *op. cit.*, II, 436; *VCH* VII, 291; HROCal. MS. F/C/256, J. Bedford to Calthorpe, 9 November 1820.
13. For full documentation, see D. Cannadine, 'The Calthorpe family and Birmingham, 1810–1910: a "conservative interest" examined', *HJ*, XVIII (1975), 734.
14. *Hansard*, new ser., 1821, IV, 350, 360; *ibid.*, 1830, XXIV, 1131–2; *Hansard*, third ser., 1831, II, 547–8.
15. *Hansard*, new ser., 1826, XIV, 1146; *ibid.*, 1820, I, 388.
16. For an edited version of their correspondence, see D. Cannadine, 'Economy, society and parliamentary reform, 1830–33: Birmingham evidence and Westminster reaction', *Bulletin of the Institute of Historical Research*, LII (1979).

17. HROCal. MS., Box 30, J. Phipson to Calthorpe, 13 October 1826.
18. EEO MS., Box 1, Calthorpe to Harris, 2 March 1831.
19. *Hansard*, third ser., 1832, xii, 456.
20. Langford, *op. cit.*, II, 546.
21. *Ibid.*, II, 571, 581.
22. Dent, *op. cit.*, 451–2; Gill and Briggs, *op. cit.*, I, 218.
23. Dent, *op. cit.*, 452.
24. D. Fraser, *Urban Politics in Victorian England*, (1976), 43–7; Langford, *op. cit.*, II, 571.
25. Gill and Briggs, *op. cit.*, I, 255; J. A. Langford, *Modern Birmingham and its Institutions* (2 vols., 1873–7), II, 269–70.
26. Langford, *Birmingham Life*, II, 580.
27. D. E. H. Mole, 'The Church of England and society in Birmingham c.1830–1866' (Ph.D. thesis, University of Cambridge, 1961), 40–1.
28. BBHS, *A Brief Summary of its History, its Finances and its Present Position* (1885), 3–5; Langford, *Modern Birmingham*, II, 176; BGH MS., Annual Report, 1844–5.
29. Langford, *Birmingham Life*, II, 516.
30. EEO MS., Box 1, Harris to Calthorpe, 4 January 1833.
31. Gill and Briggs, *op. cit.*, i, 319–62.
32. EEO MS., account books, Lord Calthorpe's subscriptions, 1851–2; Box 8, Perry subscriptions, 1860.
33. EEO MS., Box 4, memorial to Lord Calthorpe, 3 December 1851.
34. EEO MS., Parcel 3, address from the inhabitants of Birmingham and others to the Rt Hon. the Lord Calthorpe, 1862.
35. Cannadine, 'The Calthorpe family and Birmingham', 741.
36. *Hansard*, third ser., 1863, CLXIX, 66–73.
37. Gill and Briggs, *op. cit.*, I, 274–9, 410–36; A. Briggs, *Victorian Cities* (1968), 209–13.
38. E. P. Hennock, *Fit and Proper Persons: Ideal and reality in nineteenth-century urban government* (1973), 65.
39. Briggs, *Victorian Cities*, 54–5.
40. Mole, *op. cit.*, 205–7.
41. T. Ragg, *Scenes and Sketches from Life and Nature* (1847), 128, 130.
42. BBHS, *Brief Summary*, 6; BRL MS., H. J. Everson, 'Miscellaneous notes for a history of Edgbaston' (n.d.), 59, 98.
43. Min. HC SC on Birmingham Improvement Bill, 10 May 1861, 27.
44. Langford, *Modern Birmingham*, I, 411; II, 206; Mole, *op. cit.*, 51–3.
45. FGSKE MS., Register of Meetings called and held, and by whom attended, 1797–1878, 17–9; BGH MS., Annual reports, 1845–61; R. E. Waterhouse, *The Birmingham and Midland Institute 1854–1954* (1954), 183.
46. FGSKE MS., Register of Meetings, 25 March 1847 to 31 December 1863.
47. BGH MS., Board of Governors Minute Books, 1844–61.
48. Gill and Briggs, *op. cit.*, I, 415.
49. Dent, *op. cit.*, 504.
50. *Birmingham Journal*, 3 June 1857.
51. Langford, *Modern Birmingham*, I, 428.
52. Mole, *op. cit.*, 64–8.
53. *Birmingham Daily Post*, 19 December 1874.
54. J. H. Plumb, *The Growth of Political Stability in England, 1675–1725* (1969), 10.
55. FGSKE MS., Governors Order Book, 1862–6, 318; BGH MS., Board of Governors Minute Books, 1861–8.

10. FINANCIAL PROBLEMS AND MANAGERIAL DIFFICULTIES, *c*.1880–1922

1. *Birmingham Daily Gazette*, 13 February 1896; J. Bateman, *The Great Landowners of Great Britain and Ireland* (1883), 72. See also W. L. Burn, *The Age of Equipoise: A study of the mid-Victorian generation* (1964), 308.
2. EEO MS., Letter Book II, G. Edwards to Calthorpe, 1 December 1893.
3. F. M. L. Thompson, *English Landed Society in the Nineteenth Century* (1963), 291.
4. EEO MS., Letter Book II, G. Edwards to Calthorpe, 1 December 1893.
5. HROCal. MS., Box 18, valuation of property at Acle belonging to Lord Calthorpe, 23 September 1878; report to Mr T. S. Fallows, 15 June 1885.
6. HROCal. MS., Box 25, E. R. Waters to Calthorpe, 10 September 1907.
7. *Birmingham Daily Post*, 23 July 1910.
8. EEO MS., Letter Book II, G. Edwards to Calthorpe, 14 October 1893.
9. *Hants. and Berks. Gazette*, 30 July 1910.
10. EEO MS., Box 7, F. P. Lightfoot to Balden, 22 January 1908.
11. EEO MS., Box 2, Davies's application to be surveyor to G.W.R. 17 May 1892
12. EEO MS., Letter Book IV, Balden to Calthorpe, 21 January 1907.
13. EEO MS., Box 7, Calthorpe to Balden, 15 November 1909; Letter Book V, Balden to Lady Calthorpe, 23 July 1910.
14. EEO MS., File 43/2, Calthorpe to G. Edwards, 11 January 1895.
15. EEO MS., Box 7, Calthorpe to Davies, 24 March 1902, 21 June 1902.
16. *Birmingham Daily Mail*, 18 September 1903.
17. EEO MS., Letter Book, 1899–1902, Davies to Calthorpe, 22 June 1902; Box 7, Calthorpe to Davies, 23 June 1902.
18. EEO MS., Letter Book, 1899–1902, Davies to Calthorpe, 22 June 1902.
19. EEO MS., Box 7, Calthorpe to Davies, 4 September 1895.
20. EEO MS., Box 2, Calthorpe to C. F. Crowder, 3 August 1900.
21. EEO MS., Letter Book V, Balden to Lady Calthorpe, 23 July 1910.
22. HROCal. MS., Box 25, Waters to Calthorpe, 16 December 1908.
23. *Hants. and Berks. Gazette*, 30 July 1910.
24. WVH MS. D/76/3, resettlement deed, 6 March 1907.
25. BRL MS. 313,338 and 350,629; Perry sale catalogue, 1 February 1923, 14 and 15 March 1928.
26. EEO MS., Letter Book VI, Balden to F. A.-G.-Calthorpe, 22 February 1916, 24 July 1917.
27. EEO MS., Box 7, the Hon. Rachel A.-G.-Calthorpe to Balden, 15 April 1917.
28. EEO MS., Box 7, F. Lloyd-Anstruther to Balden, 14 August 1910.
29. EEO MS., Box 1, G. Edwards, SCTH, draft evidence, 1888, 4–5.
30. WVH MS. D/80/8, succession duty account, Edgbaston Estate.
31. HROCal. MS., Box 30, G. Edwards to Calthorpe, 30 April 1897.
32. Min. HCSC on Birmingham Improvement Bill, 16 April 1912, 3, 7.
33. WVH MS. D/80/8, succession duty account, Edgbaston Estate.
34. WVH MS. D/80/8, London Estate, lists of leases falling in.
35. EEO MS., Letter Book IV, Balden to Calthorpe, 25 April 1904; Box 8, Griffith, Keiling and Sherwood to Balden, 17 June 1912.
36. EEO MS., Minute Book VII, 16 May 1914, 25 May 1914.
37. *Birmingham Daily Mail*, 28 May 1914.
38. *Birmingham Daily Post*, 26 May 1914.
39. EEO MS., Box 9, the Bishop of Birmingham to the Hon. Mrs A.-G.-Calthorpe, 4 June 1914.

40. *Birmingham Daily Mail*, 12 June 1914.
41. EEO MS., Monthly Minutes, 8 September 1914.
42. EEO MS., Box 7, Calthorpe to Balden, 21 May 1909.
43. WVH MS., capital account ledgers, 1910–14, 1917–21.
44. WVH MS. D/76/3, resettlement deed, 6 March 1907; EEO MS., Letter Book v, Balden to F. Lloyd-Anstruther, 15 August 1910.
45. WVH MS. D/24/2, mortgage deed, 13 June 1911.
46. HROCal. MS., Box 27, Waters to F. A.-G.-Calthorpe, 25 January 1911, 8 February 1911.
47. WVH MS. D/26/1, Elvetham Estate: improvements and substantial repairs during the years 1911–4.
48. HROCal. MS., Box 27, Newman to Waters, 21 February 1911.
49. Thompson, *op. cit.*, 321–6.
50. WVH MS.D/76/3, resettlement deed, 6 March 1907, clause 18.
51. EEO MS., Letter Book vi, Balden to F. A.-G.-Calthorpe, 4 June 1918.
52. EEO MS., Box 6, sale catalogue of 'outlying parts of the Edgbaston Estate', for auction on 20 June 1918.
53. EEO MS., Box 7, F. A.-G.-Calthorpe to Balden, 7 March 1922.
54. EEO MS., Box 1, Guy Heaton to F. A.-G.-Calthorpe, 9 January 1930.

11. EXTERNAL THREATS AND INTERNAL WEAKNESSES, *c.* 1870–1914

1. *VCH* VII, 41.
2. EEO MS., Box 4, Calthorpe to Harris, 7 January 1825.
3. Harris to Calthorpe, 26 January 1825, quoted in *Chartered Surveyor*, lv (1973), 340.
4. EEO MS., Box 4, Calthorpe to Harris, 28 January 1825.
5. EEO MS., Box 11, J. Edwards to R. H. Milward, 17 May 1879.
6. EEO MS., File 40/14, the Hon. F. H. W. G.-Calthorpe to Whateley and Co., 2 January 1866.
7. EEO MS., File 40/14 heads of agreement between the promoters of the railway, Lord Calthorpe and his lessees, 29 March, 1866.
8. EEO MS., File 40/14, J. Edwards to G. Whateley, 29 September 1869; *VCH* VII, 13, 40.
9. EEO MS., Box 12, J. Edwards, report on proposed Birmingham and West Suburban Railway, 9 August 1870; second report on proposed Birmingham and West Suburban Railway, 24 December 1870.
10. EEO MS., Box 12, Ryland and Martineau to Whateley and Whateley, 12 January 1871.
11. EEO MS., Box 12, Lord Calthorpe's petition against the Birmingham and West Suburban Railway Bill, March 1871.
12. EEO MS., Box 12, agreement signed by J. Edwards and H. Wiggin on behalf of Lord Calthorpe and the Birmingham and West Suburban Railway.
13. Midland Railway (Additional Powers) Act (1875), clause 42.
14. EEO MS., Box 12, Milward to J. Edwards, 4 February 1876.
15. EEO MS., Box 12, Milward to G. Edwards, 27 January 1879.
16. EEO MS., Box 12, Calthorpe to Milward, 20, 27 February 1879.
17. EEO MS., Box 6, Lord Calthorpe's petition, February 1879.
18. Midland Railway (Additional Powers) Act (1879), clause 9.
19. Min. HCSC on Midland Railway (Additional Powers) Bill, 19 June 1879, 2.
20. Midland Railway (Additional Powers) Act (1881), clause 18.

21. EEO MS., Letter Book 1899–1902, Davies to Manager, National Telephone Co., 16 March 1900.
22. EEO MS., Minute Book vii, press cutting, 9 October 1913.
23. C. Gill and A. Briggs, *The History of Birmingham* (2 vols., 1952), II, 93.
24. EEO MS., File K/5, Davies to Calthorpe, 20 November 1900. In 1904, a tramway was constructed to Cotteridge, via the Pershore Road, but it trespassed on so small a part of the estate that no objection was offered.
25. EEO MS., Box 2, Calthorpe to Milward, 1 January 1874.
26. EEO MS., Box 7, Calthorpe to G. Edwards, 24 December 1885.
27. EEO MS., File K/5, Davies to Calthorpe, 15 March 1901.
28. EEO MS., Box 7, Calthorpe to Davies, 1 November 1901.
29. EEO MS., Box 7, Calthorpe to Davies, 25 and 28 November 1901.
30. EEO MS., File K/5, Davies to Calthorpe, 27 December 1901.
31. EEO MS., Letter Book iv, Balden to Calthorpe, 15 October 1904.
32. EEO MS., Letter Book iv, Balden to Calthorpe, 17 October 1906.
33. EEO MS., Letter Book iv, Balden to Calthorpe, 6 December 1906.
34. EEO MS., Box 7, Calthorpe to Balden, 8 December 1906.
35. EEO MS., Letter Book iv, Balden to Calthorpe, 19 December 1906.
36. EEO MS., Birmingham Corporation Bill, Evidence, 7–13 March 1907.
37. *Ibid.*, 13 March 1907, 69.
38. EEO MS., Letter Book iv, Balden to Calthorpe, 2 July 1907.
39. EEO MS., Birmingham Corporation Bill, Evidence, 13 March 1907, 61.
40. D. Cannadine, 'The aristocracy and the towns in the nineteenth century: a case study of the Calthorpes and Birmingham, 1807–1910' (D.Phil. thesis, University of Oxford, 1975), 325–9.
41. EEO MS., Minute Book vii, 4 April 1910.
42. *Birmingham Daily Post*, 24 July, 5 October, 27 and 30 November, 1911.
43. EEO MS., Letter Book v, Balden to F. A.-G-Calthorpe, 11 December 1911, 28 February 1912.
44. EEO MS., Letter Book v, Balden to Calthorpe, 21 April 1910.
45. *Birmingham Daily Post*, 29 November 1911.
46. *Birmingham Daily Mail*, 29 November 1911.
47. *Birmingham Daily Post*, 13 October 1911.
48. *Ibid.*, 30 November 1911.
49. *Ibid.*, 17 April 1912.
50. Min. HCSC on Birmingham Corporation Bill, 16 April 1912, 3; 17 April 1912, 78, 86–7.
51. *Ibid.*, 16 April 1912, 78, 86–7.
52. *Birmingham Daily Post*, 20 April 1912.
53. EEO MS., Letter Book v, Balden to the Hon. Mrs A.-G.-Calthorpe, 6 July 1912.
54. EEO MS., Box 7, F. A. G. Calthorpe to Balden, 12 July 1912.
55. *Birmingham Daily Post*, 2 October 1912.
56. *Ibid.*, 6 July 1912.
57. D. Cannadine, 'Victorian cities: how different?', *Social History*, ii (1977), 466.

12. THE CALTHORPES AND BIRMINGHAM, 1868–1914: A 'CONSERVATIVE INTEREST' IN DECLINE

1. A. Briggs, *Victorian Cities* (1968), 198; D. E. H Mole, 'The Church of England and society in Birmingham *c*. 1830–1866' (Ph.D. thesis, University of Cambridge, 1961), 318–19.

2. EEO MS., Box 7, Calthorpe to J. Edwards, 9 January 1885, 7 November 1886.
3. *Birmingham Daily Gazette*, 1 October 1862.
4. EEO MS., Box 6, Whateley and Whateley to Town Clerk, 23 May 1870; *The Town Crier*, September 1870.
5. *Birmingham Daily Gazette*, 5 July, 1870.
6. *Ibid.*, 21 September 1870.
7. *The Town Crier*, September 1870.
8. EEO MS., Box 6, J. Edwards to Chairman, Baths and Parks Committee, 10 January 1871.
9. E. P. Hennock, *Fit and Proper Persons: Ideal and reality in nineteenth-century urban government* (1973), 34–5, 61–2, 129.
10. Briggs, *op. cit.*, 219, 227.
11. Hennock, *op. cit.*, 143.
12. EEO MS., Box 8, Subscription list of fifth Lord Calthorpe.
13. Hennock, *op. cit.*, 174.
14. JC MS. 4/5, 57, Joseph Chamberlain, speeches on the occasion of his departure from Birmingham to Westminster, 2 and 9 November 1876; J. L. Garvin and J. Amery, *The Life of Joseph Chamberlain* (6 vols., 1932–69), I, 211.
15. C. Gill and A. Briggs, *The History of Birmingham* (1952), II, 175–7.
16. T. Wright, *The Life of Colonel Fred Burnaby* (1908), vii.
17. *Birmingham Daily Mail*, 12 December 1878.
18. *The Town Crier*, January 1879.
19. EEO MS., Parcel 6, J. Wright to Lord Calthorpe, undated letter accompanying town address, 1862.
20. *The Dart*, 6 December 1879.
21. *The Town Crier*, May 1879.
22. *Birmingham Daily Gazette*, 24 December 1878.
23. BRL MS., Sir J. B. Stone, Newspaper Cuttings Collection, vol. XXI, Conservative party election poster.
24. *Birmingham Daily Gazette*, 30 March 1880.
25. JC MS. 5/16/92–3, Chamberlain to Collings, 28 March, 9 April 1880; C. Green, 'Birmingham's politics, 1873–1891: the local basis of change', *Midland History*, II (1973), 90–1, 96.
26. *Birmingham Daily Gazette*, 22 March 1880.
27. *Ibid.*, 18 and 23 March 1880.
28. *Ibid.*, 19 March 1880.
29. *The Owl*, 25 March 1880.
30. *Birmingham Daily Gazette*, 31 March 1880.
31. *Ibid.*
32. Salisbury Papers, Hatfield, 5th Earl of Dartmouth to Salisbury, 13 February 1888. I owe this reference to Mr R. H. Trainor.
33. Briggs, *op. cit.*, 205.
34. EEO MS., Box 7, Calthorpe to Balden, 17, 24 May, 6 June 1906.
35. H. Pelling, *Social Geography of British Elections, 1885–1910* (1967), 201–3.
36. EEO MS., Box 2, Calthorpe to Milward, 11 July 1894.
37. *Birmingham Daily Post*, 23 July 1910.
38. EEO MS., Box 7, list of late Lord Calthorpe's subscriptions, 1910.
39. *Birmingham Daily Post*, 23 July 1910.
40. *Birmingham Daily Mail*, 18 November 1912.
41. R. E. Waterhouse, *The Birmingham and Midland Institute 1854–1954* (1954), 183–4.
42. FGSKE MS., list of governors, 1885.
43. BBHS MS., *Illustrated Description of Botanical Gardens*, 1910.

44. BUC MS. 4/iii/6, minutes of Canvassing Sub-Committee, 1898–9, 36–9;
    4/iii/7, minutes of Finance Sub-Comittee, 1899–1900, 1–2; 4/iii/8, minutes of
    Management Sub-Comittee, 1898–9, 2; 4/iii/9, minutes of Executive
    Committee, 2–4.
45. BUC MS. 4/iii/12, list of donations, June–October 1898; E. W. Vincent and
    P. Hinton, *The University of Birmingham: Its History and Significance* (1947), 78.
46. M. Sanderson, *The Universities and British Industry 1850–1970* (1972), 71–3; Gill
    and Briggs, *op. cit.*, II, 109–10.
47. JC MS. 12/1/1/32, Calthorpe to Chamberlain, 11 July 1900; BUC MS.
    1/i/3/1, Chamberlain to Calthorpe, 12 July 1900; Vincent and Hinton, *op. cit.*,
    85.
48. *Birmingham Daily Post*, 18 July 1900; *Birmingham Daily Gazette*, 18 July 1900.
49. EEO MS., Box 7, F. A.-G.-Calthorpe to Balden, 9 December 1911.
50. EEO MS. Box 7, F. Lloyd-Anstruther to Balden, 5 September 1910; agents
    minutes, 17 March 1915.

13. THE 'BELGRAVIA' OF BIRMINGHAM

1. D. C. Coleman, 'Gentlemen and players', *EcHR*, 2nd ser., xxvi (1973), 106.
2. A. Briggs, *Victorian Cities* (1968), 204.
3. W. Ashworth, 'Types of social and economic development in suburban
   Essex', in R. Giles (ed.), *London: Aspects of Change* (1964), 80; D. Timms, *The
   Urban Mosaic: Towards a theory of residential differentiation* (1971), 13.
4. Briggs, *op. cit.*, 204.
5. W. Barrow, 'The town and its industries', in J. H. Muirhead (ed.),
   Birmingham Institutions (1911), 48. See also: T. Anderton, *A Tale of One City*
   (1900), 48; E. P. Hennock, *Fit and Proper Persons: Ideal and reality in
   nineteenth-century urban government* (1973), 102–3; C. Gill and A. Briggs, *The
   History of Birmingham* (2 vols., 1952), II, 70.
6. W. Firey, *Land Use in Central Boston* (Cambridge, Mass., 1947), 97, 108.
7. *Idem*, 'Sentiment and symbolism as ecological variables', *American Sociological
   Review*, x (1945), 141.
8. *Ibid.*
9. H. J. Dyos and D. A. Reeder, 'Slums and suburbs', in H. J. Dyos and M. Wolff
   (eds.), *The Victorian City: Images and realities* (2 vols., 1973), I, 369.
10. D. A. Reeder, 'The making of a garden suburb: Edgbaston in the nineteenth
    century' (unpublished paper, Urban History Group Conference, 1970), 8–9.
11. This conclusion is based on an examination of the following Birmingham
    directories: *Post Office Directory of Birmingham* (1871); *Kelly's Directories of
    Birmingham* (1892, 1901 and 1911).
12. R. Glass, 'The structure of neighbourhoods', in M. Lock (ed.), *The County
    Borough of Middlesborough: Survey and plan* (1947), 156.
13. F. Brett Young, *Portrait of Clare* (1935), 496; *idem, White Ladies* (1935), 216.
14. Glass, *loc. cit.*
15. Timms, *op. cit.*, 251; H. J. Dyos, *Victorian Suburb: A study of the growth of
    Camberwell* (1961), 23, 82–3; H. Hoyt, 'The pattern of movement in
    residential neighbourhoods', in H. M. Mayer and C. F. Kohn (eds.), *Readings
    in Urban Geography* (Chicago, 1959), 501.
16. F. Brett Young, *Mr Lucton's Freedom* (1950), 14, 23–5.
17. H. Carpenter, *J. R. R. Tolkien: A biography* (1978), 46.
18. Brett Young, *Mr Lucton's Freedom*, 38, 40, 57.
19. M. Bantock, *Granville Bantock: A personal portrait* (1972), 72–9.

20. Brett Young, *Portrait of Clare*, 427–32, 449, 479.
21. *Idem, Dr Bradley Remembers* (1938), 154.
22. *Ibid.*, 162–3.
23. Brett Young, *White Ladies*, 149–65.
24. E. Edwards, *Personal Recollections of Birmingham and Birmingham Men* (1877), 89–100.
25. Gillott MS., schedule of rents received, 1862.
26. BRL MS. 8,820, Christie's sale catalogue of paintings, 19 April – 3 May 1872; Gillott MS., sale catalogue of musical instruments, 29 April 1872; Sydney Mitchell MS., sale catalogue of furniture, 4–11 June 1872; *Birmingham Daily Post*, 6 January 1872.
27. *Edgbastonia*, May 1886, 72–3; March 1891, 39–40.
28. *Ibid.*, May 1881, *passim*.
29. O. Lodge, *Past Years: An autobiography* (1931), 249–54; E. R. Dodds, *Missing Persons: An autobiography* (1977), 93, 112–13.
30. J. Whitecut, *Edgbaston High School, 1876–1976* (1976), 29–40; *Edgbastonia*, October 1897, 222–6.
31. F. Brett Young, *A Man About the House* (1942), 37.
32. *Edgbastonia*, September 1888, 135–43; January 1894, 10–4.
33. Brett Young, *White Ladies*, 163.
34. Lodge, *op. cit.*, 251, 259; BRL MS. 581,392, Edgbaston Archery and Lawn Tennis Club: list of members (1882); 579,858, Birmingham and Edgbaston Rowing Club: rules and bye-laws (1872); *Edgbastonia*, January 1882, 17; L. Duckworth, *The Story of Warwickshire Cricket* (1974), 51.
35. Lodge, *op. cit.*, 326–7.
36. J. L. Garvin and J. Amery, *The Life of Joseph Chamberlain* (6 vols., 1932–69), I, 57–64; BRL MS. 72,252, Edgbaston and Birmingham Debating Society, reports and circulars. 1886–96; J. A. L. Langford, *Modern Birmingham and its Institutions* (2 vols., 1873–7), I, 235–48.
37. *Edgbastonia*, May 1895, 123.
38. *Ibid.*, October 1884, 151–3.
39. BRL MS. 140,681, Birmingham Amateur Operatic Society programmes, 1886–1922; 259,746, Edgbaston Amateur Musical Union: concerts, 1864–90; 285,230: British and Foreign Sailors Society: An Entertainment, 15 April 1890.
40. Brett Young, *Mr Lucton's Freedom*, 20.
41. BRL MS. 238,039, *St George's Edgbaston, Parish Magazine*, August 1908; 313, 429, *St James' Parish Magazine*, December 1892; 260, 721, *Edgbaston Congregational Magazine*, May 1899.
42. *Birmingham Weekly Post*, 9 July 892.
43. *Edgbastonia*, April 1910, 61–2.
44. Calthorpe Estate Company, *Calthorpe Edgbaston Estate: Re-development Proposals* (1958), 3.
45. A. Sutcliffe and R. Smith, *The History of Birmingham*, III (1974), 14.
46. *Ibid.*, 459–6.
47. *Birmingham Post*, 2 May 1973.
48. *Ibid.*, 16 January 1971; *Birmingham Mail*, 14 September 1973; B. D. Giles, 'High status neighbourhoods in Birmingham', *West Midland Studies*, IX (1976), 11.

14. CONCLUSION: 'THE SAME WAY, BUT BY DIFFERENT STEPS'

1. D. Cannadine, 'Victorian cities: how different?', *Social History*, II (1977), 463.
2. F. M. Jones, 'The aesthetic of the nineteenth-century industrial town', in H. J. Dyos (ed.), *The Study of Urban History* (1968), 172–3.
3. F. M. L. Thompson, *Hampstead: Building a borough 1650–1964* (1974), 73–74; D. J. Olsen, *Town Planning in London in the Eighteenth and Nineteenth Centuries* (1964), 60.
4. Cannadine, *op. cit.*, 464.
5. Thompson, *op. cit.*, 241.
6. EEO MS., Box 1, Harris, Edgbaston tithe bill report, 21 May 1821.
7. J. R. Kellett, review of Olsen, *Town Planning*, in *EcHR*, 2nd ser., XIX (1966), 209.
8. M. Brock, *The Great Reform Act* (1973), 39.
9. D. Roberts, 'The paterfamilias of the Victorian governing classes', in A. S. Wohl (ed.), *The Victorian Family: Structure and stresses* (1978), 77.
10. H. R. G. Greaves, 'Personal origins and inter-relations of the Houses of Parliament', *Economica*, IX (1929), 181.
11. B. R. Mitchell and P. Deane, *Abstract of British Historical Statistics* (1962), 343–5, 471–3.
12. EEO MS., Box 1, G. Edwards, SCTH, draft evidence, 1888, 2.
13. F. M. L. Thompson, *English Landed Society in the Nineteenth Century* (1963), 247–50.
14. D. Spring, 'The English Landed estate in the age of coal and iron, 1830–1880', *Journal of Economic History*, XI (1951), 10; D. A. Reeder, 'Capital investment in the western suburbs of Victorian London, (D.Phil. thesis, University of Leicester, 1965), 236.
15. D. Cannadine, 'The aristocracy and the towns: a case study of the Calthorpes and Birmingham, 1807–1910 (Ph.D. thesis, University of Oxford, 1975), 359.
16. J. L. Garvin and J. Amery, *The Life of Joseph Chamberlain* (2 vols., 1932–69), VI, 899.

15. INTRODUCTION: THE LANDOWNERS AND THE LAND, 1782–1849

1. A. Ollivant, *One Woman: Being the second part of a romance of Sussex* (1921), 186.
2. J. Heywood, *Guide to Eastbourne* (1897), 5.
3. R. N. Wilson, *Leafy Eastbourne* (1904), 24–5.
4. A. Beckett, *The Eastbourne Pictorial* (1912), 7.
5. *EBG*, 1 February 1881; *Pike's Eastbourne Blue Book and Directory* (1910), 97.
6. *Christian World*, 1 July 1870; *Whitehall Review*, 17 August 1881; *Saturday Review*, 28 September 1881.
7. C. Hussey, 'The royal visit to Eastbourne', *Country Life*, LXXVII (1935), 137.
8. For the rise of the Devonshires, see F. Bickley, *The Cavendish Family* (1911), *passim*. For the career of Bess of Hardwick, see D. Durant, *Bess of Hardwick: Portrait of an Elizabethan dynast* 1977) and L. Stone, *The Crisis of the Aristocracy, 1558–1641* (1965), 193–4. For the later Devonshires, see J. H. Plumb, *Men and Places* (1966), 113–21; I. Leverson-Gower, *The Face without a Frown: Georgiana, Duchess of Devonshire* (1944); F. Thompson, *A History of Chatsworth* (1949); V. Markham, *Paxton and the Bachelor Duke* (1935).
9. J. C. Wright, *Byegone Eastbourne* (1898), 17.

10. CW. (Currey) MS. L/86/2, An account of purchases made by the Rt Hon. Lord George Augustus Henry Cavendish at and near Eastbourne in the County of Sussex since the time of his marriage.
11. CW. (Currey) MS. L/86/4, R. Simpson, valuation, 11 July 1821.
12. J. R. McQuiston, 'Sussex aristocrats and the county election of 1820', *EHR*, LXXXVIII (1973).
13. J. K. Walton, 'The social development of Blackpool, 1788–1914' (Ph.D. thesis, University of Lancaster, 1974), 19–22; PRO IR 29/20/289, Skegness Tithe Award, 17 July 1847.
14. J. Bateman, *The Great Landowners of Great Britain and Ireland* (1883), 183.
15. A. C. Todd, *Beyond the Blaze: A biography of Davies Gilbert* (1967), 11–17, 42, 46, 51, 165.
16. *EBG*, 29 March 1882.
17. ESRO Gib. MS. 487, C. F. Drake to Mr Gilbert, 8 December 1894; 466, N. Whitley to Mr Gilbert, 11 December 1895; CEO MS., Letter Book (Building Estate) B3, Turngood and Martin to Burke, 18 September 1913.
18. Wright, *op. cit.*, 28, 31–2.
19. R. and S. Wilberforce, *William Wilberforce: Selections from his correspondence* (2 vols., 1840), II, 165.
20. Wright, *op. cit.*, 44–5; H. C. Brookfield, 'A regional study of urban development in coastal Sussex since the eighteenth century' (Ph.D. thesis, University of London, 1950), 126–8.
21. R. J. Graham, *Eastbourne Recollections* (1888), 22; Wright, *op. cit.*, 96; G. F. Chambers, *Eastbourne Memories* (1910), 36.
22. CW. (Currey) MS. Box 61, agreement for a building lease of ground at Eastbourne in the County of Sussex, 1836.
23. CW. MS. 7 D.D., 22 January 1838.
24. *Ibid.*, 28 April 1838.
25. CW. MS. 2nd ser., 25.0, Benjamin Currey to Devonshire, 27 April 1840.
26. CW. MS. 7 D.D., 8 June 1844.
27. Chambers, *op. cit.*, 124–6.
28. CW. MS. 7 D.D., 15 June 1847.
29. *Ibid.*, 15 June 1849.

16. THE MAKING OF A HIGH-CLASS RESORT, 1849–1914

1. CW. MS. 7 D.D., 11 December 1851.
2. *Ibid.*, 6 May 1852.
3. *Ibid.*, 18 May 1854, 30 June 1855, 6 July 1855.
4. CW. (Currey) MS. Box 61, Eastbourne: builders' advances schedule.
5. J. C. Wright, *Byegone Eastbourne* (1898), 78–81.
6. CW. MS. 7 D.D., 8 July 1858.
7. Wright, *op. cit.*, 157, 244; G. F. Chambers, *Eastbourne Memories* (1910), 99.
8. *EBG*, 10 June 1863.
9. *Ibid.*, 30 March 1864.
10. CW. MS. 7 D.D., 18 May 1863.
11. ESRO Gilb. MS. 356, order of court authorizing the trustees under the will of C. D. Gilbert to grant leases, 19 March 1858; report of N. Whiteley of Truro, Cornwall, surveyor, on the desirability of laying out certain roads, drainage and other works on the Gilbert estate in the parish of Eastbourne, Sussex.
12. *EBG*, 11 November 1863.
13. Wright, *op. cit.*, 159–61.

14. CW. MS. 7 D.D., 17 March 1866.
15. *EBG*, 2 May 1877, 28 September 1881.
16. CW. MS. 7 D.D., 10 April 1873; 12 July 1876; 7 May 1877; 31 May 1878; 20 July 1880; 13 July 1883.
17. *EBG*, 21 July 1875.
18. *Homely Herbert's Popular Eastbourne Guide* (1883), 10; *EBG*, 21 March 1883.
19. ESRO Gilb. MS., 86/1, 86/2, 86/3, estate plans, 1870, 1882, 1884.
20. CW. MS. 7 D.D., 11 February 1871, 11 June 1879, 13 July 1883.
21. *EBG*, 2 January 1884.
22. ESRO Gilb. MS. Henry Currey, Eastbourne plan, 1872.
23. Wright, *op. cit.*, 246–8.
24. Chambers, *op. cit.*, 221.
25. *EBG*, 16 January 1884.
26. CW. MS. 7 D.D., 26 May 1887.
27. *EBG*, 6 October 1886.
28. *Ibid.*, 27 January 1886; 11 July 1888; 3 October 1888; 21 May 1890; 12 November 1890.
29. *Ibid.*, 23 January 1885; 17 February 1886.
30. *Ibid.*, 10 November 1886, 4 January 1888.
31. H. W. Fovargue, *Municipal Eastbourne, 1883–1933: Selections from the proceedings of the town council* (1933), 9–12.
32. *Ibid.*, 28–32.
33. *EBG*, 8 September 1886; 10 November 1886.
34. *Ibid.*, 3 March 1886, 2 June 1886.
35. CW. MS. 7 D.D., 17 July 1890; *EBG*, 19 December 1890; 22 March 1893.
36. CEO MS., Letter Book 2, G. Wallis to C. Tomkinson, 30 January 1890.
37. *EBG*, 7 June 1899.
38. *EBC*, 18 August 1900.
39. Fovargue, *op. cit.*, 173–5.
40. *EBG*, 5 April 1911.
41. *Ibid.*, 21 July 1875.

17. THE SUPERINTENDENCE OF DEVELOPMENT, 1849–1914

1. CEO MS., Letter Book, Building Estate (unnumbered), G. Wallis to C. H. Currey, 12 June 1888.
2. *Ibid.*, General Letter Book W, draft letter, 7 November 1907; Currey Letter Book v, J. P. Cockerell to F. A. Currey, 23 March 1908.
3. J. H. Powell, *Powell's Popular Eastbourne Guide* (1863), v.
4. CEO MS., Letter Book 3, G. A. Wallis to R. M. Gloyne, 15 May 1895.
5. *The Eastbourne Pictorial* (1866); *Pike's Eastbourne Blue Book and Directory* (1890), 91; A. Beckett, *The Eastbourne Pictorial* (1912), 55; *The New Guide Book to Eastbourne and its Neighbourhood* (1871), 8; R. N. Wilson, *Leafy Eastbourne*, 25.
6. *EBC*, 18 October 1913.
7. *EBG*, 18 August 1875; 5 January 1876; 13 February 1878.
8. *Ibid.*, 23 January 1885; 4 November 1885; 10 February 1886.
9. *Ibid.*, 1 January 1868.
10. CEO MS., Letter Book 1, G. A. Wallis to Mr Pettit, 26 November 1878.
11. *PP*, 1888, xxii, SCTH Q 2,767.
12. W. Hodgson and W. H. Saunders, *Eastbourne: An illustrated handbook for visitors and residents* (1919), 30–3.

13. *EBG*, 4 November 1885; 13 April 1898.
14. *Ibid.*, 21 March 1883.
15. *Ibid.*, 21 May 1890; C.E.O. MS. Letter Book 2, G. A. Wallis to J. Coster, 27 February 1889.
16. CEO MS., Letter Book 1, G. A. Wallis to builders, *passim*.
17. *Ibid.*, Letter Book 3, G. A. Wallis to M. Martin, 22 January 1895.
18. *Ibid.*, Letter Book 3, G. A. Wallis to W. H. Blackdean, 22 April 1895.
19. *Ibid.*, Letter Book 2, G. A. Wallis to Borough Surveyor, 29 July 1892.
20. *Ibid.*, Letter Book 1, G. A. Wallis to Mr Barker, 14 May 1873.
21. *PP*, xxii, 1888 SCTH QQ. 2,705, 2,817, 2,949.
22. Wilson, *op. cit.*, 39.
23. CEO MS., Agreement Book xiii, lease to Edward Foster, 26 November 1906.
24. ESRO Gilb. MS. 436, G. D. Gilbert to James Edwards, building lease, 11 October 1877.
25. CEO MS., Letter Book 3, G. A. Wallis to C. H. Currey, 9 May 1895.
26. CW. (Currey) MS. Box 61, C. H. Currey to Devonshire, 20 September 1897.
27. *Ibid.*, C. H. Currey to Devonshire, 18 July 1899, 13 January 1900.
28. CEO MS., Letter Book, Building Estate M, Coles, Sons & Tilburn to J. P. Cockerell, 11 June 1906.
29. *Ibid.*, Letter Book, Building Estate 5, U. R. Burke to Roberts, Walton & Giles, 17 July 1914.
30. *Ibid.*, Letter Book 59, U. R. Burke to F. S. Williams, 10 July 1912.
31. CW. (Currey) MS., Eastbourne File, 1897–1904, J. P. Cockerell to C. G. Hamilton, 21 October 1899.
32. *Ibid.*, J. P. Cockerell to C. G. Hamilton, 7 January 1900.
33. E.g., C.E.O. MS. Letter Books, Building Estate: C. J. Edwards to J. P. Cockerell, 25 February 1902; H. R. Barnes to J. P. Cockerell, 24 December 1903; L. F. Kingsberg to J. P. Cockerell, 18 December 1905.
34. Wilson, *op. cit.*, 44.
35. *EBG*, 21 October 1863, 4 November 1863.
36. *Ibid.*, 10 August 1887.
37. *Ibid.*, 18 June 1884.
38. 'A visitor' in *EBG*, 13 July 1864.
39. *Saturday Review*, 28 September 1881.
40. *Pike's Eastbourne Blue Book and Directory* (1890), 96.

18. THE PROVISION OF AMENITIES, 1849–1914

1. *EBG*, 8 October 1862.
2. 'A visitor' in *EBG*, 13 July 1864.
3. *EBG*, 10 May 1871, 7 January 1874, 12 January 1876, 10 January 1877, 29 September 1880, 27 April 1881.
4. *Ibid.*, 10 April 1878.
5. *Ibid.*, 10 May 1871.
6. *Ibid.*, 10 January 1877.
7. H. Perkin, *The Age of the Railway* (1970), ch. viii.
8. PRO Rail 414/65, L.B.S.C.R. Directors' Minute Books: I, 23 April 1847; II, 12 March 1849; III, 7 May 1849.
9. *EBG*, 25 August 1869.
10. *Ibid.*, 2 August 1871.
11. C. F. Dendy Marshall, *A History of the Southern Railway* (3 vols., 1963), I, 207.
12. G. F. Chambers, *Eastbourne Memories* (1910), 129–30.

13. *EBG*, 25 December 1867.
14. CW. MS. 7 D.D., 7 July 1874.
15. *Ibid.*, 30 July 1877; *EBG.*, 8 September 1880.
16. Chambers, *op. cit.*, 131–2.
17. CW. MS. 7 D.D., 30 July 1877.
18. For a fuller account of this episode, see ch. 20, section 4.
19. CEO MS. Letter Book 1, G. A. Wallis to F. Hyde, 12 June 1878.
20. CEO MS. Letter Book 1, undated memorandum on the development of the Compton Building Estate.
21. *EBG*, 9 September 1863.
22. EBLB Minute Book I, 3 July 1865; CW. MS. 7 D.D., 17 March 1866.
23. *EBG*, 29 August 1866.
24. *Ibid.*, 20 June 1866.
25. *Saturday Review*, 1 June 1867.
26. Quoted in the *Eastbourne Pictorial*, August 1886.
27. H. W. Fovargue, *Municipal Eastbourne, 1883–1933: Selections from the proceedings of the town council* (1933), xv.
28. *EBG*, 9 August 1882.
29. CW. (Currey) MS. L/54/40, N. Willard to John Simpson, 9 June 1844.
30. EBWWCo, Minute Book (unnumbered), 19 October 1857, 22 February 1858.
31. CW. MS. 7 D.D., 20 February 1857.
32. ESRO Gilb. MS. 103, Burlington to Mrs Gilbert, 12 November 1857.
33. EBWWCo, Minute Book (unnumbered), 21 December 1858.
34. CW. MS. 7 D.D., 16 July 1859.
35. CW. (Currey) MS., Box 61 memorandum by G. A. Wallis, 30 April 1889.
36. CW. MS. 7 D.D., 12 July 1876, 27 February 1880, 14 July 1883.
37. CW. (Currey) MS., Box 61, G. A. Wallis to C. H. Currey, April 1889.
38. S. Pollard, 'Barrow-in-Furness and the seventh duke of Devonshire', *EcHR*, 2nd ser., VIII (1955), 216.
39. CW. (Currey) MS., Box 61, C. H. Currey to Devonshire, 26 October 1891.
40. *Ibid.*, memorandum by G. A. Wallis, 30 April 1889.
41. *Ibid.*, C. H. Currey to Devonshire, 26 October 1891.
42. *Ibid.*, C. H. Currey to Devonshire, 8 December 1898.
43. *EBG*, 16 December 1863.
44. *Ibid.*, 26 October 1864; CW. MS. 7 D.D., 28 October 1864.
45. *EBG*, 5 April 1865.
46. *Ibid.*, 19 April 1866.
47. EBPC Minute Book 1, 2 January 1877.
48. *EBG*, 27 January 1869.
49. EBPC Minute Book 1, 24 March 1869.
50. *Ibid.*, 26 January 1867.
51. *Ibid.*, 10 February 1869.
52. *Ibid.*, 26 August 1870, 3 April 1872.
53. *Ibid.*, 18 November 1875, 16 February 1876.
54. *EBG*, 30 March 1864; CW. MS. 7 D.D., 21 July 1871.
55. EBPC, register of shares.
56. *Ibid.*, Minute Book 1, 26 August 1870, 20 March 1872, 22 May 1872, 4 June 1872.
57. *Ibid.*, 10 February 1869.
58. *EBG*, 15 June 1870.
59. *Ibid.*, 11 June 1873, 9 July 1873, 16 July 1873; EBPC Minute Book 1, 9 July 1873.

60. V. E. Allom, *Ex Oriente Salus: A centenary history of Eastbourne College* (1967), 1–2.
61. CW. MS. 7 D.D., 10 July 1865.
62. *EBG*, 20 September 1865.
63. CW. MS. 7 D.D., 19 July 1871.
64. Allom, *op. cit.*, 17–18.
65. *Ibid.*, 48–9; CW. MS. 7 D.D., 23 May 1889.
66. *EBG*, 2 January 1867.
67. CW. MS. 7 D.D., 4 October 1867.
68. Eastbourne College Minute Book, 5 November 1868.
69. *Ibid.*, 4 May 1869; Allom, *op. cit.*, 9–10; *EBC*, 12 May 1869.
70. Allom, *op. cit.*, 35–41; CW. MS. 7 D.D., 4 June 1886.
71. *EBG*, 12 May 1869.
72. CW. MS. 7 D.D., 23 May 1870.
73. *Ibid.*, 23 May 1889.
74. *EBG*, 2 January 1867.
75. Allom, *op. cit.*, 54.
76. *EBG*, 22 May 1867, 15 May 1867.
77. *Ibid.*, 6 November 1872, 13 November 1872, 18 December 1872; CW. (DP & B) MS., Box 2, *in re* the Eastbourne Baths Company Ltd: instructions to settle, 1872.
78. CW. MS. 7 D.D., 10 April 1873.
79. CW. (DP&B) MS., Box 2, *in re* the Eastbourne Baths Company Ltd, 1872.
80. *Ibid.*, Eastbourne Baths Co., minutes of Extraordinary General Meeting, 29 May 1874.
81. *EBG*, 13 May 1874.
82. CW. (DP&B) MS., Box 2, memorandum and articles of association, 16 May 1873.
83. CW. MS. 7 D.D., 9 July 1874.
84. *Ibid.*, 12 July 1896; EB.G., 26 July 1876.
85. CW. MS. 7 D.D., 7 June 1888; Pollard, *op. cit.*, 220–1.
86. *EBC*, 13 April 1907.
87. CEO MS., Account Book, Duke of Devonshire's (Eastbourne) Orchestra, 2 January 1908 to 27 January 1910.
88. *Homely Herbert's Popular Eastbourne Guide* (1871), 2.
89. *Eastbourne Official Guide* (1912), 13.
90. *EBC*, 4 June 1904.

19. THE MAKING OF A NEW TOWN: OUTLAY AND INCOME, 1849–91

1. *EBG*, 3 February 1875.
2. *Ibid.*, 5 July 1882; D. Spring, 'The English landed estate in the age of coal and iron, 1830–1880', *Journal of Economic History*, xi (1951), 19; S. Pollard, *A History of Labour in Sheffield* (1959), 221; E. J. Hobsbawm, *Industry and Empire* (1969), 107; W. A. Maguire, *The Downshire Estates in Ireland, 1801–1845* (1972), 84.
3. CW. (Currey) MS. L/82/2, Benjamin Currey, rental of Earl of Burlington's estates, 1836.
4. CW. MS. 6th duke's ser. 3326, Lord Burlington to Mrs William Cavendish, 20 May 1835.

5. D. Cannadine, 'The landowner as millionaire: the finances of the dukes of Devonshire *c*.1800–*c*.1926', *AgHR*, xxv (1977), 79–82.

6. CW. MS. 7 D.D., 26 January 1858.

7. *Ibid.*, 8 April 1840, 6 June 1840, 10 October 1840, 25 May 1842, 21 August 1842, 2 March 1858, 23 April 1858.

8. Cannadine, *op. cit.*, 84; Spring, *op. cit.*, 19.

9. *EBG*, 28 September 1881.

10. *PP*, xxii, SCTH, Q2, 954.

11. CW. MS. 7 D.D., 19 March 1851. (My italics.)

12. D. Spring, *The English Landed Estate in the Nineteenth Century: Its administration* (1963), 39.

13. CW. MS. 7 D.D., 6 July 1855.

14. *Ibid.*, 18 June 1851, 11 July 1861, 6 May 1852, 11 February 1871.

15. F. M. L. Thompson, 'The end of a great estate', *EcHR.*, 2nd ser., viii (1955), 52.

16. L. Strachy and R. Fulford (eds.), *The Greville Memoirs 1814–60* (8 vols., 1938), VII, 333.

17. CEO MS., Letter Book, Currey AA, U. R. Burke to F. A. Currey, 29 November 1912.

18. CW. MS. 7 D.D., 25 July 1877, 1 June 1887.

19. *EBG*, 20 February 1878.

20. *Ibid.*, 5 February 1873.

21. CEO MS., Report by Mr C. H. Currey and Mr Henry Currey on H. G. the Duke of Devonshire's Sussex Estates, 28 March 1895, 8.

22. *Ibid.*, C. H. Currey to Hartington, 19 December 1890.

23. CW. MS. 7 D.D., 8 July 1865.

24. D. Cannadine, 'Aristocratic indebtedness in the nineteenth century: the case re-opened', *EcHR*, 2nd ser., xxx (1977), 644.

25. *EBG*, 5 January 1881.

26. Cannadine, 'The landowner as millionaire', 86–7.

27. CW. MS. 7 D.D., 1 May 1885.

28. *Ibid.*, 27 March 1888.

29. EBLB Minute Book 2, 6 November 1865.

30. Eastbourne Improvement Act (1879), clause 52.

31. J. C. Wright, *Byegone Eastbourne* (1898), 165–6.

32. G. F. Chambers, *Eastbourne Memories* (1910), 216–20.

33. *EBG*, 10 April 1878.

20. INFLUENCE AND CONTROL: THE LOCAL OLIGARCHY, 1849–91

1. H. Leach, *The Duke of Devonshire: A personal and political biography* (1904), 23; W. L. Burn, *The Age of Equipoise: A study of the mid-Victorian generation* (1968), 310–11.

2. *Vanity Fair*, 6 June 1874.

3. *EBG*, 8 May 1867, for a full account of the day's proceedings.

4. *Ibid.*, 23 December 1863.

5. *Ibid.*, 15 June 1870.

6. *Ibid.*, 3 August 1870.

7. *Ibid.*, 26 December 1883.

8. *Ibid.*, 2 July 1881.

9. *Ibid.*, 25 July 1888.

10. Compare the impression given in A. B. Cooke and J. Vincent, *The Governing Passion: Cabinet government and party politics in Great Britain, 1885–89* (1974), 10, 15, 88–9.

11. *EBG*, 21 July 1886. There is no evidence to suggest that Devonshire at any time had a financial stake in any Eastbourne paper.

12. *Ibid.*, 2 January 1889.

13. *Ibid.*, 10 May 1882.

14. *Ibid.*, 6 January 1886.

15. *Ibid.*, 23 December 1891, 30 December 1891.

16. H. W. Fovargue, *Municipal Eastbourne, 1883–1933: Selections from the proceedings of the town council* (1933), 20; EBTC Minute Book 2, 23 December 1891.

17. *EBC*, 2 January 1892; *EBG*, 30 December 1891.

18. *EBG*, 9 October 1872.

19. *Ibid.*, 22 September 1880.

20. F. M. L. Thompson, *English Landed Society in the Nineteenth Century* (1963), 175.

21. J. D. Marshall, *Furness and the Industrial Revolution* (1958), 279–80.

22. CW. MS. 6th duke's ser., 3,037, B. Currey to Earl of Burlington, 5th June 1834.

23. Marshall, *op. cit.*, 185, 190.

24. *EBC*, 1 December 1900, obituary notice.

25. R. N. Crook, 'Henry Currey and the seventh duke of Devonshire', (unpublished R.I.B.A. dissertation, 1978), *passim*.

26. *EBG*, 2 February 1898; *EBC*, 5 February 1898.

27. Marshall, *op. cit.*, 225–6; R. G. Heape, *Buxton under the Dukes of Devonshire* (1948), 78: *EBC*, 21 December 1895, obituary notice.

28. *EBC*, 7 December 1895.

29. *EBG*, 21 February 1883.

30. *Ibid.*, 21 April 1875, 12 April 1882, 15 August 1883.

31. *Ibid.*, 18 January 1893.

32. *Ibid.*, 29 July 1863.

33. EBLB, Minute Book 2, 13 July 1863.

34. *EBG*, 6 February 1867.

35. CEO MS., Letter Book 1, G. A. Wallis to C. Tomes (Borough Surveyor), 25 March 1874, 31 May 1878, 22 August 1878, 23 July 1879.

36. *EBG*, 23 March 1881, 6 April 1881; EBLB, Minute Book 6, 21 March 1881.

37. *Ibid.*, 14 March 1883.

38. *Ibid.*, 4 July 1883, 12 September 1883, 31 October 1883, 7 November 1883.

39. *Ibid.*, 10 October 1883.

40. *Ibid.*, 26 December 1883.

41. *Ibid.*, 7 January 1885.

42. *EBC*, 21 December 1895.

43. Eastbourne Improvement Act (1879), clauses 16 and 26.

44. *EBG*, 11 February 1885, 18 February 1885.

45. CW. MS. 7 D.D., 21 July 1882.

46. CW. (Currey) MS., Box 61, Devonshire to Laing, 10 August 1882.

47. *Ibid.*, Currey to Devonshire, 1 September 1882.

48. *Ibid.*, Currey to Devonshire, 4 September 1882, 8 September 1882; Report by Wallis, 31 August 1882.

49. *Ibid.*, Devonshire to Currey, 14 September 1882.

50. *Ibid.*, Currey to Devonshire, 18 September 1882.

51. G. F. Chambers, *Eastbourne Memories* (1910), 134.

52. *EBG*, 27 December 1882.

53. CW. (Currey) MS., Box 61, Devonshire to Currey, 12 November 1882.

54. *EBG*, 27 December 1882.
55. *Ibid.,* 10 January 1883.
56. *Ibid.,* 4 April 1883; EBLB, Minute Book 6, 8 January 1883.
57. CW. MS. 7 D.D., 15 March 1883.
58. ESRO Gilb. MS., Min. HCSC on Eastbourne Railway bill, 9 April 1883, QQ 231–4.
59. CW. (Currey) MS., Box 61, Devonshire to Currey, 19 December 1883, 23 January 1884.
60. *EBG*, 10 December 1884, 30 December 1885.
61. *Ibid.,* 20 May 1885.
62. *Ibid.,* 3 June 1885, 10 June 1885.
63. *Ibid.,* 10 June 1885.
64. *Ibid.,* 24 June 1885.
65. *Ibid.,* 4 November 1885.
66. *Ibid.,* 9 December 1885; Chambers, *op. cit.,* 134.
67. *Ibid.,* 22 September 1886.
68. *Ibid.,* 6 October 1886, 3 October 1888.
69. *Ibid.,* 9 January 1884.
70. *Ibid.,* 9 September 1892; EBTC, Minute Book 2, 5 September 1892.
71. *Ibid.,* 15 August 1894.
72. *EBC*, 15 September 1894.
73. *Ibid.,* 21 December 1895; *EBG*, 25 December 1895.
74. *Ibid.,* 28 December 1895.
75. *Ibid.,* 28 March 1896, 27 June 1896; *EBG*, 11 June 1896.

21. CHANGED POLICY AND IMPROVED FORTUNES, 1891–1914

1. F. Bickley, *The Cavendish Family* (1911), 301.
2. B. Holland, *The Life of Spencer Compton, Eighth Duke of Devonshire* (2 vols., 1911), II, 223–5, 239–41.
3. *EBC*, 29 December 1900.
4. A. B. Cooke and J. Vincent, *The Governing Passion: Cabinet government and party politics in Great Britain, 1885–89* (1974), 10, 15, 24, 88–9.
5. CW. MS. 2nd ser., 340. 2537A, Lady Louisa Egerton to Devonshire, 25 January 1894.
6. *Ibid.,* 340.2551, Devonshire to Lady Egerton, 6 April 1894.
7. *Ibid.,* 340.2553, Devonshire to Lady Egerton, 23 April 1894.
8. *Ibid.,* 340.2556, Devonshire to Harcourt, 11 May 1894; 340.2557, Harcourt to Devonshire, 15 May 1894. See also Devonshire's speech at Buxton, 13 June 1894, where he stated that it might prove necessary for him to close Chatsworth, Lismore, Hardwick and Bolton Abbey: R. G. Heape, *Buxton under the Dukes of Devonshire* (1948), 121.
9. D. Cannadine, 'The landowner as millionaire: the finances of the dukes of Devonshire *c.* 1800–*c.* 1926', *AgHR*, xxv (1977), 89.
10. *Ibid.,* 90–91.
11. CW. MS. 2nd ser. 340.2553, Devonshire to Lady Egerton, 23 April 1894.
12. CEO MS., C. H. Currey to Hartington, 19 December 1890; G. A. Wallis to Hartington, 4 February 1890.
13. *Ibid.,* Farrant to Devonshire, 22 May 1894.
14. *Ibid.,* Devonshire to F. A. Currey, 20 June 1894.
15. *Ibid.,* Devonshire to C. H. Currey, June 1894.

16. *Ibid.*, Devonshire to C. H. Currey, 10 July 1894.
17. *Ibid.*, Price Waterhouse Report, 12 November 1894.
18. *Ibid.*, Farrant's Report, 11 January 1895.
19. *Ibid.*, report by Mr C. H. Currey and Mr Henry Currey on His Grace the Duke of Devonshire's Sussex estates, 28 March 1895, 19.
20. *Ibid.*
21. *Ibid.*, 10.
22. *Ibid.*, 30.
23. *Ibid.*, 31.
24. *Ibid.*, 33–4.
25. CW. MS. 7 D.D., 22 July 1878; 4 June 1886.
26. CEO MS., Letter Book 2, G. A. Wallis to C. H. Currey, 27 October 1882; CW. MS. 7 D.D., 22 July 1878.
27. *EBG*, 31 October 1883.
28. CEO MS., report by Mr C. H. Currey and Mr Henry Currey on His Grace the Duke of Devonshire's Sussex estates, 28 March 1895, 19.
29. *Ibid.*, 8.
30. CW. MS. 7 D.D., 10 June 1885.
31. *EBG*, 6 May 1908; 23 September 1908.
32. CEO MS., Duke of Devonshire File, J. P. Cockerell to Devonshire, 18 February 1902.
33. CEO MS., Devonshire Letter Book, Cockerell to Devonshire 26 February 1903, 20 February 1905, 2 February 1906, 30 January 1907.
34. *Ibid.*, Currey Letter Book T, Cockerell to F. A. Currey, 8 March 1907.
35. CW. (Currey) MS., Eastbourne 1897–1904 File, Cockerell to Devonshire, 8 March 1898.
36. CEO MS., Currey Letter Book L, Cockerell to F. A. Currey, 8 January 1903.
37. CW. (Currey) MS., Box 61, C. H. Currey to Devonshire, 14 February 1901.
38. *Ibid.*, Currey to Devonshire, 16 May 1901; Price Waterhouse to Currey, final report, 23 July 1901.
39. *Ibid.*, F. A. Currey to Devonshire, 13 June 1901.
40. *Ibid.*, Devonshire to F. A. Currey, 14 June 1901.
41. *Ibid.*, C. H. Currey to Devonshire, 24 July 1901.
42. V. E. Allom, *Ex Oriente Salus: A centenary history of Eastbourne College* (1967), 56; EBPC Minute Book 2: 17 September 1892; 6 December 1892; 10 January 1893.
43. H. W. Fovargue, *Municipal Eastbourne, 1883–1933; Selections from the proceedings of the town council* (1933), 34–5; see also ch. 22, pp. 348–51.
44. EBPC, register of shares.
45. CEO MS., Currey Letter Book M, F. A. Currey to Cockerell, 26 February 1906.
46. *EBC*, 18 May 1895; 29 December 1900; *EBG*, 25 August 1909.
47. *EBG*, 26 October 1898.
48. Fovargue, *op. cit.*, 40–2.
49. *EBG*, 25 December 1907.
50. *Ibid.*, 15 March 1905; 11 November 1903.
51. CEO MS., Town Clerk and Borough Surveyor Minute Book, H. W. Fovargue to R. Burke, 5 December 1911.
52. Fovargue, *op. cit.*, 58.
53. *EBG*, 10 October 1883.
54. *EBC*, 16 February 1895; *EBG*, 13 September 1899.
55. *EBG*, 9 November 1909.
56. Fovargue, *op. cit.*, 106–8, 116–21, 134–5, 137, 156.

22. POLITICAL CONFLICT AND SOCIAL CELEBRITY, 1891–1914

1. EBLB, Minute Book 4, 3 November 1873, 7 October 1874, 7 June 1875.
2. CEO MS., Box 61, J. P. Cockerell to R. Climpson, 7 October 1897.
3. EBTC, Minute Book 3, 3 October 1892.
4. *EBG*, 8 March 1893; 29 August 1893; 4 October 1893.
5. CEO MS., Letter Book 3, Wallis to Fovargue, 9 March 1894.
6. *Ibid.*, W. L. Wallis to C. H. Currey, 23 October 1894.
7. *EBC*, 12 January 1895.
8. *Ibid.*, 9 February 1895.
9. *Ibid.*, 20 April 1895; 11 May 1895.
10. *EBG*, 13 November 1895.
11. *Ibid.*
12. For this whole section, see H. W. Fovargue, *Municipal Eastbourne, 1883–1933: Selections from the proceedings of the town council* (1933), 28–32.
13. *EBG*, 30 October 1895.
14. Min. HLSC on Eastbourne Water bill, 11 May 1897, Q. 52.
15. *EBG*, 11 December 1895.
16. *EBC*, 21 December 1895.
17. Min. HLSC on Eastbourne Water bill, 11 May 1897, QQ. 67–70.
18. *Ibid.*, Q. 83.
19. *Ibid.*, QQ. 808–13.
20. *EBG*, 7 October 1896; 18 November 1896.
21. Min. HLSC on Eastbourne Water bill, 11 May 1897, QQ. 150–2.
22. CW. (Currey) MS., Box 61, C. H. Currey to Devonshire, 27 April 1897.
23. *EBC*, 15 May 1897.
24. *Ibid.*, 7 August 1897, for all this paragraph.
25. *Ibid.*, 14 August 1897.
26. *Ibid.*, 18 September 1897.
27. *Ibid.*, 13 November 1897.
28. *EBG*, 12 January 1898.
29. *Ibid.*, 2 February 1898.
30. *EBC*, 23 April 1898.
31. *EBG*, 26 October 1898.
32. *EBC*, 12 November 1898.
33. *EBG*, 6 October 1909.
34. *EBC*, 13 November 1897.
35. CW. (Currey) MS., Eastbourne File 1897–1904, Cockerell to Devonshire, 6 September 1897.
36. *EBC*, 13 November 1897.
37. *Ibid.*, 8 October 1898.
38. H. Leach, *The Duke of Devonshire: A personal and political biography* (1904), 300.
39. *EBC*, 1 October 1898.
40. *Ibid.*, 8 October 1898.
41. *Ibid.*, 27 October 1900.
42. *EBG*, 18 March 1903.
43. *Ibid.*, 21 August 1901.
44. *EBC*, 13 August 1904.
45. *EBG*, 16 February 1898.
46. *Ibid.*, 10 January 1906.
47. *EBC*, 5 July 1899.
48. *Ibid.*, 29 October 1910.

49. Fovargue, *op. cit.*, 65.
50. *EBC*, 28 March 1908.
51. *Ibid.*, 4 April 1908.
52. *Ibid.*, 29 October 1910.
53. *Ibid.*, 28 March 1908.
54. *Ibid.*, 19 June 1909.
55. *EBG*, 6 October 1909.
56. *EBC*, 9 October 1909.
57. *EBG*, 10 November 1909, for all this paragraph.
58. *Ibid.*, 9 February 1910, for this paragraph.
59. CEO MS., Town Clerk and Borough Surveyor Letter Book C, Fovargue to Devonshire, 5 September 1910.
60. *EBG*, 7 December 1910.
61. *Ibid.*, 9 November 1909.
62. *EBC*, 10 December 1910.
63. *Ibid.*, 29 October 1910.
64. *EBG*, 25 August 1909.
65. *Ibid.*, 4 June 1913.
66. *Ibid.*, 7 December 1910.
67. *Ibid.*, 25 August 1909.
68. *Ibid.*, 25 September 1912.
69. M. J. Daunton, *Coal Metropolis: Cardiff, 1870–1914* (1977), 198.
70. *EBC*, 6 December 1913; *EBG*, 30 July 1913; CEO MS., Currey Letter Book BB, Burke to F. A. Currey, 3 November 1914.
71. For this section, see Fovargue, *op. cit.*, 73–4, 76–8, 80.
72. *Sussex Daily News*, 2 March 1912.
73. *EBG*, 29 June 1910.
74. *Ibid.*, 7 December 1910.
75. *Ibid.*, 29 May 1912.
76. *EBC*, 2 March 1912.
77. *Sussex Daily News*, 16 March 1912.
78. EBTC, Minute Book 9, 15 November 1912.
79. *EBG*, 27 March 1912.
80. *Ibid.*, 3 April 1912.
81. CW. (DP&B) MS., Box 2, Burke to A. H. Battock, 6 January 1913.
82. EBTC, Minute Book 9, 3 March 1913.
83. CEO MS., Town Clerk and Borough Surveyor Letter Book D, Fovargue to Burke, 15 January 1914.
84. EBTC, Minute Book 8, 3 March 1913.
85. *Ibid.*, 6 October 1913.
86. *EBC*, 25 October 1913.
87. CEO MS., Currey Letter Book FF, A. H. Battock to Burke, 7 February 1914.
88. *EBC*, 7 February 1914.
89. *Ibid.*, 17 January 1914.
90. Fovargue, *op. cit.*, 89.
91. H. Nicolson, *King George V: His life and reign* (1967), 676.
92. Fovargue, *op. cit.*, supplement 1933–9, 2.
93. *EBG*, 11 May 1938; CW. (Currey) MS. L/108/83, wreaths at the funeral of the tenth duke of Devonshire, 30 November 1950.
94. EBTC, Entertainment Committee File 1320/1, draft conveyance, 25 March 1957.
95. *Ibid.*, town clerk to borough surveyor, 5 April 1955.

96.   *Eastbourne Herald,* 14 July 1973.
97.   *Hansard,* Commons, 30 June 1975, 1105–6.

23. THE 'EMPRESS OF WATERING PLACES'

1.   H. J. Perkin, 'The "Social Tone" of Victorian seaside resorts in the north-west', *Northern History,* xi (1976), 185.
2.   *EBG,* 30 August 1905.
3.   CW. (Currey) MS., Box 10, Memorandum to Devonshire, June 1865.
4.   *EBG,* 6 January 1864.
5.   CEO MS., Agreement 2712A, conveyance of Western Parades, 6 November 1902.
6.   *EBG,* 21 March 1894.
7.   *Ibid.,* 5 November 1913.
8.   H. W. Fovargue, *Municipal Eastbourne, 1883–1933; Selections from the proceedings of the town council* (1933), 20–1; *EBG,* 17 August 1892.
9.   Eastbourne Corporation Act (1902), clause xvii.
10.   Eastbourne Corporation Act (1910), clause xii, xv.
11.   *EBG,* 28 July 1886.
12.   *Ibid.,* 13 July 1890.
13.   *Ibid.,* 22 May 1907.
14.   *EBC,* 30 August 1913, quoting *Daily News and Leader.*
15.   *Ibid.,* 25 May 1912, quoting *The Standard.*
16.   *EBG,* 10 July 1901.
17.   E. Raymond, *Rossenal* (1921), chs. xv–xxiii.
18.   J. Harris, *William Beveridge: A biography* (1977), 19.
19.   P. N. Furbank, *E. M. Forster: A Life,* I, *The Growth of a Novelist (1879–1914)* (1977), 33–40.
20.   R. N. Wilson, *Leafy Eastbourne* (1904), 39.
21.   A. Ollivant, *Two Men* (1920), 159. (My italics.)
22.   S. Lynd, *The Swallow Dive* (1921), 91–2.
23.   *EBG,* 20 August 1902.
24.   *Ibid.,* 29 June 1881.
25.   L. Huxley, *Life and Letters of Thomas Henry Huxley* (2nd edn., 3 vols., 1903), III, 184, 195, 420–1.
26.   Wilson, *op. cit.,* 55.
27.   *EBG,* 9 January 1884.
28.   *Pike's Eastbourne Blue Book and Directory* (1890), 96.
29.   Wilson, *op. cit.,* 56.
30.   *EBC,* 29 December 1894.
31.   *EBG,* 27 January 1909.
32.   *Ibid.,* 16 March 1881.
33.   Lynd, *op. cit.,* 91.
34.   *EBG,* 23 August 1882.
35.   *Ibid.,* 10 January 1877.
36.   *Ibid.,* 8 March 1893.
37.   *Ibid.,* 8 October 1902, 16 January 1907.
38.   *Ibid.,* 31 August 1898.
39.   E. Newton and W. Neil, *The Christian Faith in Art* (1966), 296–7. I am grateful to Mr G. J. O. Dunstan for this reference.
40.   T. H. S. Escott, *Society in the English Country House* (1907), 53.

24. INTERNAL DIFFICULTIES AND EXTERNAL THREATS, *c*. 1890–1914

1. Throughout this section, I am much indebted to G. S. Jones, *Outcast London: A study in the relationship between classes in Victorian society* (1976), ch. II.
2. *EBG*, 12 November 1884.
3. *Ibid.*, 15 September 1887.
4. *Ibid.*, 26 January 1887.
5. R. N. Wilson, *Leafy Eastbourne* (1904), 25.
6. *EBG*, 27 October 1909.
7. *Ibid.*, 19 July 1911.
8. *Eastbourne Pictorial* (1912).
9. *EBG*, 15 March 1911.
10. *Ibid.*, 21 March 1911.
11. *Ibid.*, 22 May 1901.
12. H. Clunn, *Famous South Coast Pleasure Resorts* (1929), 28, 147, 194, 276, 310
13. *EBG*, 15 July 1896.
14. CW. (Currey) MS., Box 61, Cockerell to F. Robinson, 8 November 1897.
15. *EBG*, 24 May 1899.
16. *Ibid.*, 31 May 1899.
17. *Ibid.*, 15 November 1899.
18. *Ibid.*, 8 January 1902.
19. *Ibid.*, 5 February 1902.
20. *Ibid.*, 8 January 1902.
21. *Ibid.*, 15 January 1902.
22. *EBC*, 12 April 1902.
23. H. W. Fovargue, *Municipal Eastbourne 1883–1933: Selections from the proceedings of the town council* (1933), 173–5.
24. *EBG*, 9 September 1903.
25. *EBC*, 5 September 1903.
26. *Ibid.*, 12 November 1903.
27. *EBG*, 5 September 1906.
28. V. Bailey, 'Salvation Army riots, the "Skeleton Army" and legal authority in the provincial town', in A. P. Donajgrodzki (ed.), *Social Control in Nineteenth-Century Britain* (1977), 241.
29. *EBG*, 17 July 1872.
30. CW. (Currey) MS., Box 61, R. Sutton to Devonshire, May 1877, enclosing undated press cuttings.
31. *EBG*, 8 September 1880.
32. *Ibid.*, 6 March 1907, 16 June 1909.
33. *Ibid.*, 2 September 1885.
34. *EBC*, 24 March 1894.
35. *Ibid.*, 10 March 1894, 7 May 1898; *EBG*, 21 March 1894.
36. For this section, see Fovargue, *op. cit.*, 9–12.
37. Bailey, *op. cit.*, 241–2.
38. L. Huxley, *Life and Letters of Thomas Henry Huxley* (2nd edn., 3 vols., 1903), III, 176–83.
39. Bailey, *op. cit.*, 235–7; K. S. Inglis, *Churches and the Working Classes in Victorian England* (1963), 184–94.
40. *EBG*, 23 May 1883.
41. *Ibid.*, 23 April 1890.
42. *Ibid.*, 29 April 1891.
43. *Ibid.*, 13 May 1891.

44. *Ibid.*, 27 May 1891, 10 June 1891, 4 May 1892; Bailey, *op. cit.*, 234.
45. *EBG*, 17 June 1891.
46. Bailey, *op. cit.*, 234.
47. *EBG*, 4 April 1892, 4 May 1892.
48. *Ibid.*, 22 July 1891, 4 May 1892.
49. *Ibid.*, 3, 10 June 1891.
50. Quoted in *ibid.*, 22 July 1891.
51. Min. HLSC on Eastbourne Improvement Act (1885) Amendment, 17 June 1892, Q. 1180.
52. *EBG*, 22 July 1891.
53. *Ibid.*, 12 August 1891.
54. *Ibid.*, 9 December 1891.
55. *Ibid.*, 6 January 1892.
56. *Ibid.*, 2 March 1892.
57. *Ibid.*, 16 March 1892.
58. *Ibid.*
59. Bailey, *op. cit.*, 247–9.
60. *EBG*, 9 March 1892.
61. Clunn, *op. cit.*, 237.
62. *A Pictorial and Descriptive Guide to Eastbourne, Beachy Head, Pevensey, Herstmonceux, Lewes, Seaford, Newhaven, etc.* (1929), 1–43.
63. A. G. S. Enser (ed.), *A Brief History of Eastbourne* (1976), ch. xii.

25. CONCLUSION: 'THE DUKE'S TOWN'

1. *EBC*, 4 June 1904.
2. S. Pollard, 'Town planning in the nineteenth century: the beginnings of modern Barrow-in-Furness', *Transactions of the Lancashire and Cheshire Antiquarian Society*, LXIII (1952–3), 107–16.
3. *EBG*, 25 September 1912.
4. Lord Haldon's Estate Act (1885), 22–5.

26. THE IMPACT OF THE ARISTOCRACY ON VICTORIAN CITIES

1. C. W. Chalklin, *The Provincial Towns of Georgian England: A study of the building process, 1740–1820* (1974), 73.
2. J. R. Kellett, *The Impact of Railways on Victorian Cities* (1969), 125, 424, 521.
3. H. Perkin, *The Age of the Railway* (1970), 17.
4. D. Ward, 'The pre-urban cadester and the urban pattern in Leeds', *AAAG*, LII (1962), 151, 165.
5. M. J. Mortimore, 'Landownership and urban growth in Bradford and its environs in the West Riding conurbation, 1850–1950', *Transactions of the Institute of British Geographers*, XLVI (1969), 107, 117–18.
6. G. Rowley, 'Landownership in the spatial growth of towns: a Sheffield example', *East Midland Geographer*, VI, 1975, 220–2.
7. F. H. W. Sheppard, *London, 1808–1870: The Infernal Wen* (1971), 84–92.
8. D. Spring, *The English Landed Estate in the Nineteenth Century, its Administration*, 13; F. H. W. Sheppard (ed.), *The Survey of London*, XXXIX, *The Grosvenor Estate in Mayfair*, Part I: *General History* (1977), 1.
9. For a full list, see D. Spring, 'English landowners and nineteenth-century

industrialism', in J. T. Ward and R. G. Wilson (eds.), *Land and Industry: The landed estate and the Industrial Revolution* (1971), 39–40, 42–3.

10. Sheppard, *London, 1808–1870*, 92.
11. Quoted in Kellett, *op. cit.*, 258.
12. H. Broadhurst and R. T. Reid, *Leasehold Enfranchisement* (1885), 16.
13. F. Banfield, *The Great Landlords of London* (1888), 53–4, 72, 76, 107.
14. H. Hobhouse, *Thomas Cubitt: Master builder* (1971), 109; D. J. Olsen, *Town Planning in London in the Eighteenth and Nineteenth Centuries* (1964), 10.
15. M. J. Daunton, *Coal Metropolis: Cardiff, 1870–1914* (1977), 73; F. M. L. Thompson, 'Hampstead, 1830–1914', in M. A. Simpson and T. H. Lloyd (eds.), *Middle-Class Housing in Britain* (1977), 110–13.
16. Olsen, *op. cit.*, 6; *idem, The Growth of Victorian London* (1976), 13–14.
17. e.g. *PP*, 1886, xii, SCTH., QQ. 2,179, 2,184, 6,395.
18. e.g. *ibid.*, 7,051, 11,404.
19. S. E. Rasmussen, *London: The unique city* (1948), ch. ix; J. Summerson, *Georgian London* (1970), 40, 166.
20. A. Briggs, *Victorian Cities* (1968), 38; H. C. Prince, 'North-west London, 1814–1863', in J. T. Coppock and H. C. Prince (eds.), *Greater London* (1964), 83, 96.
21. Summerson, *op. cit.*, chs. iii, vii, xii, xiii, xiv; L. Mumford, *The City in History* (1966), 454.
22. F. M. L. Thompson, *Hampstead: Building a borough, 1650–1964* (1974), 102–3, 136, 255; H. J. Dyos, *Victorian Suburb: A study of the growth of Camberwell* (1961), fig. 20.
23. Rowley, *op. cit.*, 200.
24. Olsen, *Town Planning in London*, 199.
25. *Idem, Growth of Victorian London*, 154.
26. *Ibid.*, 82–3.
27. M. D. George, *London Life in the Eighteenth Century* (1966), 74; Sheppard, *Survey of London*, xxxix, 6.
28. Hobhouse, *op. cit.*, 116.
29. Sheppard, *Survey of London*, XXXIX, 14, 15, 30.
30. *Ibid.*, 48; Hobhouse, *op. cit.*, 119.
31. Kellet, *op. cit.*, 253.
32. Sheppard, *Survey of London*, XXXIX, 65–6.
33. Hobhouse, *op. cit.*, Ch. ix.
34. *Ibid.*, 188.
35. Kellet, *op. cit.*, 250; Olsen, *Town Planning in London*, 139–41.
36. F. H. W. Sheppard (ed.), *Survey of London*, xxxvi, *The Parish of St. Paul, Covent Garden* (1970), 49–52.
37. Olsen, *Town Planning in London*, 40, 55, 149.
38. *Idem, Growth of Victorian London*, 147.
39. *Ibid.*, 248.
40. Prince, *op. cit.*, 95–7; Kellett, *op. cit.*, 246–50; Thompson, *Hampstead: Building a borough*, 67–70.
41. Olsen, *Growth of Victorian London*, 154.
42. Kellett, *op. cit.*, 253–4.
43. Olsen, *Growth of Victorian London*, 248.
44. J. Summerson, 'Urban Forms', in O. Handlin and J. Burchard (eds.), *The Historian and the City* (Cambridge, Mass., 1966), 174.
45. Thompson, 'Hampstead, 1830–1914', 96.
46. Olsen, *Growth of Victorian London*, 247–8.
47. Thompson, 'Hampstead, 1830–1914', 87.

48. *Idem, Hampstead: Building a borough*, 260.
49. *Idem*, 'Hampstead, 1830–1914', 108–13.
50. *Idem, Hampstead: Building a borough*, 241.
51. S. B. Warner, Jr, *Streetcar Suburbs: The process of growth in Boston, 1870–1900* (Cambridge, Mass., 1962), 124.
52. *Ibid.*, 156.
53. *PP*, 1886, xii, SCTH, 677–812.
54. *The Land: The report of the Land Enquiry Committee*, II, *Urban* (1914), 349.
55. Rowley, *op. cit.*, 200.
56. K. C. Edwards, 'The Park Estate, Nottingham', in Simpson and Lloyd, *op. cit.*, 157–65.
57. M. Spiers, *Victoria Park, Manchester* (1976), ch. i.
58. R. G. Wilson, *Gentlemen Merchants: The merchant community in Leeds, 1700–1830* (1971), 204–6.
59. M. A. Simpson, 'Middle-class housing and the growth of suburban communities in the West End of Glasgow, 1830–1914' (B.Litt. thesis, University of Glasgow, 1970), 381–2.
60. *Idem*, 'The West End of Glasgow, 1830–1914', in Simpson and Lloyd, *op. cit.*, 49–51.
61. Kellett, *op. cit.*, 127.
62. *Ibid.*, 132–4.
63. R. Homan, 'Estate development in nineteenth-century Sheffield: some implications of contrasting forms of landownership' (unpublished paper, Urban History Conference, 1978), 7.
64. D. J. Olsen, 'House upon house', in H. J. Dyos and M. Wolff (eds.), *The Victorian City: Images and realities* (2 vols., 1973), I, 344.
65. Homan, *op. cit.*, 6.
66. P. H. Mann, *An Approach to Urban Sociology* (1965), 83.
67. Olsen, 'House upon house', 345.
68. J. N. Tarn, 'Sheffield', in Simpson and Lloyd, *op. cit.*, 171–8.
69. W. D. Rubinstein, 'Wealth, elites and the class structure of modern Britain', *Past and Present*, lxxvi (1977), 104–5.
70. 'London and Paris improvements', *The Saturday Review*, i (1860), 295–7.
71. M. Craig, *Dublin, 1660–1860* (1952), 187.
72. R. J. Dennis, 'Community and change in a Victorian city: Huddersfield, 1850–1880' (Ph.D. thesis, University of Cambridge, 1975), 66–71.
73. E. Jones, *A Social Geography of Belfast* (1960), 51, 238–9, 277–8; J. L. McCracken, 'Early Victorian Belfast', in J. C. Beckett and R. E. Glasscock (eds.), *Belfast: The origin and growth of an industrial city* (1967), 92; W. A. Maguire, 'Lord Donegall and the sale of Belfast: a case study from the Encumbered Estates Court', *EcHR*, 2nd ser., xxiv (1976), 582–3.
74. Daunton, *op. cit.*, 82; J. Davies, 'Glamorgan and the Bute estate, 1776–1947' (Ph.D. thesis, University of Wales, 1969), 431.
75. Daunton, *op. cit.*, 75–9, 84–6.
76. R. E. Pahl, *Whose City? And Further Essays on Urban Sociology* (1975), 249; Thompson, 'Hampstead, 1830–1914', 88.
77. *PP*, 1888, xxii, SCTH, QQ. 2,097–2,108.
78. *Ibid.*, QQ. 12,919–12,923.
79. *Ibid.*, Q. 1,272.
80. J. A. Barrett, 'The Seaside resort towns of England and Wales' (Ph.D. thesis, University of London, 1958), 48.
81. H. Carter, 'A decision-making approach to town plan analysis: a case-study

of Llandudno', in H. Carter and W. K. D. Davies (eds.), *Urban Essays: Studies in the geography of Wales* (1970), 68.

82. H. J. Perkin, 'The "social tone" of Victorian seaside resorts in the north-west', *Northern History*, xi, 186–7.

83. Olsen, *Growth of Victorian London*, 154.

84. J. Myerscough, 'The seaside holiday: industry and the urban development of the Lancashire coast' (unpublished paper, Urban History Conference, 1974), 6.

85. Perkin, *Age of the Railway*, 217–18; J. H. Sutton, 'Early Fleetwood, 1835–47: a study in the genesis and early development of the new town, port and holiday resort of Fleetwood-on-Wyre, Lancashire' (M.Litt. thesis, University of Lancaster, 1968), 224–8, 242–6.

86. R. Gurnham, 'The creation of Skegness as a resort town by the ninth earl of Scarbrough', *Lincolnshire History and Archaeology*, vii, 63; Barrett, *op. cit.*, 50.

87. Gurnham, *op. cit.*, 64–74; T. W. Beastall, *A North-Country Estate: The Lumleys and Saundersons as Landowners 1600–1900* (1975), 184, 191; R. E. Pearson, 'The Lincolnshire coast holiday region' (M.A. thesis, University of Nottingham, 1965), 13.

88. J. Lowerson and J. Myerscough, *Time to Spare in Victorian England* (1977), 40–1.

89. W. F. Pickering, 'The development of the West Brighton Estate, Hove, 1871–1900' (M.A. thesis, University of Sussex, 1970), 39.

90. H. Clunn, *Famous South Coast Pleasure Resorts* (1929), 354, 356.

91. A. Harris, 'The seaside resort towns of Westmorland and Lancashire north of the Sands in the nineteenth century', *Transactions of the Historic Society of Lancashire and Cheshire*, cxv (1963), 156–8.

92. P. J. Aspinall, 'Speculative builders and the development of Cleethorpes, 1850–1900', *Lincolnshire History and Archaeology*, xi (1976), 45, 46, 47.

93. H. J. Gayler, 'The coastal resorts of Essex: their growth and present-day function' (M.A. thesis, University of London, 1965), 87–9.

94. Barrett, *op. cit.*, 70–1, 139, 183–4, 210–14.

95. *Ibid.*, 41.

96. Hobhouse, *op. cit.*, 73.

97. Thompson, *Hampstead: Building a Borough*, 74.

98. Olsen, *Growth of Victorian London*, 247–8.

99. HROCal. MS. F/C/690, Harris to Calthorpe, 19 June 1823.

100. EEO MS., Box 1, G. Edwards, SCTH, written evidence, 1888, 2; M. J. Daunton, 'Suburban development in Cardiff: Grangetown and the Windsor Estate, 1857–75', *Morgannwg*, xvi (1972), 55; Ramsden Estate Act (1885), 3–4.

101. F. M. L. Thompson, *English Landed Society in the Nineteenth Century* (1963), 267.

102. Spring, 'English landowners and nineteenth-century industrialism', 41; Sheppard, *Survey of London*, XXXIX, 48.

103. C. Stephenson, *The Ramsdens and their Estate in Huddersfield* (1972), 21.

104. Davies, *op. cit.*, 433.

105. Gurnham, *op. cit.*, 47; Lord Haldon's Estate Act, 22–5.

106. Hobhouse, *op. cit.*, 108.

107. Olsen, *Growth of Victorian London*, 14.

27. THE ARISTOCRACY AND THE TOWNS IN THE TWENTIETH CENTURY

1. W. Ashworth, *The Genesis of Modern British Town Planning* (1954), 43.
2. F. M. L. Thompson, *English Landed Society in the Nineteenth Century* (1963), 317–26.
3. F. M. L. Thompson, 'The land market in the nineteenth century', *Oxford Economic Papers*, new ser., IX (1957), 303; D. Howell, *Land and People in Nineteenth-Century Wales* (1978), 24; *The Times*, 3 October 1885.
4. Ashworth, *op. cit.*, 90–109.
5. F. H. W. Sheppard (ed.), *The Survey of London*, XXXIX, *The Grosvenor Estate in Mayfair* Part I: *General History* (1977), 70.
6. *Idem, The Survey of London*, XXXVI, *The Parish of St. Paul, Covent Garden* (1970) 48.
7. *Ibid.*, 49–52.
8. Sheppard, *Survey of London*, XXXIX, 67, 72, 76, 78.
9. O. Marriott, *The Property Boom* (1969), 115; B. Falk, *The Berkeleys of Berkeley Square and some of their Kinsfolk* (1944), 262.
10. Thompson, *English Landed Society*, 339.
11. Duke of Portland, *Men, Woman and Things* (1937), 1–3.
12. Lord Haldon's Estate Act (1885), 17–26.
13. C. Stephenson, *The Ramsdens and their Estate in Huddersfield* (1972), 10.
14. L. R. Jones, *Metropole, Folkestone: The Old . . . The New* (1969), 35.
15. Private information.
16. J. V. N. Soane, 'The general significance of the development of the urban and social structure of Bournemouth, 1840–1940' (Ph.D. thesis, University of Surrey, 1975), 561–2, 569.
17. F. A. Bailey, *A History of Southport* (1955), 23, 217, 219.
18. Stephenson, *op. cit.*, 15–16; R. S. Churchill, *Lord Derby: 'King' of Lancashire* (1959), 96.
19. J. Davies, 'Glamorgan and the Bute estate, 1776–1947' (Ph.D. thesis, University of Wales, 1969), 351, 431.
20. T. J. Raybould, *The Economic Emergence of the Black Country: A study of the Dudley estate* (1973), 124–8.
21. C. E. B. Brett, *The Buildings of Belfast, 1700–1914* (1967), 38.
22. M. J. Mortimore, 'Landownership and urban growth in Bradford and its environs in the West Riding conurbation, 1850–1950', *Transactions of the Institute of British Geographers*, XLVI (1969), 112.
23. J. R. Kellett, *The Impact of Railways on Victorian Cities* (1969), 363.
24. BRL MS.: 313,338, 350,629: Perry sale catalogues, 1 February 1923, 14 and 15 March 1928.
25. G. Rowley, 'Landownership and the spatial growth of towns: a Sheffield example', *East Midland Geographer*, VI (1975), 207.
26. B. Gilbert, 'David Lloyd George: the reform of British landholding and the budget of 1914', *HJ*, XXI (1978), 137–41.
27. Sheppard, *Survey of London*, XXXIX, 75.
28. Stephenson, *op. cit.*, 16; Lord Haldon's Estate Act (1885), 25–6.
29. John, Duke of Bedford, *A Silver-plated Spoon* (1959), 8, 15; Sheppard, *Survey of London*, XXXVI, 49–52; M. Harrison, *Lord of London: A biography of the second duke of Westminster* (1966), 207–8; Duke of Sutherland, *Looking Back: The autobiography of the Duke of Sutherland* (1957), 86–7; D. Cannadine, 'The landowner as millionaire: the finances of the dukes of Devonshire, *c*.1800–*c*.1926', *AgHR*, XXV (1977), 90–1.
30. Thompson, *English Landed Society*, 329–33, 335–7.

31. Falk, *op. cit.*, 262.
32. H. Macmillan, *Winds of Change, 1914–1939* (1966), 189–94.
33. A. J. P. Taylor, *English History, 1914–1945* (1970), 226.
34. D. Cannadine, 'The theory and practice of the English leisure class', *HJ*, xxi (1978), 450.
35. R. R. James (ed.), *'Chips': The diaries of Sir Henry Channon* (1967), 222, 234.
36. N. Mitford, *Noblesse Oblige* (1956), 55.
37. Davies, *op. cit.*, 351.
38. Raybould, *op. cit.*, 126–9.
39. Private information.
40. Marriott, *op. cit.*, 103, 115, 116.
41. *Hansard*, 1950–1, vol. 169, 27.
42. T. Lupton and C. S. Wilson, 'The social background and connections of "Top Decision-Makers"', *Manchester School*, xxvii (1959).
43. E. Waugh, *Brideshead Revisited* (1977), 8.
44. Calthorpe Estate Company, *Window on Edgbaston* (1958), 19; Marriott, *op. cit.*, 112.
45. Sheppard, *Survey of London*, XXXIX, 79–80.
46. F. M. L. Thompson, *Hampstead: Building a borough, 1650–1964* (1974), 74.
47. Sheppard, *Survey of London*, XXXIX, 76, 100–2.
48. Private information.
49. Sheppard, *Survey of London*, XXXIX, 79.
50. A. Sutcliffe and R. Smith, *The History of Birmingham*, iii (1974), 460.

Index